ABOUT THE AUTHORS

Mia Bay, Waldo E. Martin Jr., and Deborah Gray White

Deborah Gray White (Ph.D., University of Illinois at Chicago) is Board of Governors Professor of History at Rutgers University. She is the author of many works including *Too Heavy a Load: Black Women in Defense of Themselves, 1894–1994*; *Ar'n't I a Woman? Female Slaves in the Plantation South*; and the edited volume *Telling Histories: Black Women Historians in the Ivory Tower*. She is a recipient of the John Simon Guggenheim Fellowship and the Woodrow Wilson International Center Fellowship. Her current project uses the mass marches and demonstrations of the 1990s to explore the history of the decade.

Mia Bay (Ph.D., Yale University) is professor of history at Rutgers University and the director of the Rutgers Center for Race and Ethnicity. Her publications include *To Tell the Truth Freely: The Life of Ida B. Wells* and *The White Image in the Black Mind: African-American Ideas about White People, 1830–1925*. She is a recipient of the Alphonse Fletcher Sr. Fellowship and the National Humanities Center Fellowship. Currently, she is at work on a book examining the social history of segregated transportation and a study of African American views on Thomas Jefferson.

Waldo E. Martin Jr. (Ph.D., University of California, Berkeley) is professor of history at the University of California, Berkeley. He is the author of *No Coward Soldiers: Black Cultural Politics in Postwar America* and *The Mind of Frederick Douglass* and serves as coeditor of the John Hope Franklin Series in African American History and Culture. Current projects include a forthcoming coauthored book on the Black Panther Party as well as a book on the modern black freedom struggle with an emphasis on the impact of black cultural politics.

Praise for FREEDOM ON MY MIND

"*Freedom on My Mind* is by far the best textbook on African American history that I have ever read."

— Stephanie Camp, *University of Washington*

"Pioneering and profoundly transformative, *Freedom on My Mind* has renewed my hope in the power of African American history. This will be one of the most widely used textbooks on the subject in recent time."

— Zachery Williams, *University of Akron*

"*Freedom on My Mind* is a game changer in the market of African American survey textbooks. It sets the tone for twenty-first century methods and pedagogy for those actively engaged in African American education."

— Jakobi Williams, *University of Kentucky*

"*Freedom on My Mind* is a new textbook for a new era. Displaying an impressive commitment to interdisciplinary scholarship, the authors guide us through the African American past using a broad array of sources. They supplement each chapter's narrative with insightful questions, and they demonstrate the intertwined nature of African Americans' social, cultural, political, and economic experiences. This textbook sets a new standard."

— Jonathan Holloway, *Yale University*

"The text will fill a gap that has existed far too long in the field!"

— Lee Willis, *University of Wisconsin–Stevens Point*

"*Freedom on My Mind* conveys the rich diversity of African American historical experiences in historically specific settings over time, across regions of North America, and across unfolding imperial and later national boundaries."

— Julie Saville, *The University of Chicago*

"The book is true to its mission: to present the relationship between African American history and broader American history. At every turn one can see the interplay between standard American history and the unique circumstances, accomplishments, and contributions of African Americans to the story of America."

— Marilyn Howard, *Columbus State Community College*

"The authors have done an especially good job of incorporating women and gender history throughout the text and of portraying African Americans as active agents in shaping their own lives, despite the constraints against them."

— Rebecca de Schweinitz, *Brigham Young University*

"This wonderfully conceptualized textbook effectively synthesizes labor, cultural, gender, urban, and African American history into a cohesive whole."

— Claudrena Harold, *University of Virginia*

"*Freedom on My Mind* is a well-balanced textbook with a host of primary source documents that provide students with a total learning experience in one book."

— LaTasha C. Gatling, *American Public University System*

"The authors do an excellent job bringing the African American experience to the classroom. This textbook will do much to show students that blacks were not one-dimensional players on the stage of American history."

— Rita Reynolds, *Wagner College*

"This textbook really makes the subject matter come alive through narrative, primary source readings, and images. Excellent! I would enthusiastically recommend it as head and shoulders above any other text available for this subject."

— Alyce Miller, *John Tyler Community College*

"I find the integration of the documents in the text to be such a good idea and so conducive to classroom use."

— Peter Kuryla, *Belmont University*

"The authors provide an excellent survey of African American history with a readable and comprehensive synthesis of the newest scholarship."

— Corey N. Capers, *University of Illinois at Chicago*

"*Freedom on My Mind* provides a fresh interpretation of African American history. Through its use of recent scholarship, primary documents, pictures, and media, this book provides a concise narrative history of the African American experience that is not found in comparable textbooks."

— Talitha LeFlouria, *Florida Atlantic University*

For Bedford/St. Martin's

Publisher for History: Mary V. Dougherty
Senior Executive Editor for History: William J. Lombardo
Director of Development for History: Jane Knetzger
Senior Developmental Editors: Sara Wise and Danielle Slevens
Senior Production Editor: Rosemary R. Jaffe
Assistant Production Manager: Joe Ford
Senior Marketing Manager for U.S. History: Amy Whitaker
Market Development Manager: Katherine Bates
Associate Editor: Jennifer Jovin
Editorial Assistant: Arrin Kaplan
Copy Editor: Barbara Jatkola
Map Editor: Charlotte Miller
Indexer: Leoni Z. McVey
Cartography: Mapping Specialists, Ltd.
Photo Researcher: Bruce Carson
Permissions Manager: Kalina K. Ingham
Senior Art Director: Anna Palchik
Text Designer: Boynton Hue Studio
Composition: Graphic World Inc.

Printing and Binding: RR Donnelley and Sons
Cover Designer: Marine Miller
Cover Art: Left to right: Soujourner Truth, Courtesy of Library of Congress Prints and Photographs Division; William Wells Brown, Beinecke Rare Book and Manuscript Library; *Portrait of an African* (thought to be Olaudah Equiano), c. 1757–1760 (oil on canvas), attributed to Allan Ramsay (1713–1784), Royal Albert Memorial Museum, Exeter, Devon, UK/The Bridgeman Art Library; Nat Turner, General Research and Reference Division, Schomburg Center for Research in Black Culture, The New York Public Library, Astor, Lenox and Tilden Foundations; Phillis Wheatley, Courtesy of the Library of Congress Rare Book and Special Collections Division.

President, Bedford/St. Martin's: Denise B. Wydra
Presidents, Macmillan Higher Education: Joan E. Feinberg and Tom Scotty
Director of Marketing: Karen R. Soeltz
Production Director: Susan W. Brown
Associate Production Director: Elise S. Kaiser
Managing Editor: Elizabeth M. Schaaf

Library of Congress Control Number: 2012939011

Manufactured in the United States of America.

7   6   5   4   3
f   e   d   c

For information, write: Bedford/St. Martin's, 75 Arlington Street, Boston, MA 02116   (617-399-4000)

ISBN 978-0-312-19729-2 (Combined Edition)

ISBN 978-0-312-64883-1 (Volume 1)

ISBN 978-0-312-64884-8 (Volume 2)

Volume One: To 1885

FREEDOM
ON MY MIND

A HISTORY OF AFRICAN AMERICANS

with Documents

Deborah Gray White
RUTGERS UNIVERSITY

Mia Bay
RUTGERS UNIVERSITY

Waldo E. Martin Jr.
UNIVERSTY OF CALIFORNIA, BERKELEY

Bedford / St. Martin's
Boston • New York

Preface

In his melodic ode to black history, culture, and tradition, W. E. B. Du Bois, the first professionally trained black historian, celebrated the African American's reverence for freedom. It was, as he titled the introduction to his 1903 *Souls of Black Folk*, the object of the African American's "Spiritual Strivings." "Few men ever worshipped Freedom with half such unquestioning faith as did the American Negro,"[1] wrote Du Bois of the enslaved noncitizen. Of his contemporaries, Du Bois was certain that "there are today no truer exponents of the pure human spirit of the Declaration of Independence than the American Negroes."[2] Yet, as sure as he was about freedom being the central theme of the African American's past, Du Bois also felt that the quest for it would mark his people's future and the future of the American nation; for at the turn of the twentieth century, freedom was still the "unattained ideal." Black people, wrote Du Bois, still sought "freedom of life and limb, freedom to work and think, the freedom to love and aspire"; and because black people were not free, America could not be the world's beacon of liberty. As Du Bois saw things, the freedom of black people and the American nation were codependent. Their past and indeed their destiny were inseparable.

Our Approach

Like Du Bois, we, the authors of *Freedom on My Mind*, take African Americans' quest for freedom as the central theme of African American history and explore all dimensions of that quest, situated as it must be in the context of American history. Our perspective is that African American history complicates American history rather than diverging from it. This idea is woven into our narrative, which records the paradoxical experiences of a group of people at once the most American of Americans—in terms of their long history in America, their vital role in the American economy, and their enormous impact on American culture—and at the same time the Americans most consistently excluded from the American dream. Juxtaposed against American history as a whole, this is a study of a group of Americans who have had to fight too hard for freedom, yet have been systematically excluded from many of the opportunities that allowed other groups to experience the United States as a land of opportunity. This text encourages students to think critically and analytically about African American history and the historical realities behind the American dream.

The following themes and emphases are central to our approach:

The principal role of the black freedom struggle in the development of the American state. Our approach necessitates a study of the troubled relationship between African Americans and the American democratic state. *Freedom on My Mind* underscores the disturbing fact that our democracy arose within the context of a slaveholding society but ultimately gave way to the democratic forces unleashed by the Revolution that

---

1. W. E. B. Du Bois, *The Souls of Black Folk: Essays and Sketches* (Chicago: A. C. McClurg & Co., 1903), 5.
2. Ibid., 11.

founded it and the Civil War that reaffirmed federal sovereignty. Exempt from the universalist language of the Declaration of Independence—"all men are created equal"—African Americans have been, as Du Bois insightfully noted, "a concrete test of the underlying principles of the great republic." Most vividly illustrated during the political upheavals of Reconstruction and the civil rights movement—which is often known as America's second Reconstruction—African American activism has been crucial to the evolution of American democratic institutions.

The diversity of African Americans and the African American experience. Any study of the African American freedom struggle must recognize the wide diversity of African Americans who participated in it, whether through open rebellion and visible social protest; more covert means of defiance, disobedience, and dissent; or simply survival and perseverance in the face of overwhelming odds. Complicating any conceptions students might have of a single-minded, monolithic African American collective, *Freedom on My Mind* is mindful of black diversity and the ways and means that gender, class, and ethnicity—as well as region, culture, and politics—shaped the black experience and the struggle for freedom. The book explores African Americans' search for freedom in slave rebellions, everyday resistance to slavery, the abolitionist movement, Reconstruction politics, post-Emancipation labor struggles, the Great Migration, military service, civil rights activism, and the black power movements. It shows how American democracy was shaped by African Americans' search for, as Du Bois put it, "human opportunity"—and the myriad forms and characters that this search assumed.

An emphasis on culture as a vital force in black history. *Freedom on My Mind* also illuminates the rich culture blacks established to affirm themselves and in response to their exclusion from and often adversarial relationship with American institutions—the life Du Bois metaphorically characterized as "behind the veil." The rhythms and structure of black social and religious life, the contours of black educational struggles, the music Du Bois described as the "greatest gift of the Negro people"[3] to the American nation, the parallel institutions built as a means of self-affirmation and self-defense—all these are examined in the context of African Americans' quest for freedom, escape from degradation, and inclusion in the nation's body politic.

A synthesis that makes black history's texture and complexity clear. While culture is central to *Freedom on My Mind*, we offer an analytical approach to African American culture that enables students to see it as a central force that both shaped and reflected other historical developments, rather than as a phenomenon in a vacuum. How do we process black art—poetry, music, paintings, novels, sculptures, quilts—without understanding the political, economic, and social conditions that these pieces express? When spirituals, jazz, the blues, and rap flow from the economic and social conditions experienced by multitudes of blacks, how can we not understand black music as political? Indeed, African American culture, politics, and identity are inextricably entwined in ways that call for an approach to this subject that blends social, political, economic, religious, and cultural history. Such distinctions often seem arbitrary in American history as a whole and are impossible in chronicling the experiences of African Americans. How can we separate the

---

3. Ibid., 251.

religious and political history of people whose church leaders have often led their communities from the pulpit and the political stump? Therefore, *Freedom on My Mind* sidesteps such divisions in favor of a synthesis that privileges the sustained interplay among culture, politics, economics, religion, and social forces in the African American experience.

Twenty-first-century scholarship for today's classroom. Each chapter offers a synthesis of the most up-to-date historiography and historiographical debates in a clear narrative style. So much has changed since Du Bois pioneered the field of African American history. Once relegated to black historians and the oral tradition, African American history as a scholarly endeavor flowered with the social history revolt of the 1960s, when the events of the civil rights movement drew new attention to the African American past and the social upheaval of the 1960s inspired historians to recover the voices of the voiceless. Women's history also became a subject of serious study during this era, and as a result of all of these changes, we now survey an American history that has been reconstituted by nearly a half century of sustained attention to race, class, and gender.

Drawing on the most recent scholarship, this text will not only deepen students' understanding of the interconnectedness of African American and American history, but will also link African American struggles for political and civil rights, individual autonomy, religious freedom, economic equity, and racial justice to other Americans: white, red, yellow, and brown. As Americans, all these groups shared a world subject to similar structural forces, such as environmental changes, demographic forces, white supremacy, and the devastating power of world events on the American economy in times of global economic upheaval or war. Sometimes blacks bonded with other groups, and sometimes their interests clashed. Often the experiences of other Americans ran parallel to that of African Americans, and sometimes African American resistance served as a template for the resistance of others. *Freedom on My Mind* recounts this complex historical interaction. Although more than a century has unfolded since Du Bois wrote *Souls*, we have tried to remain true to the spirit of that text and write as he did, with "loving emphasis," the history of African Americans.

The Docutext Format

We believe that the primary goals of our book—to highlight the deep connections between black history and the development of American democracy, illustrate the diversity of black experience, emphasize the centrality of black culture, and document the inextricable connections between black culture, politics, economics, and social and religious life—could not be realized to their fullest extent through narrative alone. Thus, *Freedom on My Mind*'s unique docutext structure combines a brief narrative with rich, themed sets of primary documents and visual sources, reimagining the relationship between the narrative and the historical actors who form it. The narrative portion of each chapter is followed by three sets of primary sources—two **Documents collections**, and one **Visual Sources essay**—each focused on a particular chapter topic. Each set is clearly cross-referenced within the narrative so that students can connect it to and interpret it in terms of what they've learned. Carefully developed pedagogical elements—including substantive introductions, document headnotes, and Questions for Analysis at the close of each set—help students learn to analyze primary documents and practice "doing" history.

The Documents sets are extended by the inclusion of two to three **From the Record documents** in every chapter: These primary source excerpts, each containing a headnote and a question for analysis, provide ongoing documentary evidence for students to consider and analyze as they read. In addition to the Visual Sources, the narrative is enhanced by the inclusion of **over 260 images** and **35 maps and By the Numbers graphs**, each with a substantive caption that helps students relate what they're seeing to what they've read and analyze quantitative data.

These visuals and documents showcase and examine a rich variety of African American cultural elements and underscore the abiding connections among African American political activism, religious beliefs, economic philosophies, musical genres, and literary and fine art expression. A host of pictorial source types—from artifacts, photographs, paintings, and sculpture to cartoons, movie posters, and propaganda—and documentary sources ranging from personal letters, memoirs, songs, and poetry to public petitions and newspaper accounts illuminate the primary evidence that underpins and complicates the history students learn. Taken together, documents and images as varied as slave captivity narratives, early American visual portrayals of the black body, the writings of black abolitionists David Walker and Maria Stewart, the letters of black soldiers, the artistic expression of the Harlem Renaissance, the speeches of the civil rights era, the testimonies of Million Man and Woman Marchers, the stylistic expressions of Queen Latifah, and the editorial commentary of black gay and lesbian citizens all provide students with a vivid and appealing illustration of the interplay of societal forces, as well as the centrality of African American culture to American culture.

The Documents collections also play a key role in illustrating the diversity of black experience and thought. The sources we have chosen range from slave captives, Tuskegee experiment victims, and black army wives to Reconstruction's first black politicians, prominent civil rights leaders, and contemporary black liberal and conservative commentators, representing a vast array of individual opinions and experiences. By allowing these historical actors to speak for themselves and placing them in conversation with one another, we enable students to witness firsthand the myriad variations of and nuances within individual and collective black experiences and to appreciate the points where Africans Americans have diverged, as well as where they have agreed. Together with a narrative that presents and analyzes their context, these documents facilitate students' comprehension of the textured, complicated story that is the history of African America.

Support for Students and Instructors

Freedom on My Mind includes a variety of carefully crafted pedagogical features to help students grasp, assimilate, analyze, and recall what they've learned. Each chapter opens with a **thematic vignette** that illustrates the issues confronting African Americans of that time period, and transitions to an informative **introduction** that sets out the thesis and take-away points of the chapter. A **chapter timeline** highlights the most significant events of both African American history and general United States history, providing a quick reference for students. At the end of each chapter's narrative, a **Conclusion** allows students to retrace their steps through the chapter and previews the chapter that follows. A **Chapter Review** section provides a list of key terms—all of which are bolded when first defined in the narrative and listed with their definitions in a **Glossary of Key**

Terms at the end of the book—as well as three to five **Review Questions** encouraging students to think critically about the deeper implications of each chapter section and the connections between sections.

To facilitate further research and study, we have included extensive **Notes** and a section-specific list of **Suggested References** at the close of every chapter. Finally, we have provided an **Introduction for Students** that introduces students to the work of the historian and the practice of primary source analysis, and two **Appendixes** that include a wide variety of tables, charts, and vital documents, many of them annotated to provide a deeper reference tool. We are confident that these elements will be useful not only for students, but also for instructors who wish to introduce their students to the practice of history and provide the resources students will need for research projects, further reading, and reference.

Indeed, we structured this book with the instructor in mind as well as the student: We believe that the book's docutext format provides the convenience and flexibility of a textbook and source reader in one, allowing instructors a unique opportunity to incorporate primary readings and visuals seamlessly into their classes and introduce students to primary-source analysis and the practice of history. The Documents collections and Visual Sources essays, and the pedagogy that supports them, can be used in many ways—from in-class discussion prompts to take-home writing assignments or essay questions on exams. An **Instructor's Resource Manual** for *Freedom on My Mind* provides a variety of creative suggestions for making the best use of the documents program and for incorporating rich multimedia resources into the course. ***The Bedford Lecture Kit*** and **computerized test bank** provide additional instructional support. For more information on available student and instructor resources and the wide range of books that can be packaged with this text at a discount, see the Versions and Supplements section on pp. xiii–xv.

Acknowledgments

In completing this book, we owe thanks to the many talented and generous friends, colleagues, and editors who have provided us with suggestions, critiques, and much careful reading along the way.

Foremost among them is the hardworking group of scholar-teachers who agreed to review this manuscript for us. We are deeply grateful to them for their careful readings of our early drafts, and have learned a great deal from their scholarly expertise and collective wisdom. We hope we do it justice in the book. We thank Luther Adams, *University of Washington–Tacoma*; Jennifer Baszile, *Yale University*; Justin Behrend, *SUNY Geneseo*; Michael Benjamin, *Armstrong Atlantic State University*; Laura Bergstrom, *Ivy Tech Community College*; Keith Berry, *Hillsborough Community College*; Adam Biggs, *Harvard University*; David W. Blight, *Yale University*; Christine Ellen Bohman-Cina, *Madison Area Technical College*; Martha Jane Brazy, *University of South Alabama*; Tsekani Browne, *Duquesne University*; Richard A. Buckelew, *Bethune-Cookman University*; Art T. Burton, *South Suburban College*; Stephanie Camp, *University of Washington*; Corey N. Capers, *University of Illinois at Chicago*; Court Carney, *Stephen F. Austin State University*; Dolita Cathcart, *Wheaton College*; Maceo Crenshaw Dailey, Jr., *The University of Texas at El Paso*; Spencer R. Crew, *George Mason University*; Germany Davis-Graham, *American Public University System*; Rebecca de Schweinitz, *Brigham Young*

University*; Eric D. Duke, *University of South Florida*; Benjamin Fitzpatrick, *Florida State College at Jacksonville*; Eric Foner, *Columbia University*; LaTasha C. Gatling, *American Public University System*; Aimee Glocke, *University of Wyoming*; Thavolia Glymph, *Duke University*; Aram Goudsouzian, *University of Memphis*; Joyce A. Hanson, *California State University, San Bernardino*; Claudrena Harold, *University of Virginia*; Robert Heinrich, *Brandeis University*; Sharon A. Roger Hepburn, *Radford University*; Jennifer Hildebrand, *SUNY Fredonia*; Allyson Hobbs, *Stanford University*; Jonathan Holloway, *Yale University*; Marilyn Howard, *Columbus State Community College*; Hasan Kwame Jeffries, *The Ohio State University*; Jeannette Eileen Jones, *University of Nebraska–Lincoln*; Natalie Kimbrough, *The Community College of Baltimore County*; A. Michael Kinney, *Calhoun Community College*; Tim Konhaus, *Tidewater Community College*; Peter Kuryla, *Belmont University*; Carey H. Latimore, *Trinity University*; Kara L. Lawson, *Hillsborough Community College*; Talitha LeFlouria, *Florida Atlantic University*; Eric Love, *University of Colorado*; Bobby L. Lovett, *Tennessee State University*; J. Vincent Lowery, *University of Wisconsin–Green Bay*; Lorie Maltby, *Henderson Community College*; Thomas Massey, *Cape Fear Community College*; Sharon C. Melton, *Hinds Community College*; Alyce Miller, *John Tyler Community College*; Richard Randall Moore, *Metropolitan Community College–Longview*; Keidra Morris, *Los Angeles Valley College*; William J. Moses, *Pennsylvania State University*; Earl F. Mulderink III, *Southern Utah University*; Cassandra L. Newby-Alexander, *Norfolk State University*; Andrea Oliver, *Tallahassee Community College*; Freddie L. Parker, *North Carolina Central University*; Kristen A. Petersen, *Massachusetts College of Pharmacy and Health Sciences*; Richard Pierce, *University of Notre Dame*; Rita Reynolds, *Wagner College*; Marsha R. Robinson, *Otterbein University*; Julie Saville, *The University of Chicago*; Donald R. Shaffer, *American Public University System*; Tobin Miller Shearer, *University of Montana*; John Shorey, *Iowa Western Community College*; Josh Sides, *California State University, Northridge*; Kimberly Sims, *American University*; Margaret Stevens, *Essex County College*; Jeffery Strickland, *Montclair State University*; Katrina Dyonne Thompson, *Saint Louis University*; Linda D. Tomlinson, *Fayetteville State University*; Cristy Casado Tondeur, *American Public University System*; Ahati N. N. Toure, *Delaware State University*; Robert Charles Watson, *Hampton University*; Matthew C. Whitaker, *Arizona State University*; Robert Widell, *University of Rhode Island*; Jakobi Williams, *University of Kentucky*; Zachery Williams, *University of Akron*; Lee Willis, *University of Wisconsin–Stevens Point*; Jamie J. Wilson, *Salem State University*; and Irvin D. S. Winsboro, *Florida Gulf Coast University*.

Our debts to the many brilliant editors at Bedford/St. Martin's are equally immeasurable. We are grateful to publisher Mary Dougherty and president Joan Feinberg for enlisting us to write this book and supplying us with the template for its innovative mix of historical narrative, documents, and picture essays; and we are grateful to president Denise Wydra, director of development Jane Knetzger, senior executive editor William Lombardo, senior marketing manager Amy Whitaker, market development manager Katherine Bates, former senior executive marketing manager Jenna Bookin Barry, associate editor Jennifer Jovin, editorial assistant Arrin Kaplan, and the other members of Bedford's outstanding history team for guiding its development. We also thank Ann Grogg for her developmental edits, Bruce Carson for researching and clearing the book's photographs, Kalina Ingham and Eve Lehmann for clearing the text permissions, Charlotte Miller for her work on the maps and graphs, Barbara Jatkola for copyediting the manuscript, Roberta Sobotka and Angela Morrison for proofreading, Leoni McVey for indexing, Cia Boynton for her design of the book's interior, and Marine Miller for her design of the cover.

In acknowledging the many wonderful people we worked with at Bedford/St. Martin's, we have to pause to offer especially big thanks to senior editor Sara Wise, without whose efficient leadership and endless help we simply could not have written the book. Sara is a superb reader and historical thinker, a great line editor, and a gentle voice of reason, who guided us all through our challenging early chapter drafts.

Moreover, as the book progressed, we had the pleasure of working with several of Bedford's other incredibly talented editors, who, like Sara, taught us a great deal about the art and craft of writing textbooks. Developmental editor Danielle Slevens provided us with extraordinarily painstaking, helpful, and often brilliant edits on the later drafts of our chapters, while Rosemary Jaffe, our production editor, coordinated the work of copyediting, proofing, and illustrating this book with amazing grace, good humor, and attention to detail. Thank you all for making the writing of this book such a pleasant experience.

In writing this book we have also relied on a large number of talented scholars and friends within the academy to supply us with guidance, editorial expertise, bright ideas, research assistance, and many other forms of support, and we would like to thank them here. The enormous, but by no means comprehensive, list of colleagues, friends, students, and former students to whom we are indebted includes Isra Ali, Marsha Barrett, Rachel Bernard, Melissa Cooper, John Day, Jeff Dowd, Joseph L. Duong, Ann Fabian, Jared Farmer, Larissa Fergeson, Krystal Frazier, Raymond Gavins, Mia Kissil, Sharon Harley, Nancy Hewitt, Martha Jones, Stephanie Jones-Rogers, Christopher Lehman, Thomas Lekan, Emily Lieb, Leon F. Litwack, Julie Livingston, David Lucander, Catherine L. Macklin, Jaime Martinez, Story Matkin-Rawn, Gregory Mixon, Donna Murch, Kimberly Phillips, Alicia Rodriguez, David Schoebun, Karcheik Sims-Alvarado, Jason Sokol, Melissa Stein, Ellen Stroud, Melissa Stuckey, Anantha Sudakar, Patricia Sullivan, Keith Wailoo, and Wendy Wright. Deborah would especially like to thank Maya White Pascual for her invaluable assistance with many of the document and visual essays in the last third of the book. Her insight, skill, and talent were absolutely indispensable.

Finally, all three of us are grateful to our families and loved ones for the support and forbearance that they showed us during our work on this book.

Deborah Gray White

Mia Bay

Waldo E. Martin Jr.

Versions and Supplements

Adopters of *Freedom on My Mind* and their students have access to abundant resources, including documents, presentation and testing materials, volumes in the acclaimed Bedford Series in History and Culture, and much more.

To Learn More

For more information on the offerings described below, visit the book's catalog site at **bedfordstmartins.com/graywhite/catalog**, or contact your local Bedford/St. Martin's sales representative.

Get the Right Version for Your Class

To accommodate different course lengths and course budgets, *Freedom on My Mind* is available in several different formats, including e-books, which are available at a substantial discount.

- Combined edition (chapters 1–15)—available in paperback and e-book formats
- Volume 1: To 1885 (chapters 1–8)—available in paperback and e-book formats
- Volume 2: Since 1865 (chapters 8–15)—available in paperback and e-book formats

Students can purchase the downloadable *Bedford e-Book to Go for Freedom on My Mind* from our Web site or find other PDF versions of the e-book at our publishing partners' sites: CourseSmart; Barnes & Noble NookStudy; Kno; CafeScribe; or Chegg.

Send Students to Free Online Resources

The book's companion site at **bedfordstmartins.com/graywhite** gives students a way to read, write, and study by providing plentiful quizzes and activities, study aids, and history research and writing help.

FREE Online Study Guide. Available at the companion site, this popular resource provides students with quizzes and activities for each chapter, including multiple-choice self-tests that focus on important concepts; flashcards that test students' knowledge of key terms; timeline activities that emphasize causal relationships; and map quizzes intended to strengthen students' geography skills. Instructors can monitor students' progress through an online Quiz Gradebook or receive e-mail updates.

FREE Research, Writing, and Antiplagiarism Advice. Available at the companion site, Bedford's **History Research and Writing Help** includes **History Research and Reference Sources**, with links to history-related databases, indexes, and journals; **More Sources and How to Format a History Paper**, with clear advice on how to integrate primary and secondary sources into research papers and how to cite and format sources correctly; **Build a Bibliography**, a simple Web-based tool known as *The Bedford Bibliographer* that generates bibliographies in four commonly used documentation styles; and **Tips on Avoiding Plagiarism**, an online tutorial that reviews the consequences of plagiarism and features exercises to help students practice integrating sources and recognize acceptable summaries.

Take Advantage of Instructor Resources

Bedford/St. Martin's has developed a rich array of teaching resources for this book and for this course. Most can be downloaded or ordered at **bedfordstmartins.com /graywhite/catalog**.

Instructor's Resource Manual. The instructor's manual offers both experienced and first-time instructors tools for preparing lectures and running discussions. It includes chapter-review material; lecture, discussion, and active-learning strategies; recommendations for ways to complement lectures with images, literature, film, and music; and a guide to chapter-specific supplements available for the text.

Computerized Test Bank. The test bank includes a mix of fresh, carefully crafted multiple-choice, short-answer, and essay questions for each chapter, and volume-based essay questions. It also contains the Review Questions, From the Record questions, and Questions for Analysis from the textbook, and model answers for each. All questions appear in Microsoft Word format and in easy-to-use test bank software that allows instructors to add, edit, resequence, and print questions and answers. Instructors can also export questions into a variety of formats, including Canvas and Blackboard.

The Bedford Lecture Kit: **Maps, Images, Lecture Outlines, and i>clicker Content in PowerPoint Format.** Look good and save time with *The Bedford Lecture Kit*. These presentation materials are downloadable individually from the Instructor Resources tab at **bedfordstmartins.com/graywhite/catalog** and are available on *The Bedford Lecture Kit* **Instructor's Resource CD-ROM**. They provide ready-made and fully customizable multimedia presentations in PowerPoint format that include lecture outlines with embedded maps, figures, and selected images from the textbook, and extra background for instructors. Also available are maps and selected images in JPEG and PowerPoint formats; content for i>clicker, a classroom response system, in Microsoft Word and PowerPoint formats; the Instructor's Resource Manual in Microsoft Word format; and outline maps in PDF format for quizzing or handing out. All files are suitable for copying onto transparency acetates.

Make History—**Free Documents, Maps, Images, and Web Sites.** *Make History* combines the best Web resources with hundreds of maps and images to make it simple to find the source material you need. Browse the collection of thousands of resources by course or by topic, date, and type. Each item has been carefully chosen and helpfully annotated to make it easy to find exactly what you need. Available at **bedfordstmartins .com/makehistory**.

Package and Save Your Students Money

For information on free packages and discounts up to 50%, visit **bedfordstmartins .com/graywhite/catalog** or contact your local Bedford/St. Martin's sales representative.

The Bedford Series in History and Culture. More than 150 titles in this highly praised series combine first-rate scholarship, historical narrative, and important primary documents for undergraduate courses. Each book is brief, inexpensive, and focused on a specific topic or period. For a complete list of titles, visit **bedfordstmartins .com/history/series**. Package discounts are available.

Rand McNally Atlas of American History. This collection of more than 80 full-color maps illustrates key events and eras from early exploration, settlement, expansion, and immigration to U.S. involvement in wars abroad and on U.S. soil. Introductory pages for each section include a brief overview, timelines, graphs, and photos to quickly establish a historical context. Available for $3.00 when packaged with the print text.

The Bedford Glossary for U.S. History. This handy supplement for the survey course gives students historically contextualized definitions for hundreds of terms—from *abolitionism* to *zoot suit*—that they will encounter in lectures, reading, and exams. Available free when packaged with the print text.

U.S. History Matters: A Student Guide to U.S. History Online. This resource, written by Kelly Schrum, Alan Gevinson, and the late Roy Rosenzwerg (all of George Mason University), provides an illustrated and annotated guide to 250 of the most useful Web sites for student research in U.S. history as well as advice on evaluating and using Internet sources. This essential guide is based on the acclaimed "History Matters" Web site developed by the American Social History Project and the Center for History and New Media. Available free when packaged with the print text.

Trade Books. Titles published by sister companies Hill and Wang; Farrar, Straus and Giroux; Henry Holt and Company; St. Martin's Press; Picador; and Palgrave Macmillan are available at a 50% discount when packaged with Bedford/St. Martin's textbooks. For more information, visit **bedfordstmartins.com/tradeup**.

A Pocket Guide to Writing in History. This portable and affordable reference tool by Mary Lynn Rampolla, now available as a searchable e-book, provides reading, writing, and research advice useful to students in all history courses. Concise yet comprehensive advice on approaching typical history assignments, developing critical reading skills, writing effective history papers, conducting research, using and documenting sources, and avoiding plagiarism—enhanced with practical tips and examples throughout—have made this slim reference a best seller. Package discounts are available.

A Student's Guide to History. This complete guide to success in any history course provides the practical help students need to be effective. In addition to introducing students to the nature of the discipline, author Jules Benjamin teaches a wide range of skills from preparing for exams to approaching common writing assignments, and he explains the research and documentation process with plentiful examples. Package discounts are available.

Explore Other Docutexts from Bedford/St. Martin's

Bedford/St. Martin's has been a leader in pioneering new ways to bring primary sources into the undergraduate classroom, beginning with the Bedford Series in History and Culture, described above. The "docutext" format of *Freedom on My Mind*, which combines a brief narrative with themed collections of written and visual sources, represents another innovation in making documents accessible for students. Docutexts authored by leading historians are now available from Bedford for a variety of history courses.

U.S. History Survey Find out about *Exploring American Histories: A Brief Survey with Sources*, by Nancy A. Hewitt and Steven F. Lawson, at **bedfordstmartins.com /hewittlawson/catalog**.

World History Survey Find out about *Ways of the World: A Brief Global History with Sources*, by Robert W. Strayer, at **bedfordstmartins.com/strayersources/catalog**.

U.S. Women's History Find out about *Through Women's Eyes: An American History with Documents*, by Ellen Carol DuBois and Lynn Dumenil, at **bedfordstmartins.com /duboisdumenil/catalog**.

Native American History Find out about *First Peoples: A Documentary Survey of American Indian History*, by Colin G. Calloway, at **bedfordstmartins.com/calloway /catalog**.

Twentieth-Century European History Find out about *Europe in the Contemporary World, 1900 to the Present: A Narrative History with Documents*, by Bonnie G. Smith, at **bedfordstmartins.com/smitheurope/catalog**.

Brief Contents

Contents

CHAPTER 1

From Africa to America, 1441–1808   2

CHAPTER 2 · African Slavery in North America, 1619–1739 · 54

CHAPTER 3
African Americans in the Age of Revolution, 1740–1783   **110**

CHAPTER 6   The Northern Black Freedom Struggle and the Coming of the Civil War, 1830–1860   264

CHAPTER 7 Freedom Rising: The Civil War, 1861–1865 — 322

Special Features

From the Record

By the Numbers

Maps

Introduction for Students

It is a joy to offer *Freedom on My Mind* to enhance your knowledge of both African American history and the craft of history. For us, the authors, history has never been just a series of dates and names. It is not just memorizable facts, consumed only to pass a test or complete an assignment. For us, history is adventure; it's a puzzle that must be both unraveled and put together. Being a historian is like being a time-traveling detective. To be able to use our sleuthing skills to unveil the history of African Americans, a history that for too long was dismissed but tells us so much about American democracy, is not just a delight but a serious responsibility.

The History of African American History

Although black Americans first came to North America in 1619, before the Mayflower brought New England pilgrims, the history of African American history has a relatively recent past. For most of American history black history was ignored, overlooked, exploited, demeaned, discounted, or ridiculed—much like African Americans. Worse yet, history was often used to justify the mistreatment of African Americans: The history of Africans was used to justify slavery, and the history of slavery was used to justify the subsequent disfranchisement, discrimination, rape, and lynching of African Americans.

American blacks understood this connection between a history that misrepresented them and their citizenship, and they fought not only to free themselves from bondage but also to create a legacy that future generations could be proud of: a legacy that championed their self-inspired "uplift" and that countered the negative images and history that prevailed in American society. Take just one example. D. W. Griffith's film *The Birth of a Nation* (1915) used revolutionary cinematography to disseminate a history that represented slaves as happy and race relations as rosy, until the Civil War and Reconstruction unleashed black criminals and sexual predators upon an innocent South. Many used Griffith's film to justify the lynching of black men and the segregation of the races. Indeed, President Woodrow Wilson, the historian who as president introduced segregation into Washington D.C.'s government offices, premiered the film in the White House and praised its historical accuracy.

The same year that *The Birth of a Nation* (1915) premiered, Harvard-trained black historian Carter G. Woodson founded the Association for the Study of Negro Life and History (ASNLH). Woodson's ASNLH was the culmination of what has become known as the New Negro History Movement, begun in the late nineteenth century. Its goal was to counter Griffith-type images by resurrecting a positive black history and recounting all that African Americans had done for themselves and for America. Because professional American historical journals generally did not publish black history, the ASNLH, with Woodson as editor, issued the *Journal of Negro History* and the *Negro History Bulletin*. During the 1920s, these journals and the ASNLH focused much of their attention on proving Griffith wrong.

Professionally researched articles and scholarly convention panels demonstrated that black people were not criminals or sexually dangerous. Black scholars wrote a history that showed how blacks, despite being mercilessly degraded, had in the one generation after slavery become a mostly literate people who voted responsibly and elected representatives who practiced fiscal responsibility and pursued educational and democratic reforms. Because black history was excluded from public school curricula, the ASNLH also spearheaded the movement that brought about Negro History Week (later to be a month), first in African American communities and then in the nation at large. The second week of February was chosen because it marked the birthdays of the Great Emancipator, Abraham Lincoln, and the great black freedom fighter, Frederick Douglass. Black leaders believed that a celebration of the lives of Lincoln and Douglass would evolve into the study of African Americans in general.

Black scholars did this because they understood the connection between their history and their status in America. The preeminent twentieth-century black historian, W. E. B. Du Bois, sternly warned against the erasure and/or distortion of the role played by African Americans in the building of the American nation. "We, the darker ones . . . come . . . not altogether empty-handed," he said.[1] African Americans had much to offer this country, much to teach America about humanitarianism and morality, and thus he pleaded for the study of black history and its inclusion in the national consciousness. Black history was even more important to African Americans, he instructed. Black people needed to know their history "for positive advance . . . for negative defense," and to have "implicit trust in our ability and worth." "No people that laughs at itself and ridicules itself, and wishes to God it was anything but itself ever wrote its name in history," counseled Du Bois at the turn of the twentieth century.[2] For him, black history, black freedom, and American democracy were all of a piece.

It should come as no surprise that when the freedom struggle moved on to the national stage in the mid-twentieth century, African American history became a central focus. Both black and white activists demanded not just an end to white terrorism, desegregation in all areas of American life, equality in the job market, voting rights, and the freedom to marry regardless of race; activists also demanded that non-distorted African American history and studies be included in elementary through high school public school curriculums and textbooks, as well as college courses. They insisted that colleges and universities offer degrees in African American studies and that traditional disciplines offer courses that treated black subjects as legitimate areas of study. In the 1960s, demands were made to extend black history week to a month, and in 1976, Woodson's organization, by then the Association for the Study of African American Life and History (1972), designated February as Black History Month—a move acknowledged and approved by the federal government.

---

1. W. E. B. Du Bois, *The Souls of Black Folk: Essays and Sketches* (Chicago: A. C. McClurg & Co., 1903), 13.
2. Both quoted in W. E. B. Du Bois, "The Conservation of the Races," in David Levering Lewis, ed., *W. E. B. Du Bois, A Reader* (New York: Henry Holt and Company, 1995), 25.

Debating African American History and Its Sources

Historians rely on documents written in the past. Before we can analyze a period, we must locate and unearth our sources. Primary sources originate during the period under study. Some are official and unofficial documents issued by public and private institutions; items as varied as church records, government census records, newspapers and magazines, probate records, court transcripts, and schoolbooks are exceptionally revelatory of the past. Other records come from individuals. Personal letters and diaries, bank statements, photographs, and even gravestone inscriptions help historians figure out what happened during a particular time period. Once we assemble all of our documents, we write history based on our examination and analysis of them. Our histories become part of a body of secondary sources for the period under study—secondary because they originate from someone who has secondarily written an account that relied on first, or primary, sources.

Researching African American history has always presented a challenge for scholars. During the almost 250 years of enslavement, Africans and African Americans had few belongings they could call their own; thus, they left few of the personal records that historians depend on to write history. Added to this obstacle is the fact that during slavery black literacy was outlawed. Schools for free blacks were regularly destroyed, and anyone teaching a slave to read could be arrested, fined, whipped, or jailed for corrupting a labor force that was considered most efficient when it was illiterate. Black Americans, therefore, developed a rich oral tradition. Certainly, as you will see from the sources presented in this book, some blacks, mostly those who were not enslaved, wrote letters, gave speeches, kept diaries, or wrote narratives of their experiences. However, most black communication and communion took place through personal interaction and via the spoken word. Before black history was committed to paper, it was committed to memory and passed down through folklore, art, and secular and religious music. This continued long into the twentieth century as segregation, disfranchisement, and attacks on black education forced African Americans to depend on their oral tradition.

For historians, who rely heavily on written sources, this presented a problem—as did the fact that the struggle for black freedom was often manifested in a struggle over who could and/or should write black history. This overlapped the problem of sources, because many thought it unfair to write black history using only those sources emanating from the very people and institutions responsible for the African American's second-class citizenship. For example, in his 1935 post–Civil War history, *Black Reconstruction*, Du Bois, a Harvard-trained historian, railed against the professional historians who had written about the period using only the sources that came from the defeated South. It was to be expected, argued Du Bois, that these historians, who were mostly white, male, and southern, would find fault with the freedmen; their sources were those of defeated slaveowners and others who had a stake in painting ex-slaves as unworthy of freedom. "The chief witness in Reconstruction, the emancipated slave himself, has been almost barred from the court," argued Du Bois.[3] In presenting a case

---

3. W. E. B. Du Bois, *Black Reconstruction in AmOerica, 1860–1880* (New York: The Free Press, 1998 [1935, 1962]), 721.

for using the written records of black representatives, which included the few biographies of black leaders and the unedited debates of the Reconstruction conventions, Du Bois called for true fairness: "If history is going to be scientific, if the record of human action is going to be set down with that accuracy and faithfulness of detail which will allow its use as a measuring rod and guidepost for the future of nations, there must be set some standards of ethics in research and interpretation."[4] In other words, history could not be written from just one point of view, or with sources that were highly prejudicial or exclusionary. But who was to say which sources were best and who was best qualified to write African American history? Could not those sympathetic to black causes also use history for their own purposes and bend it to their needs? And given that so many African American sources were oral and not preserved in archives, or were personal artifacts packed away in family storage, how could the existing sources be accessed to produce written history?

These issues were hotly debated during the mid-twentieth-century freedom struggle, and out of that debate came a new consensus about African American history and history in general. For as African Americans, traditionally the lowest in the American social strata, demonstrated how important their history was to them and to the nation, other Americans followed suit. Women, workers, and members of America's many ethnic groups expanded the study of their pasts and insisted on inclusion in the narrative of American history. Rather than focusing on presidents, or the nation's wars, or the institutions at the top of America's political, economic, and social systems, ordinary American citizens called for a study of America from the "bottom up." Everyone made history, these advocates argued. The daily lives of average Americans were as important for historians as the decisions made by heads of states. It was not just the rich and famous, not just men, not just whites, not just Anglo-Saxon Protestants, and not just heterosexuals who made history. As women, Native Americans, Asian Americans, Hispanics, and gay, lesbian, bisexual, and transgendered citizens demanded equal inclusion in American society, they demanded that their history be included as well. Scholars picked up the gauntlet thrown down and began to change their research methods by including different kinds of sources and asking different kinds of questions, and consequently, their histories changed. The mid-century rights movements birthed not just new and expanded citizenship rights, but a new way of thinking about and doing history. Sometimes, history from the "bottom up" looks very different from "top-down" history. Sometimes the differences are reconcilable, but often they are not. Adding the sources of rank-and-file Americans made a difference in how the past was written and understood.

The Craft of African American History

Historians of slavery pioneered the "new" African American history in the 1970s. Following the advice of Du Bois, they ceased barring the "chief witness" from their studies, integrating the experiences of former slaves into their work and writing some histories from the slave's point of view. This necessitated using different kinds of sources which, not surprisingly, were oral interviews conducted after slavery or oral testimony given to the Freedmen's Bureau, the government agency established to aid freedmen in their

---

4. Ibid., 714.

transition from slavery to freedom. Because black testimony differed significantly from most white testimony, historians were now tasked with recounting a history that looked at slavery from different vantage points.

Once historians added African American testimony, it changed the way many interpreted seemingly objective sources like census and probate records, court cases, and congressional debates. For example, Harriet Brent Jacobs's account of her master's attempt at rape and her recounting of the sexual exploitation of female slaves changed the way some historians looked at plantation lists that showed a preponderance of single females with children. This was once assumed to indicate the promiscuity of black women, but historians now had to consider the sexual profligacy of white men. Plantation records were also combed to trace black family lineages, a laborious process that revealed, for example, that not all slaves took the last names of their masters. Additionally, though the law did not recognize slave marriages, these records showed that many slaves partnered carefully and with intention—not in a willy-nilly fashion, as had previously been assumed. In the 1970s, historians studied previously excluded black folk tales and black music and art as a way to discern slaves' belief systems and culture. The new sources stimulated different answers to age-old questions and prompted serious reconsideration of previously held historical assumptions. Whereas slaveowners maintained that blacks were happy under slavery and unfit for freedom, black-originated sources spoke of ever-present black resistance to slavery. Whereas most white-originated sources gave Abraham Lincoln and other whites credit for black emancipation, black-originated sources showed how African Americans stole themselves from slavery, joined Union armies, and fought for their own freedom and for the Union cause. These new sources showed how a people who were once African became African American, and how and why a people so excluded embraced American democratic principles.

African American sources opened a window not just on slavery and more broadly the African American experience, but on the entire American experience. They allowed historians to present a total history: not just one that looked at black oppression and race relations, but a rich history that included nearly 400 years of black cultural production, black faith and religious communion, black family history, black politics, and connections to the African diaspora—that is, the dispersal and movement of peoples of African descent to different parts of the world. In the 1970s, as other groups demanded the inclusion of their own sources in the historical record, their histories grew into fields of study that challenged historians to integrate race, class, gender, and sexuality into American history. Soon, African Americans at the intersection of many of these groups—for example, African American women—also insisted that sources illuminating their history be examined and that their particular history be told. Today, many Americans object to what they see as the fractionalization of American history, preferring a more unified history that downplays difference and emphasizes the unity of the American people and the development of a unique American character. Others are comfortable with an American history that is complicated and revealing of Americans' diverse experiences.

Freedom on My Mind: History and Documents

Freedom on My Mind offers a balance between a top-down and a bottom–up approach to history. Using both primary and secondary sources, we have written a narrative of African American history and presented it in the context of American history and the evolution of American democracy. Our narrative includes the voices of blacks and whites; leaders as well as followers; men as well as women; and the well-to-do, the middle classes, and the poor. In creating this narrative, we have used both primary sources that originate in American and African American institutions and primary sources from individuals. We have used secondary sources that present the latest research and analysis of the African American past. We have shown how African Americans were represented by others, and how they represented themselves. When enabled by our sources, we have noted the different experiences and perspectives of native-born African Americans, Caribbean and African blacks, and blacks in the lesbian, gay, bisexual, and transgendered (LGBT) community.

Equal in importance to our narrative are the in-text primary sources that allow you, the student, to be a time-traveling detective and "do" history. We've offered our analysis of the sources, but we want you to be more than passive recipients of the secondary source that is this book—we want you to participate. We want you to investigate primary sources and create a narrative of your own, as if you, too, were a historian.

As you will discover, sleuthing the past is complicated. Take, for example, the narrative of Olaudah Equiano, a prominent eighteenth-century abolitionist and former slave. As a child, Equiano was stolen from Africa and enslaved, but through a unique set of circumstances, he became a free and outspoken opponent of slavery. Reading his narrative will provide you with insight into what it must have been like to be an eighteenth-century West African and allow you to empathize with those who were involuntarily separated from all that they knew and understood about life. However, you will quickly realize that being a historian requires much more than empathy. Questions will arise, such as "What does Equiano's narrative tell us about his region of Africa, and how did things change over time?" You may also ask questions like "Was Equiano typical?" or "Might Equiano have fabricated or embellished his story to gain support for abolitionism?"

Invariably, one question and answer leads to others. If you pursue your inquiry, and we encourage you to do so, you will find yourself needing additional sources, both primary and secondary. Gradually, a picture of West Africa and the slave trade will emerge—one that you have created from the sources you unearthed. If you decide to compare your study with the secondary works produced by others, you might find differences in approach and perspective. Perhaps you focused on the everyday lives of enslaved eighteenth-century Africans and wrote a "bottom-up" history, while others focused on the leaders of the abolitionist movement and used a more "top-down" approach. One thing you will note is that two historians seldom write the same exact history. This will become apparent when you and your classmates compare your answers to the questions that accompany the sources in *Freedom on My Mind*. Your stations in life, your personal identities, the time period you live in: All of these influence the questions you ask and the way you interpret the sources you read.

Freedom on My Mind includes a wide variety of sources to enable you to practice history while learning about African Americans and American democracy. This is what we think makes this text special. Although we have included many events and the names of people and places, we have tried not to overwhelm you with them; rather, we have included sources that allow you to reach conclusions on your own and thereby analyze the conclusions we have drawn. This is what excites us about our text, and we invite you to explore and get excited with us.

FREEDOM
ON MY MIND

From Africa to America,

1441–1808

IN THE SUMMER OF 1441, a Portuguese vessel under the command of Antam Goncalvez acquired ten slaves in Mauritania, a Berber kingdom on the coast of North Africa. Commissioned to explore the African coast by the Portuguese monarch Prince Henry the Navigator, Goncalvez and his crew arrived there eager to bring home captives that would satisfy the prince's curiosity about the "other dwellers of the land." After they attacked and enslaved three local "Moors," the captives, who themselves owned slaves, offered to buy their own freedom by giving the Europeans a larger group of enslaved Africans. Goncalvez agreed, receiving in payment ten Africans, male and female, from several different places in West Africa. These slaves, whom Goncalvez described as "black moors," were not only more numerous than his original captives but also of greater potential value to his mission. In particular, he hoped they would "give him news of a land much more distant," which would be of significant interest to the man who had sponsored the voyage.

Prince Henry thus opened Europe's age of exploration by sponsoring a series of voyages down the West African coast, setting the stage for Columbus's first expedition across the Atlantic in 1492. Like Columbus, Henry sought not slaves but gold, other profitable merchandise, and a passage to the Orient. Goncalvez's voyage did not achieve these goals, but it did inaugurate a lucrative trade in people. The Atlantic slave trade began only three years later when, with Henry's permission, a Portuguese merchant-adventurer dispatched another expedition to the African coast, this time specifically in search of slaves.

On August 8, 1444, the 235 enslaved Africans captured on the expedition arrived in the maritime town of Lagos, Portugal, where they were met by a crowd that included Prince Henry. Mounted on horseback, the prince looked on as the leader of the expedition paraded the captives from the docks to the town gates. The men, women, and children of all complexions and colors were distressed and disoriented as they walked through the streets of Lagos. "Some kept their heads low, and their faces [were] bathed with tears, looking upon one another," noted Henry's court chronicler, while others were "looking up to the heavens and crying out loudly, as if asking for help from the Father of nature." The spectacle ended with an auction that moved even the chronicler, a steadfast admirer of his monarch, to pity. Before their sale, the captives were divided into lots in order to help the merchants split the proceeds of their voyage—and to pay Henry the required 20 percent royal tax. The separation was bound to "increase their suffering even more," the chronicler noted, since it parted "fathers from sons, husbands from wives, and brothers. No respect was shown to either friends or relatives, but each fell down where his lot took them."[1]

Year	Event
1511–1512	Diego Velázquez employs black auxiliaries in conquest of Cuba
1513	Ponce de León lands in Florida
1516	Bartolomé de Las Casas encourages Spanish to replace Indian slaves with Africans
1518	First Africans arrive in Mexico with Hernán Cortés
1519	Ferdinand Magellan sets off to sail around world
1519–1521	Cortés conquers Aztecs
1532–1535	Francisco Pizarro conquers Peru, vanquishes Incas
1539	Hernando de Soto explores southeastern North America
1540	Francisco Vásquez de Coronado explores Southwest and Great Plains
1542	Spanish government bans enslavement of Indian peoples within its territories
1550	First slave ship lands in Brazil
1565	Spanish Florida founded
1587	Sir Walter Raleigh establishes Roanoke, first English settlement in New World
1608	French explorer Samuel de Champlain establishes Quebec
1756	Olaudah Equiano kidnapped and sold into slavery
1788	British government restricts number of slaves British ships may carry
1797	Slave women steal weapons in insurrection aboard British ship *Thomas*
1808	United States withdraws from international slave trade

3

The scene marked the beginning of an African **diaspora**, or mass dispersion of a people from their homeland, that would carry millions of Africans across the ocean in slavery under European and Euro-American masters. Although Goncalvez's captives would land in Portugal, most of this slave trade's captives ended up much farther away. With European settlement of the New World in the 1500s, a highly profitable exchange of goods and enslaved labor began to take shape between Europe, Africa, and the New World. Now known as the transatlantic slave trade, this expansive commercial enterprise involved a triangle trade: European merchants exchanged manufactured goods for enslaved Africans, shipped the slaves to the Americas to exchange for New World commodities, and used those materials to manufacture more European goods.

This immensely lucrative trade transformed both Africa and the American colonies. Although a long-standing internal slave trade had existed in West Africa prior to the arrival of Europeans, the new triangle trade both exploited and expanded it, ultimately leaving many parts of the region depopulated. Moreover, the transatlantic slave trade forever changed the lives of the millions of Africans it dispersed. Most captives hailed from vibrant West African communities that had had little contact with Europe prior to the rise of the slave trade, and most were enslaved before they ever left Africa. Once early European slave traders began to meet with armed resistance from the peoples who lived on the West African coast, they quickly turned to African traders to supply them with slaves.

Although the men, women, and children they purchased were not free in Africa, once they were swept into the transatlantic slave trade, these diasporic Africans would encounter a new kind of slavery. Crowded aboard slave ships for the long and often lethal voyage to the New World, the Africans who ended up in the Americas entered a system of bondage unlike anything that existed in Africa. Whereas slavery in Africa was often temporary and rarely heritable, in the Americas slavery was lifelong and passed from parent to child. Thus for those who survived, the transatlantic voyage marked the beginning of a captivity that would pass from one generation to the next.

Dispersed across the Americas, these slaves set about rebuilding their lives and creating new communities. As members of many different ethnic and linguistic groups, the slave trade's victims came from a variety of villages and kingdoms. Few, if any, of them thought of themselves as *Africans* when they first boarded the slave ships. Only in the Americas would they take on a collective identity imposed on them by slavery, forced migration, and the strange new world in which they found themselves.

African Origins

The ancestry of African Americans can be traced to the beginning of human history. Scientists believe that Africa was home to the ancient ancestors of all human beings, who first originated in East Africa more than a million years ago. Africa's long history witnessed the emergence of human agriculture and the rise and fall of vast civilizations in ancient Egypt and Nubia, as well as the development of a variety of states thereafter. In the fifteenth century, when the peoples of West Africa first came into sustained contact with the explorers, merchants, and traders who launched the European settlement of the New World, their region of the African continent was largely divided into small village states and kingdoms. Consequently, they spoke many different languages, belonged to a variety of ethnic groups, and would bring to America a rich heritage of customs and cultures.

One institution these societies shared, however, was the practice of slavery. They had well-established slave trading networks, which the seafaring European traders who began doing business along Africa's Atlantic coast would be quick to exploit. Out of this exploitation would come a new form of slavery that was transatlantic in scope and brutal in nature, and that forever separated millions of enslaved Africans from their homelands.

The History of West Africa

Three times the size of Europe and almost double that of the United States, Africa, at well over 11 million square miles, is the second-largest continent on earth, after Asia. Its landmass spans four hemispheres and links the rich cultural worlds of the Mediterranean, the Middle East, and sub-Saharan Africa. Throughout the ages, Africa has been populated by a diverse array of peoples, whose cultural, ethnic, and sociological differences have been shaped by the continent's varied landscape. The world's largest desert and the world's most impenetrable rain forest, as well as nearly every other kind of natural environment, are located in Africa. The prime meridian and the equator run through the continent, which encompasses climates that range from tropical to glacial and vary dramatically even within the various regions.

Not surprisingly, given its great diversity of physical environments and long history of human settlement, Africa has been home to many different societies. Ghana, the first West African state of which there is any record, sustained a powerful empire between approximately 830 and 1230. Ghana traded with the Muslim countries of the Middle East and, with a large army, ruled over many African tribes on its borders. After Ghana's collapse in the face of invading forces and internal divisions, Mali, a state within Ghana, emerged as an imperial power and controlled a large portion of western and central Africa between roughly 1230 and 1500. Thereafter, Mali's imperial rule was largely displaced by the rise of the Songhai empire, a small kingdom that broke away from Mali in 1320. Home to flourishing economies and an active international trade, Songhai reached its peak in the late 1400s and became the last of western and central Africa's three successive empires. After its collapse in 1591, following Morocco's capture of its seats of power, the region split into many small, independent kingdoms (Map 1.1).

By the time the slave trade began in the 1440s, most of Africa was populated by many small societies of people who spoke different languages, worshipped different deities, and had diverse cultures. Most practiced one of a variety of polytheistic religions that recognized many deities and spirits, as well as a more remote, all-powerful creator. Adherents of these religions saw the force of God in all things and often invoked the spirits of their ancestors, as well as a spirit world associated with their natural surroundings. But these similar beliefs did not lead West Africans to unite around a single church or religious doctrine. West Africa was also home to a small Muslim population, which rejected these indigenous beliefs and embraced a strictly monotheistic idea of God. Islam had been brought to West Africa in the tenth and eleventh centuries by traders from North Africa and the Middle East, but prior to the eighteenth and nineteenth centuries, its followers came mainly from the region's small commercial elite.

Despite their religious and regional diversity, the West African societies that supplied the transatlantic slave trade had a number of features in common. They tended to

MAP 1.1   Africa's Diverse States and Geography, 900–1800

The world's second-largest continent after Asia, Africa is bisected by the equator and subject to a variety of very different climates. This map divides the continent into eight climatic regions that range in temperature from desert to tropical rain forest to chilly highlands. The map also illustrates the geographic location of precolonial Africa's most important empires or kingdoms, many of which extended over several of the continent's climatic zones.

be of modest size: only about 30 percent of the African continent was ruled by organized states of any size; the rest was occupied by small groups of people. Moreover, the peoples who lived on Africa's west coast had a very different relationship to the Atlantic Ocean than did the seafaring Europeans who arrived on their shores in the 1400s. Unlike Europe's west coast, West Africa's treacherous coast had never been conducive to long-distance trade and travel. A mixture of coastal swamps and rocky promontories, the coastline had few natural harbors that could accommodate large boats. African maritime tradition was largely limited to the use of dugout canoes that could be carried into the water. These shallow vessels, usually carved from a single tree trunk, required no docks and were used for fishing expeditions and other trips just outside the rough surf that made the coast so hazardous. They were better suited to inland travel on the Niger, Senegal, and Gambia Rivers than to the open seas. As a result, West Africa's inland waterways sustained extensive trade networks, with canoes carrying agricultural products, lumber, fish, and slaves.

Most of the peoples along the coast lived in villages or kingdoms united by common ancestors. Property and political leadership usually passed from generation to generation along matrilineal or patrilineal lines—from mother to daughter or father to son. The governance of larger African polities such as the kingdoms of the West African interior, which tended to be ruled by confederacies of royal families, also were based on kinship affiliations. Thus the power of African rulers was often local and limited, much of it being derived from the network of kinship ties that bound individuals to their communities. The African proverb "I am because we are, and because we are therefore I am" expresses the collective nature of African social identity.[2]

African systems of landownership were also collective rather than individual. Villages held common land whose use was administered by a local official known as the grand master of the ground. People were entitled to cultivate their ancestral homelands, but they did not own them and could not pass them on to their descendants. As a result, African societies tended to figure wealth and power not in land, but in people. In these small kinship-based societies, an abundance of people helped make ruling families powerful, as did institutions that gave rulers power over people, such as slavery.

Crowned Head of an Oni
In Africa, European explorers and slave traders found a multitude of societies with long histories and rich, complex political and cultural traditions. This West African sculpture, created between the twelfth and fifteenth centuries, depicts the crowned head of an Oni, or monarch. It originated in the Yoruba city of Ife, which was founded in the seventh century B.C.E. The monarch depicted here may have been either male or female. The lines carved into the face probably represent ritual scarification. *Museum of Ife Antiquities, Lagos, Nigeria/Photograph © Andrea Jemolo.*

William Snelgrave | The *Manner* How Those People Become Slaves, 1734

William Snelgrave's *A New Account of Some Parts of Guinea, and the Slave Trade* includes the following description of how Africans were initially enslaved and then sold into the transatlantic slave trade. Captain Snelgrave was a thirty-year veteran of slaving when he wrote this work, which describes his 1727 and 1730 voyages to the slave ports of Whydah and Jakin in the kingdom of Dahomey (in the modern-day country of Benin). At that time, more captive Africans traveling on slave ships came from this area than from any other region on the African coast.

As for the *Manner* how those People become Slaves; it may be reduced under these several Heads.

1. It has been the Custom among the *Negroes*, time out of Mind, and is so to this day, for them to make Slaves of all the Captives they take in War. Now, before they had an Opportunity of selling them to the white People, they were often obliged to kill great Multitudes, when they had taken more than they could well employ in their own Plantations, for fear that they should rebel, and endanger their Masters Safety.

2*dly.* Most Crimes amongst them are punished by Mulcts [penalties such as fines] and Fines; and if the Offender has not wherewithal to pay his Fine, he is sold for a Slave: This is the Practice of the inland People, as well as of those on the Sea side.

3*dly.* Debtors who refuse to pay their Debts, or are insolvent, are likewise liable to be made Slaves; but their Friends may redeem them: And if they are not able or willing to do it, then they are generally sold for the Benefit of their Creditors. But few of these come into the hands of the *Europeans*, being kept by their Countrymen for their own use.

4*thly.* I have been told, that it is common for some inland People, to sell their Children for Slaves, tho' they are under no necessity for so doing; which I am inclined to believe. But I never observed, that the People near the Sea Coast practice this, unless compelled thereto by extreme Want and Famine. . . .

Several Objections have often been raised against the Lawfulness of this Trade, which I shall not here undertake to refute. I shall only observe in general, That tho' to traffick in human Creatures, may at first sight appear barbarous, inhuman, and unnatural; yet the Traders herein have as much to plead in their own Excuse. . . .

First, It is evident, that abundance of Captives, taken in War, would be inhumanly destroyed, was there not an Opportunity of disposing of them to the *Europeans*. . . .

Secondly, When they are carried to the Plantations, they generally live much better there, than they ever did in their own Country. . . .

Thirdly, By this means the *English* Plantations have been so much improved, that 'tis almost incredible, what great Advantages have accrued to the Nation thereby. . . .

Continued

Continued

Then as to the Criminals amongst the *Negroes*, they are by this means effectually transported, never to return again. . . .

In a word, from this Trade proceed Benefits, far outweighing all, either real or pretended Mischiefs and Inconveniencies.

SOURCE: William Snelgrave, *A New Account of Some Parts of Guinea, and the Slave Trade* (London, 1734), 158–61.

???   **What defense does Snelgrave offer of slave traders and the practice of slave trading? Consider his argument from the perspective of an African slave in the New World. How might you refute these points?**

Slavery in West Africa

In both Europe and Africa, slavery was often a by-product of war. On both continents, slave status was traditionally assigned to war captives. Conquering peoples who enslaved their enemies acquired a valuable source of labor, concubines, and trade revenues—the last of which they could accrue by selling off their most dangerous enemies to distant lands where they would no longer pose a threat. Military conflicts could foster other types of enslavement as well. European serfs, for example, acquired their unfree status during the war-torn Middle Ages, when they placed themselves voluntarily under the control of powerful warriors who offered them protection in return for their service.

But war was not the only route to enslavement. In many West African societies, slave status was assigned to those convicted of serious crimes such as adultery, murder, or sorcery. These people were not only reduced to slavery but were usually sold away from their families as well—a harsh punishment in these kinship-based societies. Debtors were also enslaved. Some were pawns, debtors who voluntarily submitted to temporary slavery in order to pay off their debts. (See From the Record: The *Manner How Those People Become Slaves.*)

Members of most of these groups could move in and out of slavery, although not all of them succeeded in doing so. Pawns, for example, could work off their debts, while female captives of war frequently became members of their owners' families via concubinage—a form of sexual slavery that typically ended in freedom if the concubine bore a freeman's child. Two other routes out of slavery were assimilation into an owner's kinship network by marriage, and manumission—a legal process that slave owners could initiate to grant freedom to a favored slave.

Within West Africa, since slave status was rarely inherited, slavery did not create a permanent class of slaves or slave owners. Indeed, prior to the arrival of Europeans in the 1440s, slave ownership and slave trading were relatively modest sources of wealth in West African societies. West Africans sold their surplus slaves to Arab slave traders who transported them across the Sahara to North Africa, for resale in the Arab world. But the expansion of slavery within West Africa was limited by the decentralized character of the region's political regimes and its lack of commerce in slave-produced goods. Agriculture was a collective pursuit dedicated to subsistence rather than trade and did not require the harsh work regimes that would come to characterize slave labor in the New World.

Slaves in African societies were socially marginal and powerless, but there were limits to their subjugation. They were generally employed in the same agricultural and domestic work that occupied other members of the community. They also retained a number of civic rights and privileges. In most African communities, slaves were permitted to educate themselves and were generally free to marry and raise children. Slavery also varied across the region, sometimes taking the form of domestic servitude, in which female slaves predominated. Larger West African polities such as Songhai employed slave soldiers and bureaucrats, whose slave status did not keep them from becoming wealthy and powerful servants of the state.

However different African slavery was from the slavery that developed in the Americas, the fact that it was an entrenched and dynamic institution would have tragic and far-reaching consequences. The European trade with sub-Saharan Africa, which began shortly before Europeans first arrived in the New World, would create a new kind of slave trade to supply the workers needed to exploit these new lands.

The Rise of the Transatlantic Slave Trade

Although Europeans and West Africans lived on neighboring continents separated only by the societies of the Middle East, they were virtual strangers prior to the fifteenth century. Small numbers of people and small quantities of goods had moved between the two continents via overland trade networks for centuries, and North African Arabs had maintained a long-standing presence in the Middle East. But prior to the expeditions pioneered by Prince Henry, Europe and West Africa were largely sealed off from each other by massive natural barriers. The Sahara desert made overland travel between the two regions difficult and dangerous, while the powerful winds and currents off the Saharan coast had long prevented sea travel between Europe and Africa. Separated by desert and sea, West Africa and western Europe were home to two distinct societies that came together abruptly in the fifteenth century—with tragic consequences. Their encounters would foster a transatlantic trade in African peoples that would last for several hundred years and depopulate many regions of West Africa.

Europe in the Age of the Slave Trade

When the Portuguese first began raiding West Africa's sub-Saharan coast, Europe was not yet the conglomeration of powerful empires it would later become. Ruled by a variety of monarchs, city-states, and feuding nobles, European societies were larger, more far-flung, and more economically interconnected than most precolonial West African societies. But they were also divided and socially unstable. European rulers, such as the Portuguese royal family, were still in the process of inventing powerful nation-states that could maintain social order—a development that would be greatly facilitated by the exploitation of Africa and the New World.

Europeans reached these regions at a time of dramatic social and political upheaval within Europe. Powerful monarchies had risen to replace Europe's feuding nobility, and Muslim incursions into eastern Europe and the Iberian Peninsula during the Crusades had allowed ambitious monarchs to expand their influence by defending Christendom and offering their subjects a more secure and politically stable social order. These rulers created royalty-based nation-states in England, France, and Iberia, securing their influence by building powerful bureaucracies and establishing standing armies and navies. But these new state powers were expensive to maintain and difficult to protect, and to sustain their influence, rulers soon needed to explore and exploit new lands.

In Africa, European monarchs such as Prince Henry hoped to find sources of gold and other luxury goods they could use to enrich their treasuries, pay their armies, and increase the commercial power of their nations. Europeans were unfamiliar with the African coast south of Cape Bojador, a headland west of the Sahara marked by treacherous winds that prevented European sailors from traveling farther down the coast. But they hoped that in crossing the unknown lands that lay south of the Cape, they would find a direct route to the riches of the Far East.

Portugal, one of Europe's earliest nation-states, pioneered the navigation of the West African coast. As the most accomplished shipbuilders in Europe, the Portuguese were the first to develop oceangoing vessels suitable for long exploratory voyages. Called **carracks** and **caravels**, these small sailing ships had two or three masts and were powered by both triangular and square sails. An innovation borrowed from the Arab dhow, the triangular sails that graced Portuguese ships allowed them to brave strong winds and travel faster and farther than any other vessels of their day. In particular, they allowed Portuguese mariners to cut through the dangerous northeasterly winds blowing off Cape Bojador, which had long prevented European sailors from traveling farther south.

Between 1418 and the 1470s, the Portuguese launched a series of exploratory expeditions that remapped the oceans south of Portugal, charting new territories that one explorer described as "oceans where none had ever sailed before."[3] They also discovered several uninhabited islands only a few hundred miles off Africa's west coast, which they began to settle and cultivate. These islands—christened Madeira, the Azores, Arguin, the Cape Verde Islands, and São Tomé and Príncipe—provided the Portuguese a stepping-off point for expeditions farther down the coast, allowing them to reach the Cape of Good Hope in 1487.

The Atlantic slave trade first took shape in conjunction with these expeditions, as Portuguese seamen began to bring back enslaved Africans to sell both in Portugal and its Atlantic islands. Spain was also active in this early trade and established its own Atlantic colony in the Canary Islands during the fifteenth century. Located off the northwest coast of Africa, the ten islands that make up the Canaries were not as easily settled as the uninhabited islands claimed by Portugal. They were home to an indigenous people known as the **Guanches**, whose ancestors likely originated among the Berber peoples of North Africa. The Guanches fought off the Spanish from 1402, when the first Spanish expedition arrived, to the 1490s, when the last of the Guanches were finally conquered. Even before that, however, the Spanish began exploiting the islands' fertile soil and temperate weather by planting sugarcane, wheat, and other crops. The Canaries proved ideal for the production of sugar, which also flourished on the Portuguese islands of Madeira and São Tomé.

Sugarcane, a valuable crop previously grown primarily in Cyprus, Sicily, and parts of southern Spain, demanded far more labor than the islands' small Guanche population could provide. First cultivated in the Pacific Rim more than 10,000 years ago, sugar was introduced to Europe in the eleventh century and became an immediate hit. It was in demand among cooks as a spice, sweetener, and preservative and was used by physicians and pharmacists as a remedy for disorders of the blood, stomach, and lungs.

As a crop requiring both warm weather and intensive labor, however, sugar was in short supply in Europe. In the Mediterranean, sugarcane was cultivated on large plantations by enslaved workers from Russia and the Balkans—traditional sources of European forced labor. But with the emergence of Portuguese and Spanish colonies in the Atlantic, this plantation system moved offshore and became increasingly dependent on the labor of enslaved Africans. By the 1490s, Madeira was the largest European sugar producer. In the sixteenth century, sugar boomed in the Azores, the Canaries, Cape Verde, and São Tomé—all of which required imported laborers.

Despite the successful slave raids that took place on some of the earliest Portuguese expeditions to Africa, kidnappings would not remain the means by which the Portuguese secured these laborers. After the early raids, West African rulers quickly organized to defend their coast. By the 1450s, Portuguese slaving expeditions along the Senegambian and Gambian coast were driven offshore by fleets of African canoe men armed with arrows and javelins. Although these African canoes lacked the firepower of the caravels, which were equipped with cannons, they could easily outmaneuver the much larger European vessels, and the canoe men could use their weapons to pick off Europeans who attempted to land. After 1456, the Portuguese crown began negotiating commercial treaties with West African rulers, who agreed to supply them with slaves in return for European goods. Thus the slave trade first emerged as a commercial relationship between coastal peoples: African merchants tapped the internal slave trade, which had existed in Africa since ancient times, to supply European traders with thousands of slaves per year.

The Enslavement of Indigenous Peoples

If the Portuguese trade in African slaves had served only Europe, the Atlantic slave trade might well have been short-lived. Europe's population boomed in the second half of the fifteenth century, making labor abundant and slave imports unnecessary. But the cultivation of Europe's Atlantic colonies created an additional labor market, which was soon complemented by similar markets in the Americas. Indeed, the first Africans arrived in the Americas either with or shortly after Columbus, who may have employed African seamen on some of his voyages. As Spaniards began to populate Hispaniola— the colony Columbus established in 1492 on the island that is now divided between Haiti and the Dominican Republic—African slaves joined them. Nicolás de Ovando, a Spanish soldier who replaced Columbus as governor of Hispaniola in 1502, brought several Iberian-born black slaves, who he hoped would both provide labor and help subdue Hispaniola's indigenous population. His hopes evidently disappointed, Ovando banned the further importation of blacks shortly thereafter, "on the grounds that they incited native rebellion."[4] But Spain's New World colonies would prove far too hungry for labor for any such ban to persist.

African workers were first used in the copper and gold mines of Hispaniola, which resumed importing them in 1505. They were needed there because Spanish attempts to exploit the labor of the island's native inhabitants, the **Taino Indians**, had met with limited success. During the first few decades of Spanish settlement, the conquistadors were able to extract forced labor from the Indians under the *encomienda* system, which permitted the Spaniards to collect tribute—in the form of labor, gold, or other goods—from the native peoples they controlled. The colonists demanded both labor and gold from the Tainos, whom they put to work mining the island's rivers and streams. But the Indians did not flourish under Spanish rule.

Some resisted working for the Spaniards and were slaughtered by them, while many more succumbed to the Old World diseases that the Spanish interlopers carried with them. Not having been exposed to common European illnesses such as influenza, smallpox, chicken pox, mumps, and measles, the Tainos possessed no resistance to these diseases and began to die in droves. By the first decade of the sixteenth century, their population had dropped from 500,000 to 60,000; by 1514 it was down to 28,000; and by 1542 there were only a few hundred Tainos left on the island.

The rapid decline of the native population in Hispaniola was repeated throughout the Americas and set the stage for the development of the transatlantic slave trade. With their settlements triggering large population losses among the hemisphere's indigenous peoples, European colonists had to look elsewhere for workers. Not surprisingly, they turned to the African slave trade to supply their needs. African slavery was already an established enterprise, offered an almost limitless supply of workers, and had several advantages over Indian slavery. Most important among them was that African peoples, who lived in the same hemisphere as the Europeans, had some immunity to Old World diseases. Moreover, African laborers were strangers to the New World, which made them more manageable than the region's native populations. Unfamiliar with the local peoples and surrounding terrain, they could not easily escape their confinement.

African slavery was also sanctioned by the Catholic Church, while the enslavement of Indians was more controversial. The Old World practice of African enslavement had received explicit license in a papal bull (formal proclamation) issued by Pope Nicholas V in 1452. Titled *Dum Diversas*, this proclamation granted the kings of Spain and Portugal permission "to invade, search out, capture, vanquish, and subdue all the Saracens [Muslims] and pagans . . . and other enemies of Christ wheresoever placed," as well as "their kingdoms, duchies, counties, principalities, [and other] possessions . . . and to reduce their persons into perpetual slavery."[5]

Issued before Columbus's voyages, *Dum Diversas* was designed to sanction European attacks on the Islamic societies of North Africa and the Middle East. It did not address the Spanish enslavement of indigenous peoples of the Americas. Troubled by Spanish mistreatment of these peoples, Dominican missionaries were quick to challenge the legitimacy of Native American slavery. "Tell me by what right of justice do you hold these Indians in such a cruel and horrible servitude?" Antonio de Montesinos, a Dominican priest stationed on Hispaniola, asked in a sermon delivered in 1511. "Why do you keep them so oppressed and exhausted, without giving them enough to eat or curing them of the sicknesses they incur from the excessive labor you give them, and they die, or rather you kill them, in order to extract and acquire gold every day."[6]

His critique was taken up by other Dominicans, most notably Bartolomé de Las Casas, who pressured both the Spanish crown and the pope to protect the Indians. Concerned about their rapidly declining populations, Las Casas, starting in 1516, encouraged the Spanish to replace Indian slaves with those imported from Africa—a position he later came to regret. He was not then aware, he explained in 1560, of "how unjustly and tyrannically Africans were taken as slaves, in the same fashion as Indians."[7]

How much Las Casas could have done to curb African slavery had he come to this realization earlier remains an open question. But as it was, his campaign put Indian rather than African slavery under contention. In 1537, Pope Paul III issued another

Black Conquistadors
Some of the first Africans in the Americas arrived with Spanish military expeditions. In Mexico, Africans initially came with Hernán Cortés, whose forces included the free black conquistador Juan Garrido. In this illustration from a sixteenth-century manuscript, Cortés is depicted meeting the Indians of the Tlaxcala region. Garrido is pictured at the far left. *Bibliothèque Nationale, Paris, France/ Scala/White Images/Art Resource, NY.*

papal bull declaring that the Indians were rational beings who should be converted rather than enslaved, and in 1542 the Spanish government banned the enslavement of Indians within its territories. Although both rulings were largely ignored by colonists and ineffective in curbing the abuses of the encomienda system, they facilitated the transatlantic slave trade's expansion, which took shape alongside European settlement of the New World and displacement of the region's indigenous peoples. (See Visual Sources: European Images of Africans in the Era of the Slave Trade, pp. 43–52.)

The First Africans in the Americas

Roughly 300,000 Africans landed in the Americas before 1620. Most came after 1550, when their numbers began to exceed those of Portuguese and Spanish migrants. By then, the Spanish conquest of the Americas had extended to include the islands of Puerto Rico, Cuba, Guadeloupe, Trinidad, and Jamaica, as well as the mainland regions of Mexico and Peru, while the Portuguese had laid claim to Brazil. Enslaved Africans supplied labor for all these colonies. The Africans' presence expanded outward from Hispaniola, which served as the staging ground for further Spanish incursions into the New World. There they worked on sugar plantations after the island's small store of precious metals had been tapped out and accompanied the Spanish on military

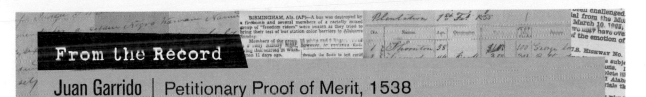

From the Record

Juan Garrido | Petitionary Proof of Merit, 1538

Among the earliest Africans in the Americas, **Juan Garrido (1487–1547)** was born in West Africa and spent some years in Lisbon before traveling to Santo Domingo in the early 1500s. As a freeman, he joined the Spanish auxiliary forces that helped invade and capture Puerto Rico and Cuba and accompanied Hernán Cortés to Mexico. Here he describes his career as a conquistador in a 1538 *probanza* (petition) for a military pension.

I, Juan Garrido, black resident . . . of this city [Mexico], appear before Your Mercy and state that I am in need of making a *probanza* to the perpetuity of the king . . . , a report on how I served Your Majesty in the conquest and pacification of this New Spain, from the time when the Marqués del Valle [Cortés] entered it; and in his company I was present at all the invasions and conquests and pacifications which were carried out, always with the said Marqués, all of which I did at my own expense without being given either salary or allotment of natives . . . or anything else. As I am married and a resident of this city, where I have always lived; and also as I went with the Marqués del Valle to discover the islands which are in that part of the southern sea [the Pacific] where there was much hunger and privation; and also as I went to discover and pacify the islands of San Juan de Buriquén de Puerto Rico; and also as I went on the pacification and conquest of the island of Cuba with the *adelantado* Diego Velázquez; in all these ways for thirty years have I served and continue to serve Your Majesty—for these reasons stated above do I petition Your Mercy. And also because I was the first to have the inspiration to sow maize here in New Spain and to see if it took; I did this and experimented at my own expense.

SOURCE: Matthew Restall, "Black Conquistadors: Armed Africans in Early Spanish America," *Americas* 57, no. 2 (October 2000): 171.

???   **What arguments does Garrido present to make his case? What does his account reveal about the Spanish treatment of black conquistadors?**

---

expeditions. The Spanish explorer Juan Ponce de León employed armed Africans to supplement his forces when he invaded Puerto Rico in 1508, while Diego Velázquez used black auxiliaries in his 1511–1512 conquest of Cuba. Likewise, the first Africans to arrive in Mexico accompanied Hernán Cortés, who in 1519–1521 conquered the Aztecs with a force that included Juan Garrido, a free black conquistador, who had fought with Ponce de León. (See From the Record: Petitionary Proof of Merit.)

Like Juan Garrido, many of the earliest Africans in the New World were *ladinos*, latinized blacks who hailed from Spain or Portugal, or from those countries' Atlantic or American colonies. Already acculturated to European ways, ladinos spoke Spanish or Portuguese and had no sympathy with the indigenous peoples of the Americas. Such attributes made them useful as domestic servants as well. Many European migrants to New Spain and Brazil brought black or mulatto (mixed-race) servants with them when they first settled these regions. The Spanish colonists began replacing their declining supply of indigenous laborers with slaves imported directly from Africa as early as 1518, and the first slave ship arrived in Portuguese Brazil in 1550.

Known in New Spain as *bozales*, these African-born slaves quickly accounted for the majority of the New World's slaves. They were also the most downtrodden, forced to do the dirtiest, most dangerous, and most demanding work. Employed to extract the silver and gold the Spanish found in Mexico and Peru, they toiled in underground tunnels that sometimes collapsed on top of them and acquired lung disease from the toxic mineral dust. Diving for pearls off the coast of Veracruz, Mexico, Africans drowned in such numbers that their bodies attracted sharks. Some worked on sugar plantations, typically laboring from dawn until dusk planting, harvesting, and refining sugar. In particular, they suffered high mortality rates due to the long hours and hazards involved in boiling the cane at high temperatures to produce sugar. The cultivation of sugarcane, one of the earliest slave-grown crops, was first introduced on Hispaniola and eventually spread throughout the Caribbean. But the largest sixteenth-century sugar producers were Brazil and Mexico, which imported tens of thousands of Africans to plant and process sugar during this period.

The demand for such labor would only increase over time, giving rise to an international slave trade that would last more than three centuries and carry approximately 12.5 million slaves to the New World. The African American population of the Americas took shape around these forced migrations.

The Business of Slave Trading

By the beginning of the seventeenth century, the Spanish and Portuguese had begun to lose their monopoly of the exploration and settlement of the New World. Drawn by the riches that their predecessors had extracted from these lands, other European powers such as the Dutch, English, and French began to claim territory in the Americas. They also followed the example set by the Spanish and Portuguese when it came to importing enslaved Africans to help build and sustain their New World settlements.

As a result, the transatlantic slave trade expanded rapidly. Average annual slave exports from Africa increased from a little over ten thousand slaves at the beginning of the seventeenth century to nearly sixty thousand by the eighteenth century. The transatlantic trade exploited and expanded upon the existing internal slave trade in Africa, pitting African leaders against one another and making the capture and enslavement of prisoners of war more profitable than ever before. Europeans also expanded the trade by traversing larger stretches of the African coast. Whereas early European traders sought their cargo largely along the Senegambian coast, the trade eventually extended south to include Guinea-Bissau, the Gold Coast, Benin, Kongo, and Angola. Some traders even did business with the East African country of Mozambique. The captives brought to these places were drawn from an expansive interior trade that extended into west-central Africa and as far east as Madagascar (Map 1.2).

For Europeans, the slave trade remained a coastal exchange that took place largely in their West African trading centers. The earliest such center was the **Elmina Castle** on the western coast of Ghana. Built as a Portuguese trading post in 1482, Elmina—the first of several forts the European powers established on the West African coast—began, by the early seventeenth century, to serve a far more enduring trade in human beings. Like later

MAP 1.2   Slave Origins and Destinations, 1501–1867

This map of the transatlantic slave trade illustrates the many routes that slave traders used to
carry millions of enslaved Africans to the Americas between 1501 and 1867. It also documents
the trading routes that took much smaller numbers of African captives to Europe and the Middle
East during this period.

European trading forts, it had been erected with the agreement or license of local rulers in exchange for access to European commodities and military support. The castles on present-day Ghana's Gold Coast offered European merchants a secure harbor for their vessels and access to African markets trading in goods as well as people. Controlled by the Dutch after 1637, the Elmina Castle remained an active slave trading post until the Dutch withdrew from the trade in 1814.

The Portuguese controlled the early transatlantic slave trade by virtue of the 1494 Treaty of Tordesillas—an agreement between Spain and Portugal granting the Western Hemisphere to Spain, and Africa and Asia to Portugal. The earliest African slaves were shipped to the New World from Lisbon and other European ports, but direct trade between Africa and European colonies in the New World began in the early 1500s under Spain's *asiento* system. Initially, the Spanish crown both regulated the slave trade and secured a portion of its profits by selling asientos (agreements) permitting individual Portuguese merchants to sell slaves in Spain's New World colonies. But as the Portuguese trade with New Spain expanded, so too did the asiento system. In 1595 Spain issued a new kind of asiento, which gave Portugal a monopoly over the transatlantic slave trade and authorized Portuguese merchants to ship enslaved Africans directly from Africa to New Spain. After Spain and Portugal became enemies in the 1640s, the Spanish transferred their business first to the Dutch and then to the British, who dominated the eighteenth-century transatlantic trade.

European slave ships carried on a **triangle trade** that began with the transport of European copper, beads, guns, ammunition, textiles, and other manufactured goods to the West African coast. After these goods were exchanged for slaves, the second leg of the triangle trade—which slave traders called the Middle Passage—began. During this most infamous and dangerous phase, slave ships transported enslaved blacks from the West African coast to the slave ports of the New World. The ships then returned to their European ports of origin laden with profitable slave-grown crops, including sugar, tobacco, rice, indigo, and later cotton (Map 1.3). This trade fueled the economic development of Europe, supplying much of the raw material and capital that propelled European powers into the industrial age. The trade was equally crucial to the economic growth of the Americas, supplying European colonists with much of the labor they needed to make the New World settlements profitable.

For Africans, however, the trade was largely tragic. Although African slave traders profited from it, most of the continent's inhabitants did not. By the early nineteenth century, Britain and other imperial powers had begun to withdraw from the slave trade—a process that started with Britain's ban on the trade in 1807 and United States' Act Prohibiting the Importing of Slaves, which took effect in 1808. Nevertheless, several hundred years of forced migration had taken a severe toll on Africa and its peoples. Generations of young people had been lost, many of them perishing as a result of the trade. The transatlantic slave trade also imposed almost unimaginable suffering on the millions of individual Africans who survived their capture and sale. (See Documents: Inside the Slave Trade, pp. 32–37.)

The Long Middle Passage

For African captives, the journey into slavery began long before they saw a European ship. Most came from regions outside the West African coast. The African communities that surrounded the European slave trading settlements rarely sold their own

MAP 1.3   The Triangle Trade

The transatlantic slave trade is known as a triangle trade because it took shape around an exchange of goods that involved ports in three different parts of the world. As illustrated in this map,
the first leg of the trade took traders from Europe to Africa, where they exchanged manufactured
goods such as cloth, copper, beads, guns, and ammunition for enslaved Africans, whom they then
sold to buyers in American ports in return for commodities such as sugar, tobacco, and cotton.

people into slavery. The trade was an African enterprise until it reached the coast; only
in Angola were Europeans ever really involved in capturing slaves themselves. Instead,
African traders acquired slaves by way of an increasingly far-flung network that extended through much of western and west-central Africa.

Separated from their families and cultures, captives endured a long trek to the coast, where they were often imprisoned for months before embarking on the horrifying transatlantic voyage. Underfed and brutally treated throughout their journey, some captives died before ever leaving Africa. Still more perished aboard the slave ships, where they were confined in filthy, overcrowded conditions. But others survived, and some even resisted their circumstances by engaging in revolts and other subversive acts on board ship. Whatever the circumstances, the transatlantic slave trade had tragic consequences and lasting effects for both the Africans who remained at home and those who endured the forced migration abroad.

Capture and Confinement

The transatlantic slave trade was a dirty and dangerous business for everyone involved. It began in the interior of Africa, where African traders purchased slaves and marched them to the coast. In addition to prisoners of war, the enslaved Africans included individuals who were kidnapped from their homes by African slave raiders. Children were especially vulnerable to such raids, as illustrated in the story of Olaudah Equiano. Born around 1745, Equiano was eleven years old when he and his sister were taken from their family compound by "robbers," who carried them off on a journey that lasted many days.[8] The children of an Igbo village leader in the kingdom of Benin, Equiano and his sister were separated long before they reached the West African coast. Like many enslaved Africans, Equiano was sold several times by African traders before he ended up in the hands of European traders on the coast.

Equiano and other African captives reached the coast by way of a long overland trek of up to a thousand miles, which often took them through parts of Africa they had never seen. Usually poorly fed and harshly treated during the journey, they marched in **coffles**, or chained groups, bound together to prevent escape. The slave traders secured the coffles using a variety of brutal restraints that included sets of iron collars and chains that strung the slaves together, as well as interconnected wooden yokes that served a similar purpose. In addition to wearing these restraints, members of the coffles were often forced to work as porters for the traders, carrying loads of food and other goods. Those who were not up to the rigors of the journey were whipped and dragged along, and captives too weak to continue were left to die by the road. (See From the Record: A Description of the Bonds Used to Control Slave Coffles.)

As many as one in ten of the captured Africans died before they reached the coast, where new dangers awaited the survivors. On the final leg of the forced march, many captives saw the ocean for the first time and had to brace themselves for a journey into the unknown. Thirteen-year-old Samuel Ajayi Crowther, who was kidnapped from his Oyo County home (in modern-day Nigeria) nearly a century after Olaudah Equiano entered the trade, had never seen a river before reaching the inland tributary where his captors loaded him on a canoe bound for Lagos, Nigeria, which was then a major slave trading port. He had originally planned to drown himself rather than be sold to the Portuguese, but he was far too frightened of the river to do so. "I had never seen anything like it in my life," he later recalled. "Nothing now terrified me more than the river and the thought of going into another world. . . . During the whole night's voyage on the canoe, not a single thought of leaping into the river had entered my mind, but on the contrary the fear of the river occupied my thoughts."[9]

Chaine d'esclaves venant de l'intérieure.

Slave Coffles and Leg Irons
In the top engraving, traders lead a slave coffle to the West African coast. The slaves are nude and bound together at the neck. Armed, fully clothed traders are positioned at the head and the end of the coffle. The bottom photograph depicts some eighteenth- and nineteenth-century slave fetters and shackles. Made of iron, these brutal restraints provided a variety of ways to secure captives and prevent escapes or rebellions during the long trek to the coast.
Top: From L'Afrique, by R. Geoffrey, 1814/Bibliothèque de L'Arsenal, Paris, France/Archives Charmet/The Bridgeman Art Library International; Bottom: The Granger Collection, NYC. All rights reserved.

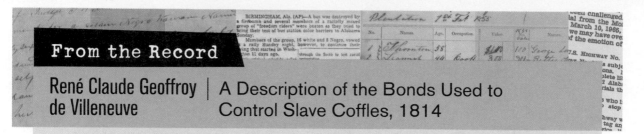

From the Record

René Claude Geoffroy de Villeneuve | A Description of the Bonds Used to Control Slave Coffles, 1814

Discussions of the mechanics of the slave trade from before 1650 are rare, but one eighteenth-century observer reported in graphic terms the brutal hardware developed to control the slave coffles. In this document, the French author **René Claude Geoffroy de Villeneuve**, who lived in Senegal during the 1780s, describes the restraints that Mandingo traders often used.

[They used] iron bolts of 15 to 18 inches long [to connect] pieces of a heavy wood, around 5 or 6 feet long, forked at one end so that the forked end can fit around the slave's neck. The two ends of the forked branch are drilled/pierced so as to permit the iron bolt, held at one end by a head, and fixed to the other end by a flexible iron blade [which passes] through a hole in the bolt. . . . When all the slaves are run through in this fashion and the traders want to start the march to the coast, they arrange the captives in a single file. One of the traders puts himself at the head of the line, loading on his shoulder the handle of the forked branch of the first black; each slave carries on his shoulder the handle of the forked branch of the person behind him. . . . During the entire route, the fork is never removed from the slaves' necks. . . . It is thus that five or six armed traders, without fear, can succeed in conveying coffles of 50 slaves, and even more, from the interior to the European coastal factory.

SOURCE: René Claude Geoffroy de Villeneuve, *L'Afrique, ou histoire, moeurs, usages et coutumes des africains: Le Sénégal* (1814), quoted in "Mandingo Slave Traders and Coffle, Senegal, 1780s," trans. Jerome S. Handler and Michael L. Tuite Jr., *The Atlantic Slave Trade and Slave Life in the Americas: A Visual Record*, http://hitchcock.itc .virginia.edu/Slavery/details.php?categorynum=3&categoryName=&theRecord=41&recordCount=43.

???   **What do the coffles and the restraints used to control them suggest about the nature of the slave trade?**

New terrors confronted the African prisoners when they reached the coast, where they were held in **barracoons**, or temporary barracks. Some barracoons were little more than exposed pens built near the European trading forts, while others were sturdier structures deep inside the forts themselves. Debilitated by the long journey, some captives succumbed to infections they developed after being exposed to European diseases for the first time. Whether confined in pens or in the dank dungeons below one of the coastal castles, the captives who survived were then put on display before African and European traders, who stripped them naked and inspected every inch of their bodies. The Portuguese were especially picky buyers, sometimes spending up to four hours scrutinizing the captives. They would sniff each captive's throat and make each

Slave Barracoon
Slaves who survived the trip to the coast found their temporary homes in barracoons, or holding areas. This engraving depicts a slave barracoon in nineteenth-century Sierra Leone. Like many barracoons, it was little more than a wooden cage with a thatched roof that left its inhabitants exposed to the elements. Slaves are lined up along the sides of the enclosure. Several guards preside outside, and one slave is getting whipped. Many slave captives died in barracoons, some as a consequence of the hardships they experienced on their journeys and some as a result of their lethal exposure to European diseases to which they had limited immunity. *The Granger Collection, NYC. All rights reserved.*

one laugh and sing to ensure that his or her lungs were sound. They also would attempt to guess each male captive's age by licking or rubbing his chin to measure the amount of facial hair.

These inspections determined which captives would be marketed to the European and American slave ships that cruised the West African coast. Certain types of slaves were unlikely to attract European buyers and were resold on the African market instead. John Barbot, an agent for the French Royal Africa Company, noted that European traders were usually willing to buy only young and relatively healthy slaves: They "rejected those above thirty-five years of age, or defective in their limbs, eyes or teeth; or grown grey, or that have the venereal disease, or any other imperfection." According to Barbot, captives who were unlucky enough to meet these requirements were "marked on the breast, with a red-hot iron, imprinting the mark of the French, English, or Dutch companies, that so each nation may distinguish their own, and to prevent their being chang'd by the natives for worse, as they are apt enough to do. In this particular, care is taken that the women, as tenderest, be not burnt too hard."[10]

Life in the barracoons was another horror of the long Middle Passage. Fed only enough to keep them alive, the captives were typically confined on the coast for several months as the traders awaited European buyers. Often stripped of their clothes, they lived in quarters that became ever more crowded as the traders accumulated potential cargo. Those in the outdoor pens escaped the elements only at night, when they were locked in filthy cells, without even a fire for warmth. The barracoons had no toilets or other facilities for human waste, so the captives also had to live with their own excrement, which covered the ground of the pens.

The slaves confined in the underground dungeons of the slave castles suffered a different but equally horrifying confinement. The imposing Cape Coast Castle—a magnificent triangular fortress, protected and adorned by elegantly designed turrets and other fortifications—housed the British merchants who lived and worked in the airy chambers located on the castle's upper floors. All but invisible then (and now) were the castle's slave quarters, which were located beneath the ground—and barely above the water. This dank "slave hole," divided into three vaulted cellars, was used to house as many as one thousand captives at a time. Carved into the rocky cliffs that supplied the castle's foundation, the slave hole was designed to protect the rest of the garrison from slave insurrections and to prepare the captives for the darkness into which they would descend once they boarded the slave ships. Shackled and confined underground, the victims were cut off from the world just as they would be in the slave ships' holds. Packed in dark, windowless rooms that received air only through narrow vents cut into the ceilings, they had little to do but listen to the ocean's waves crash against the rocks and anticipate the next stage of their journey.

The overland trek and the harsh living conditions in the barracoons killed as many as 10 percent of the captives—a figure often left unmentioned in mortality statistics. In 1684, one official at the Cape Coast Castle matter-of-factly noted that "Sundry of our slaves being lately dead and others falling sick daily makes me get to think that they are to[o] much crowded in their lodging and besides have not the benefit of Air."[11]

If they were healthy enough to do so, some captives tried to escape, but their attempts met with limited success. By the time they reached the barracoons, most of them were already far from home and could not rely on local people to shelter them even if they somehow managed to escape confinement. The towns that grew up around European settlements such as the Elmina Castle and Cape Coast Castle were populated by Africans who made their living off the slave trade and would likely return runaways to their European owners for a small fee. Fugitives who eluded immediate capture risked being reenslaved and even resold by other coastal Africans, who saw them as commodities rather than countrymen.

On the Slave Coast

The slave castles and barracoons offered little hope for successful escape. Once purchased, the slaves in the barracoons usually parted company with the African middle men and were paddled out to new prisons aboard the slave ships. Those confined in slave castles such as Elmina, the home of the famous "door of no return," exited their dungeons through doors that opened to the sea. Olaudah Equiano was terrified when he boarded the slave ship and saw its captain and crew, who he thought might have "no country, but . . . this *hollow* place." The white men and their vessel were unlike anything he had seen before, and he was convinced that he "had gotten into a world of bad spirits, and that they were going to kill me."[12]

Although Equiano was only eleven when he was kidnapped, this fear and confusion struck captives of all ages. A Muslim ironworker named Mahommah G. Baquaqua, who was kidnapped from his home as an adult in Benin almost a century later, was equally disoriented. "I had never seen a ship before," he recalled, and "my idea of it was that it was some sort of object of worship of the white man. I imagined that we were all to be slaughtered, and were being led there for that purpose."[13]

With no knowledge of the New World or the brutal **cash crop** agriculture that drove white men to travel the West African coast in search of slaves, many African captives suspected the slave traders of being cannibals who had already consumed their own people and were in search of more human flesh. African fears of cannibalism were so widespread that Portuguese slave ship owners instructed their captains to avoid letting the captives see the large metal cauldrons used to cook food, lest the Africans become convinced that they were to be boiled alive. Such fears were an expression of traditional African anxieties about dangerous foreign peoples, which often centered on fears of cannibalism. But they also speak to the social dislocation resulting from the slave trade, which produced suffering so great that some Africans associated the trade with man-eating witches or sorcerers. What else, they thought, could account for the social and physical traumas of the barracoons, or the mysterious and demoralizing future that faced the captives once they boarded the slave ships?

The ships' captains and crews had their own reasons to feel uneasy as long as their ships lingered on the West African coast. Although the captains were sometimes under instructions to bring back cargoes of slaves from specific areas, or specific proportions of men and women, they were anxious to load their ships with a full complement of marketable slaves healthy enough to survive the ocean voyage. Unless they could

Slaves on the Coast
In this eighteenth-century engraving, anguished Africans prepare to board a slave ship. Europeans were relieved to leave the coast and the many dangers it held, but their captives found themselves in a terrifying, alien world. Africans who had never before seen a ship did not know what to make of it, or of their strange new captors and the conditions under which they had been torn from their communities and their homelands. Many African slaves who left personal narratives, such as Olaudah Equiano, recalled the moment pictured here—as slaves catch their first glimpse of the imposing ship—as one filled with panic. They could not know the new horrors, psychological and physical, that awaited them on board. © *Roger-Viollet/The Image Works.*

secure a complete cargo of salable slaves at the first barracoon they visited—which was often not the case—they had to travel from port to port for several weeks, collecting human cargo along the way.

For the slave ships' largely European seamen, these sojourns along the coast were among the most dangerous phases of the triangle trade. Exposed to tropical fevers, they worried about falling sick, especially since their proximity to the coast created other hazards that required strength and awareness. While anchored in the deep waters off the coast, slave ships were targets for marauding pirates and the naval ships of hostile European powers. Slave ships anchored close to shore were sometimes attacked by African forces that accused them of kidnapping free Africans.

But internal mutiny was the slave traders' paramount concern. As long as the mainland remained in view, their terrified captives had one last hope of escape. During the dangerous days and weeks of travel along the coast, slave resistance had to be contained through the use of physical restraints that kept the captives all but immobilized in the holds of the ships. "There is put aboard . . . 30 paire of shackles and boults for such of your negers as are rebellious and we pray you be veary careful to keepe them under . . . that they ryse not against you as they have done in other ships," the Guinea Company advised the slave trader Bartholomew Hayward in 1651.[14]

Iron hand and leg cuffs known as **bilboes**, among the central tools of the trade, were always in short supply. Used primarily on male slaves, bilboes consisted of two iron shackles locked on a post and usually fastened around the ankles of two men. Joined in this way, the captives were hobbled like competitors in some macabre three-legged race. In the packed hold of a slave ship, the bilboes' heavy iron bars all but immobilized both men, making any attempt to rebel or swim to shore impossible—although they did not prevent some from throwing themselves overboard, shackles and all. Similarly, throughout the voyage, the captives required careful supervision, since suicides and other deaths caused by depression were not uncommon.

Inside the Slave Ship

Once they had gathered their cargo and caught favorable winds, the slave ship's captain and crew were happy to leave the African coast behind. The journey from Guinea to Caribbean island ports, which were generally the first stop for slave ships bound for North America, lasted fifty to ninety days. Portuguese slave ships could traverse the ocean between Angola and Brazil in thirty to sixty days. Sailing times varied based on weather, ocean currents, and the size of the ship. Advances in shipbuilding and navigation resulted in shorter crossing times.

The worst part of the long Middle Passage began as men, women, and children were packed, nearly naked, into ships designed to accommodate the maximum number of slaves in the least amount of space. Slave ships varied in size from 11-ton sloops that could accommodate only thirty slaves to 566-ton behemoths that carried up to seven hundred captives.[15] Throughout the slave trade's history, these were the most crowded oceangoing vessels in the Atlantic world.[16] By the time they were fully loaded, most ships were overflowing with naked Africans. There was some debate among shipowners over the virtues of **tight packing**, to maximize profits by packing the ship to capacity, versus "loose packing," in hopes that a slightly smaller cargo would reduce the

The Middle Passage
Slaves belowdecks lived for months in conditions of squalor and indescribable horror.
Ill health and impossibly close quarters were a perfect breeding ground for contagious
diseases. Mortality rates were high, and death made conditions belowdecks even
worse. Although the corpses of the dead were eventually thrown overboard, crew
members avoided the ship's hold, so slaves who had succumbed to sickness were not
always discovered immediately. Living slaves could remain shackled to the dead for
hours and sometimes days. *The Art Archive at Art Resource, NY.*

death rate. However, prior to 1788, when the British government restricted the number
of slaves British ships could carry, slave traders generally loaded as many slaves as they
could fit on their ships.

Throughout the slave trade, men outnumbered women by a ratio of roughly 2:1,
while children under age fifteen became increasingly common over time, probably as a
result of changes in the internal African slave trade. Before 1700, children accounted
for roughly 12 percent of slave ships' cargo, but by 1810 the proportion had risen to an
average of 46 percent. The women and children on board slave ships did not constitute
family groupings. As was the case with Olaudah Equiano and his sister, enslaved family
members were often separated long before they boarded the ships, and once aboard
the captives were segregated by gender.

Male slaves were generally kept in the ship's hold, where they experienced the
worst of the crowding. They were shackled together during much of the voyage and
often accommodated one on top of another on crudely constructed bunks, like "rows
of books on shelves."[17] The captives stationed on the floor beneath low-lying bunks
could barely move and spent much of the voyage pinned to the floorboards, which
could, over time, wear the skin on their elbows down to the bone.

The men belowdecks were the biggest worry. Mutinies were not uncommon
aboard slave ships, and male slaves were most likely to mutiny when they were on deck.

To protect themselves from their cargo, crews were often twice as large as usual. Armed crew members closely watched the shackled men whenever they were brought on deck, which was normally for only a few hours each day, primarily for meals, exercise, makeshift saltwater baths, and medical inspections. During rough or rainy weather, they stayed below all day.

During their time on deck, the captives also received exercise through a practice called "dancing the slaves." The crew forced the slaves, under close supervision, to jump or dance as best they could in their leg irons, while one of them played a drum or an African banjo, or a sailor played the bagpipes. Exercise was not optional. "If they go about it reluctantly or do not move with agility," one eighteenth-century ship surgeon observed, "they are flogged; a person standing by them all the time with a cat-o'-nine-tails in his hands for the purpose."[18]

Women and children, by contrast, were usually housed in rooms set apart from the main hold—sometimes together, sometimes separately. Generally indifferent to family ties, the slave traders honored only the relationship between infants and nursing mothers, whom they rarely separated. Regardless of where they slept, women and children—considered less dangerous than men, though they sometimes aided in slave revolts—were usually allowed to move about the ship more freely.

These arrangements also gave the seamen easy access to enslaved women, which the men regarded as one of the perks of the trade. One seaman noted that "on board some ships, the common sailors are allowed to have intercourse with such black women whose consent they can procure."[19] Other witnesses described the sexual violence inherent in such exchanges in more explicit terms. The eighteenth-century British slave trader turned abolitionist John Newton maintained that enslaved women were often "exposed to the wanton rudeness of white savages." "Naked, trembling, terrified and perhaps already exhausted with fatigue and hunger," he wrote, "the poor creatures cannot understand the language they hear, but the looks are sufficient. . . . The prey is provided on the spot and reserved till opportunity offers."[20] Though presented in an antislavery publication, Newton's description does not seem exaggerated. In a more prosaic diary entry written when he was still working in the trade, Newton recorded a sexual assault he witnessed in matter-of-fact terms: "William Cooney seduced a woman slave down into the room and lay with her brutelike in view of the whole quarter deck. . . . If anything happens to her I shall impute to him, for she is big with child. Her number is 83."[21] Likewise, witnesses such as the ex-slave Ottobah Cugoano recalled that "it was common for the dirty filthy sailors to take African women and lie upon their bodies."[22]

Such practices must have infuriated and demoralized the enslaved men confined belowdecks, as Cugoano's bitter comment suggests. But the segregation of the sexes during the Middle Passage limited interaction between African men and women. Far more mobile than men, enslaved women had better access to information on the ship's crew, fortifications, and daily routine, but little opportunity to communicate this to the men confined in the ship's hold. On the rare occasions that captive women did find ways to contact their male counterparts, they often played important roles in slave revolts. Women, for example, instigated a 1797 insurrection aboard the British ship *Thomas* by stealing weapons and passing them to the men below, and they engaged in hand-to-hand combat with slave ship crews during several other revolts.

Hardship and Misery on Board

Suicides were common both during the Middle Passage and after the captives arrived in the New World. (See Documents: The African Slave Captives, pp. 38–42.) One observer noted that captives were often "so willful and loth to leave their own country that, they have often leap'd out of canoes, boat and ship, into the sea, and kept under water till they were drowned."[23] Many were fueled by the West African religious belief that the dead join the spirits of their ancestors—a formulation that led some slave ship captains to mutilate their charges on the basis of the conviction that "many of the Blacks believe that if they are put to death and not dismembered, they shall return again to their own country, after they are thrown overboard."[24]

Suicidal thoughts among captives were no doubt influenced by depression as much as by any hope for a happier afterlife. During the ocean passage, many captives were either unwilling or unable to eat enough to stay alive, and they resisted their captors' attempts to force-feed them. The slave trader John Barbot, who considered himself "naturally compassionate," noted that he was "necessitated sometimes to cause the teeth of those wretches to be broken, because they would not open their mouths, or be prevailed upon by any entreaties to feed themselves; and thus have forced some sustenance into their throats."[25] Traders also forced slaves to exercise, which they mistakenly thought would prevent both melancholy and scurvy (a disease caused by vitamin C deficiency).

The greatest cause of death during the Middle Passage, however, was disease. Estimates of average mortality on slave ships, which rest on scholarly calculations drawn from a slave ship database that is not yet complete, currently range from 15 to 20 percent. Such figures, however, obscure the wide variation in mortality rates seen on different ships. Rates ranged from 4 percent to 55 percent, but could be even higher. In 1773, for example, the Dutch slave ship *Nooitgedacht* lost 89 percent of its 157 slaves to scurvy.[26]

The single biggest killer was dysentery, a gastrointestinal disorder that routinely swept through the packed holds. An inflammation of the intestines caused by a bacterial infection, dysentery was more evocatively known in the trade as the "bloody flux." Slaves boarded ships already malnourished and weakened by the forced march to the West African coast and their time in the barracoons, making them highly susceptible to this infection, which could also be caused or aggravated by the poor food and water on board. Highly contagious, dysentery was one of the great horrors of the voyage, even among those who survived its ravages. The holds of the slave ships had no toilets, bathing areas, or facilities set aside for the sick, so the African captives who came down with the infection had to endure the acute cramping and diarrhea caused by it while shackled to one another in airless confinement. Cooped up in these unsanitary conditions, captives also died from outbreaks of other communicable diseases, including smallpox, measles, and ophthalmia (a blinding eye infection). Any of these diseases could decimate crews and cargoes, which is one reason mortality rates on ships varied so widely.

The holds were so filthy by the time the ships docked that they gave off a stench that could be detected from the shore. The smell must have made life belowdecks even more unendurable—as did the deaths that took place there. Since the crews avoided the pestilence below as much as possible, even death did not always separate the living from the dead. Some slaves were forced to spend hours or even days chained to a dead companion. Indeed, death was an overwhelming and ubiquitous presence during the ocean voyage. Confined in close quarters, the captives watched their shipmates die in increasing numbers as the voyage progressed. High mortality rates were so common, even on voyages that escaped any major influx of disease, that contemporaries considered any slave voyage on which less than 20 percent of the slaves died to be a financial success.

The historian Stephanie Smallwood has suggested that the high mortality rates on slave ships produced "an extraordinary social crisis" among the captives because the deaths took place outside any social context that might allow the living to understand and make peace with them. The Akan captives imported to the Americas from the Gold Coast, for example, believed that mortuary rites were essential for a complete death. How could they make sense of the spiritual fate of shipmates, or even kinfolk, who perished and were summarily tossed overboard by the crew? To the Akan, their shipmates' deaths were spiritually incomplete. Surrounded by death and powerless to protect the dead, the Akan and other African captives faced what Smallwood has described as a "dual crisis: the trauma of death, and also of the inability to respond appropriately to death."[27]

The dying did not end with landfall. Even after the ships landed in Barbados, which was often their first stop, the slaves who disembarked there and at other New World ports continued to die despite the traders' attempts to revive them with fresh food and water. In the New World, the survivors of the long Middle Passage encountered more new diseases, which killed as many as 30 percent of them after they arrived. Estimates of how many Africans boarded slave ships vary, but current research suggests that upwards of twelve million were dispatched from Africa on more than forty thousand voyages that killed almost two million people.[28] Taking into account the deaths that occurred on the overland trek to the West African coast and in the barracoons—up to 10 percent of the captives—some scholars estimate that only half of the Africans destined for New World slavery survived.

CONCLUSION

The Slave Trade's Diaspora

Between the sixteenth century and the nineteenth century, when the slave trade finally ended, more than twelve million black captives departed Africa for the New World. Most came from West Africa, where they were captured or purchased by West African slave traders who sold them to European traders operating along the coast. Although the early trade was dominated by the Spanish and Portuguese, by the 1600s Dutch, French, English, Danish, Swedish, and other European traders were all visiting Africa's west coast. After 1730, traders based in North America also began to participate in the transatlantic trade. The slave trade did not take shape overnight, but instead grew in conjunction with European settlement of the New World. Approximately 3 percent of African captives arrived in the Americas before 1600; about 16 percent came in the seventeenth century, more than 50 percent in the eighteenth century, and about 30 percent in the nineteenth century.

The number of enslaved Africans in the New World began to increase in the seventeenth century as other European powers joined the Spanish and Portuguese in establishing settlements there. Intent on exploiting the hemisphere's rich resources, all of these newcomers depended on enslaved Africans for much of the labor they needed to sustain their colonies.

The forced migration of Africans to the Americas lasted for generations and created enduring African American communities throughout the hemisphere. Brought to the Americas in chains, slave trade survivors took on new identities in the New World. Whether of Igbo, Akan, Wolof, Mandinka, or other descent, slave captives were initially separated by barriers of national affiliation, ethnic group, and language. Once in the Americas, through shared experience, they would forge a collective identity as Africans—and, eventually, as African Americans.

First imported to what is now the United States to clear and cultivate early English and Dutch settlements in Virginia and New York, enslaved Africans were central to the survival and success of these early settlements. They would continue to play vital roles in many other colonies throughout the region in the coming years.

CHAPTER REVIEW

Online Study Guide ▪ bedfordstmartins.com/graywhite

Key Terms

diaspora (p. 4)	*ladinos* (p. 15)	coffles (p. 20)
carracks/caravels (p. 11)	*bozales* (p. 16)	barracoons (p. 22)
Guanches (p. 11)	Elmina Castle (p. 16)	cash crop (p. 25)
Taino Indians (p. 12)	*asiento* (p. 18)	bilboes (p. 26)
encomienda (p. 12)	triangle trade (p. 18)	tight packing (p. 26)

Review Questions

1. In what ways were African social identity, politics, and economics kinship based and collective in nature? Why might the transatlantic slave trade have been especially damaging to societies structured in this way?

2. To what factors can we attribute the initial development and eventual expansion of African slavery in Europe's New World colonies? How would you describe this progression?

3. How did traditional West African beliefs—about death, foreigners, and cannibalism, for example—serve to shape African slaves' experience of the Middle Passage?

4. Why did the diasporic Africans brought to the New World not consider themselves members of the same group? How might their shared experience have helped them form a new, collective African American identity?

5. Provide several examples of Africans' resistance to European intrusions in the early slave trade. How did Africans fight back, both individually and collectively, against slave raids, kidnappings, and their own captivity?

For Web sites, images, and documents related to topics and places in this chapter, visit **Make History** at bedfordstmartins.com/graywhite.

Inside the Slave Trade

Much of what historians know about the slave trade has been reconstructed from the records left by the traders themselves. These include ship's logs kept by slave ship captains; business records documenting profits and losses; accounts of the Middle Passage by Europeans who worked aboard the slave ships; European slave traders' assessments of the African peoples and practices they encountered in the coastal trade; and official correspondence generated by the trade.

The following four documents provide examples of these different sources. Document 1, a letter written by the Kongolese king Afonso I in the 1520s, presents an African ruler's perspective on the trade. Document 2, a ship's log from the 1670s, provides a record of African casualties during one transatlantic voyage. Documents 3 and 4 were written by James Barbot Jr. and Alexander Falconbridge, respectively, two men who worked in the slave trade. These documents provide eyewitness accounts of life aboard a slave ship.

King Afonso I (Mvemba Nzinga) | Letter to the Portuguese King João III, 1526+

The Kongolese king **Afonso I (1509–1542)** was a Christian convert who welcomed Portuguese trade, culture, and Christianity into his kingdom as a way to enhance Kongo's position as the dominant state in the region. Afonso read Portuguese and employed a Kongolese secretary, João Teixeira. Composed by the king and written by his secretary, this letter illustrates some of the problems the slave trade created for African leaders who forged alliances with slave trading European nations.

In our Kingdoms there is another great inconvenience which is of little service to God, and this is that many of our people, keenly desirous as they are of the wares and things of your Kingdoms, which are brought here by your people, and in order to satisfy their voracious appetite, seize many of our people, freed and exempt men, and very often it happens that they kidnap even noblemen and the sons of noblemen, and our relatives, and take them to be sold to the white men who are in our Kingdoms; and for this purpose they have concealed them; and

others are brought during the night so that they might not be recognized.

And as soon as they are taken by the white men they are immediately ironed and branded with fire, and when they are carried to be embarked, if they are caught by our guards' men the whites allege that they have bought them but they cannot say from whom, so that it is our duty to do justice and to restore to the freemen their freedom, but it cannot be done if your subjects feel offended, as they claim to be.

And to avoid such a great evil we passed a law so that any white man living in our Kingdoms and wanting to purchase goods in any way should first inform three of our noblemen and officials of our court whom we rely upon in this matter . . . , who should investigate if the mentioned goods are captives or free men, and if cleared by them there will be no further doubt nor embargo for them to be taken and embarked. But if the white men do not comply with it they will lose the aforementioned goods. And if we do them this favor and concession it is for the part Your Highness has in it, since we know that it is in your service too that these goods are taken from our Kingdom, otherwise we should not consent to this.

SOURCE: Basil Davidson, trans., *The African Past* (London: Curtis Brown, 1964), 192–93.

Peter Blake | An Account of the Mortality of the Slaves Aboard the Ship *James*, 1675–1676

The following ledger is from the ship's log kept by **Peter Blake**, the captain of the slave ship *James*. It chronicles the mortality among the ship's African captives on a 1675–1676 voyage from the Gold Coast to Barbados. Such accounts were used to calculate the profits and losses of a voyage. They also provide a record of the horrors of the transatlantic journey. What similarities do you notice among Blake's descriptions of the casualties aboard the *James*? What can you deduce from this evidence?

1675	Day	Men	Women	Boys	Girls	
Abbence [September]	6	1				Departed this Life suddenly.
Temenn October	28			1		Departed this life of Convulsion Fitts
Agga December	20	1				Departed this life of a feavour
Cape Corso January 1675/6	20	1				Rec'd from Wyemba thin and Consumed to Nothing and soe dyed
Ditto	26		1			Rec'd from Wyemba very thin and wasted to Nothing and soe dyed
Suckingdee February 1675/6	8	1				Rec'd from Wyemba very thin and dropsicall and soe departed this life.
Thwort of Butteren	23		1			bought to Windward and departed this life of a Consumption and Wormes.
1676						
Ditto	3	1				Rec'd from Wyembah and dep'ted this life of a dropsy.
Ditto	4	1				Rec'd of Mr. Ballwood att Amy Sea and dyed of a feavour by Lying in the Long boat, in the rain in the night which noe man knew of for hee went into her privately.
Ditto	5		1			Rec'd from Wyembah very thin and old and dep'ted this Life of the flux.
Ditto	6	1				Rec'd from Annamabooe and dep'ted this life of a flux.
Ditto	8		1			Rec'd from Wyembah with a Dropsey and departed this life of the same disease.
Ditto	9	1				bought by mee att Anamaboe and departed this life of the flux.
Ditto	12		1			Rec'd from Wyembah thin and Consumed away untill life departed from her.

Continued

Continued

1676	Day	Men	Women	Boys	Girls	
Ditto	13	1				Rec'd from Wyembah thin and dep'ted of a flux.
		1				Rec'd from Anamaboe and dyed of the Cramp in all his Joynts and all over his body being lately recovered of the flux.
		1				bought by mee dyed of the Cramp.
Att Sea May	14		2			the one rec'd from Wyembah very thin departed this life of the flux the other recd from Anamabooe and departed this life of the flux.
Ditto	16	1				Rec'd from Annamaboe and departed this life of a flux.
Ditto	20		1			bought by mee and departed this life of Convultions.
Barbados	21	1				Rec'd from Agga and departed this life of a flux.
ditto	22	1				Rec'd at Wyembah and departed this life of a flux.
ditto	23	1	1			The woman bought by mee dyed of Convultions the man rec'd att Anamabooe dyed of the flux.
ditto	29		1			Rec'd from Wyembah and dyed of a Consumption.
ditto	31		1			Rec'd ditto and dyed of a dropsy.
June ditto	1	1				
	4		1			
	6	2	1			
		28	19	4		
June 15th 1676						
In Nevis	15		1			{ both very thin and Weake when rec'd.
	16		1			
	17		1			very thin when rec'd.
	19	1				
	20		1			
	21		2			
	22		2			
		1	8			

SOURCE: Elizabeth Donnan, ed., *Documents Illustrative of the History of the Slave Trade to America* (Washington, DC: Carnegie Institution, 1930), 1:206–9.

James Barbot Jr. | General Observations on the Management of Slaves, 1700

The son and nephew of slave traders, **James Barbot Jr.** worked aboard slave ships for much of his life and recorded his experiences in several published works. Employed on the *Don Carlos* as the supercargo (officer) in charge of the slaves' purchase and sale, Barbot wrote the following description of how best to manage the captives on board. Despite the precautions described here, an onboard rebellion took place on the ship's first day at sea. At least twenty-eight captives were "lost"— either killed in battle or through suicide by drowning. Judging from this document, what did Barbot view as the most important measures to take to prevent slave insurrections?

As to the management of our slaves aboard, we lodge the two sexes apart, by means of a strong partition at the main mast; the forepart is for men, the other behind the mast for the women. If it be in large ships carrying five or six hundred slaves, the deck in such ships ought to be at least five and a half or six foot high, which is very requisite for driving a continual trade of slaves: for the greater height it has, the more airy and convenient it is for such a considerable number of human creatures; and consequently far the more healthy for them, and fitter to look after them. We build a sort of half-decks along the sides with deals and spars° provided for that purpose in *Europe*, that half-deck extending no farther than the sides of our scuttles, and so the slaves lie in two rows, one above the other, and as close together as they can be crouded. . . .

. . . The planks, or deals, contract some dampness more or less, either from the deck being so often wash'd to keep it clean and sweet, or from the rain that gets in now and then through the scuttles or other openings, and even from the very sweat of the slaves; which being so crouded in a low place,

is perpetual, and occasions many distempers, or at best great inconveniences dangerous to their health. . . .

It has been observ'd before, that some slaves fancy they are carry'd to be eaten, which makes them desperate; and others are so on account of their captivity: so that if care be not taken, they will mutiny and destroy the ship's crew in hopes to get away.

To prevent such misfortunes, we use to visit them daily, narrowly searching every corner between decks, to see whether they have not found means, to gather any pieces of iron, or wood, or knives, about the ship, notwithstanding the great care we take not to leave any tools or nails, or other things in the way: which, however, cannot be always so exactly observ'd, where so many people are in the narrow compass of a ship.

We cause as many of our men as is convenient to lie in the quarter-deck and gun-room, and our principal officers in the great cabbin, where we keep all our small arms in a readiness, with sentinels constantly at the door and avenues to it; being thus ready to disappoint any attempts our slaves might make on a sudden.

These precautions contribute very much to keep them in awe; and if all those who carry slaves duly observ'd them, we should not hear of so many revolts as have happen'd. Where I was concern'd, we always kept our slaves in such order, that we did not perceive the least inclination in any of them to revolt, or mutiny, and lost very few of our number in the voyage.

It is true, we allow'd them much more liberty, and us'd them with more tenderness than most other *Europeans* would think prudent to do; as, to have them all upon deck every day in good weather; to take their meals twice a-day, at fix'd hours, that is, at ten in the morning, and at five at night; which being ended, we made the men go down again between decks; for the women were almost entirely at their own discretion, to be upon deck as long as they pleas'd, nay even many of the males had the same liberty by turns, successively; few or none being fetter'd or kept in shackles, and that only on account of some disturbances, or injuries,

---

° Deals and spars are poles and planks.

SOURCE: James Barbot Jr., "An Abstract of a Voyage to the Congo River, or the Zair, and to Cabinde in the Year 1700" in Awnsham and John Churchill, *Collection of Voyages and Travels* (London, 1732), v. V, 546–48.

documents

offer'd to their fellow captives, as will unavoidably happen among a numerous croud of such savage people. Besides, we allow'd each of them betwixt their meals a handful of *Indian* wheat and *Mandioca*, and now and then short pipes and tobacco to smoak upon deck by turns, and some cocoa-nuts; and to the women a piece of coarse cloth to cover them, and the same to many of the men, which we took care they did wash from time to time, to prevent vermin, which they are very subject to; and because it look'd sweeter and more agreeable. Towards the evening they diverted themselves on the deck, as they thought fit, some conversing together, others dancing, singing, and sporting after their manner, which pleased them highly, and often made us pastime; especially the female sex, who being a-part from the males, on the quarter-deck, and many of them young sprightly maidens, full of jollity and good-humour, afforded us abundance of recreation; as did several little fine boys, which we mostly kept to attend on us about the ship. . . .

Much more might be said relating to the preservation and maintenance of slaves in such voyages, which I leave to the prudence of the officers that govern aboard, if they value their own reputation and their owners advantage; and shall only add these few particulars, that tho' we ought to be circumspect in watching the slaves narrowly, to prevent or disappoint their ill designs for our own conservation, yet must we not be too severe and haughty with them, but on the contrary, caress and humour them in every reasonable thing. Some commanders, of a morose peevish temper are perpetually beating and curbing them, even without the least offence, and will not suffer any upon deck but when unavoidable necessity to ease themselves does require; under pretence it hinders the work of the ship and sailors, and that they are troublesome by their nasty nauseous stench, or their noise; which makes those poor wretches desperate, and besides their falling into distempers thro' melancholy, often is the occasion of their destroying themselves.

Such officers should consider, those unfortunate creatures are men as well as themselves, tho' of a different colour, and pagans; and that they ought to do to others as they would be done by in like circumstances.

Alexander Falconbridge | An Account of the Slave Trade on the Coast of Africa, 1788

The British surgeon **Alexander Falconbridge (d. 1792)** served as a ship's surgeon on four slave trade voyages between 1780 and 1787 before rejecting the slave trade and becoming an abolitionist. He wrote *An Account of the Slave Trade on the Coast of Africa* in 1788, after his conversion. It provides an unflinching account of the brutality of the transatlantic trade.

When the ships arrive in the West-Indies, (the chief mart for this inhuman merchandize), the slaves are disposed of, as I have before observed, by different methods. Sometimes the mode of disposal,

SOURCE: Alexander Falconbridge, *An Account of the Slave Trade on the Coast of Africa* (London: J. Phillips, George Yard, 1788), 33–36.

is that of selling them by what is termed a *scramble*; and a day is soon fixed for that purpose. But previously thereto, the sick, or refuse slaves, of which there are frequently many, are usually conveyed on shore, and sold at a tavern by . . . public auction. These, in general, are purchased . . . upon speculation, at so low a price as five or six dollars a head. I was informed by a mulatto woman, that she purchased a sick slave at Grenada, upon speculation, for the small sum of one dollar, as the poor wretch was apparently dying of the flux. It seldom happens that any, who are carried ashore in the emaciated state to which they are generally reduced by that disorder, long survive their landing. I once saw sixteen conveyed on shore, and sold in the foregoing manner, the whole of whom died before I left the island, which was within a short time after. Sometimes the captains march their slaves through the town at which they intend to dispose of them, and then place them; in rows where they are examined and purchased.

The mode of selling them by scramble having fallen under my observation the oftenest, I shal[l] be more particular in describing it. Being some years ago, at one of the islands in the West-Indies, I was witness to a sale by scramble. . . .

On a day appointed, the negroes were landed, and placed altogether in a large yard, belonging to the merchants to whom the ship was consigned. As soon as the hour agreed on arrived, the doors of the yard were suddenly thrown open, and in rushed a considerable number of purchasers, with all the ferocity of brutes. Some instantly seized such of the negroes as they could conveniently lay hold of with their hands. Others, being prepared with several handkerchiefs tied together, encircled with these as many as they were able. While others, by means of a rope, effected the same purpose. It is scarcely possible to describe the confusion of which this mode of selling is productive. It likewise causes much animosity among the purchasers, who, not unfrequently upon these occasions, fall out and quarrel with each other. The poor astonished negroes were so much terrified by these proceedings, that several of them, through fear, climbed over the walls of the court yard, and ran wild about the town; but were soon hunted down and retaken. . . .

Various are the deceptions made use of in the disposal of sick slaves; and many of these, such as must excite in every humane mind, the liveliest sensations of horror. I have been well informed, that a Liverpool captain boasted of his having cheated some Jews by the following stratagem: A lot of slaves, afflicted with the flux, being about to be landed for sale, he directed the surgeon to stop the anus of each of them with oakum. Thus prepared, they were landed, and taken to the accustomed place of sale; where, being unable to stand but for a very short time, they are usually permitted to sit. The Jews, when they examine them, oblige them to stand up, in order to see if there be any discharge; and when they do not perceive this appearance, they consider it as a symptom of recovery. In the present instance, such an appearance being prevented, the bargain was struck, and they were accordingly sold. But it was not long before a discovery ensued. The excruciating pain which the prevention of a discharge of such an acrimonious nature occasioned, not being to be borne by the poor wretches, the temporary obstruction was removed, and the deluded purchasers were speedily convinced of the imposition.

Questions for Analysis

1. The slave trade involved both European and African rulers, merchants, and middlemen. Using these documents, describe and analyze the various roles Europeans and Africans played in perpetuating the trade. Did one group predominate? What evidence do you have to indicate this?

2. Most of the history of the slave trade comes from documents written by slave traders rather than by African captives. What can slave trade records such as Captain Peter Blake's account of the deaths of Africans aboard the slave ship *James*, and James Barbot's and Alexander Falconbridge's descriptions of what they witnessed aboard other slave ships tell us about the African experience of the Middle Passage? What are the limitations of such evidence?

3. Prior to the rise of an abolitionist movement dedicated to ending slavery, the use and sale of slaves was common throughout the West. In these documents, what, if any, moral concerns do European and African slave traders express about their participation in the slave trade?

The African Slave Captives

Firsthand accounts of the Middle Passage by enslaved Africans are extremely rare, because the vast majority of the millions of men, women, and children caught in that migration never had an opportunity to testify about their experiences. Moreover, few captives acquired the education needed to record their experiences in writing or were free to document their lives in any form.

The following accounts come from two eighteenth-century Africans who were enslaved as children and recorded their stories as free adults. Filtered through memory and recorded to support their authors' ambitions, both of these accounts of the authors' captivity and enslavement in Africa and their ocean voyage to the Americas may contain fictional elements. Nonetheless, they are enormously valuable as African views on life inside the trade.

Olaudah Equiano | The Interesting Narrative of the Life of Olaudah Equiano, or Gustavus Vassa, the African, 1789

Born in what is today southeast Nigeria, **Olaudah Equiano (1745–1797)** was the youngest son of an Igbo village leader in the kingdom of Benin. Kidnapped into slavery at age eleven, he was resold several times by African masters during his six-month journey to the African coast, where he was sold to a slave trader who carried him to the West Indies and into slavery in Virginia. Written after Equiano purchased his own freedom and became active in the British antislavery movement, *The Interesting Narrative of the Life of Olaudah Equiano* has long been considered the best African account of enslavement, the Middle Passage, and eighteenth-century life in an African village—although one scholar has recently suggested that Equiano's description of his African past is fictional.[29]

One day, when all our people were gone out to their works as usual, and only I and my dear sister were left to mind the house, two men and a woman got over our walls, and in a moment seized us both; and, without giving us time to cry out, or make resis-

tance, they stopped our mouths, tied our hands, and ran off with us into the nearest wood. . . . At the end of six or seven months after I had been kidnapped, I arrived at the sea coast. . . .

The first object which saluted my eyes when I arrived on the coast was the sea, and a slave-ship, which was then riding at anchor, and waiting for its cargo. These filled me with astonishment, which was soon converted into terror. . . . When I was carried on board I was immediately handled, and tossed up, to see if I were sound, by some of the crew; and I was now persuaded that I had got into a world of bad spirits, and that they were going to kill me. Their complexions too differing so much from ours, their long hair, and the language they spoke, which was very different from any I had ever heard, united to confirm me in this belief. Indeed, such were the horrors of my views and fears at the moment, that, if ten thousand worlds had been my own, I would have freely parted with them all to have exchanged my condition with that of the meanest slave in my own country. When I looked round the ship too, and saw a large furnace of copper boiling, and a multitude of black people of every description chained together, every one of their countenances expressing dejection and sorrow, I no longer doubted of my fate, and, quite overpowered

SOURCE: *The Interesting Narrative of the Life of Olaudah Equiano, or Gustavus Vassa, the African.* Written by Himself (London: printed for author, 1745), 32, 45, 46–50, 51–53, 54–55, 56.

with horror and anguish, I fell motionless on the deck and fainted. When I recovered a little, I found some black people about me, who I believed were some of those who brought me on board, and had been receiving their pay; they talked to me in order to cheer me, but all in vain. I asked them if we were not to be eaten by those white men with horrible looks, red faces, and long hair? They told me I was not; and one of the crew brought me a small portion of spirituous liquor in a wine glass; but, being afraid of him, I would not take it out of his hand. One of the blacks therefore took it from him and gave it to me, and I took a little down my palate, which, instead of reviving me, as they thought it would, threw me into the greatest consternation at the strange feeling it produced having never tasted any such liquor before. Soon after this, the blacks who brought me on board went off, and left me abandoned to despair. I now saw myself deprived of all chance of returning to my native country, or even the least glimpse of hope of gaining the shore, which I now considered as friendly: and even wished for my former slavery, in preference to my present situation, which was filled with horrors of every kind, still heightened by my ignorance of what I was to undergo. I was not long suffered to indulge my grief; I was soon put down under the decks, and there I received such a salutation in my nostrils as I had never experienced in my life: so that with the loathsomeness of the stench, and crying together, I became so sick and low that I was not able to eat, nor had I the least desire to taste any thing. I now wished for the last friend, Death, to relieve me; but soon, to my grief, two of the white men offered me eatables; and, on my refusing to eat, one of them held me fast by the hands, and laid me across, I think, the windlass, and tied my feet, while the other flogged me severely. I had never experienced any thing of this kind before; and although not being used to the water, I naturally feared that element the first time I saw it; yet, nevertheless, could I have got over the nettings, I would have jumped over the side; but I could not; and, besides, the crew used to watch us very closely who were not chained down to the decks, lest we should leap into the water; and I have seen some of these poor African prisoners most severely cut for attempting to do so, and hourly whipped for not eating. This indeed was often the case with myself. In a little time after, amongst the poor chained men, I found some of my own nation, which in a small degree gave ease to my mind. I inquired of them what was to be done with us? they gave me to understand we were to be carried to these white people's country to work for them. I then was a little revived, and thought, if it were no worse than working, my situation was not so desperate: but still I feared I should be put to death, the white people looked and acted, as I thought, in so savage a manner; for I had never seen among any people such instances of brutal cruelty; and this not only shewn towards us blacks, but also to some of the whites themselves. One white man in particular I saw, when we were permitted to be on deck, flogged so unmercifully with a large rope near the foremast, that he died in consequence of it; and they tossed him over the side as they would have done a brute. This made me fear these people the more; and I expected nothing less than to be treated in the same manner. I could not help expressing my fears and apprehensions to some of my countrymen: I asked them if these people had no country, but lived in this hollow place the ship? they told me they did not, but came from a distant one. "Then," said I, "how comes it in all our country we never heard of them?" They told me, because they lived so very far off. I then asked, where were their women? had they any like themselves? I was told they had: "And why," said I, "do we not see them?" they answered, because they were left behind. I asked how the vessel could go? they told me they could not tell; but that there were cloth put upon the masts by the help of the ropes I saw, and then the vessel went on; and the white men had some spell or magic they put in the water when they liked in order to stop the vessel. I was exceedingly amazed at this account, and really thought they were spirits. I therefore wished much to be from amongst them, for I expected they would sacrifice me: but my wishes were vain; for we were so quartered that it was impossible for any of us to make our escape. . . . At last, when the ship we were in had got in all her cargo, they made ready with many fearful noises, and we were all put under deck, so that we could not see how they managed the vessel. But this disappointment was the least of my

documents

sorrow. The stench of the hold while we were on the coast was so intolerably loathsome, that it was dangerous to remain there for any time, and some of us had been permitted to stay on the deck for the fresh air; but now that the whole ship's cargo were confined together, it became absolutely pestilential. The closeness of the place, and the heat of the climate, added to the number in the ship, which was so crouded that each had scarcely room to turn himself, almost suffocated us. This produced copious perspirations, so that the air soon became unfit for respiration, from a variety of loathsome smells, and brought on a sickness amongst the slaves, of which many died, thus falling victims to the improvident avarice, as I may call it, of their purchasers. This wretched situation was again aggravated by the galling of the chains, now become insupportable; and the filth of the necessary tubs, into which the children often fell, and were almost suffocated. The shrieks of the women, and the groans of the dying, rendered the whole a scene of horror almost inconceiveable. Happily perhaps for myself I was soon reduced so low here that it was thought necessary to keep me almost always on deck; and from my extreme youth I was not put in fetters. In this situation I expected every hour to share the fate of my companions, some of whom were almost daily brought upon deck at the point of death, which I began to hope would soon put an end to my miseries. Often did I think many of the inhabitants of the deep much more happy than myself; I envied them the freedom they enjoyed, and as often wished I could change my condition for theirs. Every circumstance I met with served only to render my state more painful, and heighten my apprehensions and my opinion of the cruelty of the whites. One day they had taken a number of fishes; and when they had killed and satisfied themselves with as many as they thought fit, to our astonishment who were on the deck, rather than give any of them to us to eat, as we expected, they tossed the remaining fish into the sea again, although we begged and prayed for some as well as we could, but in vain; and some of my countrymen, being pressed by hunger, took an opportunity, when they thought no one saw them, of trying to get a little privately; but they were discovered, and the attempt procured them some very severe floggings.

One day, when we had a smooth sea, and moderate wind, two of my wearied countrymen, who were chained together (I was near them at the time), preferring death to such a life of misery, somehow made through the nettings, and jumped into the sea; immediately another quite dejected fellow, who, on account of his illness, was suffered to be out of irons, also followed their example; and I believe many more would very soon have done the same, if they had not been prevented by the ship's crew, who were instantly alarmed. . . . At last, we came in sight of the island of Barbadoes, at which the whites on board gave a great shout, and made many signs of joy to us. We did not know what to think of this; but, as the vessel drew nearer, we plainly saw the harbour, and other ships of different kinds and sizes: and we soon anchored amongst them off Bridge Town. Many merchants and planters now came on board, though it was in the evening. They put us in separate parcels, and examined us attentively. They also made us jump, and pointed to the land, signifying we were to go there. We thought by this we should be eaten by these ugly men, as they appeared to us; and when, soon after we were all put down under the deck again, there was much dread and trembling among us, and nothing but bitter cries to be heard all the night from these apprehensions, insomuch that at last the white people got some old slaves from the land to pacify us. They told us we were not to be eaten, but to work, and were soon to go on land, where we should see many of our country people. This report eased us much; and sure enough, soon after we landed, there came to us Africans of all languages. . . . We were not many days in the merchant's custody before we were sold after their usual manner, which is this:—On a signal given, (as the beat of a drum), the buyers rush at once into the yard where the slaves are confined, and make choice of that parcel they like best. The noise and clamour with which this is attended, and the eagerness visible in the countenances of the buyers, serve not a little to increase the apprehension of the terrified Africans, who may well be supposed to consider them as the ministers of that destruction to which they think themselves devoted. In this manner, without scruple, are relations and friends separated, most of them never to see each other again.

Belinda | The Petition of Belinda, 1782

The following account of an African childhood interrupted by enslavement appears in a petition to the Massachusetts legislature written on behalf of an African-born slave known only as **Belinda**. Captured and enslaved in the 1720s, she spent much of her life as the property of Isaac Royall, a Medford, Massachusetts, resident and British loyalist during the Revolutionary War. Royall fled the colony and died in 1781. Freed after her master's death, Belinda petitioned the new state's new government for an "allowance" from the estate of her former master. Composed when she was over seventy years old, Belinda's petition was signed with an X, indicating that she was illiterate. No record of who wrote the text exists. What arguments does Belinda make on her own behalf? How does she relate slavery to current events?

To the honourable the senate and house of representatives, in general court assembled:
The petition of Belinda, an African,
    Humbly shews,
That seventy years have rolled away, since she, on the banks of the Rio de Valta, received her existence. The mountains, covered with spicy forests—the vallies, loaded with the richest fruits, spontaneously produced—joined to that happy temperature of air, which excludes excess, would have yielded her the most complete felicity, had not her mind received early impressions of the cruelty of men, whose faces were like the moon, and whose bows and arrows were like the thunder and the lightning of the clouds. The idea of these, the most dreadful of all enemies, filled her infant slumbers with horror, and her noon-tide moments with cruel apprehensions! But her affrighted imagination, in its most alarming extension, never represented distresses equal to what she has since really experienced: for before she had twelve years enjoyed the fragrance of her native groves, and ere she realized that Europeans placed their happiness in the yellow dust, which she carelessly marked with her infant footsteps—even when she, in a sacred grove, with each hand in that of a tender parent, was paying her devotion to the great Orisa, who made all things, an armed band of white men, driving many of her countrymen in chains, rushed into the hallowed shades! Could the tears, the sighs, and supplications, bursted from the tortured parental affection, have blunted the keen edge of avarice, she might have been rescued from agony, which many of her country's children have felt, but which none have ever described. In vain she lifted her supplicating voice to an insulted father, and her guiltless hands to a dishonoured deity! She was ravished from the bosom of her country, from the arms of her friends, while the advanced age of her parents, rendering them unfit for servitude, cruelly separated her from them for ever.

Scenes which her imagination had never conceived of, a floating world, the sporting monsters of the deep, and the familiar meetings of billows and clouds, strove, but in vain, to divert her attention from three hundred Africans in chains, suffering the most excruciating torment; and some of them rejoicing that the pangs of death came like a balm to their wounds.

Once more her eyes were blest with a continent: but alas! how unlike the land where she received her being! How all things appeared unpropitious. She learned to catch the ideas, marked by the sounds of language, only to know that her doom was slavery, from which death alone was to emancipate her. What did it avail her, that the walls of her lord were hung with splendor, and that the dust trodden under foot in her native country, crouded his gates with sordid worshippers! The laws rendered her incapable of receiving property: and though she was a free moral agent, accountable for her own actions, yet never had she a moment at her own disposal! Fifty years her faithful hands have been compelled to ignoble servitude for the benefit of an Isaac Royall, until, as if nations must be agitated, and the world convulsed, for the preservation of that freedom, which the Almighty Father intended for all the human race, the present war commenced. The terrors of men, armed in th

SOURCE: "Petition of an African Slave, to the Legislature of Massachusetts," *The American Museum, or Repository of Ancient and Modern Fugitive Pieces, Prose and Poetical* 1, no. 6 (June 1787): 538–40.

documents

cause of freedom, compelled her master to fly, and to breathe away his life in a land, where lawless dominion sits enthroned, pouring blood and vengeance on all who dare to be free.

The face of your petitioner is now marked with the furrows of time, and her frame feebly bending under the oppression of years, while she, by the laws of the land, is denied the enjoyment of one morsel of that immense wealth, a part whereof hath been accumulated by her own industry, and the whole augmented by her servitude.

Wherefore, casting herself at the feet of your honours, as to a body of men, formed for the extirpation of vassalage, for the reward of virtue, and the just returns of honest industry—she prays that such allowance may be made her, out of the estate of colonel Royall, as will prevent her, and her more infirm daughter, from misery in the greatest extreme, and scatter comfort over the short and downward path of their lives: and she will ever pray.

BELINDA.
Boston, February, 1782.

Questions for Analysis

1. Most of the few available African accounts of the Middle Passage relate experiences of being captured and enslaved as children but were recorded many years later. How might age and the passage of time have affected Belinda's and Olaudah Equiano's recollections of the slave trade?

2. Most captives' accounts of enslavement and the Middle Passage were addressed to white audiences; recorded, written, or edited by whites; and designed to foster opposition to the slave trade. Whom were Belinda and Olaudah Equiano addressing in their documents? To what extent do their stories seem to have been influenced by white editors or authors? How might the editors' and authors' objectives have shaped the stories?

3. Recently, the literary scholar Vincent Carretta has argued that Equiano was born in South Carolina rather than Africa.[30] Two British documents—a Royal Navy muster roll from 1773 and a baptismal record from 1759—list Equiano's birthplace as Carolina, leading Carretta to speculate that Equiano fabricated the story of his capture and forced migration from Africa to make his narrative a more effective critique of the slave trade. But historians of Africa such as Paul Lovejoy contend that Equiano's detailed knowledge of Igbo culture and language make it unlikely that he invented the story of his early childhood. They also question the importance and accuracy of the records cited by Carretta.[31] Based on your reading of Equiano's narrative, how would you assess the accuracy of his account of his early life?

European Images of Africans in the Era of the Slave Trade

Words can only go so far when it comes to reconstructing the experiences of Africans captured in the slave trade, especially since detailed firsthand accounts of their forced migration are rare. By contrast, images of the trade and its participants are far more plentiful—but they must be interpreted with great care. Like the written historical record, most of the visual artifacts chronicling the trade were crafted by European observers rather than enslaved Africans. They were not designed to record the experiences of the Africans whose lives were affected by the trade, but instead were addressed to other European viewers. The European visual record of Africans during this era contains varying images of Africa and its peoples that were shaped by the ambitions, ideas, and preconceptions of the European authors, artists, and mapmakers who created them.

Mapping Africans

West Africa was still new and not at all well known to Europeans during the era of the slave trade. Early maps of the region depicted both the continent and its inhabitants, titillating viewers with representations of the unfamiliar peoples and animals. In 1733, the British satirist Jonathan Swift commented on the blend of geography and naturalism that marked early European depictions of Africa: "So Geographers in Afric-maps / With Savage-Pictures fill their gaps / And o'er unhabitable downs / Place Elephants for want of towns."[32] The earliest available maps of Africa bear out his point.

One such map is the *Catalan Atlas*, a Spanish nautical map of the known world that dates back to 1375 (Figure 1.1). Largely devoid of geographic detail, it is adorned with pictures, including sketches of camels, as well as a large and

FIGURE 1.1
Facsimile of the *Catalan Atlas* Showing the King of Mali Holding a Gold Nugget, 1375
Erich Lessing/Art Resource, NY.

Totius Africæ tabula, & descriptio uniuersalis, etiam ultra Ptolemæi limites extensa.

FIGURE 1.2
Sebastian Münster, German Map of Africa, 1554 *From Sebastian Münster's* Cosmographia universalis *(Basel, 1554)/Historic Maps Collection, Department of Rare Books and Special Collections, Princeton University Library.*

lavish illustration of an African ruler identified as "Muse Melley," "lord of the Negroes of Guinea." This illustration likely refers to Mansa Musa, who ruled the Mali empire between 1312 and 1337, although his placement on the map is closer to North Africa than to West Africa. A devout Muslim, Musa caught the attention of the Islamic and European worlds in 1324, when he made a pilgrimage to Mecca. His opulent personal caravan included twelve hundred servants and eighty camels carrying two tons of gold, which he distributed to the needy along his route. Not soon forgotten, Musa was pictured in several fourteenth-century maps of the world. How does the drawing in Figure 1.1 reveal European mapmakers' fascination with Musa?

Later maps of Africa presented a more comprehensive view of the continent. But they still contained images of animals, references to legendary rulers, and a limited amount of geographic information. The German mapmaker Sebastian Münster, whose 1554 map of Africa is one of the earliest such maps, features an elephant at the southern end of the continent, which he designated simply "Africae Extremitas" (Figure 1.2). Münster also mapped a country designated primarily by parrots, as well as the kingdom of a mythical Christian ruler known as Prester John and the home of the Monoculi—one-eyed giants found only in European folklore.

As fanciful as it might seem, Münster's image of Africa as the home of monsters and mythical figures was no more fantastic than some European writers' descriptions of African peoples. The fourteenth-century travel writer John Mandeville, for example, insisted that Ethiopia was home to "some that have only one foot . . . [and] that foot is so big it will cover and shade all the body from the sun," as well as to "young children whose hair is white, and as they grow old their hair gets black." Not surprisingly, given the absurdity of this report, Mandeville may never have actually visited Africa. His name was fictional, as was much of his book, *The Travels of Sir John Mandeville*, which claims to describe the travels of an English knight who journeyed to Egypt, Ethiopia, India, Persia, and Turkey in the early 1320s. Neither English nor a knight, Mandeville was probably a Frenchman named Jehan à la Barbe, who perhaps never left his home country. In addition to the people with one enormous foot in Ethiopia, Mandeville said that he saw one-eyed giants in India (who looked much like the one pictured in Münster's map of Africa), where he also came across men and women with heads like dogs.[33] To four-teenth- and fifteenth-century readers, Mandeville's travels no doubt sounded much more probable than they do today. In fact, his text was carefully studied by Christopher Columbus and consulted by many European mapmakers.

Accordingly, Münster's map should not be dismissed as notably far-fetched. It should instead be read as a record of European thought about Africa in 1554. What does it tell us about how Africa was perceived? In considering this question, think not only about the giants and elephants but also about the fact that he divided Africa into distinct kingdoms (identified with the image of

FIGURE 1.3
Willem Janszoon Blaeu, *New Dutch Map of Africa*, 1644
Willem Janszoon Blaeu, "Africae nova descriptio," Amsterdam, 1644/ Bibliothèque Municipale, Auxerre, France/Erich Lessing/Art Resource, NY.

FIGURE 1.4
Page from the *Cantigas de Santa Maria*, 1252–1284
Biblioteca Monasterio del Escorial, Madrid/akg/Bildarchiv Steffens.

a crown and scepter). Based on this map, what do you think Münster saw as the differences and similarities between Europe and Africa?

Seventeenth-century European maps had far more geographic information but no fewer animals. First issued in 1630, the Dutch cartographer Willem Janszoon Blaeu's lavishly illustrated *New Dutch Map of Africa* was reprinted repeatedly over the next four decades, appearing in Latin, Dutch, French, and Spanish editions of Blaeu's atlases (Figure 1.3). Produced at a time when the Dutch and Portuguese were both active in the colonization and settlement of Africa, it captures the contours of the continent far more accurately than Münster's map and identifies thousands of towns, rivers, and other landmarks. It also details the increasing European presence on the continent. Running along the top of the map are oval views of the major cities and trading ports at the time: Tangier and Ceuta (Morocco), Algiers (Algeria), Tunis (Tunisia), Alexandria and Cairo (Egypt), Mozambique (seaport of Mozambique), Elmina Castle (Ghana), and Grand Canary (Canary Islands). Along the sides and in the map itself are images of a variety of African peoples, as well as lions, tigers, elephants, ostriches, crocodiles, and other wild animals. Such animals were intriguingly exotic to Europeans, as were, perhaps, the Africans themselves. What kind of image of Africa and Africans does this map present? What significance, if any, do you find in the fact that both people and animals are featured?

Picturing Africans

The peoples of sub-Saharan Africa were already somewhat familiar to most Europeans, so they may have seemed less of a novelty than the animals. Discussions about the appearance of Africans had long figured in ancient literature and in European travelers' tales. The ancient Greek historian Herodotus described Africans fairly prosaically as "in countenance a like black, in hayre [hair] a like frizzled," and the Roman naturalist Pliny the Younger noted that they were "all black saving their teeth, and a little of the palme of the hands." But the fairly realistic information about Africans available in ancient texts competed with the more fanciful images promoted by later writers such as John Mandeville, so it is difficult to know exactly how Europeans expected Africans to look.

Among southern Europeans, Africans were certainly too familiar to be described in fanciful terms. Under Islamic rule for much of the Middle Ages, Spanish and Portuguese Christians had had centuries of contact with a

FIGURE 1.5
The Adoration of the Magi, c. 1500 *German, museum number C.74-1919, C.75-1919. Given by J. Pierpont Morgan Jr./© Victoria and Albert Museum, London/V & A Images.*

Muslim world that included Arabs, Berbers, and "black moors" from sub-Saharan Africa. Dispersed throughout the Islamic kingdoms of North Africa by several centuries of warfare and trade, black Africans played a variety of roles in the Muslim societies that developed there and expanded into the Iberian Peninsula. As seen in Figure 1.4, a thirteenth-century depiction of Muslim soldiers attacking a Spanish city, the Islamic armies that conquered southern Europe were racially diverse. The *Cantigas de Santa Maria* (Hymns of Saint Mary), a richly illustrated collection of poems published during the reign of the Castilian king Alfonso X (1221–1284), includes panels celebrating Alfonso's victories over multicultural Islamic forces. Though prohibited from enslaving freeborn Muslims under Islamic law, Muslims enslaved captives from Europe and sub-Saharan Africa and employed free blacks and slaves in their armies.

Some evidence suggests that black slaves were held in especially low regard within the Muslim world largely because, unlike European slaves who were often ransomed or exchanged for Arab captives held by European rulers, captives from sub-Saharan Africa commanded no ransom and thus ended up working as slaves for long periods of time. Increasingly associated with slavery as a group, they were denigrated as "similar to . . . dumb animals" by at least one Islamic scholar.[34] However, the extent to which negative Arabic images of Africans influenced their early European counterparts is difficult to say, since although Europeans looked upon all Muslims as their enemies, they presented a variety of both favorable and unfavorable depictions of African peoples. Moreover, the African figures that appear in fifteenth- and sixteenth-century European art are also diverse. While black servants are not uncommon in these depictions, there are recurring images of black leaders and monarchs as well. Most notable among them is Balthazar, one of the three wise men, or Magi, who gathered in Bethlehem to pay homage to the infant Jesus. Especially in northern Europe, religious artists often represented the Magi as kings from

FIGURE 1.6
John Barbot Meeting with the King of
Sestro, 1691 *From John Barbot,* A
Description of the Coasts of North and
South-Guinea, *1732/© The British Library/
HIP/The Image Works.*

FIGURE 1.7
Negro's Cannoes, Carrying Slaves, on Board of Ships att Manfroe, seventeenth century *From John Barbot,* A
Description of the Coasts of North and South-Guinea, *1732/The New York Public Library/Art Resource, NY.*

FIGURE 1.8

Portraits of West Africans, 1679 *From John Barbot, A Description of the Coasts of North and South-Guinea, 1732/© The British Library Board, Shelf mark Add 28788 f45.*

three continents: Europe, Asia, and Africa. A stained-glass image crafted in Germany around 1500 exemplifies this tradition, featuring both a black Magus and a black (possibly female) servant, who attends to the Magus on bended knee (Figure 1.5).

European explorers and merchants who participated in the slave trade encountered Africans not only as bondmen but also as monarchs, middlemen, and ordinary people. Written in the late 1600s and first published in 1732, the British slave trader John Barbot's lavishly illustrated *A Description of the Coasts of North and South-Guinea* contained drawings of Africans in all of these roles. An illustration of Barbot's meeting with the king of Sestro (modern-day Liberia) in 1688 (Figure 1.6), for example, portrays the monarch as a dignified figure. According to Barbot, the king was "attended by twenty or twenty-two of his counselors, sitting in a semicircle on the right and left of him on fine mats."[35]

Elsewhere in his text, however, Barbot focuses on workingmen such as the canoe men of Mina (on the Gold Coast), calling them "uncommonly handsome, lusty, and strong." "Their usual employments are trade, husbandry and fishery," he noted, and "the Mina Blacks drive a great trade along the Gold Coast . . . and are the fittest and most experienc'd men to . . . paddle the canoes over the bars and breakings which render this coast . . . so perilous . . . the waves in the ocean rising in great surges"[36] (Figure 1.7).

Though ready to admire the appearance of Africans, Barbot and other European visitors to West Africa also noted the dark complexion and tightly curled hair that distinguished Africans from themselves (Figure 1.8). Most European thinkers had long maintained that differences in climate and environment were the causes of the various complexions seen in different

visual sources

FIGURE 1.9

African Slaves in the Mines, 1565

Engraving by Theodore de Bry, in Girolamo Benzoni, Historia del mondo nuovo, *1565/ Mary Evans Picture Library, London.*

NIGRITÆ IN SCRUTANDIS VENIS METALLICIS
ab Hifpanis in Infulas ablegantur.

groups. But sixteenth- and seventeenth-century European visitors to West Africa found all the peoples there to be remarkably dark, even as compared to the native peoples of the Americas. Consequently, some wondered whether their color could be fully explained by "the scorching heat of the sun."[37] One naturalist proposed that the Africans' color was a consequence of "some natural infection of the first inhabitants of that country," while others wondered how closely Europeans and Africans were related.[38] Would living in Africa turn Europeans black? How permanent were these distinctions?

By the eighteenth century, such speculations had begun to produce new notions of racial identity as a major distinction between human groups. These theories of race were also a product of the new biological theories of human development that took shape during the Enlightenment, which saw European scholars rethinking traditional understandings of the relationships between people, nature, and God. European ideas about Africans as a distinct and inferior race cannot be separated from the rise of the transatlantic slave trade. Although the first African slaves to arrive in the New World were enslaved alongside American Indians in some of the earliest European settlements, after the indigenous populations began to decline in the sixteenth and seventeenth centuries, New World slavery was largely limited to people of African descent. The system of racial slavery that emerged in the Americas created powerful and enduring links between slavery and the African body that made Europeans increasingly see Africans as naturally suited to subjugation.

Yet slavery and race were not traditionally linked in European cultures. Indeed, the origin of many European words meaning "slave" lies in the enslavement of Slavic peoples (Slavs) in the Middle Ages. With the growth of the transatlantic slave trade, however, blackness and slavery became synonymous in western Europe. African migrants were transported to the New World in chains and appear as near-naked slave laborers in early European depictions of the Americas. Published in 1565, the Italian traveler Girolamo Benzoni's *History of the New World* was one of the first works portraying Africans in this way. Benzoni's text includes engravings of enslaved laborers working in the gold mines and sugar mills of Hispaniola (present-day Haiti and the Dominican Republic) (Figure 1.9). The author notes, "When the natives of this island (*Española*) began to be extirpated, the Spaniards provided themselves with blacks (*Mori*) from Guinea . . . and they have brought great numbers thence."[39]

As the transatlantic slave trade expanded and Africans gradually replaced Indians in the slave population of the Americas, whites in both Europe and America increasingly began to associate blacks with slavery. In the New World, such associations were underscored by frequent arrivals of new shipments of enslaved blacks, as well as the development of racially discriminatory laws and customs designed to control them. Over time, black inferiority came to seem natural to Europeans, so much so that even European opponents of the slave trade were prone to representing Africans in somewhat degrading terms. The earliest image of an enslaved African created by the British antislavery movement is a case in point (Figure 1.10). Commissioned by Quaker abolitionists and produced by the famed British china manufacturer Josiah Wedgwood, who was a Quaker, this engraving shows a kneeling, shackled African man raising his hands in prayer. "Am I Not a Man and a Brother?" is the caption that invariably accompanies the image.

FIGURE 1.10

Antislavery Cameo, late eighteenth century *Wedgwood jasper medallion, 1790s/© Wilberforce House, Hull City Museums and Art Galleries, UK/The Bridgeman Art Library International.*

Widely reproduced in both Britain and America, this image perpetuated European and American associations between blackness and servitude by portraying a kneeling figure at a time when only servants typically took this position. The man also is naked, as slaves typically were aboard the slave ships, rather than wearing the crude work clothes usually allotted to slaves in the New World.

FIGURE 1.11

Group of Negros, as Imported to Be Sold for Slaves, 1796 *J. G. Stedman, from Narrative of a Five Years' Expedition against the Revolted Negroes of Surinam, 1796/Bibliothèque Nationale, Paris, France/Archives Charmet/The Bridgeman Art Library International.*

Group of Negros, as imported to be sold for Slaves.

Unclothed, often-shackled Africans appear in many antislavery depictions of the slave trade—a phenomenon suggesting that slavery's degradation, exploitation, and sexual commoditization of black bodies had a lasting impact on European images of Africans. By the eighteenth-century, West Africans no longer appeared alongside images of animals from their regions as they once had (see Figures 1.1 and 1.2). Instead they were portrayed as something less than human (Figure 1.11). Stripped of all the trappings of social autonomy, such as clothes and the freedom to speak from a standing position, enslaved African men and women were often depicted as pitiful figures with little regard for conventional sexual modesty.

Questions for Analysis

1. Describe the various images that appear in the maps of Africa (Figures 1.1, 1.2, and 1.3). What purposes do these images serve? Why would early mapmakers have embellished their maps with these images, which had nothing to do with navigation?

2. The works of art featured here include depictions of African monarchs, soldiers, servants, and slaves. Is there any consistent relationship between race and class in these images?

3. How do the images of the black body used to illustrate antislavery works (Figures 1.10 and 1.11) differ from the earlier depictions of blacks that appear in this essay? What does this tell you about changing European perceptions of Africans?

Notes

1. Gomes Eanes de Azurara, *The Chronicle of the Discovery and Conquest of the Guinea* (c. 1453), trans. Raymond Beazley and Edgar Prestage, in *Documents Illustrative of the History of the Slave Trade to America*, ed. Elizabeth Donnan (Washington, DC: Carnegie Institution, 1930), 1:206–9.

2. John S. Mbiti, *African Religions and Philosophy* (New York: Praeger, 1969), 108.

3. Luis de Camões, *Os Lusíadas*, quoted in Luis Madureira, "The Accident of America: Marginal Notes on the European Conquest of the World," *CR: The New Centennial Review* 2, no. 1 (2002): 145.

4. Matthew Restall, "Black Conquistadors: Armed Africans in Early Spanish America," *Americas* 57, no. 2 (October 2000): 176.

5. *Dum Diversas* as summarized in The Bull *Romanus Pontifex* (January 8, 1455), translated and reprinted in Francis Gardiner Davenport, ed., *European Treaties Bearing on the History of the United States and Its Dependencies to 1648* (Washington, DC: Carnegie Institution, 1917), 23.

6. Quoted in George Sanderlin, trans. and ed., *Bartolomé de Las Casas: A Selection of His Writings* (New York: Knopf, 1971), 81.

7. Quoted in Lawrence Clayton, "Bartolomé de las Casas and the African Slave Trade," *History Compass* 7, no. 6 (September 2009): 1528.

8. Olaudah Equiano, *The Interesting Narrative of the Life of Olaudah Equiano, or Gustavus Vassa, the African* (London: printed for author, 1745), 49, 51.

9. Samuel Ajayi Crowther, "Narrative of the Events in the Life of a Liberated Negro," *The Missionary Register* (London: Seeley, Jackson, & Halliday, 1837), 436.

10. John Barbot, "A Description of the Coasts of North and South-Guinea," in *Collection of Voyages and Travels*, ed. Thomas Astley and John Churchill (London: printed for Awnsham and John Churchill, 1732), v. V, 326.

11. Quoted in Stephanie E. Smallwood, *Saltwater Slavery: A Middle Passage from Africa to American Diaspora* (Cambridge: Harvard University Press, 2007), 119.

12. Equiano, *The Interesting Narrative of the Life of Olaudah Equiano*, 76, 70.

13. Mahommah Gardo Baquaqua and Samuel Moore, *Biography of Mahommah G. Baquaqua, a Native of Zoogoo, in the Interior of Africa* (Detroit: Geo. E. Pomeroy, 1854), 41.

14. Quoted in Michael A. Gomez, *Exchanging Our Country Marks: The Transformation of African Identities in the Colonial and Antebellum South* (Chapel Hill: University of North Carolina Press, 1998), 158.

15. Marcus Rediker, *The Slave Ship: A Human History* (New York: Viking, 2007), 63.

16. Herbert S. Klein, Stanley L. Engerman, Robin Haines, and Ralph Shlomowitz, "Transoceanic Mortality: The Slave Trade in Comparative Perspective," *William and Mary Quarterly*, 3rd ser., 58, no. 1 (2001): 93–118.

17. Thomas Clarkson, *History of the Rise, Progress and Accomplishment of the Abolition of the Slave Trade by the British Parliament* (London: R. Taylor, 1808), 197.

18. Alexander Falconbridge, *An Account of the Slave Trade on the Coast of Africa* (London: J. Phillips, George Yard, 1788), 23.
19. Ibid., 24–25.
20. John Newton, *Thoughts upon the African Slave Trade* (1788), in *The Works of Reverend John Newton* (New York: J. Seymour, 1811), 6:532.
21. John Newton, *Journal of a Slave Trader*, ed. Bernard Martin and Mark Spurrell (London: Epworth Press, 1962), 75.
22. Ottobah Cugoano, *Narrative of the Enslavement of Ottobah Cugoano, a Native of Africa; Published by Himself, in the Year 1788*, reprinted in Thomas Fisher, "The Negro's Memorial, by an Abolitionist" (London: printed for the author, 1825), 124.
23. Thomas Phillips, *Journal of the Voyage Made in the* Hannibal *of London, Ann. 1693, 1694*, in *Collection of Voyages and Travels*, ed. Thomas Astley and John Churchill (London: printed for Awnsham and John Churchill, 1732), 235.
24. Captain Thomas Snelgrave, quoted in Hugh Thomas, *The Slave Trade: The Story of the Atlantic Slave Trade, 1440–1870* (New York: Simon & Schuster, 1999), 427.
25. Barbot, "A Description of the Coasts of North and South Guinea," 272.
26. Neta Crawford, *Argument and Change in World Politics* (Cambridge: Cambridge University Press, 2002), 64.
27. Smallwood, *Saltwater Slavery*, 152.
28. Rediker, *The Slave Ship*, 5.
29. Vincent Carretta, *Equiano, the African: Biography of a Self-Made Man* (Athens: University of Georgia Press, 2005).
30. Vincent Carretta, "Olaudah Equiano or Gustavus Vassa? New Light on an Eighteenth-Century Question of Identity," *Slavery and Abolition* 20, no. 3 (December 1999): 96–105.
31. Paul E. Lovejoy, "Autobiography and Memory: Gustavus Vassa, Alias Olaudah Equiano, the African," *Slavery and Abolition* 27, no. 3 (December 2006): 317–47.
32. Jonathan Swift, "On Poetry: A Rhapsody" (1733). Jonathan Swift, *The Poems of Jonathan Swift, D.D.,* vol. 1. Reprint of the 1910 G. Bell and Sons edition, 2004. http://www.gutenberg.org/ebooks/14353.
33. John Mandeville, *The Travels of Sir John Mandeville* (New York: Penguin Classics, 2005), 118.
34. Ibn Khaldun, *The Muqaddimah: An Introduction to History*, trans. Franz Rosenthal (Princeton: Princeton University Press, 1967), 117.
35. Barbot, "A Description of the Coasts of North and South Guinea," 128.
36. Ibid., 157.
37. "Second Voyage to Guinea," quoted in Winthrop D. Jordan, *White over Black: American Attitudes toward the Negro, 1550–1812* (New York: Norton, 1977), 15.
38. George Best, quoted ibid.
39. Girolamo Benzoni, *History of the New World* (Boston: Adamant Media, 2001), 91.

Suggested References

African Origins

Curtin, Philip D. *Africa Remembered: Narratives by West Africans from the Era of the Slave Trade.* Prospect Heights, IL: Waveland Press, 1997.

Davis, David Brion. *The Problem of Slavery in Western Culture.* New York: Oxford University Press, 1988.

Gomez, Michael. *Diasporic Africa: A Reader.* New York: New York University Press, 2006.

Iliffe, John. *Africans: The History of a Continent.* Cambridge: Cambridge University Press, 2007.

Mbiti, John S. *African Religions and Philosophy.* New York: Praeger, 1969.

Northrup, David. *Africa's Discovery of Europe, 1450–1850.* New York: Oxford University Press, 2002.

Patterson, Orlando. *Slavery and Social Death: A Comparative Study.* Cambridge: Harvard University Press, 2007.

The Rise of the Transatlantic Slave Trade

Eltis, David. *The Rise of African Slavery in the Americas.* Cambridge: Cambridge University Press, 1999.

Green, Toby. *The Rise of the Trans-Atlantic Slave Trade in Western Africa, 1300–1589.* New York: Cambridge University Press, 2011.

Heywood, Linda M., and John K. Thornton. *Central Africans, Atlantic Creoles, and the Foundation of the Americas, 1585–1660.* New York: Cambridge University Press, 2007.

Lovejoy, Paul E. *Transformations in Slavery: A History of Slavery in Africa.* Cambridge: Cambridge University Press, 2000.

Schwartz, Stuart B. *Tropical Babylons: Sugar and the Making of the Atlantic World, 1450–1680.* Chapel Hill: University of North Carolina Press, 2004.

Thornton, John. *Africa and Africans in the Making of the Atlantic World, 1400–1800.* Cambridge: Cambridge University Press, 1998.

The Long Middle Passage

Berlin, Ira. *Many Thousands Gone: The First Two Centuries of Slavery in North America.* Cambridge: Belknap Press of Harvard University Press, 2000.

Christopher, Emma. *Slave Ship Sailors and Their Captive Cargoes, 1730–1807.* Cambridge: Cambridge University Press, 2006.

Eltis, David, and David Richardson. *Atlas of the Transatlantic Slave Trade.* New Haven, CT: Yale University Press, 2010.

Inikori, Joseph E., and Stanley L. Engerman, eds. *The Atlantic Slave Trade: Effects on Economies, Societies, and Peoples in Africa, the Americas, and Europe.* Durham, NC: Duke University Press, 1992.

Klein, Herbert S. *The Atlantic Slave Trade.* Cambridge: Cambridge University Press, 1999.

Rediker, Marcus. *The Slave Ship: A Human History.* New York: Viking, 2007.

Restall, Matthew. "Black Conquistadors: Armed Africans in Early Spanish America." *Americas* 57, no. 2 (October 2000).

St. Clair, William. *The Door of No Return: The History of Cape Coast Castle and the Atlantic Slave Trade.* New York: BlueBridge, 2007.

Smallwood, Stephanie E. *Saltwater Slavery: A Middle Passage from Africa to American Diaspora.* Cambridge: Harvard University Press, 2007.

Taylor, Eric Robert. *If We Must Die: Shipboard Insurrections in the Era of the Atlantic Slave Trade.* Baton Rouge: LSU Press, 2006.

NEGROES,
TO BE SOLD

A Parcel of young able bodied Negro Men, one of whom is a Cooper by Trade, two Negroes Wenches, and likewise two Girls, one of 12 Years old, and the other 16, the latter a good Seemitress, and can be well recommended.

CHAPTER 2

African Slavery in North America, 1619–1739

LATE IN AUGUST 1619, the Dutch warship *White Lion* docked in Jamestown, Virginia, with a cargo of "20 and odd negroes."[1] These Africans had begun their transatlantic journey in Luanda, a slave trading port in the Portuguese colony of Angola, where they were loaded onto the slave ship *São João Bautista* with more than three hundred other slaves. They survived the harrowing Middle Passage, with illness killing almost a third of them before they reached the New World. When the ship docked briefly in Jamaica to buy medicine and supplies, Captain Manuel Mendes da Cunha paused to report that he still "had many sick aboard" before hurrying on to the Mexican port of Veracruz, his final destination.[2] But the *Bautista*'s long journey was interrupted when, less than five hundred miles from Veracruz, it was captured by the *Treasurer* and the *White Lion*, two English ships sailing under the Dutch flag. Both ships were heavily armed privateers. Privateers were private warships commissioned by European powers to attack their enemies' ships and seize their cargo. Such piracy could be highly profitable; Spanish ships, for example, often carried gold. But the *Bautista* carried only African captives, so the privateers had to content themselves with seizing as many healthy slaves as they could carry.

Among them were the twenty slaves that the *White Lion*'s captain would exchange for provisions when he docked in Jamestown. The seventeen men and three women who arrived in the Chesapeake in 1619, as the first of many generations of African captives to land in English North America, have largely disappeared into history. They likely hailed from one of the African kingdoms along Angola's borders — which included Kongo, Ndongo, and Benguela— before being sold in Angola, a small coastal colony where Portuguese traders exported slaves purchased elsewhere.[3] But their exact origins are difficult to reconstruct, because the Virginia colonists who noted their arrival did not record the names or histories of their region's first black settlers. The lives they led in Virginia are also largely undocumented.

Colonial records do reveal that two men, Virginia governor George Yeardley and a prominent merchant named Abraham Pierson, purchased all twenty slaves in exchange for corn and other supplies. Both men owned large plantations, where they put their new Africans to work growing tobacco and other crops. Less clear, however, is whether all twenty of these involuntary migrants remained enslaved for life. They had landed in one of the few New World colonies where slavery had yet to take root, and individual Africans could still move from slavery to freedom with relative ease.

Slavery took several decades to develop in Virginia. The English migrants who settled there initially preferred to hire white servants, who were more familiar to them. But white laborers were not always available and often proved unwilling to work as servants for any great length of time. African slaves, who could be held in bondage for life, presented no such limitations. By the end of the seventeenth century, slave labor had become crucial to southern colonies such as Virginia and common in European settlements throughout North America.

Enslaved workers were already living in Spanish Florida when the English first arrived. They had come with the Spanish explorer Pedro Menéndez de Avilés, who imported five hundred African slaves to construct the town of St. Augustine in 1565. The Dutch entrepreneurs who settled New Netherland starting in 1625 brought in enslaved workers to clear land and help build their roads and towns, as did the French in Louisiana after 1719. European immigrants to North America were never plentiful enough to meet the colonies' labor needs, so colonists throughout the region imported enslaved Africans to provide additional labor.

With few rights under European law, African workers could be far more brutally exploited than European immigrants and were often used to perform the most grueling tasks. Once the European colonies began to take shape, slaves continued to provide much of the backbreaking labor needed to make these settlements profitable, especially in the plantation colonies that developed in the South. Meanwhile, their presence shaped the character of the communities in which they lived, creating multicultural societies in which European colonists assigned enslaved Africans a distinct and inferior legal and political status.

The character of North American slavery changed dramatically between 1619 and 1750. As African captives arrived in ever-larger numbers and racial slavery became more entrenched, it became increasingly difficult for slaves to secure their freedom or cast off the growing stigma that blackness and slavery held among the English colonists. Nevertheless, African people throughout the region slowly became African Americans. They developed a distinctive culture forged by the cross-cultural exchanges and biological intermixture that took place among Africans, Europeans, and Native Americans; by the legal and social barriers that defined their caste; and by the experience of enslavement.

Slavery and Freedom in Early English North America

Seventeenth-century English colonists did not arrive in the New World expecting to people their settlements with enslaved Africans. In fact, they hailed from a nation where slavery was no longer practiced. "As for slaves and bondsmen we have none," one English historian boasted in the 1570s. "Nay, such is the privilege of our country . . . that if anyone come hither from other realms so soon as they set foot on land they become free . . . all note of servile bondage is utterly removed from them."[4] Although enslaved Africans were not unknown in England, this claim was correct in underscoring that English common law recognized no form of slavery. Villeinage, an English form of serfdom, was extinct by the 1600s and would not be revived in the English colonies.

Instead, the earliest slaveholders in the colonies adopted a new system of racial slavery that took several decades to emerge and still longer to give rise to the plantation societies that ultimately became established in the colonial South. For much of the

1600s, Africans who arrived in these colonies entered societies where servitude was far more common than slavery, and slaves and servants occupied a similar status. But by the beginning of the eighteenth century, enslaved Africans, who had proved to be more profitable, more plentiful, and far easier to exploit than white servants, predominated in the Chesapeake colonies of Virginia and Maryland. Meanwhile, slavery appeared in New England, where the Puritans and Pilgrims held small numbers of slaves, and fueled the growth of a plantation economy in colonial Carolina.

Settlers, Servants, and Slaves in the Chesapeake

England's first successful permanent settlement in North America was founded in 1607 on Jamestown Island, about thirty miles from the mouth of Chesapeake Bay. Financed by the Virginia Company, a joint-stock company chartered by King James I in 1606 to establish an English settlement in the New World, Jamestown was not established with slavery in mind. The company's investors hoped to earn a profit on their shares, while the king hoped to expand England's imperial power.

Indeed, advocates of English colonization, such as the explorer Sir Francis Drake and the writer and armchair traveler Richard Hakluyt, had long maintained that English settlement of the New World could help rescue both blacks and Indians from the "Spanish tyranny" described by Bartolomé de Las Casas. Drake, who spent much of his career raiding the Spanish colonies for gold, undermined slavery whenever he could. For instance, he allied with a community of escaped slaves, or **maroons**, in his attack on the Spanish at Panama in 1572, and he liberated slaves when he sacked the Spanish town of St. Augustine in 1586.

The first English colonists, not unlike Drake, hoped to live off the riches of the New World. Known as "adventurers," they consisted largely of gentlemen and soldiers. But they would find no precious metals or valuable commodities in Virginia. Instead, they could barely feed themselves. Jamestown was surrounded by a fertile environment full of game and fish, but the colonists were unprepared to fend for themselves in Virginia's alien landscape. Inexperienced in hunting, fishing, or farming, they initially relied on local Indians to supply them with corn. As a result, they soon wore out their welcome among the indigenous inhabitants.

On the verge of extinction by 1611, the colony was revived by the development of a lucrative cash crop that also created a new market for labor. The colonists experimented with planting a type of tobacco imported from South America. The experiment proved so successful that when Captain Samuel Argall arrived to take over Virginia's governorship in 1617, he found "the streets, the market place and all other spare places planted with tobacco."[5] Tobacco requires constant care throughout its long growing season and must be cleaned, rolled, and dried after it is harvested. (See Visual Sources: African Labor in the Making of the Americas, pp. 97–107.) But whereas the Spanish had been able to force the Aztecs, Incas, and other indigenous populations to work for them, the English never managed to subjugate the Eastern Woodlands Indians in Powhatan's confederacy. Other Chesapeake tribes also resisted English rule and enslavement, although the colonists did acquire small numbers of Indian slaves from other regions. After 1619, they began to purchase African slaves as well, but even enslaved Africans were in short supply during the colony's early years (Map 2.1).

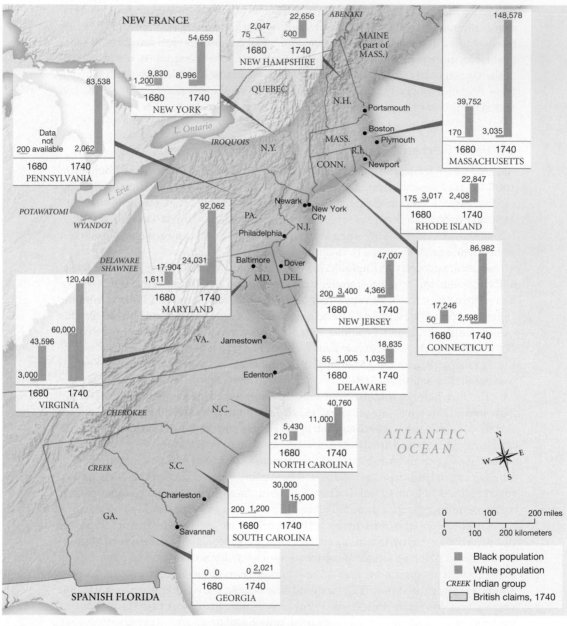

MAP 2.1   Distribution of Blacks and Whites, 1680 and 1740

This map shows the distribution of blacks and whites in British North America in 1680 and 1740.
While there were black people living throughout the colonies, by 1740, the vast majority of the
black population lived in the southern colonies of Virginia, Maryland, and the Carolinas.

White servitude, rather than black or Indian slavery, initially predominated in colonial Virginia and its close neighbor, Maryland, which English colonists founded in 1634. Both colonies were established at a time when England had an oversupply of landless rural laborers and urban paupers. Impoverished and unemployed, thousands of English and Scots-Irish servants were willing to travel abroad to cultivate tobacco in the Chesapeake. Most arrived in Virginia as **indentured servants**. As such, they were required to work for four to seven years to pay the cost of their transportation and maintenance.

The enslaved Africans who ended up in the Chesapeake arrived no more than a few dozen at a time aboard privateers and other small boats. By all evidence, these early arrivals were initially incorporated into a labor force that was at least nominally free. Slaves and servants worked and lived alongside one another, ran away together, cohabited, and even intermarried. Early colonial documents list both groups as servants, which has long made the legal status of slavery in the early Chesapeake a matter of debate. During this time, enslaved Africans moved from slavery to freedom far more easily than they would in later generations.

Planters were not legally obligated to release blacks from servitude, however, and by 1640 Virginia courts had at least tacitly recognized this fact. That year, when two white servants and one black servant were captured in Maryland after running away from a Virginia farmer, they received dramatically different sentences. All three were sentenced to thirty lashes and extended terms of service. But whereas the white servants were assigned only an additional year of servitude, the black servant—a man named John Punch—was ordered to "serve his said master or his assigns for the time of his natural Life here or elsewhere."[6]

Subsequent laws suggest that blacks began to acquire a uniquely inferior status in the colony. A 1643 law decreed that African women—who were often assigned to field work rather than domestic labor would, unlike English women, be taxed as laborers. A 1662 law made the enslaved status of black women heritable, decreeing that "all children borne in this country shall be held bond or free only according to the condition of the mother."[7] Both laws ran contrary to the patriarchal assumptions of English common law, which defined women's work as domestic, and therefore not subject to tax, and used paternity rather than maternity to determine inheritance and assign fathers legal jurisdiction over their children. But the system of **chattel slavery** under development in Virginia required a different set of assumptions. Purchased as chattel, or movable personal property, African slaves were legally equivalent to other forms of chattel, such as domestic animals and furniture. They had no rights of any kind and no legal authority over anyone—even their children, who belonged to their owners.

By using the mother's status to determine whether a child would be slave or free, Virginia legislators also resolved a number of practical questions. For instance, English law required servant women who became pregnant to work extra time to compensate their masters for the loss of their labor and expenses associated with the birth—sanctions that could not be imposed on slave women, who were already enslaved for life. Moreover, in making slavery heritable through the mother, the legislators prevented slave women from seeking liberty for their children by claiming freemen as the fathers, and they shielded white men from paternity claims. Finally, the new legislation clarified the legal status of slave women's children, which had previously been ambiguous. This ambiguity is evident in the case of Elizabeth Key, the illegitimate daughter of an enslaved mother and English father who petitioned for her freedom in 1656. Several courts ruled on her

Sex, Power, and Slavery in Virginia
Painted on the back of another painting by an anonymous artist, this piece of art is unusual in its
frank depiction of the two kinds of power white slaveholders wielded over their slaves. On the left
is an image of sexual power, which shows a well-dressed slave owner embracing a female slave.
On the right is an illustration of physical, brute power, seen as an owner or overseer prepares
to whip a male slave's bare back. Although Virginia prohibited marriage between whites and
blacks and fined white women who gave birth to mulatto children, it did not discourage sexual
relationships between white men and black women, leaving much room for slaveholders to take
advantage of female slaves. Why did the artist title the painting *Virginian Luxuries*? Virginian Luxuries,
c. 1825/Abby Aldrich Rockefeller Folk Art Museum, The Colonial Williamsburg Foundation, Williamsburg, VA.

case, handing down different verdicts. She gained her freedom only after she married her
English lawyer, who won her case before the colony's general assembly.

By the late 1660s, both Key's victory and her marriage would have been impossible. In
addition to passing the 1662 law that made slave status heritable through the mother, Virginia lawmakers in 1691 all but outlawed interracial marriage. The new law decreed that any
white person who married a "negroe, mulatto or Indian" would be forever banished from
the colony "within three months of such marriage." Ironically, though expressly designed to
prevent "that abominable mixture and spurious issue which hereafter may increase in this
dominion," this measure attacked legitimate unions between the races rather than race mixture.[8] Intermarriage became a crime, but white men were neither barred nor discouraged
from entering into sexual relationships with slave women.

As lawmakers created new laws, they also eliminated legal uncertainties that the
colony's first generation of black residents had used to seek freedom in the courts. As late

as the 1660s, for example, Chesapeake courts remained undecided about the compatibility between slavery and Christianity. Black and Indian converts became Christians with baptism, which included legal standing in colonial courts. But Christianity lost any further association with freedom in 1667, when the Virginia legislature passed an act explicitly exempting slaves from the freedoms normally extended to Christians. The "blessed sacrament of baptisme," the act noted, "doth not alter the condition of the person as to his bondage or freedome." (See Documents: Making Slaves, pp. 84–89.)

As Virginia lawmakers solidified the legal status of slavery, forces outside the colony gave the institution new economic advantages. By midcentury, Virginia's supply of white servants was declining. The colony's reputation for exploiting and abusing servants had made it increasingly unappealing to immigrants, who were also in short supply as a result of the English Civil Wars, which diverted large numbers of Englishmen into military service. Meanwhile, local supplies of enslaved Africans were slowly increasing. The Dutch, who had established settlements on the Middle Atlantic coast starting in the 1620s, took advantage of shipping disruptions caused by the English Civil Wars to secure new commercial markets in the English colonies. They began to supply slaves to the Chesapeake, where the black population soared from a few hundred in 1650 to four thousand in 1680. The English themselves entered the slave trade with the 1660 establishment of the Royal African Company, which held a monopoly over English trade with Africa until 1698, transporting between 90,000 and 100,000 slaves to English colonies in the New World. The rise of the Royal African Company and other English entities after 1698 offered English colonists a steady and affordable supply of slaves.

Chattel slavery also offered a variety of noneconomic advantages. Both slaves and servants ran away, but enslaved Africans were far easier to recover. Once they escaped beyond neighborhoods where they were known, white English-speaking servants could easily blend in with other European settlers and live as free people. By contrast, black runaways' color marked them as likely slaves, making them easy to recapture. One newly arrived African discovered this in 1739 when he was committed to the James City County Jail. According to the *Virginia Gazette*, he was "a new Negro" who could not "speak English, his name is understood to be Tom." He was soon picked up by local authorities who "suppos'd [him] to be a Runaway" and imprisoned to ensure that "his owner may have him again."[9]

Enslaved Africans offered significant long-term advantages over servant laborers. Their bondage was permanent and hereditary, which allowed slave owners to invest in a labor supply that could reproduce itself. Slaves also were subject to far stricter social controls than freemen, which made them appealing to white planters intent on maintaining their power. In contrast, by the 1670s landless white ex-servants had become a disruptive force in the Chesapeake. Largely male, young, and discontented, they competed with more established colonists for land and often drifted from county to county challenging colonial authorities, encouraging slaves to run away, and antagonizing local Indian populations by encroaching on their land.

The dangers posed by ex-servants and their allies were vividly illustrated in a 1676 upheaval in Virginia known as Bacon's Rebellion. Led by Nathaniel Bacon, a wealthy colonist who commanded the support of an army largely made up of landless freemen, servants, and slaves, the rebellion pitted land-hungry colonists against the royal authority of Governor William Berkeley. At issue was the colony's Indian policy, which was not aggressive enough to suit the many landless men who rallied around Bacon to make war on "Indians in generall," and especially nearby Native American allies.[10] Charged with treason after an attack on several such groups, Bacon and his makeshift army attacked the colony's royal government, managing to capture Jamestown and set it on fire before English troops arrived to crush the rebellion.

Bacon's Rebellion underscored the dangers of importing thousands of white male servants into a colony that held few opportunities for them. The fact that Bacon had managed to mobilize both poor whites and black bondmen also left officials worried about the common grievances uniting these two groups. Virginia's colonial government thus moved to forestall further challenges to its authority by sharpening the distinctions between servants and slaves. The legislature enacted harsh new laws allowing slave owners to kill rebellious slaves with impunity. At the same time, it curbed planters' power over white servants and freedmen by limiting the years of service that could be imposed on white servants and lowering the poll taxes that kept poor whites from voting. By empowering whites and subjecting blacks to ever-stricter systems of control, the colonial legislature took significant steps toward deepening the racial divide and creating an entrenched system of racial slavery.

The Expansion of Slavery in the Chesapeake

"They import so Many Negroes hither," the Virginia planter William Byrd wrote in 1736, "that I fear this Colony will some time or other be confirmed by the name of New Guinea."[11] Byrd's statement reflects an extraordinary demographic shift in the eighteenth-century Chesapeake. In 1680, blacks constituted approximately 7 percent of Virginia's population, but by 1750 the colony's population was 44 percent black. Maryland's black population likewise increased from 9 percent to 30 percent during the same time span. (See By the Numbers: Black and White Populations in the Seventeenth-Century Chesapeake.) Both colonies, although initially largely populated by white servants, had built plantation economies that revolved around black slavery.

The Africans who flooded the Chesapeake after 1680 had few of the opportunities afforded to early arrivals. Not many would achieve freedom, own property, or establish families. Increasingly drawn from the interior of Africa, the "new Negroes," as they were known, arrived by the boatload and were sold in small lots at numerous riverside wharfs bordering the Chesapeake. The region's farming was dispersed; even large landholders generally owned several small plantations, and few employed more than ten slaves on any single holding. Their slaves were thus widely dispersed as well, and planters usually assigned new arrivals to unskilled labor on their most remote upcountry holdings. The newcomers, who were not yet conversant in English or trained to do other work, cleared land and cultivated tobacco and other crops under the supervision of white overseers. Still ravaged by the transatlantic journey, one-quarter died within a year of arrival, and few managed to reproduce. In addition, two-thirds of the new arrivals were men, and many planters assigned their slaves to sex-segregated quarters where they had little chance to form family ties.

Drawn from different parts of Africa, the newcomers could not always converse with more acculturated slaves—or even with each other. The young Olaudah Equiano, who was shipped to Virginia in the 1750s, ended up in complete linguistic isolation. Most of his countrymen had been sold in Barbados, and he and his remaining shipmates landed in a part of Virginia where "we saw few or none of our native Africans,

BY THE NUMBERS   Black and White Populations in the Seventeenth-Century Chesapeake

This graph underscores the fact that blacks remained rare in the Chesapeake prior to the 1660s. While the number of blacks increased steadily over the decades, this region's black population nevertheless grew more slowly than its white population throughout most of the seventeenth century.

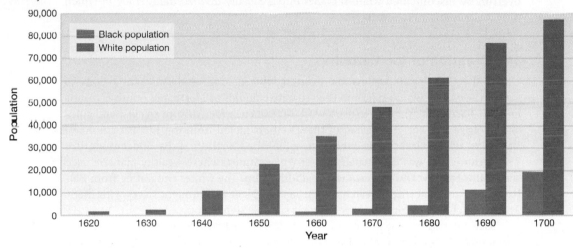

and not one soul who could talk to me."[12] Often the only English the newcomers knew were the English names assigned to them by their owners. They received no other instruction in the language.

Linguistically isolated, subjected to a harsh work regime, and forced to abandon even the names that tied them to their homelands, the newcomers struggled but somehow managed to survive. They forged a common language, which one Anglican minister described as "a wild confused medley of negro and English." These Americanized, or **creole**, forms of communication probably represented a blend of English and several African languages. Newcomers also formed close bonds within their quarters. African-born slaves were far less likely to run away than American-born ones, and they rarely ran away alone. Instead, they fled with other Africans, sometimes with the goal of creating their own communities on the frontier.

Sometimes, groups of African-born slaves conspired to revolt and escape together. When word of planned revolts in 1710 and 1722 reached the colonists, they arrested and executed the conspirators before the rebellions could take place. But one Sunday in the fall of 1730, when most plantation owners were in church, more than three hundred slaves organized into military groups and left their plantations for the Dismal Swamp—a coastal plain on Virginia's southeastern border. Taking shelter on the frontier, the runaways "did a great deal of Mischief to that Province [of Virginia]," a visitor to the colony reported, before the colonists recruited some Pasquotank Indians to hunt them down.[13]

The slaves' defiance affected the colony's free people of color, who were often suspected of fostering slave rebellions. Virginia's small free black population, mostly descended from the slaves who had secured their freedom during the colony's early years, also included **mulatto**, or mixed-race, descendants of unions between slaves and whites—some of whom had been born to a white mother and a slave father. Regardless of their origins, all lost some of their freedoms as result of the slave unrest of the early 1700s, which led white colonists to define all blacks as dangerous. The new laws that Virginia passed in the 1720s, which disarmed and disfranchised free blacks and mulattoes, reflected this conviction. With such laws, Virginia transformed a society once overrun by discontented white servants into a racially divided democracy in which only white men could be fully free.

The Creation of the Carolinas

Unlike the Chesapeake settlers, the planters who in 1663 established the colony of Carolina—which would split into the separate colonies of North and South Carolina in 1729—arrived with plans to use a workforce of enslaved Africans to clear and cultivate their settlement. About half of these settlers hailed from the English colony of Barbados, where slavery was already an established institution. By midcentury, this Caribbean island was dominated by sugar plantations, where wealthy planters used slave labor to grow and harvest the demanding crop. The whites emigrating from Barbados to Carolina came in search of new land to plant and brought slaves with them. The major challenge for them was finding a suitable staple crop.

Rice cultivation, long popular in West Africa, flourished in South Carolina largely as a result of the slaves' expertise. The crop was unfamiliar to most English planters, who nonetheless saw its potential and consulted their slaves on the possibility of growing it in Virginia as early as 1648. "The Ground and the Climate is very proper for it [rice] as our Negroes affirme," one colonist reported that year, explaining that "in their Country, [it] is most of their food."[14] Experiments in rice cultivation foundered in Virginia but were far more successful in Carolina, which by the 1720s had begun to export nearly ten million pounds of rice a year. Drawing on their own expertise, slaves grew, harvested, and processed the crop with the same equipment and techniques used in their homelands.

Rice plantation slaves worked under a **task system**, which involved minimal white supervision. Unlike slaveholders in the Chesapeake, Carolina rice planters did not employ white overseers to direct gangs of slave laborers. Instead, low-country slaves worked largely under their own direction, completing daily tasks laid out by a black **driver**—a bondman chosen to oversee the work of other slaves. Used only in rice-growing regions, the task system reflected Carolina planters' reliance on slaves' knowledge of African cultivation methods. This reliance is also evident in planters' demand for slaves from rice-growing parts of Africa, such as the Upper Guinea coast, Senegambia, and the Windward Coast. In response, slave traders promoted shipments from these regions, advertising "choice cargo[s] of Windward and Gold Coast Negroes, who have been accustomed to the planting of rice."[15]

Under the task system, slaves were assigned specific agricultural tasks each day, then were free to work on their own behalf. This small measure of independence, used as an incentive for slaves to complete their daily work quickly, was a mixed blessing. Slaves were permitted to farm small allotments of land where they could raise livestock and grow provisions to feed themselves. But with the adoption of rice culture, the practice grew increasingly exploitative. Rather than supplying rations to their slaves, planters expected them to provision themselves during whatever time they had left after completing their grueling tasks in the rice fields. While whites observed the Sabbath, most enslaved people needed to work on Sundays just to survive.

Slaves and Rice Cultivation in Carolina
Carolina planters relied on African slaves' knowledge of and experience with cultivating rice to grow this challenging and lucrative crop. The extent to which the planters valued African expertise is illustrated in advertisements placed by slave traders promoting the fact that the slaves on a particular ship came from rice-cultivating regions of Africa. This advertisement, which appeared in an eighteenth-century newspaper during a smallpox epidemic, also assured potential buyers that careful measures had been taken to keep the slaves free of the disease.

As in the Chesapeake, Carolina slave owners had little interest in providing their slaves with religious instruction. Frustrated missionaries dispatched by the Anglican Church routinely proclaimed that the slaves' seven-day workweek made conversion "scarcely possible." "The slaves had not time to be instructed by the minister on the Lord's day," reported the minister Gideon Johnston in 1713, who noted the additional difficulty of gathering slaves when "the plantations are so many and so remote in distance from one another." But he was also not sure that such gatherings would be wise, given that they would provide slaves "the opportunity of knowing their own strength and superiority from the point of view of number" and make them "tempted to recover their liberty."[16]

Carolina slaves remained isolated and numerous enough to create a distinctly African world of their own. Many lived in self-contained slave communities on plantations that housed as many as one hundred slaves. Responsible for building their own quarters, they crafted mud-walled homes with palmetto roofs using techniques and materials that were common in sub-Saharan Africa. They cooked their food in handmade earthenware pots, similar to those used in Africa, which they either made themselves or purchased from the Indians. Predominantly African-born until the 1760s, some also bore physical marks of their heritage. These included facial scars known as **country marks**, which members of some African ethnic groups received at puberty to mark their origins, and filed or clipped teeth, which often served a similar purpose. African in their speech as well as their appearance, low-country slaves rarely mastered standard English.

Carolina slaves also retained African religious traditions, although their new environment may have reshaped some of their beliefs. The religious practices of early black Carolinians are difficult to reconstruct in detail, since most white observers simply dismissed the slaves as pagans "who knew nothing of the true God."[17] Slaves often believed in magic and the existence of conjurers, who could heal the sick and kill their enemies. Such figures served as "Negro doctors" among the slaves, dispensing medicine, charms, and sometimes even poison. Conjurers were powerful figures, respected and feared even by whites, who when they fell ill sometimes accused black conjurers of having caused their illnesses.

But other beliefs accorded with those of white Christians. One Anglican missionary reported that "our negro-pagans have a notion of God and of a Devil" and interviewed a "Negro-Pagan Woman" who described her God as an omnipotent being who controlled all "all things."[18] Such a God was one feature of many West African religions, which usually recognized a multitude of lesser gods and powerful ancestral spirits as well, but slaves in the New World may have placed an increasing emphasis on the idea of a single Supreme Being. Far from their villages and sacred places, with few priests to guide them, African-born slaves and their descendants did not hold the same religious beliefs as their ancestors. Instead, they developed new, communal belief systems shaped by their experiences of exile, forced migration, and enslavement.

A brutal labor regime also shaped the character of the Carolina slave community. Throughout much of the eighteenth century, slave deaths routinely outnumbered births in Carolina. But low-country blacks, despite being worked literally to death, did not always submit to their subjugation. Like their Virginia counterparts, enslaved Carolinians sometimes escaped alone or with others to live in maroon communities on the colony's frontiers. By the early decades of the eighteenth century, however, the expansion of white settlement into North Carolina and Georgia made it increasingly difficult to avoid detection. As in Virginia, Carolina planters paid Indian slave catchers to capture and return runaways. Planters also instituted measures intended to prevent runaways or rebellions. In 1690, South Carolina adopted the Barbadian slave code, which provided that slaves who ran away or defied their masters more than once could be whipped, slit through the nose, and branded with a hot iron. Three-time offenders could be castrated or hamstrung (have their leg tendons cut). Such punishments were not uncommon, according to one Huguenot missionary, who noted that South Carolina slaves were often crippled or disfigured for "small faults."[19]

Africans in New England

The New England colonies, first settled in the 1620s and 1630s, never became home to a large number of slaves or relied on slave labor to sustain their economies. The region's cold climate and short growing season prohibited the cultivation of labor-intensive crops such as sugar, tobacco, and rice, resulting in little need for enslaved workers. Instead, most New England agriculture took the form of small family farms dedicated to the production of crops and livestock that could be tended by household members. Prior to 1700, blacks constituted less than 1 percent of the region's population (or fewer than one thousand people), and they never amounted to more than 3 percent.

These limits to slavery's growth in New England were more a result of geography than of antislavery measures. The Pilgrims and Puritans who established the New England colonies came to the Americas to escape religious persecution in Europe, but their religious ideals did not preclude slave ownership. They looked to the Bible for guidance in establishing exemplary Protestant communities and accepted the slavery of both prisoners of war and foreign peoples as practices sanctioned by the Scriptures.

Accordingly, the Puritans and Pilgrims, who were frequently at odds with their Indian neighbors, enslaved Native Americans whenever they could. Early New England communities, which comprised a collection of coastal settlements, were also drawn into African slavery as a result of their commercial relationships with slaveholding colonies in the Caribbean. New Englanders shipped provisions such as wheat, beef, butter, fish, and cheese to these island colonies and received molasses, sugar, indigo, and other slave-grown goods in return. Occasionally, they purchased slaves as well.

In addition, New England colonists also acquired black slaves in exchange for Native American prisoners-of-war, whom they often shipped off to slavery in the Caribbean. These exchanges required New Englanders to address slavery's legality earlier than other English colonists. Massachusetts became the first North American colony to legally recognize chattel slavery, which was sanctioned in the Body of Liberties the colonists compiled in 1641. (See From the Record: The Massachusetts Body of Liberties.) This document, an enumeration of colonists' rights, permitted them to enslave "Captives taken in just warres" and purchase "such strangers as willingly selle themselves or are sold to us." With the formation of the New England Confederation in 1643, the Plymouth, Connecticut, and New Haven colonies legally recognized slavery as well. New Hampshire, under the legal jurisdiction of Massachusetts until 1679, also began importing small numbers of slaves. Only Rhode Island, founded as a haven for religious dissenters in 1636, hesitated. Rhode Island colonists initially rejected permanent bondage, passing a law that limited the servitude of both blacks and whites to ten years. But the law was never enforced, and Rhode Island went on to import more slaves per capita than any other New England colony.

By the beginning of the eighteenth century, Boston's slave population had grown large enough to trouble some Puritans. "Numerousness of Slaves at this day in the Province, and the Uneasiness of them under their Slavery, hath put many upon thinking whether the Foundation of it be firmly and well laid," wrote the wealthy Boston merchant and judge Samuel Sewall, who had presided over the Salem witch trials in 1692–1693. The only one of three Salem judges to publicly regret his role in the conviction and execution of nineteen accused witches, Sewall issued a formal apology in 1697. But after quieting his conscience on that score, he became increasingly uneasy with himself for having "long neglected doing anything" about slavery.[20] In 1700, he issued the first antislavery tract published in America, a pamphlet entitled *The Selling of Joseph: A Memorial*, which questioned the morality of slavery. (See Documents: British Colonists Debate the Merits of Slavery, pp. 90–96.)

Most of Sewall's contemporaries ignored his pamphlet. Even the colony's Puritan clergy were confident that Massachusetts provided slaves "all the liberties and Christian

From the Record

The Massachusetts Body of Liberties, 1641

Adopted in 1641, the Massachusetts Body of Liberties was New England's first legal code. Drafted by the Puritan lawyer Nathan Ward of Ipswich, it drew on both English common law and biblical law to define the rights of the region's European colonists. Enslaved "Forreiners and Strangers," however, were not entitled to freedom under the Body of Liberties.

Liberties of Forreiners and Strangers.

89. If any people of other Nations professing the true Christian Religion shall flee to us from the Tiranny or oppression of their persecutors, or from famyne, warres, or the like necessary and compulsorie cause, They shall be entertayned and succoured amongst us, according to that power and prudence, god shall give us.

90. If any ships or other vessels, be it freind or enemy, shall suffer shipwrack upon our Coast, there shall be no violence or wrong offered to their persons or goods. But their persons shall be harboured, and relieved, and their goods preserved in safety till Authoritie may be certified thereof, and shall take further order therein.

91. There shall never be any bond slaverie, villinage or Captivitie amongst us unles[s] it be lawfull Captives taken in just warres, and such strangers as willingly selle themselves or are sold to us. And these shall have all the liberties and Christian usages which the law of god established in Israell concerning such persons doeth morally require. This exempts none from servitude who shall be Judged thereto by Authoritie.

SOURCE: Charles W. Eliot, ed., *American Historical Documents, 1000–1904,* The Harvard Classics (New York: P. F. Collier & Son, 1910), 43:79.

???   **On what grounds does this document sanction slavery? What limits does it place on the practice of slavery?**

usages which the law of god established in Israell concerning such persons doeth morally require." Though subject to some forms of segregation, enslaved Africans were permitted to legally marry, were entitled to a trial by jury when accused of a crime, and were welcome to join New England churches. The influential Puritan minister Cotton Mather claimed that as long as slave owners were conscientious about providing religious instruction to slaves, Christianity "wonderfully dulcifies, and mollifies and moderates the circumstances of [slavery]." A slave owner himself, Mather supplied special catechisms that other slave owners could use to guide enslaved Africans toward salvation and told them to promise their slaves that "*if they serve God patiently and cheerfully in the Condition which he orders for them,*" they will be rewarded by "*Eternal Happiness*" in heaven. Mather also

A Young Domestic Slave

Young slaves often assumed domestic roles, sometimes tending to children in a planter's household. In this painting, Henry Darnall III, the young son of a wealthy Maryland planter, is shown with a black boy about the same age as he. Darnall stands in front of a balustrade, holding a bow and arrow; his young servant stands behind it, holding a dead bird. Notice the differences in the two figures' dress, positions, and activities. What does this tell us about the training of young slaves and their relationships with the members of their masters' households, including the children? *Portrait, Henry Darnall III, 1702–c. 1787, oil on canvas by Justus Engelhardt Kühn, c. 1710. Museum Department/Courtesy of the Maryland Historical Society, image ID 1912.1.3.*

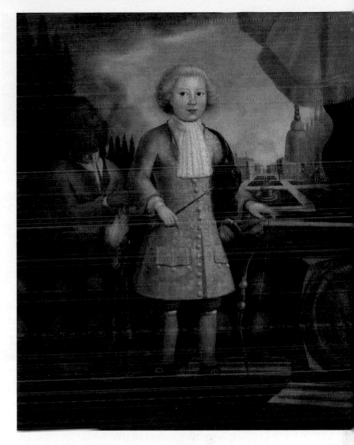

took pains to reassure slave owners that "the *Law of Christianity*" did not set the "*Baptized slave at Liberty*."[21]

Though sanctioned by spiritual authorities such as Mather, the practice of slaveholding grew only modestly in New England. Few slaves were imported into the region by New England slave merchants, who typically delivered their shipments to the lucrative slave markets of the Caribbean or the American South rather than to northern slave trading ports. Instead, New England remained a secondary market for slaves, where traders disposed of a small number of blacks who were too young, old, or sick to be sold elsewhere. Known in the trade as "refuse slaves," most of them arrived in the region after their shipmates had been sold in the Caribbean.

Venture Smith, a native of Guinea who was captured and sold into slavery at age eight, was imported to Barbados with approximately 260 other African captives, only 200 of whom survived after smallpox broke out on board ship. All but four of the survivors attracted West Indian buyers; the rest sailed on to Rhode Island. Purchased and employed by the steward of the slave ship that brought him there, Smith was typical of the slaves who ended up in New England: He was too young to appeal to planters in the West Indies or in Britain's southern colonies, who sought brawny adult laborers for plantation work. Bought for four gallons of rum and a piece of calico, he was a speculative investment on the part of the ship's steward, who named him Venture and sent him home to his family to work as a domestic servant.

Young slaves such as Venture Smith, who were more affordable than adults, were welcome in northern markets. Buyers sometimes expressed a preference for young slaves—"the younger the better if not quite children," one buyer specified.[22] These slaves were often trained to perform domestic service and skilled work. Young Africans were in a better position to learn English, achieve a measure of acculturation, and

Venture Smith's Gravestone
After being kidnapped and sold into slavery as a child, Venture Smith grew into a successful, industrious adult who was able to purchase his own and his family's freedom. He eventually provided a narrative of his life to a schoolteacher, who transcribed and published it. The words on Smith's gravestone provide some insight into the aspects of his life that his family was most proud of: "Sacred to the Memory of Venture Smith an African tho the son of a King he was kidnapped & sold as a slave but by his industry he acquired Money to purchase his Freedom, who Died Sept 19 1805 in the 77th Year of his Age." © *David C. Nelson.*

master domestic tasks and other new skills than the adult field hands the planters preferred. Young Venture's masters put him to work carding wool and pounding dried corn into meal until he grew old enough for farmwork; then he switched to working both in and out of doors.

Venture Smith grew up to be a strong, healthy, and hardworking man who married, fathered three children, and ultimately managed to purchase his own and his family's freedom. But many blacks in New England did not share his fate. Mortality rates were high and birthrates low among the region's black population during the eighteenth century. Those who survived had trouble finding partners and establishing families, because most were male, and they tended to be employed by different households scattered across the region, which limited their contact with other blacks.

Even slaves who were lucky enough to marry often lived in different households and may have hesitated to have children because they could not raise a family together. Slave children were not prized by northern masters, whose households were rarely large enough to accommodate slave families. Enslaved women were sometimes sold because of their reproductive potential, as one Connecticut ad for a sixteen-year-old girl indicates. Her owner wished to dispose of her "for no other fault but because she is like[ly] to be a good breeder."[23] Although some black men found African or Indian spouses, marriage between blacks and whites was outlawed in Massachusetts in 1705 and discouraged virtually everywhere else.

Slavery in the Middle Atlantic Colonies

The settlement of North America's Middle Atlantic coast was pioneered by the Dutch, who began importing slave workers to the region in 1626, just a few years after the first white settlers arrived. Known as New Netherland, the region the Dutch settled included large portions of present-day New York, Connecticut, Delaware, and New Jersey, as well as parts of Pennsylvania. This land remained under Dutch rule only until 1664, when England, at war with the Dutch throughout much of the seventeenth century, seized the colony and opened the region to English settlement. Slavery continued and became more repressive under English rule.

Slavery and Half-Freedom in New Netherland

The Dutch colonization of New Netherland was led by the West India Company, a group of Dutch merchants who held a royal monopoly over Dutch trade in the Caribbean and the Americas, as well as dominion over Dutch participation in the African slave trade. Chartered in 1621, the West India Company established its North American headquarters on the island of Manhattan in 1625. The settlement, known as New Amsterdam, was designed as a fur trading center that also supplied timber for Dutch ships and developed farms to feed Dutch settlers and sell food to the Netherlands. Anxious to reduce their tiny nation's need to import food from other European powers, the company's directors hoped that Dutch farmers would lead the agricultural settlement of New Netherland. But such hopes were dashed when the colony attracted only itinerant fur traders. In 1626, the West India Company began importing slaves to build New Amsterdam, the colony's capital. Owned by the company, the enslaved laborers were drawn from various Dutch slave trading regions and included individuals from Angola, Kongo, the Caribbean, and Brazil.

These laborers were crucial to New Netherland's survival. They cleared land and built New Amsterdam's fort, church, warehouses, sawmills, and farms. Unable to attract European migrants willing to clear, cultivate, and occupy their colony, the company's directors soon resolved that "Negroes would accomplish more work for their masters and at less expense, than farm servants, who must be bribed to go thither by a great deal of money and promises."[24] After 1629, the company's attempts to attract white immigrants included a promise "to supply the colonists with as many Blacks as they conveniently can."[25] The offer encouraged slaveholding settlers to fan out throughout the lower Hudson valley, creating settlements in what would later become Manhattan's five boroughs and moving across the river to present-day New Jersey as well. (See From the Record: Correspondence regarding Slave Shipments.) Slavery was even adopted by the Swedish colonists who established settlements along Delaware Bay in 1638. New Netherland's widely dispersed slave population grew steadily, rising to approximately 25 percent of the colony's population by midcentury.

Many of the colony's slaves were the property of the West India Company rather than individual owners, which complicated their status under Dutch law and left the terms of their service open to challenge. Company slaves were quick to take advantage of this ambiguity and began petitioning for wages and suing for their freedom as early as the 1630s. Their litigation had mixed results: It won them wages but not freedom, and it further confused the legal status of slavery in the colony. But their efforts did establish that enslaved blacks had the right to petition colonial authorities and gain access to Dutch courts. Between 1635 and 1664, black colonists in New Netherland took legal action to allow them to earn money, buy land, and petition for freedom.

In the 1640s, such petitions led to a status called **half-freedom**. Primarily allotted to blacks who had helped defend the colony against Indian attacks, half-freedom

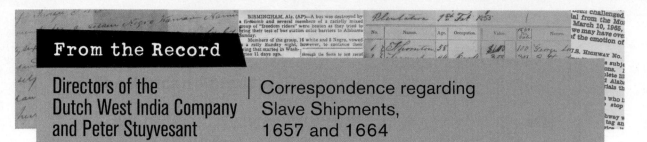

From the Record

Directors of the Dutch West India Company and Peter Stuyvesant | Correspondence regarding Slave Shipments, 1657 and 1664

In the following selections, the **Directors of the Dutch West India Company** write to **Peter Stuyvesant**, Director-General of New Netherland, in 1657 to tell him they have not been able to send him all the skilled tradesmen that he requested and to suggest that he purchase slaves to be trained for skilled work; Stuyvesant writes the Directors in 1664 about a shipment of slaves that he received from them. The property of the Dutch West India Company, these slaves were to serve as a supply of both labor and revenue for company officials such as Stuyvesant. But Stuyvesant found some of the slaves unsalable and too feeble to be useful. What do these documents tell us about the role that slave labor played in the colony, and about the kinds of slaves the colonists preferred?

[April 7, 1657] The Directors to Peter Stuyvesant: We would have liked to send you now two masons and as many ship carpenters, if they could have been engaged at fair wages, but we had to defer it until the departure of the next ships, when you may certainly expect them. We are in doubt however, whether instead of ship carpenters you do not mean house carpenters, who we think are more required, because of the small shipping owned there by the Company. To engage such people is expensive for the Company and therefore trades as carpentering, brick-laying, blacksmithing and others ought to be taught to the negroes, as it was formerly done in *Brazil* and now is in *Guinea* and other Colonies of the Company; this race has sufficient fitness for it and it would be very advantageous; therefore we recommend it to you most earnestly.

[June 10, 1664] Peter Stuyvesant to the Directors: This day fortnight arrived here your Honors' Vessel, the *Musch* [*Sparrow*], with forty head of slaves, sent to us by Vice Director Beck to procure provisions and all sorts of timber work, fix ox carts and a new . . . [mill]. The negroes and negresses have all arrived safely and in health, but were, on an average, quite old, and as the skipper alleges, rejected by the Spaniards. The product of the greater part appears by the accompanying account of the public vendue [auction]. They would have brought more, had they not been so old. Five of the negro women, who were, in our opinion, unsalable, have been kept back and remain unsold. In like manner, six negroes also, to help to cut the required timber and to perform some other necessary work for the honorable company.

SOURCES: Edmund B. O'Callaghan, ed., *Documents Relative to the Colonial History of the State of New York* (Albany: Weed, Parsons and Company, 1854), 3:387; Elizabeth Donnan, ed., *Documents Illustrative of the History of the Slave Trade to America* (Washington, DC: Carnegie Institution, 1930), 3:429.

???   **Why do the Directors of the Dutch West India Company see slave labor as especially advantageous to the developing colony?**

liberated adult slaves but not their children. These adults maintained obligations to the West India Company and were required to serve as wage laborers for the company when needed, but they were free to work for themselves at all other times, provided they paid a yearly tribute of "one hog, 23 bushels of corn, wampum or fur pelts worth 20 guilders" to the company.[26]

Half-freedom was exploitative in that it exempted the Dutch West India Company from having to take responsibility for the adult slaves it freed, while retaining the labor of their children and requiring slave families to pay corporate tribute. But it ultimately enhanced black liberty in the Middle Atlantic region, because many half-free blacks successfully petitioned the company for full freedom shortly before the English took over New Netherland in 1664. Anxious to retain their allegiance, the company freed the blacks' children and removed all other restrictions on their liberty. Some petitioners even received small plots of farmland. The legacy of half-freedom enabled one in five New Netherland blacks to claim freedom when the Dutch surrendered the colony to the English.

Slavery in England's Middle Colonies

In 1664, the English seized New Netherland from the Dutch, laying permanent claim to New York, New Jersey, Delaware, and land that would later be incorporated into Pennsylvania. Since slavery was already well established in Dutch America, this acquisition greatly expanded the geographic and demographic scope of slavery throughout England's northern colonies. New Netherland was home to approximately 300 slaves and 75 free blacks, who constituted approximately 20 percent of the colony's 1,500 inhabitants. When the English took over, they continued to rely on enslaved Africans to supply much of the region's labor. King Charles II granted control of the colony to his brother James, Duke of York, renaming the colony New York in his honor.

Eager to develop New York as a market for slaves, James—who held a controlling interest in the Royal African Company—developed policies that favored the purchase of slaves from the company, such as the abolition of any property tax on slaves and the imposition of tariffs on domestic slave imports. James also put the colony under the control of English administrators, who made few efforts to attract European workers and permitted the Royal African Company to sell large cargoes of African slaves directly to New Yorkers at fixed prices. When New Yorkers proved to be more interested in buying seasoned and acculturated slaves from the West Indies, the company accommodated their preferences by exchanging locally grown provisions for Caribbean slaves. New York's slave population grew steadily as a result of these measures, increasing at a faster pace than the colony's white population between 1698 and 1738.

Slavery in the other Middle Atlantic colonies developed along much the same lines. New Jersey and Delaware had slave populations when the English arrived and continued to import slaves thereafter. New Jersey, which was initially controlled by English proprietors appointed by Charles II, sought to encourage the settlement and cultivation of farmland by offering sixty acres per slave to any colonist who imported slaves. New Jersey maintained a similar policy even after it became a formal colony in 1702. At this time, England's Queen Anne, who saw slavery as crucial to the success of the North American colonies, instructed the royal governors of all the colonies to make sure that the colonists had access to "a constant and sufficient supply of merchantable Negroes at moderate prices."[27]

NEGROES, TO BE SOLD

A Parcel of young able bodied Negro Men, one of whom is a Cooper by Trade, two Negroes Wenches, and likewise two Girls, one of 12 Years old, and the other 16, the latter a good Seemſtreſs, and can be well recommended.

Northern Slave Markets
Britain's Middle Atlantic colonies became lucrative markets for slaves in the eighteenth century. Northern slaves proliferated in port cities, where they performed a variety of skilled and unskilled jobs. They also played an important role in developing and cultivating the region's agricultural areas. This advertisement for a New York slave auction, which was published in the *New York Journal or General Advertiser*, announces the availability of five slaves, one a cooper by trade and another a seamstress. *The Granger Collection, NYC. All rights reserved.*

New York, New Jersey, Delaware, and Pennsylvania, which was founded by the Quaker leader William Penn in 1681, all contained agricultural areas where Dutch and English farmers used a mixture of slave and servant workers to grow a variety of crops. Farms throughout the region were small and largely dedicated to the production of wheat, corn, and other provisions, rather than tobacco, rice, or any of the other labor-intensive crops that predominated in the slave South. Even in Delaware, where tobacco production flourished during the late seventeenth and early eighteenth centuries, large slaveholders remained rare. Most of the colony's tobacco was grown by small farmers who owned only a few slaves.

In addition to working in the fields, Middle Atlantic slaves cleared land; tended livestock; chopped wood; pressed cider; maintained fences, buildings, and grounds; and served as domestic workers as needed. Like the indentured servants with whom they often worked, they did not have their own quarters, but were relegated to the household's back rooms, attics, closets, kitchens, and outbuildings. Slaves usually occupied the least appealing spaces, as noted in a 1742 advertisement for a Long Island estate whose farmhouse included "a room of 14 by 16 foot for white servants, over it lodging rooms and a back stairs; behind it a kitchen with a room fit for negroes."[28]

Despite the importance of slave labor in these agricultural areas, port cities remained the largest slaveholding communities in both the Middle Atlantic and New England colonies.

Founded in 1681 with the establishment of the Commonwealth of Pennsylvania, Philadelphia is a case in point. Both the city and the commonwealth were the brainchild of William Penn, an English-born **Quaker**, or member of the egalitarian English Protestant sect also known as the Religious Society of Friends. Penn and other Quakers embraced religious freedom as one of the commonwealth's founding principles. But they were slower to embrace other universal freedoms, so slave laborers soon proliferated in the port city of Philadelphia, which was home to a lively trade with

England's Caribbean colonies. Among the many Philadelphia Quakers who owned and employed slaves was Penn himself, who noted that he preferred black slaves to white indentured servants, "for then a man has them while they live."[29]

But slavery became controversial among the Quakers even during Penn's lifetime, which may help explain why Penn, who died in 1718, freed his slaves in his will. A group of Germantown Quakers issued the first American antislavery petition in 1688. Its authors were a group of four Dutch-speaking Quakers who had left Europe to escape religious persecution. Dismayed to hear that some of their Quaker neighbors had decided to use slave labor, they drafted a petition deploring what they called "the traffik of men-body." "Is there any that would be done or handled at this manner?" they wrote in a document that displayed remarkable empathy for the slaves. "We should do to all men like as we will be done ourselves; making no difference of what generation, descent, or colour they are. . . . To bring men hither [to America], or to rob and sell them against their will, we stand against. In Europe there are many oppressed for conscience-sake; and here there are those oppressed which are of a black colour."[30]

This early petition did not gain a broad audience or wide support. Instead, slavery continued to flourish in Philadelphia, where many Quaker merchants owned slaves, and imports of enslaved Africans helped sustain Pennsylvania's economic growth during periods when European wars curtailed white immigration.

Frontiers and Forced Labor

In the early eighteenth century, slavery began to extend farther west and south into the frontier colonies located on the periphery of European settlement. These colonies, which included French Louisiana and Spanish Florida, were short of labor but too isolated and sparsely settled to maintain a secure slave labor force. Between 1717 and 1731, thousands of slaves were imported into the Mississippi valley, where the French had claimed a vast stretch of land known as Louisiana. But Louisiana planters were neither numerous enough nor powerful enough to establish a well-regulated plantation society, and they struggled to maintain control of their slaves.

Colonists in Spanish Florida, founded in 1565, took a less ambitious approach by permitting slavery but never establishing plantations. The colony was instead founded as a military outpost to defend Spain's New World empire, and by the eighteenth century it had also become a haven for fugitive slaves from Carolina. The Spanish permitted these maroons to establish free black communities; in return, the runaways joined the colony's militia and helped protect its borders.

The British colony of Georgia, founded in 1732, was likewise founded to protect Britain's New World colonies and initially prohibited slavery for that reason. Georgia was meant to serve as a buffer zone between Carolina and Spanish Florida, and its crown-appointed trustees believed that slavery would threaten its military security. They banned slavery until 1750, when they reversed the ban in response to a sustained campaign among the colonists to legalize slavery.

The early history of slavery in these three frontier settlements illustrates the immense importance of enslaved African laborers in the settlement of the American South, as well as the security risks such workers posed.

Slavery in French Louisiana

France's Louisiana colony, situated on the western frontier of most European settlements in the New World, extended from the Gulf of Mexico to the Canadian border. Claimed by the French explorer Robert de La Salle, who traveled down the Mississippi River in 1682, the colony attracted few European immigrants, but facilitated a lucrative fur trade with the region's Indian nations. By 1700, French investors and the French crown were eager to set up plantation settlements. They had established profitable sugar colonies on the West Indian islands of Guadeloupe, Martinique, and Saint Domingue during the seventeenth century and hoped to grow lucrative crops in Louisiana as well.

At this time, however, Louisiana lacked the manpower to sustain commercial agriculture. As of 1706, the colony had fewer than one hundred French and Canadian inhabitants, most of whom were fur traders and soldiers. The Company of the West Indies, which was granted a trade monopoly in the colony by France's King Louis XV in 1719, needed workers to clear land; build fortifications, roads, levees, and irrigation works; and cultivate the plantations that the company hoped to establish. But few French men and women were willing to immigrate to this frontier outpost. Virtually the only white migrants to the region were a few thousand convicts exiled from France for serious crimes, but even with these new additions, the colony's white population remained well under two thousand throughout the 1720s. Mortality rates among the immigrants were high, and those who survived often fled. Meanwhile, experiments with Native American labor were disappointing. The Indians of the region, who maintained an indigenous slave trade of their own, supplied Louisiana with more than two hundred slaves during its early years. But the Indian slaves provided "very little service," a French official complained in a 1709 letter to the French Ministry of the Colonies, adding that "they are not appropriate for hard labor like the blacks."[31]

With the colony teetering on the brink of collapse, France responded to the colonists' complaints by sending them shiploads of slaves directly from Africa. Most of these ships originated in Senegal, where the French controlled the slave trade, and they delivered almost six thousand slaves to Louisiana between 1719 and 1731. These forced migrants were crucial to the colony's survival. Approximately two-thirds came from Senegambia, where they had cultivated many of the same crops they would be required to grow in Louisiana. Officials from the Company of the West Indies were aware that rice cultivation was practiced in Africa, and they capitalized on the slaves' expertise in this regard. They instructed the captains who delivered the colony's first shiploads of slaves to deliver several barrels of rice seed as well and to make sure their human cargo included captives who knew how to grow rice. Within a year, rice was growing along large stretches of the Mississippi River. Slaves from Senegambia were also likely crucial to the success of Louisiana's indigo and tobacco plantations. (See Visual Sources: African Labor in the Making of the Americas, pp. 97–107.)

Despite these successes, the future of Louisiana remained far from secure. Nearly one-third of the Africans died, and the remainder proved hard to control. Louisiana's black majority outnumbered the colonists by a ratio of 2:1 and never fully accepted French rule. Some ran away and formed fugitive communities in Louisiana's dense woods and tidal wetlands; others sought refuge among their Natchez Indian neighbors, who were hostile to the French. Blacks fought on both sides of the Natchez uprising against the French in 1729–1730, and they plotted their own uprising shortly after the French defeated the Natchez. In 1730, a group of approximately four hundred Bambara slaves (members of a Malinke-speaking people whose homeland was on the northern banks of the Senegal River) conspired to kill the French and take over the colony, but their plot was discovered. Even after the leaders of the conspiracy were publicly executed, however, slavery in Louisiana remained a disturbing force. Slave imports all but ceased after 1731, when the Company of the West Indies resigned its monopoly over the region. The colony's slave population eroded further when colonists established a free black militia to secure the colony from slave uprisings and Indian attacks.

Thus, instead of becoming a lucrative plantation society, French Louisiana remained a chaotic frontier settlement. Consequently, its racial hierarchies remained somewhat fluid. As a French colony, Louisiana had strict slave laws known as the **Code Noir**, or "Black Code," which had been issued in 1685 by Louis XIV for use throughout France's empire. Under the code, slaves who ran away three times were subject to capital punishment, but the French colonists were too few and too poor to kill off their workers—or even capture their slaves when they ran away. Many fugitives ended up living out their lives in Bas du Fleuve, a maroon community located on the outskirts of New Orleans. One of the colony's fastest-growing settlements, Bas du Fleuve housed almost a third of Louisiana's slaves by 1763. These fugitives, subservient to no one, made their living farming and supplying lumber to New Orleans sawmills.

Black Society in Spanish Florida

Like French Louisiana, Spanish Florida never developed large-scale plantation agriculture. The thinly populated military outpost had been established with the help of slaves supplied by the Spanish crown, but its enslaved population remained small after that. Given its military purpose, Spanish Florida needed soldiers more than field hands. Slaves constructed and maintained the region's forts, grew their own food, were assigned tasks as needed, and served in the colony's militia, which also enlisted free blacks. But free blacks and slaves alike had a high degree of autonomy in Spanish Florida, which made the colony an attractive destination for runaway slaves from Carolina. The first arrived in 1687, just a few decades after Carolina was founded. That year, eight men, two women, and a nursing child made their way to St. Augustine in a stolen canoe, requesting baptism in the "true faith" of the Catholic Church.

These fugitives successfully appealed to the church, which claimed religious authority over the lives of all its members, both free and enslaved. The Spanish governor Diego de Quiroga y Losada welcomed them and refused to return them to their English owners, maintaining that they were religious refugees and even offering to buy them from the Carolina official who traveled to St. Augustine to reclaim them. When word of these negotiations spread to slaves back in Carolina, they began making their way to the Spanish colony in greater numbers. In 1690, Carolina's governor complained to the Spanish that his colony's slaves ran off "dayly to your towns."[32] He received little satisfaction. Intent on defending their own colony, and more than willing to undermine English colonies in the New World, the Spanish continued to welcome the refugees. In 1693, Spain's King Charles II issued a royal proclamation granting liberty to all

Slaves in St. Augustine
This 1673 engraving shows black slaves engaged in a variety of tasks, including escorting the
Spanish to their ships. A little over a decade later, the first recorded runaway slaves from Carolina
would successfully seek sanctuary in Spanish Florida, where they were welcomed by Spanish
officials. Spanish authorities refused to return such fugitives to the English, which made
St. Augustine a prime destination for those fleeing slavery. *The Granger Collection, NYC. All rights reserved.*

fugitive slaves who wished to convert to Catholicism. Not surprisingly, this policy infuriated English officials in Carolina, who launched military assaults on St. Augustine in
1702 and 1728. The Spanish colony was able to draw on its growing population of fugitives to rebuff these attacks and to retaliate against the English.

Runaways from Carolina also joined and sometimes even led raids on their former
owners, whose slaves they freed and brought back to St. Augustine. They also fought
for their own freedom and autonomy in Florida. Fugitives were initially subject to
reenslavement by Spanish colonists who ignored the king's promise to free slaves seeking religious sanctuary. After petitioning colonial officials for decades, the runaways
finally received a grant of unconditional freedom in 1738. That year, they also established their own settlement, the town of Gracia Real de Santa Teresa de Mose, which
became known as Fort Mose. Located two miles outside St. Augustine, this free black
settlement served the interests of both the free blacks and the Spanish crown. It was
strategically situated to warn St. Augustine residents of any foreign attack, and it offered
the refugees a comfortable home on land where they could support themselves. Surrounded by fertile fields and forests, Fort Mose was bisected by a saltwater river with
an abundant supply of fish and shellfish. The ex-slave sanctuary would not survive
for long, however. Captured and destroyed by the British in 1739 during the War of
Jenkins's Ear—a dispute between Britain and Spain over land claims—the fort was
resettled only briefly in the 1750s.

Slavery and Servitude in Early Georgia

Just north of Spanish Florida lay yet another frontier colony designed to act as a buf
fer and protect its founders' imperial interests. Georgia's colonization was led by a
group of British trustees who envisioned a colony populated by lower-class whites.
Indentured servants were welcome, but slaves were not, since they could not be
expected to defend the colony against its Indian and Spanish enemies. If slavery was
permitted in Georgia, one of the colony's founders noted in 1732, "there would not
be 50 out of 500 remain[ing] in two months time, for they would fly to the Spaniards
[in Florida]."[33] Royal officials agreed, instituting a ban on slavery. But few of Georgia's early settlers ended up supporting the ban. No whites could be found to perform the backbreaking work required to clear Georgia's land for production. Even
the indentured servants fled to South Carolina and other British colonies rather than
serve out their terms in Georgia. Meanwhile, the settlers who stayed lobbied relent-
lessly to end the ban on slave labor.

Other than the trustees, the only colonists in favor of maintaining the ban were the
Salzburgers, a group of approximately three hundred German speaking Protestants
who migrated to Georgia in 1734. The Salzburgers hailed from the Catholic principal-
ity of Salzburg, Austria, which expelled its Protestant population in 1731. This small,
hardworking community of friends and relatives, who came to Georgia with the support of the region's trustees, saw no reason to object to the ban even after their British
neighbors told them that it was "impossible and dangerous for white people to plant
and manufacture rice, being a work only for Negroes." Instead, to prove that the colony
could prosper without forced labor, they planted rice and soon mastered its cultivation
to the point of producing a surplus.

Their opposition to slavery, however, was more practical than moral. They worried that it would weaken their close-knit sect by scattering its members across large
plantations. They were also alarmed by reports of black uprisings in the West Indies,
which convinced them that slavery was a dangerous institution. Shortly after the
Salzburgers arrived in America, their pastor, Johann Martin Bolzius, heard that slaves
on St. John in the Virgin Islands had massacred "all the white people on the island,"
and he wondered whether the "great convenience" of slave labor was not offset by the
dangers that it posed. His worries were compounded a few weeks later when one of
the Salzburgers' supporters in South Carolina lent them a dozen slaves to help them
clear land and build roads in their settlement of Ebenezer, Georgia. Bolzius was dismayed by the violent conflicts between the slaves and the white overseer who was
sent to supervise them. He objected when the overseer whipped several slaves and
was still more horrified when one slave threatened the overseer with an ax. "The
departure of the Negroes has deprived us of some advantage," Bolzius wrote after the
slaves returned to South Carolina, "but it has also freed us of much disquietude and
worry."[34]

The Stono Rebellion

In 1739, the Salzburgers' fears were borne out by a slave uprising that began near the
Stono River in St. Paul's Parish, South Carolina, and took the lives of about twenty
whites and more than forty African Americans. On the morning of Sunday, September
9, approximately twenty slaves gathered on the banks of the Stono. They broke into a

nearby store that sold guns and ammunition, killed the shopkeepers, and armed them-selves with guns, axes, and clubs. They then headed south, killing the whites they encountered and burning their homes to the ground. The rebels spared the life of a local tavern owner who was known to be kind to his slaves and overlooked one planter who was hidden by his slaves, but they were otherwise merciless, massacring entire families. Joined by other slaves as they marched, the rebels were approximately sixty strong and ten miles from home when they were finally tracked down by a hastily assembled patrol of armed whites late that afternoon. More than forty slaves were killed before the **Stono rebellion** was finally suppressed. Most of those who escaped were eventually captured or killed. (See From the Record: South Carolina Governor's Report to the Royal Council on the Stono Rebellion.)

The rebels, who were executed without trial, left little evidence of what had inspired the largest slave uprising in the British colonies. The rebellion occurred at the end of a long, hot summer marked by a malaria epidemic in Charleston, and amid heightened political tensions between Britain and Spain. Exhausted by the heat, depleted by the epidemic, and apprehensive about a possible war with Spain, the colo-ny's white population was unusually troubled, which may have influenced the timing of the rebellion. The early eighteenth century's traffic in black Christians from Kongo also could have played a role. The kingdom of Kongo, once ruled by a Catholic king and his son, had collapsed by the 1710s, leaving many Catholic converts in its wake. Slaves brought to South Carolina from this region would have been alert to Spanish procla-mations offering freedom and sanctuary to Catholics. The rebels also may have seized on colonial troubles as an opportunity to fight their way to refuge in St. Augustine. Few made it that far, but their rebellion was a wake-up call to white colonists across the South. "Evil brought home to us, within our very Doors, awaken'd the Attention of the most Unthinking," a committee of South Carolina legislators noted, summarizing the impact of the rebellion.[35]

However, the colonists' commitment to slavery remained unshaken. Colonial offi-cials were convinced that "the *Negroes* would not have made this Insurrection had they not depended on *St. Augustine* for a Place of Reception afterwards," which allowed them to blame the Spanish. The officials moved quickly to pass a slave code to discour-age further uprisings.[36] South Carolina's 1740 Negro Act was designed to keep slaves in "due subjection and obedience" and underscored that whites were free to kill rebellious slaves without a trial. It also allowed colonists to keep slaves under constant surveil-lance by empowering all whites to police their slaves' movements. After 1740, slaves could no longer travel beyond the boundaries of their masters' plantations without a ticket or pass granting permission. All whites were authorized to investigate and whip slaves caught without a pass and to "lawfully" kill any slave who physically resisted interrogation or punishment.[37]

The Stono rebellion was not British America's first slave revolt, nor would it be the last. "Freedom wears a cap that Can without a Tongue, Call together those who wish to shake of[f] the fetters of slavery," Lieutenant Governor Alexander Spotswood warned Virginia planters in 1710 after they hanged, quartered, and decapitated two slaves who had conspired to revolt. The planters divided the miscreants' corpses over several counties to ensure that their body parts were on display in all of the "most publick places"—reserving the head of one rebel for exhibition in the colony's capital. Their

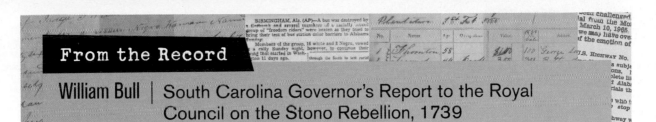

From the Record

William Bull | South Carolina Governor's Report to the Royal Council on the Stono Rebellion, 1739

In the aftermath of the Stono rebellion, **Lieutenant Governor William Bull (1683–1755)** wrote to the British king's Royal Council to inform them about the revolt. In his letter, he describes the "daring" actions of the determined Stono rebels, as well as the measures the militia took to subdue the rebellion. He also proposed that the Council employ Indian slave hunters to track down runaway slaves.

My Lord,

　　. . . I had the Honour some time ago to lay before your Grace, some account of Our Affairs in regard to the desertion of Our Negroes[;] . . . on the Ninth of September last at night a Great number of Negroes arose in rebellion, broke open a store where they got arms, killed twenty one White Persons, and were marching in a daring manner out of the Province, killing all they met and burning the Houses on the Road through which they passed[;] returning in my way from the Southward with four Gentlemen, I met these Rebels at Eleven o'clock in the Forenoon, so that I fortunately diserned the danger time enough to avoid it and to give notice to the Militia, who on the Occasion behaved with so much expedition and bravery as by four o'clock the same day to come up with them, and killed and took so many as put a stop to any further mischief at that time. Forty four of the Rebels have been killed & Executed, some few yet remain concealed in the Woods and expecting the same Fate seem desperate. . . .

　　It was the Opinion of His Majestys Council with several other Gentlemen, that one of the most effectual means that could be used at present, to prevent such desertion of Our Negroes is to encourage some Indians by a suitable reward to pursue and if possible to bring back the deserters, and while the Indians are thus employed they would be in the way ready to intercept others that might attempt to follow, and I have sent for the Chicasaws living at New Windsor and the Catabaw Indians for that purpose.

SOURCE: William Bull to the Royal Council, October 5, 1739, South Carolina Department of Archives and History, Columbia.

???　**What does Bull's description reveal about the nature of the rebellion?**

goal was to "inspire such a terror in the other Negroes, as will keep them from forming such designs for the future," but Spotswood was not convinced that violence alone could secure the safety of the colonists. After all, even the "babel of languages" spoken among African slaves had not prevented them from conspiring to revolt. The colonists must suppress all "consultations" among black people, Spotswood argued, lest they come together around a common love of liberty.[38]

CONCLUSION

Regional Variations of Early American Slavery

The first half of the eighteenth century saw slavery become ever more entrenched in British America. Though unfamiliar to the continent's earliest English settlers, slavery was eventually adopted by colonists from New England to Georgia, who employed slaves to perform many different kinds of work. Slave labor was most vital to sustaining the settlement and growth of the southern colonies, where slave owning landowners built a plantation economy dedicated to the production of lucrative **cash crops**. Colonists farther north were less dependent on slave labor, but slaves were common in the region's port cities and most productive agricultural areas.

Africans in early America led lives that were shaped by the regional economies in which they found themselves. Culturally isolated New England slaves were more likely to learn English and adopt European ways than their counterparts in Georgia and South Carolina, who often lived in African enclaves on remote plantations and retained many of their West African cultural practices and beliefs. Most slaves in the southern colonies worked as field hands, while those in New England and the Middle Atlantic were as likely to perform domestic service as farmwork.

Regardless of region, however, slave life remained a struggle. Male slaves predominated in many areas, and not all of them were able to find mates or establish families. New shipments of captive Africans became increasingly common in the southern colonies, bringing in men and women for whom the traumas of the Middle Passage were still fresh. Moreover, both recent arrivals and native-born slaves were increasingly subjected to harsh discipline and careful surveillance. Faced with a growing slave population, colonial legislatures across British America enacted strict slave codes that outlawed slave gatherings, punished slave rebellions, and instituted armed slave patrols. Only in sparsely populated frontier settlements such as French Louisiana and Spanish Florida, where whites relied on people of color to help them defend their borders, did slaves and free blacks retain some degree of freedom.

Even so, throughout the colonies, enslaved Africans proved difficult to control. The strict slave codes introduced in Carolina and other British colonies did little to suppress slave resistance. Instead, during the second half of the eighteenth century, freedom would only become more alluring to African Americans. As the social and political turmoil of the Revolutionary era disrupted slavery and the slave trade, it offered large numbers of individual bondmen and bondwomen opportunities to escape their condition. The era's debates over slavery, liberty, and the rights of man would supply enslaved Africans throughout the colonies with an even more dangerous weapon: a revolutionary rhetoric that could be mobilized against all forms of tyranny, including slavery.

CHAPTER REVIEW

Online Study Guide ▪ bedfordstmartins.com/graywhite

Key Terms

maroons (p. 57)

indentured servants (p. 59)

chattel slavery (p. 59)

creole (p. 63)

mulatto (p. 63)

task system (p. 64)

driver (p. 64)

country marks (p. 66)

half-freedom (p. 71)

Quaker (p. 74)

Code Noir (p. 77)

Stono rebellion (1739) (p. 80)

cash crops (p. 82)

Review Questions

1. Describe the regional variations of slavery throughout Britain's North American colonies. How did the development of and attitudes toward the institution differ in each area?

2. How and why did the nature of slavery change in the Middle Atlantic colonies after the English seized the region from the Dutch?

3. What tactics did slaves in the frontier colonies use to win their freedom? Why were the slaves in these regions more difficult for slaveholders and colonial governments to control?

4. How did the character of slavery change throughout colonial North America between 1619 and 1739? What factors were responsible for these changes?

For Web sites, images, and documents related to topics and places in this chapter, visit **Make History** at bedfordstmartins.com/graywhite.

Making Slaves

To transform African captives into chattel slaves, the English colonists developed legal codes that regulated who could be enslaved, and assigned both slaves and free blacks a distinctive legal status. Virginia, one of the first colonies to codify slavery, led the way by passing laws determining how slavery would pass from parent to child and establishing that enslaved Africans who converted to Christianity would not be entitled to the same freedoms as other Christians. The colony's law books also include several rulings that some historians have read as clear evidence that the English colonists always disapproved of interracial sex. Other scholars have suggested that cases such as the 1630 ruling sanctioning Hugh Davis for "lying with a negro" might have been judgments against extramarital sex or homosexuality. Since the legal proceedings were not recorded, the specific circumstances they addressed remain unknown. How much definitive information can we draw from such legal cases?

By the beginning of the eighteenth century, many colonies had passed laws regulating every aspect of slave behavior, which also permitted slave owners to use virtually unlimited force in disciplining their slaves. These laws governed the behavior of whites as well and typically included sanctions against interracial marriage, measures prohibiting whites from sheltering runaway slaves, and provisions requiring slave owners to supply food and clothing to slaves. Though frequently disregarded by both masters and slaves, the legal codes regulating slavery gave slave owners license to govern their slaves and almost unlimited powers of discipline.

The following documents include excerpts from laws developed by English colonists to regulate the slave systems in Virginia, New Jersey, and South Carolina.

The Codification of Slavery and Race in Seventeenth-Century Virginia, 1630–1680

Determining the legal status of blacks in early Virginia remains controversial because laws regulating slavery do not appear in the colony's legal statutes prior to the 1660s—more than forty years after the first African slaves arrived. However, cases prosecuted in Virginia in 1630 and 1640 suggest that Africans may not have received equal justice even before then, while excerpts from laws passed in the 1660s and beyond are clearly discriminatory. The relatively gradual appearance of such laws has led some historians to argue that racial prejudice was crucial to the development of black slavery.

SOURCE: William Waller Hening, *Statutes at Large; Being a Collection of All the Laws of Virginia* (Richmond, VA: Samuel Pleasants, 1810), 1:146, 552; 2:170, 260, 267, 270, 280–81.

[1630]

September 17th, 1630. Hugh Davis to be soundly whipped, before an assembly of Negroes and others for abusing himself to the dishonor of God and shame of Christians, by defiling his body in lying with a negro; which fault he is to acknowledge next Sabbath day.

[1640]

October 17, 1640. *Whereas Robert Sweat* hath begotten with child a negro woman servant belonging unto Lieutenant *Sheppard, the court hath therefore ordered* that the said negro woman shall be whipt at the whipping post and the said *Sweat* shall tomorrow in the forenoon do public penance for his offence at *James City* church in the time of divine service according to the laws of *England* in that case provided.

[1662]

WHEREAS some doubts have arisen whether children got by any Englishman upon a negro woman should be slave or free, *Be it therefore enacted and declared by this present grand assembly,* that all children borne in this country shall be held bond or free only according to the condition of the mother, *And* that if any christian shall commit fornication with a negro man or woman, he or she so offending shall pay double the fines imposed by the former act.

[1667]

WHEREAS some doubts have risen whether children that are slaves by birth, and by the charity and piety of their owners made pertakers of the blessed sacrament of baptisme, should by vertue of their baptisme be made free; *It is enacted and declared by this grand assembly, and the authority thereof,* that the conferring of baptisme doth not alter the condition of the person as to his bondage or freedome; that diverse masters, freed from this doubt, may more carefully endeavour the propagation of christianity by permitting children, though slaves, or those of greater growth if capable to be admitted to that sacrament.

[1668]

WHEREAS some doubts, have arisen whether negro women set free were still to be accompted [accounted] tithable according to a former act, *It is declared by this grand assembly* that negro women, though permitted to enjoy their freedome yet ought not in all respects to be admitted to a full fruition of the exemptions and impunities of the English, and are still lyable to payment of taxes.

[1669]

WHEREAS the only law in force for the punishment of refractory servants (*a*) resisting their master, mistris or overseer cannot be inflicted upon negroes, nor the obstinacy of many of them by other then [than] violent meanes supprest, *Be it enacted and declared by this grand assembly,* if any slave resist his master (or other by his masters order correcting him) and by the extremity of the correction should chance to die, that his death shall not be accompted [accounted] felony, but the master (or that other person appointed by the master to punish him) be acquit from molestation, since it cannot be presumed that prepensed malice (which alone makes murther felony) should induce any man to destroy his owne estate.

[June 1670]

WHEREAS it hath beene questioned whither Indians or negroes manumited, or otherwise free, could be capable of purchasing christian servants, *It is enacted* that noe negroe or Indian though baptised and enjoyed their owne freedome shall be capable of any such purchase of christians, but yet not debarred from buying any of their owne nation.

An Act for Regulating of Slaves in New Jersey, 1713–1714

Colonial statutes regulated the status of individual slaves and the workings of the slave system as a whole. New Jersey legislators enacted the following law to prohibit the colony's citizens from engaging in any kind of commercial transaction with slaves without first securing the permission of the slave's owner. It also prohibited citizens from sheltering slaves who might be fugitives or from freeing their own slaves without pledging "security" funds to the colony should the former slaves ever require public support.

[§1] *Be it Enacted by the Governour, Council and General Assembly, and by the Authority of the same,* That all and every Person or Persons within this Province, who shall at any time after Publication hereof, buy, sell, barter, trade or traffick with any *Negro, Indian* or *Mullatto Slave,* for any Rum, Wine, Beer, Syder, or other strong Drink, or any other Chattels, Goods, Wares or Commodities whatsoever, unless it be by the consent of his, her or their Master or Mistress, or the person under whose care they are, shall pay for the first Offence *Twenty Shillings,* and for the second and every other Offence, *forty Shillings,* Money according to the Queens Proclamation, the one half to the Informer, the other half to the use of the Poor of that Place where the Fact is committed, to be recovered by Action of Debt before any one of Her Majesties Justices of the Peace.

[§2] *And be it further Enacted by the Authority aforesaid,* That all and every Person or Persons within this Province, who shall find or take up any Negro, Indian or Mulatto Slave or Slaves, five Miles from his, her or their Master or Mistresses habitation, who hath not leave in writing from his, her or their Master or Mistress, or are not known to be on their service, he, she or they, so taken up, shall be Whipt by the party that takes them up, or by his order, on the bare back, not exceeding Twenty Lashes; and

the Taker up shall have for his reward Five Shillings, Money aforesaid, for every one taken up as aforesaid, with reasonable Charges for carrying him, her or them home, paid him by the Master or Mistress of the Slave or Slaves so taken up; and if above the said five Miles, *six pence per Mile* for every Mile over and above, to be recovered before any one Justice of the Peace, if it exceeds not Forty Shillings, and if more, by Action of Debt in the Court of Common Pleas in the County where the fact shall arise. . . .

[§12] *Be it further Enacted by the Authority aforesaid,* That no Person or Persons whatsoever shall hereafter imploy, harbour, Conceal or entertain other Peoples Slaves at their Houses, Out-Houses or Plantation, without the consent of their Master or Mistress, either signified to them Verbally, or by Certificate in writing under the said Master or Mistresses Hand, excepting in Distress of Weather, or other extraordinary Occasions, upon the forfeiture of *Forty Shillings* for every Time they are so entertained and concealed, to be paid to the Master or Mistress of such Slave or Slaves (so that the Penalty for entertaining such Slave exceeds not the Value of the said Slave) And if any Person or Persons whatsoever shall be found guilty [of] so harbouring, entertaining or concealing of any Slave, or assisting to the conveying them away, if such Slave shall happen to be lost, Dead, or otherways rendered Unserviceable, such Person or Persons so harbouring, entertaining, concealing, assisting or conveying them away, shall be also liable to pay the value of such Slave to the Master or Mistress, to be recovered by Action of Debt in any Court of Record within this Province. . . .

[§14] *And Whereas* it is found by experience, that Free Negroes are an Idle Sloathful People, and prove very often a charge to the Place where they are,

Be it therefore further Enacted by the Authority aforesaid, That any Master or Mistress, manumitting and setting at Liberty any Negro or Mullatto Slave, shall enter into sufficient Security unto Her Majesty, Her Heirs and Successors, with two Sureties, in the Sum of *Two Hundred Pounds,* to pay yearly and every year

SOURCE: "An Act for Regulating of Slaves," in *The Law of Slavery in New Jersey,* comp. Paul Axel-Lute, rev. October 8, 2009, New Jersey Digital Legal Library, http://njlegallib.rutgers.edu/slavery/acts/A13.html.

to such Negro or Mullatto Slave, during their Lives, the Sum of *Twenty Pounds*. And if such Negro or Mullatto Slave shall be made Free by the Will and Testament of any Person deceased, that then the

Executors of such Person shall enter into Security, as above, immediately upon proving the said Will and Testament, which if refused to be given, the said Manumission to be void, and of none Effect.

The South Carolina Slave Code, 1740

Punishment was another important function of slave law. In the aftermath of the Stono rebellion, the South Carolina legislature strengthened its already severe code of slave punishment by passing the following legislation. How did this statute attempt to safeguard against future rebellions?

AN ACT FOR THE BETTER ORDERING AND GOVERNING [OF] NEGROES AND OTHER SLAVES IN THIS PROVINCE

4. *Whereas* in his majesty's plantations in America, slavery has been introduced and allowed; and the people commonly called negroes, Indians, mulattoes and mestizos, have been deemed absolute slaves, and the subjects of property in the hands of particular persons; the extent of whose power over such slaves, ought to be settled and limited by positive laws, so that the slaves may be kept in due subjection and obedience, and the owners and other persons having the care and government of slaves, may be restrained from exercising too great rigour and cruelty over them; and that the public peace and order of this province may be preserved.

* * *

7. *Provided*, that in any action or suit to be brought in pursuance of the direction of this act, the burthen of the proof shall lay upon the plaintiff, and it shall be always presumed, that every negro, Indian, mulatto and mestizo, is a slave, unless the contrary can be made appear. (The Indians in amity with this government excepted) in which case the burthen of the proof shall lie on the defendant.

* * *

12. If any slave, who shall be out of the house or plantation where such slave shall live or shall be usually employed, or without some white person in company with such slave, shall refuse to submit to or undergo the examination of any white person, it shall be lawful for any such white person to pursue, apprehend and moderately correct such slave; and if such slave shall assault and strike such white person, such slave may be lawfully killed.

* * *

20. . . . *Be it therefore enacted*, that the several crimes and offences herein after particularly enumerated, are hereby declared to be felony without the benefit of the clergy, *that is to say*, if any slave, free negro, mulatto, Indian or mestizo, shall wilfully and maliciously burn or destroy any stack of rice, corn or other grain, of the product, growth or manufacture of this province; or shall willfully and maliciously set fire to, burn or destroy any tar kiln, barrels of pitch, tar, turpentine or rosin, or any other [of] the goods or commodities of the growth, produce or manufacture of this province; or shall feloniously steal, take or carry away any slave, being the property of another, with intent to carry such slave out of this province; or shall wilfully and maliciously poison, or administer any poison to any person, freeman, woman, servant or slave; every such slave, free negro, mulatto, Indian, (except as before excepted) and mestizo, shall suffer death as a felon.

21. Any slave who shall be guilty of homicide of any sort, upon any white person, except by misadventure, or in defence of his master or other person under whose care and government such slave shall be, shall upon conviction thereof as aforesaid suffer death.

SOURCE: Joseph Brevard, *An Alphabetical Digest of the Public Statute Law of South-Carolina* (Charleston, SC: John Hoff, 1816), 2:229–31, 233, 238, 240–41, 243.

22. And every slave who shall raise or attempt to raise an insurrection in this province, *or shall endeavour to delude or entice any slave to run away and leave this province; every such slave and slaves, and his and their accomplices, aiders and abettors, shall upon conviction as aforesaid suffer death.*

* * *

35. *And whereas* several owners of slaves do suffer their slaves to go and work where they please, upon conditions of paying to their owners certain sums of money agreed upon between the owner and slave; which practice has occasioned such slaves to pilfer and steal, to raise money for their owners, as well as to maintain themselves in drunkenness and evil courses; for prevention of which practices for the future, *Be it enacted,* That no owner, master or mistress of any slave, after the passing of this act, shall permit or suffer any of his, her or their slaves to go and work out of their respective houses or families, without a ticket in writing, under pain of forfeiting the sum of ten pounds, current money, for every such offence.

* * *

41. And for that as it is absolutely necessary to the safety of this province, that all due care be taken to restrain the wanderings and meetings of negroes and other slaves, at all times, and more especially on Saturday nights, Sundays and other holidays, and their using and carrying wooden swords, and other mischievous and dangerous weapons, or using or keeping of drums, horns, or other loud instruments, which may call together or give sign or notice to one another of their wicked designs and purposes; and that all masters, overseers and others may be enjoined diligently and carefully to prevent the same:

42. *Be it enacted,* That it shall be lawful for all masters, overseers and other persons whomsoever, to apprehend and take up any negro or other slave that shall be found out of the plantation of his or their master or owner, at any time, especially on Saturday nights, Sundays or other holidays, not being on lawful business, and with a letter from their master or a ticket, or not having a white person with them, and the said negro or other slave or slaves correct by a moderate whipping. . . .

43. *And whereas* cruelty is not only highly unbecoming those who profess themselves Christians, but is odious in the eyes of all men who have any sense of virtue or humanity; therefore to restrain and prevent barbarity being exercised towards slaves, *Be it enacted,* That if any person or persons whosoever, shall wilfully murder his own slave, or the slave of any other person, every such person shall upon conviction thereof, forfeit and pay the sum of seven hundred pounds current money, and shall be rendered, and is hereby declared altogether and for ever incapable of holding, exercising, enjoying or receiving the profits of any office, place or employment civil or military within this province. . . .

* * *

45. And if any person shall, on a sudden heat [of] passion, or by undue correction, kill his own slave or the slave of any other person, he shall forfeit the sum of three hundred and fifty pounds current money. And in case any person or persons shall wilfully cut out the tongue, put out the eye, castrate, or cruelly scald, burn, or deprive any slave of any limb or member, or shall inflict any other cruel punishment, other than by whipping or beating with a horse-whip, cow-skin, switch or small stick, or by putting irons on, or confining or imprisoning such slave; every such person shall for every such offence, forfeit the sum of one hundred pounds current money.

46. That in case any person in this province, who shall be owner, or who shall have the care, government or charge of any slave or slaves shall deny, neglect or refuse to allow such slave or slaves under his or her charge, sufficient cloathing, covering or food, it shall and may be lawful for any person or persons, on behalf of such slave or slaves, to make complaint to the next neighbouring justice in the parish where such slave or slaves live or are usually employed; . . . and shall and may set and impose a fine or penalty on any person who shall offend in the premises, in any sum not exceeding twenty pounds current money, for each offence.

* * *

52. *And whereas* many owners of slaves, and others who have the care, management and overseeing of

slaves, do confine them so closely to hard labour, that they have not sufficient time for natural rest; *Be it therefore enacted,* That if any owner of slaves, or other person who shall have the care, management or overseeing of any slaves, shall work or put any such slave or slaves to labour, more than fifteen hours in twenty-four hours, from the twenty-fifth day of March to the twenty-fifth day of September, or more than fourteen hours in twenty-four hours, from the twenty-fifth day of September to the twenty-fifth day of March; every such person shall forfeit any sum not exceeding twenty pounds, nor under five pounds current money, for every time he, she or they shall offend herein, at the discretion of the justice before whom the complaint shall be made.

53. *And whereas* the having of slaves taught to write, or suffering them to be employed in writing, may be attended with great inconveniencies; *Be it enacted,* That all and every person and persons whatsoever, who shall hereafter teach, or cause any slave or slaves to be taught to write, or shall use or employ any slave as a scribe in any manner of writing whatsoever, hereafter taught to write; every such person and persons shall, for every such offence, forfeit the sum of one hundred pounds current money.

Questions for Analysis

1. What was the legal status of people of African descent in colonial Virginia? How were blacks distinguished from other Virginians?

2. What powers of punishment and control did Virginia, New Jersey, and South Carolina slave laws give to white colonists? To what extent did slave regulations vary over time and place?

3. What kind of legal obligations did colonial slave statutes impose on whites in South Carolina? Why might these have been viewed as important in preventing future slave insurrections?

documents

British Colonists Debate the Merits of Slavery

As slavery became increasingly common throughout the British colonies, some colonists had second thoughts. The Puritan merchant and magistrate Samuel Sewall questioned the morality of the institution, while the trustees who first established the Georgia colony thought slavery would endanger the safety of white settlers. Colonists who insisted that slavery was a useful and profitable institution disputed these objections. The following documents include a debate over slavery between Samuel Sewall and another Boston merchant and magistrate, John Saffin, and an exchange between Georgia's colonists and trustees.

Boston Merchants Samuel Sewall and John Saffin Clash over Slavery

The first antislavery tract published in New England, *The Selling of Joseph*, condemned both African slavery and the slave trade in North America. Written by **Samuel Sewall (1652–1730)**, who had long been uneasy about slavery, it may have been inspired by the freedom struggles of a slave named Adam, who belonged to **John Saffin (1626–1710)**. Saffin had promised that he would give Adam his freedom after hiring out his labor to a nearby farmer for a term of seven years, but Saffin later reneged, forcing Adam to petition for his freedom and inspiring white Bostonians to circulate a petition on his behalf. Sewall's antislavery tract does not take up Adam's case, but instead contests the legitimacy of slavery as an institution by invoking the biblical tale of Joseph, who was sold into slavery by his jealous brothers. Saffin's reply provides biblical support for slavery, while also attacking the character of Africans as a race.

Samuel Sewall | The Selling of Joseph: A Memorial, 1700

FOR AS MUCH *as* Liberty *is in real value next unto* Life: *None ought to part with it themselves, or deprive others of it, but upon most mature Consideration.*

The Numerousness of Slaves at this day in the Province, and the Uneasiness of them under their Slavery, hath put many upon thinking whether the Foundation of it be firmly and well laid; so as to sustain the Vast Weight that is built upon it. It is most certain that all Men, as they are the Sons of *Adam*, are Coheirs; and have equal Right unto Liberty, and all other outward Comforts of Life. *GOD hath given the Earth* [with all its Commodities] *unto the Sons of* Adam, *Psal* 115. 16. *And hath made of One Blood, all Nations of Men, for to dwell in all the face of the Earth, and hath determined the Times before appointed, and the bounds of their habitation: That they should seek the Lord. Forasmuch then as we are the Offspring of GOD* &c. Act 17.26, 27, 29.° Now although the Title given by the last ADAM, doth infinitely better Mens Estates, respecting GOD and themselves; and grants them a most beneficial and inviolable Lease under the Broad Seal of Heaven, who were before only Tenants at Will: Yet through the Indulgence of GOD to our First Parents after the Fall, the outward Estate of all and every of their Children, remains the same, as to one another. So that Originally, and Naturally, there is no such thing as Slavery. *Joseph* was rightfully no more a Slave to his Brethren, than they were to him: and they had no more Authority to *Sell* him, than they had to

---

SOURCE: Samuel Sewall, *The Selling of Joseph: A Memorial* (Boston: Bartholomew Green and John Allen, 1700).

° Sewall cites Psalm 115 and Acts 17 to prove the common origins of all men and women.

Slay him.° And if *they* had nothing to do to Sell him; the *Ishmaelites*° bargaining with them, and paying down Twenty pieces of Silver, could not make a Title. Neither could *Potiphar* have any better Interest in him than the *Ishmaelites* had.° *Gen.* 37. 20, 27, 28. For he that shall in this case plead *Alteration of Property*, seems to have forfeited a great part of his own claim to Humanity. There is no proportion between Twenty Pieces of Silver, and LIBERTY. . . . 'Tis pity there should be more Caution used in buying a Horse, or a little lifeless dust; than there is in purchasing Men and Women: Whenas they are the Offspring of GOD, and their Liberty is,

—*Auro pretiosior Omni.*°

And seeing GOD hath said, *He that Stealeth a Man and Selleth him, or if he be found in his hand, he shall surely be put to Death.* Exod. 12. 16. This Law being of Everlasting Equity, wherein Man Stealing is ranked amongst the most atrocious of Capital Crimes: What louder Cry can there be made of that Celebrated Warning,

Caveat Emptor!°

And all things considered, it would conduce more to the Welfare of the Province, to have White Servants for a Term of Years, than to have Slaves for Life. Few can endure to hear of a Negro's being made free; and indeed they can seldom use their freedom well; yet their continual aspiring after their forbidden Liberty, renders them Unwilling Servants. And there is such a disparity in their Conditions, Colour & Hair, that they can never embody with us, and grow up into orderly Families, to the Peopling of the Land: but still remain in our Body Politick as a kind of extravasat

Blood.° . . . Moreover it is too well known what Temptations Masters are under, to connive at the Fornication of their Slaves; lest they should be obliged to find them Wives, or pay their Fines. It seems to be practically pleaded that they might be Lawless; 'tis thought much of, that the Law should have Satisfaction for their Thefts, and other Immoralities; by which means, *Holiness to the Lord*, is more rarely engraven upon this sort of Servitude. It is likewise most lamentable to think, how in taking Negros out of *Africa*, and Selling of them here, That which GOD has joyned together men do boldly rend asunder; Men from their Country, Husbands from their Wives, Parents from their Children. How horrible is the Uncleanness, Mortality, if not Murder, that the Ships are guilty of that bring great Crouds of these miserable Men, and Women. Methinks, when we are bemoaning the barbarous Usage of our Friends and Kinsfolk in *Africa*: it might not be unreasonable to enquire whether we are not culpable in forcing the *Africans* to become Slaves amongst our selves. And it may be a question whether all the Benefit received by *Negro* Slaves, will balance the Accompt [account] of Cash laid out upon them.

[Sewall refutes four common justifications for slavery.]

Obj. 1. *These Bluckamores*° *are of the Posterity of Cham,*° *and therefore are under the Curse of Slavery.* Gen. 9. 25, 26, 27.

Answ. . . . For *Canaan* is the Person Cursed three times over, without the mentioning of *Cham*. Good Expositors suppose the Curse entaild on him, and that this Prophesie was accomplished in the Extirpation of the *Canaanites*, and in the Servi-

---

° The story of Joseph appears in the Old Testament (Gen. 37–50). The favorite son of his father, Jacob, Joseph was sold into slavery in Egypt by his jealous older brothers.

° Joseph's first purchasers, the Ishmaelites, were descendants of Ishmael. Ishmael was the eldest son of Abraham, the father of the Hebrews, or Jews.

° Potiphar was a member of the Egyptian pharaoh's guard, who purchased Joseph from the Ishmaelites.

° *Auro pretiosior Omni* is Latin for "More precious than all the gold in the world."

° *Caveat Emptor* is Latin for "Let the buyer beware."

° *Extravasat blood* is an archaic medical term describing blood from a ruptured artery or vein filling the body cavity.

° *Blackamore* is an archaic term used to describe black or dark-skinned people.

° One of Noah's three sons, Cham—better known as Ham—is cursed for disrespecting his father in Genesis 9:25. The punishment singles out Cham's son Canaan, who is condemned to be a "servant of servants." This story was a common scriptural explanation for slavery, which Sewall goes on to reject.

tude of the *Gibeonites.* . . .° Whereas the Black-mores are not descended of *Canaan,* but of *Cush.* Psal. 68. 31. *Princes shall come out of Egypt* [Miz-raim] *Ethiopia* [Cush] *shall soon stretch out her hands unto God.* Under which Names, all *Africa* may be comprehended; and their Promised Conversion ought to be prayed for. *Jer.* 13. 23. *Can the Ethiopian change his skin?* This shews that Black Men are the Posterity of *Cush:* Who time out of mind have been distinguished by their Colour. . . .°

Obj. 2. *The Nigers° are brought out of a Pagan Country, into places where the Gospel is Preached.*

Answ. Evil must not be done, that good may come of it. The extraordinary and comprehensive Benefit accruing to the Church of God, and to *Joseph* personally, did not rectify his brethrens Sale of him.

Obj. 3. *The Africans have Wars one with another: Our Ships bring lawful Captives taken in those Wars.*

Answ. For ought is known, their Wars are much such as were between *Jacob's* Sons and their Brother *Joseph.* If they be between Town and Town; Provincial, or National: Every War is upon one side Unjust.

° The Gibeonites—residents of Gibeon, an ancient city north of Jerusalem—were conquered and enslaved by the biblical hero Joshua in the Old Testament book of Joshua (6:3–27).

° In rejecting the idea that blacks were subject to the curse of Cham, Sewall notes that only Cham's son Canaan was cursed and that the curse could never have applied to black Africans, who descend not from Canaan, but from his older brother Cush. The king of Ethiopia, Cush led the settlement of black Africa.

° Black Africans, or people from the West African region of Niger.

An Unlawful War can't make lawful Captives. And by Receiving, we are in danger to promote, and partake in their Barbarous Cruelties. I am sure, if some Gentlemen should go down to the *Brewsters°* to take the Air, and Fish: And a stronger party from *Hull°* should Surprise them, and Sell them for Slaves to a Ship outward bound: they would think themselves unjustly dealt with; both by Sellers and Buyers. And yet 'tis to be feared, we have no other kind of Title to our *Nigers. Therefore all things whatsoever ye would that men should do to you, do ye even so to them: for this is the Law and the Prophets.* Matt. 7. 12.

Obj. 4. Abraham *had Servants bought with his Money, and born in his House.*

Answ. Until the Circumstances of *Abraham's* purchase be recorded, no Argument can be drawn from it. In the mean time, Charity obliges us to conclude, that He knew it was lawful and good.

. . . Our Blessed Saviour has altered the Measures of the Ancient Love-Song, and set it to a most Excellent New Tune, which all ought to be ambitious of Learning. *Matt.* 5. 43, 44. *John* 13. 34. These *Ethiopians,* as black as they are; seeing they are the Sons and Daughters of the First *Adam,* the Brethren and Sisters of the Last ADAM, and the Offspring of GOD; They ought to be treated with a Respect agreeable.

° The Brewsters is likely a reference to a cluster of islands in Boston Harbor known as Great Brewster, Little Brewster, Middle Brewster, and Outer Brewster.

° Hull is a town near Boston.

documents

John Saffin | **A Brief and Candid Answer to a Late Printed Sheet, Entituled, The Selling of Joseph, 1701**

THAT Honourable and Learned Gentleman, the Author of a Sheet, Entituled, *The Selling of Joseph, A Memorial*, seems from thence to draw this conclusion, that because the Sons of *Jacob* did very ill in selling their Brother *Joseph* to the *Ishmaelites,* who were Heathens, therefore it is utterly unlawful to Buy and Sell Negroes, though among Christians; which Conclusion I presume is not well drawn from the Premises, nor is the case parallel; for it was unlawful for the *Israelites* to Sell their Brethren upon any account, or pretence whatsoever during life. But it was not unlawful for the Seed of *Abraham*° to have Bond men, and Bond women either born in their House, or bought with their Money, as it is written of *Abraham, Gen.* 14. 14 & 21. 10 & *Exod.* 21. 16 & *Levit.* 25. 44, 45, 46. . . .

. . . So God hath set different Orders and Degrees of Men in the World, both in Church and Common weal. Now, if this Position of parity should be true, it would then follow that the ordinary Course of Divine Providence of God in the World should be wrong, and unjust, (which we must not dare to think, much less to affirm) and all the sacred Rules, Precepts and Commands of the Almighty which he hath given the Son of Men to observe and keep in their respective Places, Orders and Degrees, would be to no purpose; which unaccountably derogate from the Divine Wisdom of most High, who hath made nothing in vain, but hath Holy Ends in all his Dispensations to the Children of men. . . .

Our Author doth further proceed to answer some Objections of his own framing, which he supposes some might raise.

Object. 1. *That these Blackamores are of the Posterity of* Cham, *and therefore under the Curse of Slavery. Gen.* 9. 25, 26, 27. That which the Gentleman seems to deny, saying, *they were the Seed of Canaan that were Cursed, &c.*

Answ. Whether they were so or not, we shall not dispute: this may suffice, that not only the seed of *Cham* or *Canaan,* but any lawful Captives of other Heathen Nations may be made Bond men as hath been proved.

Obj. 2. *That the Negroes are brought out of Pagan Countreys into places where the Gospel is Preached.* To which he Replies, *that we must not doe Evil that Good may come of it.*

Answ. To which we answer, That it is no Evil thing to bring them out of their own Heathenish Country, where they may have the Knowledge of the True God, be Converted and Eternally saved.

Obj. 3. *The Africans have Wars one with another;* our Ships bring lawful Captives taken in those Wars.

To which our Author answers Conjecturally, and Doubtfully, *for ought we know,* that which may or may not be; which is insignificant, and proves nothing. He also compares the Negroes Wars, one Nation with another, with the Wars between *Joseph* and his Brethren. But where doth he read of any such War? . . .

By all which it doth evidently appear both by Scripture and Reason, the practice of the People of God in all Ages, both before and after the giving of the Law, and in the times of the Gospel, that there were Bond men, Women and Children commonly kept by holy and good men, and improved in Service: and therefore by the Command of God, *Lev.* 25, 44, and their venerable Example, we may keep Bond men, and use them in our Service still; yet with all candour, moderation and Christian prudence, according to their state and condition consonant to the Word of God.

[Saffin's reply concludes with the following poem.]

The Negroes Character.

Cowardly and cruel are those Blacks Innate,
Prone to Revenge, Imp of inveterate hate.
He that exasperates them, soon espies
Mischief and Murder in their very eyes.
Libidinous, Deceitful, False and Rude,
The Spume Issue of Ingratitude.
The Premises consider'd, all may tell,
How near good Joseph *they are parallel.*

° "Seed of Abraham" refers to his descendants.

SOURCE: John Saffin, *A Brief and Candid Answer to a Late Printed Sheet, Entituled, The Selling of Joseph,* 1701. Reprinted in George Henry Moore, *Notes on the History of Slavery in Massachusetts* (New York: D. Appleton & Co., 1866), 251–52, 254, 256.

documents

Georgia Trustees and Settlers Disagree over Slavery

The British crown–appointed trustees who founded Georgia banned slavery in 1735 as a matter of public policy. Though not opposed to slavery on principle, they believed that the adoption of slavery in Georgia would compromise the military security of the colony and discourage white settlers from immigrating there. But many of the colonists who settled in Georgia, convinced that they could not prosper without slaves, repeatedly petitioned the trustees to reverse their ban. One such petition is presented here, followed by the trustees' reply.

Georgia Settlers | The Settlers' Petition, 1738

To the Honourable the Trustees for Establishing the Colony of *Georgia* in *America*.

May it please your Honours,

We, whose Names are under-written, being all Settlers, Freeholders, and Inhabitants of the Province of *Georgia*, and being sensible of the great Pains and Care exerted by you, in endeavouring to settle this Colony, since it has been under your Protection and Management, do unanimously join to lay before you, with the utmost Regret, the following Particulars. . . .

. . . The Land . . . , not being able to maintain the Settlers here, they must unavoidably have recourse to, and depend upon, Trade; but to our woeful Experience likewise, the same Causes that prevent the first, obstruct the latter; for though the Situation of this Place is exceeding well adapted for Trade, and, if it were encouraged, might be much more improved by the Inhabitants, yet the Difficulties and Restrictions which we hitherto have and at present do labour under, debar us of that Advantage.

SOURCE: Peter Force, *Tracts and Other Papers, Relating Principally to the Origin, Settlement, and Progress of the Colonies in North America, from the Discovery of the Country to the Year 1776* (Washington, DC: Peter Force, 1836), 1:37–41.

Timber is the only Thing we have here which we can Export, and notwithstanding we are obliged to fall it in planting our Land, yet we cannot manufacture it fit for a Foreign Market, but at double the Expence of other Colonies; as for Instance the River of *May*, which is but Twenty Miles from us, with the Allowance of Negroes, load Vessels with that Commodity at one half of the Price that we can do; and what should induce Persons to bring Ships here, when they can be loaded with one Half of the Expence so near us? Therefore the Timber on the Land is only a continual Charge to the Possessors of it, though of very great Service in all the Northern Colonies, where Negroes are allowed, and consequently Labour cheap. We do not in the least doubt, but that in Time Silk and Wine may be produced here, particularly the former; but since the Cultivation of Lands with White Servants only cannot raise Provision for our Families, as before mentioned, therefore it is likewise impossible to carry on these Manufactures according to the present Constitution. It is very well known that *Carolina* can raise every thing that this Colony can, and they having their Labour so much cheaper, will always ruin our Market, unless we are in some measure on a Footing with them; and as in both, the Land is worn out in Four or Five Years, and then fit for nothing but Pasture, we must be always at a great deal more Expence than they in clearing new Land for Planting. . . .

But we, for our parts, having intirely relied on, and confided in, your good Intentions, believing you would Redress our Grievances that should appear, and now, by our long Experience from Industry and continual Application to Improvement of Land here, do find it impossible to pursue it, or subsist ourselves any longer, according to the present nature of the Constitution: And likewise believing you will agree to those Measures which are found by Experience, capable to make this Colony succeed, and to promote which we have consumed our Money, Time and Labour; we do, from a sincere and true Regard to its Welfare, and in Duty both to you and ourselves, beg leave to lay before your immediate Consideration, the Two following chief Causes of these our present Misfortunes, and this deplorable State of the Colony; and which, we are certain, if Granted, would be an infallible Remedy for both.

1. The want of a Free Title or Fee Simple [full ownership] to our Lands, which, if Granted, would occasion great Numbers of new Settlers to come among us, and likewise encourage those who remain here, chearfully to proceed in making further Improvements, as well to retrieve their sunk Fortunes, as to make Provision for their Posterity.

2. The want and use of Negroes with proper Limitations, which, if Granted, would both induce great Numbers of White People to come here, and also render us Capable to subsist ourselves by raising Provisions upon our Lands, until we could make some Produce of it for Export, and in some measure to balance our Importation. We are very sensible of the Inconveniences and Mischiefs that have already, and do daily arise from an unlimited use of Negroes; but we are as sensible that these might be prevented by a due Limitation, such as, so many to each White Man, or so many to such a Quantity of Land, or in any other Manner which your Honours shall think most proper.

By Granting us, Gentlemen, these Two particulars, and such other Privileges as his Majesty's most dutiful Subjects in *America* enjoy, you will not only prevent our impending Ruin, but we are fully satisfied, also, will soon make this the most flourishing Colony possessed by his Majesty in *America*, and your Memories will be perpetuated to all future Ages, our latest Posterity sounding your Praises as their first Founders, Patrons and Guardians: But if, by Denying us those Privileges, we ourselves and Families are not only Ruined, but even our Posterities likewise, you will always be mentioned as the Cause and Authors of all their Misfortunes and Calamities; which we hope will never happen.

We are, with all due Respect,
Your Honours most Dutiful,
and Obedient Servants.

Georgia Trustees | **Answer of the Trustees, 1739**

To the Magistrates of the Town of Savannah, *in the Province of* Georgia. . . .

. . . The Trustees are the more confirmed in their opinion of the Unreasonableness of this Demand, [now] that they have received Petitions from the *Darien* [a frontier town in Georgia], and other Parts of the Province, representing the Inconvenience and Danger, which must arise to the good People of the Province from the Introduction of Negroes. And as the Trustees themselves are fully convinced, that besides the Hazard attending that *Introduction*, it would destroy all Industry among the white Inhabitants; and . . . the Colony would soon be too like its Neighbours, void of white Inhabitants, filled with Blacks, and reduced to be the precarious Property of a Few, equally exposed to Domestick Treachery, and Foreign Invasion; and therefore the Trustees cannot be supposed to be in any Disposition of granting this Request; and if they have not before this signified their Dislike of it, this Delay is to be imputed to no other Motives, but the Hopes they had conceived, that Time and Experience would bring the Complainants to a better Mind: And the Trustees readily join Issue with them in their Appeal to Posterity, who shall judge between them, who were their best Friends; *Those*, who endeavoured to preserve for them a Property in their Lands, by tying up the Hands of their unthrifty Progenitors; or *They*, who wanted a Power to mortgage or alien them: Who were the best Friends to the Colony, *Those* who with great Labour and Cost had endeavoured to form a Colony of His Majesty's Subjects, and persecuted *Protestants* from other Parts of *Europe*, had placed them on a fruitful Soil, and strove to secure them in their Possessions, by those Arts which naturally tend to keep the Colony full of useful and industrious People, capable both

SOURCE: Peter Force, *Tracts and Other Papers, Relating Principally to the Origin, Settlement, and Progress of the Colonies in North America, from the Discovery of the Country to the Year 1776* (Washington, DC: Peter Force, 1836), 1:51–53.

to cultivate and defend it; or *Those*, who, to gratify the greedy and ambitious Views of a few Negroe Merchants, would put it into their Power to become sole Owners of the Province, by introducing their baneful Commodity; which, it is well known by sad Experience, has brought our Neighbour Colonies to the Brink of Ruin, by driving out their white Inhab-itants, who were their Glory and Strength, to make room for Black, who are now become the Terror of their unadvised Masters.

*Signed by Order of the Trustees,
this 20th Day of June, 1739.*
Benj. Martyn, *Secretary.*

Questions for Analysis

1. What roles do religion and morality play in these eighteenth-century debates over slavery?

2. What practical arguments for and against slavery are presented in these debates?

3. According to John Saffin and the Georgia settlers, what specific traits do black people possess? How do the writers use these assertions to advance their arguments?

African Labor in the Making of the Americas

By the time the first slaves arrived in Virginia, African workers were already supplying much of the labor needed to sustain the European settlement of the New World. Slaves' labor was unpaid and often unrecorded. But it figures prominently in the art and artifacts produced in many New World colonies, which contain images documenting the prominent role black workers played in building and maintaining European settlements.

African Labor and Expertise

Slave laborers cleared the land for many of the plantations on which future generations of enslaved workers would toil and grew most of the profitable crops that fostered the rapid expansion of European settlements throughout the Americas. Enslaved workers also constructed roads and buildings in early urban settlements such as New Amsterdam, which would later become New York City. Though rarely mentioned in modern-day histories of Manhattan, black laborers can be seen in one 1640s depiction of New Amsterdam (Figure 2.1). This engraving is dominated by a Dutch woman, who appears to be holding a tray of fruits and vegetables, and a Dutch man holding a sheaf of tobacco. The image contains an early view of New Amsterdam in the background, along with several busy black figures. How would you describe these figures' activities and general depictions? What does this portrayal convey about slavery in the colony?

FIGURE 2.1
Nieu Amsterdam, c. 1642–1643
New York Public Library, USA/The Bridgeman Art Library International.

97

FIGURE 2.2
Lucy Parke Byrd, c. 1716 *Oil on canvas by studio of Sir Godfrey Kneller/Lent anonymously to the Virginia Historical Society, Richmond, VA/The Bridgeman Art Library International.*

Slave workers also served as domestics throughout the Americas and were ubiquitous enough to figure in portraits of their owners, as seen in Sir Godfrey Kneller's portrait of Lucy Parke Byrd (Figure 2.2). From a prominent Virginia family, Lucy Parke married wealthy tobacco planter William Byrd II in 1706 and became the mistress of a household that included hundreds of slaves. This portrait features a well-dressed black servant in the background. While Kneller's painting documents the widespread use of domestic slaves in early America, it can also be read as evidence of how the slaveholding gentry of Virginia chose to represent themselves. Why might there be a slave present? What does his presence and appearance tell you about how Lucy Parke Byrd hoped to be portrayed?

Though often assigned to menial work or domestic service, African migrants also brought distinctive skills to the New World. Many came from regions where fishing, swimming, and the use of small boats were common, and they were often more comfortable in the water than Europeans. Early European visitors to the Gold Coast noted that people there "can swim very

FIGURE 2.3

Canoe for Pearl Fishing, c. 1586 Histoire Naturelle des Indes (The Natural History of the Indies), *"Drake" manuscript, fol. 57. 29.2 x 20 cm. Bequest of Clara S. Peck, 1983; MA 3900, fol. 57/The Pierpont Morgan Library, New York, NY, USA/Art Resource, NY.*

fast, generally easily outdoing people of our nation in swimming and diving."[39] Later colonists found ways to put such skills to use. During the seventeenth century, enslaved Africans harvested pearls off Venezuela's Pearl Coast. Brought in to replace Native American divers after the region's indigenous population declined, black pearl divers initially worked alongside Native Americans, who likely helped them master the art of pearl diving. Enslaved divers usually worked in crews of four to six and spent their days at sea diving from canoes, as can be seen in Figure 2.3—although the drawing erroneously features a sailboat rather than a canoe. Pearl diving was one of the most dangerous forms of slave labor in the New World. Frequently killed or injured in shark attacks, divers also suffered from acute decompression sickness, or the bends, a sometimes fatal blood and tissue disorder caused by rising too rapidly from a dive. Not surprisingly, many black pearl divers tried to escape, so pearl diving trips were usually supervised by an armed white overseer.

Tome II, page 8.   *Représentation d'un Esquif, ou Tent-Boote, avec huit Negres qui Rament.*   Planche III.

FIGURE 2.4

Tent Boat, 1769   *Schomburg Center, NYPL/Art Resource, NY.*

Enslaved laborers also worked on the water as fishermen and manned many of the boats and barges used to transport people and goods in the plantation societies of the New World. Figure 2.4 shows slave watermen powering one of the "tent boats" used to carry wealthy whites through the Dutch colony of Suriname in South America. A society made up of large plantations where enslaved workers produced sugar, coffee, and cocoa, Suriname was most easily traversed by its inland waterways. While planters in this colony traveled in luxurious boats where they could find shelter from the sun in a tent, six to eight black paddlers and a black helmsman rowed them from one place to another. Also pictured in this illustration is a slave passenger, possibly a female domestic servant, on the roof of the tent. Travelers in colonial Virginia and Maryland likewise rode in boats manned by black watermen, although in considerably less comfortable conditions. When the Englishman Edward Kimber visited the Chesapeake in 1746, he found himself traveling in a "very small dangerous sort of canoa, liable to be overturned by the least motion of the sitters in it. The Negroes manage them very dexterously, with a Paddle."[40]

Due to their many different kinds of work, enslaved Africans mastered a wide variety of new skills while in bondage. On self-contained eighteenth-century plantations such as the tidewater estates of Virginia, and on Barbados's sugar plantations, slaves worked as carpenters, coopers, sawyers, blacksmiths, tanners, curriers, shoemakers, weavers, and knitters. They became skilled workers through careful training. Usually assigned to such occupations by their owners, most learned their trades by apprenticing with more senior tradesmen, often for several years. Some, however, had mastered their trades in Africa.

African Plantation Labor and Products

Agriculture was the single most common form of work performed in the plantation economies of the New World, so most slaves were field workers rather than artisans. The use of enslaved workers in the skilled trades declined over time in many slave societies as free artisans became increasingly reluctant to share their trade secrets with slaves for fear of undercutting the economic value of such skills.

Still, even plantation agriculture demanded skills that were passed on to generations of slaves, who sometimes drew on African farming and plant-processing methods to cultivate and process their owners' commercial crops. Plantation commodities such as sugar and tobacco required more than just planting and picking. These valuable commercial products had to be carefully grown, processed, and packed by slave laborers who understood how to refine sugarcane and cure tobacco. African labor and expertise became closely associated with the production of these products.

The earliest New World slave crop was sugar, which enslaved Africans planted and processed on the Atlantic islands of Madeira and São Tomé off the west coast of Africa as early as the sixteenth century. With the Portuguese colonization of Brazil in the seventeenth century, slaves from these islands were imported to work on the new sugar plantations there. Soon supplemented by additional enslaved Africans, black laborers helped transform the colony into the world's leading sugar producer. Black workers also came to be used as living symbols of sugar production, as can be seen in Figure 2.5, a map of the Pernambuco region in northeast Brazil, which fell under Dutch control between 1630 and 1654.

Created by the Dutch cartographer Johannes Blaeu, the map focuses on the coastline of the region. The interior is occupied by a drawing of a sugar refinery that shows blacks milling sugarcane and performing a variety of other jobs. A more detailed image of the sugar production process can be seen in another image created for an early history of the French West Indies (Figure 2.6). It shows slave workers feeding stalks of sugarcane into an ox-powered mill designed to grind them up and release the raw sugar inside them. Slaves in the foreground are boiling the sugarcane juice down to make refined sugar.

African workers were also closely associated with the cultivation of tobacco. In the Chesapeake area, this highly profitable crop was initially grown by white and Native American laborers, but it became a slave crop during the seventeenth century. More easily controlled than indentured servants or the often hostile Eastern Woodlands Indians whom they replaced, African slaves were also adept at growing tobacco. Most of the slaves brought to Maryland and Virginia in the seventeenth century came from the Bight of Biafra, Senegambia, the Gold Coast, or west-central Africa—regions where, as one European traveler observed, "tobacco is planted about every man's house."[41] They were, therefore, accustomed to growing and planting tobacco seedlings, which they grew alongside corn and beans, as was also customary among Native Americans. African laborers were experienced in curing and packing tobacco as well, and they helped expand the production of commercial tobacco

FIGURE 2.6
Slaves Producing Sugar, 1681
Charles de Rochefort, Histoire naturelle et morale des îles Antilles de l'Amérique/*Private Collection/The Bridgeman Art Library International.*

FIGURE 2.7
Engraving of a Virginia Tobacco Farm, 1725 *Pierre Pomet,* A Complete History of Drugs, *London, 1725 edition/Image Select/Art Resource, NY.*

in the Chesapeake, using African woodworking skills to improve on the design of the barrels in which it was exported.

Figure 2.7 shows several slaves working in a tobacco shed. Tobacco leaves, which must be cured, or dried, before processing, hang above them, and the slaves prepare these dried leaves for the market. At the far end of the shed, a slave woman and child are pulling down the tobacco leaves. In the foreground, another woman strips the leaves off the stems. Behind her, a man rolls the leaves flat for shipping. To his left, another man cuts pieces of rope to tie up the leaves. Missing from this picture is any white overseer or supervisor. Is this a deliberate omission on the part of the artist? What role did whites play in the production of sugar and tobacco?

In addition to being exploited for their labor, enslaved Africans were used to market Virginia's famously sweet-scented tobacco. A premium product sold under a variety of names in tobacco shops throughout Britain, Virginia tobacco was almost always promoted with engravings featuring black figures as the producers and consumers of it. African figures appear on the trade cards tobacco merchants passed around to advertise their wares, as well as on the labeled paper that they used to wrap the tobacco. Sometimes the Africans portrayed on these cards and papers sport Native American headdresses, seemingly standing in for Indians as well (Figure 2.8). In other cases, they can be seen curing and packing the crop, with a white smoker nearby (Figure 2.9).

Exactly why black figures were so important in the marketing of tobacco is difficult to say. What do these figures suggest about the character or labor of the workers who produced the crop? In what ways might they underscore the imperial power of the British planters?

Other prominent slave crops such as rice and indigo, although they were tended by slaves, did not generate similar images. (In the 1940s, however, an African American rice farmer called Uncle Ben lent his name to a commercially produced converted rice product that is still on the market today.) The production of indigo and rice, traditionally sold without advertising or branding, depended on African expertise, a fact that has remained largely invisible to historians until recent years. In the Caribbean, as in West Africa, black workers cultivated, harvested, and processed indigo — the source of a powerful blue textile dye most famously used for coloring denim. The leafy subtropical shrub can be seen next to some kind of cactus in Figure 2.10. Originally used to illustrate a history of the French West Indies, this sketch depicts the process by which slave workers turned the leaves of the indigo plant into dye. Grown as an export product on Saint Domingue, Guadeloupe, and Martinique starting in the seventeenth century, indigo was processed with techniques similar to those used in Africa, though adapted for the larger-scale production of the New World.

Indigo could be cultivated and harvested by unskilled field hands, but transforming it into dye required skilled workers. The grueling process began

FIGURE 2.10
Slaves Making Dye from Indigo, 1748 *Pierre Pomet, A Complete History of Drugs, London, 1748 edition, image ID SIL7-33-01/Courtesy of the Smithsonian Institution Libraries, Washington, DC.*

FIGURE 2.11
Processing Indigo Dye, 1757 (detail) *William DeBrahm, A Map of South Carolina and a Part of Georgia, 1757. Area Table 75 1780 Faden/Tracy W. McGregor Library of American History, Special Collections, University of Virginia Library.*

with field hands loading bundled stalks of indigo into the first of three stepped vats (see Figure 2.10), which they covered with stones or logs to submerge them in water. After the leaves began to dissolve into a foul-smelling greenish soup, which usually took 12 to 24 hours, skilled workers took over. They processed the rotting plants, which drew hordes of flies, by releasing the liquid into the second vat, where it could be paddled, or stirred, until the fermented indigo began to separate from the water and form a thick mud on the bottom of the vat. After the water was drained off, the indigo sludge was transferred into the third vat. From there, workers spooned it into small cloth bags, which were left in a shed to dry overnight.

Once the indigo dried into a paste, it was pressed into molds and dried again until it was solid enough to be cut into blocks of pure dye. Figure 2.11 shows a South Carolina slave cutting slabs of indigo into blocks and loading them into a barrel for shipping.

"Tobacco, cotton, rice, hemp, indigo, the improvement of Indian corn and many other important products, are all the result of African skill and labor," noted the nineteenth-century African American intellectual and former slave Martin Delany. Born in Virginia, Delany escaped slavery at an early age but had an abiding respect for the skills possessed by enslaved workers. "It is notorious that in the planting states, the blacks themselves are the only successful cultivators," he maintained, "the proprietor knowing little or nothing about the art, save that which he learns from the African husbandman, while his ignorant white overseer, who is merely there to see that work is attended to knows a great deal less."[42] His views were likely shared by the slaves themselves, whose work songs sometimes indicated that their owners were wholly dependent on their labor: "De big bee flies high," they sang in one such song, "De little bee makes de honey / De black man raise de cotton / An' de white man gets de money."[43]

Questions for Analysis

1. Slaves rarely figure prominently in traditional accounts of the settlement of the Americas. How could the images presented here be used to challenge such accounts? What kinds of stories do they tell?

2. What kinds of work were associated with forced labor? What role did whites play in such work?

3. What do the images that would have been viewed or displayed publicly—such as the portrait in Figure 2.2 or the tobacco label in Figure 2.9—tell you about depictions of black slaves in art and advertising? How accurate were these depictions? What response were they meant to evoke in viewers?

Notes

1. John Rolfe, "A Letter to Sir Thomas Sandys, Jan. 1619/20," in *The Records of the Virginia Company of London*, ed. Susan Myra Kingsbury (Washington, DC: Government Printing Office, 1933), 3:243.

2. Tim Hawshaw, *The Birth of Black America: The First African Americans and the Pursuit of Freedom at Jamestown* (New York: Carroll and Graf, 2007), 69.

3. John Thornton, "The African Experience of the '20, and Odd Negroes' Arriving in Virginia in 1619," *William and Mary Quarterly* 55, no. 3 (1998): 421–24.

4. Raphael Holinshed, William Harrison and Others, *Holinshed's Chronicles of England, Scotland, and Ireland* (1577; repr. London: J. Johnson, 1807), 275.

5. Quoted in Anthony S. Parent, *Foul Means: The Formation of a Slave Society in Virginia, 1660–1740* (Chapel Hill: University of North Carolina Press, 2003), 16.

6. Meeting minutes, July 9, 1640, in *Minutes of the Council and General Court of Colonial Virginia* (Richmond, VA: Colonial Press, 1924), 466.

7. William Waller Hening, ed., *Statutes at Large; Being a Collection of All the Laws of Virginia* (Richmond, VA: Samuel Pleasants, 1810), 2:170.

8. William Waller Hening, ed., *The Statutes at Large; Being a Collection of All the Laws of Virginia from the First Session of the Legislature, in the Year 1619* (New York: R. & W. & G. Bartow, 1823), 3:87.

9. *Virginia Gazette* (Williamsburg), November 2, 1739.

10. "Bacon's 'Manifesto,'" *Virginia Magazine of History and Biography* 1 (1893), quoted in Warren Billings, ed., *The Old Dominion in the Seventeenth Century: A Documentary History of Virginia, 1606–1689* (Chapel Hill: University of North Carolina Press, 1975), 277–79.

11. William Byrd to John Perceval, Earl of Egmont, July 12, 1736, in *Documents Illustrative of the History of the Slave Trade to America*, ed. Elizabeth Donnan (Washington, DC: Carnegie Institution, 1930), 4:131–132.

12. Olaudah Equiano, *The Interesting Narrative of the Life of Olaudah Equiano, or Gustavus Vassa, the African* (London: printed for author, 1745), 90.

13. John Bricknell, *Natural History of Carolina* (1737), quoted in Anthony S. Parent, *Foul Means: The Formation of a Slave Society in Virginia, 1660–1740* (Chapel Hill: University of North Carolina Press, 2003), 161.

14. Quoted in Daniel Littlefield, *Rice and Slaves: Ethnicity and the Slave Trade in Colonial South Carolina* (Baton Rouge: LSU Press, 1981), 100.

15. Advertisement, *Charleston Evening Gazette*, July 11, 1785, quoted in Judith Ann Carney, *Black Rice: The African Origins of Rice Cultivation in the Americas* (Cambridge: Harvard University Press, 2001), 90.

16. Gideon Johnston, "Instructions of the Clergy of the South Carolina, Given to Mr. Johnston" (1713), in *Carolina Chronicle: The Papers of Commissary Gideon Johnston, 1707–1716*, ed. Frank J. Klingberg, University of California Publications, vol. 35 (Berkeley: University of California Press, 1946), 123, 124.

17. Henry Melchior Muhlenberg, *The Journals of Henry Melchior Muhlenberg*, trans. Theodore G. Tappert and John W. Doberstein (Philadelphia: Muhlenberg Press, 1942), 1:58.

18. Quoted in Albert J. Raboteau, *Slave Religion: The "Invisible Institution" in the Antebellum South* (New York: Oxford University Press, 1978), 122.

19. Francis Le Jau, *The Carolina Chronicle of Dr. Francis Le Jau, 1706–1717* (Berkeley: University of California Press, 1980).

20. Samuel Sewall, *Diary of Samuel Sewall*, June, 19, 1700, Collections of the Massachusetts Historical Society, v. VI (Boston: Published by the Society, 1878), 16.

21. Cotton Mather, *The Negro Christianized*, ed. Paul Royster, Electronic Texts in American Studies, paper 28, UNL Digital Commons@University of Nebraska-Lincoln, 16, http://digitalcommons.unl.edu/cgi/viewcontent.cgi?article=1028&context=etas.

22. Quoted in William Dillon Piersen, *Black Yankees: The Development of an Afro-American Subculture in Eighteenth-Century New England* (Amherst: University of Massachusetts Press, 1988), 5.

23. *Connecticut Courant*, February 23, 1733.

24. Quoted in Thelma Wills Foote, *Black and White Manhattan: The History of Racial Formation in Colonial New York City* (New York: Oxford University Press, 2004), 36.

25. "Freedoms and Exemptions Granted by the Board of Nineteen of the West India Company to All Patroons, Masters or Private Persons, Who Will plant Colonies in New Netherland" (1630), in *Documents Relative to the Colonial History of the State of New York*, ed. Edmund B. O'Callaghan (Albany: Weed, Parsons and Company, 1856), 1:555.

26. Ibid., 39.

27. See, for example, "Instructions for Robert Hunter, Governor of New York" (1709), *Documents Relative to the Colonial History of the State of New York*, ed. Edmund B. O'Callaghan (Albany: Weed, Parsons and Company, 1855), 5:136.

28. *New York Weekly Journal*, June 21, 1742.

29. William Penn quoted in Samuel Macpherson Janney, *The Life of William Penn: With Selections from His Correspondence and Autobiography* (Philadelphia: Hogan, Perkins and Company, 1852), 422.

30. The Germantown Protest (1688), quoted in David Brion Davis, "Slavery and Emancipation in Western Culture," in *Slavery and Freedom in American History and Memory*, Gilder Lehrman Center for the Study of Slavery, Resistance, and Abolition, Yale University, http://www.yale.edu/glc/aces/germantown.htm.

31. Nicolas de la Salle to the French Ministry of the Colonies, Fort Lewis, August 29, 1709, trans. and quoted in Gwendolyn Midlo Hall, *Africans in Colonial Louisiana: The Development of Afro-Creole Culture in the Eighteenth Century* (Baton Rouge: LSU Press, 1995), 57.

32. Quoted in Jane Landers, *Black Society in Spanish Florida* (Urbana: University of Illinois Press, 1999), 25.

33. Quoted in Patrick Riordan, "Finding Freedom in Florida: Native Peoples, African Americans, and Colonists, 1670–1816," *Florida Historical Quarterly* 75, no. 1 (1996): 30–31.

34. Salzburger Petition 91739, quoted in James Van Horn Melton, "From Alpine Miner to Low-Country Yeoman: The

Transatlantic Worlds of a Georgia Salzburger, 1693 1761," Past and Present 201, no. 1 (2008): 128.

35. "Statements Made in the Introduction to the Report on General Oglethorpe's Expedition to St. Augustine" (1741), in *Historical Collections of South Carolina,* ed. Bartholomew Rivers Carroll (New York: Harper & Bros., 1836), 359.

36. "Report of the Committee Appointed to Inquire into the Causes of the Disappointment of Success in the Late Expedition against St. Augustine" (1742), in *Stono: Documenting and Interpreting a Southern Slave Revolt,* ed. Mark Michael Smith (Columbia: University of South Carolina Press, 2005), 28.

37. Joseph Brevard, *An Alphabetical Digest of the Public Statute Law of South-Carolina* (Charleston: John Hoff, 1816), 229, 231.

38. Quoted in Parent, *Foul Means,* 155, 153, 154.

39. Pieter de Marees, *Description and Historical Account of the Gold Kingdom of Guinea* (1602), trans. and ed. Albert van Dantzig and Adam Jones (New York: Published for The British Academy by Oxford University Press, 1987), 187.

40. Edward Kimber, *Itinerant Observations in America* (1746; repr., Newark: University of Delaware Press, 1998), 118.

41. William Finch, a British merchant who visited Sierra Leone in 1607, quoted in Alexander Peter Kup, *A History of Sierra Leone, 1400–1787* (New York: Cambridge University Press, 1961), 160.

42. Martin R. Delany, *The Condition, Elevation, Emigration, and Destiny of the Colored People of the United States* (1852; repr., New York: Arno Press, 1968), 64.

43. William Wells Brown, *My Southern Home,* in *From Fugitive Slave to Free Man: The Autobiographies of William Wells Brown* (New York: New American Library, 1993), 66.

Suggested References

Slavery and Freedom in Early English North America

Berlin, Ira. *Generations of Captivity: A History of African-American Slaves.* Cambridge: Belknap Press of Harvard University Press, 2004.

Breen, T. H., and Stephen Innes. *Myne Owne Ground: Race and Freedom on Virginia's Eastern Shore, 1640–1676.* New York: Oxford University Press, 1982.

Brown, Kathleen M. *Good Wives, Nasty Wenches, and Anxious Patriarchs: Gender, Race, and Power in Colonial Virginia.* Chapel Hill: University of North Carolina, 1996.

Carney, Judith Ann. *Black Rice: The African Origins of Rice Cultivation in the Americas.* Cambridge: Harvard University Press, 2001.

Gomez, Michael A. *Exchanging Our Country Marks: The Transformation of African Identities in the Colonial and Antebellum South.* Chapel Hill: University of North Carolina Press, 1998.

Greene, Lorenzo Johnston. *The Negro in Colonial New England, 1620–1776.* Bowie, MD: Heritage Books, 1998.

Knight, Frederick. *Working the Diaspora: The Impact of African Labor on the Anglo-American World, 1650–1850.* New York: New York University Press, 2010.

Morgan, Jennifer L. *Laboring Women: Reproduction and Gender in New World Slavery.* Philadelphia: University of Pennsylvania Press, 2004.

Morgan, Philip D. *Slave Counterpoint: Black Culture in the Eighteenth-Century Chesapeake and Lowcountry.* Chapel Hill: University of North Carolina Press, 1998.

Parent, Anthony S. *Foul Means: The Formation of a Slave Society in Virginia, 1660–1740.* Chapel Hill: University of North Carolina Press, 2003.

Wood, Peter H. *Black Majority: Negroes in Colonial South Carolina from 1670 through the Stono Rebellion.* New York: Norton, 1996.

Slavery in the Middle Atlantic Colonies

Berlin, Ira, and Leslie Harris. *Slavery in New York.* New York: New Press, 2005.

Essah, Patience. *A House Divided: Slavery and Emancipation in Delaware, 1638–1865.* Charlottesville: University of Virginia Press, 1996.

Foote, Thelma Wills. *Black and White Manhattan: The History of Racial Formation in Colonial New York City.* New York: Oxford University Press, 2004.

Harris, Leslie M. *In the Shadow of Slavery: African Americans in New York City, 1626–1863.* Chicago: University of Chicago Press, 2004.

Hodges, Graham Russell. *Root and Branch: African Americans in New York and East Jersey, 1613–1863.* Chapel Hill: University of North Carolina Press, 1999.

———. *Slavery and Freedom in the Rural North: African Americans in Monmouth County, New Jersey, 1665–1865.* Lanham, MD: Rowman & Littlefield Publishers, 1997.

Williams, Oscar. *African Americans and Colonial Legislation in the Middle Colonies.* London: Routledge, 1998.

Williams, William H. *Slavery and Freedom in Delaware, 1639–1865.* Lanham, MD: Rowman & Littlefield Publishers, 1999.

Frontiers and Forced Labor

Deagan, Kathleen A., and Darcie A. MacMahon. *Fort Mose: Colonial America's Black Fortress of Freedom.* Gainesville: University Press of Florida, 1995.

Hall, Gwendolyn Midlo. *Africans in Colonial Louisiana: The Development of Afro-Creole Culture in the Eighteenth Century.* Baton Rouge: LSU Press, 1995.

Hoffer, Peter Charles. *Cry Liberty: The Great Stono River Slave Rebellion of 1739.* New York: Oxford University Press, 2010.

Landers, Jane. *Black Society in Spanish Florida.* Urbana: University of Illinois Press, 1999.

Smith, Mark Michael, ed. *Stono: Documenting and Interpreting a Southern Slave Revolt.* Columbia: University of South Carolina Press, 2005.

Usner, Daniel H. "From African Captivity to American Slavery. The Introduction of Black Laborers to Colonial Louisiana." *Louisiana History* 20, no. 1 (January 1, 1979).

Wood, Betty. *Slavery in Colonial Georgia, 1730–1775.* Athens: University of Georgia Press, 2007.

Young, Jeffrey Robert. *Domesticating Slavery: The Master Class in Georgia and South Carolina, 1670–1837.* Chapel Hill: University of North Carolina Press, 1999.

CHAPTER 3

African Americans in the Age of Revolution,
1740–1783

DURING THE WINTER OF 1741, British colonists were quick to blame a series of fires that swept lower Manhattan on a massive slave conspiracy. In the wake of a recent maroon war in Jamaica and slave revolts in Antigua and South Carolina (the Stono rebellion; see chapter 2), white New Yorkers were nervous about the two thousand slaves who made up one-fifth of the city's population. New York slaves had good reason to be discontented during that unusually cold winter, when food and fuel were scarce. The first fire took place inside Fort George, which contained Lieutenant Governor George Clarke's mansion. Soldiers stationed there rescued Clarke and his family, and citizens gathered with buckets to douse the flames. But onlookers were disturbed to note that although some blacks pitched in to help, not all of them tried to fight the fire. One slave confided to another that he "wished the Governor had been burnt in the middle of it," while a slave named Cuffee danced as the fire spread.[1]

The Fort George fire was only the first in a series of conflagrations. One week later, flames scorched a nearby house, and a week after that a warehouse burned to the ground. The first week of April saw seven fires, one next to the house of Captain Jacob Sarly. The captain owned a slave named Juan de la Silva, who along with several of his shipmates had been captured and sold into slavery after an attack on a Spanish ship. All of the men swore that they were sailors rather than slaves and "free subjects of Spain" as well. They had also publicly threatened to roast John Lush, the privateer who had captured their ship, like "a side of beef." Moreover, de la Silva had vowed to burn Sarly's house as well. After the fire at Sarly's neighbor's house broke out, some New Yorkers assumed that de la Silva and his shipmates had started all the fires in a plot to "ruin the city." A cry swept through the city: "Take up all the Spanish Negroes."[2] But even as de la Silva and his compatriots were rounded up and dragged off to City Hall, another fire broke out in a warehouse on New Street. Cuffee, the slave who had danced while Fort George burned, was seen leaving the building. A huge mob chased him down and carried him to the city jail, shouting, "The Negroes are rising!"[3]

More than one hundred blacks and several whites were arrested and imprisoned as authorities investigated the alleged conspiracy, coercing confessions from the men and women they tried and convicted. By the end of the trials, 17 blacks and 4 whites had been hanged, 13 blacks had been burned at the stake, and 70 blacks and 7 whites had been banished from the colony. How many of them were guilty of arson— or anything else—remains an open question. The trials took place at a moment when New Yorkers were alert to the dangers of slave rebellion, embroiled in an imperial war with Spain, and suffering the economic effects of a deep recession. One witness reported that blacks planned "to burn the town, kill

1776	Thomas Paine publishes *Common Sense*, arguing for independence
	Continental Congress adopts Declaration of Independence
1777–1820s	Northern states begin to abolish slavery
1778	British adopt southern strategy
1779	Philipsburg Proclamation promises to free slaves serving Britain in any capacity
1781	Colonists adopt Articles of Confederation
	British surrender at Yorktown, Virginia
1783	United States and Great Britain sign Treaty of Paris
	Virginia law directs attorney general to seek manumission for all slave soldiers still held in bondage
	Massachusetts Supreme Court rules that slavery is incompatible with state constitution

111

the white men, and take their wives and daughters as mistresses." Others maintained that the fires had been set by blacks and poor whites who had united against the wealthier classes. But once the hysteria of the trials died down, many New Yorkers wondered whether they had been caught in "the merciless Flames of an Imaginary Plot."[4]

Planned or not, the fires provoked fears that illuminated the dangers of slavery, as well as the dangers of interracial freedom struggles in colonial America. Trial testimony reveals a world of discontented slaves, servants, and white workers, whose grievances could easily swell into outright rebellion. Most of the accused were men and women who worked on New York's racially mixed waterfront, where they socialized together, slept together, and shared a common resentment toward more prosperous New Yorkers and the city's social order. But such allegiances did not prevent blacks from becoming the primary scapegoats. Some of the alleged ringleaders, such as the dancing Cuffee, were criminals whose traffic in stolen goods may have made them easy targets of property owners. Others, such as the hapless "Spanish Negroes," were men who were primarily focused on securing their own freedom.

As the eighteenth century progressed and American colonists battled for independence from Britain, freedom-seeking blacks would become important foot soldiers in what one historian has described as "the motley crew" of the American Revolution.[5] Discontented blacks, with no property or privileges to preserve, saw the Revolution as an opportunity to win their own freedom. They fought on both sides of the conflict and participated in all of the Revolution's major battles. White patriots were initially reluctant to enlist black soldiers, fearing a slave revolt, but after the British began enlisting slaves in 1775, most of the colonies followed suit. While securing black freedom was not among the colonists' Revolutionary goals, they and the British usually freed slaves who served in their armed forces. African Americans on both sides of the conflict were quick to embrace these opportunities.

The Revolutionary era offered African Americans other routes to freedom as well. The religious revivals of the Great Awakening fostered a spirit of egalitarianism that was appealing to both blacks and whites. Moreover, as white Americans struggled to free themselves from British domination, many began to question the legitimacy of slavery. Whites manumitted, or freed, more than twenty thousand slaves during the final decades of the eighteenth century. Some were inspired to do so by their religious convictions, while others were influenced by the Revolution's democratic ideals.

Thus the American Revolution fueled the freedom dreams of African Americans, who took advantage of the war's social and political dislocation to join the patriot or British forces, run away, or challenge the terms of their enslavement in court. Their actions helped to erode slavery in America, resulting in a new nation where slavery was permitted in some states but not in others.

African American Life in Eighteenth-Century North America

During the 1741 slave trials, New York chief justice Daniel Horsmanden warned slaveholders that they had "enemies of their own household," who should be replaced and "replenished with white people."[6] But New York slaveholders proved no more willing to relinquish their slaves than had their counterparts in South Carolina, even in the wake of the bloody Stono rebellion. As the supply of white workers shrank, North America's British colonies imported even more captive Africans. Sixty percent of all the African-born slaves imported into the American colonies, most of whom ended up in the South, arrived between the 1720s and the 1780s. In the North, the newcomers joined an existing black population in which American-born blacks predominated. English-speaking and comfortable living among whites, many American-born black northerners had become Christians as well. During these years, African Americans forged a distinct and evolving identity, combining the contributions of the continuous flow of African newcomers with those of the large population of American-born blacks.

Slaves and Free Blacks across the Colonies

By the mid-eighteenth century, white laborers were in short supply throughout the colonies, especially after Europe's Seven Years' War of 1756–1763 reduced the flow of European indentured servants and increased the rate of military enlistment in Europe. This shortage led colonists to embrace slavery with greater enthusiasm than ever before. Whereas the total number of slaves shipped from Africa to North America between 1700 and 1720 was roughly 20,000, colonists imported more than 50,000 captives per decade in the 1740s and 1750s and maintained similar rates, with only a slight drop-off, in the years immediately preceding the Revolution. Most of these newcomers ended up in the southern colonies, but slave imports in the North increased as well, enlarging and Africanizing the region's small black population.

In the South, the newcomers populated an expanding plantation frontier. Georgia, which was founded with a ban of slave imports, was home to only 500 slaves in 1750. That year, however, its trustees agreed to lift the ban as of January 1, 1751, and after that, the colony quickly became a slave society. Its slave population soared, reaching 18,000 in 1775. South Carolina also resumed massive imports of slaves in the 1750s, bringing in 56,000 between 1751 and 1775, even as the colony's slave population began to expand by natural increase. Only in the Chesapeake, which was already home to almost half a million people of African descent, did slave imports slow. As a result of robust rates of natural increase, most Chesapeake planters could expect slave families to grow on their own. Planters did continue to bring enslaved Africans to recently settled areas, such as the Virginia Piedmont and western Maryland, but those imports declined over time and amounted to less than one thousand per year by the 1770s.

By contrast, the enslaved population in the northern colonies was never self-sustaining. Northern employers had to import slaves to meet their labor needs. Scattered across the region, northern slaves were rarely able to find partners, so their numbers were not replenished by reproduction. Although the slave population in the North remained modest in comparison to that in the South, between 1732 and 1754 slaves made up a third of all immigrants (voluntary or involuntary) entering New York City, and black New Yorkers accounted for almost 20 percent of the city's population. Likewise, one in five Philadelphia laborers and one in ten of all Bostonians were enslaved by midcentury. Massachusetts as a whole saw its black population increase by 50 percent during each decade between 1700 and 1750.

During the mid-eighteenth century, the use of enslaved labor expanded into new occupational sectors in New England and the middle colonies. Slaves had long been common in northern port cities such as New York, Boston, and Philadelphia, where they served as domestic and maritime workers. But urban artisans who had tradition-ally employed white apprentices now began to train black slaves to work in their shops. Increasing numbers of enslaved Africans were also employed in agriculture, both in southern New England and in the grain-producing regions of the middle colonies, areas that had previously relied on white immigrant workers. Landowners in slave owning regions such as Narragansett County, Rhode Island, became more dependent on slave labor, while farmers in Pennsylvania, northern New Jersey, the Hudson Valley, and Long Island began to import large numbers of enslaved Africans for the first time.

As slaves became integral to the northern labor force, both American and African American society changed. Since slave birthrates remained extremely low in the North, slavery there was sustained by "a continual supply . . . from Africa," as Benjamin Franklin noted.[7] As his observation indicates, by the 1740s northern merchants had begun to import boatloads of West African slaves. Prior to 1741, 70 percent of the slaves shipped to New York originated in the Caribbean, and only 30 percent came directly from Africa. After 1741, the proportions were reversed.[8] Changes in both demand and supply shaped this shift in the composition of slave imports. As the demand for slaves rose in northern cities, the slave market there could no longer rely on the small-scale trade in "refuse slaves" from the West Indies. At the same time, in 1720 the British crown eliminated duties on slaves imported directly from Africa, making it easier for American merchants to buy shiploads of African slaves.

As slavery expanded in eighteenth-century America, black freedom contracted. Both the northern and southern colonies had long been home to small numbers of free blacks, whose populations were increasingly dwarfed by the steady influx of enslaved migrants. By 1775, one observer recalled, "the number of free negroes [in Virginia] was so small that they were seldom to be met with."[9] Free blacks were even scarcer in South Carolina. Laws discouraging manumission and requiring African Americans who did gain freedom to leave the state also limited the free black population in the South. Free blacks were somewhat more common in the North, where such restrictions were rare, but as of 1760 they still totaled only 10 percent of the region's small black population— or a few thousand people.

Shaping an African American Culture

The steady importation of thousands of West African captives ensured that African culture shaped the lives of blacks throughout the colonies, even as the American-born black population also increased. The cultural impact of these migrants varied by region: It was most striking in areas where American- and Caribbean-born blacks predomi-nated, such as the Northeast, and weakest in the colonies of the Lower South, where African-born slaves had long formed a majority.

African American communities in the North were transformed when shiploads of Africans began docking in northeastern port cities in the 1740s. The newcomers infused African culture into these increasingly acculturated black communities, made up of English-speaking slaves who had long lived and worked among whites and main-tained only limited ties to their African roots. But northern blacks were sufficiently set apart from the white world to enjoy their own evolving culture. Both African and American, they welcomed the new migrants and embraced their African traditions. By midcentury, blacks across the North began to adopt a self-consciously African identity, which shaped the naming of early black organizations such as the African Lodge No. 1, a black Masonic lodge founded in 1776.

During this period, Africans and African Americans in the North united across cultural and linguistic divides in a boisterous annual celebration known as **Negro Election Day**. Largely a New England phenomenon, Negro Election Day combined the Puritan tradition of an election day holiday with African rituals of festive role reversals, in which the powerless temporarily played the role of the powerful. This holiday saw black New Englanders elect their own kings and governors in elaborate ceremonies that included royal processions, political parades, and inaugural parties. Those ceremonies, which partly spoofed white behavior on official election days, were often regarded with amused disdain by whites, who tended not to grasp the extent to which Negro Election Day parodied its white counterpart. In fact, white municipal authorities sanctioned the festivities. On this day, one white observer noted, "all the various languages of Africa, mixed with broken and ludicrous English, filled the air, accompanied with music of the fiddle, tambourine, the banjo, drum, etc."[10]

But the elections were at least semiserious in their public recognition of local black leaders' authority. Black governors and kings were often African-born men of royal lineage, and many had the added distinction of serving wealthy and powerful white men, who supplied them with the food, liquor, and elegant clothing required to compete for these offices. Although these were primarily ceremonial positions, some black governors and kings were authorized to speak on behalf of their communities and were called on to preside over informal trials of slaves accused of petty crimes.

Black northerners also came together for African-influenced funeral ceremonies, which struck white observers as alarmingly pagan. Drawing on West African mortuary rites that celebrated the dead with music and song designed to ease their journey into the spirit world, black funerals confounded white New Englanders. "They did not express so much sorrow at the funeral," a white observer named William Benton wrote of a black funeral in Salem, Massachusetts, "as real gratification at appearing so well, a greater sympathy with living happily than the bereaved."[11] Such celebrations made far more sense to the black men and women who participated in them. Benton's comments suggest that, while white northerners found African religious traditions alien, black northerners did not. Instead, such traditions were a shared point of connection between African newcomers and blacks who had spent many years in America.

The brisk slave trade in the Chesapeake ensured that slaves there, like their northern counterparts, did not become wholly estranged from their African cultural heritage. At midcentury, blacks who lived in the Chesapeake tended to be highly acculturated as a result of sustained contact with whites, with whom they shared modest-sized plantations and urban dwellings. Between 1720 and the 1770s, however, the planters who settled in the Virginia Piedmont imported approximately fifteen thousand African captives. Most of these settlers came from the tidewater region on Virginia's eastern coast, where decades of tobacco production had exhausted the soil, forcing planters to seek more fertile land farther west. As the settlers fanned out, they carved new plantations out of the wilderness using the labor of both American blacks and recent African migrants, who worked and lived together. The African-born slaves helped sustain African cultural practices and beliefs among the American-born blacks throughout the region. In turn, the American blacks helped the newcomers assimilate.

Over time, the two groups blended and intermixed, creating a slave culture that was simultaneously African and American.

This blended culture was also evident in linguistic patterns that developed in the Upper South, where blacks spoke English but also continued to use African idioms and syntax. According to John Smyth, an Englishman who immigrated to Virginia shortly before the Revolution, these cultural hybrids "spoke a mixed dialect between the Guinea and English."[12] Local whites, who in turn adopted some of the black idioms, called the regional variation of English spoken by Chesapeake blacks "Virginian," a term that recognized the influence of the blend of African and American culture on the region as a whole.

African cultural beliefs and customs also remained common in the Upper South. Like northern blacks, even highly acculturated southern blacks often insisted on honoring the dead by singing, dancing, and rejoicing at funerals. They also honored traditional African beliefs in the power of **conjure**. Rooted in West African religious traditions and rituals recognizing the existence of magic and the influence of ancestral spirits and other occult powers in daily life (see chapter 2), conjure was also influenced by the surroundings in which it took shape in North America, drawing on Native American knowledge of natural remedies. Conjurers, who could be men or women, were also known as "root doctors" or "Negro doctors" and were often skilled in the use of botanical medicines. Black and white southerners alike consulted them to heal the sick with spells and charms as well as roots and herbs. Conjurers also created love potions and were thought to be able to predict the future. On a more sinister note, many people believed that they poisoned their enemies.

Conjure and other African traditions were most entrenched in the Lower South, where acculturation was minimal. Most blacks in eighteenth-century South Carolina, for example, lived in an increasingly Africanized world. Slave birthrates remained low there for much of the century, forcing the colony's planters to import thousands of West African slaves each year to meet the needs of the growing plantation economy. The new arrivals reinforced African cultural practices and spiritual beliefs among low-country slaves, even after the number of American-born blacks in the region slowly began to increase.

Many low-country blacks never mastered the English language. Isolated on large plantations and put to work under the supervision of black drivers, they had little contact with English speakers. As a result, even the region's native-born blacks often spoke a creole language known as **Gullah**, which whites found difficult to understand. Gullah speakers mixed English with West African syntax and words. For instance, using a term from the Efik-Ibibio language spoken by many people in what is today southeastern Nigeria, they referred to white people as "backra" or "buckra," meaning "he who surrounds or governs."[13]

The Slaves' Great Awakening

The enduring influence of African traditions and beliefs and the influx of new arrivals limited the spread of Christianity among African Americans in the eighteenth century. So, too, did the lack of enthusiasm that many slave owners expressed toward slave conversion. But the period also saw the slow beginnings of Afro-Christianity in both the North and the South, inspired by the **Great Awakening**, a wave of religious revivals

The Creation of an African American Culture
This late-eighteenth-century painting, *The Old Plantation*, depicts a group of slaves on a South Carolina plantation. The slaves' activities strongly suggest the persistence of West African cultural traditions and practices in the Lower South. This painting may depict a wedding, which sometimes featured the tradition of "jumping the broom," or it may depict a dance. Many of the participants' accoutrements—the women's head ties and the players' instruments, for example—are West African in origin. But the other garments shown are typical of American working-class attire during this period, and the slave cabins and other plantation buildings remind us of the setting in which this distinctly African American culture was taking shape.
The Old Plantation, attributed to John Rose, Beaufort County, South Carolina, c. 1785–1790/Abby Aldrich Rockefeller Folk Art Museum, The Colonial Williamsburg Foundation, Williamsburg, VA.

that began in New England in the mid-1730s and spread south during the Revolutionary era. This multidenominational movement was led by evangelical ministers from various Protestant sects, attracting Presbyterian, Congregationalist, Baptist, and Methodist participants, as well as members of German and Dutch Reformed churches. These ministers, known as **New Lights**, rejected Protestantism's traditional emphasis on doctrine and ritual in favor of emotional sermons that urged listeners to repent and find spiritual salvation in Christ. New Lights did not seek out black converts, but they welcomed black and Indian congregants, and their emotional preaching drew spectators of all colors and faiths.

Their message was also appealing. New Light ministers stressed that the liberating effects of faith were open to all. "You that are our servants," Benjamin Colman of Boston's Brattle Street Church told his congregants in 1740, "the meanest of our servants,

Phillis Wheatley

Poet and antislavery activist Phillis Wheatley published her first book of poems, *Poems on Various Subjects, Religious and Moral*, in 1773 at age twenty. The title page and frontispiece, shown here, feature an engraving of a dignified, intellectual Wheatley engaged in her craft. The frame around her portrait identifies her as "Phillis Wheatley, Negro Servant to Mr. John Wheatley, of Boston." Later that year, John Wheatley would free her. *Title page and frontispiece to* Poems on Various Subjects, Religious and Moral *by Phillis Wheatley (1753–1784), published in London, 1773 (engraving)/ © Massachusetts Historical Society, Boston, MA, USA/The Bridgeman Art Library International.*

even our poor Negroes, chuse you the Service of CHRIST; he will make you his Freemen; The SON OF GOD, shall make you free, and you shall be free indeed."[14] At revival meetings, ministers encouraged blacks and women to relate their conversion experiences and serve as religious examples for other worshippers, opening up new religious roles for both groups. "Women and girls; yea Negroes, have taken it upon them to the business of preachers," one hostile observer complained in 1743.[15] (See Documents: The Great Awakening in the South, pp. 140–44.)

The Great Awakening's egalitarian spirit fostered the education, conversion, and eventual manumission of several notable black northerners, including the famous poet Phillis Wheatley. Wheatley, who was seven or eight years old when she was sold into slavery in the Senegal/Gambia region, was converted and educated by the devout family who purchased her from a slave ship in 1761. Her pious mistress, Susannah Wheatley, loved the "spellbinding sermon[s]" of evangelical leaders and took their message to heart, encouraging her daughter, Mary, to teach their young slave to read, write, and commit much of the Bible to memory. Phillis Wheatley began writing poetry in her teens, publishing her first book of poems in London when she was twenty years old. *Poems on Various Subjects, Religious and Moral* won her a following among British antislavery activists and also helped her win her own freedom. Later that year, Wheatley's owner freed her "at the desire of [his] friends in England."[16] (See Documents: African American Patriots, pp. 145–48.)

Wheatley's path to freedom was not uncommon. As the Great Awakening moved south, it inspired thousands of slaveholders to take a new interest in slaves' religious education and triggered a wave of manumissions among devout masters. But the revival movement posed only a limited challenge to slavery as an institution. Although New Light ministers welcomed black worshippers, few challenged slavery. In fact, the movement's leading luminaries, the Connecticut Congregationalist Jonathan Edwards and George Whitefield, an itinerant Anglican minister from Gloucester, England, both owned slaves themselves.

These evangelical leaders had little trouble reconciling slavery with their religious faith. Edwards, who owned several domestic slaves, criticized slave owners who mistreated their slaves, but he also maintained that slaves flourished under the guidance of a good Christian master. Whitefield, once he moved from England to preach in Savannah, Georgia, developed similar convictions. Although he openly chided some Georgia slave owners who abused their slaves, calling them "Monsters of Barbarity,"[17] he also remained convinced that slavery was compatible with Christianity as long as slave owners were careful to attend to their slaves' spiritual needs. He seems to have been terrified by the prospect of a slave revolt, having traveled through South Carolina shortly after the Stono rebellion in 1739. Whitefield encouraged enslaved blacks to "stay in your calling at all costs . . . [and] give up the thought of seeking freedom from your masters." He also "pray[ed] God, they may never be permitted to get the upper hand."[18]

In the Chesapeake, where white colonists outnumbered black slaves, there was less opposition to black participation in the revivals. Virginia and Maryland slaves, who were primarily native-born and spoke English, had no trouble understanding the evangelical movement's message and were drawn to its emotional style of worship. Evangelical revival services, which often took place in tent encampments, usually included songs and testimonials as well as prayer. They were more lively and open to innovation than the highly ritualized services offered in the Chesapeake's traditional churches, and they provided black participants with opportunities to incorporate African music and styles of expression. Although some white ministers deplored the "groans, cries, screams, and agonies" heard from blacks and other enthusiastic worshippers, most welcomed such congregants. "Ethiopia has . . . stretched forth her hands to God," the Presbyterian revivalist Samuel Davies declared after more than a hundred African Americans attended a revival he held in Hanover County, Virginia, in 1751. Anxious to instruct slaves in the Christian faith, Davies distributed Bibles and other religious literature at his revivals. Many of his slave congregants, hungry for literacy as well as salvation, spent "every leisure hour" learning to read.[19]

By the late eighteenth century, black lay preachers were leading conversions of their own. Many kept their calling largely silent and led congregations that met in secret. Slave preachers and their followers were members of a multidenominational black church that one historian has called the "invisible institution."[20] The product of an era when slaves were generally forbidden to hold public gatherings, slave congregations often met only under the veil of night. As a result, the activities of enslaved preachers are not well documented.

Even free black preachers were often forbidden to lead public forms of worship, as the Virginia-born John Marrant found out. A lay preacher, he was eager to share his religious faith with the slaves on the Charleston, South Carolina, plantation where he worked as a carpenter, but the plantation's mistress objected. She insisted that Christianity would only result in "negroes ruined," Marrant later recalled. He defied her wishes by leading covert prayer meetings, until her husband launched a surprise raid on one such meeting, bringing in neighbors and employees who helped him flog the congregants until "blood ran from their backs and sides to the floor to make them leave off praying." Thereafter, Marrant's followers prayed only in secret.[21]

Despite white opposition, African Americans' "invisible institution" flourished, offering worshippers a buffer against the white racism they faced on a daily basis. Whereas the South's white evangelicals hoped that Christianity would school blacks in obedience and submission to make them better slaves, black converts took other lessons from their newfound faith. Drawn in by the egalitarian spirit of the evangelical movement, they embraced Christianity's message that all men and women are equal before God, and they saw in the Bible's promises of spiritual deliverance some hope of eventually achieving freedom on earth as well as in heaven. In doing so, they crafted a distinctly Afro-Christian religious faith that helped them survive slavery while praying for freedom.

The African American Revolution

The Revolutionary era was a time of remarkable ideological ferment among African Americans. The Great Awakening offered both a new religious faith and educational opportunities to many black converts, who often found a critique of slavery in the revivalists' message of religious equality. African Americans found the egalitarian principles on which the colonists based their struggles against the British to be equally liberating. The American Revolution took place during the Enlightenment, a time when thinkers throughout the Americas and western Europe questioned traditional institutions, customs, and morals. The discontented colonists framed their complaints in terms of philosophical principles with far-reaching implications.

The colonists' rift with Britain took shape over the taxes, import duties, and other obligations the British Parliament imposed on the American colonies. But the colonists went beyond financial disputes to insist that all men had a natural right to self-government. In doing so, they opened up new questions about the legitimacy of slavery. The Revolutionary leader James Otis Jr. maintained that "the colonists are by the law of nature freeborn, as indeed all men are, white or black," and many of Otis's fellow patriots opposed American participation in the African slave trade.[22] But the Revolution's leaders avoided direct attacks on American slavery for fear that internal controversies might derail their attempts to unite the colonies in the common cause. African Americans did not share these fears and approached the Revolution as an antislavery struggle from the outset. They drew on both Revolutionary ideology and the social and political chaos of war to challenge slavery by petitioning for freedom, running away, and fighting for their own liberty on both sides of the conflict.

The Road to Independence

The American colonists' discontent with British rule began in the early 1760s, when the British Parliament levied a new series of taxes on the colonies. The taxes, designed to raise money to pay off British debts incurred during the French and Indian War (1754–1763), when British troops were deployed to protect the colonists' land, were not excessive. But they represented a shift from Britain's previous policy of benign neglect toward the colonies. Colonists had long controlled their own affairs and paid only local taxes. They also had no say in British imperial policy and no political representation in Parliament, which they felt entitled to as British subjects. In particular, they insisted that they should not be subject to "taxation without representation." Taxes imposed on the colonies by Parliament, the rebellious colonists maintained, deprived them of their property without their consent, making them little better than slaves.

African Americans were largely unaffected by British taxes because most blacks were either enslaved or impoverished, and therefore had little access to the goods that were taxed. But colonists' protests against British tyranny nonetheless held a powerful appeal for African Americans. White patriots cast their opposition to British authority as a struggle for freedom, denouncing the "vile, ignominious slavery" imposed on them by Britain's new policies.[23] Their protests drew on the natural rights philosophy articulated by thinkers such as Britain's own John Locke, who maintained that "men being . . . by nature all free, equal, and independent, no one can be put out of this estate and subjected to the political power of another without his own consent."[24]

Though rarely intended to challenge slavery, white colonists' rhetoric gave slaves a powerful new political language with which to address their own condition. When white colonists in Charleston protested passage of the Stamp Act of 1765—which required colonists to print most documents on a special stamped paper that was issued and taxed by the British government—with chants of "Liberty! Liberty and stamp'd paper," local slaves also called for "Liberty, liberty," much to the horror of white observers. A South Carolina politician, recording the incident, dismissed the slaves' chant as "a thoughtless imitation" of whites.[25] But slave unrest mounted throughout the years leading up to the Revolution, as the conflict inspired African Americans to stage freedom struggles of their own.

In the pre-Revolution years, as American colonists boycotted British goods; protested taxes on stamped documents, sugar, and tea; and scuffled with British soldiers stationed on American soil, slaves across the colonies took advantage of the unrest to escape from their owners. In Georgia and South Carolina, they fled to swamplands and other unsettled frontier areas to form maroon communities. In the more densely populated North, they often headed for urban areas. According to Boston patriot John Adams, some of the slaves already living in northern cities took advantage of the social disorder to free themselves. As the colonies moved toward declaring their independence, he later recalled, Boston slaves pushed for their own freedom by becoming "lazy, idle, proud, vicious and at length wholly useless to their masters, to such a degree that the abolition of slavery became a measure of economy."[26]

Other black northerners publicly embraced the Revolutionary struggle. In 1772, while still a slave herself, Phillis Wheatley wrote a poem dedicated to the Earl of Dartmouth, the British king's newly appointed secretary of state for North America—and a man who the colonists hoped might remedy their discontent. In verses linking the patriots' tribulations with those of the black slaves, Wheatley heralded Dartmouth's appointment as a sign that New England would once more see "Freedom's charms unfold." She went on to explain that having been "young in life" when she was "snatch'd from Afric's fancy'd happy seat," she knew the pain of slavery all too well and could "but pray / Others may never feel tyrannic sway." After her emancipation, Wheatley continued publicly to question how the colonists could reconcile their "cry of liberty" with "the exercise of oppressive power over others." (See Documents: African American Patriots, pp. 145–48.)

Most of Wheatley's black contemporaries did not possess her writing skills, but some managed to take such questions to the courts by initiating **freedom suits** that challenged local magistrates and colonial legislatures to recognize their natural rights. "Attended Court; heard the trial of an action of trespass, brought by a mulatto woman, for damages, for restraining her of her liberty," John Adams wrote in his diary in 1766 after witnessing a freedom suit brought by Jenny Slew of Ipswich, Massachusetts. "This is called suing for liberty; the first action that ever I knew of the sort, though I have heard there have been many."[27] As the daughter of a free white woman, Slew claimed her liberty as a birthright, but later slave litigants claimed freedom as a natural right, sometimes winning their liberty as a result.

Some of the impetus for the freedom suits came from events in Britain rather than America. The **Somerset case**, which freed an American slave named James Somerset in 1772, inspired new challenges to slavery throughout the British empire. Somerset was born in Africa and sold into slavery in Virginia, where he lived until his owner, Charles Stewart, brought him to London while traveling on business. Somerset ran away but was caught and imprisoned on a ship bound for Jamaica, where Stewart planned to sell him. The British antislavery activist Granville Sharp, a municipal official, hired lawyers who issued a writ of **habeas corpus** challenging Stewart's right to detain Somerset. Designed to prevent false imprisonment, writs of habeas corpus (Latin for "you should have the body") request the legal review of prisoners detained without trial. The Somerset case ended up in the court of Britain's lord chief justice William Murray, Earl of Mansfield, who was aware that it could challenge the legal status of British slavery. He nonetheless ruled in favor of freeing Somerset, although his ruling was carefully worded to apply only to Somerset's case.

The Somerset case did not make slavery illegal in Britain or even address its status anywhere else, but when British antislavery activists celebrated Somerset's release, slaves in Britain and the Americas drew on the case to make their own claims to liberty. In January 1773, Massachusetts blacks petitioned the colony's governor and legislature as a group for the first time. Signed by one author, Felix [Holbrook], but written on behalf of slaves throughout Massachusetts, the document appealed to legislators to relieve the "unhappy state and condition" of the enslaved. Invoking the Somerset case as a precedent for their own emancipation, petitioners noted that "men of Great note and Influence . . . pleaded our cause with arguments which we hope will have weight in this honorable court."[28] Meanwhile, in Virginia, news of the Somerset case may have prompted a slave named Bacchus to begin a long journey to England in 1774. (See From the Record: Runaway Ad for Bacchus.)

What became of Bacchus is unknown, but the Massachusetts legislature tabled Felix's petition. They received another petition a month later. The new petition listed several authors: Peter Bestes, Sambo Freeman, Felix Holbrook, and Chester Joio. It also bypassed the colony's unpopular governor to speak directly to the patriots in the rebellious house of representatives. "We expect great things from men who have made

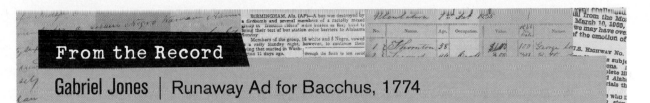

From the Record

Gabriel Jones | Runaway Ad for Bacchus, 1774

A slave named Bacchus was among the African Americans inspired to seek freedom in the wake of the Somerset case. His departure is recorded by his owner, the Virginia lawyer **Gabriel Jones**, who describes both Bacchus's appearance and his possible paths of escape in some detail.

AUGUSTA, *June 18, 1774.*

Run away the 16th Instant, from the Subscriber, a Negro Man named BACCHUS, about 30 Years of Age, five Feet six or seven Inches high, strong and well made; had on, and took with him, two white *Russia* Drill Coats, one turned up with blue, the other quite plain and new, with white figured Metal Buttons, blue Plush Breeches, a fine Cloth Pompadour Waistcoat, two or three thin or Summer Jackets, sundry Pairs of white Thread Stockings, five or six white Shirts, two of them pretty fine, neat Shoes, Silver Buckles, a fine Hat cut and cocked in the Macaroni Figure, a double-milled Drab Great Coat, and sundry other Wearing Apparel. He formerly belonged to Doctor *George Pitt*, of *Williamsburg*, and I imagine is gone there under Pretence of my sending him upon Business, as I have frequently heretofore done; he is a cunning, artful, sensible Fellow, and very capable of forging a Tale to impose on the Unwary, is well acquainted with the lower Parts of the Country, having constantly rode with me for some Years past, and has been used to waiting from his Infancy. He was seen a few Days before he went off with a Purse of Dollars, and had just before changed a five Pound Bill; most, or all of which, I suppose he must have robbed me off [*sic*], which he might easily have done, I having trusted him much after what I thought had proved his Fidelity. He will probably endeavour to pass for a Freeman by the Name of *John Christian*, and attempt to get on Board some Vessel bound for *Great Britain*, from the Knowledge he has of the late Determination of *Somerset*'s Case. Whoever takes up the said Slave shall have 5£ Reward, on his Delivery to . . . GABRIEL JONES.

SOURCE: *Virginia Gazette*, June 30, 1774.

??? Although Bacchus's owner authored this document, how can we mine it for evidence about Bacchus himself? What does it suggest about Bacchus's plans and the strategies he used to orchestrate his escape?

such a noble stand against the design of their *fellow-men* to enslave them," they wrote, before requesting the representatives' "assistance in our peaceable and lawful attempts to gain our freedom . . . which we, as men, have a natural right to."[29] Framed in the Revolutionary rhetoric of the day, the petitioners' request echoed the expansive natural rights philosophy celebrated by Massachusetts patriots such as James Otis Jr. But Otis never even freed his own slave manservant, and Massachusetts legislators proved equally unwilling to link the petitioners' freedom struggles to their own. They ignored the second petition and several subsequent appeals.

Black Patriots

Despite such disappointments, many black northerners joined the patriot cause. Once the conflict began, fugitives could often secure their freedom through military service. More than five thousand African Americans are estimated to have fought alongside American forces during the Revolution, while other blacks sided with the patriots without actually enlisting. Among the best known of these unofficial patriots is Crispus Attucks, a fugitive slave who became the American Revolution's first casualty.

After his 1750 escape from a farm in Framingham, Massachusetts, Attucks may have kept a low profile to avoid capture. But as a sailor and dockworker who lived and worked on the Boston waterfront when he was not at sea, Attucks was among the many Bostonians who resented the growing British military presence in New England's premier port city. The British "redcoats" were especially unpopular among men in Attucks's profession, because they often supplemented their meager military salaries by working part-time at lower wages than American workers were willing to accept. The soldiers' presence on the docks also discouraged the brisk business in smuggled goods that had long allowed colonial shippers to avoid British taxes. Finally, the British troops threatened the liberty of American sailors and dockworkers, who were often impressed or forced into service in the British navy. These discontented American workers figured prominently in igniting what became known as the Boston Massacre.

The conflict took place on the afternoon of March 5, 1770, in a tavern on Boston's waterfront when a group of men that one observer described as a "motley rabble of saucy boys, Negroes and mulattoes, Irish teagues (a derogatory term for Catholics) and outlandish Jacktars (sailors)" encountered a British soldier who came in to inquire about part-time work.[30] Later that day, outraged by this intrusion onto their turf, more than thirty men from the bar gathered outside the port's customhouse to taunt and heckle the British soldiers stationed outside. The scuffle ended only when the redcoats fired on the crowd, killing five men and wounding eleven more.

The first to die was Attucks, a forty-seven-year-old man of African and Nantucket Indian descent. More than six feet tall and powerfully built, Attucks was one of the mob's leaders. He may not have been fighting for freedom, but as a member of a close-knit community of workingmen, he was willing to defend his livelihood and died a hero as a result. Attucks and the massacre's other martyrs were honored with a funeral procession that attracted ten thousand mourners, and they were buried together in a common grave. (See Visual Sources: Freedom's Fight, pp. 149–57.)

The Boston Massacre rallied men and women across the thirteen colonies to the patriot cause. In Boston, it set the stage for the Boston Tea Party in 1773. In an open rebellion against the British Tea Act, colonists dressed as Indians boarded British ships and dumped boxes of tea into Boston harbor. The conflict escalated when Britain passed a series of laws known as the Intolerable Acts. These included the Massachusetts Government Act and the Administration of Justice Act, which curtailed the colonial government's power; the Boston Port Act, which closed Boston's port until its citizens reimbursed British officials for the tea they had destroyed; and the Quartering Act, which stationed British troops in Boston. The British hoped that this punitive legislation would isolate the

LA DESTRUCTION DE LA STATUE ROYALE A NOUVELLE YORCK.

Die Zerstorung der Koniglichen Bild Saule zu Neu Yorck | La Destruction de la Statue royale a Nouvelle Yorck

African Americans in the Revolution

On July 9, 1776, a group of New York patriots pulled down and destroyed an equestrian statue of Britain's King George III. This French print shows one artist's attempt to depict the event. Although the image has some flaws—rather than being mounted on horseback as he was in the actual statue, for example, the king is shown standing in the print—it is significant in its portrayal of the patriots, most of whom appear to be slaves. Black northerners, free and slave, were a vital force in the patriot struggle. They hoped that in casting off British rule, the colonists would also renounce African slavery. La déstruction de la statue royale à Nouvelle York/Die Zerstorung der Koniglichen Bild Saule zu Neu Yorck, *published in Paris, 1777/Library of Congress LC-USZC4-1476.*

Massachusetts rebels, but instead it united the American colonists in outrage. In 1774, they organized the First Continental Congress to lobby Britain for the reversal of the Intolerable Acts. The congress threatened to boycott British goods if the acts were not repealed and pledged to support Massachusetts in the event of a British attack, which was not long in coming. On April 19, 1775, the British marched on the towns of Lexington and Concord in a surprise attack designed to subdue the rebellious colony's leaders. Instead, it started a war.

Black northerners were among the patriots who rallied against the British, often joining the struggle in hopes of encouraging the colonists to reject African slavery as well as British tyranny. For instance, a free black resident of Massachusetts named Lemuel Haynes joined the Granville minutemen and fought in several battles before he fell ill. Horrified when the British invaded Lexington and Concord, the twenty-two-year-old Haynes had recently been freed from indentured servitude and saw the Battle of Lexington as a fight between "tyrants" and the "Liberty [for which] each freeman strives."[31] He also wished to expand the boundaries of that freedom. Although the Declaration of Independence, issued in 1776, maintained that "all men are created equal," it did not free the slaves, an omission that inspired the studious Haynes, who became a Congregationalist minister, to write his own addendum to it later that year. Titled "Liberty Further Extended," Haynes's unpublished manuscript called for the abolition of slavery in the American colonies. (See Documents: African American Patriots, pp. 145–48.)

As Haynes's actions illustrate, even before the Second Continental Congress met in May 1775 to organize the war effort, colonial militias mobilized all over New England, enlisting blacks as well as whites. The Massachusetts Safety Committee, formed in the summer of 1774 to protect citizens from British tyranny, had initially barred slave enlistment as "inconsistent with the principles [of freedom] that are to be supported."[32] But bans had little practical effect after the British marched on Lexington. As the redcoats approached, Peter Salem, a local slave, was freed to help defend the town. Militia rosters across New England soon listed men such as "Joshua Boylston's Prince" and "Isaac Gardner's Adam," whose names suggest that they, too, had only recently been freed from slavery.[33]

Haynes hoped that military service would win black Americans their "*undeniable right to . . . liberty*," and many slave combatants clearly shared his hope.[34] Slaves enlisted in large numbers after northern colonies from Rhode Island to New York passed legislation pledging to free blacks willing to serve for the duration of the conflict. Shortly before the war, the Connecticut slave Boyrereau Brinch, whose autobiography later recorded his ambivalence about fighting "to liberate freemen, my tyrants," was drafted into the Sixth Connecticut Regiment while still enslaved. He fought for five years before finally receiving his freedom.[35]

For other black northerners, military service brought immediate freedom. In Rhode Island, where slavery was entrenched, the promise of freedom prompted blacks to enlist at twice the rate of whites—despite their owners' warnings that the British would ship them off to the West Indies if they were captured. Undeterred, slaves abandoned their masters to enlist until the state began offering masters up to £120 for each slave they liberated for military service. In addition to paying for slave soldiers, northern states encouraged slave enlistments by allowing owners to send slave substitutes into battle rather than fight themselves.

Black patriots were far less common in the South, where widespread opposition to slave soldiers prohibited black enlistments during the early years of the conflict. As the war began, white southerners understandably questioned slaves' loyalty to the cause. As early as 1774, slaves in Virginia had conspired to run away in groups when British troops arrived, convincing slave owners that they would side with the British. "If America & Britain come to a hostile rupture," Virginian James Madison worried, "an Insurrection among the slaves may and will be promoted."[36]

Appointed commander in chief of the newly established Continental army on June 15, 1775, General George Washington shared Madison's sentiments. When he traveled to Cambridge, Massachusetts, to assume command of the patriot forces, he was horrified to find armed black men among them. He issued general orders barring their enlistment, which he renewed in December. But there is little evidence that Washington's prohibitions, which he later reversed, had a significant effect on blacks' service. Many New England troops were integrated from the start of the conflict, and after 1776 other colonies used slave soldiers to fill enlistment quotas. Only South Carolina and Georgia never mobilized their black populations.

The slaveholding colonists who resisted the use of black soldiers feared slave insurrections and were also afraid of losing their human property. As the Revolution spread south, both outcomes quickly became real possibilities. In 1775, long before the southern colonies had begun to enlist enslaved blacks, the British organized their first regiment of runaway slaves. They also encouraged runaways to join their armies throughout the conflict. In doing so, they created thousands of black **loyalists**, as those who remained loyal to the British were called. In this war, African Americans sought freedom on both sides of the conflict (Map 3.1).

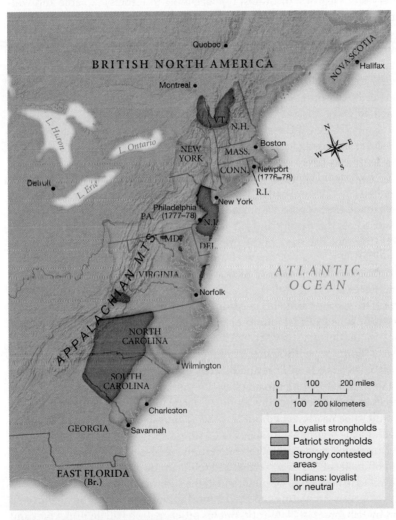

MAP 3.1 Patriots and Loyalists

The American Revolution divided the eastern seaboard's inhabitants into loyalists and patriots, whose sympathies varied from place to place. Patriots were in the majority in most of the colonies; loyalists were widely dispersed, but their strongholds were limited. These political allegiances were hard to track and shifted often, making it difficult to pinpoint the exact numbers of patriots and loyalists at any given point.

Black Loyalists

Approximately fifteen thousand black loyalists served with the British. They first entered the war early at the request of Virginia's royal governor John Murray, the Earl of Dunmore, whom patriot forces had driven out in June 1775. Determined to recapture the colony, Dunmore took refuge on a British ship patrolling the waters outside Yorktown. With only three hundred men at his disposal, he desperately needed reinforcements. On November 7, he reached out to local allies by issuing what became known as **Lord Dunmore's Proclamation**. This published broadside offered freedom to all "indentured Servants, Negroes, or others, (appertaining to Rebels) . . . able and willing to bear Arms" for the British.

Like other British officials, Dunmore realized that many blacks would serve on whichever side would allow them to fight for their own freedom. He had begun receiving slave volunteers as early as April 1775—many months before he issued his proclamation. He knew that by enlisting slaves, he would also deprive rebellious planters of their workers—and send some rebel soldiers scurrying home to guard their slaves. But he still hesitated to enlist enslaved soldiers for fear of alienating loyal colonists. By November, he had no choice and issued the carefully worded proclamation, designed to recruit only slaves belonging to rebels.

But his message may have reached a larger audience. Lord Dunmore's Proclamation unleashed a massive tide of slave unrest that fundamentally reshaped the character of the war. Between late 1775 and early 1776, some eight hundred male slaves and many of their families made their way to Dunmore's floating headquarters, while thousands more fanned out across the swamplands in an effort to reach Dunmore or seize their freedom some other way. The wave of runaways disrupted slave agriculture and forced Virginia slaveholders to wage a war on two fronts: In addition to defeating the British, they had to battle armed slave rebels and devote additional manpower to patrolling their remaining slaves.

Meanwhile, Dunmore secured his position by organizing the fittest of the fugitives into a military unit called Lord Dunmore's Ethiopian Regiment—possibly the first black regiment in the history of British America. Members of the regiment were rumored to wear uniforms with sashes reading "Liberty for Slaves," although this rumor was likely false, since Dunmore could barely outfit his existing troops. The men spent much of their time foraging for supplies. They also saw battle, making up half of Dunmore's forces in his victory over the Virginia militia at Kemp's Landing on November 16, 1775, only to be nearly wiped out less than a month later when patriot forces decimated much of the regiment. Replenished with new fugitive slaves, black troops accompanied Dunmore's men as they retreated to the shores of Chesapeake Bay, but smallpox killed off many of the new recruits and their families.

Dunmore failed to hold on to Virginia, and in the summer of 1776, just as the Continental Congress began circulating the Declaration of Independence, he abandoned Virginia to join British forces in New York. But his proclamation had an important and enduring effect on patriot military policy. The prospect of Virginia slaves fighting for the British convinced General Washington that the outcome of the war now depended on "which side can arm the Negroes faster," and with his support, the congress declared all blacks eligible for service in the Continental army a week after Dunmore issued his proclamation.[37]

Lord Dunmore's Proclamation also attracted freedom-seeking black loyalists from as far away as New York and New Jersey. One was a twenty-two-year-old slave named Titus, who ran away from a farmer in Monmouth County, New Jersey, to join the Ethiopian Regiment. He was shipped out when Dunmore retreated to New York and soon ended up less than a hundred miles from his home. Undeterred, Titus joined New Jersey's loyalist troops and fought in the Battle of Monmouth County in June 1778, capturing the head of the Monmouth militia. Although he was never officially commissioned as an officer, Titus earned the name "Colonel Tye" for his successful raids. He organized his own commando unit, known as the Black Brigade, with New Jersey blacks who knew the countryside well. The brigade raided the homes of slaveholding farmers, making off with their cattle, horses, and slaves. Tye and his men turned their captives over to the British and sold the British the food and supplies that they seized. By the spring of 1780, Tye had New Jersey patriots so terrified that they prevailed on their governor to declare martial law—to little avail. Tye's men continued to terrorize New Jersey until the fall of that year, when Tye died after being wounded in battle.

Lord Dunmore's Proclamation had its most significant impact in the South. Most of the blacks who served with loyalist forces were southerners, and the proclamation also triggered a mass exodus of fugitive slaves, who escaped their plantations by crossing British lines. Historians estimate that 80,000 to 100,000 southern slaves fled their masters during the Revolution. Not all remained with the British, however. Some freed themselves and headed to places where they were likely to remain free, such as cities and towns with large free black populations or frontier areas where slavery had yet to take hold. Moreover, the British did not offer shelter to all the runaways who crossed their lines. British officers were obliged to return any fugitives who had escaped from loyalist owners, and some British officers sold slaves who had escaped from patriot owners.

Despite such risks, the chance to find freedom with the British appealed to African Americans throughout the war. Most refugees did not end up in British uniforms, because British commanders had little time to train new troops and were often unable to supply their black volunteers with food and shelter, let alone arms. So they put the refugees to work foraging for food and supplies. Although such duties frequently required the fugitives to carry arms and fight any patriots they encountered, they did so without recognition or military pay. Refugees worked behind the lines as well, building fortifications, transporting munitions, cooking for troops, and doing their laundry. British commanders also employed refugees as domestic servants, often supplying their officers with an entire staff of black domestics.

Black refugees were entitled to a "certificate of freedom" for their work but received few other benefits and often had to provide food and shelter for themselves. They also faced other dangers. Not only were food and clean water often in short supply, but disease remained endemic in the British camps. Thousands escaped slavery only to die of smallpox and what contemporaries called "camp fever," which was likely typhus. Despite these harrowing conditions, many African Americans took their chances with the British, who offered them their only opportunity to achieve freedom. (See From the Record: Memoirs of a Black Loyalist.)

The service of these runaways was crucial to Britain's war effort and helped reshape British military strategy—and not a moment too soon. In 1778, after three years' worth of military action in the North, the British had yet to win a decisive victory. Worse still

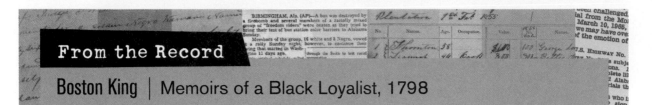

From the Record

Boston King | Memoirs of a Black Loyalist, 1798

Born on a plantation near Charleston, South Carolina, **Boston King (c. 1760–1802)** joined the loyalists rather than return to the carpenter to whom his master had apprenticed him and who beat him brutally. The following excerpt describes King's experiences with British and American forces in South Carolina.

To escape [my master's] cruelty, I determined to go to Charles-Town, and throw myself into the hands of the English. They received me readily, and I began to feel the happiness of liberty, of which I knew nothing before, altho' I was much grieved at first, to be obliged to leave my friends, and reside among strangers. In this situation I was seized with the small-pox, and suffered great hardships; for all the Blacks affected with that disease, were ordered to be carried a mile from the camp, lest the soldiers should be infected, and disabled from marching. This was a grievous circumstance to me and many others. We lay sometimes a whole day without any thing to eat or drink; but Providence sent a man, who belonged to the York volunteers whom I was acquainted with, to my relief. He brought me such things as I stood in need of; and by the blessing of the Lord I began to recover.

By this time, the English left the place; but as I was unable to march with the army, I expected to be taken by the enemy. However when they came, and understood that we were ill of the small-pox, they precipitately left us for fear of the infection. Two days after, the waggons were sent to convey us to the English Army, and we were put into a little cottage, (being 25 in number) about a quarter of a mile from the Hospital.

Being recovered, I marched with the army to Chamblem [Camden, New Jersey]. . . . Upon returning to the camp, to my great astonishment, I found all the English were gone, and had left only a few [loyalist] militia. I felt my mind greatly alarmed, but Captain Lewes, who commanded the militia, said, "You need not be uneasy, for you will see your regiment before 7 o'clock to-night." This satisfied me for the present, and in two hours we set off. As we were on the march, the Captain asked, "How will you like me to be your master?" I answered that I was Captain Grey's servant. "Yes," said he; "but I expect they are all taken prisoners before now; and I have been long enough in the English service, and am determined to leave them." These words roused my indignation, and I spoke some sharp things to him. But he calmly replied, "If you do not behave well, I will put you in irons, and give you a dozen stripes every morning." I now perceived that my case was desperate, and that I had nothing to trust to, but to wait the first opportunity for making my escape. The next morning, I was sent with a little boy over the river to an island to fetch the Captain some horses. When we came to the Island we found about fifty of the English horses, that Captain Lewes had stolen from them at different times while they were at Rockmount [Rocky Mount]. Upon our return to the Captain with the horses we were sent for, he immediately set off by himself. I stayed till about 10 o'clock and then resolved to go to the English army.

SOURCE: "Memoirs of the Life of Boston King, a Black Preacher," *Methodist Magazine*, March 1798, 107–8.

???   **What actions did King take to secure and preserve his own freedom?**

for the British, after patriot forces defeated General John Burgoyne's army at Saratoga, New York, in 1777, the French entered the war on the side of the Americans, raising fears that Spain would join their cause as well. France and Spain were Britain's chief imperial rivals, and both countries saw the American rebellion as a chance to challenge Britain's power in America and the Caribbean. With an increasingly international war now under way, Britain's military resources were overextended. Even the mighty British navy could not defend the Caribbean as long as Britain devoted most of its military resources to subduing the die-hard patriots.

Slaves, Soldiers, and the Outcome of the Revolution

As the Revolutionary War dragged on, Britain's decision to free slaves in exchange for service angered slave owners and weakened loyalist support in the South. When the British abandoned the American colonies in defeat, they also abandoned many black allies who had fought valiantly in hopes of gaining their freedom. The American Revolution set the northern states on a path to ending slavery—immediately (1777) in some states and more gradually in others, until it was almost entirely eliminated by the 1820s. The free black population of both the North and the Chesapeake increased significantly throughout this period. Only elsewhere in the South did slavery remain entrenched.

American Victory, British Defeat

Toward the end of 1778, the British Parliament adopted a new battle plan known as the **southern strategy**. Its goal was to crush the rebellion by retaking the South, which was home to far more loyalists than the Northeast and would therefore, the British hoped, be far easier to conquer. The plan depended partly on enlisting help from the region's slaves, whose loyalties lay with the British rather than the patriots. Moving the war south also allowed the British to monitor French and Spanish activities in the Caribbean, as well as to blockade southern ports to prevent the delivery of French aid to the patriots.

Britain's southern strategy initially paid off. British troops captured Savannah in 1778 and Charleston in 1779. Black loyalists were crucial to their efforts from the start. In Georgia, a black sailor named Samson guided the British fleet over shoals at the mouth of the Savannah River. When British troops disembarked, they discovered that the patriots had destroyed a bridge leading to the city and guarded the only remaining road. An elderly slave named Quamino Dolly approached a lieutenant colonel with his plans for an alternative approach and showed troops a route through a nearby swamp, which allowed the British to stage a surprise attack and capture Savannah.

Sir Henry Clinton, who became commander in chief of the British forces later that year, was eager to enlist similar slave support. In June 1779, as he prepared for an assault on Charleston, he issued the Philipsburg Proclamation. It expanded Lord Dunmore's Proclamation by promising to free all slaves willing to serve in any capacity, rather than just those who joined the fighting. It also recognized the growing importance of African American patriot combatants by declaring that any blacks found serving the patriots would be sold for the benefit of the crown.

In the end, however, Britain's southern strategy failed. The vast geographic scope of the southern states ensured that the British would never have enough manpower to defend the areas they conquered, while the loyalist support they had hoped for failed to materialize. Instead of finding allies among the former colonists, the British were thwarted by determined opposition from patriot forces. In addition, the embattled new nation had no crucial center of power that British forces could capture and subdue. Even though the British twice seized Philadelphia, the new nation's original capital, they could not derail the Americans.

Moreover, the growing presence of black soldiers in the Continental army often undermined British attempts to use the patriots' own slaves against them. In the summer of 1781, for example, a black patriot spy double-crossed the British by infiltrating their headquarters on behalf of the Marquis de Lafayette, a French volunteer who became a general in George Washington's army. Lafayette was desperate to drive the British general Charles Cornwallis out of Virginia and had been trying for months, without success, to gain advance information about his troop movements. He finally succeeded when he dispatched an ex-slave named James Armistead, who easily infiltrated Cornwallis's camp at Yorktown by posing as a refugee looking for work. Armistead won the trust of Cornwallis, who invited him to spy for the British, at which point Armistead became a double agent. He supplied true information to the Americans and false information to the British, remaining undiscovered until the day the defeated Cornwallis encountered Armistead in Lafayette's camp and realized that he had been duped.

Still more fatal to Britain's southern strategy was the distinctly mixed success of the British policy of freeing the rebels' slaves. Although the British desperately needed manpower, by enlisting slave support, both Dunmore and Clinton eroded their loyalist support in the South and stiffened the resolve of southern patriots. Many southerners were ambivalent about independence when the fighting began, but after Dunmore issued his proclamation, the British never commanded the widespread southern support they envisioned. Clinton's Philipsburg Proclamation only compounded the problem. In the Carolinas and Georgia especially, where most whites owned slaves, loyalists were regarded as traitors to public safety and patriots were as dedicated to protecting slavery as they were to achieving independence. With support for the war wavering at home, the British abandoned America to the patriots rather than continue the fight. Cornwallis's 1781 surrender at Yorktown was the beginning of the war's end and set the stage for a military retreat that largely devastated Britain's black allies.

The Fate of Black Loyalists

At the siege of Yorktown, Britain's first major defeat, Cornwallis provided no protection for the thousands of African Americans serving in his forces. Under a sustained assault from French and American forces that began in late September 1781, his headquarters were crowded, ravaged by smallpox, and cut off from British supply lines. Desperately short of food by mid-October, he first slaughtered his horses to prevent them from starving and then issued orders expelling his African American allies to fend for themselves. "It is not to be done," mourned the senior British officer who took the orders and was all too aware that the refugees would be reenslaved. "We drove back to the enemy all of our black friends," another soldier later reflected. "We had used them to good advantage and set them free and now, with fear and trembling they had to face the reward of their cruel masters."[38] The British surrendered a week later, evacuating their troops and leaving their black allies behind. As the British boarded their boats, American troops patrolled the banks of the York River to ensure that no African Americans escaped.

Other loyalist troops held their positions as late as 1783. In 1782, Lord Dunmore and other "fight-to-the-end" generals who still hoped to reverse the Yorktown defeat made desperate appeals for ten thousand black troops. But Britain's military leaders remained unwilling to make full use of their black allies, even as defeat stared them in the face. Parliament had never intended to abolish American slavery—or to compromise Britain's investment in the slave trade and its West Indian sugar colonies. The British statesman Edmund Burke warned Parliament that freeing the slaves to fight might unleash a conflict even more dangerous than the American bid for independence. Once armed, he argued, the slaves would keep fighting until they "made themselves the masters of the houses, goods, wives, and daughters of their lords."[39] Unable to win the war and unwilling to jeopardize British investments, the House of Commons voted to begin peace talks with the former colonists in the spring of 1782.

The British retreat dealt a cruel blow to their black allies. The Royal Navy eventually managed to evacuate fifteen thousand black loyalists, whom they transported to England or resettled in Britain's remaining colonies in Canada, Jamaica, the Bahamas, South Africa, and Australia. But they left at least as many behind. In Charleston, the navy had to ship out thousands of slaves belonging to white loyalists—who were unwilling to leave their human property behind—and at the same time find room for the ex-slaves whose service entitled them to freedom.

Unable to accommodate all the refugees, the British left behind the families of many slave allies, who faced reenslavement. As the British fleet filled up, African Americans dove into Charleston harbor and swam out to longboats loading the navy's vessels in desperate hopes of securing a berth. Most were beaten back with cutlasses by the British soldiers who manned the boats. Some clung to the boats until their fingers were sliced off their hands. Even the blacks who made it aboard faced an uncertain future. Many former slaves were resold into slavery in Jamaica and other British colonies, while some free fugitives found themselves claimed as property by unscrupulous British soldiers and subject to reenslavement or sale.

For most refugees, the prospect of returning to slavery in the South was more fearsome than the uncertainties of relocation. When the British evacuation of New York in 1783 inspired rumors that the slaves who fought with the British would be returned to their masters, ex-slaves were terrified. As Boston King, the fugitive slave from South Carolina who fought with the British in New York, later recalled, "Many of the slaves had very cruel masters, so that the thought of returning home with them embittered life to us. For some days, we lost our appetite for food, and sleep departed from our eyes."[40] To King's great relief, loyalists in New York offered more generous shelter than their southern counterparts: Between three thousand and four thousand blacks accompanied the British troops when they left.

Black Patriots and Loyalists

African Americans served valiantly on both sides of the Revolution, often allying themselves with the side they felt provided the best opportunity for securing their own freedom. The black soldier-musician in the image on the right is a member of a French expeditionary corps that fought with the patriots. The woodcutter in the image below is a loyalist who sought refuge in Canada after the war. When the British retreated, black loyalists scrambled to avoid reenslavement. Many resettled in British colonies in Canada, Jamaica, the Bahamas, South Africa, and Australia. *First image: Gouache by Nicolas Hoffmann, 1780/The Granger Collection, NYC. All rights reserved; Second image: William Booth,* A Black Wood Cutter at Shelburne, *1788. Library and Archives Canada/W. Booth/W. H. Coverdale Collection of Canadiana, Manoir Richelieu Collection/C-040162.*

Other black loyalists continued to defend their territory in the low-country swamps as late as 1786—three years after the Treaty of Paris, the agreement that formally ended the war and recognized the United States. On Bear Creek, which runs through the Savannah River marshes that once divided South Carolina and Georgia along the coast, fugitive slaves built a fortified village one mile long and four hundred feet wide. From there, they raided nearby plantations in both states until May 1789, when the South Carolina governor dispatched a coalition of troops from South Carolina and Georgia, as well as some Catawba Indians, to destroy the settlement. Vanquished after a four-day battle, the Bear Creek settlers, who called themselves "the King of England's Soldiers," were branded a gang of common criminals by the governor.[41]

Closer to Freedom

Despite the crushing losses suffered by black loyalists, the American Revolution brought African Americans closer to freedom. Most of the five thousand blacks who served among the American forces ended up free, although some struggled to achieve their freedom. James Armistead, the double agent who spied for Lafayette, was briefly reenslaved after the British left. Despite supplying invaluable intelligence, he never held an official position in the patriot forces and did not qualify for manumission. He was not freed until 1786, after Lafayette wrote a letter of commendation for him that he used to secure his freedom. Black patriots on the muster rolls were not generally subject to reenslavement, even in the southern states—with the notable exception of Virginia, where some slaveholders tried to retain the slave substitutes who had fought for them during the war. This caused a public outcry and inspired a 1783 legislative decree that declared the actions of such slaveholders "contrary to principles of justice and to their own solemn promise" and directed the state's attorney general to seek manumission for any enslaved former soldiers.[42]

Black veterans formed only part of the greatly enlarged free black community that emerged in the decades following the war. Concentrated largely in the North and Upper South, free blacks, who had numbered only a few thousand in 1760, reached 60,000 in 1790 and 110,000 in 1800 (Map 3.2). These remarkable increases reflect a number of developments. Thousands had seized their liberty during the war by running away or pursuing successful freedom suits. In 1780, Mum Bett, a slave in Sheffield, Massachusetts, filed a suit that helped push her state toward abandoning slavery for good. Having endured years of physical abuse at the hands of her master's wife, she sued for her freedom after hearing public discussions of the Declaration of Independence and the Massachusetts state constitution. "I heard that paper read yesterday that says, all men are born equal, and that every man has a right to freedom. I am not a dumb critter; won't the law give me my freedom?" Bett asked a local lawyer named Theodore Sedgwick, who agreed to represent her in court.[43] Bett's successful suit transformed her into Elizabeth Freeman, a name she took as a symbol of her liberty. Three years later, her lawsuit provided a precedent for the state's final freedom suit—the Quock Walker case of 1783, in which the Massachusetts Supreme Court ruled that slavery was incompatible with the state's new constitution.

After the war, the number of free blacks in the new nation increased steadily through the abolition of slavery in the northern states. Vermont, which had never had

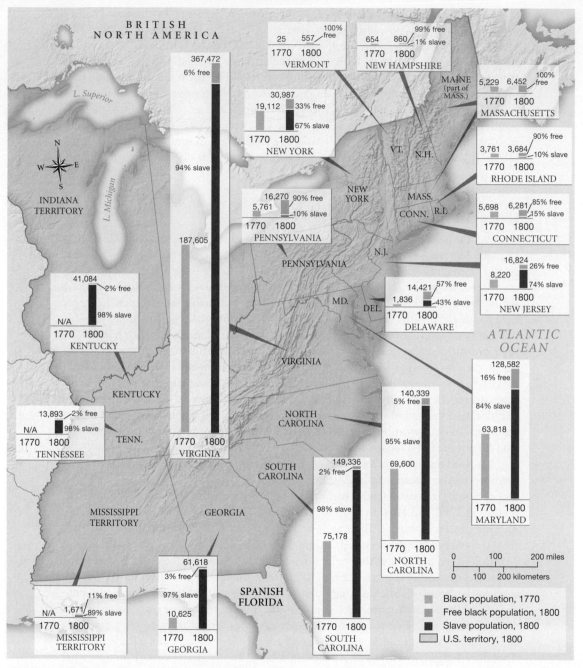

BRITISH
NORTH AMERICA

VERMONT
25 / 557 / 100% free
1770 / 1800

NEW HAMPSHIRE
654 / 860 / 99% free / 1% slave
1770 / 1800

MAINE (part of MASS.)

MASSACHUSETTS
5,229 / 6,452 / 100% free
1770 / 1800

NEW YORK
30,987
19,112 / 33% free / 67% slave
1770 / 1800

RHODE ISLAND
3,761 / 3,684 / 90% free / 10% slave
1770 / 1800

PENNSYLVANIA
16,270 / 90% free
5,761 / 10% slave
1770 / 1800

CONNECTICUT
5,698 / 6,281 / 85% free / 15% slave
1770 / 1800

NEW JERSEY
16,824 / 26% free
8,220 / 74% slave
1770 / 1800

DELAWARE
14,421 / 57% free
1,836 / 43% slave
1770 / 1800

VIRGINIA
367,472 / 6% free
187,605 / 94% slave
1770 / 1800

KENTUCKY
41,084 / 2% free / 98% slave
N/A
1770 / 1800

TENNESSEE
13,893 / 2% free / 98% slave
N/A
1770 / 1800

MARYLAND
128,582 / 16% free / 84% slave
63,818
1770 / 1800

NORTH CAROLINA
140,339 / 5% free / 95% slave
69,600
1770 / 1800

SOUTH CAROLINA
149,336 / 2% free / 98% slave
75,178
1770 / 1800

GEORGIA
61,618 / 3% free / 97% slave
10,625
1770 / 1800

MISSISSIPPI TERRITORY
11% free
N/A / 1,671 / 89% slave
1770 / 1800

SPANISH FLORIDA

INDIANA TERRITORY

MISSISSIPPI TERRITORY

ATLANTIC OCEAN

0 — 100 — 200 miles
0 — 100 — 200 kilometers

- Black population, 1770
- Free black population, 1800
- Slave population, 1800
- U.S. territory, 1800

MAP 3.2 African Americans across the Developing Nation, 1770 and 1800

This map illustrates the varying regional distribution of the new nation's black population. The gold bars show each state's black population in 1770. The red and pink bars show each state's slave population and free black population in 1800. The bar graphs underscore the rapid expansion of the slave populations in the southern states during these years, as well as the increasing predominance of free blacks in the North.

a large slave population, banned slavery in 1777. Pennsylvania began planning to end slavery shortly thereafter, although its Act for the Gradual Abolition of Slavery of 1780 was far from generous. It freed only slaves born after 1780, who had to pay for their freedom by serving their owners for the first twenty-eight years of their lives. Still, this groundbreaking law advanced the cause of freedom in the new nation and set the stage for gradual abolition in other northern states, which was largely complete by the 1820s.

The free black population in the South also increased dramatically, largely as a result of manumissions in the Upper South between the 1750s and 1790s. The Great Awakening, combined with antislavery sentiments inspired by the American Revolution, prompted slaveholders across the region to free large numbers of slaves. American Quakers abandoned slavery during this period, and they encouraged non-Quakers to do so as well. Manumissions were also facilitated by the declining profitability of plantation agriculture in the Chesapeake during the second half of the eighteenth century, which reduced the profits to be gained from slave labor. Whereas free blacks had constituted a tiny percentage of the region's black population for much of the century, by the 1790s about 10 percent of Chesapeake blacks were free. Only in the Lower South did free blacks remain a rarity (see Map 3.2).

Freedom Suits

After suffering ongoing physical abuse as a slave, Mum Bett, depicted here, worked with lawyer Theodore Sedgwick to win her freedom in a 1781 court case. Between 1781 and 1783, her case served as a precedent for a series of cases involving a slave named Quock Walker. Adjudicated by the Massachusetts Supreme Court in 1783, the final Quock Walker case ruled that slavery was incompatible with the state's new constitution. *Portrait of Elizabeth "Mumbet" Freeman (c. 1742–1829), watercolor on ivory, Sedgwick, Susan Anne Livingston Ridley III (fl. 1811)/© Massachusetts Historical Society, Boston, MA, USA/The Bridgeman Art Library International.*

Free black communities across the nation gained strength after the Revolution. Although free blacks continued to be persecuted in the South, their swelling numbers provided more allies and stronger claims to a status separate from that of their enslaved brethren. In the North, the abolition of slavery allowed blacks to live in free territory for the first time in American history. To be sure, newly freed blacks were poor and subject to racial discrimination, but once emancipated, they could form autonomous families and communities for the first time in their history.

The Revolution was only one step toward black freedom, however. The majority of African Americans were still permanently enslaved in regions where no end to slavery was in sight. African American slaves constituted 92 percent of the nation's black population in 1790. The slave population continued to increase in the decades that followed due to slave imports and high rates of reproduction. By the start of the Civil War in 1861, the United States would be home to millions of slaves.

CONCLUSION

The American Revolution's Mixed Results for Blacks

The American Revolution was a watershed in African American history, but it produced mixed results for blacks. On one hand, the gradual demise of slavery across the northern states and the expansion of black freedom in the Upper South marked a great victory for blacks in these regions. Few white Americans were willing to make the abolition of slavery a central goal, but black northerners sought to make the American rebellion against British rule an end to the tyranny of slavery as well, and they were largely successful in doing so—at least in the North. On the other hand, the Revolution's outcome was far less rewarding for black southerners, who faced longer odds and gained much less ground. Most sided with the loyalists, suffering great hardships during the war for little compensation. Some achieved freedom by enlisting with the patriots, escaping to the North, or leaving the country with the British, but the majority remained trapped in a region still deeply committed to slavery.

African Americans continued to fight for freedom long after the war ended. Among slaves, freedom remained a goal even as plantation slavery expanded across the South. Among free blacks, the persistence of southern slavery marked the limits of the freedom that they had achieved and the battles that still lay ahead. Many of their friends, relatives, and countrymen remained enslaved, and in the years to come, free blacks would struggle to emancipate their enslaved brothers and sisters, while also fighting to fully secure their own freedom.

In these struggles, blacks throughout America would continue to embrace the egalitarian principles of both the Great Awakening and the patriot cause. In the years to come, slaves and free blacks continued to join evangelical churches and embrace an Afro-Christian faith that stressed the equality of all men and women before God. Free black communities established their own churches, which became central to the antislavery movement that took shape among northern free blacks. So, too, did the democratic principles of the American Revolution, as post-Revolutionary African American leaders stressed that their "fathers fought, bled and died for the liberty neither they nor their children have received."[44]

CHAPTER REVIEW

Key Terms

Negro Election Day (p. 115)

conjure (p. 116)

Gullah (p. 116)

Great Awakening (p. 116)

New Lights (p. 117)

freedom suits (p. 122)

Somerset case (1772) (p. 122)

habeas corpus (p. 122)

loyalists (p. 127)

Lord Dunmore's Proclamation
  (1775) (p. 128)

southern strategy (p. 131)

Review Questions

1. What role did religion—both traditional West African beliefs and practices and the spread of Christianity—play in the shaping of an African American culture during the eighteenth century?

2. How did African Americans on both the patriot and loyalist sides use the Revolution to pursue and secure their own freedom? How did they draw on the conflict's ideology to do so? Choose several examples from the chapter to support your argument.

3. Overall, how would you assess African Americans' gains and losses during the Revolutionary era? Consider the outcomes for patriots and loyalists, northerners and southerners, and free blacks and slaves. Who benefited the most and the least? What factors were responsible for these results?

4. How did African Americans' participation on both sides of the war change its course? How might the progression or outcome of the conflict have been different had blacks been barred from service?

For Web sites, images, and documents related to topics and places in this chapter, visit **Make History** at bedfordstmartins.com/graywhite.

The Great Awakening in the South

The Great Awakening challenged the staid religious practices of Anglican and Congregationalist ministers, whose flocks were shrinking as Americans became increasingly "unchurched." Evangelical preachers such as George Whitefield delivered highly emotional sermons that urged all Americans to seek a place in the kingdom of God. They also underscored that all men were equal before God, a message that attracted African American converts.

But black and white evangelicals expressed different understandings of Christianity, as can be seen in the following set of documents. In the first document, George Whitefield takes the inhabitants of Maryland, Virginia, and the Carolinas to task for physically mistreating their slaves and neglecting their spiritual education. The second document records the religious message preached by David Margate, a black British minister who did not last long in Georgia. The third document describes the early life and Christian conversion of David George, who escaped from slavery to become a Baptist minister.

George Whitefield | A Public Letter to Slaveholders, 1740

The British minister **George Whitefield (1714–1770)** was tremendously popular in the American colonies, where his visits helped sustain and expand the religious enthusiasm of the Great Awakening. He spent several months as a parish priest in Savannah, Georgia, where he saw slavery firsthand. Whitefield did not object to the practice of slavery and later owned slaves himself, but on his first visit to the southern colonies, he was appalled to see how poorly the slaves were treated. He wrote this public letter to slaveholders in Maryland, Virginia, and the Carolinas, urging them to change their ways.

Savannah, Jan. 23, 1740.

As I lately passed through your provinces, in my way hither, I was sensibly touched with a fellow-feeling of the miseries of the poor negroes. Could I have preached more frequently among you, I should have delivered my thoughts to you in my public discourses: but, as business here required me to stop as little as possible on the road, I have no other way to

Source: George Whitefield, *The Works of the Reverend George Whitefield, M.A.* (London: Edward and Charles Dilly, 1771), 4:37–39.

discharge the concern which at present lies upon my heart, than by sending you this letter. . . . I must inform you, in the meekness and gentleness of CHRIST, that I think GOD has a quarrel with you, for your abuse of and cruelty to the poor negroes. Whether it be lawful for christians to buy slaves, and thereby encourage the nations from whence they are brought to be at perpetual war with each other, I shall not take upon me to determine; but sure I am it is sinful, when bought, to use them as bad as, nay worse than brutes: and whatever particular exceptions there may be, (as I would charitably hope there are some) I fear the generality of you that own negroes, are liable to such a charge; for your slaves, I believe, work as hard, if not harder, than the horses whereon you ride.

These, after they have done their work, are fed and taken proper care of; but many negroes, when wearied with labour in your plantations, have been obliged to grind their own corn after they return home.

Your dogs are caressed and fondled at your tables; but your slaves, who are frequently stiled [styled] dogs or beasts, have not an equal privilege: they are scarce permitted to pick up the crumbs which fall from their masters tables, nay, some, as I have been informed by an eye-witness, have been, upon the most trifling provocation, cut with knives, and have had forks thrown into their flesh: not to mention what numbers have been given up to the inhuman usage of cruel task-masters, who by their unrelenting scourges have ploughed upon their backs, and made long furrows, and at length brought them even to death itself.

'Tis true, I hope, there are but few such monsters of barbarity suffered to subsist amongst you: some, I hear, have been lately executed in *Virginia* for killing slaves; and the laws are very severe against such who at any time murder them.

And perhaps it might be better for the poor creatures themselves, to be hurried out of life, than to be made so miserable as they generally are in it. And indeed, considering what usage they commonly meet with, I have wondered, that we have not more instances of self-murder among the negroes, or that they have not more frequently risen up in arms against their owners. *Virginia* has

been once, and *Charles Town* more than once, threatened in this way.

And though I heartily pray GOD, they may never be permitted to get the upper hand; yet, should such a thing be permitted by providence, all good men must acknowledge the judgment would be just. For is it not the highest ingratitude, as well as cruelty, not to let your poor slaves enjoy some fruits of their labour?

When passing along, whilst I have viewed your plantations cleared and cultivated, many spacious houses built, and the owners of them faring sumptuously every day, my blood has frequently almost run cold within me, to consider how many of your slaves had neither convenient food to eat, nor proper raiment to put on, notwithstanding most of the comforts you enjoy, were solely owing to their indefatigable labours. The scripture says, "Thou shalt not muzzle the ox that treadeth out the corn." Does GOD take care of oxen? And will he not take care of the negroes also? Undoubtedly he will.

James Habersham and William Piercy | Papers on David Margate, 1775

The seminarian David Margate was born in Africa and educated at Trevecca College in South Wales. The Countess of Huntingdon, who founded the college, sent Margate to minister to the slaves at Bethesda, an orphanage in Savannah, Georgia. Bethesda was originally established by George Whitefield, who bequeathed it to the Countess in his will. After Whitefield's death in 1770, the Countess took over Bethesda and staffed it with students and clergy from Trevecca. Margate did not stay at Bethesda long because he soon became convinced that God wished him to deliver his people from slavery. Warned by sympathetic whites to avoid discussing slavery, Margate nonetheless publicly condemned the institution and had to flee Georgia to avoid being arrested for inciting a slave revolt. Margate left no written record of his stay, but

the story of his trip and the sense of alarm that his ideas provoked are captured in a series of letters about Margate written by concerned whites. **James Habersham**, a friend of Whitefield's, and **William Piercy**, an English curate whom the Countess of Huntington had appointed to serve as Bethesda's president, wrote the following letters in the spring of 1775.

James Habersham to the Countess of Huntingdon
April 19, 1775

I hope that your black man David may be blessed, as he seems to be very anxious to be instrumental of good to your ladyship's negroes, and, as far as I can learn, conducts himself very well, and I am only afraid that the kind notice he has met with in England, will make him think too highly of himself. I have hinted this to Mr Piercy and I hope he has cau-

SOURCE: Mark M. Smith et al., eds., *Slavery in North America: From the Colonial Period to Emancipation* (London: Pickering & Chatto, 2009), 1:294–96.

tioned him to avoid splitting upon this rock [self-destructing]. This work of instructing the negroes, if it should have the desired effect, I am persuaded will meet with all the opposition and reproach that men and Devils can invent. . . .

William Piercy to the Countess of Huntingdon
May 6 and 7, 1775

What has been indeed lately a great hindrance was the imprudent conduct of poor David while here, which I wrote you in a former letter. He spoke & acted so rashly that bench warrants have been issued out against him ever since; & had he not instantly retired to Georgia privately he would have been taken up & hanged by the negro laws of the province. This circumstance I mentioned to him as soon as I saw him, as did Cosson [John Cosson, Bethesda's Chaplain] & his wife with Mr Habersham, with much tenderness & informed him that his situation was very critical here & that if he did not conduct himself properly he would lose his life as well as ruin my usefulness & the credit of the [Trevecca] college. For a few days it seem'd to have its desired effect as I wrote you word; but he was soon led again by the Devil into the same snare. Nothing could have happened of a more distressing nature, we are so surrounded with blacks, or have given me greater pain as my soul so much longed for the instruction & salvation of your slaves. I dont indeed know what judgement to form either of his works or conduct since he has been at Bethesda; but the whole has been the most alarming & brought me into the greatest reproach as well as censure from the Governor & all the white people. We have been under a continual apprehension of an insurrection among the slaves from his conduct & discourses to the negroes. And this upon such strong grounds as have almost distressed me to death both day & night. About a fortnight I think after he came to Bethesda, the Devil put it in his head that he was sent here to be a second Moses & should be called to deliver his people from slavery. This shocking delusion he spoke of & told

my Bro'r [brother] that God told him so & appointed the time. This alarmed the whole family, but still I hoped by talking to him to convince him of his error & hoped to see him humbled for his sin before God. . . . I am continually in fear lest some dreadful scheme s'd [should] be formed by him to poison all the white people. But Mr H[abersham] feels so much that I expect to hear that he has dismissed him & that things will again be put right. But nothing could be done with him among the slaves nor any instruction given by my Bro'r or Mr Cosson[;] some how or other I can't help thinking that a great part of David's wicked conduct arises from his pride & Cosson seems of my opinion. His pride seems so great, that he can't bear to think of any of his own color being slaves, tho' he has confessed that he was only a runaway slave himself. The whole of this affair gives me such uneasiness & pain & much more so as I so earnestly pressed you with letters upon the subject till he came that my heart is quite overwhelmed with sorrow & I feel myself incapable to write any more to you at present. . . .

Monday May 7. . . . A gentleman has been to inform me that the people are determined to send a party of men to Georgia & take David & should they lay hold of him he will certainly be hanged for what he has delivered, as all the laws are against him. The people are continuously apprehensive of an insurrection among the slaves & insist upon it that he was the first cause. In all their town meetings this affair has been upon the carpet & they seem more and more terrified with the consequences. I am going immediately to send off a dispatch to Mr Habersham by Mr Cosson for him instantly to put David on board of some ship that his life may be saved. I am afraid he should be gone from Bethesda & that by that means the people should lay hold of him. There is no making him sensible of the state of the blacks in this country & think in all his words & conduct he goes against the laws. If there should be a ship directly sailing for England I have begged on Mr H, without delay, to put him privately on board & he may get off with his life.

David George | A Fugitive Slave's Early Life and Religious Conversion, 1785

Born in Virginia to African parents, **David George (c. 1740–1810)** was a slave who escaped from his master several times before evacuating with the British when they shipped out of Charleston. His account of his years as a fugitive slave describes his slow conversion to Christianity. A friend of the black Baptist minister George Liele, George became a minister after he resettled in Nova Scotia and later established a black Baptist church in Sierra Leone.

An Account of the Life of Mr. DAVID GEORGE, from Sierra Leone in Africa; given by himself in a Conversation with Brother RIPPON of London, and Brother PEARCE of Birmingham.

I was born in Essex county, Virginia, about 50 or 60 miles from Williamsburg, on Nottaway river, of parents who were brought from Africa, but who had not the fear of God before their eyes. The first work I did was fetching water, and carding of cotton; afterwards I was sent into the field to work about the Indian corn and tobacco, till I was about 19 years old. My father's name was John, and my mother's Judith. I had four brothers, and four sisters, who, with myself, were all born in slavery: our master's name was Chapel—a very bad man to the Negroes. My oldest sister was called Patty; I have seen her several times so whipped that her back has been all corruption, as though it would rot. My brother Dick ran away, but they caught him, and brought him home; and as they were going to tie him up, he broke away again, and they hunted him with horses and dogs, till they took him; then they hung him up to a cherry-tree in the yard, by his two hands, quite naked, except his breeches, with his feet about half a yard from the ground. They tied his legs close together, and put a pole between them, at one end of

which one of the owner's sons sat, to keep him down, and another son at the other. After he had received 500 lashes, or more, they washed his back with salt water, and whipped it in, as well as rubbed it in with a rag; and then directly sent him to work in pulling off the suckers of tobacco. I also have been whipped many a time on my naked skin, and sometimes till the blood has run down over my waistband; but the greatest grief I then had was to see them whip my mother, and to hear her, on her knees, begging for mercy. She was master's cook, and if they only thought she might do any thing better than she did, instead of speaking to her as to a servant, they would strip her directly, and cut away. I believe she was on her death-bed when I got off, but I have never heard since. Master's rough and cruel usage was the reason of my running-away. Before this time I used to drink, but not steal; did not fear hell, was without knowledge; though I went sometimes to Nottaway, the English church, about eight or nine miles off. I left the plantation about midnight, walked all night, got into Brunswick county, then over Roanoak river, and soon met with some White travelling people, who helped me on to Pedee river. When I had been at work there two or three weeks, a hue and cry found me out, and the master [George's new employer] said to me, there are 30 guineas offered for you, but I will have no hand in it: I would advise you to make your way towards Savannah river. I hearkened to him, but was several weeks going. . . .

[George was recaptured and escaped from slavery again. He lived for several years with Creek and Natchez Indians before moving to Silver Bluff, South Carolina, where he married.]

After my wife was delivered of our first child, a man of my own color, named Cyrus, who came from Charlestown, South Carolina, to Silver Bluff, told me one day in the woods, That if I lived so, I should never see the face of God in glory. (Whether he himself was a converted man or not, I do not know.)

SOURCE: *An Account of the Life of Mr. David George*, in *The Baptist Annual Register for 1790, 1791, 1792, and Part of 1793* (London, [1793?]), 473–76.

This was the first thing that disturbed me, and gave me much concern. I thought then that I must be saved by prayer. . . . Soon after I heard brother George Liele preach, . . . *Come unto me all ye that labour, and are heavy laden, and I will give you rest.* When it was ended, I went to him and told him I was so; That I was weary and heavy laden, and that the grace of God had given me rest. . . . About this time more of my fellow-creatures began to seek the Lord. . . . There were eight of us now who had found the great blessing and mercy from the Lord, and my wife was one of them, and brother Jesse Gaulfin . . . was another. Brother [Wait] Palmer [a white Baptist preacher from Connecticut who had traveled South to spread the gospel] appointed a Saturday evening to hear what the Lord had done for us, and the next day he baptized us in the Mill-stream. Some time afterwards, when Brother George Liele came again, and preached in a corn field, I had a great desire to pray with the people myself, but I was ashamed, and went to a swamp and poured out my heart before the Lord. I then came back to Brother George Liele, and told him my case. He said, In the intervals of service you should engage in prayer with the friends. At another time, when he was preaching, I felt the same desire, and after he had done, I began in prayer—it gave me great relief, and I went home with a desire for nothing else but to talk to the brothers and sisters about the Lord. Brother Palmer formed us into a church, and gave us the Lord's supper at Silver Bluff. Then I began to exhort in the church, and learned to sing hymns. The first I learned out of book was a hymn of that great writing man, [Isaac] Watts, [an English hymn writer and theologian] which begins with "Thus saith the wisdom of the Lord." Afterwards the church advised with Brother Palmer about my speaking to them, and keeping them together; I refused, and felt I was unfit for all that, but Brother Palmer said this word to me, "Take care that you don't offend the Lord." Then I thought that he knew best, and I agreed that I would do as well as I could. So I was appointed to the office of an Elder and received instruction from Brother Palmer how to conduct myself. I proceeded in this way till the American war was coming on, when the Ministers were not allowed to come amongst us lest they should furnish us with too much knowledge. The Black people all around attended with us, and as Brother Palmer must not come, I had the whole management, and used to preach among them myself. Then I got a spelling book and began to read. As Master was a great man, he kept a White schoolmaster to teach the White children to read. I used to go to the little children to teach me a, b, c. They would give me a lesson, which I tried to learn, and then I would go to them again, and ask them if I was right? The reading so ran in my mind, that I think I learned in my sleep as really as when I was awake; and I can now read the Bible, so that what I have in my heart, I can see again in the Scriptures. I continued preaching at Silver Bluff, till the church, constituted with eight, increased to thirty or more, and till the British came to the city of Savannah and took it.

Questions for Analysis

1. George Whitefield, James Habersham, and William Piercy believed that Christianity and slavery were compatible. What roles and responsibilities do they assign to Christian slaveholders in these documents?

2. Why were Habersham and Piercy discontented with David Margate? What did they and other whites such as George Whitefield hope for and expect from black Christians?

3. What inspired David George to convert to Christianity? Did he find Christianity compatible with slavery? Why or why not?

African American Patriots

African Americans fought for their own freedom with the pen and the sword during the American Revolution. Black soldiers joined both the patriot and loyalist forces, and both free blacks and slaves were drawn into the natural rights debates engendered by the Revolution. Slaves petitioned for freedom by articulating claims to the "Natural and Unaliable [inalienable] Right to that freedom which the Grat Parent of the Unavers hath Bestowed equalley on all menkind," while a handful of literate blacks also wrote poems and essays describing these claims.[45]

Freed in 1773, the poet Phillis Wheatley was one early black commentator. Though still a teenager when the war began to take shape, she kept a close eye on the Revolution's ideological conflicts. In 1772, a year before she was emancipated, she wrote a poem addressed to King George's secretary of state for North America, the Earl of Dartmouth, that supported the patriot cause while also mourning the freedom that blacks had not yet won. Two year later, she expressed similar sentiments as a free woman in a letter written to the Indian leader Samson Occum. Both pieces are included here.

Wheatley's compositions are followed by an essay by Lemuel Haynes, a free black who was born in Connecticut and raised in Massachusetts and who served with both the minutemen and the Continental army. Although he fought with the patriots, Haynes was dissatisfied with the new nation's political principles and called for Americans to extend liberty to blacks as well as whites.

Phillis Wheatley | A Poem to the Earl of Dartmouth, 1772

Born in Gambia, **Phillis Wheatley (c. 1753–1784)** was only seven or eight years old when she was sold into slavery. Her masters encouraged her to learn how to read and write and were so impressed by her intelligence that they permitted her to devote her time largely to her education and to develop her gift for poetry. Wheatley wrote and published her first poems as a teenager, attracting attention and controversy as an early black author who spoke on behalf of a people whom many whites saw as illiterate by nature. What was Wheatley trying to accomplish with this poem, addressed to Britain's secretary of state for North America? How does she go about it in the poem?

SOURCE: Phillis Wheatley, *Poems on Various Subjects, Religious and Moral* (1773; repr., Denver: W. H. Lawrence, 1887), 66–68.

TO THE RIGHT HONORABLE WILLIAM, EARL OF DARTMOUTH.
His Majesty's Principal Secretary of State for North America, etc.

Hail, happy day, when smiling like the morn,
Fair Freedom *rose New England to adorn;*
The northern clime beneath her genial ray,
Dartmouth congratulates thy blissful sway;
Elate with hope her race no longer mourns,
Each soul expands, each grateful bosom burns,
While in thine hand with pleasure we behold
The silken reins, and Freedom's charms unfold.
Long lost to realms beneath the northern skies
She shines supreme, while hated faction dies;
Soon as appeared the Goddess long desir'd,
Sick at the view, she languish'd and expir'd;

documents

Thus from the splendor of the morning light
The owl in sadness seeks the caves of night.

No more America, in mournful strain
Of wrongs, and grievance unredress'd complain,
No longer shall thou dread the iron chain,
Which wanton Tyranny with lawless hand
Had made, and with it meant to enslave the land.
Should you, my lord, while you peruse my song,
Wonder from whence my love of Freedom *sprung,*
Whence flow these wishes for the common good,
By feeling hearts alone best understood,
I, young in life, by seeming cruel fate
Was snatch'd from Afric's fancy'd happy seat;
What pangs excruciatingly must molest,
What sorrows labour in my parent's breast?
Steel'd was that soul and by no misery mov'd

That from a father seized his babe belov'd;
Such, such my case. And can I then but pray
Others may never feel tyrannic sway?

For favors past, great Sir, our thanks are due,
And thee we ask thy favors to renew,
Since in thy pow'r, as in thy will before,
To sooth the griefs, which thou didst once deplore.
May heav'nly grace the sacred sanction give
To all thy works, and thou forever live
Not only on the wings of fleeting Fame,
Though praise immortal crowns the patriot's
*   name,*
But to conduct to heav'n's refulgent fane
May fiery coursers sweep th' etherial plain,
And bear thee upwards to the blest abode,
Where, like the prophet, thou shalt find thy God.

Phillis Wheatley | Letter to the Reverend Samson Occom, 1774

Phillis Wheatley's letter to the Reverend Samson Occom, a Mohegan Indian and ordained minister with whom she had a correspondence, was in response to a piece that Occom had written in condemnation of Christian ministers who owned slaves. It was first printed in the *Connecticut Gazette* on March 11, 1774. What sort of a future does Wheatley foresee for slavery in the letter? What justifications does she offer for her views?

Boston, February 11th, 1774.

Rever'd & Honoured Sir,

I this day received your kind obliging epistle, and am greatly satisfied with your reasons respecting the Negroes, and think highly reasonable what you offer in vindication of their natural rights. Those that invade them cannot be insensible that the divine light is insensibly chasing away the thick darkness which broods over the land of Africa, and

the chaos which has reigned so long is converting into beautiful order, and reveals more and more clearly the glorious dispensation of civil and religious liberty, which are so inseparably united, that there is little or no enjoyment of one without the other; otherwise the Israelites had been less solicitous for their freedom from Egyptian slavery. I do not say they would have been contented without it—by no means: for in every human breast God has implanted a principle which we call, love of freedom. It is impatient of oppression, and pants for deliverance; and, by the leave of our modern Egyptians, I will assert that the principle lives in us—God grant deliverance in his own way and time, and get him honour upon all those whose avarice compels them to countenance and help forward the calamities of their fellow creatures. This I desire not for the hurt, but to convince them of the strange absurdities of their conduct whose words and actions are so diametrically opposite. How well the cry of liberty and the reverse disposition for the exercise of oppressive power over others agree, I humbly think it does not require the penetration of a philosopher to determine.

SOURCE: *Connecticut Gazette*, March 11, 1774, 188.

Lemuel Haynes | Liberty Further Extended, 1776

Born in Connecticut, **Lemuel Haynes (1753–1833)** was abandoned by his white mother and African father. He grew up in Massachusetts, where he was bound out as an indentured servant at the age of six months. He joined the Granville minutemen and fought with patriot forces until 1776, when he caught typhus and had to return home. That year, he wrote the following unpublished and recently discovered manuscript. Probably composed shortly after the publication of the Declaration of Independence, it expands on that document by calling for an antislavery revolution. Haynes was self-educated and became ordained as a Congregationalist minister. How does he use the principles of the Declaration of Independence to argue his point here?

We hold these truths to be self-Evident, that all men are created Equal, that they are Endowed By their Creator with Ceartain unalienable rights, that among these are Life, Liberty, and the pursuit of happyness.

    Congress.

The Preface [of the Declaration of Independence]. As *tyrony* had its Origin from the infernal regions: so it is the Deuty, and honner of Every son of freedom to repel her first motions. But while we are Engaged in the important struggle, it cannot Be tho't impertinent for us to turn one Eye into our own Breast, for a little moment, and See, whether thro' some inadvertency, or a self-contracted Spirit, we Do not find the monster Lurking in our own Bosom; that now while we are inspir'd with so noble a Spirit and Becoming Zeal, we may Be Disposed to tear her from us. If the following would produce such an Effect the auther should rejoice. . . .

    Liberty, & freedom, is an innate principle, which is unmovebly placed in the human Species; and to see a man aspire after it, is not Enigmatical, seeing

SOURCE: Ruth Bogin, ed., "'Liberty Further Extended': A 1776 Antislavery Manuscript by Lemuel Haynes," *William and Mary Quarterly* 40, no. 1 (January 1983): 94–96.

he acts no ways incompatible with his own Nature; consequently, he that would infring upon a mans Liberty may reasonably Expect to meet with oposision, seeing the Defendant cannot Comply to Nonresistance, unless he Counter-acts the very Laws of nature.

    Liberty is a Jewel which was handed Down to man from the cabinet of heaven, and is Coaeval [originated at the same time] with his Existance. And as it proceed from the Supreme Legislature of the univers, so it is he which hath a sole right to take away; therefore, he that would take away a mans Liberty assumes a prerogative that Belongs to another, and acts out of his own domain.

    One man may bost a superorety above another in point of Natural previledg; yet if he can produse no convincive arguments in vindication of this preheminence his hypothesis is to Be Suspected. To affirm, that an Englishman has a right to his Liberty, is a truth which has Been so clearly Evinced, Especially of Late, that to spend time in illustrating this, would be But Superfluous tautology. But I query, whether Liberty is so contracted a principle as to be Confin'd to any nation under Heaven; nay, I think it not hyperbolical to affirm, that Even an affrican, has Equally as good a right to his Liberty in common with Englishmen.

    I know that those that are concerned in the Slavetrade, Do pretend to Bring arguments in vindication of their practise; yet if we give them a candid Examination, we shall find them (Even those of the most cogent kind) to be Essencially Deficient. We live in a day wherein *Liberty* & *freedom* is the subject of many millions Concern; and the important Struggle hath alread caused great Effusion of Blood; men seem to manifest the most sanguine resolution not to Let their natural rights go without their Lives go with them; a resolution, one would think Every one that has the Least Love to his country, or futer posterity, would fully confide in, yet while we are so zelous to maintain, and foster our own invaded rights, it cannot be tho't impertinent for us Candidly to reflect on our own conduct, and I doubt not But that we shall find that subsisting in the midst of us, that may with propriety be stiled *Opression*, nay, much greater opression, than that which Englishmen seem so much to spurn at. I mean an oppression which they, themselves, impose upon others. . . .

. . . There is Not the Least precept, or practise, in the Sacred Scriptures, that constitutes a Black man a Slave, any more than a white one.

Shall a mans Couler Be the Decisive Criterion whereby to Judg of his natural right? or Becaus a man is not of the same couler with his Neighbour, shall he Be Deprived of those things that Distuing-sheth [Distinguisheth] him from the Beasts of the field?

I would ask, whence is it that an Englishman is so far Distinguished from an Affrican in point of Natural privilege? Did he recieve it in his origenal constitution? or By Some Subsequent grant? Or Does he Bost of some hygher Descent that gives him this pre-heminance? for my part I can find no such revelation. It is a Lamantable consequence of the fall, that mankind, have an insatiable thurst after Superorety one over another: So that however common or prevalent the practise may be, it Does not amount, Even to a Surcomstance, that the practise is ~~Legal~~° warrentable.

° The strikethrough is part of the original document.

Questions for Analysis

1. What do these documents reveal about their authors' hopes for the war's outcome?

2. What role does religion play in the antislavery arguments made by Wheatley and Haynes?

3. How do Wheatley and Haynes link the political issues under dispute during the American Revolution with their calls for black freedom?

Freedom's Fight

During the American Revolution, black soldiers were welcomed for their manpower. But once the fighting stopped, their contributions were all but forgotten until the 1850s, when abolitionists began to commemorate Crispus Attucks and other black patriots. The works of European and American artists who depicted the Revolution provide an uneven and incomplete record of African American participation. Many works of art record the presence of black men whose roles in the Revolutionary struggle might otherwise have been forgotten. The artists tend to downplay their contributions, however, by depicting them as servants rather than soldiers. Any historical reading of these images requires a careful analysis of the artistic conventions, political motivations, and nationalist visions that shaped the works in which they appear.

The Double Death of Crispus Attucks

Lauded as "the first to defy, the first to die" when British soldiers fired on a mob of unruly colonists in 1770, Crispus Attucks was commemorated by his fellow Bostonians as a martyr for freedom.[16] A man of mixed Indian and African ancestry who may have been a fugitive slave, Attucks was an unlikely hero whose race was rarely mentioned in Revolutionary-era commemorations of the Boston Massacre. Indeed, the famous silversmith and engraver Paul Revere chose to omit Attucks from his popular engraving depicting the event (Figure 3.1). His engraving captures the first casualty of the conflict, but the figure lying in the foreground is white—even in the color prints of the engraving created by Christian Remick, the artist Revere employed to colorize his broadside. Revere's image has other factual errors as well. It portrays the conflict as having taken place during the daytime, though it occurred at night, and it shows the British soldiers advancing in military formation on a crowd of docile Bostonians, when in fact the conflict began with a scuffle. Were errors such as these accidental? What does the omission of Attucks signify?

FIGURE 3.1
Paul Revere, *The Bloody Massacre*, 1770 *Library of Congress LC-DIG-ppmsca-01657.*

Crispus Attucks, the First Martyr of the American Revolution, King (now State) Street, Boston, March 5th, 1770. Page 16.

FIGURE 3.2
Crispus Attucks, the First Martyr of the American Revolution, 1855 *From William Cooper Nell's The Colored Patriots of the American Revolution, with Sketches of Several Distinguished Colored Persons (Boston, 1855)/Art Resource, NY.*

Revere's engraving was widely distributed and helped erase the memory of Crispus Attucks. By the mid-nineteenth century, historians of the Revolution had all but forgotten him until the black abolitionist William Cooper Nell revived his memory in *The Colored Patriots of the American Revolution* (1855), which contained yet another depiction of the Boston Massacre (Figure 3.2). Published at a time when black abolitionists seemed to be losing their antislavery struggle, the book reminded readers that "but for the blow struck at the right time by a black man, the United States, with all that it boasts of right and justice, might not have been an independent republic."[47] This same sentiment was expressed the following year in a dramatic lithograph showing the colonists fighting the British (Figure 3.3). Attucks is at the center of the conflict with a club in his hand and a British bayonet at his throat. What changes in public sentiment do these two images suggest? How do Figures 3.1, 3.2, and 3.3 reflect the specific viewpoints of the artists who created them?

The Disappearance of Peter Salem

Nell also recovered the images of other black patriots, such as Peter Salem, an ex-slave from Framingham, Massachusetts, once famous for his role in the war's

FIGURE 3.3
Lithograph of the Boston
Massacre, 1856 *The Granger
Collection, NY. All rights reserved.*

Battle of Bunker Hill. During the Revolutionary era, Salem was widely credited with firing the shot that killed the unpopular British leader Major John Pitcairn.[48] Exactly who killed Pitcairn remains a matter of debate, because the major was shot four times in a pitched battle that involved thousands of men, including another black soldier named Salem Poor. But by the 1850s, Peter Salem had disappeared from most accounts of the Battle of Bunker Hill, much to the bemusement of the white abolitionist Theodore Parker, who wrote to the historian George Bancroft in 1858 to complain: "In the engravings of the battle when I was a boy, the black man, Peter Salem, appears in the act of shooting Major Pitcairn; but now-a-days a white man is put in his place."[49] Parker's claim is difficult to document because, outside of Nell's revisionist history, there are no surviving images of the Battle of Bunker Hill that depict the death of Major Pitcairn. But the fact that a black soldier killed Pitcairn was certainly mentioned more often in early accounts of the battle than eighty years later, in Parker's day.

Images produced during the Revolutionary War call into question whether black fighting men such as Peter Salem would have been depicted in their own era. John Trumbull's *The Death of General Warren at the Battle of Bunker's Hill*, painted by a patriot artist who actually participated in the battle, commemorates a popular

FIGURE 3.4
John Trumbull, *The Death of General Warren at the Battle of Bunker's Hill, 17th June 1775,* c. 1815–1831 (after the 1786 version) *John Trumbull (1756–1843). Oil on canvas/Museum of Fine Arts, Boston, Massachusetts, USA/Gift of Howland S. Warren/The Bridgeman Art Library International.*

Massachusetts patriot who vowed to fight to the death. An early and much-mourned casualty of the war, General Joseph Warren is depicted in his dying moments in Trumbull's painting, which also features a black man standing behind a white soldier at the far right edge of the frame (Figure 3.4). This black man has been routinely mistaken for Peter Salem. But as his noncombative posture might suggest, he is not the black soldier who shot Pitcairn. He is Asaba Grosvenor, the enslaved manservant of Lieutenant Thomas Grosvenor of Connecticut, who accompanied his master into battle. Asaba Grosvenor was one of the approximately one hundred patriots of color who served during the Battle of Bunker Hill—but most of them were fugitive or free black soldiers rather than enslaved servants. Why did Trumbull choose to include Asaba Grosvenor in his painting? Why is Grosvenor depicted standing behind his master holding a rifle that is pointed upward rather than toward the enemy?

The Service of William Lee and James Armistead Lafayette

Such imagery of subordination is also evident in the many Revolutionary-era depictions of William "Billy" Lee, George Washington's favorite slave and valet. Lee remained in bondage until after Washington's death, when he was freed by the terms of Washington's will. Lee fought closely beside Washington and was

FIGURE 3.5
John Trumbull, *George Washington*, 1780 *John Trumbull (1756–1843). Oil on canvas, 36 x 28 in. (91.4 x 71.1 cm). Bequest of Charles Allen Munn, 1924 (24.109.88). © The Metropolitan Museum of Art, New York, NY, USA/Art Resource, NY.*

a constant presence in his life. Lee appears in a number of portraits of Washington, including a 1780 portrait also painted by John Trumbull (Figure 3.5).

Although Lee and Washington spent a great deal of time together, Lee's frequent appearance in depictions of Washington are not drawn from life. Black servants enlivened the background of many eighteenth-century European and American paintings, often appearing partially hidden—like the black youth in Trumbull's *The Death of General Warren* (see Figure 3.4). Another nonmilitary portrait of Washington by the American engraver and portrait artist Edward Savage features the same convention and underscores its purpose (Figure 3.6). Savage completed this portrait of the Washington family surveying a

FIGURE 3.6
Edward Savage, *The Washington Family*, 1789–1796 *Oil on canvas. Andrew W. Mellon Collection/Image courtesy of the National Gallery of Art, Washington, 1940.1.2.*

visual sources

FIGURE 3.7
Jean-Baptiste Le Paon, *General Lafayette at Yorktown, Attended by James Armistead*,
c. 1783   *Marie-Joseph Paul Yves Roch Gilbert Motier (1757–1834), Portrait of the Marquis de Lafayette
with an Aide-de-Camp during the American War of Independence, oil on canvas, 18th century/Musée
de la Ville de Paris, Musée Carnavalet, Paris, France/Archives Charmet/The Bridgeman Art Library
International.*

plan for the new national capital between 1789 and 1796. Washington and his
family were drawn from life; they sat for Savage three times as he roughed out his
portrait. Sometimes misidentified as William Lee, the slave in the background is
instead a stock figure added by Savage as he completed his painting. Nearly
featureless, he is simply an artistic convention.

Such conventions frequently distorted the role of African Americans who
made major contributions to the patriot cause, as can be seen in Jean-Baptiste
Le Paon's portrait of General Lafayette, attended by James Armistead, at
Yorktown (Figure 3.7). The ex-slave, who later renamed himself James
Armistead Lafayette in the general's honor, served as a double agent against the

FIGURE 3.8
John Blennerhassett Martin, *James Armistead Lafayette*, c. 1824 *The Granger Collection, NY. All rights reserved.*

British under the avowedly antislavery Lafayette. But the black man is nonetheless portrayed as a servant in Le Paon's portrait of General Lafayette. He holds Lafayette's horse and appears in an elaborate costume that owes more to European portraiture than to the subtleties of espionage.

This painting contrasts starkly with a portrait of Armistead Lafayette by John Blennerhassett Martin, painted after the ex-slave and the French general were reunited in Richmond, Virginia, during Lafayette's triumphal tour of the United States in 1824 (Figure 3.8). Through news reports, Armistead Lafayette caught the attention of Martin, a recent immigrant from Ireland, who produced both a painting and an engraved likeness of the black hero that year. Martin's portrait of Armistead Lafayette may reflect the fact that he was not yet indoctrinated in the prejudices that caused so many artists to reduce African Americans to stock figures. How does his portrayal of Armistead Lafayette differ from that of Jean-Baptiste Le Paon in Figure 3.7?

Similar portraits of Revolutionary-era black soldiers in uniform are rare, despite the fact that African American soldiers themselves were numerous. *The Death of Major Peirson* is perhaps the only Revolutionary-era picture

visual sources

FIGURE 3.9
John Singleton Copley, *The Death of Major Peirson, January 6, 1781,* 1783   *John Singleton Copley (1738–1815). Oil on canvas/Tate, London/Art Resource, NY.*

that includes an image of a uniformed black man actually in battle (Figure 3.9). Completed by the Massachusetts loyalist John Singleton Copley in the early 1780s, it portrays the death of a fellow loyalist, Major Francis Peirson, who was killed at the Battle of Jersey in the Channel Islands, far from the Revolution's main theater of operations. The work shows a black soldier in a plumed hat defending the British soldiers supporting Major Peirson's dying body.

The British island of Jersey, located off the coast of Normandy, France, was a privateering base for the British and French, which France sought to capture during the Revolution. Although France's 1781 invasion of Jersey was unsuccessful, Peirson was killed shortly before the French surrendered. The black soldier in Copley's painting, dressed in the uniform of the Ethiopian Regiment, could not have participated in the battle, however, because the Ethiopian Regiment was not there. Copley no doubt knew of the regiment from his time in Boston, before he was forced to flee to Britain. Why would he have included a member of this regiment in his rendition of the battle?

Moreover, why is Copley's black soldier perhaps the only uniformed black man shown firing a gun in all the late-eighteenth-century depictions of the war? Perhaps black men with guns were best relegated to obscure British islands off the coast of France. The eighteenth century was a tumultuous era of political instability in both Europe and the Americas. It saw two maroon wars in Jamaica, as well as slave rebellions across the New World. The most terrifying slave rebellion of all, the Haitian Revolution of 1791–1804, greatly amplified Euro-American fears of black men as soldiers. Thus it is not surprising that many white Americans were unwilling to commemorate or even remember the Revolution's black patriots. The memory of the Revolution's black soldiers was ultimately preserved by northern free blacks. As founders of the free black communities that took shape in the North after the war, these veterans would be commemorated by their descendants, who would campaign against slavery in the South. "Our fathers fought for freedom not from the yoke of liberty, but from the yoke of American slavery," one antislavery activist maintained, taking inspiration from the memory of the Revolution's black patriots as he continued the same fight.[50]

Questions for Analysis

1. What do the images in this essay suggest about the relationship between military service and citizenship?

2. Which of these images can be described as propaganda? What causes do those images promote, and what messages do they convey? Who would have been the intended audience?

3. What is the relationship between race and masculinity in these paintings? Provide specific examples to support your argument.

Notes

1. Daniel Horsmanden, *The New York Conspiracy: or, A History of the Negro Plot with the Journal of the Proceedings against the Conspirators at New-York in the Years 1741–2* (New York: Southwick and Pelsue, 1810), 24.

2. Ibid., 155.

3. Quoted in Jill Lepore, *New York Burning: Liberty, Slavery, and Conspiracy in Eighteenth-Century Manhattan* (New York: Knopf, 2005), 50, 51.

4. Leopold S. Launitz-Schurer Jr., "Slave Resistance in Colonial New York: An Interpretation of Daniel Horsmanden's New York Conspiracy," *Phylon* 41 (1980): 137–52.

5. Marcus Rediker, "A Motley Crew of Rebels: Sailors, Slaves, and the Coming of the American Revolution," in Hoffman and Albert, eds., *The Transforming Hand of Revolution: Reconsidering the American Revolution as a Social Movement* (Charlottesville: University of Virginia Press, 1995), 155.

6. Quoted in Thelma Wills Foote, *Black and White Manhattan: The History of Racial Formation in Colonial New York City* (New York: Oxford University Press, 2004), 46.

7. Quoted in Gary B. Nash and Jean R. Soderlund, *Freedom by Degrees: Emancipation in Pennsylvania and Its Aftermath* (New York: Oxford University Press, 1991), xii.

8. Leslie M. Harris, *In the Shadow of Slavery: African Americans in New York City, 1626–1863* (Chicago: University of Chicago Press, 2003), 47.

9. Quoted in Philip D. Morgan, *Slave Counterpoint: Black Culture in the Eighteenth-Century Chesapeake and Lowcountry* (Chapel Hill: University of North Carolina Press, 1998), 490.

10. Quoted in William Dillon Piersen, *Black Yankees: The Development of an Afro-American Subculture in Eighteenth-Century New England* (Amherst: University of Massachusetts Press, 1988), 121.

11. Quoted ibid., 77.

12. Quoted in Morgan, *Slave Counterpoint*, 572.

13. Morgan, *Slave Counterpoint*, 567.

14. Quoted in Thomas S. Kidd, *The Great Awakening: The Roots of Evangelical Christianity in Colonial America* (New Haven: Yale University Press, 2007), 216.

15. Charles Chauncey, *Seasonable Thoughts on the State of Religion in New England* (Boston: Rogers and Fowle, 1743), 226.

16. Mukhtar Ali Isani, "Phillis Wheatley in London: An Unpublished Letter to David Wooster," *American Literature* 51, no. 2 (1979): 257.

17. Quoted in Stephen J. Stein, "George Whitefield on Slavery: Some New Evidence," *Church History* 42, no. 2 (1973): 243–56.

18. George Whitefield, *The Works of the Reverend George Whitefield, M.A.* (London: printed for Edward and Charles Dilly, 1771), 38.

19. "Davies' Account of the Negroes" (1756), reprinted in William Henry Foote, *Sketches of Virginia, Historical and Biographical* (Philadelphia: W. S. Martien, 1850), 290.

20. Albert J. Raboteau, *Slave Religion: The "Invisible Institution" in the Antebellum South* (New York: Oxford University Press, 2004).

21. John Marrant, *A Narrative of the Lord's Wonderful Dealings with John Marrant, a Black, (Now Going to Preach the Gospel in Nova-Scotia) Born in New-York, in North-America* (London: R. Hawes, 1785), 30–33.

22. James Otis, *The Rights of the British Colonists, Asserted and Proved* (1761), reprinted in *Pamphlets of the American Revolution, 1750–1776*, ed. Bernard Bailyn (Cambridge: Harvard University Press, 1965), 444.

23. Quoted in Patricia Bradley, *Slavery, Propaganda, and the American Revolution* (Jackson, MS: University Press of Mississippi, 1999), 3.

24. John Locke, *The Second Treatise of Civil Government* (1689; repr., Amherst, NY: Prometheus Books, 1986), 54.

25. Quoted in Sylvia R. Frey, *Water from the Rock: Black Resistance in a Revolutionary Age* (Princeton: Princeton University Press, 1993), 15.

26. Quoted in John Wood Sweet, *Bodies Politic: Negotiating Race in the American North, 1730–1830* (Philadelphia: University of Pennsylvania Press, 2006), 253.

27. John Adams, November 5, 1766, in *Diary and Autobiography of John Adams* (Cambridge, MA: Belknap Press, 1966), 1:322.

28. John Adams, *The Works of John Adams, Second President of the United States: With a Life of the Author, Notes and Illustrations* (Boston: Charles C. Little, and James Brown, 1850), 2:200.

29. "Transcription of a Freedom Petition Submitted by Four Slaves in Boston to the Massachusetts Legislature" (1773), in Herbert Aptheker, ed., *A Documentary History of the Negro People in the United States* (New York: Citadel Press, 1951), 7.

30. Quoted in David McCullough, *John Adams* (New York: Simon and Schuster, 2008), 67.

31. Ruth Bogin, "'The Battle of Lexington': A Patriotic Ballad by Lemuel Haynes," *The William and Mary Quarterly* 42, no. 4. Third Series (October 1, 1985): 501, 503.

32. Quoted in Michael Stephenson, *Patriot Battles: How the War of Independence Was Fought* (New York: HarperCollins, 2008), 184.

33. Margaret Elisabeth May, *Brookline in the Revolution*, Publications of the Brookline Historical Publication Society, 1st–2nd ser. (Brookline, MA: Riverdale Press, 1897), 30.

34. Ruth Bogin, "'Liberty Further Extended': A 1776 Antislavery Manuscript by Lemuel Haynes," *The William and Mary Quarterly* 40, no. 1. Third Series (January 1, 1983): 92.

35. Boyrereau Brinch, *The Blind African Slave, or Memoirs of Boyrereau Brinch* (St. Albans, VT: printed for Harry Whitney, 1810), 156.

36. Quoted in Sidney Kaplan and Emma Nogrady Kaplan, *The Black Presence in the Era of the American Revolution* (Amherst: University of Massachusetts Press, 1989), 254.

37. Quoted in Robin Blackburn, *The Overthrow of Colonial Slavery, 1776–1848* (New York: Verso, 1988), 112–13.

38. Quoted in Simon Schama, *Rough Crossings: The Slaves, the British, and the American Revolution* (New York: HarperCollins, 2007), 123.

39. Quoted in Peter A. Dorsey, *Common Bondage: Slavery as Metaphor in Revolutionary America* (Knoxville: University of Tennessee Press, 2009), 131.

40. "Memoirs of the Life of Boston King, a Black Preacher," *Methodist Magazine* 21 (April 1798): 15.
41. Schama, *Rough Crossings*, 127.
42. Quoted in Henry Wiencek, *An Imperfect God: George Washington, His Slaves, and the Creation of America* (New York: Macmillan, 2004), 248.
43. Quoted in Catharine Maria Sedgwick, "Slavery in New England," *Bentley's Miscellany* 34 (1853), 424.
44. Jeremiah Asher, *Incidents in the Life of J. Reverend Asher* (1850; repr., Freeport, NY: Books for Libraries Press, 1971), 18.
45. "Petition for Freedom to the Massachusetts Council and the House of Representatives" (January 1777), in *Collections of the Massachusetts Historical Society*, 5th Series (Boston: The Massachusetts Historical Society, 1877), 3:436.
46. The quote is from a poem by John Boyle O'Reilly that appears on the Crispus Attucks Memorial on Boston Common.
47. Letter from George T. Dowling to William Cooper Nell (March 3, 1960), reprinted in *William Cooper Nell, Nineteenth-Century African American Abolitionist, Historian, Integrationist: Selected Writings from 1832–1874*, eds. Dorothy Porter Wesley and Constance Porter Uzelac (Baltimore: Black Classic Press, 2002), 471.
48. Benjamin Quarles, *The Negro in the American Revolution* (Chapel Hill: University of North Carolina Press, 1996), 10–11.
49. Theodore Parker to George Bancroft, 1858, in *Life and Correspondence of Theodore Parker*, ed. John Weiss and Goldwin Smith (New York: D. Appleton & Company, 1884), 235.
50. Asher, *Incidents in the Life of J. Reverend Asher*, 18.

Suggested References

African American Life in Eighteenth-Century North America

Gomez, Michael A. *Exchanging Our Country Marks: The Transformation of African Identities in the Colonial and Antebellum South.* Chapel Hill: University of North Carolina Press, 1998.

Hodges, Graham Russell. *Root and Branch: African Americans in New York and East Jersey, 1613–1863.* Chapel Hill: University of North Carolina Press, 1999.

Lepore, Jill. *New York Burning: Liberty, Slavery, and Conspiracy in Eighteenth-Century Manhattan.* New York: Knopf, 2005.

Morgan, Philip D. *Slave Counterpoint: Black Culture in the Eighteenth-Century Chesapeake and Lowcountry.* Chapel Hill: University of North Carolina Press, 1998.

Olwell, Robert. *Masters, Slaves, and Subjects: The Culture of Power in the South Carolina Low Country, 1740–1790.* Ithaca, NY: Cornell University Press, 1998.

Piersen, William Dillon. *Black Yankees: The Development of an Afro-American Subculture in Eighteenth-Century New England.* Amherst: University of Massachusetts Press, 1988.

Sidbury, James. *Becoming African in America: Race and Nation in the Early Black Atlantic.* New York: Oxford University Press, 2009.

Sweet, John Wood. *Bodies Politic: Negotiating Race in the American North, 1730–1830.* Philadelphia: University of Pennsylvania Press, 2006.

The African American Revolution

Bradley, Patricia. *Slavery, Propaganda, and the American Revolution.* Jackson: University Press of Mississippi, 1999.

Countryman, Edward. *Enjoy the Same Liberty: Black Americans and the Revolutionary Era.* Lanham, MD: Rowman & Littlefield Publishers, 2012.

Egerton, Douglas R. *Death or Liberty: African Americans and Revolutionary America.* Oxford: Oxford University Press, 2009.

Gates, Henry Louis, Jr. *The Trials of Phillis Wheatley: America's First Black Poet and Her Encounters with the Founding Fathers.* New York: Basic Civitas Books, 2003.

Holton, Woody. *Black Americans in the Revolutionary Era: A Brief History with Documents.* Boston: Bedford/St. Martin's, 2009.

Kaplan, Sidney, and Emma Nogrady Kaplan. *The Black Presence in the Era of the American Revolution, 1770–1800.* Amherst: University of Massachusetts Press, 1989.

Nash, Gary B. *The Forgotten Fifth: African Americans in the Age of Revolution.* Cambridge: Harvard University Press, 2006.
——— *The Unknown American Revolution: The Unruly Birth of Democracy and the Struggle to Create America.* New York: Penguin, 2006.

Saillant, John. *Black Puritan, Black Republican: The Life and Thought of Lemuel Haynes, 1753–1833.* New York: Oxford University Press, 2003.

Wiencek, Henry. *An Imperfect God: George Washington, His Slaves, and the Creation of America.* New York: Macmillan, 2004.

Slaves, Soldiers, and the Outcome of the Revolution

Frey, Sylvia R. *Water from the Rock Black Resistance in a Revolutionary Age.* Princeton: Princeton University Press, 1993.

Gilbert, Alan. *Black Patriots and Loyalists: Fighting for Emancipation in the War for Independence.* Chicago: University of Chicago Press, 2012.

Hochschild, Adam. *Bury the Chains: Prophets and Rebels in the Fight to Free an Empire's Slaves.* New York: Mariner Books, 2006.

Jasanoff, Maya. *Liberty's Exiles: American Loyalists in the Revolutionary World.* New York: Knopf, 2011.

Piecuch, Jim. *Three Peoples, One King: Loyalists, Indians, and Slaves in the Revolutionary South, 1775–1782.* Columbia: University of South Carolina Press, 2008.

Pulis, John W. *Moving On: Black Loyalists in the Afro-Atlantic World.* London: Routledge, 1999.

Pybus, Cassandra. *Epic Journeys of Freedom: Runaway Slaves of the American Revolution and Their Global Quest for Liberty.* Boston: Beacon Press, 2007.

Quarles, Benjamin. *The Negro in the American Revolution.* Chapel Hill: University of North Carolina Press, 1996.

Schama, Simon. *Rough Crossings: The Slaves, the British, and the American Revolution.* New York: HarperCollins, 2007.

CHAPTER

4

Slavery and Freedom in the New Republic,

1783–1829

NEGRO.

IN 1791, A THIRTY-EIGHT-YEAR-OLD black man named Benjamin Banneker composed a carefully worded letter to Thomas Jefferson, the new nation's first secretary of state. Born free, Banneker owned a small farm just outside Baltimore, where he made his living growing fruit and raising cattle and bees. He was also a self-educated scientist, inventor, and author who had recently published an almanac, which he sent to Jefferson along with his letter. Although he enjoyed the "blessings of free and unequalled liberty," Banneker told Jefferson, he was well aware that most of his fellow black Americans remained enslaved. After winning a war dedicated to protecting their own liberties, white Americans had offered few rights to blacks. Instead, they dismissed them, Banneker complained, as "a race of beings" more "brutish than human, and scarcely capable of mental endowments." Banneker appealed to Jefferson to help African Americans "eradicate that train of absurd and false ideas and opinions, which so generally prevails with respect to us."[1]

As a Virginia planter who owned hundreds of slaves, Jefferson might seem to have been an unlikely choice of correspondents. But Banneker addressed Jefferson as a revolutionary rather than a planter, reminding him that he had once had reservations about the injustices of slavery. Indeed, when faced with the "arms and tyranny of the British crown," Banneker wrote, Jefferson had composed the Declaration of Independence, asserting that "all men are created equal, that they are endowed by their Creator with certain unalienable rights, [and] that among these are life, liberty, and the pursuit of happiness."[2]

Jefferson's brief reply to Banneker was courteous but noncommittal. "Nobody wishes more than I do," he wrote, "to see such proofs as you exhibit, that nature has given to our black brethren talents equal to those of the other colors of men; and that the appearance of the want of them, is owing merely to the degraded condition of their existence, both in Africa and America." He even forwarded Banneker's almanac to the French Academy of Sciences as evidence of one black man's accomplishments.[3] But Jefferson did not address Banneker's critique of his support for slavery. The Virginia planter had never managed to reconcile slavery with the egalitarian ideals that he articulated in the Declaration of Independence, so he had good reason to ignore Banneker's charges against him.

Instead, Jefferson's reply centered on the question of black racial inferiority, which would become a central issue in the post-Revolutionary debate over slavery, liberty, and equal rights. He told Banneker that while he, too, hoped to see conditions for blacks improve, he remained unsure that the race could rise very far. In *Notes on the State of Virginia* (1785), Jefferson advanced the "suspicion" that blacks were "inferior to the whites in the endowments both of body and mind," and he would never admit otherwise.[4] In a private letter written to a friend in 1809,

1791–1804 Haitian Revolution

1792–1821 New slave states established: Kentucky, Tennessee, Louisiana, Mississippi, Alabama, and Missouri

1793 Fugitive Slave Act establishes legal mechanisms for capture and return of escaped slaves

Eli Whitney invents cotton gin

1794 African Methodist Episcopal (AME) Church established

1798 Alien and Sedition Acts tighten restrictions on aliens in United States, limit speech criticizing government

1800 Gabriel's rebellion

1803 Louisiana Purchase doubles size of United States

1804 Ohio passes black laws

1806 Virginia imposes new restrictions on manumission

1808 International slave trade ends

1812–1815 War of 1812

1815 Paul Cuffe takes thirty-eight black Bostonians to Sierra Leone

1816 American Colonization Society (ACS) first meets in Washington, D.C.

1823 Monroe Doctrine warns against future European colonization in Western Hemisphere

Jefferson even questioned Banneker's intellect, writing, "I have had a very long letter from Banneker which shows him to have a mind of very common stature indeed."[5]

Both Banneker's 1791 letter and Jefferson's response speak to the limits of black freedom in the new nation. The Revolution marked the beginning of slavery's abolition in the northern states and provided many African Americans throughout the country with the possibility of freedom through military service, manumission, or escape. But slavery still persisted throughout the South. Fueled by the production of cotton and sugar, the region's plantation economy expanded west and south into new territories. As Jefferson's guarded response to Banneker indicates, although he and other slave-holders of his era often deplored slavery, they were even more opposed to emancipation and questioned whether blacks were fit for freedom. For example, Jefferson's friend and fellow Founding Father James Madison, who deemed slavery "the most oppressive dominion ever exercised by man over man," nevertheless considered blacks "degraded" and abolition impractical.[6]

Not all Americans agreed with Jefferson and Madison. In the aftermath of the Revolution, thousands of white southerners liberated their slaves, while white north-erners began eliminating slavery altogether. Massachusetts and Vermont abolished slavery during the Revolution, and New Hampshire had fewer than fifty slaves by 1786. The citizens of Pennsylvania, Connecticut, Rhode Island, New York, and New Jersey also enacted gradual emancipation laws between 1780 and 1804. These laws dictated an emancipation process that was far from swift, however. They freed only those born after the laws were passed, and these slaves were emancipated only after they had served their masters for decades.

Moreover, free blacks in the North and the South did not have the same liberties as whites. Once the political idealism that ran high during the Revolution died down, many whites proved unwilling to embrace free blacks as their political or social equals. Whites, as citizens of a republic in which most free blacks were ex-slaves and hundreds of thousands of African Americans were still in slavery, tended to associate blackness with slavery and degradation. To combat these prejudices, free blacks established sepa-rate black churches, schools, and social organizations and focused their efforts on building their own communities.

Both prejudice and slavery persisted in the Republic, calling into question whether blacks would ever be granted the liberties enshrined in the Declaration of Independence. This question remained largely unresolved during the Republic's early decades, which saw both black slavery and black freedom expand and the Founders adopt a Constitution that neither endorsed nor outlawed slavery. The result left African Americans, both slave and free, on the fringes of American democracy.

The Limits of Democracy

The circumscribed nature of black freedom in the post-Revolutionary era was bitterly disappointing to African Americans, who during and immediately after the Revolution had some reason to hope that slavery might collapse. Between 1776 and 1787, all but three of the new nation's thirteen states banned the importation of slaves from outside the United States—although South Carolina only suspended the trade for three years. Among the three states that did not ban the trade, only Georgia, which had suffered massive slave losses during the war, resumed the trade uninterrupted. North Carolina, which also had no ban, nevertheless discouraged participation in the slave trade by putting prohibitive duties on slave imports. New Hampshire had no ban because it did not import enough slaves to need one.

Yet the politicians who met to draft the U.S. Constitution in 1787 extended both slavery and the slave trade by agreeing that the United States would not withdraw from the international slave trade prior to 1808 and by creating few checks on the institution within the United States. Slavery quickly rebounded in Georgia and South Carolina and expanded rapidly across the Lower South starting in the 1790s, as planters developed lucrative new **cash crops**. The expansion of slavery was also facilitated by a vast expanse of new land that the United States acquired when it bought Louisiana from the French in 1803.

The Status of Slavery in the New Nation

In the decade following the Revolution, even the new nation's federal government seemed willing to take action to prohibit slavery's growth. When the Congress of the Confederation, which served as the country's governing body prior to the ratification of the Constitution in 1790, met in July 1787 to organize the U.S. territories northwest of the Ohio River into prospective states (and auction off some of the land to pay its debts), leaders from across the nation agreed to ban slavery in these territories, which included the present-day states of Illinois, Indiana, Michigan, Ohio, and Wisconsin, as well as part of Minnesota. The Congress approved the resulting legislation, known as the **Northwest Ordinance**, when it met to draft the Constitution a month later. But the Northwest Ordinance was not an antislavery triumph. It lent tacit approval to slavery south of the Ohio River, giving the institution license to expand there and specifying that slaves who escaped to those territories should be "lawfully reclaimed and conveyed" to their owners (Map 4.1).

Moreover, the Constitutional Convention put no further constraints on slavery. The framers of the Constitution left slavery's status within the existing states under the jurisdiction of the state legislatures. The fifty-five delegates were charged with strengthening the new nation's first system of government rather than addressing the issue of slavery, and they were willing to compromise on divisive issues in order to form a viable federal union. Accordingly, they rejected Pennsylvania delegate Gouverneur Morris's suggestion for a compensated gradual emancipation, which would have required owners to free their slaves after a set number of years and used federal funding to reimburse them for the loss of their property. With Georgia's and South Carolina's delegates threatening to leave the Union if the Constitution included such a measure, the delegates crafted a document that made no explicit reference to slaves or slavery and included several measures to preserve both.

The Founders protected the interests of the slave states with a clause forbidding all states to shelter or emancipate fugitive slaves—or, as termed in the Constitution, "Person[s] held to Service or Labour." This **fugitive slave clause** was later reinforced by the Fugitive Slave Act of 1793, which established the legal mechanisms by which escaped slaves could be seized and returned. The Constitution also offered slaveholders federal aid to subdue slave rebellions in a clause providing federal protection against "domestic violence" within a state's borders.

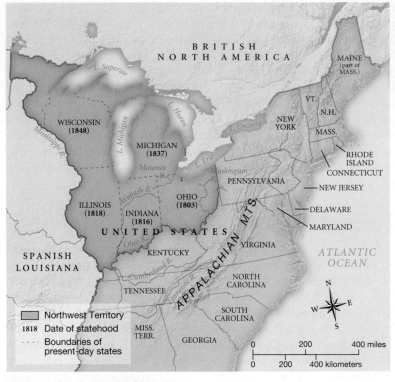

MAP 4.1   The Northwest Ordinance

Passed by the Congress of the Confederation on July 13, 1787, the Northwest Ordinance organized U.S. lands north and west of the Ohio River and east of the Mississippi River into a region known as the Northwest Territory. The Northwest Ordinance also prohibited slavery in this region.

The delegates balanced the opposing interests of slaveholding and nonslaveholding states when it came to the thorny issue of how slaves would be counted toward each state's federal representation and tax burden. Would slaves be enumerated in the tallies that determined the number of political representatives allotted to each state? Would slaves be taxed? Representatives from slave states wanted their slaves counted for the purposes of representation but left untaxed; delegates from the other states wanted slaves to be taxed but not represented. The **Three-Fifths Compromise** split the difference: Three-fifths of each state's slave population would be counted in determining each state's tax burden and representation in the House of Representatives. The compromise was spelled out in the three-fifths clause of the Constitution.

The result was more generous to the southern states than the Founders had intended. In the decades following the Constitutional Convention, southern congressional representation soared as the region's slave population increased. The number of slaves grew from 694,207 in 1790 to 3,953,760 in 1860—almost all of whom lived in the South. As a result, southerners dominated the House of Representatives and controlled the presidency and the Supreme Court for much of the antebellum era (the period before the

Civil War). But most of the delegates who met in 1787 did not foresee the long-term consequences of the three-fifths clause.

When the Founders met in Philadelphia, the future of slavery was far from certain. A wave of manumissions had swept through the Upper South during the Revolutionary era, increasing the number of free blacks and underscoring the declining economic viability of slavery in the region. By the 1780s, tobacco production was declining in Virginia and Maryland, two of the largest slave states, and many Chesapeake planters were beginning to grow wheat, which required fewer full-time workers. The slackening demand for slaves was one reason Constitutional Convention delegates agreed to set a twenty-year limit on states participating in the foreign slave trade. This potentially controversial measure had the support of Upper South delegates, such as James Madison, who claimed to oppose the slave trade on humanitarian principles but who was also aware that his region did not need more slaves. Among the thirteen states that ratified the Constitution, only Georgia and South Carolina had expanding slave economies.

Slavery's Cotton Frontiers

Although slavery seemed to be shrinking in 1787, the southern economy was soon transformed in ways the Founders could not have anticipated. In the 1790s, southern planters developed two new cash crops, sugar and cotton, that secured the future of slavery and turned the South into a growing Slave Power. As Florida and Louisiana came under U.S. control, American planters expanded into those regions, which became the nation's primary sugar-producing areas. But these developments were really fueled by the 1793 invention of Eli Whitney's cotton gin, a machine that facilitated the processing of cotton. Cotton became the most widely cultivated slave-grown crop, flourishing throughout the lower Mississippi Valley and beyond and leading to the establishment of new slave states, including Kentucky (1792), Tennessee (1796), Louisiana (1812), Mississippi (1817), Alabama (1819), Missouri (1821), and Arkansas (1836).

The cultivation of cotton was not new to the Lower South. During the first half of the eighteenth century, Carolina's early proprietors and Georgia's colonial trustees had encouraged the colonists to diversify the emerging plantation economy by growing cotton, hemp, flax, and foodstuffs, rather than producing only cash crops such as rice and indigo. But most planters took little interest in what was then a garden crop, rather than an export staple. Slaves and small farmers tended small cotton patches, but the fibrous cotton bolls, or seedpods, that they yielded took much of the winter to clean, card, and spin. Only slaves and whites too poor to buy ready-made British textiles bothered to produce homespun cotton fabric. Cotton farming had little commercial appeal because salable cotton required far too much work to be cost-effective.

Southern landowners became more interested in producing cotton and other textiles in the years leading up to the Revolution. As the conflict took shape, rebellious colonists began to boycott British goods. Once a badge of poverty, homespun clothing became a symbol of patriotism. It was a necessity during the war, when British imports were no longer available and British warships blockaded the southern colonies, cutting off most of their exports of rice, tobacco, and indigo. Cotton thus became more marketable and useful than ever before, expanding even before Whitney patented his famous gin and soaring thereafter.

BALING COTTON.

GINNING COTTON BY STEAM.

PICKING COTTON.

Slaves Processing Cotton
This image depicts early-nineteenth-century slaves picking, baling, and ginning cotton. Cotton, and the invention of the cotton gin, transformed the American South and rendered its economy ever more dependent on slave labor. As you examine this image, consider what the artist chose to depict and how he chose to depict it. What is included, and what has been left out? What is the general feeling of the image, and where do its accuracies and/or inaccuracies lie?
© *North Wind Picture Archives/Alamy.*

The commercial cultivation of cotton first took hold in the Sea Islands of coastal Georgia and South Carolina, where the weather was consistently warm enough to support the cultivation of long-staple, or long-fibered, cotton—an easily cleaned, premium variety. But only a short-staple variety known as "upland cotton," whose fuzzy green seeds had to be carefully combed out, flourished on the mainland. The cotton gin, which used wire spikes, brushes, and a pair of rollers to separate the cotton from its seeds, revolutionized cotton production by transforming mainland cotton into a commercial crop. Whereas cleaning a pound or two of cotton had once taken a full day, the cotton gin allowed a single worker to clean as many as fifty pounds in that time. Upland cotton was also a hardy plant that could be grown throughout much of the South, and as a labor-intensive, profitable crop with a long growing season, it quickly proved to be an ideal crop for slave labor.

The South's upland cotton production skyrocketed from 150,000 pounds a year in 1793 to 6.5 million pounds in 1795, and by 1815 the region was producing well over

BY THE NUMBERS   The Growth of Slavery and Cotton, 1820–1860

Slave laborers played a crucial role in the production of U.S. cotton crops. As this figure indicates, cotton production expanded tremendously as the slave population grew. As slavery fostered the growth of cotton, cotton also promoted the expansion of slavery: The demanding crop required forced labor to clear the land and plant, cultivate, and prepare the cotton for sale. White migrants to the expanding cotton frontiers brought slaves with them and purchased both foreign and domestic slaves to meet their growing needs.

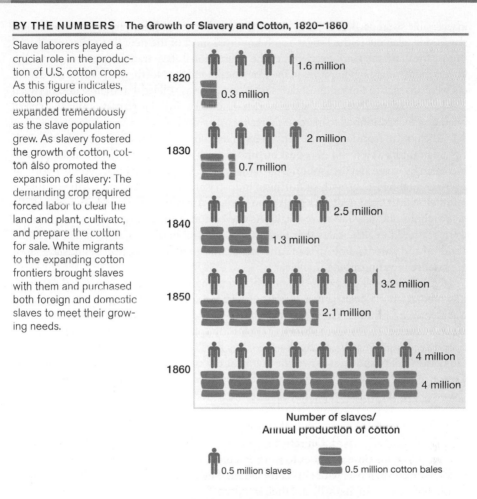

Number of slaves/
Annual production of cotton

0.5 million slaves   0.5 million cotton bales

100 million pounds annually. Because its cultivation depended on slave labor, cotton sustained slavery as well, creating an enduring demand for slaves throughout the Lower South. The quest for cotton profits drove slaveholding settlers farther south and west in search of new land, creating an expanding frontier where forced labor predominated. Between 1790 and 1820, more than 250,000 white migrants from Virginia and Maryland settled in the backcountry regions of South Carolina and Georgia and on the frontiers of Alabama, Mississippi, Louisiana, and Missouri. The wealthiest settlers brought hundreds of slaves with them; others used the profits from growing cotton to buy foreign and domestic slaves. (See By the Numbers: The Growth of Slavery and Cotton, 1820–1860.)

As the cotton boom began, slaves were especially in demand in Georgia and South Carolina, which had both been short of slaves even before the boom. Georgia had lost two-thirds of its slave population during the Revolutionary War, while South Carolina may have lost up to one-quarter. To recoup their losses, planters in these states tracked down wartime fugitives who had escaped to other states and used their militias and Native American slave catchers to hunt down maroon communities living in the region's backwoods and most inaccessible swamps. Before 1808, when the United States withdrew from the international slave trade, planters in the Lower South imported most of the new slaves they purchased from Africa and the Caribbean. But as the international slave trade came to an end, such buyers increasingly sought slaves in the Chesapeake and the North, where many slave owners were anxious to unload their slaves while slavery was still legal in their states. Between 1790 and 1820, nearly 170,000 slaves were transferred to frontier plantations in an internal migration that continued to increase thereafter.

The cotton frontier provided planters in the Upper South, whose slaves were multiplying rapidly as a result of robust birthrates, with a profitable market for slaves, who increasingly exceeded the labor needs of the region. Cotton also enriched the nation as a whole, fueling the growth of northern industry and quickly becoming the country's premier export crop. Cotton's impact on African Americans in the South was equally far-reaching but also far more tragic. As the cotton frontier expanded west, families were scattered in slave sales that forever separated siblings, husbands and wives, and children and parents. For African Americans consigned to the cotton fields, slave labor grew more mind-numbing than ever.

Unlike other skilled or seasonal work, tending cotton crops demanded unremitting menial labor. Clearing new land was backbreaking, and planting and raising cotton was nearly as arduous. Cotton has a 180- to 200-day growing season, and once the plants matured, slaves spent several more months picking the cotton, carefully ginning it, and pressing it into bales. By the time they finished, it was almost time to return to the cotton fields and beat down the stems of the old plants to prepare the new crop. Cotton planters typically planted and harvested corn during breaks in the cotton-growing season, which ensured that slaves worked all year round.

This unrelenting regime left little time for slaves to cultivate their own food or take care of their families. Thus, while their official workday ended at nightfall, their labors continued long afterward. On returning home, the average slave, one observer noted, "does not lose his time. He goes to work at a bit of land which he has planted with provisions for his own use, while his companion, if he has one, busies herself in preparing [some food] for him, herself, and their children."[7]

Between sundown and sunrise, plantation slaves also had to build new communities. Newly imported African- and Caribbean-born slaves were far from home, and American-born slaves from the Upper South or the North had little hope of reconnecting with their kin. Planters who migrated to the new cotton frontiers sometimes brought all the slaves they owned, but they were usually more selective and often ended up separating married couples and breaking up families. Planter migrants needed strong slaves who could clear their new land and survive the rigors of the long trip south, often made on foot. As a result, planters favored young adults over their parents and grandparents, and left young children and nursing mothers behind.

Slave families in the Upper South also were broken up by slave sales. One example is the family of Charles Ball, who lived in Calvert County, Maryland, until age four. After his master died in the 1780s, his mother and all of his siblings were sold to separate purchasers, including a Georgia trader who drove Ball's mother away from him with a rawhide whip. Ball survived his childhood and went on to have a family of his own. But in 1805, he, too, was sold to a Georgia trader without warning and never saw his wife and children again.[8] (See From the Record: Charles Ball Describes Being Sold

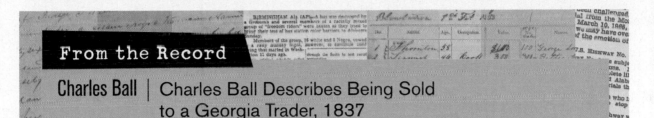

From the Record

Charles Ball | Charles Ball Describes Being Sold to a Georgia Trader, 1837

Slave owners frequently did not inform their slaves that they had been sold, because the information was likely to inspire protests or even attempts to escape. Instead, slaves were simply transferred abruptly to new owners and marched away in chains. In the following excerpt from **Charles Ball's** *Fifty Years in Chains* (1859), Ball, who was sold and forced to leave his home in Maryland in 1805, recounts the experience.

This man came up to me, and, seizing me by the collar, shook me violently, saying I was his property, and must go with him to Georgia. At the sound of these words, the thoughts of my wife and children rushed across my mind, and my heart beat away within me. I saw and knew that my case was hopeless, and that resistance was vain, as there were near twenty persons present, all of whom were ready to assist the man by whom I was kidnapped. I felt incapable of weeping or speaking, and in my despair I laughed loudly. My purchaser ordered me to cross my hands behind, which were quickly bound with a strong cord; and he then told me that we must set out that very day for the South. I asked if I could not be allowed to go to see my wife and children, or if this could not be permitted, if they might not have leave to come to see me; but was told that I would be able to get another wife in Georgia.

My new master, whose name I did not hear, took me that same day across the Patuxent [River], where I joined fifty-one other slaves, whom he had bought in Maryland. Thirty-two of these were men, and nineteen were women. The women were merely tied together with a rope, about the size of a bed-cord, which was tied like a halter round the neck of each; but the men, of whom I was the stoutest and strongest, were very differently caparisoned. A strong iron collar was closely fitted by means of a padlock round each of our necks. A chain of iron, about a hundred feet in length, was passed through the hasp of each padlock, except at the two ends, where the hasps of the padlock passed through a link of the chain. In addition to this, we were handcuffed in pairs, with iron staples and bolts, with a short chain, about a foot long, uniting the handcuffs and their wearers in pairs. In this manner we were chained alternately by the right and left hand; and the poor man, to whom I was thus ironed, wept like an infant when the blacksmith, with his heavy hammer, fastened the ends of the bolts that kept the staples from slipping from our arms. For my own part, I felt indifferent to my fate. It appeared to me that the worst had come that could come, and that no change of fortune could harm me.

SOURCE: Charles Ball, *Fifty Years in Chains, or The Life of an American Slave* (New York: H. Dayton, 1859), 28–30.

??? Why does Ball describe himself as "incapable of weeping or speaking" and "indifferent to [his] fate"? How did his circumstances inspire these feelings?

to a Georgia Trader.) Ball ended up in Georgia, along with numerous other slaves who had left behind families in the Chesapeake. He eventually escaped from slavery and settled in Pennsylvania, where he wrote his memoir and remained "fearful, at this day, to let my place of residence be known."[9]

Slavery and Empire

The United States' westward expansion was limited by Spanish, French, and Native American claims to much of the continent's interior. At the turn of the century, the new nation took advantage of imperial conflicts in Europe and the Caribbean to expand its national boundaries. The most notable of these conflicts was the Haitian Revolution in the French colony of Saint Domingue, which had far-reaching effects for France's New World empire. This massive slave rebellion scared slaveholders across the hemispheres and provided African American populations with an enduring vision of political freedom. It also reshaped the New World's commodity markets and imperial borders in ways that helped expand slavery in the United States.

The Haitian Revolution (1791–1804) took place in the wake of the French Revolution (1789), when France's grasp on its colonies was already weakened by internal

The Haitian Revolution
The Haitian Revolution (1791–1804) in the French colony of Saint Domingue inspired slaves internationally and terrified their owners. The frontispiece of this 1815 history of the revolution conveys slaveholders' greatest fears, depicting white men, women, and children running helplessly from armed blacks. Note, in particular, how the women are portrayed. There are many mothers with small children, a wife mourning her collapsed husband, an elderly woman with a cane, and a young woman who appears to be partially naked from the waist up. How is white womanhood used here to illustrate the dangers of a slave revolt and perhaps to justify slaves' bondage? *Schomburg Center, NYPL/Art Resource, NY.*

turmoil. Slave rebels, who numbered 100,000, burned their plantations, executed their owners, and shut down sugar production in Haiti, then one of the world's largest sugar producers. Their actions reverberated across the Atlantic world, with sugar in short supply and whites fleeing Haiti. Many of Haiti's sugar planters took refuge in the lower Mississippi Valley and began to cultivate sugar there. Meanwhile, France never regained control of Haiti. The powerful French general Napoleon Bonaparte, who unseated France's revolutionary leaders at the beginning of the nineteenth century, tried to reenslave Haiti's former slaves. But even after he captured their leader, Toussaint-Louverture, who died in a French jail in 1803, Haiti's black population resisted reenslavement and declared the country's independence in 1804. The loss of this most lucrative New World colony caused Napoleon to reevaluate how many colonies France could maintain. He decided to sell off some of its least valuable assets, including Louisiana.

Thomas Jefferson, elected president in 1800, profited from France's shrinking imperial ambitions. In 1802, Jefferson dispatched James Monroe to offer to buy the port city of New Orleans, which was vital to U.S. trade. Jefferson authorized Monroe to pay $10 million for the city, along with as much land west of the Mississippi River as the French government could be persuaded to surrender. When Monroe arrived in France, he found Napoleon's foreign minister willing to sell all of Louisiana for the bargain price of $15 million. "They ask for only one town of Louisiana," Napoleon said, "but I already consider the whole colony as completely lost."[10] Monroe was quick to agree, for the purchase would give the United States dominion over a vast section of North America's interior, extending from the Gulf of Mexico to the Canadian border and including large swaths of land on the western banks of the Mississippi River.

The **Louisiana Purchase** (1803) doubled the size of the United States, adding 828,000 square miles of land, and fostered the spread of slavery in what Jefferson called the "empire for liberty." It included territory that would later become the slave states of Arkansas and Missouri, as well as present-day Oklahoma and portions of Texas (Map 4.2). This new land was well suited to the cultivation of cotton, adding millions of acres to the South's growing cotton frontier. Southeastern Louisiana contained land suitable for the cultivation of sugar, an even more profitable cash crop. This purchase spurred new waves of westward migration among the planters of the Upper South and offered lucrative new markets for the domestic slave trade, adding to the thirty thousand slaves already living in Louisiana. New Orleans quickly became a principal port for the resale of African slaves. (To evade the congressional ban on importing foreign slaves into New Orleans, traders first sold the slaves in South Carolina, then resold them in New Orleans.)

Slavery and Freedom outside the Plantation South

If cotton gave slavery a new lease on life in the plantation South, the status of slavery elsewhere was more mixed. In southern cities, slavery first expanded and then contracted after the Revolution. The acquisition of New Orleans greatly enlarged the South's enslaved urban population, as did the rapid growth of other urban areas.

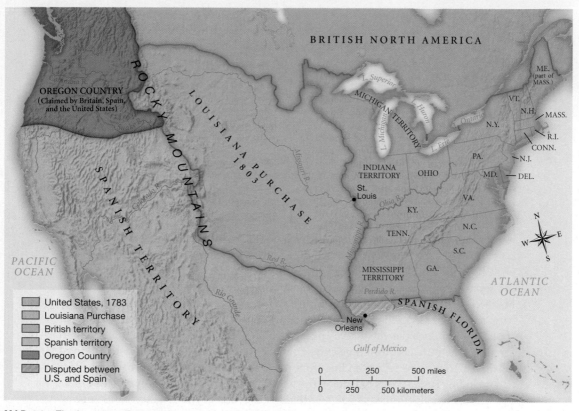

MAP 4.2   The Louisiana Purchase

The 828,000 square miles of land that the United States purchased from France in 1803 extended from the Gulf of Mexico to Canada and included all of present-day Arkansas, Missouri, Iowa, Oklahoma, Kansas, and Nebraska, most of North and South Dakota, and parts of Minnesota, New Mexico, Texas, Colorado, and Louisiana. The acquisition, which doubled the size of the United States, also had a tremendous impact on slavery: It opened new lands for the cultivation of slave-grown cotton and sugar crops and sparked a westward migration of planters, facilitating the growth of the slave trade.

Thriving markets for cotton and other slave-grown crops fueled the growth of these cities, which shipped the commodities out of their harbors. Urban businessmen employed slaves to haul, load, and unload goods and to build the barrels, crates, and storehouses that contained them. Slaves also worked in port cities as tradesmen's assistants and domestics.

But slavery never became as entrenched in urban areas as it did in the countryside, and over time the use of free black workers became increasingly common in southern cities. Urban slaves were more expensive to maintain than free workers and potentially more dangerous. They often achieved a greater degree of independence than plantation slaves, which made southerners uneasy—especially in the wake of Gabriel's rebellion, an abortive slave plot that took place in Richmond, Virginia, in 1800.

Meanwhile, in the North, slavery was outlawed in every state in the decades following the Revolution. But slavery was slow to die, because several states adopted gradual emancipation laws that kept African Americans enslaved well into the early decades of the nineteenth century. Moreover, not all slave owners honored these laws, and some slaves were forced to seek their freedom in court.

Urban Slavery and Southern Free Blacks

The slave population in most nineteenth-century southern cities either declined or leveled off over time. Most of the slaves who passed through the commercial hubs and major slave trading centers such as New Orleans and Charleston were sold to rural slave owners. Southern cities tended to be sites of exchange rather than industry, and did not require a large population of enslaved laborers. One major exception was Richmond, which became Virginia's state capital in 1780 and produced a variety of manufactured goods. The success of industrial slavery in Richmond was widespread enough to sustain a growing population of enslaved laborers, but the city was unusual in this regard.

Blacks did not disappear from such cities, however. Instead, in cities where slave populations declined, the number of free blacks usually increased. In Baltimore, which saw the earliest and most dramatic shift of this kind, slavery boomed in the decades immediately after the Revolution and declined after 1810. But the city's free black population soared thereafter.

During the Revolution, Baltimore expanded when Maryland planters abandoned tobacco, which no longer fetched high prices, in favor of wheat and other grains. The city profited enormously from this shift and became a center for milling grain into flour. Baltimore workers also produced the barrels used to store the flour and supplied the labor needed to transport, package, and ship all of Maryland's agricultural exports, as well as to construct roads, warehouses, and other buildings. Between 1790 and 1810, the city's slave population expanded rapidly as a result of these developments. "Surplus" slaves brought in from the surrounding countryside were cheap and plentiful in a region where tobacco no longer occupied most of the labor force, and they initially supplied much of the labor needed to sustain the city's economic growth. But the rise of cotton, combined with the closing of the international slave trade in 1808, soon made such slaves increasingly expensive. Maryland planters with surplus slaves began selling them to planters on the cotton frontier rather than to local buyers, and Baltimore's slave population shrank.

Meanwhile, free blacks flocked to Baltimore. The city's growing free black population, like its economic growth, was a product of forces in the countryside. The declining labor needs of Maryland's planters inspired a wave of manumissions, especially among Baptist and Methodist planters. Many still chose to sell rather than free their surplus slaves, however, and the fear of being sold inspired some slaves to free themselves—either by working to purchase their freedom or by escaping. Fugitive slaves and free blacks alike migrated to Baltimore, where jobs were plentiful and the large free black population could provide a community for freemen and shelter runaways. Maryland slave masters often suspected that missing slaves were in Baltimore passing as free blacks. In 1789, one owner ran a newspaper ad seeking the whereabouts of a missing slave named Charity. His ad maintained that he was all but certain she "is in or near

Baltimore-town, passes for a free woman, practices midwifery, and goes by the name of Sarah Dorsey, or Dawson the Granny."[11]

The economics of slavery in urban areas were never as clear-cut as they were in the rural South. On one hand, the rise of the domestic slave trade after 1808 ensured that urban slaves commanded a good price, which encouraged owners to retain their slaves as investments. On the other hand, urban slaves tended to be less productive than their agricultural counterparts. Whether they worked as domestic laborers or served under tradesmen, city slaves were rarely subjected to the unremitting labor regime that prevailed in the countryside. Moreover, urban slaves could become a drain on their owner's finances if they were not fully employed, because they were more expensive to clothe, house, and feed in the city than on the plantation.

Thus a system of **hiring out** was developed to exploit urban slaves' labor, allowing some owners to make a good living by contracting out their slaves. The practice allowed businessmen who could not afford to buy slaves or needed their labor for only a short time to employ enslaved workers for anywhere from one day to one year. Unlike slave owners, these employers had no obligation to house their workers or supervise them after they left work. Although slaves who were hired out for domestic jobs might live in their employers' homes, many others lived independently. They were allowed to keep a portion of their earnings to cover their room and board and were given the freedom to find their own lodging. This practice, known as **living out**, evolved because many urban employers had no place to house slave workers.

The hiring-out system gave slaves a degree of freedom that often worried white southerners, who enacted but rarely enforced laws banning the system. Slaves who were hired out in southern cities typically made their own work arrangements, remained largely unsupervised, and were often in close contact with free blacks. This could reduce their value, as one slave owner discovered when he tried to sell a slave family he had long hired out. His slaves attracted no offers because other owners were wary of purchasing slaves who had known independence. By contrast, this autonomy benefited enslaved men and women, who sometimes accumulated enough money to buy their freedom by living cheaply and working extra hours. It could also tempt them to free themselves by either running away or rebelling.

Gabriel's Rebellion

Although city life offered some degree of freedom, it was not enough for an urban slave known as Prosser's Gabriel, who led a plot to overturn slavery in Richmond in the summer of 1800. Gabriel's rebellion testified to slaves' abiding discontent, but it was also inspired by recent events. At a time when the memory of the American Revolution was very much alive, the more recent Haitian Revolution underscored the possibility that an enslaved people could overthrow their oppressors. Gabriel was among the black Virginians who embraced this possibility. An enslaved blacksmith, he lived outside Richmond with his brothers, Solomon and Martin, on a tobacco plantation belonging to his owner, Thomas Prosser. Aware that divisions among the French had helped set the stage for the Haitian Revolution, Gabriel hoped that Virginia's slaves could exploit the social and political tensions among whites in their state, which were then running high in anticipation of the election of 1800.

With the aid of his brothers and other enslaved confederates, Gabriel planned to enlist about a thousand slaves to attack Richmond's wealthy citizens, while sparing the city's poor whites. He hoped that these discontented Virginians, as well as anti-slavery whites such as the city's Methodists and Quakers, would join the rebels and help them take control of the state. Most of Gabriel's slave recruits worked in or around Richmond and were American-born and highly acculturated. Many were artisans whose labor was not closely supervised. They saw themselves as working-men united around a cause, much as the colonists had been a quarter century earlier. Gabriel even planned to carry a flag reading "Death or liberty," evoking well-known Revolutionary-era language. Gabriel and his followers took advantage of their free-dom of movement to hold secret planning meetings in local taverns and shops and even traveled to the countryside to recruit rural followers at barbecues and revival meetings. They were also able to amass a small cache of weapons, which they hoped to use to seize more weapons in Richmond.

In the end, Gabriel's plot collapsed. As word of the revolt spread to hundreds of slaves across the Virginia countryside, two disclosed the plot to their master, who alerted Virginia governor James Monroe. Between this betrayal and a torrential storm that delayed implementation of the plan, the rebellion failed. Six of the ringleaders were captured immediately, and a militia assembled by the governor tracked down the remaining twenty. Among the last to surrender was Gabriel, who eluded the militia for almost three weeks before he was captured and taken back to Richmond in chains. There he was tried and executed along with the twenty-five others. More slaves also were indicted, but by mid-October a state law requiring Virginia to compensate owners of slaves convicted of capital crimes made the executions prohibitively expensive. The state had paid $8,899.91 to the owners of the condemned men, and many more sus-pects awaited trial. Governor Monroe suspended the executions after Thomas Jefferson suggested that the rebels might instead be sold outside the United States.

Even though Gabriel's rebellion failed, white Virginians lived in fear of an uprising, especially after another slave plot was uncovered in 1802. Some members of the Vir-ginia General Assembly even contemplated abandoning slavery completely, commis-sioning the governor to confer with President Jefferson about locating a place where "such negroes or mulattoes, as may be emancipated, may be sent or choose to remove as a place of asylum."[12] Instead, most slave owners called for laws that would discourage slave revolts.

Virginia authorities responded by eliminating much of the independence and mobility that urban blacks enjoyed. In Richmond, Monroe secured the state capital's arsenals and public buildings by instituting a nightly police patrol. The officers were responsible for rounding up any slaves caught on the street after nine o'clock. Accord-ing to the law, these slaves would receive "as many stripes" as the officer "might see proper to inflict."[13] In addition, African American laborers were regulated much more carefully than before. Although it was already illegal, slaves' hiring out of their own time was outlawed once more, and this time the legislature mandated stiff fines for slave owners and severe whippings for slaves who broke the law. The general assembly also cracked down on the "unlawful assemblages" of slaves who gathered to relax after work or on Sundays, ordering the state's justices of the peace to break up all such gath-erings and to punish slaves who participated in them. Even attending church became difficult, because slaves could no longer go anywhere without a written pass from their masters, who were often unwilling to supply one.

Free blacks found themselves more confined in the aftermath of Gabriel's rebellion as well. Although none were implicated, free blacks were suspected of helping the rebels promote their plot and steal from their owners. Moreover, many white Virginians were convinced that free blacks' very existence endangered slavery. "If blacks see all their color as slaves," one lawmaker explained, "it will seem to them a disposition of Providence, and they will be content. But if they see others like themselves free, and enjoying the rights they are deprived of, they will repine."[14] So when the state assembly clamped down on the network of black boatmen who had helped spread word of the planned revolts of 1800 and 1802, it targeted both free blacks and slaves. An 1802 law banned any "negro or mulatto" from obtaining a ship pilot's license, and black pilots whose licenses were issued prior to the law were confined to their boats as they traveled through Virginia. As slave patrols proliferated, free blacks came under scrutiny in their own neighborhoods. They could no longer survive without papers and had to register with their towns as "Free Negroes & Mulattoes."[15]

In the wake of Gabriel's rebellion, opportunities to pass from slavery to freedom began to decrease across the South. In 1806, Virginia legislators reversed the liberal manumission law the state had adopted during the Revolutionary era, which made manumission a private matter, and replaced it with a new law that made manumission very difficult. The law also required newly emancipated slaves to leave the state within twelve months or forfeit their freedom and become subject to reenslavement and sale. Newly freed blacks and their owners could petition the legislature to exempt individuals from the law, but self-purchase and manumission no longer offered Virginia slaves a direct route to lasting freedom. To be legally free, Virginia slaves now had to migrate north and forever separate themselves from their enslaved family and friends. Not surprisingly, many were unwilling to leave on these terms. By 1815, the state legislature was so overwhelmed by petitions from free blacks who wanted to remain in Virginia that they authorized the county courts to permit any black freed for "extraordinary merit" to stay.[16]

Achieving Emancipation in the North

In addition to expanding the boundaries of America's slave South, the Louisiana Purchase added more land to the free territory of the Old Northwest. The Northwest Ordinance had banned slavery in U.S. territories north of the Ohio River and east of the Mississippi River. But in the short term, the ban did not prevent some early settlers from keeping slaves in those areas: It did not apply to slaves already living there and did not keep some settlers from importing more. But the gradual emancipation of slaves in the northern states discouraged such imports, paving the way for the creation of other free states throughout the region.

By 1804, every northern state had either abolished slavery outright or passed a plan to eliminate slavery over time, and the new states that emerged in the Old Northwest followed suit. But black freedom was not easily gained or maintained in these states. In Indiana Territory, which included much of the upper Mississippi valley, gradual emancipation meant brutal forms of indentured servitude for up to thirty years before slaves became free. To avoid becoming a haven for fugitive slaves, Ohio, which became a free state in 1803, policed the border along the Ohio River between the slave

South and the free North. In 1804, Ohio passed **black laws** requiring all free blacks to supply legal proof of their free status and post a $500 bond to guarantee their good behavior. Indiana, which became a state in 1816, and Illinois, which gained statehood in 1818, also entered the Union as free states with similar laws. Though not uniformly enforced, such laws were common in the western states and imposed bond requirements for free blacks that eventually reached $1,000—a sum well beyond the reach of most African Americans.

Federal legislation passed during the early national period also solidified the limits on black freedom. The nation's first immigration law, the **Naturalization Act of 1790**, instituted residence and racial requirements for potential citizens. Naturalization was available to "free white person[s]" who had been in the United States for at least two years. Free blacks, by contrast, were not classified as full citizens under the laws of the Republic: They were barred from joining the national militia, carrying federal mail, or holding elected office in the District of Columbia. Moreover, the Constitution did not protect blacks from racially discriminatory laws imposed by individual states. Emancipation would not bring full freedom for black northerners, and just achieving emancipation was a struggle for many blacks.

Throughout the North, former slaves were liberated on terms that were neither swift nor generous. Slavery was outlawed in Massachusetts and Vermont during the Revolution, and abolished by means of gradual emancipation laws in the other northern states—with the exception of New Hampshire, which passed no abolition law and instead let its tiny slave population dwindle to nothing through manumission and attrition. The first state to adopt a gradual emancipation law was Pennsylvania. Passed in 1780, Pennsylvania's Act for the Gradual Abolition of Slavery provided a model for similar laws in Connecticut and Rhode Island in 1784, New York in 1799, and New Jersey in 1804. The laws applied only to slaves born after they were passed—those born before generally remained enslaved for life—and specified that slaves were to be freed in their mid- to late twenties, after they had labored long enough, in effect, to pay for their own freedom. As a result, despite their efforts to speed the application of these laws, thousands of black northerners remained in bondage through the 1820s.

Many slave owners were reluctant to emancipate slaves even after they had completed the terms of service required. Isabella Baumfree, who later renamed herself Sojourner Truth, was one of many black northerners who struggled to achieve the freedom promised her by law. Born in upstate New York in 1797, two years too early to qualify for gradual emancipation, Baumfree had little hope of freedom before 1817. That year, the New York legislature revised state law, setting July 4, 1827, as the date by which all New York slaves would achieve freedom regardless of birth date. This revision did not release slave children born before that date from their service obligation, but it reduced the term to twenty-one years. Baumfree, who endured several abusive owners and many hardships as a slave, was understandably eager to be freed, and she no doubt welcomed the law's reduction of her five children's terms of service. As 1827 approached, she even managed to get her owner, John Dumont, to agree to release her one year early if she behaved well and served him faithfully. But July 4, 1827, came and went, and Baumfree remained enslaved. Dumont insisted that Baumfree owed him more time because she had worked less than usual that year due to a "badly diseased hand."[17]

That fall, Baumfree freed herself by sneaking out of Dumont's house early one morning with a baby in one arm and her clothing in the other. She left behind her husband, whom Dumont had picked for her, and the rest of her children, who still owed Dumont many years of labor. But she did not travel far from her family. She took refuge with two antislavery neighbors, Maria and Isaac Van Wagenen, who sheltered Baumfree despite her owner's objections. When Dumont tried to drag Baumfree and her baby back to his home, Isaac Van Wagenen told his neighbor that even though he had "never been in the practice of buying and selling slaves; [and] he did not believe in slavery," he would buy out the remainder of Baumfree's time rather than see her return. Dumont accepted his offer of $20 for Baumfree's freedom and $5 for her baby's. Baumfree, who could hardly believe her good fortune, initially assumed that she had changed hands once more. Only after Van Wagenen assured her that "there is but *one* master; and he who is *your* master is *my* master" did she believe that she was free.[18] Baumfree still had to fight to free her other children, who remained with Dumont, and even took him to court to achieve that end. (See Documents: Slavery's Children, pp. 190–93.)

Gradual emancipation laws gave northern slaveholders many years to devise ways to sell their slaves out of state rather than set them free. Unscrupulous owners sold thousands of black northerners illegally in the South. Northern blacks resisted such sales and sought the support of antislavery whites in recovering friends and family members who had been sold illegally. In Pennsylvania, reports of illegal slave sales helped inspire the birth of the nation's first antislavery organization, the Pennsylvania Society for Promoting the Abolition of Slavery and for the Relief of Free Negroes Unlawfully Held in Bondage. Founded in 1784, it was a white organization with a predominantly Quaker membership. White New Yorkers founded the New York Manumission Society the same year to address similar concerns. Its members protested the kidnapping of blacks, both slave and free, that took place in the years immediately following the Revolution and pushed the legislature to prevent New Yorkers from evading gradual emancipation by exporting their slaves. But such practices were difficult to police.

Over time, however, the illegal sale and exportation of northern slaves ended along with slavery itself. Although some slave owners managed to evade gradual emancipation, northern emancipation statutes also provided many of the region's slaves with unprecedented opportunities for negotiation. Slave owners were most willing to offer early emancipation to very young and very old slaves, who were their least profitable workers, but eventually they had to free all their slaves and were sometimes willing to free them early. The region was home to almost 50,000 slaves in 1770, but that number declined rapidly thereafter. By 1820, fewer than 20,000 slaves, most of whom lived in New York and New Jersey, remained in the North. By 1840, the North was home to a little over 1,000 slaves.

Free Black Life in the New Republic

As northern blacks achieved emancipation, free black communities took shape across the region. Whereas free blacks in the North never numbered more than a few thousand during the colonial era, by 1810 there were 50,000 of them. That number doubled by 1820 and reached 170,728 in 1840. Most were located in port cities, which had long had large black communities even during the colonial era. No longer bound to rural masters, the ex-slave population congregated in major northern cities such as New York, Philadelphia, and Boston, all of which also attracted fugitive slaves. City life offered safety in numbers to escaped slaves and held significant advantages, such as greater opportunities for independence and employment, for free blacks as well. With their new freedom, African Americans sought to build their own households and sustain larger black communities that could support churches, schools, and social organizations.

Free Black Organizations

Black life in the larger northern cities was not without promise for ambitious ex-slaves such as Absalom Jones and Richard Allen of Philadelphia. Both were born in Delaware, a state where slavery declined to very low levels after the Revolution but was never formally abolished. The two men, both Methodist converts owned by evangelical masters who allowed them to purchase their freedom in the early 1780s, met in Philadelphia and became lifelong friends and allies. They also prospered in business: Jones was a shoemaker, and Allen owned a chimney-sweeping business. They became prominent members of Philadelphia's rapidly growing free black community and founded the city's first black **mutual aid society** in 1787. Members of the Free African Society pledged to support one another "in sickness and for benefit of their widows and fatherless children."[19]

The Free African Society was one of several similar free black organizations established during the late eighteenth and early nineteenth centuries. Others included Providence, Rhode Island's African Union Society, established in 1780; the Brown Fellowship Society of Charleston, South Carolina, founded in 1790; Boston's African Society, organized in 1796; New York's African Society for Mutual Relief, established in 1808; and the Resolute Beneficial Society of Washington, D.C., founded in 1818. All of these organizations were funded by dues and other fees collected from their members, which they used to provide a social safety net for their community. The specific benefits offered varied by organization, but they typically included sickness and disability benefits, burial insurance, and pensions to widows and orphans. Mutual aid societies also helped free blacks establish other institutions that proved crucial to their community's well-being. Most notable among these were black churches.

Although many early members of the black mutual aid societies initially belonged to white churches, they often ended up establishing their own—a move usually inspired by the prejudices they encountered. Richard Allen, Absalom Jones, and other early members of Philadelphia's Free African Society, for example, attended St. George's Methodist Church. Allen, who was a gifted preacher, even led special services for African Americans there. But as Allen's sermons drew more black worshippers to St. George's, these congregants became increasingly unwelcome. White leaders began to segregate them, asking them first to sit along the walls, then moving them to seats in the balcony. "You must not kneel here," a church trustee told Absalom Jones when he and several others defied this segregated seating plan, claiming seats on the first floor and kneeling to join the rest of the congregation in prayer one Sunday morning in 1792.[20] Heads still bowed, Jones and his followers refused to move until the prayer was over, at which point the trustee summoned several white men to help him force the

Bethel AME Church
Black churches such as the Bethel AME Church in Philadelphia provided far more than church services. They met a variety of needs for their communities and congregations, also serving as schools, meetinghouses, clubhouses, lecture halls, and sites for social and political gatherings. Black churches flourished in northern cities during the early nineteenth century, serving both African Americans who were already well established and the recently arrived migrants and newly freed slaves who came in need of education, work, and community support.
Schomburg Center, NYPL/Art Resource, NY.

Bethel A. M. E. Church, the first Colored Methodist Church in Philadelphia, Established in 1787

black congregants to the balcony. Disgusted, St. George's black members got up and walked out of the church.

"We never entered it again!" remembered Allen, who had been soliciting funds for the creation of a separate black church in Philadelphia even before the walkout.[21] The group worshipped in a rented storefront until July 29, 1794, when the African Methodist Episcopal (AME) Church—led by Allen and later renamed the Bethel AME Church—finally opened its doors. Bethel AME joined several other black Methodist churches to form an independent AME denomination in 1816, at which point the new denomination's congregants elected Allen to serve as the AME's first bishop. But not all African Americans who had attended St. George's joined Bethel AME. Some abandoned Methodism altogether, registering a permanent protest against the segregationist policies of white Methodists. Among them was Absalom Jones, who with help from Allen and other members of the Free African Society founded the African Episcopal Church of St. Thomas, the nation's first African American Episcopal church, and became an ordained Episcopal minister in 1804.

Black churches, mostly Methodist or Baptist, proliferated in other cities as well during the early 1800s. Many were funded and built with help from black mutual aid societies, with which they often remained closely affiliated. Boston's first black Baptist church, the African Meeting House, was founded in 1805 with the help of Boston's African Benevolent Society and the city's oldest black fraternal order, the Prince Hall Masonic Lodge. Early black churches hosted mutual aid society meetings, public lectures, protest meetings, and other gatherings and served the needs of newly freed men and women who came in search of educational opportunities and economic assistance as well as Sunday services. Virtually all early black churches also served as schools at various points in their history. Richard Allen founded the nation's first black Sunday school in his church in 1795, and he opened a night school for adults a few years later. Meanwhile, the African Union Society of Providence built its African Union Meeting House in 1821 to serve as both a school and a Baptist church.

Free Black Education and Employment

Black northerners emerged from slavery eager to support themselves, and the difficulties they often faced in finding work made them doubly anxious to educate their children. The gradual emancipation acts passed in Pennsylvania, Connecticut, Rhode Island, New York, and New Jersey freed slaves only after they had devoted many of their most productive years to working without pay or any opportunity to educate themselves or acquire property. In an era when most people started working in their teens and did not live much past forty, these ex-slaves began their lives as free adults far poorer than even the poor whites beside whom they often worked. Some ex-slaves became destitute and swelled the rolls of northern poorhouses.

Even young and healthy free blacks had great difficulty finding anything but low-paying menial jobs. Whereas slaves had once been used in a variety of occupations, the slow progress of gradual emancipation allowed former slave owners and working-class whites time to craft racially discriminatory statutes and practices designed to keep blacks at the bottom of the northern labor market. As slaves, black northerners had not competed directly with white workers for paying jobs. Now white workers saw them as a threat. Many whites were unwilling to work alongside blacks, and many white employers were reluctant to hire former slaves for anything other than menial labor, so even highly skilled ex-slaves had difficulty securing well-paying jobs. Instead, free blacks were welcome only in service trades that were closely associated with slavery. Black women worked as washerwomen, seamstresses, and cooks, while black men were employed as laborers, mariners, barbers, coachmen, porters, and bootblacks. Northern whites were quick to blame free blacks' poverty and low occupational status on inherent racial inferiority rather than social forces, which only compounded the discrimination that free blacks faced.

Still, black northerners remained hopeful that education would improve the status of their race and help their children to succeed in life, and they worked hard to create educational opportunities for their offspring. Most northern municipalities did not

The New York African Free School

The New York African Free School, established in 1787 by the New York Manumission Society, began as a one-room schoolhouse with forty students, most of whose parents were slaves. In 1835, it was incorporated into the New York City public school system. The African Free School had by then graduated more than fourteen hundred students, many of whom went on to achieve distinction in a variety of professions and to advance the cause of abolitionism. The building depicted here is most likely the replacement for the original schoolhouse, which was destroyed in a fire in 1814. *Drawing of the exterior of the New York African Free School with Penmanship.* Manuscripts Penmanship and Drawing Book, *AFS, 1822, vol. 4, p. 6, negative #59134/Collection of the New-York Historical Society.*

have public schools until the 1830s, however, and the ones that existed were not always welcoming to black children. Boston established a public school system as early as the 1790s, but the African Americans who attended were treated poorly. The black minister Hosea Easton, who attended school in Boston in the early 1800s, later recalled his teachers' blatant racism. Pupils who misbehaved, black or white, were banished to the "nigger seat," while those who did not complete their lessons were deemed as "poor and ignorant as a nigger" or as "having no more credit than a nigger." According to Easton, this training had a "disastrous [effect] upon the minds of a community having been instructed from youth to look upon the black man in no other light but as a slave." It also drove black parents in Boston to establish their own African School in 1798.[22]

In Philadelphia, African Americans who wished to educate their children faced different obstacles. The city had no public schools prior to 1818, and although the Pennsylvania Antislavery Society (PAS), a white philanthropic organization, founded a private school for black children at the beginning of the nineteenth century, many parents could not afford to pay the tuition. The fact that PAS leaders decided not to fund schools taught by black teachers—withdrawing the support they had once provided to Richard Allen's church—may have alienated black parents as well, and many continued to send their children to Allen's church to be educated.

In New York, the New York Manumission Society (NYMS) established the New York African Free School in 1787, creating perhaps the most successful early black school established by white reformers. Its distinguished graduates included Ira Aldridge, who became a renowned black actor, and James McCune Smith, the first African American to receive a medical degree. But the NYMS's ideas about education were not always in accord with those of black parents and teachers, and they highlighted the divisions separating early-nineteenth-century blacks from their white allies.

The NYMS, an exclusively white organization founded by some of New York's wealthiest men, had relatively modest antislavery goals. It supported the education and careful supervision of New York's free black population in the hope of fostering public support for abolition. The organization's members resolved to "keep a watchful eye over the conduct of such Negroes as have been or may be liberated; and . . . to prevent them from running into immorality or sinking into idleness." In 1788, they even established the Committee for Preventing Irregular Conduct Among Free Negroes. The New York African Free School set similar goals for both its pupils and their parents, to the point where school administrators reserved the right to place former pupils in jobs or apprenticeships rather than letting them "waste their time in idleness . . . [or] mingle in bad company" once they left school.[23]

Even in cities with black schools, securing an education remained a challenge. These schools were chronically underfunded and short of books and supplies. In addition, not all black parents could afford to send their children to school. Many black youngsters had to work to support their families, while others stayed home because their parents had no money for school clothing or shoes.

Education was a double-edged sword even for those black northerners lucky enough to attend school. Subject to the same racial prejudices as other African Americans, educated blacks were shut out of most jobs, both skilled and unskilled. "What are my prospects?" the valedictorian of the New York African Free School's class of 1819 asked rhetorically when he addressed his fellow classmates. "Shall I be a mechanic? No one will employ me; white boys won't work with me. Shall I be a merchant? No one will have me in his office; white clerks won't associate with me."[24] But education would nevertheless be crucial. During the early decades of the nineteenth century, black schools educated important black leaders whose speeches and publications helped sustain their community's struggle for abolition and civil rights. (See Documents: Free Black Activism, pp. 194–98.)

White Hostility

Ironically, African Americans faced more rather than less racial hostility as they moved from slavery to freedom. Many whites continued to see blacks as an economic threat and a social menace. Emancipated blacks, concentrated in urban areas and often impoverished, formed a highly visible underclass in northern cities, where they performed much of the noisiest, dirtiest work. White New Yorkers complained that the "army of black sweeps" left the city filled with dust, that black street vendors were the source of New York's most hideous and outlandish crimes, and that the black tubmen who emptied New York's privies left the houses they passed "filled with stinking stench."[25] Even the activities of more prosperous blacks made many northern whites nervous. Blacks' establishment of their own institutions, as well as the public events they staged to celebrate emancipation, suggested that blacks were beginning to succeed in raising their social status. Consequently, whites regarded free blacks with alarm and subjected them to relentless hostility, mockery, and violence.

Blacks met "daily insults . . . in the streets of Boston," the Revolutionary War veteran Prince Hall complained in 1797. These only escalated on "public days of recreation," when drunken white ruffians celebrated special occasions such as Independence Day by beating black men and stripping "helpless old women."[26] Such actions finally forced African Americans to move their own Independence Day celebrations from July 4 to July 5. Racial violence increased over time, as early-nineteenth-century white troublemakers and mobs began targeting black institutions, disrupting services at black churches, and sometimes even attacking black congregations. They also began to mock emancipation itself. Racist broadsides made fun of black gatherings to commemorate

Racism and White Hostility

Like many other racist broadsides that appeared in the early nineteenth century, *Dreadful Riot on Negro Hill!* parodies free blacks' speech, activities, and attempts to achieve success in the North. This document, which is billed as a "copy of an intercepted letter from PHILLIS, to her sister in the country," describes a riot in a black urban neighborhood. The text, written in unflattering poetic verse, and the name "Phillis" (which appeared in a number of broadsides), are meant to mock the poet Phillis Wheatley. Consider this image alongside the engraving of Wheatley in chapter 3 (p. 118). How does this portrayal speak to that one? *1827 broadside/Library of Congress LC-USZ62-34025.*

the abolition of slavery by calling these events **Bobalition** (a deliberate garbling of *abolition*) celebrations. (See Visual Sources: The Black Body in Early American Culture, pp. 199–207.)

Northern free blacks and their white allies did not always agree on how best to combat growing prejudice and the persistence of slavery elsewhere in the nation. Members of early white antislavery organizations such as the PAS and NYMS, convinced that prejudice could only be addressed by reforming African Americans, sponsored schools dedicated to young blacks' moral and religious education and urged African Americans to avoid any behavior that might offend whites. Moreover, these white reformers remained cautious about challenging other Americans' property rights and condemned slavery without calling for slaveholders to free their slaves. Instead, they supported the United States' withdrawal from the international slave trade and gradual emancipation within their home states.

By contrast, as early as 1797, black activists appealed to Congress to end what one petition called slavery's "unconstitutional bondage." (See From the Record: Free Black Petition to Congress.) African American leaders parted company with white antislavery reformers in identifying white racism as one of the greatest obstacles facing the antislavery movement. Richard Allen and Absalom Jones addressed this in a 1794 protest pamphlet, condemning the racist arguments that whites used to justify slavery. "Will you . . . plead our incapacity for freedom, and our contented condition under oppression, as sufficient cause for keeping us under the grievous yoke?" they asked.[27]

By the beginning of the nineteenth century, black leaders had reason to fear that racism would undermine black freedom even in the North. As the egalitarian spirit of

From the Record

Absalom Jones | Free Black Petition to Congress, 1797

In 1788, North Carolina passed a law permitting the recapture and reenslavement of free blacks who had been manumitted without court approval. The law forced ex-slaves whose former owners had not consulted the courts to flee to a free state for safety. In 1797, four North Carolina exiles who had settled in Philadelphia submitted a petition to the U.S. Congress protesting their exile. Written for Jupiter Nicholson, Jacob Nicholson, Joe Albert, and Thomas Pritchet by the African American abolitionist and clergyman **Absalom Jones (1746–1818)**, the petition also protested slavery itself.

The Petition and Representation of the under-named Freemen, respectfully showeth:

That, being of African descent, late inhabitants and natives of North Carolina, to you only, under God, can we apply with any hope of effect, for redress of our grievances, having been compelled to leave the State wherein we had a right of residence, as freemen liberated under the hand and seal of humane and conscientious masters, the validity of which act of justice, in restoring us to our native right of freedom, was confirmed by judgment of the Superior Court of North Carolina, wherein it was brought to trial; yet, not long after this decision, a law of that State was enacted, under which men of cruel disposition, and void of just principle, received countenance and authority in violently seizing, imprisoning, and selling into slavery, such as had been so emancipated; whereby we were reduced to the necessity of separating from some of our nearest and most tender connexions, and of seeking refuge in such parts of the Union where more regard is paid to the public declaration in favor of liberty and the common right of men, several hundreds, under our circumstances, having, in consequence of the said law, been hunted day and night, like beasts of the forest, by armed men with dogs, and made a prey of as free and lawful plunder. . . .

If, notwithstanding all that has been publicly avowed as essential principles respecting the extent of human right to freedom; notwithstanding we have had that right restored to us, so far as was in the power of those by whom we were held as slaves, we cannot claim the privilege of representation in your councils, yet we trust we may address you as fellow-men, who, under God, the sovereign Ruler of the Universe, are intrusted with the distribution of justice, . . . who can admit that black people (servile as their condition generally is throughout this Continent) have natural affections, social and domestic attachments and sensibilities; and that, therefore, we may hope for a share in your sympathetic attention while we represent that the unconstitutional bondage in which multitudes of our fellows in complexion are held, is to us a subject sorrowfully affecting. . . . We are far from considering all those who retain slaves as wilful oppressors, being well assured that numbers in the State from whence we are exiles, hold their slaves in bondage, not of choice, but possessing them by inheritance, feel their minds burdened

Continued

Continued

under the slavish restraint of legal impediments to doing that justice which they are convinced is due to fellow-rationals. May we not be allowed to consider this stretch of power, morally and politically, a Governmental defect, if not a direct violation of the declared fundamental principles of the Constitution; and finally, is not some remedy for an evil of such magnitude highly worthy of the deep inquiry and unfeigned zeal of the supreme Legislative body of a free and enlightened people?

Source: *Annals of the Congress of the United States,* 4th Cong., 2nd sess. [March 1795–March 1797] (Washington, DC: Gales and Seator, 1849), 6:2015–2018.

???   **What arguments do the petitioners present to explain why the government should be interested in their plight?**

the Revolutionary era waned, African American civil rights contracted. Black soldiers served in the War of 1812 (a conflict in which Britain opposed U.S. expansion into British and Indian lands in the Northwest and the United States fought against British trade restrictions and the forcible enrollment of American sailors into the British Royal Navy) and hoped their patriotism would help them win full citizenship. But even after black troops helped American forces fortify Philadelphia, defend New York, and win the Battle of New Orleans, their civil rights continued to erode. New Jersey blacks lost the right to vote in 1807, even before the war. Blacks also were disfranchised in Connecticut in 1814 and Pennsylvania in 1838. Even in states where free blacks retained the franchise, they faced voter discrimination. New York, for example, imposed prohibitively high property requirements on black voters, even after abolishing all such requirements for white voters in 1821.

The Colonization Debate

Given the abiding prejudices facing African Americans during the post-Revolutionary era, some members of both races began to question blacks' long-term prospects for success in the United States. Blacks occasionally contemplated abandoning the United States altogether, fearing that they would never achieve full citizenship. Some whites expressed great enthusiasm for their departure, proposing **colonization** schemes designed to send African Americans back to Africa.

During the late eighteenth century, when many blacks were still relatively recent arrivals, some were eager to return to the land of their ancestors. In 1787, a group of Massachusetts blacks petitioned the state legislature to help them migrate to Africa. They asked for help in raising money to "procure lands to settle upon; and to obtain a passage for us and our families."[28] Their petition was never answered, but the idea resurfaced in 1815, when a wealthy black businessman and ship captain named Paul Cuffe, or Cuffee, took thirty-eight black Bostonians to the West African colony of Sierra Leone.

Sierra Leone, founded in 1787 by the British reformer Granville Sharp as a refuge for some of London's black poor, was also home to approximately twelve hundred black loyalists from Nova Scotia, many of whom had fled slavery in the United States.

PAUL CUFFE   CAPTAIN

1812.

From a Drawing by John Pole, M. D. of Bristol, Eng.

The Colonization Movement

Born free to a West African father and a Native American mother, Paul Cuffe grew up to become one of the richest African Americans of his day. After working aboard whaling ships, he rose to the position of captain and eventually acquired a small fleet. This 1812 engraving depicts his planned conveyance of a group of emigrants to Sierra Leone. Cuffe's silhouette looms large over the lush, tranquil shores, where Africans play music and wait in welcome for the approaching ship. What does this image reveal about early black colonizationists' hopes for their endeavor? *1812 engraving/Library of Congress LC-USZ62-26174.*

Although the main intent of the colony was the repatriation of former slaves to West Africa, it was of interest to Cuffe because his father, Cuffe Slocum, had been born in West Africa. After visiting Sierra Leone in 1811, Cuffe began to consider taking "to Africa some Sober Stedy habited peopel of Colour in order to incourage Sobriety and industry and to interduce culteriantion and Commersce."[29] Cuffe knew a number of African-born men and women who wished to return to the continent, and in 1812 he began to make arrangements to transport a group of them to the colony.

Cuffe's voyage in 1815, however, was not a success. His commercial plans were foiled by British officials who refused to allow him to unload the cargo he had hoped to sell to finance the trip, leaving him $1,700 in debt. He had never planned to lead a mass movement of blacks back to Africa and vowed not to travel there again without assurances that British officials would be more cooperative in the future. He also cautioned other colonization supporters that Sierra Leone was unlikely to welcome large numbers of American expatriates. Cuffe himself never returned to Sierra Leone; he became sick in the summer of 1817 and died that fall.

Although Cuffe's expedition had the support of black leaders such as Absalom Jones, it did not foster a colonization movement among American blacks. Instead, it captured the imagination of white reformers, whose enthusiasm soon had free black communities across the North worried about a forced migration. Reform-minded whites had long "indulged a hope that . . . free people of color be removed to the coast of Africa with their own consent," the Presbyterian minister Robert Finley wrote Cuffe as he embarked on his journey, appealing to the ship captain to help him plan a mass migration.[30] With Cuffe's voyage standing as testimony to colonization's practical possibility, Finley founded a national organization to promote the colonization of free blacks.

The American Society for Colonizing the Free People of Color in the United States, more popularly known as the American Colonization Society (ACS), first met in Washington, D.C., in 1816. Made up of prominent white clergymen, lawyers, financiers, and politicians—including Speaker of the House Henry Clay—the ACS appealed to both slaveholders and those opposed to slavery. Although Finley hoped colonization would eventually bring an end to slavery, the ACS planned to colonize free blacks only. Its members agreed to avoid the "delicate question" of emancipation, instead assuring southerners that colonization would help secure their slave property by ridding the region of free blacks.[31] Meanwhile, antislavery advocates believed that colonization would facilitate manumissions, allowing planters to free their slaves without enlarging the region's already unpopular free black population or violating the states' manumission laws. By 1819, the ACS's influential white supporters included President James Monroe, who helped the organization secure a congressional appropriation of $100,000 for its cause. In 1821, the ACS used the money to establish the colony of Liberia on the west coast of Africa and to recruit potential migrants.

Most of the blacks the ACS shipped to Liberia were former slaves liberated by the organization in order to allow their emigration. Although the ACS was eager to recruit free blacks, most were both unwilling to move and deeply suspicious. Less than a month after the first ACS meeting in 1816, three thousand free blacks gathered in Richard Allen's Philadelphia church to adopt a set of resolutions denouncing colonization as an "unmerited stigma attempted to be cast upon the reputation of the free people of color." Many were American-born blacks with few ties to Africa, and many suspected that colonization was merely a plan to prop up slavery by shipping America's free blacks out of the United States. They issued a statement saying, "We will never separate ourselves voluntarily from the slave population of the country." Although the black leader James Forten, who presided over the meeting and recorded these resolutions, had previously supported Cuffe's voyage to Sierra Leone on the grounds that black Americans might "never become a people untill they com[e] out from amongst the white people," black Philadelphians' mass opposition to the ACS changed his mind.[32]

Most African Americans remained suspicious of colonization throughout the antebellum era. But white enthusiasm for the idea did not depend on black support, so the American Colonization Society continued to attract white members.

CONCLUSION

African American Freedom in Black and White

Faced with the threat of forced removal, northern free blacks saw the idea of colonization as an assault on their community. Like Benjamin Banneker several decades earlier, they were convinced that African Americans were entitled to the rights and freedoms that Americans had defended during the Revolution, and they believed that immediate emancipation was the only way to end slavery in the United States.

After 1817, northern free blacks drew on the network of mutual aid societies and churches they had founded as they fought their way out of slavery. The anticolonization campaign that they mounted linked the future of all African Americans, both slave and free, to a freedom struggle that would not end until slavery was abolished throughout the United States. Laying new and stronger claims to the United States as "the land of our nativity," northern blacks drew on their own recent history to insist that slavery could be defeated. "Every year, many of us have restored to us by the gradual, but certain march of the cause of abolition—Parents from whom we have long been separated—Wives and Children whom we had left in servitude—and Brothers, in blood as well as in early sufferings, from whom we had long been parted," Philadelphia's anticolonization blacks maintained.[33]

The new Republic's black southerners, by contrast, had much less cause for optimism. Although free black communities expanded in some parts of the South during the nation's early decades, slavery experienced more spectacular gains with the growth of plantation agriculture. Slavery was protected by federal laws mandating the return of fugitive slaves and sanctioned in the Constitution, which gave slaveholders additional political representation under the three-fifths clause. With the acquisition of Louisiana from France, the United States further guaranteed slavery's institutional strength by acquiring vast new territories that would soon become home to slaveholding settlers. As slavery's cotton frontier expanded into Louisiana, Mississippi, and Alabama during the first half of the nineteenth century, the expansion of plantation agriculture brought wealth and power to the region's slaveholders and tremendous anguish to the slaves. Once the United States ceased importing slaves from Africa in 1808, most of the slaves who cleared the land and cultivated the crops in these new states were American-born. The majority hailed from the Chesapeake or the northern states and had to leave behind families, friends, and neighbors as they embarked on the forced migration to plantations in the deep South.

CHAPTER REVIEW

Online Study Guide ▪ bedfordstmartins.com/graywhite

Key Terms

cash crops (p. 163)

Northwest Ordinance (1787) (p. 163)

fugitive slave clause (p. 163)

Three-Fifths Compromise (p. 164)

Louisiana Purchase (1803) (p. 171)

hiring out (p. 174)

living out (p. 174)

black laws (p. 177)

Naturalization Act of 1790 (p. 177)

mutual aid society (p. 179)

Bobalition (p. 184)

colonization (p. 186)

Review Questions

1. Describe the fate of slavery in the post-Revolutionary years and the various factors—political, social, and economic—that contributed to this state of affairs. Would it have been possible to predict in 1783 that things would turn out this way? Why or why not? How might things have been different if political, social, or economic circumstances had been different?

2. Describe the various freedoms allowed, and the restrictions placed on, urban slaves, southern free blacks, northern slaves, and newly emancipated northern free blacks. What limits to their freedom and mobility did each group experience? Which groups were the most and the least restricted and why?

3. Why did whites grow increasingly hostile toward African Americans as they moved from slavery to freedom? How did the proliferation of free black organizations help African Americans combat this hostility?

4. How did the colonization effort change from a small, black-led initiative to a large, white-led movement? What initial appeal did colonization have for its black supporters? How was this different from the appeal it held for whites, both slaveholders and abolitionists?

For Web sites, images, and documents related to topics and places in this chapter, visit **Make History** at bedfordstmartins.com/graywhite.

Slavery's Children

The gradual emancipation laws passed in several northern states kept slave-born children in bondage well into adulthood and left them vulnerable to resale and separation from their parents. Slave children in the South had still less hope of freedom. Southern manumission laws discouraged even the slave owning fathers of mixed-race children from emancipating their progeny by requiring all manu-mitted blacks to leave the state immediately.

These two accounts tell the stories of two slave children who eventually achieved freedom. Six-year-old Peter Baumfree, who was the son of Isabella Baumfree (later renamed Sojourner Truth) and her husband, Robert, was illegally sold into slavery in Alabama by Baumfree's former master. He gained his freedom only through his mother's perseverance and determination. Madison Hemings, who was the son of Thomas Jefferson and his slave maid Sally Hemings, grew up in Jefferson's Monticello slave quarters. Though well treated by Jefferson, Hemings notes that Jefferson "was not in the habit of showing partiality or fatherly affection" to him. He was freed by Jefferson's will at age twenty-one.

Sojourner Truth | A Former Slave's Fight to Free Her Son, 1850

Though entitled to freedom at age twenty-one under New York's gradual emancipation law, Isabella Baumfree's son Peter ended up in Alabama after her former owner, John Dumont, sold the boy to his brother, who shipped him out of state. He might well have remained enslaved there all his life but for his mother's battle to free him. Following is a passage from the *Narrative of Sojourner Truth*, which **Isabella Baumfree (1797–1883)**, who changed her name to Sojourner Truth in 1843, dictated to Olive Gilbert in 1850. In discussing Truth's life prior to her name change, Gilbert refers to her as Isabella or Isabel Baumfree. What does Baumfree's story reveal about the relationships between slaves and slaveholders?

When Isabella heard that her son had been sold South, she immediately started on foot and alone, to find the man who had thus dared, in the face of all law, human and divine, to sell her child out of the State; and if possible, to bring him to account for the deed.

Source: Sojourner Truth, *Narrative of Sojourner Truth*, ed. Olive Gilbert (Boston: printed for author, 1850), 44–45, 50, 53–54.

Arriving at New Paltz, she went directly to her former mistress, Dumont, complaining bitterly of the removal of her son. Her mistress heard her through, and then replied—"*Ugh! a fine* fuss to make about a little *nigger!* Why, haven't you as many of 'em left as you can see to, and take care of? A pity 'tis, the niggers are not all in Guinea!! Making such a halloo-balloo about the neighborhood; and all for a paltry nigger!!!" Isabella heard her through, and after a moment's hesitation, answered, in tones of deep determination—"*I'll have my child again.*" "Have *your child* again!" repeated her mistress—her tones big with contempt, and scorning the absurd idea of her getting him. "How can you get him? And what have you to support him with, if you could? Have you any money?" "No," answered [Isa]Bell, "I have no money, but God has enough, or what's better! And I'll have my child again." These words were pronounced in the most slow, solemn and determined measure and manner. And in speaking of it, she says, "Oh my God! I know'd I'd have him agin. I was sure God would help me to get him. Why, I felt so *tall within*—I felt as if the *power of a nation* was with me!" . . .

[Isabella sought assistance from the Quakers, who helped her to file a legal complaint that forced Dumont's brother to return Peter from Alabama. On Peter's return six months later, Isabella was told that she'd have to wait several more months until the next court session to complete her case.]

"What! wait another court! wait *months?*" said the persevering mother. "Why, long before that time, he can go clear off, and take my child with him—no one knows where. I *cannot* wait; I *must* have him *now*, whilst he is to be had." "Well," said the lawyer, very coolly, "if he puts the boy out of the way, he must pay the $600—one half of which will be yours"; supposing, perhaps, that $300 would pay for a "heap of children," in the eye of a slave who never, in all her life, called a dollar her own. But in this instance, he was mistaken in his reckoning. She assured him, that she had not been seeking money, neither would money satisfy her, it was her son, and her son alone she wanted, and her son she must have. Neither could she wait court, not she. The lawyer used his every argument to convince her, that she ought to be very thankful for what they [the court and her lawyer] had done for her . . . [and] she should now wait patiently the time of the court. . . .

[Unwilling to do so, Isabella found a lawyer to expedite her case and successfully appealed to her Quaker friends to pay him. She was reunited with Peter less than twenty-four hours later. To Isabella's dismay, however, her son refused to acknowledge her.]

. . . At sight of her the boy cried aloud, and regarded her as some terrible being, who was about to take him away from a kind and loving friend. He knelt, even, and begged them, with tears, not to take him away from his dear master, who had brought him from the dreadful South, and been so kind to him.

When he was questioned relative to the bad scar on his forehead, he said, "Fowler's horse hove [me]." And of the one on his cheek, "That was done by running against the carriage." In answering these questions, he looked imploringly at his master, as much as to say, "If they are falsehoods, you bade me say them; may they be satisfactory to you, at least."

The justice, noting his appearance, bade him forget his master and attend only to him. But the boy persisted in denying his mother, and clinging to his master, saying his mother did not live in such a place as that. However, they allowed the mother to identify her son; and Esquire Demain [Baumfree's lawyer] pleaded that he claimed the boy for her, on the ground that he had been sold out of the State, contrary to the laws in such cases made and provided—spoke of the penalties annexed to said crime, and of the sum of money the delinquent was to pay, in case any one chose to prosecute him for the offence he had committed. Isabella, who was sitting in a corner, scarcely daring to breathe, thought within herself, "If I can but get the boy, the $200 may remain for whoever else chooses to prosecute—*I* have done enough to make myself enemies already"—and she trembled at the thought of the formidable enemies she had probably arrayed against herself helpless and despised as she was. When the pleading was at an end, Isabella understood the Judge to declare, as the sentence of the Court, that the "boy be delivered into the hands of the mother—having no other master, no other controller, no other conductor, but his mother." This sentence was obeyed; he was delivered into her hands, the boy meanwhile begging, most piteously, *not* to be taken from his dear master, saying she was not his mother, and that his mother did not live in such a place as that. And it was some time before lawyer Demain, the clerks, and Isabella, could collectively succeed in calming the child's fears, and in convincing him that Isabella was not some terrible monster, as he had for the last months, probably, been trained to believe; and who, in taking him away from his master, was taking him from all good, and consigning him to all evil.

documents

Madison Hemings | Life among the Lowly, 1873

The son of Thomas Jefferson and Sally Hemings, **Madison Hemings (1805–1877)** grew up on Jefferson's Monticello estate. When Jefferson died in 1826, he freed Madison and his brother Eston in his will. The brothers were allowed to stay in Virginia as a result of a petition to the legislature that Jefferson submitted before his death, and they remained there until their mother died in 1835. The Hemings children were descended from slave owners on their mother's side as well. Sally Hemings was fathered by John Wayles, Jefferson's father-in-law—which made her Jefferson's wife Martha's half sister and made Wayles her children's paternal grandfather. In 1873, Madison Hemings shared his family history with S. F. Wetmore, a reporter for Ohio's *Pike County Republican*.

Elizabeth Hemings [Madison's grandmother] grew to womanhood in the family of John Wales [*sic*], whose wife dying she (Elizabeth) was taken by the widower Wales as his concubine, by whom she had six children—three sons and three daughters, viz: Robert, James, Peter, Critty, Sally and Thena. These children went by the name of Hemings.

Williamsburg was the capital of Virginia, and of course it was an aristocratic place, where the "bloods" of the Colony and the new State most did congregate. Thomas Jefferson, the author of the Declaration of Independence, was educated at William and Mary College, which had its seat at Williamsburg. He afterwards studied law with Geo. Wythe, and practiced law at the bar of the general court of the Colony. He was afterwards elected a member of the provincial legislature from Albemarle county. Thos. Jefferson was a visitor at the "great house" of John Wales, who had children about his own age. He formed the acquaintance of his daughter Martha (I believe that was her name, though I am not positively sure,) and an intimacy sprang up between them which ripened into love,

and they were married. They afterwards went to live at his country seat, Monticello, and in course of time had born to them a daughter whom they named Martha. About the time she was born my mother, the second daughter of John Wales and Elizabeth Hemings was born. On the death of John Wales, my grandmother, his concubine, and her children by him fell to Martha, Thomas Jefferson's wife, and consequently became the property of Thomas Jefferson, who in the course of time became famous, and was appointed minister to France during our revolutionary troubles, or soon after independence was gained. About the time of the appointment and before he was ready to leave the country his wife died, and as soon after her interment as he could attend to and arrange his domestic affairs in accordance with the changed circumstances of his family in consequence of this misfortune (I think not more than three weeks thereafter) he left for France, taking his eldest daughter with him. He had sons born to him, but they died in early infancy, so he then had but two children—Martha and Maria. The latter was left home, but afterwards was ordered to follow him to France. She was three years or so younger than Martha. My mother accompanied her as a body servant. When Mr. Jefferson went to France Martha was just budding into womanhood. Their stay (my mother's and Maria's) was about eighteen months. But during that time my mother became Mr. Jefferson's concubine, and when he was called back home she was *enceinte* [pregnant] by him. He desired to bring my mother back to Virginia with him but she demurred. She was just beginning to understand the French language well, and in France she was free, while if she returned to Virginia she would be re-enslaved. So she refused to return with him. To induce her to do so he promised her extraordinary privileges, and made a solemn pledge that her children should be freed at the age of twenty-one years. In consequence of his promise, on which she implicitly relied, she returned with him to Virginia. Soon after their arrival, she gave birth to a child, of whom Thomas Jefferson was the father. It lived but a short time. She gave birth to four others,

SOURCE: S. F. Wetmore, "Life among the Lowly, No. 1," *Pike County (Ohio) Republican*, March 13, 1873.

and Jefferson was the father of all of them. Their names were Beverly, Harriet, Madison (myself), and Eston—three sons and one daughter. We all became free agreeably to the treaty entered into by our parents before we were born. We all married and have raised families.

Beverly left Monticello and went to Washington as a white man. He married a white woman in Maryland, and their only child, a daughter, was not known by the white folks to have any colored blood coursing in her veins. Beverly's wife's family were people in good circumstances.

Harriet married a white man in good standing in Washington City, whose name I could give, but will not, for prudential reasons. She raised a family of children, and so far as I know they were never suspected of being tainted with African blood in the community where she lived or lives. I have not heard from her for ten years, and do not know whether she is dead or alive. She thought it to her interest, on going to Washington, to assume the role of a white woman, and by her dress and conduct as such I am not aware that her identity as Harriet Hemings of Monticello has ever been discovered.

Eston married a colored woman in Virginia, and moved from there to Ohio, and lived in Chillicothe several years. In the fall of 1852 he removed to Wisconsin, where he died a year or two afterwards. He left three children.

As to myself, I was named Madison by the wife of James Madison, who was afterwards President of the United States. Mrs. Madison happened to be at Monticello at the time of my birth, and begged the privilege of naming me, promising my mother a fine present for the honor. She consented, and Mrs. Madison dubbed me by the name I now acknowledge, but like many promises of white folks to the slaves she never gave my mother anything. I was born at my father's seat of Monticello, in Albemarle county, Va., near Charlottesville, on the 18th day of January, 1805. My very earliest recollections are of my grandmother Elizabeth Hemings. That was when I was about three years old. She was sick and upon her death bed. I was eating a piece of bread and asked if she would have some. She replied: "No, granny don't want bread any more." She shortly afterwards breathed her last. I have only a faint recollection of her.

Of my father, Thomas Jefferson, I knew more of his domestic than his public life during his life time. It is only since his death that I have learned much of the latter, except that he was considered as a foremost man in the land, and held many important trusts, including that of President. I learned to read by inducing the white children to teach me the letters and something more; what else I know of books I have picked up here and there till now I can read and write. I was almost 21½ years of age when my father died on the 4th of July, 1826.

About his own home he was the quietest of men. . . . He was not in the habit of showing partiality or fatherly affection to us children. We were the only children of his by a slave woman. He was affectionate toward his white grandchildren, of whom he had fourteen, twelve of whom lived to manhood and womanhood.

Questions for Analysis

1. What do the childhood experiences of Peter Baumfree and Madison Hemings reveal about family ties under slavery? What kind of authority did slave parents have over slave children?

2. How did Isabella Baumfree counter and overcome the obstacles she faced? What do the white people's reactions to Baumfree reveal about their attitudes toward African Americans?

3. Did Sally Hemings's children benefit from having Thomas Jefferson as their father? Why or why not?

Free Black Activism

While the American Revolution greatly enlarged the size of the free black population, the rights that free blacks obtained were never secure. Free blacks could not testify on their own behalf in southern courts, which meant that they had no legal means to free themselves if they were abducted by slave traders, and even in northern states such as Pennsylvania, they were required to document their freedom. By the early nineteenth century, many whites had begun to embrace colonization rather than civil rights as a remedy for the discrimination that free blacks faced, forcing free blacks to fight for a place in the United States.

The following documents include a 1791 memorial in which South Carolina free blacks appealed to the state legislature to repeal discriminatory laws that made it difficult for them to find justice in the state's courts; a 1799 petition to Congress composed by the Philadelphia clergyman Absalom Jones, which protested the fact that the federal government's fugitive slave law made free blacks vulnerable to illegal enslavement; an 1813 oration commemorating the end of the slave trade; and an 1817 petition to Congress regarding colonization, issued by free blacks in Richmond. Taken together, these texts show free blacks' efforts to secure their status by expressing their views on colonization and the end of the slave trade.

Thomas Cole and Other Free Blacks | A Memorial to the South Carolina Senate, 1791

A group of freemen of color appealed to the South Carolina Senate to repeal some of the provisions against free blacks contained in the former colony's slave codes. Passed in the aftermath of the Stono rebellion, the 1740 Negro Act denied free blacks the right to trial by jury and prohibited them from testifying under oath. It also permitted slaves, who could testify under oath, to present informal testimony against free blacks. These authors called their document a "memorial," which at the time meant a written statement of facts or a petition presented to a legislative body. What arguments do the memorialists advance for their citizenship?

SOURCE: Thomas Cole and Other Free Blacks, "Petition Asking That They May Be Exempt from the Negro Act of 1740 and Enjoy Any Rights and Privileges of Free Citizens," Records of the General Assembly, Petitions, 1791, no. 181, South Carolina Department of Archives and History, Columbia.

To the Honorable David Ramsay Esquire President and to the rest of the Honorable New Members of the Senate of the State of South Carolina.

The Memorial of Thomas Cole Bricklayer, P. B. Mathews and Matthew Webb Butchers on behalf of themselves & other Free Men of Colour.

Humbly sheweth That in the Enumeration of Free Citizens by the Constitution of the United States for the purpose of Representation of the Southern States in Congress, Your Memorialists have been considered under that description as part of the Citizens of this State. Although by the Fourteenth and Twenty Ninth Clauses in an Act of Assembly made in the Year 1740 and intitled an Act for the better Ordering and Governing Negroes and other Slaves in this Province commonly called The Negroe Act now in force, Your Memorialists are deprived of the Rights and Privileges of Citizens by not having it in their power to give Testimony on Oath in prosecutions on behalf of the State from which cause many Culprits have escaped the Punishment due to their Atrocious Crimes (nor can they give their Testimony in recovering Debts due to them, or in establishing Agreements made by them within the meaning of the Statutes of Frauds and Perjuries in force in this State except in cases where Persons of Colour are concerned, whereby they are subject to great Losses and repeated Injuries without any means of redress).

That by the said Clauses in the said Act, They are debarred of the Rights of Free Citizens by being subject to a Trial without the benefit of a Jury and subject to Prosecution by testimony of Slaves without Oath by which they are placed on the same footing.

Your Memorialists shew that they have at all Times since the Independence of the United States contributed and do now contribute to the support of government by chearfully paying their Taxes proportionable to their Property with others who have been during such period, and now are in full enjoyment of The Rights and Immunities of Citizens Inhabitants of a Free Independent State.

That as your Memorialists have been and are considered as Free-Citizens of this State they hope to be treated as such. They are ready and willing to take and subscribe to such Oath of Allegiance to the States as shall be prescribed by this Honorable House, and are also willing to take upon them any duty for the preservation of the Peace in the City or any other occasion if called on.

Your Memorialists do not presume to hope that they shall be put on an equal footing with the Free White Citizens of the State in general. They only humbly solicit such indulgence as the Wisdom and Humanity of this Honorable House shall dictate in their favor by Repealing the Clauses [in] the Act beforementioned and substituting such a Clause as will effectually Redress the grievances which your Memorialists humbly submit in this their Memorial but under such restrictions as to your Honorable House shall seem proper.

May it therefore please your Honors to take your Memorialists Case into tender consideration, and make such Acts or insert such Clauses for the purpose of relieving your Memorialists from the unmeritted grievance they now Labour under as in your Wisdom shall seem meet. And as in duty bound your Memorialists will ever pray.

Absalom Jones and Others | Petition to Congress on the Fugitive Slave Act, 1799

The following petition is one of the earliest surviving free black petitions to the U.S. Congress. Written by **Absalom Jones** and signed by more than seventy others, it was submitted on December 30, 1799. Its authors contend that the Fugitive Slave Act of 1793, which was passed to enforce the Constitution's fugitive slave clause and allowed slave catchers to detain slaves and free blacks, threatened the lives and welfare of African Americans. The petitioners sought protection for free blacks abducted by slave catchers and challenged the constitutional basis of slavery. Congress ignored their appeal. How do the petitioners use the Constitution to make their argument?

SOURCE: John Parrish, *Remarks on the Slavery of the Black People* (Philadelphia: Kimber, Conrad, 1806), 49–51.

To the President, Senate, and House of Representatives.

The Petition of the People of Colour, free men, within the City and Suburbs of Philadelphia, humbly sheweth,

That, thankful to God, our Creator, and to the Government under which we live, for the blessings and benefits granted to us in the enjoyment of our natural right to liberty, and the protection of our persons and property, from the oppression and violence which so great a number of like colour and national descent are subject to, we feel ourselves bound, from a sense of these blessings, to continue in our respective allotments, and to lead honest and peaceable lives, rendering due submission unto the laws, and exciting and encouraging each other thereto, agreeable to the uniform advice of our friends, of every denomination; yet while we feel impressed with grateful sensations for the Providential favour we ourselves enjoy, we cannot be insensible of the condition of our afflicted brethren, suffering under various circumstances, in different parts of these states; but deeply sympathizing with them, are incited by a sense of social duty, and humbly conceive ourselves authorized to address and petition you on their behalf, believing them to be objects of your representation in your public councils, in common with ourselves and every other class of citizens within the jurisdiction of the United States, according to the design of the present Constitution, formed by the General Convention, and ratified in the different states, as set forth in the preamble thereto in the following words, viz. "We, the people of the United States, in order to form a more perfect union, establish justice, insure domestic tranquillity, provide for the common defence, and to secure the blessings of liberty to ourselves and posterity, do ordain, &c." We apprehend this solemn compact is violated, by a trade carried on in a clandestine manner, to the coast of Guinea, and another equally wicked, practised openly by citizens of some of the southern states, upon the waters of Maryland and Delaware; men sufficiently callous to qualify them for the brutal purpose, are employed in kidnapping those of our brethren that are free, and purchasing others of such as claim a property in them: thus, those poor helpless victims, like droves of cattle, are seized, fettered, and hurried into places provided for this most horrid traffic, such as dark cellars and garrets, as is notorious at Northwest-fork, Chestertown, Eastown, and divers other places. After a sufficient number is obtained, they are forced on board vessels, crouded under hatches, without the least commiseration, left to deplore the sad separation of the dearest ties in nature, husband from wife, and parents from children; thus packed together, they are transported to Georgia and other places, and there inhumanly exposed to sale. Can any commerce, trade, or transaction, so detestably shock the feeling of man, or degrade the dignity of his nature

equal to this? And how increasingly is the evil aggravated, when practised in a land high in profession of the benign doctrines of our Blessed Lord, who taught his followers to do unto others as they would they should do unto them. Your petitioners desire not to enlarge, though volumes might be filled with the sufferings of this grossly abused part of the human species, seven hundred thousand of whom, it is said, are now in unconditional bondage in these states: but conscious of the rectitude of our motives in a concern so nearly affecting us, and so effectually interesting to the welfare of this country, we cannot but address you as guardians of our rights, and patrons of equal and national liberties, hoping you will view the subject in an impartial, unprejudiced light. We do not ask for an immediate emancipation of all, knowing that the degraded state of many, and their want of education, would greatly disqualify for such a change; yet, humbly desire you may exert every means in your power to undo the heavy burdens, and prepare the way for the oppressed to go free, that every yoke may be broken. The law not long since enacted by Congress, called the Fugitive Bill, is in its execution found to be attended with circumstances peculiarly hard and distressing; for many of our afflicted brethren, in order to avoid the barbarities wantonly exercised upon them, or through fear of being carried off by those menstealers, being forced to seek refuge by flight, they are then, by armed men, under colour of this law, cruelly treated, or brought back in chains to those that have no claim upon them. In the Constitution and the Fugitive Bill, no mention is made of black people, or slaves; therefore, if the Bill of Rights, or the Declaration of Congress are of any validity, we beseech, that as we are men, we may be admitted to partake of the liberties and unalienable rights therein held forth; firmly believing that the extending of justice and equity to all classes, would be a means of drawing down the blessing of Heaven upon this land, for the peace and prosperity of which, and the real happiness of every member of the community, we fervently pray.

George Lawrence | Oration on the Abolition of the Slave Trade, 1813

The abolition of the international slave trade on January 1, 1808, was commemorated annually by early-nineteenth-century black northerners. Speakers typically deplored the abuses of the trade and celebrated its abolition, while also discussing the ongoing problems that African Americans still faced. **George Lawrence** presented the following oration at the African Methodist Episcopal Church in New York City on January 1, 1813. Nothing further is known about Lawrence, who gave no other recorded speeches.

We now celebrate the fifth anniversary of the Abolition of the Slave Trade, and a partial restoration of one of those rights most congenial to the human heart. . . . We rejoice for the abolition of the slave trade; and our joy overflows when we reflect that this heaven born plant shall bring forth the full fruits of emancipation, and divulge that bright genius so long smothered in slavery. . . .

My brethren, the land in which we live gives us the opportunity rapidly to advance the prosperity of liberty. This government founded on the principles of liberty and equality, and declaring them to be the free gift of God, if not ignorant of their declaration, must enforce it; I am confident she wills it, and strong forbodings of it is discernable. The northern sections of the union is fast conceding, and the southern must comply, although so biased by interest, that they have become callous to the voice of reason and justice; yet as the continual droppings of water has a tendency to wear away the hardest and most flinty substance, so likewise shall we, abounding in good works, and causing our examples to shine forth as the sun at noon day, melt their callous hearts, and render sinewless the arm of sore oppression. My brethren, you who are enroled and proudly march under the banners of the Mutual Relief . . . Societies, consider your important standings as incorporated bodies, and walk worthy of the name you bear, cling closely to the paths of virtue and morality, cherish the plants of peace and temper-

ance; by doing this you shall not only shine as the first stars in the firmament, and do honor to your worthy patrons, but immortalize your names. Be zealous and vigilant, be always on the alert to promote the welfare of your injured brethren; then shall providence shower down her blessings upon your heads, and crown your labors with success. It has been said by your enemies, that your minds were not calculated to receive a sufficient store of knowledge, to fit you for beneficial or social societies; but your incorporation drowned that assertion in contempt. . . . In vain they fostered a hope that our unfavorable circumstances would bear them out in their profane insinuations. . . .

There could be many reasons given, to prove that the mind of an African is not inferior to that of an European; yet to do so would be superfluous. It would be like adding hardness to the diamond, or lustre to the sun. There was a time whilst shrouded in ignorance, the African was estimated no higher than beasts of burthen, and while their minds were condensed within the narrow compass of slavery, and all their genius damped by the merciless power of cruel masters, they moved in no higher sphere. Their nature was cramped in infancy, and depraved in riper years, vice was showed them for virtue, and for their labor and industry, the scourge was their only reward. Then did they seem dead to a better state, but it was because they were subject to arbitrary power; and then did their proud oppressors assert, though against their better judgment, that they were destined by nature to no better inheritance. But their most prominent arguments are lighter than vanity, for vacuous must the reasons of that man have been, who dared to assert that genius is confined to complexion, or that nature knows difference in the immortal soul of man: No! the noble mind of a Newton could find room, and to spare, within the tenement of many an injured African. . . .

Then Fathers, Brethren and Friends, although depressed under many grievances, yet the strong fibres of that pressure must give way, and the time is not far distant when our tree of liberty shall reach the sun, and its branches spread from pool to pool. Then let us stand firm in union, let us transmit to

SOURCE: George Lawrence, *Oration on the Abolition of the Slave Trade* (New York: Hardcastle and Van Pelt, 1813), 5, 6, 11, 12–13, 15.

ages yet to come, deeds that shall bear record with time and not find their rival; let us cultivate the minds of youth; let your examples clothed with wisdom be strewed in their paths; by you let their tender minds be impressed with humane principles; let your virtues shine conspicuously before them, as lamps that shall light them to a glorious victory over their enemies, and conduct them to the haven of immortal bliss; let malice and hatred be far from your doors; let your hearts be linked in the chain that bids defiance to the intrigues of your enemies; let not the cries of the widow and the orphan pass you unnoticed: although this happy land abounds with humane institutions, yet has your individual aid, opportunities to alleviate the miseries of thousands; many are the miseries of our exiled race in this land, and dark are the clouds that shrouds them in woe. O! then, let us call forth our every power.

Free People of Color of Richmond, Virginia | Petition to Congress on Colonization, 1817

In 1817, free blacks in Richmond, Virginia, met to discuss the American Colonization Society's plans for sending African Americans back to Africa. Though willing to move away from Virginia, they were not willing to leave North America and petitioned the U.S. Congress to grant them land somewhere on the continent where they could resettle.

Whereas a Society has been formed at the seat of government, for the purpose of colonizing, with their own consent, the free people of color of the United States; therefore we, the free people of color of the city of Richmond, have thought it advisable to assemble together under the sanction of authority, for the purpose of making a public expression of our sentiments on a question in which we are so

deeply interested. We perfectly agree with the Society, that it is not only proper, but would ultimately tend to the benefit and advantage of a great portion of our suffering fellow creatures, to be colonized; but while we thus express our approbation of a measure laudable in its purposes, and beneficial in its designs, it may not be improper in us to say, that we prefer being colonized in the most remote corner of the land of our nativity, to being exiled to a foreign country—and whereas the president and board of managers of the said Society have been pleased to leave it to the entire discretion of Congress to provide a suitable place for carrying these laudable intentions into effect—Be it therefore

Resolved, That we respectfully submit to the wisdom of Congress whether it would not be an act of charity to grant us a small portion of their territory, either on the Missouri river, or any place that may seem to them most conducive to the public good and our future welfare, subject, however, to such rules and regulations as the government of the United States may think proper to adopt.

SOURCE: William Lloyd Garrison, *Thoughts on African Colonization, or An Impartial Exhibition of the Doctrines, Principles and Purposes of the American Colonization Society. Together with the Resolutions, Addresses and Remonstrances of the Free People of Color* (Boston: Garrison and Knapp, 1832), 63.

Questions for Analysis

1. What were the specific goals of the free blacks represented in these documents? What common problems did they share, and what solutions did they seek?

2. To what communities and authorities did the petitioners and letter writers appeal in their quest for racial justice?

3. Why were free blacks in Virginia reluctant to leave the United States?

4. How might the regions in which these petitioners and letter writers lived have influenced their outlooks and their arguments?

The Black Body in Early American Culture

By the turn of the eighteenth century, there were many images of people of African descent in circulation. While printed matter was relatively scarce in colonial America, post-Revolutionary improvements in printing technology and the establishment of the U.S. Post Office made it cheaper and easier to produce and distribute books, pamphlets, and periodicals. Americans no longer had to import the bulk of their reading material from Britain, as printers proliferated, producing printed matter covering a range of topics and depicting the new nation's inhabitants. As a result, African Americans were pictured in more detail than ever before. Antislavery advocates, both black and white, created some of these images. Others illustrated discussions of racial difference, treating the black body as a scientific curiosity. A third broad category of images can only be described as caricatures, designed to lampoon the physical appearance and social aspirations of blacks.

Antislavery Images of Blacks

Both blacks and whites produced antislavery images featuring the black body, but the images created by the two groups differed vastly. African Americans' efforts to improve the image of their race largely took the form of self-representation. Early African American authors, for example, often promoted both their own work and the concept of black literacy by including pictures of themselves in published pieces. Benjamin Banneker featured a dignified portrait of himself on the cover of several editions of his almanac (Figure 4.1). Crafted by an unknown artist, the portrait in his 1795 almanac shows a thoughtful, well-dressed man clad in somber Quaker garb. Banneker was not a Quaker, but his choice of clothing may reflect his admiration for this antislavery sect. The picture also told readers that he was, as he wrote to Thomas Jefferson in 1791, "of the African race; and in that color which is natural to them of the deepest *dye*."[34] The almanac's preface, probably written by the printers, emphasized the same point by asking readers, "Is a Black capable of composing an Almanac?" and then reassuring them, "It is no less strange than true; and what a clever longheaded wise black he is." How would eighteenth-century readers have received such reassurances? Would they have bought Banneker's almanac, which was a commercial success, because of his race—or in spite of it?

FIGURE 4.1
Cover of Benjamin Banneker's Almanac, 1795 *Holding Institution, Special Collections/Maryland Historical Society, image ID MS2700.*

FIGURE 4.2
Samuel Jennings, *Liberty Displaying the Arts and Sciences, or the Genius of America Encouraging the Emancipation of the Blacks,* 1792 *Oil on canvas/The Library Company of Philadelphia. Gift of the artist, 1792.*

Antislavery whites also addressed the question of black literacy, but they focused on less accomplished black figures. The imagery they produced often emphasized that education could improve the African race. These philanthropists believed that freedom and literacy went hand in hand, as can be seen in a 1792 painting by Samuel Jennings (Figure 4.2) commissioned by the leaders of the Library Company of Philadelphia, many of whom were also members of the Pennsylvania Antislavery Society. *Liberty Displaying the Arts and Sciences* depicts liberty as a woman in white, offering the fruits of Western culture to a group of freed slaves.

Consider the dress, postures, facial expressions, and relative sizes of the figures in the painting. What is happening in this interaction, and what message is the painter trying to convey? Does this imagery challenge or reinforce eighteenth-century racial hierarchies? The subservient pose of the blacks leaves them poorly positioned to appreciate the gifts that Liberty displays, but it is one of the most common poses assumed by blacks in antislavery art and artifacts.

The image of a kneeling (often near-naked) slave, first adopted as a symbol of antislavery in Britain in the 1780s, was widely used in the United States and inspired the poet John Greenleaf Whittier to compose the famous poem "Our Countrymen in Chains!" Written in 1837, Whittier's poem called for Americans to liberate their nation's "crouching . . . writhing slaves," whom he described as the embodiment of the antislavery figure of the kneeling slave.[35] The membership certificate for the New Jersey Society for Promoting the Abolition of Slavery included the image of a kneeling slave (Figure 4.3). In what ways does this figure echo the imagery used in *Liberty Displaying the Arts and Sciences*? How does it compare to the portrait of Benjamin Banneker in Figure 4.1? What does this tell us about the different types of images put forth by antislavery whites and blacks?

Scientific Images of Blacks

Antislavery activists of both races emphasized black literacy in their imagery because they realized that many of their contemporaries attributed black illiteracy not to slavery, but to the innate deficiencies of the black race. Color, most whites suspected, was simply the outward manifestation of the deeper racial differences that separated blacks and whites. Yet even the leading thinkers of the day were not sure exactly what those differences were. Thomas Jefferson, in making his case for black inferiority in *Notes on the State of Virginia* (1785), theorized that blacks were less intelligent than whites; he also believed that they smelled different than whites and needed less sleep. Other writers, such as the well-known British surgeon Charles White, argued that blacks and whites were anatomically distinct and did not belong to the same species. Published in 1799, White's *An Account of the Regular Gradation in Man, and in Different Animals and Vegetables* contended that rather than sharing common ancestors, each race had been divinely created for its own region. However, he did not see the races as separate but equal. Instead, he ranked all the species, singling out whites as the most fully developed and Africans "as nearer to brute creation than any other species." As Figures 4.4 and 4.5 illustrate, he believed that anatomy was the key to "progress in civilization," and he used anatomical comparisons to show that whites were more distinct from animals than other races.[36] What anatomical features does he emphasize in these illustrations?

FIGURE 4.3
New Jersey Society for Promoting the Abolition of Slavery's Membership Certificate, 1792 *Haverford College Library, Haverford, PA, Special Collections, Quaker Collection, Coll. No. 988E-R.*

visual sources

FIGURE 4.4
Charles White's Illustrations of
the Anatomical Features of
Animals and Humans, 1799
*Courtesy of the Waring Historical
Library, MUSC, Charleston, SC.*

White was ahead of his time. Prior to the rise of the virulent scientific racism of the mid-nineteenth century, few scientific authorities in either Britain or America believed that blacks constituted a distinct branch of the human family. Most took their account of the genesis of mankind from the Bible, which maintains that "of one blood, God hath created all the races of men" (Acts 17:26). Typical in this regard was the British naturalist Oliver Goldsmith, whose book *A History of the Earth and Animated Nature* (first published in 1774) was widely reprinted in the United States during the first half of the nineteenth century. Goldsmith maintained that all humans "sprung from one common parent" and attributed the variations in the human family to the influence of climate, custom, and culture. However, he did assume that mankind was originally white and that other races had degenerated from "the original perfection" still seen in the European race.[37] Otherwise dedicated to cataloging species of animals, birds, and plants, his book contained a frontispiece with a picture of all the races—except the European race (Figure 4.6). Why did he leave out Europeans? What kind of scientific information might this image be designed to convey?

Even Americans who accepted the biblical account of human creation sometimes wondered how the races had come to be so distinct. In answering this question, they usually focused on the black body, questioning not how whites came to be white, but how blacks came to be black. For instance, the well-respected Philadelphia physician Benjamin Rush conjectured that "the Black Color (as it is called) of the Negroes Is Derived from the LEPROSY."[38] Rush developed this idea after meeting a black man named Henry Moss, who marketed himself as a "GREAT CURIOSITY" in Philadelphia and other

FIGURE 4.5
(Left) Charles White's *Comparisons of Humans and Other Primates*, 1799 *Courtesy of the Waring Historical Library, MUSC, Charleston, SC.*

FIGURE 4.6
(Below) Oliver Goldsmith, *A History of the Earth and Animated Nature*, 1774 *(Reprinted Philadelphia, 1795). Courtesy American Antiquarian Society/The Bridgeman Art Library International.*

AMERICAN.   NEGRO.   HOTTENTOT.   LAPLANDER.   CHINESE.

FIGURE 4.7
The True Picture of Mary-Sabina,
c. 1744 Portrait of Mary-Sabina
(b. 1736), unsigned, c. 1744, object
number RCSSC/P 256/© The Royal
College of Surgeons of England.

American cities during the 1790s.[39] Probably afflicted with vitiligo, a condition causing the depigmentation of patches of skin, Moss entertained visitors who were willing to pay half a shilling to see a man whose complexion was slowly changing from black to white.

Moss was not the only "spotted Negro" to attract an audience. Mary-Sabina, who was born into slavery on a Jesuit plantation in Cartagena, Colombia, in the 1730s, was well known in Victorian medical circles as "Our Variegated Little Damsel." Discolored by a medical condition known as piebaldism, which is a form of albinism, Sabina was portrayed in both a widely circulated portrait and engravings that appeared in the French naturalist George Louis Leclerc de Buffon's massive thirty-two-volume *Histoire naturelle, générale et particulière* (Figure 4.7). A Jamaican youth with similar coloring was displayed in London in the 1790s, where he attracted the attention of a German naturalist who featured him in a publication titled *The Natural Varieties of Mankind.*[40]

The spectacle of an individual who was both black and white attracted special interest in the United States, where Henry Moss inspired several prominent thinkers to hope that blackness might be a reversible condition. Benjamin Rush was convinced that nature was spontaneously curing Moss of the leprosy that had turned him black, and he looked forward to other such cures. Staunchly antislavery, Rush believed that if the coloring of the African race could be proved to be the mark of a disease, all claims of white superiority were baseless.

Black Caricatures

To most African Americans, the decreasing incidence of dark skin among blacks had more obvious explanations. Widespread race mixture in the North and South was lightening the complexion of many African American children without bridging the social divide between blacks and whites. Most common in the slave South, where many slave owners and overseers took slave mistresses, such relationships were an open secret in early America. Considered normal but rarely publicized, they came to light only when they led to court cases or public controversy. The relationship between Thomas Jefferson and his slave maid, Sally Hemings, is a case in point. Still controversial today, it was first publicized in 1802 when the *Richmond Recorder* reported that Jefferson "kept, as his concubine, one of his own slaves." Written by the journalist James Callender, who disliked Jefferson and hoped to derail his reelection in 1804, the report fleshed out local rumors of a liaison between Jefferson and one of his slaves. "Her name is Sally," noted Callender, who alleged that Jefferson had "several children" by her. Jefferson denied the allegation.[41] Federalist writers repeatedly mocked Jefferson for succumbing to what they called Sally's "sooty charms."[42] This is illustrated in a widely circulated image titled *A Philosophic Cock* (Figure 4.8).

The only surviving image of Hemings, it portrays her as a hen standing behind Jefferson, who is depicted as a rooster. The cartoon mocks Jefferson's lust for his slave mistress, while also making fun of his enthusiasm for French philosophy. In the cartoon Jefferson says, "'Tis not a set of features or complexion or tincture of a skin that I admire." But its depiction of Hemings is less obviously amusing, and more difficult to interpret. Known as "Dashing Sally," Hemings was by all accounts a beautiful woman. How is she portrayed in this caricature? How does this differ from the representation of Jefferson?

A PHILOSOPHIC COCK

FIGURE 4.8
James Akin, *A Philosophic Cock*, c. 1804 *Hand-colored aquatint, Newburyport, Massachusetts/Courtesy American Antiquarian Society/The Bridgeman Art Library International.*

visual sources

FIGURE 4.9
Bobalition Broadside, 1825
Boston Public Library/Rare Books.

While Hemings was perhaps not the major figure of ridicule in this cartoon, blacks were clearly parodied in other images from the same period. Indeed, the first few decades of the nineteenth century saw the emergence of a distinct genre of publications lampooning the appearance and behavior of free blacks. Published at a time when black northerners had just begun to leave slavery behind and were celebrating their emancipation by founding schools and churches to educate and improve themselves, "Bobalition" broadsides made fun of their freedom struggles and aspirations (Figure 4.9). These professionally printed documents usually purported to announce black gatherings to celebrate abolition between 1816 and 1832. They originated in Boston, where they mocked the speech and manners of the black Bostonians who participated in such gatherings. Written in nearly incomprehensible prose, they portrayed blacks as illiterate and ignorant.

The proliferation of Bobalition broadsides just as slavery was ending throughout the northern states suggests that free blacks carried the social stigma of slavery into freedom and that racist ideas about blacks' intellectual inferiority were on the rise in the North. But it also suggests that popular perceptions of black inferiority required reinforcement. What might the anonymous author of the Bobalition broadside in Figure 4.9 have been trying to accomplish?

As all these images indicate, post-Revolutionary Americans were presented with a variety of competing portrayals of blacks and the black body. The combined effect of these images is difficult to calculate. How did viewers make sense of portrayals of blacks as kneeling slaves, scientific curiosities, dignified authors, or cartoonish characters? Perhaps the most important common theme among these images is racial difference. Whether they were presented as surprisingly wise, submissive, foolish, or physically odd, blacks were portrayed as distinct from, and sometimes opposed to, their white counterparts.

Questions for Analysis

1. Which of the images in this essay can be described as racial stereotypes? What makes an image stereotypical? What specific visual cues convey these stereotypical messages?

2. Compare the white figures in Figures 4.2, 4.3, and 4.8 with the black figures that appear in those images. What are the similarities and differences in their appearance, demeanor, and relationship to one another? What comparisons can you make across images?

3. Discuss the various kinds of clothing worn by blacks in these images. Were blacks associated with any particular style of dress? How did artists use clothing to convey racial difference?

Notes

1. Benjamin Banneker to Thomas Jefferson, Letter to Thomas Jefferson, August 19, 1791, reprinted in John H. B. Latrobe, "Memoir of Benjamin Banneker," *African Repository and Colonial Journal* 11 (November 1845): 330.
2. Ibid.
3. Thomas Jefferson to Benjamin Banneker, August 30, 1791, in Paul Leicester Ford, ed., *The Works of Thomas Jefferson* (New York: G. P. Putnam's Sons, 1904), 6:310.
4. Thomas Jefferson, *Notes on the State of Virginia* (London: printed for John Stockdale, 1787), 239.
5. Thomas Jefferson to Joel Barlow, October 8, 1809, in Ford, ed., *The Works of Thomas Jefferson*, 11:121.
6. James Madison, speech, Constitutional Convention, June 1787, in *The Debates in the Several State Conventions on the Adoption of the Federal Constitution*, ed. Jonathan Elliott (New York: Lippincott, 1876), 5:162.
7. Quoted in Ira Berlin, *Generations of Captivity: A History of African-American Slaves* (Cambridge: Harvard University Press, 2003), 151.
8. Ibid., 29.
9. Charles Ball, *Fifty Years in Chains, or The Life of an American Slave* (New York: H. Dayton, 1859), 347.
10. Quoted in Thomas J. Fleming, *The Louisiana Purchase* (Hoboken, NJ: John Wiley and Sons, 2003), 110.
11. Quoted in Seth Rockman, *Scraping By: Wage Labor, Slavery, and Survival in Early Baltimore* (Baltimore: Johns Hopkins University Press, 2008), 36.
12. "Proceedings of the Virginia Legislature on the Subject of African Colonization," *African Repository and Colonial Journal* 3, no. 4 (June 1832): 104.
13. Douglas R. Egerton, *Gabriel's Rebellion: The Virginia Slave Conspiracies of 1800 and 1802* (Chapel Hill: University of North Carolina Press, 1993), 164.
14. Quoted in Ira Berlin, *Slaves without Masters: The Free Negro in the Antebellum South* (New York: New Press, 2007), 89.
15. Revisors of the Laws, Virginia, *Draughts of Such Bills as Have Been Prepared by the Revisors of the Laws* (Richmond: Ritchie, Trueheart & Du-Val, and Shepherd & Pollard, 1817), 263.
16. Berlin, *Slaves without Masters*, 147.
17. Sojourner Truth, *Narrative of Sojourner Truth*, ed. Olive Gilbert (Boston: printed for author, 1850), 29.
18. Ibid., 43.
19. "Preamble of the Free African Society," in Reverend William Douglass, *Annals of the First African Church in the United States of America Now Styled the African Episcopal Church of St. Thomas*, Philadelphia (Philadelphia: King & Baird, 1862), 15.
20. Quoted in Richard Newman, *Freedom's Prophet: Bishop Richard Allen, the AME Church, and the Black Founding Fathers* (New York: New York University Press, 2009), 64.
21. Ibid.
22. Hosea Easton, *A Treatise on the Intellectual Character, and Civil and Political Condition of the Colored People of the U. States* (Boston: Isaac Knapp, 1937), 43.
23. *An Address to the Parents and Guardians of the Children Belonging to the New York African Free School* (New York: Samuel Wood and Sons, 1818), 20–21.
24. Quoted in Charles C. Andrews, *The History of the New-York African Free-Schools* (New York: Mahlon Day, 1830), 132.
25. *New York Evening Post*, September 22, 1826.
26. Quoted in the *Proceedings of the One Hundredth Anniversary of the Granting of Warrant 459 . . . by Freemasons, African Lodge No. 459* (Boston: Franklin Press, 1883), 15.
27. Absalom Jones and Richard Allen, *A Narrative of the Proceedings of the Colored People in Philadelphia During the Awful Calamity in the Year of 1793, and Refutation of Some Censures Thrown upon Them in Some Late Publications* (Philadelphia: printed for authors by William W. Woodward, 1794), 23.
28. Prince Hall and the African Lodge No. 459, "Petition for Repatriation to Africa" (1787), in *The African American Experience: Black History and Culture through Speeches, Letters, Editorials, Poems, Songs, and Stories*, ed. Kai Wright (New York: Black Dog, 2009), 101.
29. Paul Cuffe to Nathan G. M. Sterner, March 1, 1814, in *Captain Paul Cuffe's Logs and Letters, 1808–1817: A Black Quaker's "Voice from within the Veil,"* ed. Rosalind Cobb Wiggins (Washington, DC: Howard University Press, 1996), 276.
30. Quoted in Julie Winch, *A Gentleman of Color: The Life of James Forten* (New York: Oxford University Press, 2003), 188.
31. Prince Hall and the African Lodge No. 459, "Petition for Repatriation to Africa," 101.
32. Resolution of Assembled Free Blacks, Bethel AME Church, Philadelphia, January 15, 1817, quoted in Winch, *A Gentleman of Color*, 196.
33. American Convention for Promoting the Abolition of Slavery and Improving the Condition of the African Race, *Minutes of the Proceedings of a Special Meeting of the Fifteenth American Convention for Promoting the Abolition of Slavery and Improving the Condition of the African Race Assembled at Philadelphia, on the Tenth Day of December, 1818* (Philadelphia: printed for convention by Hall & Atkinson, 1818), 70.
34. Benjamin Banneker to Thomas Jefferson, Letter to Thomas Jefferson, August 19, 1791, 331.
35. John Greenleaf Whittier, "Our Countrymen in Chains!," broadside (New York: Anti-Slavery Office, 1837), American Memory Collection, Library of Congress.
36. Charles White, *An Account of the Regular Gradation in Man, and in Different Animals and Vegetables; and from the Former to the Latter* (London: printed for C. Dilly, 1799), 43.
37. Oliver Goldsmith, *A History of the Earth and Animated Nature* (Philadelphia: R. Wright, 1825), 2:18–19.
38. Benjamin Rush, "Observations Intended to Favour a Supposition That the Black Color (As It Is Called) of the Negroes Is Derived from the Leprosy," *Transactions of the American Philosophical Society* 4 (January 1, 1799): 289.
39. Quoted in Kariann A. Yokota, "Not Written in Black and White: American National Identity and the Curious Color Transformation of Henry Moss," *Common-Place* 4, no. 2 (January 2004), http://www.common-place.org/vol-04/no-02/yokota/.
40. Jessie Dobson, "Mary Sabina, the Variegated Damsel," *Annals of the Royal College of Surgeons* 22, no. 4 (April 1958): 273–78.

41. *Richmond Recorder*, September 1, 1802.
42. Quoted in Robert M. S. McDonald, "Race, Sex, and Reputation: Thomas Jefferson and the Sally Hemings Story," *Southern Cultures* 4, no. 2 (2000): 48.

Suggested References

The Limits of Democracy

Berlin, Ira. *Generations of Captivity: A History of African-American Slaves*. Cambridge: Belknap Press of Harvard University Press, 2004.

Dain, Bruce. *A Hideous Monster of the Mind: American Race Theory in the Early Republic*. Cambridge: Harvard University Press, 2003.

Fischer, Sibylle. *Modernity Disavowed: Haiti and the Cultures of Slavery in the Age of Revolution*. Durham, NC: Duke University Press, 2004.

Kornblith, Gary J. *Slavery and Sectional Strife in the Early American Republic, 1776–1821*. Lanham, MD: Rowman & Littlefield, 2009.

Mason, Matthew. *Slavery and Politics in the Early American Republic*. Chapel Hill: University of North Carolina Press, 2008.

Morrison, Michael A. *Race and the Early Republic: Racial Consciousness and Nation Building in the Early Republic*. Lanham, MD: Rowman & Littlefield, 2002.

Rothman, Adam. *Slave Country: American Expansion and the Origins of the Deep South*. Cambridge: Harvard University Press, 2007.

Van Cleve, George William. *A Slaveholders' Union: Slavery, Politics, and the Constitution in the Early American Republic*. Chicago: University of Chicago Press, 2010.

Waldstreicher, David. *Slavery's Constitution: From Revolution to Ratification*. New York: Hill and Wang, 2010.

Slavery and Freedom outside the Plantation South

Berlin, Ira. *Slaves without Masters: The Free Negro in the Antebellum South*. New York: New Press, 2007.

Curry, Leonard P. *The Free Black in Urban America, 1800–1850: The Shadow of the Dream*. Chicago: University of Chicago Press, 1986.

Egerton, Douglas R. *Gabriel's Rebellion: The Virginia Slave Conspiracies of 1800 and 1802*. Chapel Hill: University of North Carolina Press, 1993.

Horton, James Oliver, and Lois E. Horton. *Black Bostonians: Family Life and Community Struggle in the Antebellum North*. Rev. ed. New York: Holmes & Meier, 2000.

King, Wilma. *The Essence of Liberty: Free Black Women during the Slave Era*. Columbia: University of Missouri Press, 2006.

Litwack, Leon F. *North of Slavery: The Negro in the Free States, 1790–1860*. Chicago: University of Chicago Press, 1961.

Melish, Joanne Pope. *Disowning Slavery: Gradual Emancipation and "Race" in New England, 1780–1860*. Ithaca, NY: Cornell University Press, 2000.

Painter, Nell Irvin. *Sojourner Truth: A Life, a Symbol*. New York: Norton, 1997.

Rockman, Seth. *Scraping By: Wage Labor, Slavery, and Survival in Early Baltimore*. Baltimore: Johns Hopkins University Press, 2008.

Wade, Richard C. *Slavery in the Cities: The South, 1820–1860*. New York: Oxford University Press, 1967.

Zilversmit, Arthur. *The First Emancipation: The Abolition of Slavery in the North*. 3rd ed. Chicago: University of Chicago Press, 1969.

Free Black Life in the New Republic

Alexander, Leslie M. *African or American? Black Identity and Political Activism in New York City, 1784–1861*. Urbana: University of Illinois Press, 2008.

Dunbar, Erica Armstrong. *A Fragile Freedom: African American Women and Emancipation in the Antebellum City*. New Haven: Yale University Press, 2008.

Horton, James Oliver. *In Hope of Liberty: Culture, Community and Protest among Northern Free Blacks, 1700–1860*. New York: Oxford University Press, 1998.

Nash, Gary B. *Forging Freedom: The Formation of Philadelphia's Black Community, 1720–1840*. Cambridge: Harvard University Press, 1991.

Newman, Richard. *Freedom's Prophet: Bishop Richard Allen, the AME Church, and the Black Founding Fathers*. New York: New York University Press, 2009.

———. *The Transformation of American Abolitionism: Fighting Slavery in the Early Republic*. Chapel Hill: University of North Carolina Press, 2002.

Sweet, John Wood. *Bodies Politic: Negotiating Race in the American North, 1730–1830*. Philadelphia: University of Pennsylvania Press, 2006.

White, Shane. *Stories of Freedom in Black New York*. Cambridge: Harvard University Press, 2007.

Winch, Julie. *A Gentleman of Color: The Life of James Forten*. New York: Oxford University Press, 2003.

CHAPTER

5

Black Life in the Slave South,

1820–1860

WILLIAM WELLS BROWN WAS BORN into slavery on a Kentucky plantation in 1814. His early experiences as a slave were varied and painful. Until he was twelve, he lived in rural Missouri, where his master, Dr. Young, moved his household of forty slaves shortly after Brown was born. Young employed Brown's mother and four older siblings on a tobacco and hemp plantation outside St. Louis, where Brown observed the brutal discipline imposed on plantation field hands. As an infant, he often rode on his mother's back while she worked in the fields because she was not allowed to leave the fields to nurse. As a young boy, he was routinely awakened by the sounds of the whippings that Young's overseer gave field hands—including Brown's mother and siblings—who were not at work by 4:30 a.m. He was close enough to the fields to "hear every crack of the whip, and every groan and cry," and he wept at the sounds.[1] More sorrow lay ahead after Young sold Brown's mother and siblings but kept Brown himself because he was the son of Young's cousin and fellow planter George Higgins.

Young hired the boy out to a variety of masters, leaving him with a broad understanding of enslaved life and labor in the antebellum South. His first employer, a tavern owner named Major Freeland, was short-tempered, unstable, and prone to lashing out at his slaves without warning. To punish disobedient slaves, Freeland employed a technique he had learned in his home state of Virginia. Brown recalled that "he would tie them up in the smoke-house, and whip them; after which, he would cause a fire to be made of tobacco stems, and smoke them. This he called '*Virginia play*.'"[2] Brown was so terrified of Freeland that he ran away and hid in the woods, where another local slaveholder who kept a pack of bloodhounds for this purpose recaptured him. On his return to Freeland's tavern, Brown, too, was whipped and smoked.

After Freeland's business failed, Brown was promptly hired out again. He ended up working as a steward for a slave trader named Mr. Walker, who employed Brown to tend to the slave cargo he shipped from St. Louis to New Orleans. Brown's twelve months in Walker's employ, which he called "the longest year I ever lived," left him with a renewed determination to escape. On the journey south, Brown worried that he would be sold himself once the boat reached New Orleans, and he loathed his duties, which included preventing Walker's slaves from escaping whenever the boat stopped. One woman who had been sold away from her husband and children committed suicide by flinging herself into the Mississippi River. Brown was also in charge of doling out rations during the journey and preparing the slaves for market once the boat docked. After shaving the old men and blackening their whiskers to make them look younger, Brown had to have them all "dressed and driven out into the yard," where "some

1830	Indian Removal Act
1831	William Lloyd Garrison founds abolitionist newspaper the *Liberator*
	Nat Turner's rebellion
1835	Eight hundred Black Seminoles help Seminole tribe repel U.S. troops
	Gag rule prohibits reading of antislavery petitions in Congress
1836	Texas settlers clash with Mexican troops at Alamo and San Jacinto
	Arkansas admitted as slave state
1837	Panic of 1837
1838	Trail of Tears
1841	U.S. Supreme Court frees *Amistad* rebels
	Solomon Northup kidnapped and sold into slavery
1843	*Creole* insurrection
1845	Texas annexed, admitted as slave state
	Florida admitted as slave state
1848	Ellen and William Craft escape from slavery
1849	Harriet Tubman and Henry "Box" Brown escape from slavery
1854	*John v. State* rules that any killing of a white person by a slave is murder

211

were set to dancing, some to jumping, some to singing, and some to playing cards" to make them appear cheerful and happy.[3] Brown eventually escaped from Walker, but he was forever haunted by what he had witnessed and became an abolitionist who fought to end slavery.

Brown was a captive spectator to the rapid expansion of a system built around the brutal forced migration and sale of enslaved blacks. With the closing of the international slave trade in 1808, American slaves became a predominantly U.S.-born population. They maintained a robust rate of reproduction, growing in number from a little over 1.5 million in 1820 to almost 4 million in 1860. And they continued to be bought and sold in an expanding domestic slave trade that supplied black workers to the new slave states and territories taking shape in the South.

Slave labor predominated throughout the South, which maintained a largely agricultural economy even as industrialization moved many northern workers from fields to factories. As a result, the North and South became increasingly distinct and divided by the 1820s, especially with regard to the expansion of slavery. But strong economic ties also connected the regions. The South was crucial to American industrialization: Enslaved African Americans cultivated and harvested many of the raw materials used in northern factories. Likewise, the South depended on the North for textiles and manufactured goods—and provided the North with a lucrative market for those goods.

Enslaved African Americans rarely profited from their labor. In addition to working for their masters from sunup to sundown, they had to sustain themselves and their families. They also nurtured their communities and forged a distinctive culture within the confines of an oppressive system of bondage. Successful escapes were rare, and slave uprisings still more so. Slaves fought back by means of truancy, malingering, theft, and outright defiance under the watchful eyes of their owners and overseers. They also followed the sectional debates that divided the slave and free states. Those debates encouraged them to pray for freedom and hope that northern opposition would help topple the slave system. But until that day came, they would have to settle for survival.

The Expansion and Consolidation of Slavery

By 1820, slavery was all but dead in the North and banned throughout the Old Northwest. But it never came close to dying out completely, as many of the Founding Fathers had once predicted. Instead, the rise of cotton cultivation in the 1790s fostered the steady expansion of southern plantation agriculture. Moreover, during the first half of the nineteenth century, the Louisiana Purchase, Spain's cession of Spanish Florida, and the annexation of Texas opened new territory to American settlement and expanded the region within which slavery could be practiced. The expansion of the southern states took place at the expense of the Indian inhabitants of the Southeast, whom white settlers pushed off their land. As white settlers moved into this territory, southern slavery became more entrenched.

The domestic slave trade expanded as the Upper South sold its surplus slaves in the Lower South, displacing hundreds of thousands of African Americans and tearing apart black families and communities. The South's most lucrative crops required a large supply of enslaved workers, which strengthened white southerners' commitment to slavery in an era when many northerners were increasingly committed to free labor.

These regional differences became a source of major sectional conflict during the late 1810s, when Missouri's petition for statehood threatened to upset the balance between slaveholding and nonslaveholding states, and they remained divisive throughout the antebellum era.

Slavery, Cotton, and American Industrialization

By the 1820s, stark regional differences were emerging between the North and South. Although these years saw the start of a transportation revolution that would link both regions to a shared national market, the new railroads, turnpikes, and shipping routes connected two increasingly distinct societies. With gradual emancipation all but complete, the North was committed to free labor, while the South's investment in slavery only increased over time. Both regions expanded steadily, adding new people and new territory. Whereas population growth in the South relied primarily on natural increase, however, growth in the North also resulted from immigration. Between 1815 and 1860, more than five million Europeans immigrated to the United States, but less than one-eighth of them settled in southern slave states.

Slavery itself discouraged immigration to the South, because there were few jobs for white immigrants. Although a majority of white southerners did not own slaves, nonslaveholding whites were largely small farmers with no employees. The region's major employers and wealthiest men were planters who favored slaves over white workers. In addition to the labor they provided, slaves were a profitable investment: Their prices rose steadily throughout the antebellum era, as did the return that slave owners could expect when slaves reproduced. Slaves also could be forced to do any type of work, including the grueling year-round labor needed to produce the South's lucrative **cash crops.**

The production of tobacco, rice, sugar, hemp, and above all cotton sustained the South's economy. By 1850, 55 percent of the South's slaves worked on cotton plantations, where they grew 75 percent of the world's supply of cotton (Map 5.1). Their labor enriched both the South and the nation as whole: That year, cotton constituted more than 50 percent of all U.S. exports. Sugar, produced primarily in Louisiana, was another highly profitable crop. Used throughout the United States, Louisiana sugar was also exported, making up as much as one-quarter of the world's sugar production during years when the crop flourished.

Southern businessmen used slave labor in the region's small industrial sector as well. Enslaved workers produced chewing tobacco in Richmond and Petersburg, Virginia; salt in western Virginia; and iron in a variety of ironworks located along Virginia and Maryland's waterways. They also staffed lumber camps in forests and swamps across the South.

The North, by contrast, was home to a much larger nonagricultural sector. The first half of the nineteenth century saw northern farmers adopt new machinery that allowed them to increase production while reducing the number of workers they employed. Moreover, they took advantage of the reduced transportation costs and increased shipping speeds resulting from the transportation revolution to expand their markets. Food no longer had to be grown locally. Instead, large commercial farms in the Midwest began to monopolize the North's agricultural sector, while other parts of the region industrialized. Major manufacturing centers emerged in Boston, New York, and

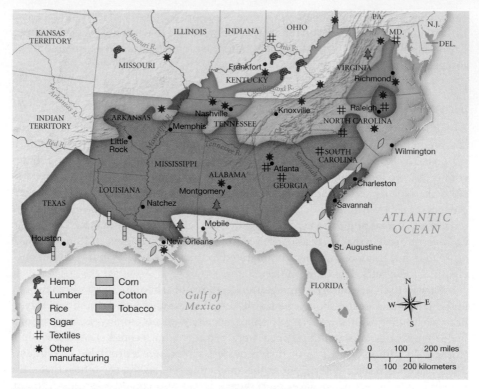

MAP 5.1   Agriculture and Industry in the Slave South, 1860

The antebellum South's economy was dominated by cotton production, but southern planters also cultivated corn and tobacco in the Upper South, sugar in parts of Louisiana and Texas, and rice along the coasts of North and South Carolina, Georgia, and Louisiana. In addition, southern workers also produced hemp, lumber, textiles, and small quantities of other kinds of manufactured goods.

Philadelphia, and factory towns sprang up across the Northeast. Wages were high enough in these industrial areas to attract European immigrants, providing the northern states with a rapidly expanding free white labor force.

The different regional economies that emerged in the North and South were by no means autonomous. Southerners produced few manufactured goods and relied on the North—and, to a lesser extent, Europe—to supply them with furniture, tools, clothing, shoes, and other products. Likewise, northern industrialists imported raw materials such as cotton and indigo from the South. They used these materials to produce textiles, including fabrics manufactured specifically for the southern market, such as "negro cloth," a coarse cotton fabric used for slaves' clothing. Northern manufacturers also imported other crucial raw materials from the South. The most important was lumber, which factories used to make furniture, paper, buttons, bobbins, and many other household items and supplies that were then shipped to the South as finished products.

Despite such ties, the North and South had different economic and political interests. As the regions' economies diverged, northerners favored government measures designed to support American industrial production, such as protective tariffs on manufactured goods. Southerners, who produced few manufactured goods and imported many from abroad, opposed tariffs. Underlying such divergent interests were even deeper divisions over slavery.

The Missouri Compromise Crisis

With Alabama already scheduled for admission as a slave state in 1819, the nation was made up of eleven free states and eleven slave states. The admission of Missouri threatened to upset the balance. Missouri Territory had no restrictions on slavery, and some of its most fertile farmland had been settled by slaveholders such as William Wells Brown's owner. By 1818, when Missouri applied for statehood, the territory was already home to more than two thousand slaves. Nevertheless, northern congressmen were reluctant to admit Missouri as a slave state. The admission of another slave state would increase the South's power in Congress at a time when northern politicians had already begun to regret the Constitution's Three-Fifths Compromise (see chapter 4).

Although more than 60 percent of white Americans lived in the North, by 1818 northern representatives held only a slim majority of congressional seats. The additional political representation allotted to the South as a result of the Three-Fifths Compromise gave southerners many more seats in the House of Representatives than they would have had if the number of representatives had been based on just the free population. Moreover, since each state had two Senate seats, Missouri's admission as a slave state would result in more southern than northern senators.

Many northern legislators also had misgivings about the westward expansion of slavery. One of them was New York representative James Tallmadge, who proposed a radical amendment to Missouri's statehood bill banning slavery in Missouri and requiring that all slaves already in the region be freed by age twenty-five. Tallmadge's amendment set off a storm of sectional controversy that the elderly Thomas Jefferson likened to a "fire bell in the night," because it raised alarming new questions about whether the United States would remain united.[4]

The "Missouri question" inspired the nation's first extended debate over the expansion of slavery, which engaged both black and white Americans. Anxious to see whether Congress would take action against slavery, free blacks living in Washington, D.C., crowded the galleries of the House and Senate, while white southerners threatened to secede from the Union, and northern politicians embraced federal action against slavery for the first time.

Tallmadge's amendment was narrowly approved in the House of Representatives, but it stalled in the Senate. The question went unresolved until 1820, when a group led by Kentucky senator Henry Clay embraced a compromise in which Missouri would be admitted as a slave state alongside the new free state of Maine, which had split off from Massachusetts to form an independent territory in 1819. The **Missouri Compromise**, as it became known, retained the balance of power between the regions, but it also included a major concession to antislavery northerners: Congress agreed that slavery throughout the rest of the Louisiana Purchase would be prohibited north of latitude 36°30′, which runs along Missouri's southern border (Map 5.2). Slavery would not travel north, as many northern whites feared. But the Missouri Compromise was deeply disappointing to African Americans in both regions.

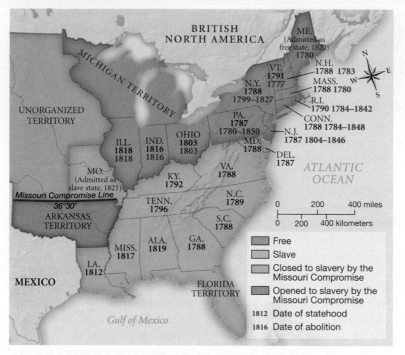

MAP 5.2   The Missouri Compromise

Passed in 1820, the Missouri Compromise prohibited slavery north of the parallel 36°30′ north, except within the boundaries of the state of Missouri. As Map 5.2 shows, the passage of the Missouri Compromise solidified the sectional divide between the slaveholding states of the South and the free states of the North, which all passed abolition laws well before 1820. The year in which these laws were passed is also indicated, along with the year in which slavery actually ended in states that used gradual emancipation laws to abolish slavery.

It stopped the southward progression of gradual emancipation at Missouri's southern border and shored up slavery in the South.

Slavery Expands into Indian Territory

The relentless expansion of the slave South also had a devastating effect on the region's Native American peoples. White settlers and federal officials used a combination of treaties, warfare, and forced migration to drive the Cherokee, Creek, Choctaw, Chickasaw, and Seminole tribes from their homelands. Known among whites as the Five Civilized Tribes, because they had adopted European institutions in an attempt to live peacefully alongside their white neighbors, these tribes occupied large amounts of land that became increasingly appealing to settlers as the South's plantation economy expanded. The conflicts that white encroachment created culminated in the federal government's passage of the **Indian Removal Act** in 1830, which forced Indians living east of the Mississippi River to relocate to Indian Territory (present-day Oklahoma).

This act came on the heels of several decades of conflict, most of which involved disputes over the Indians' traditional homelands, which were coveted by white settlers. But the Seminole tribe, which lived in northern Florida, also clashed with state and federal authorities on the issue of slavery. Although the Seminoles owned slaves, their system of bondage differed dramatically from that of the other four tribes, whose slave owning practices resembled those of southern whites. Seminole slaves were adopted as kin: They could not be sold to whites, and they rarely passed their enslaved status on to their children. The tribe also allied with runaway slaves and sheltered entire communities of fugitives. Known today as Black Seminoles, the members of these maroon communities remained free by paying their Seminole hosts an annual tribute in livestock or crops, and they helped the Seminoles defend their land from white squatters.

By the late 1820s, all five tribes were having trouble holding on to their land. As white settlers proliferated, they drove the Indians out by squatting on their territory, stealing their livestock, and burning their towns. The Indians complained to both state and federal officials, who resolved the conflict by dispossessing the Indians. The Indian Removal Act of 1830 was designed by Andrew Jackson, who had been elected president in 1828, and called for the Five Civilized Tribes to sign treaties giving up their homelands in the Southeast in return for payments and new land in the West. The army forcibly displaced Indians who refused to relocate. Among them were most of the Cherokees, who remained on their land until 1838, when federal troops marched them west on a brutal journey known as the Trail of Tears. As the tribes moved west, they took their slaves with them.

The Seminoles were the only tribe to resist with force. Their slave and maroon allies helped them repel the U.S. troops who arrived to drive them out of Florida in 1835. The Seminoles themselves numbered only 4,000, but they had 800 Black Seminole allies who fiercely opposed relocation. Some of the Black Seminoles were runaways who knew they would be returned to

Black Seminoles
Slaves and maroons played a vital role in helping the Seminole tribe to resist the incursions of U.S. troops. Black Seminole leaders such as John Horse, pictured here, gathered recruits and spearheaded efforts to drive the troops out of Florida. In the years immediately following his relocation to Oklahoma, Horse continued to work on behalf of the Seminoles and served as an interpreter. In 1849, he emigrated to Mexico and became a captain in the Mexican army. This engraving, titled *Gopher John, Seminole Interpreter*, first appeared in an 1848 history of the Second Seminole War.
Courtesy P. K. Yonge Library of Florida History, George A. Smathers Libraries, University of Florida.

their owners if the tribe agreed to move. Others feared that relocation would reenslave all Black Seminoles. Black Seminole leaders such as John Horse, fighting alongside Seminole leaders such as Osceola, enlisted several hundred rebellious plantation slaves to join the Seminole cause. When Osceola's forces were defeated in the spring of 1838, Horse was forced west along with most of his Seminole allies. Several hundred

Seminoles remained behind in the Florida swamps, however, and they waged another war to resist displacement between 1855 and 1858.

The Domestic Slave Trade

Most enslaved African Americans were owned by white southerners. Louisiana and Alabama joined the Union in 1812 and 1819, respectively, further expanding the South's cotton belt. Cotton planters migrated into the territories of Arkansas and Missouri and also established settlements in Spanish Florida, which Spain ceded to the United States in the 1819 Adams-Onís Treaty. (The agreement took effect two years later, in 1821.) Slaveholding settlers also began arriving in Texas as early as the 1820s, when the region still belonged to Mexico, which had abolished slavery. They supported Texas's war for independence in the 1830s and the U.S. annexation of Texas in 1845, which brought Texas into the Union as a slave state. As the last of the four new slave states to enter the Union between 1820 and 1860, Texas followed Missouri (1821), Arkansas (1836), and Florida (1845).

Slavery was most important in the Lower South. Between 1820 and 1860, 1.2 million African Americans moved from the Upper South to the Lower South in a mass migration that relocated almost half of the region's slave population. Approximately one-third of these involuntary migrants belonged to Upper South slaveholders who took their slaves with them as they migrated west and south to establish new plantations in South Carolina, Georgia, Alabama, Mississippi, Louisiana, Florida, Arkansas, and Texas. The remaining two-thirds were bought, transported, and resold in the Lower South by slave traders (Map 5.3).

Most slaves made the grueling journey on foot, in coffles that could contain anywhere from thirty to three hundred men, women, and children. The men were usually chained together in handcuffed pairs, while the women and children trailed behind them or were carried in wagons. Traders on horseback, with whips and guns, accompanied the coffles. After walking twenty to twenty-five miles during the day, the slaves often slept outdoors, sometimes under tents or just huddled together on the ground. As the South's transportation network improved, traders shipped their slaves south on steamships that chugged down the Mississippi or on oceangoing ships that docked in New Orleans. By the 1850s, transporting slaves by rail was also common. Lyman Abbott, a northerner who visited the region in 1856, found that "every train going south has . . . slaves on board . . . twenty or more, and [has] a 'nigger car,' which is generally also the smokers' car, and sometimes the baggage car."[5]

Regardless of how the slave migrants traveled, the journey represented a new middle passage for them. Slaves dreaded being "sold down the river" to the Lower South, knowing, above all, that such sales usually meant permanent separation from their families and friends. The majority of slaves who entered the trade were under thirty; most left their parents behind, although very young children were usually sold with their mothers. The trade also split up many young slave couples, disrupting one in five slave marriages in the Upper South, and divided siblings, extended families, and friends. These losses were all the more devastating because they came without warning: Owners usually sold slaves in secret to avoid giving them a chance to object. Charity Bowery's mistress, for example, made sure that Bowery was out running errands when she sold Bowery's twelve-year-old son. "She didn't want to be troubled

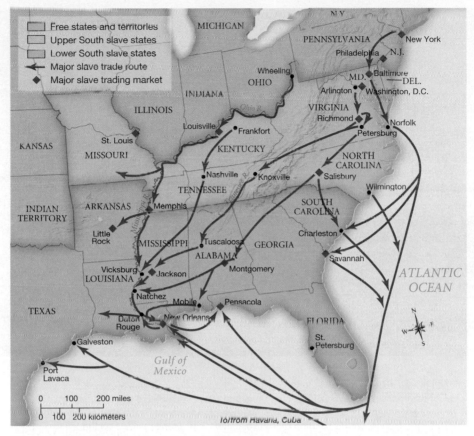

MAP 5.3 The Domestic Slave Trade, 1808–1865

With the termination of the international slave trade in 1808, an extensive domestic slave trade developed to transfer slaves from the North and Upper South, where free labor was increasingly predominant, to the Lower South's ever-expanding plantation frontier. This map illustrates the various routes by which the forced migrants traveled south: Some were carried in railroad cars, while others were loaded onto riverboats and oceangoing vessels and shipped to slave ports such as New Orleans. Many more made the long journey on foot, marching south under the supervision of armed slave traders. SOURCE: *The Atlas of African American History and Politics: From the Slave Trade to Modern Times,* by Arwin Smallwood and Jeffrey Elliot. Copyright © 1998 The McGraw-Hill Companies, Inc. Used by permission of McGraw-Hill.

with our cries," Bowery later remembered.[6] Slave owners routinely used the ever-present threat of sale to control their slaves and suppress dissent. According to one slave, his master would threaten "that if we didn't suit him he would put us in pocket quick—meaning that he would sell us."[7]

Once in the Lower South, slaves faced new traumas. On arrival, they were marketed at auction houses and slave trading centers across the region. Prospective buyers appraised them as if they were farm animals, inspecting their bodies for signs of illness or other physical weakness and scars from frequent whippings, which might indicate a rebellious nature. Virtually all buyers were men, since even widowed white women often bought their slaves through male intermediaries rather than entering into the

Slave Auction

Slaves experienced tremendous degradation in the process of their auction and sale. Potential buyers, almost all of whom were white men, inspected them bodily and subjected them to questioning. Slave couples and parents of slave children were burdened with the additional fear of having their families torn asunder. In this painting of a slave auction, one woman stands on the auction block before a group of bidders, while potential buyers question and examine the other slaves, most of whom are women and small children. *Friedrich Schulz (1823–1875), The Slave Market, 19th century, oil on canvas/Hirshhorn Museum and Sculpture Garden, Washington, DC, USA/The Bridgeman Art Library International.*

trade themselves. Prospective buyers subjected slaves to a level of scrutiny considered too indelicate for white women to witness. Men examined slaves' teeth to determine their age and pushed back their clothes to look at their muscles. They also "felt all over the women folks," one ex-slave recalled, to try to determine whether they were fertile.[8] Not surprisingly, slaves found the whole procedure deeply degrading. But some also tried to shape its outcome. Henry Bibb, whose Kentucky master punished him for being a chronic runaway by selling his entire family to a slave trader, was so intent on keeping his family together that he told a prospective buyer he had run away only once.

Black Challenges to Slavery

As slavery expanded, black discontent heightened. In 1820, the disappointing outcome of the Missouri crisis helped inspire a free black named Denmark Vesey to denounce slavery and exhort South Carolina slaves to rebel. Divine inspiration, alternatively, moved a slave preacher named Nat Turner to lead a bloody attack on slavery in Southampton, Virginia, in 1831. Neither succeeded in overturning slavery, but both men's actions had an enduring impact. Within the region, Vesey and Turner inspired new repressive measures to forestall any future rebellions. Outside the South, their actions fueled black abolitionist critiques of slavery. In particular, David Walker, a free black man who fled the South after Vesey's planned revolt was suppressed, insisted that slave rebels were heroes and called for others to follow in their footsteps.

Denmark Vesey's Plot

Originally named Telemarque, Denmark Vesey hailed from St. Thomas in the Danish West Indies. As a teenager, he relocated to Charleston, South Carolina, with his owner in 1793. Fluent in both French and English, the young slave had taught himself to read and write by the time he reached Charleston, where his owner employed him as a clerk and domestic servant. As a highly skilled and valuable slave, Vesey might have remained in bondage all his life but for an extraordinary stroke of good luck in 1799. That year, he purchased a lottery ticket—likely with money earned from taking on extra work during his free hours—and won the princely sum of $1,500. He used $600 of it to purchase his own freedom and the remainder to move out of his master's house and establish a carpentry business.

Vesey continued to socialize and identify with slaves, and he became increasingly eager to see all of his enslaved friends set free. In 1819, when congressional debates over the status of Missouri appeared in the Charleston newspapers, Vesey was delighted to see slavery under attack. His plot took at least some inspiration from these debates, the news of which reached black communities across the country. As one Charleston slaveholder complained, "By the Missouri question, our slaves thought, there was a charter of liberties granted them by Congress."[9]

By 1820, with the help of several enslaved friends, Vesey had begun planning a rebellion. They spent more than a year recruiting other men. Armed with stolen guns and knives, they planned to raid Charleston's Meeting Street Arsenal and a nearby shop to gather additional weapons for their supporters, whom they expected to number in the thousands. Vesey was a lay preacher in Charleston's African Methodist Episcopal (AME) church, and he reviewed the details of the plot at religious classes held in his home, in which he likened the planned rebellion to the delivery of the children of Israel from Egyptian slavery.

The conspirators dreamed of freeing themselves and sailing off to Haiti, but more than a month before the scheduled rebellion, two Charleston slaves divulged the plan to their owners. Local authorities swiftly suppressed the uprising. Over the next month, officials arrested 131 slaves and free blacks, 72 of whom were tried, convicted, and sentenced to death. More died in custody, and 27 were ultimately released. Vesey was hanged on July 2, 1822, with 5 other men in a public spectacle that drew thousands of black and white Charlestonians. The event was followed by several other mass hangings that month.

The rebels were deliberately denied funerals or proper burials. Aware that Africans and African Americans cherished funeral rites as a way to free the spirit of the deceased, Charleston authorities had the rebels cut down and dismembered after they were hanged. As the death toll mounted, however, it became clear that the costly executions could not proceed indefinitely. The loss of slave property and labor imposed a severe economic burden on both the slaves' owners and the state. By late July, Carolinians were ready to see the hangings come to an end. As a lawyer told one of Charleston's magistrates, "You must take care and save enough negroes for the Rice crop."[10] The remaining 37 rebels were transported to slave societies outside the United States at their owners' expense.

Neither death nor deportation could erase the memory of Vesey's plot, however, and like Richmond whites in the aftermath of Gabriel's rebellion in 1800 (see chapter 4), white South Carolinians moved quickly to limit the mobility and autonomy of their slaves. (See Documents: Managing the Slaves, pp. 242–44.) State officials banned slaves from hiring themselves out, and they forbade free blacks to hire slaves. The City of Charleston took the additional precaution of hiring a permanent force of 150 guardsmen to patrol the city around the clock. Any slave caught on the street after 9 p.m. without a written pass could be arrested and whipped or, worse, assigned to walk on a prison treadmill installed at the Charleston jail in 1823. The treadmill consisted of a wheel with steps, which was propelled by a group of manacled slaves, who climbed the rotating steps under the supervision of a driver brandishing a cat-o'-nine-tails. The mill was used to grind corn sold to offset the jail's daily expenses, but even when there was no grain to grind, prisoners could be assigned to hard labor on the treadmill.

Bitterly aware that Vesey and most of his key collaborators could read and write, South Carolina officials reinforced existing laws against teaching slaves to read, and the state legislature adopted new legislation forbidding free black education. In the fall of 1822, municipal authorities also razed the AME church where Vesey had preached, although they could find no evidence that church leaders had participated in the plot. As one nineteenth-century commentator later noted, the church was threatening because it "tended to spread the dangerous infection of the alphabet."[11]

Free blacks were also subject to new legislation and surveillance designed to make them feel unwelcome in the state. One law required all free black males over age fifteen to find white guardians willing to post bonds for their good behavior, and it barred free blacks who left the state from returning. The state also began to require free black sailors who worked on ships that docked in South Carolina to be jailed until their vessels left the state. The City of Charleston levied a $50 annual tax on its free black residents, who also had to register with municipal officials twice a year.

David Walker's Exile

Even as Charleston whites moved to ensure that no new Vesey would threaten their safety, Vesey's memory lived on. Among the free blacks who fled Charleston in the wake of the plot was David Walker, who moved north and made a name for himself as the most militant black abolitionist of his era. The rising hostility toward free blacks in Charleston had convinced him that "if I remain in this bloody land . . . I will not live long."[12] By 1825, the forty-year-old Walker had resettled in Boston, where he ran a used clothing store near the harbor, outfitting the sailors and other mariners who passed through the city. In Boston, Walker found a lively black community, married, and joined the African Lodge of the Honorable Society of Free and Accepted Masons. Members included local leaders such as the Reverend Thomas Paul, the minister of Boston's First African Baptist Church.

But moving to Massachusetts did not allow Walker to escape white oppression. He found most African American northerners "ignorant and poor" and unable "to obtain the comforts of life, but by cleaning their [white people's] boots and shoes, old clothes, [and] waiting on them." He also found African Americans hard-pressed to secure their position in the face of the American Colonization Society's (ACS's) plans.[13]

The ACS, though opposed by blacks, had become steadily more popular among whites. At their most polite, ACS members continued to champion colonization as a step toward the eradication of slavery. But after founding the West African colony of Liberia in 1821 (see chapter 4), they began to focus their attention on free blacks. While many blacks were not opposed to emigration in theory, they questioned the motives of the ACS and believed that the organization's propaganda hurt black prospects for freedom in America. ACS members rejected the views of an earlier generation of antislavery whites who embraced black education as the road to self-improvement. Instead, colonizationists such as ACS secretary Elias Caldwell contended that improving the condition of African Americans would only give them more "relish for those privileges which they can never attain."[14]

David Walker was appalled by the ACS, viewing colonization as a doctrine designed to perpetuate slavery by banishing free blacks. Walker advocated abolition instead of emigration and denounced colonization as a proslavery plot. Convinced that all blacks should fight for freedom within the United States, he sheltered fugitive slaves in his home and became a contributor to the nation's first black newspaper, *Freedom's Journal* (founded in 1827), which opposed both colonization and slavery. Like the *Journal*'s editors, Walker was convinced that African Americans could not defeat slavery and racism without pleading their own cause. This conviction inspired him to publish an abolitionist manifesto of his own in 1829, titled *Walker's Appeal . . . to the Coloured Citizens of the World.* (See From the Record: Slavery and Colonization.)

The controversial pamphlet was influential on several counts. It galvanized a new generation of radical blacks who would lobby for abolition and civil rights for many years to come (see chapter 6). Among whites, it helped shift the focus of the antislavery movement from colonization to emancipation. Walker's call for slave violence was widely condemned by white abolitionists, most of whom were political moderates who supported the ACS, but these reformers proved more open to his critique of colonization. The influential white abolitionist William Lloyd Garrison, who still held moderate views when he first encountered Walker's pamphlet, criticized "the spirit and tendency of this *Appeal*" but also acknowledged that it contained many "valuable truths."[15] Shortly after its publication, Garrison renounced colonization and dedicated himself to the immediate abolition of slavery.

In the South, *Walker's Appeal* made whites even more determined to suppress black dissent. By 1830, the pamphlet had reached Virginia, North Carolina, Georgia, Louisiana, and Alabama, where whites discovered copies in the hands of black seamen and slaves. Terrified by its message, they offered a $3,000 bounty for Walker's death and a $10,000 reward for anyone willing to kidnap Walker and deliver him alive. His pamphlet was the subject of special meetings of several southern state legislatures, and it inspired new laws restricting the rights of slaves and free blacks in Georgia and North Carolina.

In the midst of this controversy, Walker was found dead in the doorway of his home in June 1830, just after the publication of the third edition of his *Appeal*. He probably succumbed to tuberculosis, which was rampant in nineteenth-century Boston. But given the size of the reward that Walker's enemies offered to see him dead, many

From the Record

David Walker | Slavery and Colonization, 1829

Walker's Appeal . . . to the Coloured Citizens of the World, the most radical antislavery document of its era, was written by **David Walker (1796/97–1830)** in 1829. It is a fiery protest against slavery and colonization that lambasts white people for enslaving and oppressing people of color, while also critiquing blacks for acquiescing to white domination.

Are we [blacks] MEN!!—I ask you, O my brethren! are we MEN? Did our Creator make us to be slaves to dust and ashes like ourselves? Are they [whites] not dying worms as well as we? . . . How we could be so *submissive* to a gang of men, whom we cannot tell whether they are *as good* as ourselves or not, I never could conceive. . . .

. . . Oh! my coloured brethren, all over the world, when shall we arise from this deathlike apathy?—And be men!! You will notice, if ever we become men, (I mean *respectable* men, such as other people are,) we must exert ourselves to the full. For remember, that it is the greatest desire and object of the greater part of the whites, to keep us ignorant, and make us work to support them and their families.—Here now, in the Southern and Western sections of this country, there are at least three coloured persons for one white, why is it, that those few weak, good-for-nothing whites, are able to keep so many able men, one of whom, can put to flight a dozen whites, in wretchedness and misery? . . .

Do the colonizationists think to send us [free blacks] off without first being reconciled to us? Do they think to bundle us up like brutes and send us off . . . ?

. . . Do they think to drive us from our country and homes, after having enriched it with our blood and tears, and keep back millions of our dear brethren, sunk in the most barbarous wretchedness, to dig up gold and silver for them and their children? Surely, the Americans must think that we are brutes, as some of them have represented us to be. They think that we do not feel for our brethren, whom they are murdering by the inches, but they are dreadfully deceived. I acknowledge that there are some deceitful and hypocritical wretches among us, who will tell us one thing while they mean another, and thus they go on aiding our enemies to oppress themselves and us. But I declare this day before my Lord and Master, that I believe there are some true-hearted sons of Africa, in this land of oppression, but pretended *liberty!!!!!*—who do in reality feel for their suffering brethren, who are held in bondage by tyrants.

SOURCE: David Walker, *Walker's Appeal, in Four Articles; Together with a Preamble, to the Coloured Citizens of the World, but in Particular, and Very Expressly, to Those of the United States of America, Written in Boston, State of Massachusetts, September 28, 1829*, rev. ed. (Boston: published by author, 1830), 16, 74, 78, 79.

??? **According to Walker, how do the same mechanisms serve to oppress both slaves and free blacks? How does Walker relate the plights of both groups to each other?**

free blacks were convinced that he was the victim of foul play. Either way, Walker's death did not end his influence. His pamphlet had shown that slavery had enemies throughout the nation.

Nat Turner's Rebellion, the *Amistad* Case, and the *Creole* Insurrection

Walker's message received additional support just a few years later when an enslaved lay preacher named Nat Turner led one of the bloodiest slave rebellions in American history. Born in 1800, Turner was a lifelong resident of Southampton County, Virginia, and grew up during a time when many blacks and whites in the Upper South were embracing evangelical Christianity. The first few decades of the nineteenth century saw the **Second Great Awakening**, similar to the Great Awakening of the eighteenth century. Once again, a wave of Baptist and Methodist revivals swept through the nation. But black and white congregants often understood the message of religious equality quite differently, especially in the South.

Raised in a Methodist household, Turner was a pious young man who spent much of his spare time praying and fasting. He experienced powerful religious visions, which eventually convinced him that "the great day of judgment" was at hand. Turner bided his time for years, waiting for "signs in the heavens that it would make known to me when I should commence the great work." On the evening of August 21, 1831, he struck, accompanied by a small band of fellow slaves who shared his vision of "slay[ing] my enemies with their own weapons."[16]

Armed with axes and hatchets, Turner and his men began by murdering Turner's owner, Joseph Travis, and his family and stealing their small cache of guns. They then moved from plantation to plantation freeing slaves; killing white men, women, and children; and gathering more weapons and recruits. Turner's force grew to more than 50 slaves and free blacks, who managed to kill 60 whites before a Virginia militia tracked them down two days later. The rebels scattered but were pursued by a growing force of armed whites, who went on a killing spree that lasted more than two weeks and resulted in the deaths of more than 100 blacks—all of whom died without trial. An additional 48 suspects were captured, tried, and executed by the state, including Turner himself, who managed to evade capture for three months until a white farmer discovered him in hiding.

Turner's rebellion terrified whites across the South. Turner was soon rumored to have an army of 1,200 coconspirators located as far away as North Carolina. In Virginia, as one plantation mistress put it, fears of revolt were "agonizing." Virginia legislators were even willing to consider the abolition of slavery rather than continue to contemplate "the horrors of servile war which will not end until . . . the slaves and the whites are totally eliminated."[17] They debated a gradual emancipation plan but quickly decided that emancipation was not the solution.

Convinced that Turner's uprising was caused by the abolitionist agitation of men such as David Walker, Virginia's leaders instead revised the state's legal code to bar slaves and free blacks from preaching or even attending religious meetings without white supervision. Virginia legislators also targeted free blacks with a colonization bill, which allocated new funding to remove them, and a police bill that denied free blacks trial by jury and made any free blacks convicted of a crime subject to sale and relocation.

HORRID MASSACRE IN VIRGINIA·

The Scenes which the above Plate is designed to represent, are—Fig. 1. a Mother intreating for the lives of her children.—2. Mr. Travis, cruelly murdered by his own Slaves.— 3. Mr. Barrow, who bravely defended himself until his wife escaped.—4. A comp. of mounted Dragoons in pursuit of the Blacks.

Nat Turner's Rebellion

For many slaveholders, Nat Turner's rebellion was the realization of their greatest fears. This image, which is annotated at the bottom with descriptions of the scene's various parts, is an illustration from the *Authentic and Impartial Narrative of the Tragical Scene Which Was Witnessed in Southampton County* (New York: Warner and West, 1831), a pamphlet about the revolt written by white Virginian Samuel Warner. According to the annotations, Figure 1 represents "a Mother intreating for the lives of her children"; Figure 3 shows "Mr. Barrow, who bravely defended himself until his wife escaped." Why would such depictions have resonated with slaveholders?
F & A Archive/The Art Archive at Art Resource, NY.

Lawmakers also took precautions that were unprecedented in scope. In 1835, southern legislators silenced congressional debates over slavery for almost a decade by passing a **gag rule** prohibiting the reading of antislavery petitions in Congress. Former president John Quincy Adams, now a representative from Massachusetts, tirelessly opposed this rule, believing that it imposed unconstitutional limitations on petitioners' freedom of speech. He also saw congressional support for the rule as evidence that the nation was falling under the control of a dangerous "slavocracy" led by wealthy southern slaveholders. Known as "Old Man Eloquent" for his rhetorical skills, Adams called for rescinding the gag rule every year until 1844, when he finally prevailed.

Still, no gag rule or law could fully suppress black dissent. Instead, in the years following Nat Turner's rebellion, two slave insurrections at sea intensified whites' fears and called the security of the slave system into question. In 1839, a group of Africans who had just been kidnapped and enslaved seized control of the Spanish slave ship *Amistad* in international waters near Cuba. The U.S. navy captured the ship and made the rebels prisoners of the U.S. government, at which point Spain demanded their return. But the rebels' enslavement violated treaties prohibiting the international slave trade, so their status had to be determined in court. The **Amistad case** became a widely publicized abolitionist cause and ultimately reached the U.S. Supreme Court, which freed the rebels in 1841.

A similar revolt in 1843 had a comparable outcome. Led by Madison Washington, slaves aboard the *Creole*, an American ship engaged in the internal slave trade, seized the vessel, sailed to British waters, and declared themselves free. The British accepted the slaves' emancipation declaration, enabling them to go free in the Bahamas. Speaking for the U.S. government, Secretary of State Daniel Webster honored the rebels' claims to freedom in the **Creole insurrection** but insisted unsuccessfully that the British government compensate the slaves' owners for their lost property.

Although both incidents took place at sea, the *Amistad* and *Creole* revolts reinforced the insecurity that southern slaveholders felt. Like the actions of Denmark Vesey, David Walker, and Nat Turner, these slaves' endeavors suggested that black dissent could never be fully subdued. Moreover, the fact that the rebels went on to win their freedom in U.S. courts underscored the limited support slavery enjoyed outside the South.

Everyday Resistance to Slavery

Both external and internal opposition to slavery unnerved white southerners, whose control over their slave population was precarious and hard-won. Although they used repressive slave codes, vigilant slave patrols, brutal punishments, and the threat of sale to keep their bondmen and bondwomen subdued, they could never eradicate black resistance to slavery. Instead, individual resistance was nearly an everyday occurrence. Organized rebellions became rare in the wake of Nat Turner's revolt, but slave discontent remained ubiquitous. Enslaved African Americans protested their condition in many ways, including stealing plantation property, feigning illness, refusing to work, defying their owners, and running away.

Disobedience and Defiance

Theft was perhaps the most common form of disobedience, although few slaves regarded it as a crime. "Po' nigger had to steal back dar in slav'y eben to git 'nuff to eat. . . . Ef it hadn't been fo' dem [whites], nigger wouldn't know nothin' 'bout stealin'," explained one ex-slave from Virginia. The former South Carolina slave Rosa Barnwell reported that her owners expected slaves to survive on a weekly allowance of approximately eight quarts of corn and four quarts of sweet potatoes. Given no meat, they sometimes took "a hog on their own account." Louisa Gause, who was also enslaved in South Carolina, concluded, "If [a slave] did [steal], he never take nothin' but what been belong to him."

Slaves also feigned illness to avoid unpleasant work assignments. Planters often complained of slaves who were "lazy . . . and affected to be sick," and some even employed doctors to determine whether their slaves were "really ill or merely 'playing possum.'"[18] Such determinations were not always possible, however, and some ex-slaves reported success by refusing to eat for days and pretending to be too weak to stand up.

Harriet Tubman
Harriet Tubman, born Araminta "Minty" Ross, endured a brutal childhood and young adulthood in slavery. Following her final, permanent escape in 1849, she helped many more slaves—including members of her own family—escape to freedom and spoke out against the horrors of the institution. During the Civil War, she served the Union as a cook, nurse, teacher, scout, and spy. *Library of Congress, LC-USZ62-7816.*

Slaves also defied their owners by running away and hiding to avoid punishment or other harsh measures. Mostly temporary, such escapes were often propelled by despair and fear rather than being carefully planned. Araminta "Minty" Ross, who later renamed herself Harriet Tubman, fled her mistress in terror at age seven after stealing a lump of sugar. Miss Susan, the brutal mistress for whom Tubman worked as a nursemaid, was a merciless taskmaster who beat Tubman every day, lashing out at the girl every time the baby she tended cried. Caught in the act of stealing, Tubman was afraid to face whatever punishment this far graver transgression might bring. When she saw her mistress grab her rawhide whip, she ran as far as she could and then took shelter in a pigpen, where she hid for five days, braving the muck of the pen and competing with the pigs for scraps to eat. She stayed there until hunger and her increasing fear of the adult pigs drove her to return home and face the wrath of her mistress. Not until 1849, two decades later, did she finally manage to escape permanently.

In escaping from slavery only temporarily, the seven-year-old Tubman became what slaveholders deemed a **truant**—a slave who absconded for a matter of days, weeks, or sometimes months. Although truants were generally adults, many were like Tubman in that they fled to avoid punishment. Others sought to escape especially onerous work assignments or abusive treatment, and they would sometimes agree to return after negotiating better conditions with their owners. Truants often hid in local swamps or woods—a form of resistance also known as **lying out**. In many cases, such runaways received support from other slaves who brought them food and supplies, and sometimes even hid the truants in their homes. But truants also included more short-term escapees, who left to visit loved ones or attend religious meetings, dances, or other social events.

Some slaves countered harsh treatment with outright resistance. The famous fugitive Frederick Douglass almost lost his life at age sixteen when he physically resisted a whipping from a particularly brutal master. Born on a Maryland plantation, Douglass spent much of his youth in Baltimore working as a house servant. But when he became an unruly teenager, Douglass's owner sent him out of the city to work for a poor white farmer named Mr. Covey, who was known for his ability to subdue even the most recalcitrant slaves. Covey subjected Douglass to a brutal work regime and terrible weekly beatings that left Douglass feeling utterly "broken in body, soul, and spirit." One day, however, he found himself fighting back against his tormentor. "From whence came the spirit I don't know," Douglass later recalled. The two men exchanged blows until both were exhausted, and thereafter Douglass recovered his "long-crushed spirit." He took no more beatings from Covey and "let it be known . . . that the white man who expected to succeed in whipping, must also succeed in killing me."[19]

Douglass was lucky to survive this resolution, but slaves who physically resisted risked death. They had no right to self-defense under southern law, which gave white people uncontrolled authority over slaves' bodies. Even whites who supervised rather than owned slaves had this authority, as the North Carolina judge Thomas Ruffin ruled in the influential 1829 case *State v. Mann*. (See From the Record: *State v. Mann*.) Ruffin overturned the slave owning widow Elizabeth Jones's attempt to impose criminal sanctions on John Mann, to whom she had hired out her slave Lydia. When Lydia disobeyed Jones, he whipped her, and when she tried to escape, he shot and killed her. Jones's acquittal shored up the power of southern whites who employed or even supervised slaves. Subsequent rulings across the South reinforced these principles. Georgia's Supreme Court ruled in *John v. State* (1854) that any slave accused of killing a white person had to be charged with murder, even if he or she had acted in self-defense (an act that would normally carry a manslaughter charge).[20]

Runaways Who Escaped from Slavery

Successful permanent escapes were rare. Whites patrolled plantation districts on a nightly basis, severely punishing slaves who left their quarters. "Run Nigger, run, Patty Roller will catch you . . . I'll shoot you with my flintlock gun," enslaved African Americans would sing, sometimes in an effort to warn others that patrollers were nearby.[21] Some of slavery's successful fugitives, such as Frederick Douglass, William Wells Brown, and Harriet Tubman, went on to provide eloquent testimony about the brutality of slavery and become among the nation's most influential antislavery activists. Although most runaways were caught before they made it out of the South, even unsuccessful escape attempts had an impact on the slave system, because they cost slave owners time and money and reminded southern whites that African Americans were held in bondage against their will.

One difficulty of permanent escape was that although runaways could hide in nearby woods or swamps with relative ease, they could not travel on roads without a pass. A few exceptionally enterprising fugitives learned to read and write so that they could forge their own passes, but even procuring paper and ink could be a challenge. Solomon Northup, a free black man from New York, learned this firsthand when he was kidnapped and sold into slavery in 1841. Northup was drugged and ended up in a slave pen after traveling to Washington, D.C., with two white men who had offered him a job as a musician. The men sold him to a slave trader, who believed, despite Northup's protests to the contrary, that he was a runaway slave from Georgia. Neither the trader nor any of Northup's subsequent owners had any incentive to believe that he was free, and he was eventually sold as far south as Louisiana, where he toiled on cotton plantations for many years.

From the Record

Judge Thomas Ruffin | *State v. Mann*, 1829

In *State v. Mann* (1829), the North Carolina Supreme Court ruled that masters could not be punished for assaulting their slaves. The case came about after John Mann first whipped, and then shot and killed, a rented slave named Lydia, who had disobeyed him and tried to flee his whip. Charged with assault and battery in Lydia's death, Mann was acquitted by **Judge Thomas Ruffin**, who maintained that "the power of the master must be absolute, to render the submission of the slave perfect." Note, however, that the judge also expressed some regrets about his ruling.

The Court is compelled to express an opinion upon the extent of the dominion of the master over the slave in North Carolina.

The indictment charges a battery on Lydia, a slave of Elizabeth Jones. . . . Here the slave had been hired by the defendant, and was in his possession; and the battery was committed during the period of hiring. . . . The inquiry here is, whether a cruel and unreasonable battery on a slave, by the hirer, is indictable. . . . Our laws uniformly treat the master or other person having the possession and command of the slave, as entitled to the same extent of authority. The object is the same—the services of the slave; and the same powers must be confided. . . .

. . . The power of the master must be absolute, to render the submission of the slave perfect. I most freely confess my sense of the harshness of this proposition: I feel it as deeply as any man can. And as a principle of moral right, every person in his retirement must repudiate it. But in the actual condition of things, it must be so. There is no remedy. This discipline belongs to the state of slavery. . . .

. . . I would gladly have avoided this ungrateful question. But being brought to it, the Court is compelled to declare, that while slavery exists amongst us in its present state, or until it shall seem fit to the legislature to interpose express enactments to the contrary, it will be the imperative duty of the judges to recognize the full dominion of the owner over the slave, except where the exercise of it is forbidden by statute. And this we do upon the ground, that this dominion is essential to the value of slaves as property, to the security of the master, and the public tranquillity, greatly dependent upon their subordination; and in fine, as most effectually securing the general protection and comfort of the slaves themselves.

. . . Let the judgment below be reversed, and judgment entered for the defendant.

SOURCE: James Bradley Thayer, ed., *Cases on Constitutional Law* (Cambridge, MA: University Press, John Wilson and Son, 1894), 473–76.

??? **What are Ruffin's views on slavery, and why does he resist offering slaves any protection from lethal violence?**

Literate and legally free, Northup had white friends in New York who could vouch for his identity, but plantation life made it almost impossible for him to write or mail a letter. He explained his difficulty in his autobiography, *Twelve Years a Slave*: "In the first place, I was deprived of pen, ink, and paper. In the second place, a slave cannot leave his plantation without a pass, nor will a post-master mail a letter for one without written instructions from his owner. I was in slavery nine years, and always watchful and on the alert, before I met with the good fortune of obtaining a sheet of paper." Even after that, Northup had to figure out how to make ink to write his letter and find a white man he trusted to mail it.[22]

Geographic distance created another obstacle. Slaves who lived in Texas sometimes managed to escape to Mexico, but fugitives from other regions generally made their way north. Those who attempted to leave the Lower South faced a trek of hundreds of miles and had to navigate their way through vast expanses of strange territory without getting lost. Uneducated and for the most part illiterate, fugitive slaves had no maps and had to hide during the day and travel at night, guided only by the **North Star**. (See Visual Sources: The Art of the Plantation, pp. 250–61.)

Skilled slaves had slightly better opportunities to escape. They could blend in with free blacks more easily in southern cities than could scantily dressed field hands, which gave them opportunities to travel north by boat or train. Although steamboats were often inspected for runaways, and blacks on trains had to carry passes or papers documenting their free status, successful fugitives, such as the slave couple Ellen and William Craft, found ingenious ways to evade detection. The Crafts, who left a plantation in Macon, Georgia, in 1848, escaped by passing the light-skinned Ellen off as a sickly young slave master traveling north to seek medical attention. Her husband played the role of the young invalid's faithful attendant. With Ellen swathed in bandages and pretending to be too ill to speak, the couple rode by train to Savannah, where they boarded a steamship bound for Philadelphia. A year later, the enslaved tobacco factory worker Henry "Box" Brown made an equally daring escape from Richmond. With help from a sympathetic white shopkeeper, Brown had himself shipped to Philadelphia in a large wooden crate, which traveled by steamboat, rail, ferry, and delivery wagon before finally arriving at its destination twenty-seven hours later. Such escapes were well publicized, leaving white southerners ever more vigilant.

Slaves who lived in or traveled through border states and territories had the best chance to escape because of their proximity to free soil. Slaves in Kentucky could cross the Ohio River to seek freedom to the north, while those in Missouri could try their luck in Iowa or Illinois. These slaves were also much closer to the **underground railroad**, a network of black and white antislavery activists who routinely sheltered escaped slaves. But to contact the underground railroad, slaves first had to elude patrollers, slave catchers, and the hunting dogs white southerners used to track them down.

Moreover, family ties kept many slaves from attempting escape. Most successful fugitives were young men from the Upper South and border states who, in addition to being strong enough to withstand the trek, were either childless or already separated from their families due to sale or migration. They also had a better chance of traveling undetected, because planters typically employed young male slaves to run errands. Women, by contrast, were far less likely to be given jobs that took them away from their owners' property. Childbearing and motherhood limited their options even further. Slave women bore an average of seven children, beginning in their late teens, and spent much of their twenties and thirties

THE RESURRECTION OF HENRY BOX BROWN AT PHILADELPHIA.
Who escaped from Richmond Va in a Box 3 feet long 2½ ft deep and 2 ft wide.

Henry "Box" Brown
The Virginia slave Henry "Box" Brown's daring escape, in which he had himself shipped to Philadelphia in a crate, serves as one of the more creative and surprising examples of slaves' determination to be free. After winning his freedom, Brown published an autobiography and became a popular abolitionist speaker and entertainer. Some abolitionists, however, including Frederick Douglass, disapproved of Brown's disclosure of his escape method, feeling that it prevented other slaves from escaping by similar means. *Library of Congress, LC-USZCN4-225.*

either pregnant or nursing. They maintained close ties with their children through to adulthood and frequently cared for grandchildren when they became too old to work in the fields. Few women were willing to escape without their offspring, and few fugitives made it far when accompanied by children. Female fugitives who traveled with children could not "walk so far or so fast as the scores of *men* who are constantly leaving," one underground railroad volunteer observed, while another estimated that such women were three times more likely to be caught than men who traveled alone.[23]

Survival, Community, and Culture

Since permanent escape was not a viable option for most slaves, they increasingly turned to Christianity to help them bear slavery's hardships. They also counted on fellow slaves. Most nineteenth-century slaves lived and worked on holdings large enough to sustain small slave communities. As of 1850, 73.4 percent of all slaves were owned by planters who owned ten or more slaves, and 51.6 percent belonged to planters owning more than twenty. Work took up much of their time and fostered bonds among enslaved laborers, who often worked in gender-segregated work gangs. Meanwhile, even though African American families were often scattered by sale, kinship remained central to slaves' cultural and social life, and family ties were extensive and resilient. Slaves sustained loving relationships with relatives and created new connections with nonrelatives to endure life under slavery and seek refuge from complete domination by their owners.

Slave Religion

By the early 1800s, many enslaved communities had embraced evangelical Christianity, but young slaves received much of their religious education in the slave quarters rather than in church. Drawn to the emotional forms of worship common in Baptist and Methodist revivals and churches, African Americans continued to favor these denominations over Presbyterian and Episcopal churches, where Sunday services tended to be more restrained. They rarely relied solely on white religious leaders for guidance, however. In rural areas, many blacks lacked access to religious services, and even in areas where churches were more plentiful, slave owners did not always permit slaves to attend church. (See Documents: Slave Testimony, pp. 245–49.)

Even blacks who worshipped alongside whites or received religious instruction from their masters tended to distrust white Christianity. Relegated to segregated pews or sometimes required to listen to the minister's sermon from outside the church, African Americans had few opportunities to worship on equal terms. In the "white folks' church," one former slave remembered, the slaves "couldn't do nuthin'—jes sit dere. Dey could sing, an' take de sacrement; but didn't have no voice—jes like animals!"[24] The character of the religious instruction that slaves received made matters worse. White ministers often stressed obedience and humility, with popular teachings centering on scriptural passages such as "Servants be obedient to their masters" and "Let as many servants as are under the yoke count their own masters worthy of all honor." Slaves understood the obvious self-interest animating such teachings. As the ex-slave Wes Brady recalled, "You ought to have heard that 'Hellish' preaching. . . . 'Obey your Master and Mistress, don't steal chickens, don't steal eggs and meat,' and nary word 'bout having a soul to save."[25]

Rather than accepting this instruction, enslaved blacks across the South often belonged to what historians have termed the **invisible church**. Slave Christianity stressed the equality of all men under God, drawing on the Bible as inspiration for spirituals that expressed slaves' own humanity, capacity for freedom, and hope of justice for an oppressed people. Slaves also embraced scriptural stories that held out the promise of liberation under a just God. Their favorite was the Old Testament's book of Exodus, which tells of how Moses freed the children of Israel from slavery in Egypt. This story was celebrated in slave spirituals such as "Go Down, Moses." (See From the Record: Go Down, Moses.)

Slaves gathered in their homes to hold their own religious ceremonies or assembled in secret "hush harbors" in the woods. Often led by slave elders, these ceremonies might incorporate African spiritual practices such as juju and voodoo. Most common was the **ring shout**, often known simply as the "shout." In this form of worship,

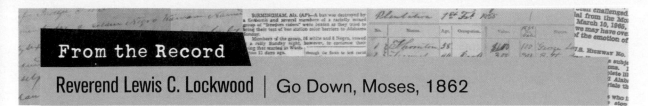

From the Record

Reverend Lewis C. Lockwood | Go Down, Moses, 1862

One of the first slave spirituals to be published, this song was transcribed by
the **Reverend Lewis C. Lockwood (1815–1904)** at Fort Monroe, Virginia, in 1862.
Lockwood, who learned the song from the ex-slaves he was ministering to at the fort,
noted that it had been popular among enslaved African Americans for almost a decade.
Also known as "Let My People Go," this song is notable for the direct parallel it draws
between the enslavement of African Americans and the enslavement of the Israelites in
the biblical story of the Exodus.

The Lord, by Moses, to Pharaoh said: Oh! let my people go;
If not, I'll smite your first-born dead—Oh! let my people go.
  Oh! Go down, Moses,
  Away down to Egypt's land,
  And tell King Pharaoh
  To let my people go.

No more shall they in bondage toil—Oh! let my people go;
Let them come out with Egypt's spoil—Oh! let my people go.

Haste, Moses, till the sea you've crossed—Oh! let my people go;
Pharaoh shall in the deep be lost—Oh! let my people go.

The sea before you shall divide—Oh! let my people go;
You'll cross dry-shod to the other side—Oh! let my people go.

Fear not King Pharaoh or his host—Oh! let my people go;
For they shall in the sea be lost—Oh! let my people go.

They'll sink like lead, to rise no more—Oh! let my people go;
An' you'll hear a shout on the other shore—Oh! let my people go.

The fiery cloud shall lead the way—Oh! let my people go;
A light by night, a shade by day—Oh! let my people go.

Jordan shall stand up like a wall—Oh! let my people go;
And the walls of Jericho shall fall—Oh! let my people go.

Your foes shall not before you stand—Oh! let my people go;
And you'll possess fair Canaan's land—Oh! let my people go.

Oh! let us all from bondage flee—Oh! let my people go;
And let us all in Christ be free—Oh! let my people go.

Continued

Continued

> *This world's a wilderness of woe—Oh! let my people go;*
> *Oh! let us all to glory go—Oh! let my people go.*
>   *Oh! Go down, Moses,*
>   *Away down to Egypt's land,*
>   *And tell King Pharaoh*
>   *To let my people go.*

SOURCE: *Continental Monthly*, July 1862, 112–13.

??? **How is this song emblematic of the slaves' invisible church? How does its message contrast with the messages conveyed to slaves in white churches?**

congregants formed a circle and moved counterclockwise while shuffling their feet, clapping, singing, calling out, or praying aloud. Practiced in both the West Indies and North America, the ring shout combined West African–based music and dance traditions with the passionate Protestantism of the Second Great Awakening to create a powerful new ritual that offered emotional and physical release. The former slave Mose Hursey, who witnessed these ceremonies as a child in Red River, Texas, recalled, "I heard them [slaves] get up with a powerful force of spirit, clappin' they hands and walking around the place. They'd shout, 'I got the glory. I got the old time religion in my heart.'"[26] The expressive, rhythmic music produced during the shouts lives on today in musical genres such as the blues and gospel.

Gender, Age, and Work

In communities forbidden any form of formal education, family structures allowed slaves to pass on wisdom, knowledge, and skills from one generation to the next. Slave elders usually played a vital role in schooling their communities. Few could teach their young people to read or write, because slave literacy was discouraged or banned in the southern states. But elderly slaves passed on other valuable lessons to youngsters, such as how to handle their owners, negotiate with overseers and other white authorities, and resolve disputes within their quarters. Generally respected for their extensive life experience, many served as the spiritual leaders of their communities as well.

Older slaves taught younger ones the agricultural techniques used to cultivate the planters' crops and the gardens that sustained slave families. They also helped young people master other survival skills. Adult men taught young boys how to fish, hunt, and forage for food, while women taught girls how to cook, sew, clean, take care of children, and even help deliver babies. These tasks were not strictly divided by gender. Frederick Douglass recalled that his grandmother was not only a skilled nurse but also "a capital hand at making nets for catching shad and herring" and equally good at using her nets to catch these fish.[27] Children of both sexes performed housework and took care of other children. But once they were old enough for adult labor, typically at puberty, girls and boys often worked separately and learned different tasks.

Although slave men and women both worked in the fields on plantations, tasks were commonly divided by gender. Field hands were usually split into sex-segregated work gangs and assigned different work regimes. Women were classified as three-quarters of a hand (rather than as a full hand), and on plantations with sufficient male workers, women were spared some of the most physically taxing labor. During planting season, women hoed while men plowed, and when slave workers erected fences, the men split the rails while the women assembled the fences.

When additional labor was needed, however, female slaves might be assigned to any task. On Louisiana sugar plantations, for example, female work gangs toiled along-side male gangs. They worked sixty to seventy hours per week under conditions that compromised their capacity to conceive, deliver, and nurture healthy children. Whereas slave populations grew swiftly throughout the rest of the South, in southeastern Louisiana the natural growth rate among slaves declined by 13 percent per decade. During the grinding season, when slaves of both sexes worked almost around the clock cutting cane for the sugar mills, and during planting, which involved hand-planting thousands of seed cane stems, women had trouble conceiving and carrying babies to term. In addition, the cane workers' spare diet of salt pork, molasses, and corn bread did not supply women with enough calories or vitamins to have healthy babies or, in some cases, even sustain their fertility. Stillborns and miscarriages were common, and many infants died.

Such losses were psychologically devastating for slave women, whose numerous pregnancies and miscarriages also taxed their physical health. One woman named Rachel, who worked on Joseph Kleinpeter's Variety Plantation in Louisiana, gave birth to nine children between 1836 and 1849, only four of whom survived. "My ma die[d] 'bout three hours after I was born," noted the former slave Edward De Bieuw. She was hoeing cane when she went into labor, he explained, and even though "she told the driver she was sick; he told her to just hoe-right-on. Soon I was born, and my ma die[d] a few minutes after dey brung her to the house."[28]

Wealthy Louisiana sugar planters could afford to purchase new slaves when theirs did not reproduce, but planters elsewhere generally had a vested interest in encouraging slave reproduction. Some slaveholders reduced the daily work required of pregnant and nursing women, reclassifying them as one-half hands rather than three-quarter ones and assigning them to lighter tasks. Generous masters also increased their food allotment. Such measures helped maintain a robust rate of reproduction throughout much of the antebellum South.

Many slave owners and overseers were convinced that black women were naturally immune to the rigors of pregnancy, which often kept white women confined to their beds for months. One Mississippi planter told a northern visitor that the exercise that black women received performing field work spared them "the difficulty and danger which attended the women of better classes in giving birth to offspring." Such beliefs often made masters quick to suspect pregnant slaves and nursing mothers of faking or "playing the lady" when they complained of pain or fatigue.[29] Some even whipped pregnant slaves, and such whippings were common enough that owners developed a special method for administering them. According to one former slave, pregnant slaves "were made to lie facedown in a specially dug depression in the ground," which protected the fetus while the mother was abused.[30]

Sent back to work shortly after giving birth, slave women then had to juggle infant care and the grueling labor regime. Some field workers, such as William Wells Brown's mother, were allowed no time to nurse and thus forced to carry their infants with them in the fields. Even when pregnant or nurturing newborns, slave women faced many hours of domestic work upon returning home, where they had to feed their families, take care of their children, and tend to domestic tasks such as sewing and housecleaning. Slave men often supplemented their families' meager diets by catching game and fish, raising vegetables, and keeping domestic animals such as pigs and chickens. But women performed much of the domestic labor in the slave quarters.

Slave women shouldered their burdens by taking care of one another and developing a sense of independence that made them more similar to their husbands than were most antebellum wives. Whereas freemen of that era had considerable power over their wives' behavior and possessions, enslaved men had virtually no authority over slave women. Slave men were not breadwinners and often performed the same kind of work as their wives. Gender norms in the quarters, therefore, tended to recognize black men and women as equal partners with similar abilities.

Marriage and Family

Southern courts never recognized slave marriages because, according to slave codes, chattel slaves were "not ranked among sentient beings, but among things, and things do not marry."[31] In practice, however, slaves courted, loved, and formed lasting unions. Enslaved couples came together and remained together largely at the discretion of their owners, many of whom had little interest in their happiness. Owners were anxious for female slaves to reproduce and for male slaves to be tied down by family loyalties, and they generally encouraged their slaves to marry informally, often conducting the ceremonies themselves.

"The marsters married slaves without any papers," an ex-slave named John Bectom remembered. "All they did was say . . . Frank, I pronounce you and Jane man and wife."[32] Some slave owners hosted big slave weddings, even hiring preachers to lead the ceremonies. Such weddings were popular among the slaves, who regarded them as occasions for celebration. Many years after slavery ended, the ex-slave Richard Moring still had good memories of the weddings held on his master's North Carolina plantation. "When there was a wedding there was fun for all," he recalled. "Dey wus all dressed up in new clothes, an' the marster's dinin' room wus decorated with flowers fer de occasion. . . . De preacher married dem up good an' tight just like he done the white folks."[33] But wedding ceremonies were not always officiated by slaveholders, and some took place within the slave quarters.[34]

However they were celebrated, slave unions lacked the sanctity, and sometimes even the consensual character, of marriages among whites. Sexual partners could be imposed on slaves in appallingly brutal ways. Louisa Everett's marriage began when her owner came into her cabin with a male slave named Sam and forced Sam to undress. According to Louisa, he then asked her, "Now, 'do you think you can stand this big nigger?' He had that old bull whip flung across his shoulder, and Lawd, that man could hit so hard! So I jes said 'yassur, I guess so,' and tried to hide my face so I couldn't see Sam's nakedness, but he made me look at him anyhow. Well, he told us what we must git busy and do in his presence, and we had to do it. After that we were considered man and wife. Me and Sam was a healthy pair and had fine, big babies, so I never had another man forced on me, thank God. Sam was kind to me and I learnt to love him."[35] Of course, not all slave women could say the same. When Rose Williams was sixteen, she was told to share a cabin occupied by a slave named Rufus, whose sexual advances she did not welcome. When she complained to her master, he threatened to beat her if she did not have sex with Rufus. He paid "big money" for her, he said, "cause I want you to raise me childrens."[36]

Moreover, all enslaved women, single or married, were vulnerable to sexual abuse, and slave men could offer them little protection from white men's sexual advances. "WHY does the slave ever love?" wrote the fugitive slave Harriet Jacobs when she learned that, in order to keep her as his mistress, her master had rebuffed the free black carpenter who wished to marry her and buy her freedom.[37] Such abuses were so common that one critic of slavery charged that "one of the reasons why wicked men in the South uphold slavery is the facility it affords for a licentious life."[38] These violations also complicated the family ties between slave couples and their children. Slave men ended up with children who were not their own, and fatherless children were all too common. Henry Bibb never knew his father, Kentucky state senator James Bibb, but he grew up knowing that he and his seven brothers were all children of slaveholders, none of whom prevented any of them from being bought and sold.

Not all slave families were the products of an owner's coercion, however. The prevalence of marriages between slaves on different plantations, known as **abroad marriages**, suggests that many owners allowed slaves to choose their own partners. Though never particularly popular with slave owners, such marriages may have accounted for as many as a third of all slave marriages in mid-nineteenth-century South Carolina.[39] Abroad marriages required a strong commitment, because enslaved men had to secure their masters' permission to visit their wives and then brave the slave patrols en route. "My pa would have to git a pass to come see my mammy. He sometimes come without a pass," recalled the ex-slave Millie Barbie.[40] But these marriages had the advantage of sheltering spouses from witnessing their loved ones' harsh treatment. Newly married Henry Bibb was initially happy to be purchased by Mr. Gatewood, who owned his wife, Malinda, but he soon found himself "much discontented," because "to live where I must be eye witness to her insults, scourgings and abuses, such as are common to be inflicted upon slaves, was more than I could bear."[41]

Parenthood posed similar dilemmas for slaves, whose children could be disciplined or brutalized by their owners. The abuse of Bibb's daughter Mary Frances made his family life under slavery still more unbearable. Once the child grew old enough to be weaned, her parents were no longer permitted to look after her during the day. Instead, they had to work in the fields, leaving their little girl in the home of a cruel and impatient plantation mistress who would often "slap with her hand the face of little Frances, for crying after her mother, until her little face was left black and blue." As much as he loved his daughter, Bibb also regretted fatherhood, stating that he "could never look upon the dear child without being filled with sorrow and fearful apprehensions, of being separated by slaveholders, because she was a slave, regarded as property."[42]

Such apprehensions were common even among slaves who did not have the opportunity to raise their own children. Although African American family members were frequently scattered by sale, family units remained important even when

Slave Punishment
Slaves of all ages, male and female, endured a wide range of horrific abuses. Difficult as these were to bear individually, they were made all the worse when slaves had to witness the cruel treatment of their loved ones. This early-nineteenth-century engraving depicts a group of slaves of all ages enduring different kinds of physical abuse, suffering alone as well as witnessing others' pain. At the far right, a young man—perhaps a father, like Henry Bibb—tries to shield two children from the whip, attempting to halt their tormentor with a gesture. *Culver Pictures/The Art Archive at Art Resource, NY.*

their members were not united by blood. African Americans who lost their kinfolk to sale or migration often created new family connections by embracing nonrelatives as **fictive kin**. Orphaned children were taken in by nonrelatives, as young Laura Clark learned when she and her mother were sold to different owners. Although bereft at the loss of her daughter, Laura's mother acted quickly to secure a substitute parent. According to Laura, her mother asked a woman who had been sold to the same owner to "take keir of my baby Chile . . . and if fen I never sees her no mo' raise her for God."[43] Young migrant teenagers likewise claimed older slaves as foster parents and grandparents. When such migrants had children of their own, they named them after both the family members they had left behind and their adopted relatives. These new family ties eased, but did not erase, the pain felt by slaves separated from their families by sale.

CONCLUSION

Surviving Slavery

Whether a matter of blood or otherwise, families helped African Americans survive and endure slavery. These powerful social ties united an enslaved people who had originated in many different West African societies and survived the Middle Passage, only to form new communities that also fell prey to slavery and sale. As one prominent scholar has put it, throughout "generations of captivity," African Americans endured by building communities strong enough to overcome these adversities.[44] Slave communities nurtured their children, cherished their elders, passed down African traditions, and provided members with a supportive environment.

No amount of community, however, could spare enslaved blacks from slavery's worst sorrows. Slave families lived in constant fear of separation by sale. Most slaves faced terrible hardships on a daily basis, working long hours under grueling conditions. They were subjected to brutal corporal punishment meted out not only by their owners but also by other whites, such as overseers and employers. Enslaved parents could not protect their children from such punishment or other forms of mistreatment, and enslaved spouses could not defend each other in the face of whippings and sexual abuse.

Slaves often resisted such abuses, but their resistance was usually covert. Slave rebels who offered direct physical opposition to their oppressors rarely survived their confrontations. Truancy as well as more serious escape attempts were common, as were stealing and avoiding work. Supervised by their owners and overseers during the day, and watched by armed patrollers at night, most slaves had few opportunities to plan any form of organized resistance, and those who attempted it were often caught in the act. Still, African American resistance to slavery could never be completely suppressed. Successful slave insurrections or advanced plots, when they did occur, further illuminated the impossibility of completely silencing black dissent.

Antebellum slave communities sustained their hopes for freedom by embracing an egalitarian form of Christianity assuring them that all men were equal under God. In addition to providing spiritual comfort and emotional release, slave religion nourished freedom dreams by emphasizing biblical texts such as the book of Exodus. As sectional struggles increasingly pitted the free North against the slave South, enslaved African Americans began to cherish more secular hopes for freedom as well. Joined by a growing cadre of black abolitionists in the North, they kept a close, hopeful watch on the widening rift between white northerners and southerners, and they stood ready to cast off their chains should freedom ever come.

CHAPTER REVIEW

Key Terms

Online Study Guide ▪ bedfordstmartins.com/graywhite

cash crops (p. 213)

Missouri Compromise (1820) (p. 215)

Indian Removal Act (1830) (p. 216)

Second Great Awakening (p. 225)

gag rule (p. 226)

Amistad case (p. 227)

Creole insurrection (p. 227)

truant (p. 228)

lying out (p. 228)

North Star (p. 231)

underground railroad (p. 231)

invisible church (p. 233)

ring shout (p. 233)

abroad marriages (p. 238)

fictive kin (p. 239)

Review Questions

1. Discuss the deepening political, economic, social, and slavery-related divisions between the North and South in the years 1820–1860. How was each region becoming more distinctive, and how were both regions becoming more opposed to each other? In spite of this, in what ways did the two regions remain linked?

2. How did the actions of Denmark Vesey, Nat Turner, David Walker, and the slaves aboard the *Amistad* and *Creole* resonate throughout the country? Compare the effects of their actions in the North and South, and the implications for both slaves and free blacks. What does this tell you about the state of the nation during this period?

3. Discuss the various types of slave resistance. How did individual slaves' circumstances— age, gender, location, or skill level, for example—make it more or less difficult to defy their masters or escape permanently?

4. How did gender affect slaves' experiences? In what ways were slave women's hardships different from slave men's? In what ways were slave women and men arguably more equal than white women and men of this period?

For Web sites, images, and documents related to topics and places in this chapter, visit **Make History** at bedfordstmartins.com/graywhite.

Managing the Slaves

For white southerners, enslaved African Americans were enormously valuable but also difficult to control. As chattel that could be bought and sold, they were many planters' major source of wealth and power, and they provided poorer slave owners with a potentially profitable labor force. But they were also human beings who resented their enslavement and often defied their owners' wishes. Since only productive slaves were valuable, slave owners struggled to institute a system of plantation management that would keep their bondmen and bond-women at work, while all white southerners lived in fear of a slave uprising. The following documents illustrate two white southerners' concerns about managing and maintaining control of the region's slave population.

Thomas Pinckney [Achates] | Reflections, Occasioned by the Late Disturbances in Charleston, 1822

Writing under the pen name Achates, **Thomas Pinckney (1750–1828)**, a seventy-two-year-old Revolutionary War hero and former South Carolina congressman, published a pamphlet on the Denmark Vesey conspiracy shortly after it was suppressed. In this selection, he analyzes the causes of the planned rebellion and offers suggestions on how future slave unrest might be prevented.

Previous to the proposal of any plan for preventing the recurrence of similar danger, it may be useful to advert to the causes which produced the late conspiracy. The following may be assigned as some of the most obvious:—1st, The example of St. Domingo, and (probably) the encouragement received from thence.—2dly, The indiscreet zeal in favor of universal liberty, expressed by many of our fellow-citizens in the States north and east of Maryland; aided by the Black population of those States.—3dly, The idleness, dissipation, and improper indulgences permitted among all classes of the Negroes in Charleston, and particularly among the domestics: and, as the most dangerous of those indulgencies, their being taught to read and

Source: Thomas Pinckney [Achates], *Reflections, Occasioned by the Late Disturbances in Charleston* (Charleston, SC: A. E. Miller, 1822), 6–7, 22–23.

write: the first bringing the powerful operation of the Press to act on their uninformed and easily deluded minds; and the latter furnishing them with an instrument to carry into execution the mischievous suggestions of the former.—4th, The facility of obtaining money afforded by the nature of their occupations to those employed as mechanics, draymen, fishermen, butchers, porters, hucksters, &c.—5th, The disparity of numbers between the white and black inhabitants of the City. No effort of ours can remove some of these causes, but over others we may exercise control. . . .

[Pinckney goes on to suggest that Charleston officials secure the city by replacing its black tradesmen and domestics with free white workers, who would be more efficient and economical and also "exempt from the degrading vices of the slave."]

. . . If, in the place of 22,432 coloured persons now maintained there, only half the number of white inhabitants were introduced; as all the mechanics, the draymen, the fishermen, and the porters, would of course be males, more than five thousand effective men would be added to our muster-roll; whereby, not only Charleston would be perfectly secure, but all thoughts of servile insurrection in the country, would be forever banished.

P. C. Weston | Management of a Southern Plantation, 1857

documents

On rice plantations in Georgia and South Carolina, slave laborers worked individually on a set of daily tasks rather than in gangs under the direct supervision of an overseer. But their work was still carefully managed by their owner, as noted in the instructions that the rice planter **P. C. Weston** issued to his overseer in 1856. The following year, his rules were published in *De Bow's Review*, a widely circulated magazine dedicated to the "agricultural, commercial, and industrial progress" of the American South.

The Proprietor, in the first place, wishes the Overseer *most distinctly* to understand that his first object is to be, under all circumstances, the care and well being of the negroes. The Proprietor is always ready to excuse such errors as may proceed from want of judgment; but he never can or will excuse any cruelty, severity, or want of care towards the negroes. For the well being, however, of the negroes, it is absolutely necessary to maintain obedience, order, and discipline; to see that the tasks are punctually and carefully performed, and to conduct the business steadily and firmly, without weakness on the one hand, or harshness on the other. For such ends the following regulations have been instituted:

Lists—Tickets.—The names of all the men are to be called over every Sunday morning and evening, from which none are to be absent but those who are sick, or have tickets [passes]. When there is evening Church, those who attend are to be excused from answering. At evening list, every negro must be clean and well washed. No one is to be absent from the place without a ticket, which is always to be given to such as ask it, and have behaved well. All persons coming from the Proprietor's other places should show their tickets to the Overseer, who should sign his name on the back; those going off the plantation should bring back their tickets signed. The Overseer is every now and then to go round at night and call at the houses, so as to ascertain whether their inmates are at home.

Allowance—Food.—Great care should be taken that the negroes should never have less than their regular allowance: in all cases of doubt, it should be given in favor of the largest quantity. The measures should not be *struck* [filled only to the top], but rather heaped up over. None but provisions of the best quality should be used. If any is discovered to be damaged, the Proprietor, if at hand, is to be immediately informed; if absent, the damaged article is to be destroyed. The corn should be carefully winnowed before grinding. The small rice is apt to become sour: as soon as this is perceived it should be given out every meal until finished, or until it becomes too sour to use, when it should be destroyed. . . .

Work, Holidays, &c.—. . .

No negro is to leave his task until the driver has examined and approved it, he is then to be permitted immediately to go home; and the hands are to be encouraged to finish their tasks as early as possible, so as to have time for working for themselves. Every negro, except the sickly ones and those with suckling children, (who are to be allowed half an hour,) are to be on board the flat [a flat-bottomed boat] by sunrise. One driver is to go down to the flat early, the other to remain behind and bring on all the people with him. He will be responsible for all coming down. The barn-yard bell will be rung by the watchman two hours, and half an hour, before sunrise.

Punishments.—It is desirable to allow 24 hours to elapse between the discovery of the offence, and the punishment. No punishment is to exceed 15 lashes: in cases where the Overseer supposes a severer punishment necessary, he must apply to the Proprietor, or to ———, Esq., in case of the Proprietor's absence from the neighborhood. Confinement (*not* in the stocks) is to be preferred to whipping: but the stoppage of Saturday's allowance, and doing whole task on Saturday, will suffice to prevent ordinary offences. Special care must be taken to prevent any *indecency* in punishing women. No Driver, or other negro, is to be allowed to punish any person in any way, except by order of the Overseer, and in his presence. . . .

Finally.—The Proprietor hopes the Overseer will remember that a system of *strict justice* is

SOURCE: *De Bow's Review*, 3rd ser., 2 (January 1857): 38, 40–44.

necessary to good management. No person should ever be allowed to break a law without being punished, or any person punished who has not broken a well known law. Every person should be made perfectly to understand what they are punished for, and should be made to perceive that they are not pun-

ished in anger, or through caprice. All abusive language or violence of demeanor should be avoided: they reduce the man who uses them to a level with the negro, and are hardly ever forgotten by those to whom they are addressed.

Questions for Analysis

1. Thomas Pinckney's pamphlet lists the causes of Denmark Vesey's planned rebellion in hopes of forestalling similar rebellions in the future. What events and circumstances does the author say inspired Vesey? How would this knowledge have helped slave owners in Charleston prevent future uprisings?

2. What were the major goals of the system of slave management outlined in P. C. Weston's rules for his rice plantation? How might these goals have differed from those of a Louisiana sugar planter?

3. Do Pinckney and Weston argue that slaves could be completely controlled if properly managed? Do the management techniques that they suggest seem likely to allow slave owners such control? What kinds of slave behavior do these authors wish to prevent?

Slave Testimony

Enslaved African Americans had few opportunities to express their views on slavery. Rarely permitted to learn to read or write, they were usually unable to record their stories even after slavery was abolished. Some former slaves, such as William Wells Brown and Frederick Douglass, published autobiographies known as fugitive slave narratives. Often written with the help of white editors, these book-length works constitute some of the richest testimony we have about the slave experience. Such narratives must, however, be read with caution, always keeping in mind what influence white editors might have had on the black authors.

Similar interpretive issues relate to shorter documents that shed light on the slave experience. The first document excerpted here is a journalist's summary of the life of a fugitive slave named Francis Henderson, drawn from a conversation with Henderson. The second is from a letter written or dictated by a slave named Vilet Lester to her former mistress seeking information about her daughter and other family members. The last document is from an interview with the ex-slave Mary Reynolds, one of more than 2,300 former slaves interviewed between 1936 and 1938 under the Federal Writers' Project. Part of the federally funded Works Progress Administration (WPA), this depression-era initiative employed mostly white writers and journalists, whom the elderly former slaves often regarded with suspicion. Even so, the interviews provide a crucial record of more than two thousand individuals' perspectives on slavery.

Francis Henderson | A Fugitive's Story, 1856

The following account of daily life under slavery was recorded by the abolitionist editor Benjamin Drew, who traveled through eastern Canada in the mid-1850s collecting the life stories of slaves who had escaped to freedom in the North. **Francis Henderson**, of London, Ontario, grew up on a plantation near Washington, D.C., where slavery was not abolished until 1862. How does Henderson describe the relationship between slaves and poor nonslaveholding whites?

I worked on a plantation from about ten years old till my escape [at age nineteen]. They raised wheat, corn, tobacco, and vegetables,—about forty slaves on the place. My father was a mulatto, my mother

Source: Benjamin Drew, *A North-Side View of Slavery: The Refugee, or the Narratives of Fugitive Slaves in Canada* (Boston: John Jewett, 1856), 154–57.

dark; they had thirteen children, of whom I was the only son. On that plantation the mulattoes were more despised than the whole blood blacks. I often wished from the fact of my condition that I had been darker. My sisters suffered from the same cause. I could frequently hear the mistress say to them, "you yellow hussy! you yellow wench!" etc. The language to me generally was, "go do so and so." But if a hoe-handle were broken or any thing went wrong, it would be every sort of a wicked expression—so bad I do not like to say what—very profane and coarse.

Our houses were but log huts—the tops partly open—ground floor,—rain would come through. My aunt was quite an old woman, and had been sick several years: in rains I have seen her moving about from one part of the house to the other, and rolling her bedclothes about to try to keep dry,—every

documents

thing would be dirty and muddy. I lived in the house with my aunt. My bed and bedstead consisted of a board wide enough to sleep on—one end on a stool, the other placed near the fire. My pillow consisted of my jacket,—my covering was whatever I could get. My bedtick [a mattress covered in a cloth case] was the board itself. And this was the way the single men slept,—but we were comfortable in this way of sleeping, *being used to it*. I only remember having but one blanket from my owners up to the age of 19, when I ran away.

Our allowance was given weekly—a peck of sifted corn meal, a dozen and a half herrings, two and a half pounds of pork. Some of the boys would eat this up in three days,—then they had to steal, or they could not perform their daily tasks. They would visit the hog-pen, sheep-pen, and granaries. I do not remember one slave but who stole some things,—they were driven to it as a matter of necessity. I myself did this,—many a time have I, with others, run among the stumps in chase of a sheep, that we might have something to eat. If colored men steal, it is because they are brought up to it. . . . In the summer we had one pair of linen trousers given us—nothing else; every fall, one pair of woollen pantaloons, one woollen jacket, and two cotton shirts.

My master had four sons in his family. They all left except one, who remained to be a driver. He would often come to the field and accuse the slaves of having taken so and so. If we denied it, he would whip the grown-up ones to make them own it. Many a time, when we didn't know he was anywhere round, he would be in the woods watching us,—first thing we would know, he would be sitting on the fence looking down upon us, and if any had been idle, the young master would visit him with blows. I have known him to kick my aunt, an old woman who had raised and nursed him, and I have seen him punish my sisters awfully with hickories from the woods.

The slaves are watched by the patrols, who ride about to try to catch them off the quarters, especially at the house of a free person of color. I have known the slaves to stretch clothes lines across the street, high enough to let the horse pass, but not the rider: then the boys would run, and the patrols in full chase would be thrown off by running against the lines. The patrols are poor white men, who live by plundering and stealing, getting rewards for runaways, and setting up little shops on the public roads. They will take whatever the slaves steal, paying in money, whiskey, or whatever the slaves want. They take pigs, sheep, wheat, corn,—any thing that's raised they encourage the slaves to steal: these they take to market next day. It's all speculation—all a matter of self-interest, and when the slaves run away, these same traders catch them if they can, to get the reward. If the slave threatens to expose his traffic, he does not care—for the slave's word is good for nothing—it would not be taken. There are frequent quarrels between the slaves and the poor white men. About the city on Sundays, the slaves, many of them, being fond of dress, would appear nicely clad, which seemed to provoke the poor white men. I have had them curse and damn me on this account. They would say to me, "Where are you going? Who do you belong to?" I would tell them,—then, "Where did you get them clothes? I wish you belonged to me—I'd dress you up!" Then I have had them throw water on me. One time I had bought a new fur hat, and one of them threw a watermelon rind, and spoiled the hat. Sometimes I have seen them throw a slave's hat on the ground, and trample on it. He would pick it up, fix it as well as he could, put it on his head, and walk on. The slave had no redress, but would sometimes take a petty revenge on the man's horse or saddle, or something of that sort.

Vilet Lester | Letter to Patsey Patterson, 1857

Vilet Lester wrote or dictated the following letter to her former mistress, Patsey Patterson, in the summer of 1857. Little information is available about Lester's life, but the letter suggests that the Patterson family had sold Lester away from her North Carolina home several years earlier. Lester lists the series of owners she has lived with since she "was constrained" to leave North Carolina and expresses how much she misses her family and her former owner. She is also anxious to locate her daughter, whom her new owner has agreed to purchase.

Georgia Bullock Co August 29th 1857

My Loving Miss Patsey

I hav long bin wishing to imbrace this presant and pleasant opertunity of unfolding my Scans [scenes?] and fealings Since I was constrained to leav my Long Loved home and friends which I cannot never gave my Self the Least promis of returning to. I am well and Injoying good hlth and has every Since I Left Randolph. whend I Left Randolf I went to Rockingham and Stad there five weaks and then I left there and went to Richmon virgina to be Sold and I Stade there three days and was bought by a man by the name of Groover and braught to Georgia and he kept me about Nine months and he being a trader Sold me to a man by the Name of Rimes and he Sold me to a man by the Name of Lester and he has owned me four years and Says that he will keep me til death Siperates us without Some of my old north Caroliner friends wants to buy me again. my

Dear Mistress I cannot tell my fealings nor how bad I wish to See you and old Boss and Miss Rahol and Mother. I do not [k]now which I want to See the worst Miss Rahol or mother I have thaugh[t] that I wanted to See mother but never befour did I [k]no[w] what it was to want to See a parent and could not. I wish you to gave my love to old Boss[,] Miss Rahol and bailum and gave my manafold love to mother brothers and Sister and pleas to tell them to Right to me So I may here from them if I cannot See them and also I wish you to right to me and Right me all the nuse. I do want to [k]now whether old Boss is Still Living or now [not] and all the rest of them and I want to [k]now whether bailum is maried or no. I wish to [k]now what has Ever become of my Presus little girl. I left her in goldsborough with Mr. Walker and I have not herd from her Since and Walker Said that he was going to Carry her to Rockingham and gave her to his Sister and I want to [k]no[w] whether he did or no[t] as I do wish to See her very mutch and Boss Says he wishes to [k]now whether he will Sell her or now [not] and the least that can buy her and that he wishes a answer as Soon as he can get one as I wis[h] him to buy her and my Boss being a man of Reason and fealing wishes to grant my trubled breast that mutch gratification and wishes to [k]now whether he will Sell her or now [not]. So I must come to a close by Escribing my Self your long loved and well wishing play mate as a Servant until death

Vilet Lester of Georgia
to Miss Patsey Padison of North Caroliner

My Bosses Name is James B Lester and if you Should think a nuff of me to right me which I do beg the faver of you as a Servant direct your leter to Millray Bullock County Georgia. Pleas to right me So fare you well in love.

SOURCE: Vilet Lester to Patsey Patterson, August 29, 1857, Joseph Allred Papers, David M. Rubenstein Rare Book & Manuscript Library, Duke University, Durham, NC.

documents

Mary Reynolds | The Days of Slavery, 1937

The daughter of a free black father and an enslaved mother, **Mary Reynolds** grew up on the Kilpatrick family plantation in Black River, Louisiana. Although her father was willing to buy Reynolds's mother and children, their owner refused to sell them, so the family remained enslaved until the Union army took control of Louisiana during the Civil War. Reynolds told her story in the mid-1930s to a writer working for the Federal Writers' Project of the Works Progress Administration. Interviewed in the Dallas County (Texas) Convalescent Home, she claimed to be over one hundred years old, and although she appeared feeble and frail, her memories of slavery were vivid.

M assa Kilpatrick wasn't no piddlin' man. He was a man of plenty. He had a big house with no more style to it than a crib, but it could room plenty people. He was a medicine doctor and they was rooms in the second story for sick folks what come to lay in. It would take two days to go all over the land he owned. He had cattle and stock and sheep and more'n a hundred slaves and more besides. He bought the bes' of niggers near every time the spec'lators come that way. He'd make a swap of the old ones and give money for young ones what could work.

He raised corn and cotton and cane and 'taters and goobers,° 'sides the peas and other feedin' for the niggers. I 'member I helt a hoe handle mighty onsteady when they put a old woman to larn me and some other chillun to scrape the fields. That old woman would be in a frantic. She'd show me and then turn 'bout to show some other li'l nigger, and I'd have the young corn cut clean as the grass. She say, "For the love of Gawd, you better larn it right, or

Solomon will beat the breath out you body." Old man Solomon was the nigger driver.

Slavery was the worst days was ever seed in the world. They was things past tellin', but I got the scars on my old body to show to this day. I seed worse than what happened to me. I seed them put the men and women in the stock with they hands screwed down through holes in the board and they feets tied together and they naked behinds to the world. Solomon the overseer beat them with a big whip and massa look on. The niggers better not stop in the fields when they hear them yellin'. They cut the flesh most to the bones and some they was when they taken them out of stock and put them on the beds, they never got up again. . . .

The times I hated most was pickin' cotton when the frost was on the bolls. My hands git sore and

Mary Reynolds, Age 105, at the Dallas County Convalescent Home, Texas, c. 1937
Library of Congress, Manuscript Division. WPA Slave Narrative Project (Texas Narratives, vol. 16, part 3), Federal Writers' Project, U.S. Works Progress Administration (USWPA).

° 'Taters and goobers are potatoes and peanuts. The word *goober* probably comes from *n-guba,* a Kongolese or Kimbundu term for "peanut."

Source: Ex-slave Stories (Texas): Mary Reynolds, in *Born in Slavery: Slave Narratives from the Federal Writers' Project, 1936–1938,* American Memory, Library of Congress, 238–40, http://lcweb2.loc.gov/cgi-bin/query/S?ammem/mesnbib:@field(AUTHOR+@od1(Reynolds,+Mary)).

crack open and bleed. We'd have a li'l fire in the fields and iffen the ones with tender hands couldn't stand it no longer, we'd run and warm our hands a li'l bit. When I could steal a 'tater, I used to slip it in the ashes and when I'd run to the fire I'd take it out and eat it on the sly.

In the cabins it was nice and warm. They was built of pine boardin' and they was one long rom [room] of them up the hill back of the big house. Near one side of the cabins was a fireplace. They'd bring in two, three big logs and put on the fire and they'd last near a week. The beds was made out of puncheons [wooden posts] fitted in holes bored in the wall, and planks laid 'cross them poles. We had tickin' mattresses filled with corn shucks. Sometimes the men build chairs at night. We didn't know much 'bout havin' nothin', though. . . .

Once in a while they'd give us a li'l piece of Sat'day evenin' to wash out clothes. . . . When

they'd git through with the clothes . . . the niggers which sold they goobers and 'taters brung fiddles and guitars and come out and play. The others clap they hands and stomp they feet. . . .

We was scart of Solomon and his whip, though, and he didn't like frolickin'. He didn't like for us niggers to pray, either. We never heared of no church, but us have prayin' in the cabins. We'd set on the floor and pray with our heads down low and sing low, but if Solomon heared he'd come and beat on the wall with the stock of his whip. He'd say, "I'll come in there and tear the hide off you backs." But some [of] the old niggers tell us we got to pray to Gawd that he don't think different of the blacks and the whites. I know that Solomon is burnin' in hell today, and it pleasures me to know it.

Questions for Analysis

1. All three of these accounts raise a variety of questions about slaves' views of white people. How do white people figure into Francis Henderson's and Mary Reynolds's accounts of slavery? How does Vilet Lester's relationship with Patsey Patterson compare with these accounts? What did Lester hope to achieve in writing to Patterson, and how might this have affected how she worded her letter?

2. The documents describing the experiences of Henderson and Lester date to the antebellum era, whereas Reynolds remembers slavery many years after emancipation. How might slaves' and ex-slaves' perspectives on the institution of slavery have changed over time, and why might this have been the case?

3. Most slave testimony, including Henderson's and Reynolds's accounts, was not recorded by the slaves themselves. Instead, slaves' stories were recorded by white contemporaries who often guided and reshaped their statements. To what extent do Henderson's and Reynolds's accounts seem to be direct transcriptions of these individuals' own thoughts about slavery? How and where can you detect the presence of another person?

4. Compare and contrast the slave testimony in these documents with slaveholders' ideas about slave management in Documents: Managing the Slaves, pp. 242–44. What forms of white control did these slaves experience? Did they encounter slave owners with attitudes like Thomas Pinckney [Achates] or rules like P. C. Weston's?

The Art of the Plantation

Enslaved black southerners left few visual records of their lives. They composed haunting slave spirituals and syncopated work songs that have had a formative effect on American music and left an enduring record of their creative gifts. But slavery offered few opportunities to create other works of art portraying visual images of slave life from the slaves' perspective. As a result, what we know about African American life in the plantation South comes from other sources, such as slave crafts, paintings, drawings and etchings of southern life by white artists, and early photographs of black southerners.

One of the antebellum South's most famous slave craftsmen was a potter known simply as Dave. Born around 1801 on a North Carolina plantation owned by Harry Drake, Dave spent most of his life working on plantation pottery in Edgefield, South Carolina. After emancipation, he took the last name of his first owner and became David Drake. Best known for his ability to produce massive, beautifully shaped, 25- to 40-gallon jugs and jars, Dave is also remembered for writing on his pottery. In an era when most slaves were forced to be illiterate and anonymous, Dave signed his pots, leaving behind more than one hundred signed and dated vessels. He also wrote poems on a number of his creations. "Put every bit all between / surely this jar will hold 14," he wrote on a 14-gallon jar created in 1834. Other verses are more self-referential. "Dave belongs to Mr. Miles / Wher the oven bakes & the pot biles," he wrote on a pot crafted in 1840, commenting on his new owner, Lewis Miles, who had purchased him in the late 1830s. Some of his poems might even be considered subversive. The 25-gallon jar in Figure 5.1, for example, seems to speak of losing family members to sale. Dated 1857, it reads, "I wonder where is all my relations / Friendship to all—and every nation."[45]

A similar jar features a more cryptic inscription: "The sun, moon and stars / in the west are plenty of bears."[46] Dave's juxtaposition of astronomy and animals in this poem may be a carefully veiled reference to the constellation of stars known as Ursa Major, or the Big Bear. Also called the Big Dipper and known among African American slaves as "the drinking gourd," this ladle-shaped group of stars points to the North Star, which enslaved fugitives often used to navigate their way to freedom. The constellation's importance to runaways was even com-

FIGURE 5.1
Detail of a Jar by Dave, 1857
Storage jar, 1857 (glazed stoneware), Dave Drake (Dave the Potter) (c. 1800–1870)/Museum of Fine Arts, Boston, Massachusetts, USA/Harriet Otis Cruft Fund and Otis Norcross Fund/The Bridgeman Art Library International.

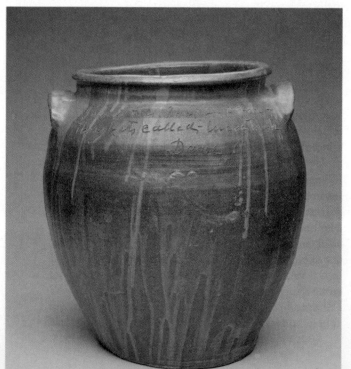

memorated in one slave spiritual, which instructs slaves, "Follow the Drinking Gourd / For the old man is a-waiting for to carry you to freedom."[47] Why would Dave have inscribed this information on a pot?

Other expressive works of art include the quilts produced by slave women. Striking for their intricate designs and exquisite use of color, slave-made quilts are sometimes thought to have contained secret codes to guide slaves to freedom along the underground railroad. But the idea of "quilt codes" is a myth that originated in the 1980s, when a post-Bicentennial revival of folk art created new interest in African American quilts. Antiques dealers and quilters capitalized on this enthusiasm by claiming that slave-made quilts played a role in aiding escaped slaves. The quilts sewn by slave women do contain symbols and other meaningful imagery, but the quilt-making process was far too laborious to lend itself to the creation of coded messages.

Often commissioned to make quilts for their owners, slave women spent many hours stitching together the three layers of cloth that make up quilts. These layers typically consisted of a pieced or appliquéd top, a middle layer of filling, and a bottom lining. When sewing for themselves, enslaved women had to save up the fabric before they could start. Although they bought new cloth such as calico, broadcloth, or gingham when they had money to spend, many quilts were partially or wholly constructed from carefully saved bits of fabric from their old clothes, their owners' hand-me-downs, or material left over from fabric allowances. They pulled leftover thread off looms, saved gunnysacks used to carry grain and potatoes, and sometimes even picked sheep's wool out of briar patches to assemble enough material. They often colored the fabric they collected with plant dyes made from berries and bark to achieve the designs they desired on the tops of their quilts.

In assembling the quilts, slave women used figures and patterns influenced by what they saw and believed, and by a blend of African and Anglo-American sewing and design traditions. "My mother wove that white cloth an' the thread it's quilted with," one ex-slave noted about a particular quilt, and she got the pattern by "goin' out into the woods an' getting a leaf to cut it by. . . . This quilt is about ninety years old, an' it was made when people was smart an' went out to [the] woods to get their patterns."[48] Very few antebellum-era quilts survive, but the slave-made oak leaf panel seen in Figure 5.2 confirms this ex-slave's account of the influence of natural shapes on their design. The patterned quilt in Figure 5.3, by contrast, incorporates a popular design called the Star of Bethlehem.

FIGURE 5.2
Oak Leaf Panel from a Slave Quilt, 1857–1858 *Courtesy of Michigan State University Museum.*

visual sources

Slave quilters also incorporated African design elements, such as snakes—which connote fertility in African mythology—into their creations. The appliqué style of quilting they favored, in which decorative pieces are applied to the quilt's surface, also may have originated in the cultures of West Africa. Appliqué is a prominent feature of the traditional tapestries of Benin, where many African Americans came from. These tapestries evoke stories from oral tradition and history, as does the work of some African American quilters. Most notable in this regard is Harriet Powers, a quilter of extraordinary talent who was born into slavery in Georgia in 1837. Only two of her quilts survive, both crafted after emancipation. They show how slaves blended African quilting techniques with Christian and African symbolism to create works of outstanding artistry.

Powers used her quilts to dramatize and commemorate the Bible tales that sustained African Americans during slavery, as well as scenes from her own life. The Bible quilt pictured in Figure 5.4 begins with a panel of Adam and Eve in the Garden of Eden and continues with a panel that includes their son Cain. This is followed by a panel that Powers called "Satan in de Seven Stars" (apparently a reference to seven stars that represent the angels of the seven churches in Revelation 1:20).[49] The middle row of the quilt contains two panels of Cain and Abel (Cain killing his brother Abel and Cain going into the land of Nod to get a wife), as well as a panel depicting the popular Bible story of the Israelite patriarch Jacob's vision of a ladder to heaven, which came to him in a dream when he was tired, homeless, and sleeping on the ground. The last five panels of the quilt depict the life of Christ: The last panel in the middle row features Christ's baptism, while the bottom row represents (from left to right) the Crucifixion, Judas Iscariot and the thirty pieces of silver, the Last Supper, and the Holy Family.

Both Powers's choice of biblical scenes and the imagery with which she represents them are unconventional and distinctive. Why did Powers feature these scenes in her Bible quilt? What role does color play in the religious symbolism of the quilt? How might you relate her experience as a black southerner to the different-colored figures that appear in her quilt?

FIGURE 5.3
Slave Quilt with Star of Bethlehem Pattern Variation, c. 1837–1850 *Makers: Ellen Morton Littlejohn (1826–1899), Margaret Morton Bibb (c. 1832–c. 1900–1910), United States, Kentucky, Russellville ("The Knob"). Silk and cotton, 88¼ x 87⅛ in. (224.2 x 221.3 cm)./Gift of Roger Morton and Dr. Paul C. Morton, 1962 (62.144)/The Metropolitan Museum of Art, New York, NY, USA/Image © The Metropolitan Museum of Art/Art Resource, NY.*

FIGURE 5.4
Harriet Powers, Bible Quilt, 1886   *Object ID TE*T14713, Gift of Mr. and Mrs. H. M. Heckman/National Museum of American History, Smithsonian Institution.*

For more literal representations of the slave South, we must turn to the works of white artists who painted plantation life. Such artists, however, frequently omitted slaves completely from their works. Commissioned by planters to showcase their properties or painted to honor famous slaveholders such as George Washington, these works depict the planters' magnificent homes and surrounding landscape, leaving out the slaves and fields that sustained these estates (Figure 5.5). What does the absence of slaves suggest about the ways in which planters hoped to represent themselves and their homes? Many of the most famous plantation scenes that do include slaves were painted after emancipation in 1865. What does this tell us?

Still, slavery generated enough controversy to require representation as well as omission, especially within the pro- and antislavery literature of the antebellum era. This period saw a propaganda war between abolitionists and proslavery southerners, both of whom mobilized popular fiction to present their arguments and underscored their stories with illustrations of slave life. Antislavery images stressed the brutality of slavery, while proslavery images

FIGURE 5.5
Francis Jukes, *Mount Vernon in Virginia*, 1800 *Francis Jukes (1745–1812). Aquatint, 1800/The Granger Collection, NY. All rights reserved.*

often portrayed slaves relaxing in peaceful rural settings—in marked contrast to the urban spaces in which free blacks often dwelled.

Harriet Beecher Stowe's famous antislavery novel *Uncle Tom's Cabin* (1852) was an example of the former and included terrifying scenes of ragged slaves being hunted and beaten. Created for Stowe by the internationally known English illustrator George Cruikshank, who never visited the United States, the engraving in Figure 5.6 is set in Louisiana and depicts the capture of Scipio, a runaway slave who was pursued by a party of armed white men. Augustine St. Clare, the Louisiana aristocrat whose brother owns Scipio, is on hand to keep the patrollers from "shooting him, in the flush of success," and can be seen in the center of Cruikshank's engraving fending off the hunting party. How realistic is Cruikshank's depiction of the capture? What view of slavery does it communicate?

Henry Bibb, who witnessed the abuse of his wife and child as a slave, supplemented his account of their suffering with a pair of pictures illustrating the special hardships slavery imposed on black women (Figure 5.7). They are accompanied by captions drawn from the Scriptures. "Can a mother forget her

FIGURE 5.6
Scipio Hunted, "As Men Hunt a Deer!," from *Uncle Tom's Cabin, or Life among the Lowly,* 1852
© *Bettmann/Corbis.*

suckling child?" comes from Isaiah 49:15, which stresses God's love of all his children. The second caption quotes Proverbs 12:10, which maintains, "A righteous man regardeth the life of his beast; but the tender mercies of the wicked are cruel." How are African American women's experiences under slavery depicted in these two scenes, and what message might Bibb have wanted to communicate in these illustrations? How do Bibb's captions relate to the images they describe? Why might he have chosen to use captions derived from the Bible?

Proslavery apologists countered such works with their own propaganda, which invariably stressed that slaves were both well treated and happy and which included illustrations designed to prove these points. In response to *Uncle Tom's Cabin,* proslavery novels about plantation life proliferated in the 1850s and contained similar illustrations. All omitted whippings or any forms of discipline; in fact, they rarely even featured slaves at work. Instead, works such as Maria H. Eastman's *Aunt Phillis's Cabin, or Southern Life as It Is* (1852) and W. L. G. Smith's *Life at the South, or "Uncle Tom's Cabin" as It Is* (1852) showed slaves napping, standing idle in the fields, and relaxing in their cabins. Smith's book even had pictures of slave children attending Sunday school (Figure 5.8) and having lessons with the schoolmaster (Figure 5.9).

FIGURE 5.7
Black Women Slaves from *Narrative of the Life and Adventures of Henry Bibb, an American Slave, Written by Himself,* 1849–1850 *Schomburg Center, NYPL/Art Resource, NY.*

Can a mother forget her suckling child?

The tender mercies of the wicked are cruel.

More common proslavery imagery avoided the controversial subject of slave education in favor of plantation scenes that included dancing slaves, as in the opening of Eastman's book (Figure 5.10).

Most proslavery apologists portrayed slavery as a benign, paternalistic institution in which solicitous slave owners looked after childlike slaves, whom they regarded as members of the family. Their illustrations frequently showed slave owners tending to elderly or ailing slaves with great care. *Frank Freeman's Barber Shop* (1852) is a cautionary tale by the southern minister Baynard R. Hall. The title character is a fugitive slave unwise enough to be tricked by abolitionists into running away and starting a business of his own, which fails. Hall's story also calls into question Frank Freeman's decision to leave his former owners, the Leamingtons, through a scene showing the couple

SUNDAY SCHOOL.

FIGURE 5.8
Slave Children in Sunday School from *Life at the South, or "Uncle Tom's Cabin" as It Is,* 1852 Sunday School, *by John William Orr (1815–1887), 1852/Schomburg Center, NYPL/Art Resource, NY.*

FIGURE 5.9
Slave Children and Schoolmaster from *Life at the South, or "Uncle Tom's Cabin" as It Is,* 1852 The Schoolmaster, *by John William Orr (1815–1887), 1852/Schomburg Center, NYPL/Art Resource, NY.*

visual sources

visual sources

NEGRO VILLAGE ON A SOUTHERN PLANTATION.

FIGURE 5.10
Slaves Dancing from *Aunt Phillis's Cabin, or Southern Life as It Is,* 1852 Aunt Phillis's Cabin, or Southern Life as It Is/ *Eastman (PS646.F53.E27A8 1852). Clifton Walker Barrett Library of American Literature, Special Collections, University of Virginia Library.*

lavishing loving care on an elderly slave named Dinah as she lies on her deathbed (Figure 5.11). Summoned to Dinah's cabin, they solicitously hover over her. "Mrs. L. sobbed . . . convulsively," while her husband offered his hand to Dinah, who "raised [it] to her lips and kissed [it] most affectionately" and said with dying breath "'Farewell!—most kind Massa! I going home, Massa! I soon see *you* dar!'" What point was Hall trying to make with this dialogue? How does the illustration support his proslavery message?

The photographic record of slavery, by contrast, presents slave subjects in more everyday situations than proslavery and antislavery depictions of the institution do. Photography began as early as the late 1830s with daguerreotypes, but these fragile photographic images burned on metal plates could only capture still figures that remained in place for several minutes, so they were used primarily for portraits. Nannies are among the slaves who appear most frequently in daguerreotypes, where they are literally on the job, holding their charges in place for the photographic process. Created by an unknown North Carolina photographer about 1855, Figure 5.12 shows a young slave holding on to her still younger charge.

FIGURE 5.11
Death of Dinah from *Frank Freeman's Barber Shop,* 1852
Frank Freeman's Barber Shop: A Tale *(PS1774.H455.F7 1852).*
University of Virginia Library.

FIGURE 5.12
A Child and Her Nanny, c. 1855 *Library of Congress,
LC-USZC4-S251.*

visual sources

FIGURE 5.13
A Slave Family in a Georgia Cotton Field, c. 1860   *Private Collection/Peter Newark American Pictures/The Bridgeman Art Library International.*

By 1860, American photographers were using faster photographic techniques that allowed them to capture scenes from everyday life. Although
African Americans do not figure prominently in antebellum-era photography, a
few striking images of black life before the war do exist. Among them is a
photograph of a slave family in a Georgia cotton field taken by an unknown
photographer about 1860 (Figure 5.13). They stand facing the camera and
appear to have paused in their work for the photographer, but they are clearly
far from finished for the day. Workers in the cotton fields typically labored until
sundown, especially during cotton-picking season. What can we tell about the
family's work life from this photograph?

The visual record of slavery captured in these early photographs should not be assumed to be objective, since the slave subjects were selected, situated, and possibly even posed by the unknown photographers. But it is worth noting that photographs of slaves depict neither the happy-go-lucky subjects often seen in proslavery propaganda (Figure 5.10) nor the cowering, pitiful creatures featured in antislavery illustrations (Figure 5.6). Instead, many photographs capture black southerners performing the work they were purchased to perform. Slave labor is also documented in the huge pots thrown by Dave and in the careful needlework of slave quilters, but it figures far less prominently in plantation paintings, and it rarely plays a role in pro- or antislavery propaganda.

Questions for Analysis

1. What do slave crafts tell us about slaves' creativity and resourcefulness? How does this knowledge mesh with the fictional depictions of slaves we see in Figures 5.6 through 5.11?

2. What are the limitations of the images of black southerners included here? How can we interrogate these sources to discern where their biases or inaccuracies lie? When examined critically, do they provide us with a visual record of slavery we can trust? Why or why not?

3. Compare and contrast the black figures that appear in antislavery publications (Figures 5.6 and 5.7) with those featured in proslavery works (Figures 5.8 through 5.11). In what ways do the photographs (Figures 5.12 and 5.13) resemble or contradict these illustrations?

4. Do the photographs provide a more objective or powerful record of their subjects than the images that precede them? If so, why are the more obviously biased or fictionalized images still important to the visual record of slave life?

visual sources

Notes

1. William Wells Brown, *Narrative of William W. Brown, a Fugitive Slave, Written by Himself* (Boston: Anti-Slavery Office, 1849), 15.

2. Ibid., 20.

3. Ibid., 61, 44.

4. Thomas Jefferson to John Holmes, April 22, 1820, in *Thomas Jefferson: Writings*, ed. Merrill D. Peterson (New York: Library of America, 1984), 1433–35.

5. Lyman Abbott, *Reminiscences* (New York: Houghton Mifflin, 1915), 102.

6. Interview with Charity Bowery, in John W. Blassingame, *Slave Testimony: Two Centuries of Letters, Speeches, Interviews, and Autobiographies* (Baton Rouge: LSU Press, 1977), 265.

7. Quoted in Benjamin Drew, *Refugees from Slavery* (Mineola, NY: Courier Dover, 2004), 19.

8. Interview with Carrie E. Davis, in *The WPA Oklahoma Slave Narratives*, ed. T. Lindsay Baker and Julie P. Baker (Norman: University of Oklahoma Press, 1996), 102.

9. Robert James Turnbull [Brutus], *The Crisis, or Essays on the Usurpations of the Federal Government*, no. 26 (Charleston, SC: A. E. Miller, 1827), 133.

10. Quoted in Douglas Edgerton, *He Shall Go Out Free: The Lives of Denmark Vesey* (Madison: Madison House, 1999), 198.

11. Thomas Wentworth Higginson, "Denmark Vesey," *Atlantic*, June 1861, 735.

12. David Walker, *Walker's Appeal, in Four Articles; Together with a Preamble, to the Coloured Citizens of the World, but in Particular, and Very Expressly, to Those of the United States of America, Written in Boston, State of Massachusetts, September 28, 1829*, rev. ed (Boston: published by author, 1830), 5.

13. Ibid., 41.

14. Quoted in ibid., 63.

15. William Lloyd Garrison, "Walker's Appeal," *Liberator* (January 8, 1831): 1; William Lloyd Garrison, "Walker's Pamphlet," *Liberator* (January 29, 1831): 4.

16. Nat Turner, *The Confessions of Nat Turner, the Leader of the Late Insurrection in Southampton, Va.* (Baltimore: Thomas R. Gray, 1831), 10, 11.

17. Both quoted in Kenneth S. Greenberg, ed., *Nat Turner: A Slave Rebellion in History and Memory* (New York: Oxford University Press, 2003), 156.

18. Bush v. Jackson (1854), quoted in Paul Finkelman, *Slavery and the Law* (Lanham, MD: Rowman & Littlefield, 2002), 319; Robert Vaughan and Henry Allon, "Stirling's Letters from the Slave States," *British Quarterly Review* 26 (July and October 1857): 617.

19. Frederick Douglass, *Narrative of the Life of Frederick Douglass, an American Slave, Written by Himself* (Boston: Anti-Slavery Office, 1845), 63, 71, 73.

20. John v. State, 16 GA 203 (1854).

21. Quoted in Sally E. Haddon, *Slave Patrols: Law and Violence in Virginia and the Carolinas* (Cambridge: Harvard University Press, 2001), 120.

22. Solomon Northup, *Twelve Years a Slave: Narrative of Solomon Northup, a Citizen of New-York, Kidnapped in Washington City in 1841, and Rescued in 1853* (Auburn, NY: Derby and Miller, 1853), 230.

23. Quoted in Deborah Gray White, *Ar'n't I a Woman? Female Slaves in the Plantation South*, rev. ed. (New York: Norton, 1999), 72.

24. Interview with Anna Morgan, in *The American Slave: A Composite Autobiography, North Carolina and South Carolina Narratives*, ed. George P. Rawick, suppl., 1st ser., vol. 11, part 1 (Westport, CT: Greenwood Press, 1978), 149.

25. Interview with Wes Brady, in *The American Slave: A Composite Autobiography, Texas Narratives*, ed. George P. Rawick, suppl., 2nd ser., vol. 2, part 1 (Westport, CT: Greenwood Press, 1979), 401.

26. Interview with Mose Hursey, in *The American Slave: A Composite Autobiography, Texas Narratives*, ed. George P. Rawick, suppl., 2nd ser., vol. 4, part 2 (Westport, CT: Greenwood Press, 1979), 170–71.

27. Frederick Douglass, *My Bondage and My Freedom* (New York: Miller, Orton & Mulligan, 1855), 35.

28. Quoted in Richard Follett, "Heat, Sex, and Sugar: Childbearing in the Slave Quarters," *Journal of Family History* 28 (October 2003): 528.

29. White, *Ar'n't I a Woman?*, 112.

30. Paul D. Escott, *Slavery Remembered* (Chapel Hill: University of North Carolina Press, 1979), 43.

31. William Goodell, *The American Slave Code in Theory and Practice* (New York: American and Foreign Antislavery Society, 1853), 90.

32. Quoted in Rebecca J. Fraser, *Courtship and Love among the Enslaved in North Carolina* (Jackson: University Press of Mississippi, 2007), 89.

33. Quoted in T. E. Will, "Weddings on Contested Grounds: Slave Marriages in the Antebellum South," *Historian* 62, no. 1 (1999): 111.

34. Ibid., 110.

35. Interview with Louisa Everett, in *Far More Terrible for Women: Personal Accounts of Women in Slavery*, ed. Patrick Neal Minges (Winston-Salem, NC: John F. Blair, 2006), 16.

36. Quoted in White, *Ar'n't I a Woman?*, 103.

37. Harriet Ann Jacobs, *Incidents in the Life of a Slave Girl* (Boston: printed for author, 1861), 58.

38. Quoted in Edward D. C. Campbell Jr. and Kim S. Rice, *Before Freedom Came: African-American Life in the Antebellum South* (Charlottesville: University of Virginia Press, 1997), 62.

39. Emily West, "The Debate on the Strength of Slave Families: South Carolina and the Importance of Cross-Plantation Marriages," *Journal of American Studies* 33, no. 2 (1999): 225.

40. Interview with Millie Barbie, in *The American Slave: A Composite Autobiography, South Carolina Narratives*, ed. George P. Rawick, vol. 2, part 1 (Westport, CT: Greenwood Press, 1973), 39.

41. Henry Bibb, *Narrative of the Life and Adventures of Henry Bibb, an American Slave, Written by Himself* (New York: published by author, 1849), 42.

42. Ibid., 43, 44.

43. Quoted in Ira Berlin, *The Making of African America: The Four Great Migrations* (New York: Penguin, 2010), 119.

44. This phrase is drawn from the title of Ira Berlin's *Generations of Captivity: A History of African-American Slaves* (Cambridge: Belknap Press of Harvard University Press, 2004).

45. Quoted in Jill Beute Koverman, ed., *I Made This Jar . . . : The Life and Works of the Enslaved African-American Potter Dave* (McKissick Museum: University of South Carolina, 1998), 25, 33, 24.

46. Ibid., 91.

47. Quoted in Steven Cornelius, *Music of the Civil War Era* (Westport, CT: Greenwood Press, 2004), 119.

48. Quoted in Gladys-Marie Fry, *Stitched from the Soul: Slave Quilts from the Antebellum South* (Chapel Hill: University of North Carolina Press, 2002), 46.

49. Gladys-Marie Fry, "A Sermon in Patchwork: New Light on Harriet Powers," in *Singular Women: Writing the Artist*, ed. Kristen Frederickson and Sarah E. Webb (Berkeley: University of California Press, 2003), 88.

Suggested References

The Expansion and Consolidation of Slavery

Baptist, Edward E. *Creating an Old South: Middle Florida's Plantation Frontier before the Civil War.* Chapel Hill: University of North Carolina Press, 2002.

Campbell, Randolph B. *Empire for Slavery: The Peculiar Institution in Texas, 1821–1865.* Baton Rouge: LSU Press, 1991.

Deyle, Steven. *Carry Me Back: The Domestic Slave Trade in American Life.* New York: Oxford University Press, 2006.

Follett, Richard. *The Sugar Masters: Planters and Slaves in Louisiana's Cane World, 1820–1860.* Baton Rouge: LSU Press, 2007.

Forbes, Robert Pierce. *The Missouri Compromise and Its Aftermath: Slavery and the Meaning of America.* Chapel Hill: University of North Carolina Press, 2009.

Johnson, Walter. *Soul by Soul: Life inside the Antebellum Slave Market.* Cambridge: Harvard University Press, 2001.

Morrison, Michael A. *Slavery and the American West: The Eclipse of Manifest Destiny.* Chapel Hill: University of North Carolina Press, 1997.

Rothman, Adam. *Slave Country: American Expansion and the Origins of the Deep South.* Cambridge: Harvard University Press, 2007.

Black Challenges to Slavery

Aptheker, Herbert. *American Negro Slave Revolts.* 5th ed. New York: International Publishers, 1983.

Dillon, Merton L. *Slavery Attacked: Southern States and Their Allies, 1619–1865.* Baton Rouge: LSU Press, 1991.

Egerton, Douglas R. *He Shall Go Out Free: The Lives of Denmark Vesey.* Lanham, MD: Rowman & Littlefield, 2004.

Greenberg, Kenneth S. *Nat Turner: A Slave Rebellion in History and Memory.* New York: Oxford University Press, 2003.

Hinks, Peter P. *To Awaken My Afflicted Brethren: David Walker and the Problem of Antebellum Slave Resistance.* University Park: Penn State University Press, 1996.

Jones, Howard. *Mutiny on the Amistad: The Saga of a Slave Revolt and Its Impact on American Abolition, Law, and Diplomacy.* New York: Oxford University Press, 1997.

Rucker, Walter C. *The River Flows On: Black Resistance, Culture, and Identity Formation in Early America.* Baton Rouge: LSU Press, 2007.

Wood, Peter H., J. Vernon Cromartie, and Rodger Lyle Brown. *The Invisible War: African American Anti-Slavery Resistance from the Stono Rebellion through the Seminole Wars.* Atlanta: Clarity Press, 2006.

Everyday Resistance to Slavery

Berry, Daina. *"Swing the Sickle for the Harvest Is Ripe": Gender and Slavery in Antebellum Georgia.* Urbana: University of Illinois Press, 2010.

Camp, Stephanie M. H. *Closer to Freedom: Enslaved Women and Everyday Resistance in the Plantation South.* Chapel Hill: University of North Carolina Press, 2004.

Franklin, John Hope, and Loren Schweninger. *Runaway Slaves: Rebels on the Plantation.* New York: Oxford University Press, 2000.

Glymph, Thavolia. *Out of the House of Bondage: The Transformation of the Plantation Household.* Cambridge: Cambridge University Press, 2008.

Jones, Norrece T. *Born a Child of Freedom, Yet a Slave: Mechanisms of Control and Strategies of Resistance in Antebellum South Carolina.* Middletown, CT: Wesleyan University Press, 1991.

McLaurin, Melton A. *Celia, a Slave.* New York: Avon, 1999.

Rivers, Larry Eugene. *Rebels and Runaways: Slave Resistance in Nineteenth-Century Florida.* Urbana: University of Illinois Press, 2012.

Schermerhorn, Calvin. *Money over Mastery, Family over Freedom: Slavery in the Antebellum Upper South.* Baltimore: Johns Hopkins University Press, 2011.

Webber, Thomas L. *Deep Like the Rivers.* New York: Norton, 1980.

Survival, Community, and Culture

Blassingame, John W. *The Slave Community: Plantation Life in the Antebellum South.* Rev. ed. New York: Oxford University Press, 1979.

Fett, Sharla M. *Working Cures: Healing, Health, and Power on Southern Slave Plantations.* Chapel Hill: University of North Carolina Press, 2002.

Irons, Charles F. *The Origins of Proslavery Christianity: White and Black Evangelicals in Colonial and Antebellum Virginia.* Chapel Hill: University of North Carolina Press, 2008.

Kaye, Anthony E. *Joining Places: Slave Neighborhoods in the Old South.* Chapel Hill: University of North Carolina Press, 2009.

Levine, Lawrence W. *Black Culture and Black Consciousness: Afro-American Folk Thought from Slavery to Freedom.* New York: Oxford University Press, 1978.

Raboteau, Albert J. *Slave Religion: The "Invisible Institution" in the Antebellum South.* Oxford: Oxford University Press, 1980.

Schwartz, Marie Jenkins. *Born in Bondage: Growing Up Enslaved in the Antebellum South.* Cambridge: Harvard University Press, 2001.

West, Emily. *Chains of Love: Slave Couples in Antebellum South Carolina.* Urbana: University of Illinois Press, 2004.

White, Deborah Gray. *Ar'n't I a Woman? Female Slaves in the Plantation South.* Rev. ed. New York: Norton, 1999.

6

The Northern Black Freedom Struggle and the Coming of the Civil War, 1830–1860

IN JANUARY 1849, twenty-five-year-old Mary Ann Shadd weighed in on the enduring debate among free blacks in the North about how best to advance their cause. A veteran schoolteacher who had benefited from her private education and her family's political activism, Shadd spoke in a self-confident and independent voice. She was also impatient. "We have been holding conventions for years—have been assembling together and whining over our difficulties and afflictions, passing resolutions on resolutions . . . but it does really seem that we have made but little progress, considering our resolves." Her solution was clear and pointed: "We should do more, and talk less."[1]

Shadd was both a doer and a talker. Despairing of African American prospects in the United States, she left her teaching job in New York City in 1851 and moved to Canada. In Windsor, Ontario, where African Americans had already formed a small community, she took another teaching job and soon also became cofounder and editor of the *Provincial Freeman*, a weekly black newspaper whose masthead announced its devotion "to anti-slavery, temperance, and general literature." Attending the 1855 National Negro Convention in Philadelphia as one of only two female delegates, she gave a speech that electrified the audience. An observer described it as "one of the most convincing and telling speeches in favor of Canadian emigration I ever heard."[2]

Teacher, journalist, abolitionist, proponent of emigration to Canada, and women's rights activist, Mary Ann Shadd (later Cary) represents many of the different liberation paths that African Americans pursued after 1830. In the 1830s and 1840s, free blacks in northern cities focused on building their own communities and on promoting moral reform, education, and black unity to beat back antiblack prejudice and discrimination. Increasingly, leading men and women formed organizations to accomplish the paired goals of securing equal rights in the North and ending slavery in the South. They met in local, regional, and national conventions to debate their goals and strategies, and they established and wrote for black newspapers that linked communities and ideas throughout the North. The former fugitives among them described the horrors of slavery to persuade whites to join their efforts. Some black activists mounted legal challenges to the discrimination they endured even in states that had abolished slavery. Some participated in petition campaigns and, though generally barred from voting, joined new political parties that aimed to prohibit the spread of slavery to new territories in the West.

Black activists pushed abolition onto the national agenda, and in the 1840s and 1850s the issue of slavery in the territories increasingly threatened to tear the nation apart. Activists deliberately disobeyed a strict new fugitive slave law, continuing to shepherd fugitive slaves to freedom by way of the underground railroad. Increasingly, that meant fleeing to Canada,

1848	Douglass attends women's rights convention in Seneca Falls, New York
1849	*Roberts v. City of Boston* upholds segregated schools in Massachusetts
1850	Compromise of 1850
	Fugitive Slave Act
1851	Christiana Resistance
	Mary Ann Shadd emigrates to Canada
1852	Harriet Beecher Stowe's *Uncle Tom's Cabin* published
	Martin Delany advocates establishing black nation outside United States
1854	Elizabeth Jennings sues New York streetcar company to end segregated seating
	Kansas-Nebraska Act
	Republican Party founded
	Fugitive slave Anthony Burns captured and returned to slavery
1855	Massachusetts becomes first state to prohibit segregation by race in public schools
1856	Violence erupts in Kansas between proslavery and antislavery settlers
1857	Black community of Seneca Village razed to make way for Central Park in New York City
	Dred Scott v. Sandford decision denies African American citizenship
1859	Delany begins search for site of African American emigrant settlement in Africa
	John Brown's raid on Harpers Ferry, Virginia
1860	Abraham Lincoln elected president
	South Carolina secedes from Union

as in the 1850s a growing number of free blacks came to believe there was no place for them in the United States. Others chose to stay and to confront injustice directly, a few through violent resistance and even insurrection. By 1860, black activism had helped force a catastrophic national showdown over slavery. As the states of the slave South and the free North grew increasingly discontented, each convinced that the other was conspiring to take over the federal government, the sectional struggle descended into disunion and civil war.

The Boundaries of Freedom

In the three decades before the Civil War, free black people in the North sought to make viable lives for themselves and their children even as their communities fought against increasing white hostility. Prejudice, law, and custom increasingly limited black opportunities for participation in the political, economic, and social life of the Republic. As a consequence, black communities turned inward to focus on building attitudes and institutions that would make them self-reliant. Yet their very success often provoked an angry, even violent, white response. More and more, free blacks in the North saw their struggle for self-improvement and full citizenship as inseparable from the struggle of enslaved blacks to end their bondage.

Racial Discrimination in the Era of the Common Man

By 1830, slavery existed almost exclusively in the South. Starting in the 1780s, northern states had abolished slavery, primarily through gradual emancipation laws that freed slaves after they reached a certain age. In 1830, New Jersey was the only northern state with a significant number of slaves: 2,254. By 1850, that number was 236, and slavery in the North was fast becoming a distant memory.

Yet the end of slavery brought an increase, not a decrease, in antiblack prejudice, discrimination, and even violence. "The prejudice of race," noted the French writer and visitor to the United States Alexis de Tocqueville in 1831, "appears to be stronger in the states that have abolished slavery than in those where it still exists; and nowhere is it so intolerant as in those states where servitude has never been known."[3] There are several explanations for this intensification of racial hostility. With blacks no longer enslaved, their lower status could no longer be taken for granted. Whites created structures of exclusion, segregation, and repression to enforce black submission. Increasingly, they viewed blacks as racially inferior, and studies in the emerging social sciences investigating human origins reinforced their views. In the 1820s and 1830s, Dr. Samuel G. Morton of Philadelphia collected human skulls from all over the world and classified them according to race. Measuring skull cavities, he proposed in *Crania Americana* (1839) that Europeans had the most brain capacity, Africans the least. His studies in craniology claimed to prove racial hierarchies popularized in studies such as *Types of Mankind, or Ethnological Researches* (1854) by Josiah Clark Nott and George Robins Gliddon, with a contribution by Louis Agassiz. Agassiz, a Swiss zoologist and geologist who taught at Harvard, lectured widely on the separate origins of the races and their distinguishing characteristics.

Throughout the nineteenth century, leading scholars in Europe and America investigated and debated racial origins and character. For American slaveholders, these early studies in the field that would become anthropology helped justify the enslavement of

African Americans. For white northerners, these ideas fed notions of white supremacy and suggested reasons to view free blacks as a problem population. Many favored schemes to remove this problem by colonizing African Americans outside the United States, but the American Colonization Society's efforts to sponsor the emigration of free blacks to Liberia were largely unsuccessful. Most free blacks opposed the idea of colonization, as they believed that the United States was their home. A group of Rochester blacks asserted, "We do not consider Africa to be our home, any more than the present whites do England, Scotland, or Ireland."[4]

Unable to pressure or force free blacks to leave the country, whites circumscribed African Americans' freedom and undermined their impact through segregation and exclusion. Black laws discouraged or forbade blacks from entering or settling in Ohio, Indiana, and Illinois—free states bordering on slave states—as well as in Wisconsin and the slave state of Missouri. By law and by custom, whites severely restricted blacks' access to jobs, public institutions and accommodations, and white neighborhoods. Black passengers on stagecoaches, steamboats, trains, streetcars, and omnibuses were required to sit in separate sections or relegated to separate cars.

The legal system, too, discriminated against blacks. Law enforcement officers routinely left black life, liberty, and property unprotected, and blacks had little redress in the courts. A white Cincinnati lawyer admitted to Tocqueville that the lack of legal protection for local blacks often led to "the most revolting injustices."[5] Blacks were also imprisoned at far higher rates than whites for all kinds of offenses—real and imagined, minor and major—in part because of racist views that held them prone to criminality. Because blacks could not serve on juries or function as witnesses or lawyers, blacks accused of crimes were more likely to be convicted and sentenced than whites similarly accused. Not until the late 1850s were blacks permitted to serve on juries, and then only in Massachusetts.

For whites, this was the era of the common man. Universal white male suffrage became the norm after 1830, while black men lost the right to vote. In 1837, Pennsylvania disfranchised black men, and every state that entered the Union after 1819, except Maine, prohibited black suffrage. In 1860, black men could vote only in Maine, New Hampshire, Vermont, Massachusetts, and Rhode Island. Blacks constituted just 6 percent of the population in these five states.

Black political exclusion solidified white male supremacy. Fearing that voting by allegedly ignorant and untrustworthy black men would pollute the political system, white men and white laws effectively removed black interests from democratic representation. Whites degraded the status of blacks and then punished them for it. Excluding blacks from political life also had the effect of marginalizing them in the nation's economic life. Thrown into competition with American-born working-class whites and new white immigrants looking to establish themselves, free blacks were often the targets of a hostility that flared into violence. Racially motivated riots were almost commonplace in northern cities, as white mobs attacked black neighborhoods with much loss of property and even loss of life.

A series of riots in Cincinnati offers an example. Directly across the Ohio River from the slave state of Kentucky, Cincinnati was where southern blacks who had been emancipated or had purchased their freedom often relocated. It was also a destination for fugitive slaves. The city's black population grew so rapidly as to alarm its white population, and in late June 1829 local officials announced that they would rigorously apply Ohio's black laws. Even as the city's blacks began to investigate the possibility of resettling in Canada, white mobs attacked them. Over the summer, half the black population was driven from the city. Some two hundred eventually settled in Upper Canada, where they named their new community Wilberforce, after the British abolitionist William Wilberforce, who led the effort to end slavery in Britain's colonies. His goal was accomplished in 1833 when Parliament passed a compensated emancipation law that applied to the entire British empire.

But the violence was not over in Cincinnati. In 1836, white mobs destroyed the shop that printed an abolitionist newspaper and moved on to destroy houses and churches belonging to African Americans. In 1841, fights between unemployed black and white dockworkers escalated into a battle in which blacks mobilized to protect their neighborhood. After police and militiamen disarmed these blacks, the whites returned, leading to more loss of life and more devastation of property.

Boston, New York, and Providence, Rhode Island, also experienced antiblack riots, but no city had more than Philadelphia, which, not coincidentally, had the largest black population. Riots rocked the city in 1820, 1829, 1834, 1835, 1838, 1842, and 1849.

Destruction by Fire of Pennsylvania Hall,
On the night of the 17th May, 1838

The Destruction of Pennsylvania Hall
Arson has historically been a common form of antiproperty violence, often associated with frenzied mobs. In May 1838, arsonists torched Philadelphia's Pennsylvania Hall, a building tied to abolitionism and the elevation of free blacks. The primitive state of fire prevention and firefighting at this time typically meant that arson exacted a heavy toll in lives lost and property destroyed.
Hand-colored lithograph by J. C. Wild, 1838/The Library Company of Philadelphia.

During the 1834 riot, both prosperous and poor blacks were attacked, many died, and hundreds fled the city. Roving white mobs vandalized the African Presbyterian Church and devastated a black Methodist church. They attacked white supporters of black rights as well. In 1838, a mob assaulted black and white abolitionists meeting in Philadelphia's Pennsylvania Hall, which had just been dedicated to the cause of abolitionism, and burned it to the ground. The year before, proslavery activists in Alton, Illinois, hurled the printing presses of a white antislavery newspaper into the Mississippi River, burned the print shop, and murdered the editor, Elijah P. Lovejoy. These race riots, which targeted white abolitionists as well as blacks, formed part of a larger pattern of racial and ethnic hostility that was also evident in politics. During the 1840s and 1850s, anti-immigrant, anti-Catholic Know-Nothings, so-called for the secret nature of their party organization, won local and state offices in New England, New York, and Pennsylvania. The era of the common man was also an era of intense nativism that defined the United States as Anglo-Saxon and Protestant, a land in which free black people had no place. (See Visual Sources: Minstrel Shows, pp. 309–13.)

Black Communities in an Era of Expansion

Racial hostility, economic discrimination, political exclusion, and violence had severe consequences for black communities in the North in the decades after 1830. These forces constrained the efforts of northern free blacks to make a living and improve themselves

The Results of Abolitionism!
According to those opposed to abolitionism, it upset the racial status quo, it promoted free black labor dominance in the guise of racial equality, and it subordinated the interests of whites, especially white workers, to the interests of blacks. Some believed that black workers were, wittingly or unwittingly, collaborating with white capitalists, whose primary goal was to divide and conquer all workers, white and black. In this engraving, a white capitalist supervises black workers: "Sambo hurry up the white laborers." The black workers then supervise the white workers: "White man hurry up them bricks." "Bring up the mortar you white rascals." "You bog-trotters [a term for Irish immigrants] come along with them bricks." Irish immigrants were also objects of discrimination at this time, partly because many of them were Catholic. There was also significant antiblack racism among them, in part because of widespread job competition between blacks and Irish immigrants.
Wood engraving, artist unknown, c. 1835/The Library Company of Philadelphia.

and undermined their communities. The jobs available to black people were primarily unskilled and paid the lowest wages. Often the work was seasonal, with periods of unemployment. Between 1820 and 1860, the percentages and relative numbers of black men in skilled and semiskilled jobs actually declined, as these jobs increasingly went to native-born whites and the growing numbers of white immigrants. Between 1830 and 1860, the U.S. population increased from 13 million to 32 million, almost 5 million of whom were immigrants. Most newcomers settled in the cities of the North, where their numbers increased competition for scarce jobs. Serious economic downturns in each decade between 1830 and 1860 further eroded the already declining economic status of northern blacks.

Black women formed a little more than half the population in urban black communities. The shorter life expectancy of black males—owing to disease as well as both overwork and poverty from lack of work—and the consistently high demand for black women as domestic servants help explain their greater numbers. There were more widows than widowers in the black communities in Philadelphia, Boston, and Cincinnati, and the number of female-headed households grew. These households were generally poorer than dual-headed households.

Blacks had shorter life expectancies and higher death rates than whites due to accidents and disease. They had higher infant mortality rates and fewer children. After 1840, urban black families in the North were smaller in size than rural black families in the North and southern black families in general. In the short term, smaller families had a positive impact, as that meant fewer demands on limited family budgets. In the longer term, smaller families had a more negative impact, for there were fewer young people to contribute to the family income.

Yet overall, the number of free blacks in the North continued to grow through natural increase, the migration of free blacks from the South, and the arrival of fugitives from slavery. By 1860, half the nation's free black population (226,152) lived in cities in the North. In 1860, Boston had 2,261 blacks, New York 12,472, and Philadelphia 22,185. As a proportion of the population, however, these black communities were shrinking, for the white population was rising more rapidly due to the influx of immigrants, especially from Ireland, which suffered from widespread famine in the 1840s. Increasingly, the newer cities of the West, such as Pittsburgh and St. Louis, also had large black populations. Cincinnati, for example, counted 3,737 blacks in 1860.[6] (See By the Numbers: Percent Change in Free Black Population, 1830–1860.)

In northern cities, black neighborhoods evolved close to, but mostly separate from, white neighborhoods. Cities were still small and densely settled, and blacks, as one observer noted, found themselves "crammed into lofts, garrets and cellars, in blind alleys and narrow courts." Some neighborhoods were racially diverse, with blacks living among poor and working-class whites, especially recent immigrants. The inhabitants of New York City's Five Points district in lower Manhattan were made up "of all colors, white, yellow, brown and ebony black."[7] Some affluent blacks lived in predominantly white areas, but more white neighborhoods were closed to them. Where the black population was larger, as in "Nigger Hill," on the lower slopes of Boston's Beacon Hill, clusters of white households developed within largely black areas. Black neighborhoods almost everywhere were crowded and lacked clean

BY THE NUMBERS   Percent Change in Free Black Population, 1830–1860

As this figure illustrates, in the vast majority of northern states, the free black population rose significantly during the period from 1830 to 1860. Despite these increases, however, free black representation in the general population decreased during this same period, owing largely to the influx of white European immigrants to the United States. While the northern slave population became statistically insignificant during these years, it is important to remember that most blacks remained enslaved—and that most free blacks still lived in the South.

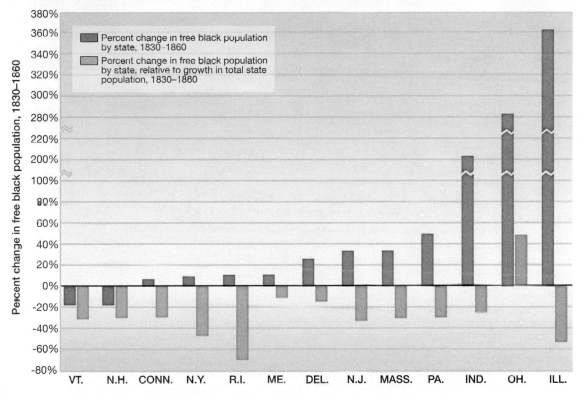

streets and public services such as police and fire protection. Poor sanitation was one reason life expectancies for blacks were shorter than for whites.

Although the economic and physical security of black communities generally declined from 1830 to 1860, some individuals and families succeeded in pulling themselves out of poverty, primarily by establishing small businesses that grew into larger enterprises. The Forten family of Philadelphia is one example. At the end of the eighteenth century, James Forten, a second-generation free black, purchased a sail loft from the man with whom he had apprenticed. By the 1830s, his sail-making business was highly respected and prosperous, with twenty to thirty employees.[8] Forten was a wealthy man, who was able to give his daughters and granddaughters a good education. Most became teachers, and all were active abolitionists and strong advocates of free black **uplift**: the idea, especially popular among the elite, that black self-help, leadership, and autonomy were necessary to elevate the race as a whole. Like Forten, the free blacks who prospered usually came from families that had been free for more than one generation.

FIVE POINTS, 1827.

Five Points

This notorious neighborhood in lower Manhattan featured a racially diverse population, with a sizable number of blacks. It also included a significant number of poor and working-class residents. The interracial socializing here, especially in its taverns and bawdy houses, was a cause for alarm among whites, including city officials and travelers. High rates of crime and disease marred the community. For these reasons, Five Points was seen as dangerous and immoral.

The Five Points, Junction of Baxter, Worth and Park Streets, New York, *hand-colored engraving by George Catlin (1796–1872),* © *Museum of the City of New York, USA/The Bridgeman Art Library International.*

Ironically, the very success of black entrepreneurs attracted the animosity of whites, and successful communities were often victims of violence. Seneca Village, in upper Manhattan, was a thriving black community in the 1830s and 1840s, with churches, schools, businesses, cemeteries, and various community institutions. Wealthy blacks invested in it because of its promise; poorer blacks lived there because of its affordability and welcoming atmosphere. Community gardens, with "cabbage, and melon patches, with hills of corn and cucumbers, and beds of beets and parsnips,"[9] sustained those who lived there. Known as a haven for runaway slaves, Seneca Village was also a center of abolitionism and growing agitation for black rights. In 1857, city officials razed it to make way for Central Park.

Black Self-Help in an Era of Moral Reform

The day-to-day struggles of northern blacks to overcome oppression created an internal focus on self-improvement and community building. Excluded from the political, economic, and social worlds of whites, blacks looked to one another for emotional and spiritual support as well as material and institutional resources. Their sense of racial unity built on a growing commitment to self-help—the belief that they themselves must take responsibility for their destinies, regardless of external forces. As the influential black journalist, doctor, and writer Martin R. Delany observed in 1852, "Our elevation must be the result of self-efforts, and work of our own hands. No other human power can accomplish it. If we but determine it shall be so, it will be so."[10]

Mutual aid societies, independent black churches, and black schools knit black communities together. A range of benevolent institutions for women and men, including male lodges and fraternal orders, as well as their women's auxiliaries, helped individuals look out for one another. Female benevolent societies aimed especially to assist the many widows in black communities. By 1840, there were more than sixty such societies in Philadelphia alone. Black orphanages took care of children whose parents had died or could not support them. In New York City, the Colored Orphan Asylum, set up by white Quaker women in 1836, quickly became an important black community institution that provided education, apprenticeships, and job opportunities. In 1846, James McCune Smith was appointed its medical director. Denied admission to American colleges, he had received his medical training in Scotland but had returned to the United States to serve African Americans. His commitment was typical of the way privileged black men and women helped support their communities.

Independent black churches, too, sustained their communities with a range of services. Philadelphia's Mother Bethel AME Church was among the most active. Like other black churches, Mother Bethel sponsored schools in the belief that education would both improve the lives of future generations and decrease white hostility. "If we ever expect to see the influence of prejudice decrease and ourselves respected," maintained one spokesman in 1832, "it must be by the blessings of an enlightened education."[11] Attending schools with white children was rarely an option, as white families, associating integrated schools with abolition and racial mixing, vigorously opposed them. Sunday schools, which enhanced religious education with basic training in reading, writing, and arithmetic, helped advance black literacy and numeracy.

Northern black communities pushed for separate black public schools and created private schools, often with the assistance of supportive whites, especially Quakers and abolitionists. Yet even white assistance brought little assurance of success. In 1832, when Prudence Crandall, a young Quaker teacher in Canterbury, Connecticut, admitted an African American girl to her female academy, white parents withdrew their students. Crandall responded by closing her school, then reopening it for black girls only. Local opposition escalated, and Connecticut passed a law that made the school illegal. Crandall was arrested, and her school was vandalized and eventually burned. Under pressure from abolitionists, Connecticut repealed the law, but Miss Crandall's School for Young Ladies and Little Misses of Color never reopened.

Though appreciative of the commitment of white teachers, blacks increasingly sought to establish their own schools, with black teachers who could more closely identify with their students. By the 1830s, the New York African Free School had more than fourteen hundred students. Yet most black schools were poorly equipped, lacking books and unable to pay teachers the salaries white teachers received. An assessment in 1848 concluded that the state of black education "has been shamefully limited."[12] Slowly, however, the spread of the common school movement—the effort to create public schools open to all—and court challenges to discrimination in education opened some public schools to African Americans. In Cincinnati, for example, blacks created a community-based black high school in the face of extreme white opposition. The city later built a black public high school.

To meet the expanding need for teachers, black secondary education throughout the North focused on teacher training. The Institute for Colored Youth in Philadelphia trained teachers, as did Charles Avery's Allegheny Institute, established near Pittsburgh in 1849. Avery's school emphasized vocational training, but in the 1850s two new black colleges focused on the arts and sciences. In Chester County, Pennsylvania, the Ashmun Institute opened in 1854 to provide a higher education "for male youth of African descent"; it was renamed Lincoln University after the Civil War. In Ohio, the Methodist Church founded Wilberforce University, named for the British abolitionist, in 1856. Also in Ohio, Oberlin College, founded by abolitionists in 1833, had been open to both African Americans and women for twenty years.

Teaching attracted the most talented black women of the era because it was one of the few professions open to women. Sarah Mapps Douglass, for example, born into a comfortable black Philadelphia family and educated by private tutors, founded a high school for girls that included training in science, atypical of education for girls in the period. In 1853, she began running the girls' department of the Institute for Colored Youth. After taking classes at the Female Medical College of Pennsylvania and Penn Medical University in the late 1850s, she began a series of medical education classes for women in her home.

Douglass was committed to black uplift, and her uplift activities are representative of educated black women. They were generally deeply religious and deeply engaged in the reform spirit of the era. These were the years in which evangelicals, especially women evangelicals, sought to reform and even perfect society by promoting virtuous living. Using women's role as guardian of the family and home, these women argued for temperance to end the abuses of alcoholism. They also called for an end to prostitution and for more humane treatment of prisoners and the mentally ill. For black women, social reform had the particular aim of improving black communities and elevating the status of blacks. (See Documents: Elite Black Women Speak Out on Education, Citizenship, and Slavery, pp. 298–302.)

Among the first to articulate this message was Maria W. Stewart, who, in Boston in the early 1830s, was the first American woman, white or black, to speak before a mixed audience of men and women—at the time a brave and highly controversial act. She had been influenced by David Walker (see chapter 5), who encouraged her brief but electrifying public speaking career. Intensely religious, Stewart rejected Walker's call for violence, promoting the moral reform of the black community instead. Beginning in 1831, in speeches, essays, and editorials, she stressed the importance of education, especially that of girls, and black elevation generally. "How long shall the fair daughters of Africa be compelled to bury their minds and talents beneath a load of iron pots and kettles?" she asked. She also urged African American women to understand their duty as mothers "to create in the minds of your little girls and boys a thirst for knowledge." She implored men to "flee from the gambling board and the dance-hall; for we are poor, and have no money to throw away. . . . Let our money, instead . . . be appropriated for schools and seminaries of learning for our children and youth."[13] (See From the Record: Lives of Continual Drudgery and Toil.)

From the Record

Maria W. Stewart | Lives of Continual Drudgery and Toil, 1832

Maria W. Stewart (1803–1879) was no stranger to hard work. Born free in Connecticut, she was orphaned at age five and bound in servitude until age fifteen. After that, she continued working as a domestic servant, educating herself by attending Sunday school. Widowed at age twenty-six, she began writing and speaking on Christian morality and black self-improvement. Negative responses to a February 1833 speech that decried the lack of ambition among black men contributed to her abandonment of her speaking career. Earlier speeches show a deep understanding of the constraints on black lives. In this one, delivered in Boston on September 21, 1832, she describes the combined effects of ignorance, drudgery, and destitution on the lives of free blacks.

I have heard much respecting the horrors of slavery; but may Heaven forbid that the generality of my color throughout these United States should experience any more of its horrors than to be a servant of servants, or hewers of wood and drawers of water! Tell us no more of southern slavery; for with few exceptions, although I may be very erroneous in my opinion, yet I consider our condition but little better than that. Yet, after all, methinks there are no chains so galling as those that bind the soul, and exclude it from the vast field of useful and scientific knowledge. . . .

Few white persons of either sex, who are calculated for anything else, are willing to spend their lives and bury their talents in performing mean, servile labor. And such is the horrible idea that I entertain respecting a life of servitude, that if I conceived of [there] being no possibility of my rising above the condition of servant, I would gladly hail death as a welcome messenger. O, horrible idea, indeed! to possess noble souls aspiring after high and honorable acquirements, yet confined by the chains of ignorance and poverty to lives of continual drudgery and toil. Neither do I know of any who have enriched themselves by spending their lives as house-domestics, washing windows, shaking carpets, brushing boots, or tending upon gentlemen's tables. . . .

. . . The whites have so long and so loudly proclaimed the theme of equal rights and privileges, that our souls have caught the flame also, ragged as we are. As far as our merit deserves, we feel a common desire to rise above the condition of servants and drudges. I have learnt, by bitter experience, that continual hard labor deadens the energies of the soul, and benumbs the faculties of the mind; the ideas become confined, the mind barren, and, like the scorching sands of Arabia, produces nothing; or like the uncultivated soil, brings forth thorns and thistles. . . .

. . . Do you ask, why are you wretched and miserable? I reply, look at many of the most worthy and most interesting of us doomed to spend our lives in gentlemen's kitchens. Look at our young men, smart, active and energetic, with souls filled with ambitious fire; if they look forward, alas! What are their prospects? They can be nothing but the humblest laborers, on account of their dark complexions; hence many of them lose their

Continued

Continued

ambition, and become worthless. Look at our middle-aged men, clad in their rusty plaids and coats; in winter, every cent they earn goes to buy their wood and pay their rents; the poor wives also toil beyond their strength, to help support their families. Look at our aged sires, whose heads are whitened with the frosts of seventy winters, with their old wood-saws on their backs. Alas, what keeps us so? Prejudice, ignorance and poverty.

SOURCE: Maria Stewart, "Lecture Delivered at the Franklin Hall," September 21, 1832, in *Maria W. Stewart, America's First Black Woman Political Writer: Essays and Speeches*, ed. Marilyn Richardson (Bloomington: Indiana University Press, 1987), 45–49.

???   **According to Stewart, how did servitude affect the lives of blacks as a whole—what Stewart calls "the generality of my color throughout these United States"?**

Stewart believed that black moral and intellectual improvement would decrease white prejudice,[14] and other black leaders made similar arguments. Writing in the *Colored American*, the Pittsburgh AME minister and educator Lewis Woodson held that deportment and dress reflect inner character: "Every one must agree that the moral effect of mean dress is, to degrade us in our own eyes and in the eyes of all who behold us." Articulating a common concern among black women and men, Woodson maintained that "colored females should be extremely attentive to cleanliness and neatness of dress" because "of the prejudices which exist against them in the community in which they live; and they should consider how imprudent it is, by neglecting their personal appearance, to heighten and aggravate that prejudice."[15]

But most black leaders recognized that it was not only black people who needed improving. In 1836, James Forten and others founded the Christian-inspired American Moral Reform Society. The Society was dedicated to the equality of all, including blacks, whites, and women, and promoted various initiatives—such as public education, peace activism, and temperance—to elevate all Americans regardless of race. They proposed to advance African Americans' struggle as a way of "improving the condition of mankind."[16] Thus they sought an end to slavery and urged members to boycott goods produced by slave labor. The society's program was indicative not only of antebellum reform generally, but also of the peculiar situation of a free people striving to work with white allies to achieve respect and dignity in a nation that sanctioned black enslavement.

Forging a Black Freedom Struggle

Increasingly, the commitment of northern black communities to self-improvement and moral reform was linked to the abolition of slavery. Free blacks recognized that they could not elevate their own people unless all black people in the nation were free. This understanding compelled black activism, as black leaders began to work together outside their communities as well as within them. Only a concerted effort could bring about fundamental change in the nation's conscience, laws, and practices. Through speeches, meetings, annual conventions, and newspapers, black leaders formed networks that connected their communities and sharpened their message of moral reform to address the nation's conscience. Casting slavery as an evil institution, they wrote and lectured on the ways it debased individual lives and corrupted the nation as a whole. They argued for the importance of equal rights, not only for blacks but also for women, and they challenged blacks' status in the courts. The arrival of fugitive slaves brought new and powerful voices to strengthen their ranks. Black activists generally participated in and supported the white abolitionist organizations founded in this era, but they also operated independently. Although largely disfranchised, they engaged in political actions to advance the uplift of free blacks as well as abolitionism.

Black Communities Connect

In September 1830, Bishop Richard Allen called black clergy and other leaders to gather at Philadelphia's Mother Bethel AME Church to consider the issues that beset their communities, including abolitionism. Some forty responded, from nine states, including the slave states of Delaware, Maryland, and Virginia. The First National Negro Convention was the first in a series of gatherings that constituted the **black convention movement**. In national meetings called annually through 1835 and occasionally thereafter, and especially in a far more prolific series of state and local conventions, black leaders built networks. They discussed and debated the state of their communities and what they could do to improve them. They framed resolutions and undertook projects that sought to elevate the status of free blacks and to promote abolitionism. Many were ministers, and their proposals reflected Christian values and the importance of an upright moral character.

The first convention, in 1830, set an agenda for future meetings. In light of the recent Cincinnati riots, migration to Canada was under discussion, as was black education, especially black vocational schools. At the early conventions, attendees expressed support for programs that enhanced blacks' job prospects and looked for ways to move blacks from menial to vocational jobs, although a proposal for a manual labor school for black boys never materialized. They went on record as promoting cooperative economic enterprises, such as black businesses and mutual savings banks. They also promoted the moral virtue of farm life. In fact, churchgoing and righteous living—including temperance, sexual morality, and thrift—would, they argued, ensure the social and moral reform of individual lives that would benefit the community as a whole.

In the 1840s, conventions met in other cities, including Cleveland, New York City, and Rochester and Troy in upstate New York. Discussions were increasingly political and militant. A new generation of leaders was emerging, men and women who had formerly been slaves and whose frank descriptions of slave life riveted audiences and were winning converts to abolition among reform-minded white men and women. Speaking at the 1843 convention in Buffalo, New York, were two former slaves from Maryland. Henry Highland Garnet, minister of the Liberty Street Presbyterian Church in Troy, called openly for a slave rebellion, while Frederick Douglass, a lecturer on the abolitionist circuit, advocated a more tempered response, believing it would be better to appeal to the conscience of the nation and to end slavery peaceably. (See Documents: Former Slaves Speak Out on Slavery, pp. 303–8.)

These black conventions, especially the national ones, helped create a sense of African Americans as a distinct people. Although debates were often spirited and proposals ranged from conservative to radical, they strengthened black identity through a unity of purpose. These conventions amounted to a significant and alternative black political movement with a core agenda that united free black uplift and abolition. Meeting in Rochester in 1853, one convention stressed this powerful sense of African American peoplehood: "We are as a people, chained together. We are one people—one in general complexion, one in common degradation, one in popular estimation. As one rises, all must rise, and as one falls all must fall."[17]

The black press was also a vital element in the growing network of black leaders and institutions with a unified purpose. In 1827, John Russwurm and Samuel Cornish began publishing *Freedom's Journal*, the nation's first African American newspaper. It was, the first issue announced, "devoted to the dissemination of useful knowledge among our brethren, and to their moral and religious improvement." The *Journal* continued, "We wish to plead our own cause. Too long have others spoken for us."[18] The paper lasted only two years, and in 1829 Cornish began publishing *The Rights of All*, primarily to argue against colonization. This paper, too, was short-lived, its brief run indicative of how difficult it was to sustain any newspaper at this time, but especially a black one. Agents were required to distribute copies and enlist subscribers. Most black papers survived long-term only with the help of wealthy patrons as well as white and black subscribers.

Nevertheless, between 1830 and 1860, more than forty black newspapers provided a weekly or monthly perspective on current events and a forum for discussing the fight for abolition as well as issues relevant to free black uplift, such as suffrage, jobs, housing, schools, and fair treatment on public transportation. Because copies were passed from one person to another, the papers had a widespread influence. Stories in one were reprinted in others, building a sense of black unity and contributing to the emergence of a powerful national black press tradition. (See From the Record: A Disfranchised People.)

The most influential newspaper was published by Frederick Douglass. In 1847, he launched the *North Star* as an explicitly abolitionist paper aiming to "attack slavery in all its forms and aspects; advocate Universal Emancipation; exact the standard of public morality; promote the moral and intellectual improvement of the colored people; and to hasten the day of freedom to our three million enslaved fellow countrymen."[19] The *North Star* attracted white readers as well as black. In 1851, it merged with the *Liberty Party Paper* to become *Frederick Douglass' Paper*, which continued publication until 1863. Its longevity both derived from and contributed to Douglass's stature as the preeminent black leader of his day. The paper also published contributions from well-known correspondents, such as James McCune Smith, who in 1855 argued for race pride. "We must learn to love, respect and glory in our Negro nature," he asserted.[20]

Black Activists and Activism

In addition to the influential role Frederick Douglass played in the newspaper business, he was a powerful lecturer who captivated white audiences by recounting the realities of his life as a slave. He had escaped from slavery in 1838 and settled in New Bedford, Massachusetts, where he worked as a day laborer. In 1841, while attending an antislavery meeting in Nantucket, he agreed to say a few words. The audience was riveted, and the meeting's organizers urged him to begin lecturing regularly for the abolitionist

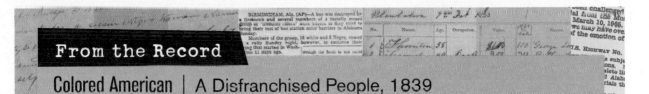

From the Record

Colored American | A Disfranchised People, 1839

In 1837, the *Colored American* began publication in New York City, with Samuel Cornish, Charles B. Ray, and Philip A. Bell as editors. A weekly, it was subsidized by Arthur Tappan and published until 1842. It promoted abolition, opposed colonization, and sought the elevation of free blacks. This editorial examines the effects of disfranchisement on character. The second part of the editorial, on the effects of disfranchisement on the conduct of whites toward blacks, is no longer extant.

This is the only distinction which universally attends our people in these United States; and it is an adequate source for all our woe. The want of the franchise affects us first in its direct influence in our character, and secondly, indirectly in its influence in the conduct of the whites towards us.

1st. Its influence on our character. It is a truth with regard to mind as well as to the corporal organization of man that there are certain functions (an essential point of its being) co-eval with its existance, which, if duly performed, contribute to the health and vigor of the possessor, but which if left unemployed, results in a mind diseased. One of their functions, entailed in the human mind, by its destiny, is an exercise of its faculties for the general good: man was not created to live alone, but in communities. Thence, in addition to these faculties which are requisite to enable him to provide for the necessaries of life, there are other and nobler ones where legitimate direction is for the benefit of the community of which he is a part. A full exercise of their faculties by all its members is productive of the greatest good to a community. It would indeed be a wide diffusion of political power, which would lead to parties and strife; but their parties and strife are a safety valve through which the exuberant spleen and passions of men find vent, and party strife would elicit principles and strike out improvements, which in the end conduce to the general good.

If these things be true, our disfranchisement may be said in a measure to dehumanise us; it debars us from the exercise of faculties which our Maker has incorporated with our being.

But these faculties, shut out from their legitimate sphere, cannot remain inactive; prevented from doing good, they must do harm to our selves, and those among whom we live.

Source: "A Disfranchised People," *Colored American*, October 12, 1839, Black Abolitionist Archive, University of Detroit Mercy.

??? According to the writer, how would the black vote improve the condition of both African Americans and the nation as a whole?

Engraved by J. C. Buttre.

Frederick Douglass

This engraving of a smartly dressed young Douglass vividly captures his self-confidence and middle-class bearing. Douglass's emergence as the preeminent black leader and black abolitionist of his era owed significantly to his intelligence, hard work, and ambition. His rise to prominence also owed to his uncanny ability to articulate not only his people's cause but also how that cause shaped America's past, present, and future. As a social reformer dedicated to a wide range of issues, including woman suffrage, Douglass helped bring people together across barriers of race, gender, and class.

cause. One of these organizers was the prominent white abolitionist William Lloyd Garrison, who soon encouraged Douglass to make lecturing a career and to publish the story of his life.

In 1845, Douglass published *Narrative of the Life of Frederick Douglass, an American Slave.* It sold more than 30,000 copies in its first five years in print, and in 1855 he published an expanded version, *My Bondage and My Freedom.* These books reached a wide range of readers and today exemplify the whole genre of slave narratives that emerged in this era as the most original and significant form of African American literary expression. Addressed largely to white audiences, these narratives charted individual yet representative journeys from southern slave to free black person. By revealing the details of what it meant to be a slave, they affirmed the humanity of enslaved African Americans. Notable narratives of slavery and escape were written by William Wells Brown, Henry "Box" Brown, and Henry Bibb (see chapter 5). Harriet Jacobs, in *Incidents in the Life of a Slave Girl* (published later, in 1861), revealed the sexual exploitation of slave women by white masters.[21]

This outpouring of African American literature was in a real sense a renaissance. Jarena Lee, a member of Mother Bethel, wrote a spiritual autobiography (originally published in 1836; expanded and updated in 1849) that recorded her struggles in the male-dominated world of preaching. Frances Ellen Watkins (later Harper) published *Poems on Miscellaneous Subjects* (1854), a collection that included "The Slave Mother," which examined the unique pain enslaved mothers endured. Frederick Douglass and Martin Delany published novels with plots centered on slave insurrections, while William Wells Brown's novel *Clotel* (1853) helped establish the character type of the "tragic mulatta," a white-looking black woman whose mixed-race identity typically led to tragedy. Both Clotel, allegedly Thomas Jefferson's daughter, and her mother, Currer, Jefferson's alleged mistress, were tragic mulattas. In *Our Nig, or Sketches from the Life of a Free Black* (1859), Harriet E. Wilson explored prejudice in the North through a coming-of-age narrative remarkably like her own life story. James W. C. Pennington wrote both a slave narrative and a study of the history of black people in the United States, while William Cooper Nell recorded the contributions of black soldiers to the nation's wars. Hosea Easton published his challenge to racism in *A Treatise on the Intellectual Character, and Civil and Political Condition of the Colored People of the U. States* (1837).

These works exhibited significantly less of the deference to white leadership that had marked the writings of the first post-Revolutionary generation. Pioneering this increasing black militancy, David Walker's *Appeal* (1829; see chapter 5) had called on slaves to revolt, and Robert Alexander Young's pamphlet *The Ethiopian Manifesto* (1829) had warned slave owners of a terrible punishment from God unless they freed their slaves and sought God's forgiveness. The new generation of black leaders carried forward this militant approach. They sought to reform not only the black community but also the nation. Their strategy of **moral suasion** aimed to convince the white majority that slavery and the oppression of free blacks were immoral, offensive to God, and contrary to the nation's ideals.

Frederick Douglass was certainly the most well-known African American speaker on the abolitionist lecture circuit, but Sojourner Truth may have been the most compelling. Born a slave named Isabella Baumfree, she had achieved freedom and secured custody of her son, who had been sold illegally, through a lawsuit (see chapter 4). In 1843, she transformed herself by taking a new name and occupation. As a lecturer-spiritualist-preacher, she was both outspoken and plainspoken, powerful and fearless. In 1847, before a packed audience in Boston's Faneuil Hall, she challenged even Douglass, who had despaired of God's

I Sell the Shadow to Support the Substance.
SOJOURNER TRUTH.

Sojourner Truth
One of the most famous and influential black women of the nineteenth century, Sojourner Truth (born Isabella Baumfree) both embodied and spoke powerfully to the intersection of the struggles of blacks, women, and the dispossessed. Truth's wide-ranging influence and popularity owed heavily to her piercing intelligence, Christian spirituality, striking speaking ability, and commanding sense of herself. Notwithstanding her illiteracy, Truth's voice resonated with insight and the power of personal witness. This image was printed on a small card. The caption underneath it, "I Sell the Shadow to Support the Substance," illustrates her willingness to help support herself however she could. *Library of Congress, LC-USZC4-6165.*

ability to bring about a peaceful end to slavery. Truth stood up and asked, "Frederick, is God dead?" The audience enthusiastically shouted support for her position.[22]

For Truth, as for many of her religiously motivated reform colleagues, the abolition of slavery was both part of God's divine plan and necessary for America to realize its democratic ideals. But as a woman, Truth also argued for women's rights. In an 1851 speech in Akron, Ohio, she made a case for women's equality: "I have plowed and reaped and husked and chopped and mowed. . . . I can carry as much as any man, and can eat as much, too, if I can get it."[23] Truth did not present herself as a respectable middle-class reformer who argued for abolition and equality in the abstract. Her words grew out of her own experience as a slave, a wage earner, and a mother. Her directness won both followers and detractors. In an 1858 speech in a small Indiana town, when hecklers questioned whether so forceful a speaker could actually be a woman, Truth bared her breast.[24]

The experience and approach of Sarah Parker Remond was entirely different. She was born into an affluent free black family in Salem, Massachusetts, but when she was barred from attending a girls' academy there, her family moved to Newport, Rhode Island, where she received an education. She chose a career as an antislavery lecturer, speaking locally, then nationally, and eventually traveling to England to push forward a global campaign against slavery. Remond and other female abolitionist speakers braved strong opposition to women speaking in public. (See Documents: Elite Black Women Speak Out on Education, Citizenship, and Slavery, 298–302.) Their perseverance is testimony to their commitment to the abolitionist crusade and offers insight into their support for women's rights.

Elizabeth Jennings, a teacher in New York City's black schools who had also lectured on behalf of black women, took her activism to a new level when, in 1854, she was forcibly removed from a streetcar on her way to church. The Third Avenue Railroad, she was told, had separate cars for black customers. With the support of her congregation, she sued the railroad company, claiming that as public conveyances, streetcars could not refuse to serve passengers on the basis of race. The jury ruled in her favor and awarded her damages. The Third Avenue Railroad stopped segregating its cars, and the case, reported in *Frederick Douglass' Paper*, received considerable attention.[25]

This case, and a few others in the 1840s and early 1850s, seemed to signal that free blacks could use the courts to end discrimination. Benjamin Roberts initiated one of the most important legal cases. In 1848, Roberts sued the city of Boston on behalf of his daughter Sarah, who was forced to attend a mediocre all-black school when there was a better all-white school closer to the family's home. Robert Morris, one of the nation's first black lawyers, and the white lawyer Charles Sumner, later a U.S. senator, argued the *Roberts* case. In *Roberts v. City of Boston* (1849), the Massachusetts Supreme Court upheld Boston's public school statute requiring racially segregated schools. But the argument presented by Sumner, that "a school, exclusively devoted to one class, must differ essentially, in its spirit and character, from that public school . . . where all classes meet together in equality,"[26] did not go unheeded. Boston blacks organized the Equal School Rights Committee to continue the fight for integrated public schools locally and statewide, and in 1855 Massachusetts became the first state to prohibit segregation of public schools on the basis of race.

The Abolitionist Movement

Black abolitionists were innumerable and varied and often operated independently of any organization. From many different perspectives—female and male, former slave and freeborn—they urged their own communities and Americans in general to reform themselves and to perfect society by ensuring equal rights and ending slavery. Some cooperated with sympathetic white men and women who also organized against slavery. Some broke away from white organizations. Regardless, the agendas of black activists helped shape the growing **abolitionist movement**, which was increasingly commanding the attention of ordinary white citizens, politicians, and the national government.

In the 1830s, the momentum of abolitionism shifted away from groups advocating gradual emancipation, compensating slaveholders for freeing their slaves, and colonizing blacks outside the United States. The new abolitionist movement sought to end slavery immediately, rather than gradually, and without compensation, through moral suasion and **political action**—working within the political system. Despite their exclusion from political life, black activists supported the latter as well as the former. Indeed, blacks continued to mount a vigorous and widespread opposition to slavery, working within their own organizations as well as within more influential and better-funded mostly white abolitionist groups.

William Lloyd Garrison led the moral suasion wing of the abolitionist movement, while the wealthy brothers Arthur and Lewis Tappan led the political action wing. Together they founded the American Anti-Slavery Society in 1833. Among the sixty-three delegates from eleven states at the first meeting in Philadelphia were three African Americans: Robert Purvis, James McCrummell, and James G. Barbadoes. The delegates framed two goals: "the entire abolition of slavery in the United States" and the elevation of "the character and condition of the people of color."[27]

Garrison's moral suasion approach had been shaped by the arguments of black abolitionists, and in 1831, with their support, he began publishing the *Liberator*, the most famous antislavery newspaper of the era. James Forten signed up subscribers in Philadelphia and sent Garrison's Boston office an advance payment on their subscriptions. Writing as "A Colored Philadelphian," he was also a frequent contributor to the paper's early issues.[28] Garrison worked well with black activists and counted them among his friends. He published Maria Stewart's speeches in the *Liberator* and promoted the speaking career of Frederick Douglass, writing a preface to Douglass's slave narrative.

In the pages of the *Liberator*, Garrison condemned slavery as immoral and contrary to Christian principles, and he called for immediate, uncompensated emancipation. He stated his opposition to colonization, and he promoted many of the era's reforms, including women's rights, prison reform, and temperance. Garrison believed that slavery could be ended and society perfected through a change in the human heart, not through political action. In fact, he perceived the Constitution as a proslavery document and the federal government as fouled by its proslavery connections.

The Tappan brothers, by contrast, saw the Constitution as an antislavery document. Consequently, they fought to end slavery through political action, including electing antislavery candidates and creating antislavery political parties. They believed it best to work within the political system to build a climate favorable to abolition. Political abolitionists gained growing influence as increasing numbers of northern politicians took a stand against slavery. Their strong support for the antislavery wing of the national Whig Party enhanced their impact, and they were actively involved in two antislavery parties—the Liberty Party, founded in 1839, and the Free-Soil Party, founded in 1848, which absorbed the Liberty Party in that year.

Although black men and all women were excluded from the nation's political life, they were active in abolitionist organizations. Women worked through women's auxiliaries of the American Anti-Slavery Society, which set up numerous regional affiliates. They also formed separate organizations. In 1833, the white Quaker abolitionist Lucretia Mott founded the Philadelphia Female Anti-Slavery Society; among its members were the black activist Grace Douglass and her daughter Sarah Mapps Douglass, as well as women from the Forten family. There was also a Female Anti-Slavery Society in Boston. Women in these organizations signed petitions, distributed literature, sponsored bazaars to raise money, and vigilantly supported the cause of fugitive slaves. Many participated in the free produce movement, which encouraged boycotting goods raised by slave labor. Female abolitionists often felt a special empathy for slave families torn apart by slave sales, and their concern for the plight of slave women, especially slave mothers, informed their antislavery arguments.

Women's participation in the abolitionist movement contributed significantly to the emergence of the women's rights movement. As women organized petition campaigns and formulated antislavery arguments, they gained confidence in their ability to work in the public arena and felt more keenly the limitations male abolitionist organizers placed on their participation. Women were usually prohibited from speaking in public and routinely denied leadership positions. The issue of women's role became so contentious that in 1840, when Garrison appointed a woman to the executive committee of the American Anti-Slavery Society, the organization split in two. The Tappans and a group of black ministers, including Henry Highland Garnet, founded the rival American and Foreign Anti-Slavery Society (AFAS), which was committed to political abolitionism and to male leadership at the top levels. At an international meeting of abolitionist organizations in London that June, the AFAS joined with like-minded British abolitionists to prohibit women from participating in policymaking. Lucretia Mott, representing the Philadelphia Female Anti-Slavery Society, had to observe the proceedings from a railed-off space reserved for women. Eight years later, in Seneca Falls, New York, Mott and Elizabeth Cady Stanton organized the nation's first women's rights convention. Frederick Douglass was in attendance, and some black male activists, including the former slave Jermain W. Loguen, lent their support to women's rights, notably woman suffrage.

By this time, the abolitionist movement was further divided by a split between Garrison and Douglass, who came to agree with Garnet that political action was the most effective means of mobilizing public opposition to slavery. Douglass's decision in 1847 to publish his own newspaper, the *North Star*, also indicated his increasing independence from his mentor. Even the most zealous white abolitionists, including Garrison, did not always treat black activists as equals. Many seemed more committed to freeing slaves than to securing equal rights for free blacks.

Though fraught with divisions, the abolitionist movement won converts to its cause, especially among white evangelical northerners. For many, Christian principles seemed synonymous with concern for the slave. In the 1830s and 1840s, the Baptist, Methodist, and Presbyterian Churches forbade their members to own slaves, and the issue caused proslavery southern churches to withdraw from these denominations and organize separately. In 1846, several white abolitionist missionary societies merged with the black Union Missionary Society to form the **American Missionary Association**. With widespread support from black leaders and members, including Samuel

Cornish, Henry Highland Garnet, Jermain Loguen, James Pennington, and Mary Ann Shadd, it promoted not only abolition but Christian education for African Americans as well. The abolitionist movement also succeeded in pushing slavery onto the national political agenda. In 1846, when war with Mexico began, the contest over whether slaves should be allowed in the West intensified, giving the slavery issue an urgent and decidedly political cast.

The Slavery Question and National Crisis

What to do about the existence of slavery in a democratic nation that professed freedom and equality was a question that would not go away. Delegates at the Constitutional Convention in 1787 had devised a series of compromises that protected slavery even as some states took steps to end it. As the nation expanded, another compromise in 1820 protected slavery in territories south of the southern border of Missouri while prohibiting it to the north. In the 1850s, a new compromise sought to hold the increasingly disaffected North and South together. But as a consequence, the Missouri Compromise was undone, first by a new plan for letting the people themselves decide whether the territory in which they lived would be slave or free, and then by a U.S. Supreme Court ruling that Congress did not have, and had never had, the authority to prohibit slavery in the territories. Northerners feared that a vast southern slaveholder, or "Slave Power," conspiracy had triumphed, taking away their rights and allowing the detested slave system to undercut their free labor system. With the election of Abraham Lincoln as president in 1860, southerners feared that the incoming Republican administration would implement a vast northern conspiracy to end the slave system. Politics and compromise could no longer hold the Union together. African Americans had more than a political stake in the tumultuous events of the 1850s, as their protections and rights increasingly eroded. Some responded with resistance, even violence. Some saw emigration as the only solution. And some hoped that war, if it came, would end slavery altogether.

Westward Expansion and Slavery in the Territories

Between 1830 and 1860, hundreds of thousands of Americans moved west, including black slaves and Native Americans who were forcibly relocated (see chapter 5). While the issue of which regions would permit slavery and which would not had been settled for the Louisiana Territory by the Missouri Compromise, American incursions into Mexican territory raised the issue anew. By 1830, the more than 20,000 Americans who had settled in Mexican Texas had reintroduced slavery—and 2,000 slaves—into an area where Mexico had formally abolished it. In 1836, these proslavery Americans seceded from Mexico, declared themselves the Lone Star Republic, and sought annexation to the United States. They were at first refused, but in 1845 Texas was admitted to the Union as a slave state. Northerners' opposition to a move they perceived as growing evidence of a Slave Power conspiracy invigorated the Liberty Party, which in 1844 received nearly nine times the number of votes it had in 1840—62,000 of the more than 2.5 million votes cast.

By this time, many Americans enthusiastically supported the notion that it was the "manifest destiny" of the nation to rule the continent from the Atlantic to the Pacific.

The provisional government of the Oregon Territory, which had been created by white settlers, abolished slavery in 1844, even before the United States recognized the Oregon Territory in 1848. Prior to official Oregon territorial recognition, the Oregon Treaty of 1846 between the United States and Great Britain had settled a boundary dispute in the area, clearing the way for such recognition. Congressional wrangling over whether to forbid slavery in the Oregon Territory, as the Oregon provisional government had already done, had slowed official territorial recognition by the United States.

Northern and southern politicians closely watched the number of potential slave and free states, lest one section dominate the other in Congress. Even before the Oregon negotiation with Great Britain was settled, however, the United States was at war with Mexico, following a failed attempt to purchase the Mexican provinces of Upper California and New Mexico. The prospect that these areas would become U.S. possessions ignited the issue of slavery in the territories once again. In the House of Representatives, Pennsylvania Democrat David Wilmot introduced a proviso that "neither slavery nor involuntary servitude shall ever exist in any part" of any territory gained from the Mexican-American War. Wilmot was against slavery, but he was not pro-black. He aimed to keep slavery out of the territories, so that free white labor would have a chance to thrive there, and to prevent blacks from coming into the area. The **Wilmot Proviso** failed to pass the Senate, but the angry debate it sparked intensified tensions between the North and South.

In 1848, the Treaty of Guadalupe Hidalgo sealed the U.S. victory over Mexico. In the treaty, Mexico ceded what became the territories of California, New Mexico, and Utah, as well as all of Texas north of the Rio Grande. Meanwhile, the discovery of gold in California drew so many prospectors to that territory (including more than four thousand free blacks) that in 1850 it applied for admission to the Union as a free state. If admitted, California would tip the balance in the Senate to the free states.

The vote on California statehood was one of the issues that was finally settled by the **Compromise of 1850**, which consisted of a series of separate bills. Neither side got all it wanted. Antislavery northerners succeeded in abolishing the slave trade in the District of Columbia, while southerners prevented the abolition of slavery there. California entered the Union as a free state, but the decision regarding whether slavery would be allowed in the territories of New Mexico and Utah was left up to the people living in those areas, a policy known as **popular sovereignty**. The federal government assumed the debt contracted by the Lone Star Republic, and as a concession to the South, a new fugitive slave law was enacted.

The **Fugitive Slave Act** of 1850 made it easier for fugitive slaves to be captured and returned to their owners by strengthening federal authority over the capture and return of runaway slaves. Many northerners had long objected to the actions of slave catchers, and some northern states had passed **personal liberty laws** forbidding the kidnapping and forced return of fugitives. These laws were ruled unconstitutional in *Prigg v. Pennsylvania* (1842), but in its decision the U.S. Supreme Court also affirmed that the return of fugitives was a federal matter, in which state officials could not be required to assist. Northern states had then passed new personal liberty laws that forbade state officials to assist in fugitive cases and prohibited the use of state courts and jails for alleged fugitives. Under the Fugitive Slave Act of 1850, federal marshals were required to pursue alleged runaway slaves, and federal commissioners were appointed to oversee runaway cases. The fees these officials received—$10 for a runaway returned to the claimant, $5 for a runaway set free—reflected the law's bias. But it was the authorizing of federal marshals to call on citizen bystanders to aid in the capture of alleged runaways that especially angered northerners. Citizens who refused or who in any way aided an alleged fugitive could be fined $1,000 and sent to prison for six months. Many in the North who had not given much thought to slavery now felt that the federal government had far exceeded its powers. They perceived the federal effort to protect slave property as an attack on their own personal liberty, forcing them to act against their conscience. Wisconsin challenged the constitutionality of the law, and a Massachusetts statute sought to nullify it.

For black Americans, however, the implications of the law were far more menacing. Those who had escaped slavery, even years before, were no longer safe in the North. They were subject to arrest, denied jury trials, and forbidden to testify on their own behalf. A statement by an owner making a claim, together with an identification of the runaway, was all that was needed to return a person to slavery. Increasing numbers of former fugitives left the United States for Canada, Mexico, Europe, and elsewhere. Given the provisions of the law, free blacks were also at risk, as there was little to prevent slave hunters from seizing and enslaving them. An unknowable number of free blacks as well as fugitive slaves suffered enslavement or reenslavement at the hands of slave hunters. During the 1850s, 296 of 330 fugitives formally arrested, or 90 percent, suffered reenslavement.[29]

The Fugitive Slave Crisis

Northern black communities, where many fugitives lived, responded to the Fugitive Slave Act of 1850 with protest meetings, resolutions, and petitions. Blacks and their white allies demanded repeal of the act and mounted vigorous resistance against it. Jermain Loguen, born a slave in Tennessee, exclaimed, "I will not live a slave, and if force is employed to reenslave me, I shall make preparations to meet the crisis as becomes a man."[30]

As a young man, Loguen had escaped to freedom on the underground railroad (Map 6.1). In the North, **vigilance committees**, an aboveground arm of the underground railroad, assisted arriving fugitives by providing temporary shelter, food, clothing, and sometimes legal assistance and jobs. The black printer David Ruggles led the New York Vigilance Committee, which was widely admired for its militancy and effectiveness. Abolitionist Quakers joined the effort, but in the 1830s and 1840s vigilance committees consisted primarily of blacks. After the Fugitive Slave Act was passed in 1850, however, northern white support for the underground railroad grew, and vigilance committees became increasingly interracial. They expanded the networks of cellars, attics, church basements, and other safe spaces where fugitives could take refuge before being shepherded to freedom, often in Canada. Although their operations were of necessity covert, because they were illegal, they helped an untold number of people. For example, the Boston Vigilance Committee acknowledged helping sixty-nine fugitives to escape in 1851 alone.

The best-known "agent" on the underground railroad was William Still. As head of the Philadelphia Vigilance Committee, he kept records on the fugitive slaves he assisted and later published their stories in *The Underground Railroad* (1872). The most famous "conductor" was Harriet Tubman, who escaped from slavery in 1849. She returned to the South at least fourteen times to lead, directly and indirectly, some 130 slaves to freedom. She was known for her strict discipline and carefully developed plans and reputedly never lost a fugitive. Deeply revered in northern abolitionist circles, where

MAP 6.1   The Underground Railroad

As this map illustrates, the reach of the underground railroad was extensive and international in scope. Although these locations remained secret at the time, we now know that the underground railroad consisted of an intricate network of people, routes, and safe places that allowed thousands of slaves to achieve freedom. After 1850, the growing number of organizations and individuals committed to abolitionism caused an increase in the number of fugitive slaves that continued through the Civil War. Escaping from slavery required the utmost secrecy, organization, and coordination, and freedom fighters such as Harriet Tubman placed themselves—and their own freedom—at great risk to help others reach the North.

she was hailed as "the Moses of Her People," Tubman was intensely hated in the South, where there was a $40,000 bounty (more than $1 million today) for her capture.[31]

Those who aided fugitive slaves or refused to help in their capture engaged in **civil disobedience**—refusal to obey a law that one considers unjust—a form of protest with a long history among African Americans. Their resolve was soon tested. On September 11, 1851, William Parker, an escaped slave who lived with his wife, Eliza, also an escaped slave, near Christiana, Pennsylvania, refused to allow a U.S. marshal and a party of Maryland slaveholders led by Edward Gorsuch to search the Parker home for recent fugitives from his plantation. Eliza sounded a large dinner horn, summoning more than seventy-five local supporters. In the fight that followed, Gorsuch was killed and his son wounded. The Parkers and the other fugitive slaves they were hiding escaped to Canada, but in the

HEAVY WEIGHTS—ARRIVAL OF A PARTY AT LEAGUE ISLAND
(Fifteen escaped in this Schooner.)

Escaping Slavery via the Underground Railroad
In this engraving, a group of exhausted slaves, including a mother and infant, arrive at League
Island, Philadelphia, from Norfolk, Virginia. Carriages stand by as volunteers help them up the
hill to safety. The engraving is a compelling illustration of slave resistance: the lengths to which
the slaves themselves went in their quest for freedom. It also shows their committed and courageous allies in the struggle against slavery. Indeed, the underground railroad has come to
symbolize the extraordinary difficulties of the fight for both human rights and black freedom.
Newberry Library, Chicago, IL, USA/The Bridgeman Art Library International.

wake of what became known as the Christiana Resistance, thirty-five blacks and three
white Quakers were arrested for treason and conspiracy under the Fugitive Slave Act of
1850. Their cause attracted nationwide attention. Support came from as far away as
Columbus, Ohio, where a meeting of free blacks adopted a resolution praising "the victo-
rious heroes at the battle of Christiana."[32] Pennsylvania congressman Thaddeus Stevens
assisted in their defense, and eventually the charges were dropped.

Boston became a hotbed of resistance to the hated law. In early 1851, slave hunters
seized Shadrach Minkins (also known as Frederick Wilkins), an escaped slave working
at a coffeehouse, and dragged him to a federal courthouse. Almost instantly, the Boston
Vigilance Committee mobilized, and a crowd surrounded the courthouse while a
group of black men liberated Minkins and sent him on to freedom in Canada. In late
May 1854, a similar effort to save Anthony Burns, another local African American who
had been seized and jailed as a fugitive slave, failed. President Franklin Pierce sent federal troops to Boston, and as they escorted Burns to the wharf for his return to slavery,

some 50,000 protesters lined the streets and draped Boston's buildings in black. Eventually, although he was returned to slavery, Boston abolitionists raised enough money to purchase his freedom.

The fugitive slave crisis intensified the conflict between the North and South over slavery. Southerners perceived the confrontations as part of a well-orchestrated northern campaign to defy the law and destroy slavery and the southern way of life that depended on it. For northerners, the confrontations forced an awareness of the reality of slavery and its impact on their lives. So did publication of the best-selling novel **Uncle Tom's Cabin** in 1852. Its white evangelical author, Harriet Beecher Stowe, crafted a sentimental yet graphic depiction of slavery's devastating effects on families, building empathy with slavery's victims in order to increase support for abolition.

Confrontations in Kansas and the Courts

In 1854, Illinois senator Stephen A. Douglas, who had engineered passage of the Compromise of 1850, reopened the issue of slavery in the territories by promoting popular sovereignty for Kansas and Nebraska. By the terms of the **Kansas-Nebraska Act**, the people who settled those territories would vote to determine whether, as states, they would be slave or free (Map 6.2). The result was a series of violent confrontations between proslavery and antislavery settlers. In May 1856, when proslavery forces from Missouri

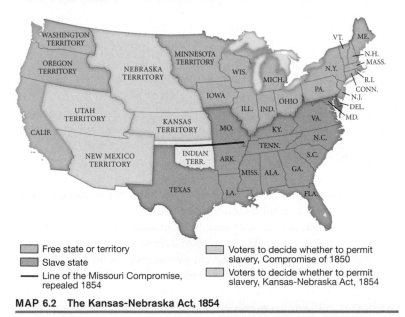

Free state or territory

Slave state

Line of the Missouri Compromise, repealed 1854

Voters to decide whether to permit slavery, Compromise of 1850

Voters to decide whether to permit slavery, Kansas-Nebraska Act, 1854

MAP 6.2   The Kansas-Nebraska Act, 1854

This map shows the free and slave states following the passage of the Kansas-Nebraska Act, as well as the areas where both this act and the Compromise of 1850 allowed popular sovereignty to rule the day. As the map indicates, the Kansas-Nebraska Act promoted the increasingly stark sectional divide between the slave South and the free North. From this point forward, maintaining a balance between the number of free and slave states proved no less essential to preserving the Union than under the Missouri Compromise of 1820, which the act superseded.

attacked the antislavery town of Lawrence, Kansas, John Brown, the self-appointed "captain" of antislavery forces, took revenge by murdering five proslavery settlers at Pottawatomie Creek. The furor over "Bleeding Kansas" also brought violence to the floor of the Senate when South Carolina representative Preston S. Brooks beat Massachusetts senator Charles Sumner into unconsciousness at his desk. Brooks claimed to be upholding the honor of his kinsman, South Carolina senator Andrew P. Butler, whom Sumner had singled out for insult in an earlier speech on "The Crime against Kansas."

The national political system and the methods of civil debate, negotiation, and compromise proved increasingly ineffective in managing the slavery question. The issue eventually split the Whig Party, and it disintegrated. After 1856, the Democratic Party, ever more wedded to proslavery interests, was the only national political party left. Meanwhile, a number of sectional parties related to the slavery issue had merged. The abolitionist Liberty Party, formed in 1839, had called for an end to slavery in the District of Columbia and to the domestic slave trade. In 1848, it became part of the Free-Soil Party, founded that year. With the motto "Free Soil, Free Speech, Free Labor, Free Men," this party announced its opposition to the extension of slavery into the territories. To discourage the spread of plantation agriculture, the party also supported a homestead law that would distribute federal land in small plots to settlers (preferably whites) who would actually farm it, rather than to speculators. Although the party's motivations were often racist and many members were not abolitionists, it did attract influential abolitionist politicians and supporters of civil rights for free blacks, such as Charles Sumner. Free-Soilers, black and white, helped Massachusetts blacks in their successful battles against discrimination in schools and transportation and in overturning state laws prohibiting interracial marriage.

In 1854, Free-Soilers joined with northern opponents of the Kansas-Nebraska Act and others opposed to the spread of slavery to form the Republican Party. Like the Liberty and Free-Soil Parties, the Republican Party was a solely northern party, with no southern support. Its 1856 presidential election slogan, "Free Soil, Free Labor, Free Speech, Free Men, Frémont" (for Republican presidential candidate John Frémont), highlighted its opposition to the extension of slavery into the territories, but it made no commitment to end slavery itself. Nevertheless, Frederick Douglass and a growing number of blacks joined the party, believing it could energize the abolitionist crusade. Through the Republican Party, the northern black political struggle connected with the national political system. White southerners, observing black support for the Republicans, feared that the party was conspiring to destroy slavery.

Meanwhile, a case making its way through the courts addressed the issue of slavery in the territories head-on. In 1846, slaves Dred and Harriet Scott sued for their freedom because they had lived with their master in Wisconsin Territory, where slavery was forbidden, before he moved them back to the slave state of Missouri. After a series of technical issues and split decisions in the Missouri courts, the U.S. Supreme Court took the case and in 1857 rendered its decision. In **Dred Scott v. Sandford**, the Court ruled against Scott, and by extension his wife, Harriet. First, said the Court, Scott was not entitled to sue in the courts of Missouri because he was not a citizen. No person of African descent could be a citizen of the United States. Further, from the time of the nation's founding, "negroes of the African race" had been "regarded as beings of an inferior order, and altogether unfit to associate with the white race, either in social or political relations; and so far inferior, that they had no rights which the white man was

Dred and Harriet Scott
Harriet and Dred Scott, the enslaved plaintiffs in *Dred Scott v. Sandford* (1857), met and married around 1836. Shortly thereafter, they had two daughters, Eliza and Lizzie. In 1846, they filed separate petitions for freedom in the St. Louis circuit court, which the court subsequently combined, with Dred as the plaintiff. In fact, the ruling applied to all the Scotts, including the girls. Although they were freed almost immediately after the U.S. Supreme Court announced its decision, Dred died of tuberculosis a year later. Harriet died in 1876.   *Library of Congress, LC-USZ62-79305.*

bound to respect."[33] Slaves were legally protected property, and under the Constitution, Congress had no authority to deny the right of property. Thus it could not forbid slaveholding anywhere. All laws that forbade slavery in the territories were unconstitutional, including the Missouri Compromise of 1820.

Emigration and Insurrection

The effect of the *Dred Scott* decision was instantaneous and inflammatory. Not only abolitionists but also many northerners generally saw the decision as more evidence of a massive Slave Power conspiracy, now authorized by the courts to extend slavery into new territories. There was nothing to prevent southern slave labor from undermining northern free labor. Like the Fugitive Slave Act of 1850, *Dred Scott* turned an increasing number of northerners, even whites opposed to abolition and black civil rights, against the Supreme Court's position on slavery, which they saw as eroding their personal liberties.

For black men and women, the decision was devastating. Their citizenship denied and their status declared inferior, they began to question more seriously their ties to the nation in which they lived. Robert Purvis declared that he owed no allegiance to a nation in which black men possessed no rights that whites must respect. Frederick Douglass blasted the decision as "judicial wolfishness." Speaking to African Americans from Canada, Mary Ann Shadd Cary exclaimed, "Your national ship is rotten and sinking, why not leave it?"[34]

The *Dred Scott* decision clearly diminished blacks' prospects for a viable life and meaningful future in the United States. They also had more reason than ever to fear for their personal safety. Many decided to leave the country, most going to Canada. By 1860, several thousand former African Americans lived in communities there. Proponents of emigration to Canada included H. Ford Douglas, a prominent black leader from Ohio, and Mary Ann Shadd Cary, who had emigrated shortly after Congress passed the Fugitive Slave Act of 1850. Also residing in Canada in the late 1850s was the family of Martin R. Delany.

Thoroughly disillusioned with the United States, Delany became the era's most prominent champion of emigration. He spoke for a loose-knit yet committed group that promoted emigration to Canada, Central and South America, the West Indies, and West Africa. In a series of national emigration conventions, the first and most important in Cleveland in 1854, Delany tapped into an emigrationist sentiment that grew stronger and more vocal by the end of the 1850s. In speeches and especially in his influential book *The Condition, Elevation, Emigration and Destiny of the Colored People of the United States* (1852), he turned the idea of black self-reliance into black self-determination, proposing the establishment of a black nation outside the United States. In this regard, he can be considered the father of **black nationalism**: the belief that African Americans were a nation within a nation that required some form of self-determination. (See From the Record: Political Destiny of the Colored Race on the American Continent.)

Toward the end of the decade, Delany focused on the prospects for black emigration to West Africa, where he hoped to establish an unnamed though "thriving and prosperous Republic." Africa was "the native home of the African race," he argued, "and there he can enjoy the dignity of manhood, the rights of citizenship, and all the advantages of civilization and freedom."[35] In 1859 and 1860, joined by Robert Campbell, a Jamaican chemist, Delany explored the Niger River valley in search of a site for a black American emigrant settlement. Like most such efforts, the enormous financial, political, and logistical difficulties of this plan led to its failure, and Delany returned to the United States.

Interest in emigration remained widespread, however. In the 1850s, the American Colonization Society sponsored the migration of several thousand blacks to Liberia (see chapter 4), while the black press featured a vigorous debate on Liberia's benefits and drawbacks. Proponents stressed black self-rule; opponents stressed Liberia's high mortality rate and inefficient government. Henry Highland Garnet came out in favor of emigration and worked on a plan—ultimately unsuccessful—to establish an emigrant black American colony in West Africa funded by whites. The Episcopal priest and missionary James Theodore Holly promoted emigration to Haiti, and in 1861 he led a group of 101 people to an ill-fated and short-lived settlement there. But most northern blacks remained in the United States. Despite the intensification of racial hostility and legal exclusion, they dared to hope that, as William Still expressed it, "great evils must be consummated that good might come."[36]

Some were not content to wait. In 1859, upon learning that John Brown secretly planned to incite a slave insurrection, five black men joined his effort. Brown's plan was to seize arms and ammunition at the federal arsenal at Harpers Ferry, Virginia, thereby inspiring local slaves to join in an uprising that would trigger a series of slave revolts

Martin R. Delany | Political Destiny of the Colored Race on the American Continent, 1854

Martin R. Delany (1812–1885) was born free in Virginia and later moved with his family to Pittsburgh, where the reformist message of the Reverend Lewis Woodson influenced him. Having studied medicine under several doctors, Delany was accepted to attend Harvard Medical School, but when most of the white students objected, he was dismissed. He began to believe there was no place for African Americans in the United States and emigrated to Canada. In the 1850s, he became a great proponent of emigration and black nationalism. The following excerpt is from a speech to a convention on emigration that he organized in Cleveland in 1854.

No people can be free who themselves do not constitute an essential part of the *ruling element* of the country in which they live. . . . The liberty of no man is secure, who controls not his own political destiny. . . .

A people, to be free, must necessarily be *their own rulers*. . . .

. . . We have fully discovered and comprehended the great political disease with which we are affected, the cause of its origin and continuance; and what is now left for us to do, is to discover and apply a sovereign remedy—a healing balm to a sorely diseased body— a wrecked but not entirely shattered system. We propose for this disease a remedy. That remedy is Emigration. . . .

Our friends in this and other countries, anxious for our elevation, have for years been erroneously urging us to lose our identity as a distinct race, declaring that we were the same as other people. . . .

The truth is, we are not identical with the Anglo-Saxon or any other race of the Caucasian or pure white type of the human family, and the sooner we know and acknowledge this truth, the better for ourselves and posterity. . . .

We have then inherent traits, attributes—so to speak—and native characteristics, peculiar to our race—whether pure or mixed blood—and all that is required of us is to cultivate these and develope [*sic*] them in their purity, to make them desirable and emulated by the rest of the world. . . .

. . . The great issue, sooner or later, upon which must be disputed the world's destiny, will be a question of black and white; and every individual will be called upon for his identity with one or the other. The blacks and colored races are four-sixths of all the population of the world; and these people are fast tending to a common cause with each other. The white races are but one-third of the population of the globe—or one of them to two of us—and it cannot much longer continue, that two-thirds will passively submit to the universal domination of this one-third.

SOURCE: Martin R. Delany, "Political Destiny of the Colored Race on the American Continent," in *Proceedings of the National Emigration Convention of Colored People, Held at Cleveland, Ohio, . . . on the 24th, 25th and 26th of August, 1854* (Pittsburgh: A. A. Anderson, 1854), 35, 37, 39–41.

??? What is "the great political disease" that Delany describes, and why was emigration the remedy?

throughout the South and destroy the institution. On the night of October 16, Brown and his band of twenty-one men slipped into Harpers Ferry from a nearby farm, where they had been hiding out and planning. Poorly conceived, the plan unraveled as quickly as it unfolded. In the federal troops' hastily organized counterattack, ten of Brown's comrades were killed, including two of his sons. Five others escaped; seven, including Brown, were captured.

News of **John Brown's raid** on Harpers Ferry inflamed the conspiratorial views that the slave South and free North increasingly had of each other. Proslavery forces saw Brown as a madman. They perceived the botched though frightful insurrection as evidence of a "Black Republican Conspiracy" bent on destroying slavery and the southern way of life. Yet abolitionists, particularly black abolitionists, even those opposed to violence as a means of emancipation, viewed Brown and his comrades as martyrs. Frances Ellen Watkins called Brown "the hero of the nineteenth century." Frederick Douglass praised him as "a human soul illuminated with divine qualities." A group of Providence blacks applauded him as an "unflinching champion of liberty."[37]

Yet at the time, most Americans supported the restoration of order, swift and harsh justice for the guilty, and renewed efforts to moderate the slavery crisis. As a result, Brown's speedy trial and treason conviction were a relief. On December 2, he went calmly to his hanging death, but not before he handed a note to a jail guard, offering this prediction:

Charlestown, Va. 2nd, December, 1859.

I John Brown am now quite certain that the crimes of this guilty, land: will never be purged away; but with Blood. I had as I now think: vainly flattered myself that without verry [sic] much bloodshed; it might be done.[38]

The next year, when Republican Abraham Lincoln won the presidency, the slavery question seemed less likely than ever to be resolved. Lincoln's appeal was clearly sectional: All his electoral votes came from the free states of the North and West. Most of the electorate voted against him. In a four-way race, with northern and southern wings of the Democratic Party running separate candidates and a hastily organized Constitutional Union Party offering yet another choice, Lincoln won just 39 percent of the popular vote. Although he repeatedly stated that neither he as president nor the Republican Party would disturb slavery where it already existed, the slave states of the South made plans to withdraw from the Union.

CONCLUSION

Whose Country Is It?

Who belongs in the United States of America? When the slavery question reached a crisis with the election of Abraham Lincoln, it was the slave states that believed they did not belong. But throughout the preceding three decades, it was the free black people of the North who debated that question. Most felt they were Americans, and they resisted efforts by white advocates of colonization to resettle them in Africa. But they also struggled to maintain their allegiance to a nation that circumscribed and excluded them.

At the beginning of the 1830s, northern black communities turned inward. In the face of racial prejudice that cast them as inferiors, they sought to be self-reliant. They cared for one another through mutual aid societies; they built independent churches and supported black schools. Black leaders promoted moral reform, arguing that Christian ideals and virtuous living would strengthen their communities and win the approval of whites. But to no avail. Only by freeing the enslaved, they concluded, could the free elevate themselves.

So blacks turned outward, dedicating themselves to abolition. At conventions, they debated strategies. Through newspapers, they built networks. They formed organizations. They boycotted goods produced by slave labor. The arrival of fugitive slaves magnified the voices of black abolitionists and emboldened them. They asserted that white attitudes and practices toward blacks urgently needed to be reformed. They lectured and wrote books. They petitioned the government and sued for equal treatment in schools and on public conveyances. Yet they continued to be hemmed in by laws and practices that denied them representation in the nation's political life and pushed them to the margins of its economic life. Segregation and black exclusion from white circles was the social norm. Studies in the emerging social sciences outlined racial hierarchies that placed blacks at the bottom. Most whites avoided them, fearing contamination.

In the 1850s, black prospects for a future in the United States constricted further. A new law meant that fugitive slaves could not be secure in the free states, and a U.S. Supreme Court ruling asserted that African Americans could not be, and never had been, citizens of the land of their birth. Many concluded that they no longer belonged in such a nation, and some emigrated—to Canada, Africa, Haiti, and elsewhere.

Yet black claims to equality and freedom had pushed the slavery issue onto the national agenda, and the very crisis that undermined their allegiance to the nation also split the nation apart. Following the election of a president whose support was entirely in the North, the states of the South began to withdraw. The coming civil war would prove that African Americans, as free people, indeed belonged in the United States. In fact, that war would redefine the very nature of the nation. Frederick Douglass understood this. In 1849, he wrote, "We deem it a settled point that the destiny of the colored man is bound up with that of the white people of this country. . . . *We are here*, and here we are likely to be. . . . This is *our* country; and the question for the philosophers and statesmen of the land ought to be, What principles should dictate the policy of action toward us?"[39] That question would not, however, be settled by the war. It would continue to be asked, again and again.

CHAPTER REVIEW

Online Study Guide ▪ bedfordstmartins.com/graywhite

Key Terms

uplift (p. 271)]

black convention movement (p. 277)

moral suasion (p. 281)

abolitionist movement (p. 283)

political action (p. 283)

American Missionary Association (p. 284)

Wilmot Proviso (1846) (p. 286)

Compromise of 1850 (p. 286)

popular sovereignty (p. 290)

Fugitive Slave Act (1850)
 (p. 286)

personal liberty laws
 (p. 286)

vigilance committees
 (p. 287)

civil disobedience (p. 288)

Uncle Tom's Cabin (1852) (p. 290)

Kansas-Nebraska Act (1854)
 (p. 290)

Dred Scott v. Sandford (1857)
 (p. 291)

black nationalism (p. 293)

John Brown's raid (1859) (p. 295)

Review Questions

1. In what ways did the end of slavery in the North bring about an increase in antiblack prejudice? What strategies did free black northerners develop to combat discrimination and fortify their communities?

2. How did free black northerners begin to link their plight to that of enslaved southerners?

3. What techniques did free blacks employ, and what organizations and institutions did they found, to advance the developing black freedom movement?

4. Describe the various legal and political battles surrounding slavery during the years 1850–1860. How did black northerners respond? What impact did these events have on the black freedom struggle?

5. How did the events of 1830–1860 fuel the mounting tensions between the North and South?

For Web sites, images, and documents related to topics and places in this chapter, visit **Make History** at bedfordstmartins.com/graywhite.

Elite Black Women Speak Out on Education, Citizenship, and Slavery

The majority of black women in the antebellum North were poor, working-class, and illiterate. Written records of their attitudes and experiences are rare. It is possible, however, to learn something of the attitudes and experiences of black women from the few who were well educated and whose family backgrounds and opportunities afforded them elite status. The speeches of Sarah Mapps Douglass, Elizabeth Jennings, Lucy Stanton, and Sara G. Stanley offer such insights.

What emerges most tellingly in the following documents is that these women's status did not keep them from recognizing the common concerns of their race and sex. They sought to promote the improvement of all blacks and women and to advance the struggle against slavery and discrimination. In the 1830s and 1840s, women generally, and black women in particular, did not speak in public, and especially not before audiences that included men. As you read the following speeches, consider the audience to which each woman was speaking, and pay attention to how she shaped her argument.

Sarah Mapps Douglass | To Make the Slaves' Cause Our Own, 1832

Sarah Mapps Douglass (1806–1882) was a founding member of the Female Literary Society of Philadelphia and the Philadelphia Female Anti-Slavery Society. A well-regarded lecturer and political essayist, she also established a high school for black girls and taught at the Institute for Colored Youth. Her life and activism reflected her deep commitment to Quakerism. In the speech excerpted here, which she gave at one of the first meetings of the Female Literary Society, she describes the awakening of her compassion for enslaved blacks.

My friends—my sisters: How important is the occasion for which we have assembled ourselves together this evening, to hold a feast, to feed our never-dying minds, to excite each other

to deeds of mercy, words of peace; to stir up in the bosom of each, gratitude to God for his increasing goodness, and feeling of deep sympathy for our brethren and sisters, who are in this land of christian light and liberty held in bondage the most cruel and degrading—to make their cause our own!

An English writer has said, "We must feel deeply before we can act rightly; from that absorbing, heart-rendering [sic] compassion for ourselves springs a deeper sympathy for others, and from a sense of our weakness and our own upbraidings arises a disposition to be indulgent, to forbear, to forgive." This is my experience. One short year ago, how different were my feelings on the subject of slavery! It is true, the wail of the captive sometimes came to my ear in the midst of my happiness, and caused my heart to bleed for his wrongs; but, alas! the impression was as evanescent as the early cloud and morning dew. I had formed a little world of my own, and cared not to move beyond its precincts. But how was the scene changed when I beheld the

SOURCE: *The Black Abolitionist Papers*, ed. C. Peter Ripley (Chapel Hill: University of North Carolina Press, 1991), 3:122–23.

oppressor° lurking on the border of my own peaceful home! I saw his iron hand stretched forth to seize me as his prey, and the cause of the slave became my own. I started up, and with one mighty effort threw from me the lethargy which had covered me as a

------

° She may be referring to a slave hunter or to discussions in the Pennsylvania legislature regarding the return of fugitives.

mantle for years; and determined, by the help of the Almighty, to use every exertion in my power to elevate the character of my wronged and neglected race. One year ago, I detested the slaveholder; now I can pity and pray for him. Has not this been your experience, my sisters? Have you not felt as I have felt upon this thrilling subject? My heart assures me some of you have.

Elizabeth Jennings | On the Cultivation of Black Women's Minds, 1837

Elizabeth Jennings was a member of the Ladies Literary Society of New York, founded in 1834 by the city's elite black women to promote self-improvement through reading, discussion, and community activities. Jennings gave the speech excerpted here at the society's third annual meeting, which was also attended by a number of supportive men. Jennings's topic, the importance of black women improving their minds, was a consistent theme among elite black women.

It is now a momentous time, a time that calls us to exert all our powers, and among the many of them, the mind is the greatest, and great care should be taken to improve it with diligence. We should cultivate these powers and dispositions of the mind, which may prove advantageous to us. It is impossible to attain to the sphere for which we were created, without persevering. It is certain we were formed for society, and it is our duty and interest to cultivate

------

SOURCE: Philip S. Foner and Robert James Branham, eds., *Lift Every Voice: African American Oratory, 1787–1900* (Tuscaloosa: University of Alabama Press, 1998), 167–68.

social qualities and dispositions to endeavor to make ourselves useful and pleasing to others—to promote and encourage their happiness—to cherish the friendly affections, that we may find in them the source of the greatest blessings this world can afford.

But, alas! society too often exhibits a far different scene, and this is in consequence of neglect of cultivation, which certainly is much more fatal than we can imagine. Neglect will plunge us into deeper degradation, and keep us grovelling in the dust, while our enemies will rejoice and say, we do not believe they (colored people) have any minds; if they have, they are unsusceptible of improvement. My sisters, allow me to ask the question, shall we bring this reproach on ourselves? Doubtless you answer NO, we will strive to avoid it. . . . Why sleep thus? Awake and slumber no more—arise, put on your armor, ye daughters of America, and start forth in the field of improvement. You can all do some good, and if you do but little it will increase in time. The mind is powerful, and by its efforts your influence may be as near perfection, as that of those which have extended over kingdoms, and is applauded by thousands.

documents

Lucy Stanton | Slavery and Abolition as War, 1850

Lucy Stanton (1831–1910) was one of the first black women to receive an undergraduate degree from an American college, graduating in 1850 from Oberlin. She took the "Ladies' Course," a two-year program that led to a diploma but was separate from the four-year "Gentlemen's Course." Stanton delivered this speech to the Oberlin Ladies' Literary Society, of which she was the president.

When I forget you, Oh my people, may my tongue cleave to the roof of my mouth, and may my right hand forget her cunning!° Dark hover the clouds. The Anti-Slavery pulse beats faintly. The right of suffrage is denied. The colored man is still crushed by the weight of oppression. He may possess talents of the highest order, yet for him is no path of fame or distinction opened. He can never hope to attain those privileges while his brethren remain enslaved. Since, therefore, the freedom of the slave and the gaining of our rights, social and political, are inseparably connected, let all the friends of humanity plead for those who may not plead their own cause.

Reformers, ye who have labored long to convince man that happiness is found alone in doing good to others, that humanity is a unit, that he who injures one individual wrongs the race;—that to love one's neighbor as one's self is the sum of human virtue—ye that advocate the great principles of Temperance, Peace, and Moral Reform will you not raise your voice in behalf of these stricken ones!—will you not plead the cause of the Slave?

Slavery is the combination of all crime. It is War. Those who rob their fellow-men of home, of liberty, of education, of life, are really at war against them as though they cleft them down upon the bloody field. It is intemperance; for there is an intoxication when the fierce passions rage in man's breast, more fearful than the madness of the drunkard, which if let

loose upon the moral universe would sweep away everything pure and holy, leaving but the wreck of man's nobler nature. Such passions does Slavery foster—yea, they are a part of herself. It is full of pollution. Know you not that to a slave, virtue is a sin counted worthy of death? That many, true to the light within, notwithstanding the attempts to shut out the truth, feeling that a consciousness of purity is dearer than life, have nobly died? Their blood crieth to God, a witness against the oppressor.

Statesmen, you who have bent at ambition's shrine, who would leave your names on the page of history, to be venerated by coming generations as among those of the great and good, will you advocate the cause of the down-trodden, remembering that the spirit of liberty is abroad in the land? . . .

Woman, I turn to thee. Is it not thy mission to visit the poor? to shed the tear of sympathy? to relieve the wants of the suffering? Where wilt thou find objects more needing sympathy than among the slaves!

Mother, hast thou a precious gem in thy charge, like those that make up the Savior's jewels? Has thy heart, trembling with its unutterable joyousness, bent before the throne of the Giver with the prayer that thy child might be found in his courts? Thou hast seen the dawning of intelligence in its bright eye, and watched with interest the unfolding of its powers. . . . Now thou canst feel for the slave-mother who has bent with the same interest over her child, whose heart is entwined around it even more firmly than thine own around thine, for to her it is the only ray of joy in a dreary world. . . .

Sister, have you ever had a kind and loving brother? . . . You saw him suddenly stricken by the destroyer. Oh! How your heart ached!

Mother, sister, by thy own deep sorrow of heart; by the sympathy of thy woman's nature, plead for the downtrodden of thy own, of every land. Instill the principles of love, of common brotherhood, in the nursery, in the social circle. Let these be the prayer of thy life.

Christians, you whose souls are filled with love for your fellow men, whose prayer to the Lord is, "Oh! that I may see thy salvation among the children of men!" Does the battle wax warm? dost thou

---

° Stanton is paraphrasing Psalm 137.
Source: Philip S. Foner and Robert James Branham, eds., *Lift Every Voice: African American Oratory, 1787–1900* (Tuscaloosa: University of Alabama Press, 1998), 221–23.

faint with the burden and heat of the day? Yet a little longer; the arm of the Lord is mighty to save those who trust in him. Truth and right must prevail. The bondsman shall go free. Look to the future! Hark! the shout of joy gushes from the heart of earth's freed millions! It rushes upward. The angels on heaven's outward battlements catch the sound on their golden lyres, and send it thrilling through the echoing arches of the upper world. How sweet, how majestic, from those starry isles float those deep inspiring sounds over the ocean of space! Softened and mellowed they reach earth, filling the soul with harmony, and breathing of God—of love—and of universal freedom.

Sara G. Stanley | A Call to Action! Black Women Support Black Male Vote in Ohio, 1856

In 1856, **Sara G. Stanley (1837–1918)**, a twenty-year-old black schoolteacher, represented the Ladies' Anti-Slavery Society of Delaware, Ohio, at an Ohio convention of black men gathered to petition the state legislature to permit black men to vote. Unable to address the all-male convention directly because she was a woman, Stanley arranged for one of the male delegates to read her statement, excerpted here, which thrilled the convention. She expressed black women's support for the black male vote in the strongest possible terms, but the appeal to the Ohio legislature failed. During and after the Civil War, Stanley would go on to become a teacher of freedpeople.

A s the song of Freedom verberates and reverberates through the northern hills, and the lingering symphony quivers on the still air and then sinks away into silence, a low deep wail, heavy with anguish and despair, rises from the southern plains, and the clank of chains on human limbs mingles with the mournful cadence.

What to the toiling millions there, is this boasted liberty? What to us is this organic body—this ideal reduced to reality—this institution of the land?—A phantom, shadowy and indistinct—a disembodied form, impalpable to our sense or touch. In the broad area of this Republic there is no spot, however small or isolated, where the colored man can exercise his God-given rights. Genius of America! How art thou fallen, oh Lucifer, son of the morning how art thou fallen!

In view of these things, it is self-evident, and above demonstration that we, as a people, have every incentive to labor for the redress of wrongs. On our native soil, consecrated to freedom, civil liberties are denied us, and we are by compulsion subject to an atrocious and criminal system of political tutelage deleterious to the interest of the entire colored race, and antagonistical to the political axioms of this Republic.

Intuitively, then, we search for the panacea for the manifold ills which we suffer. One, and only one, exists; and when each individual among us realizes the absolute impossibility for him to perform any work of supererogation° in the common cause, the appliances will prove its own efficacy; it is embodied in one potent word—ACTION. Let unanimity of action characterize us; let us reject the absurd phantasy of non-intervention; let us leave conservatism behind, and substitute a radical, utilitarian spirit, let us cultivate our moral and mental faculties, and labor to effect a general diffusion of knowledge, remembering that "ascendancy naturally and properly belongs to intellectual superiority." . . .

Continued and strenuous effort is the basis of all greatness, moral, intellectual, and civil. . . .

To you, gentlemen, as representatives of the oppressed thousands of Ohio, we look hopefully. This convening is far from being nugatory or unimportant. "Agitation of thought is the beginning of truth," and furthermore, by pursuing such a line of

SOURCE: Philip S. Foner and Robert James Branham, eds., *Lift Every Voice: African American Oratory, 1787–1900* (Tuscaloosa: University of Alabama Press, 1998), 286–87.

° Going beyond the call of duty.

policy as you in your wisdom may deem expedient, *tending toward that paramount object*, the results may transcend those attending similar assemblies which have preceded it. Sure, you are numerically small; but the race is not always gained by the swift, nor the battle by the strong, and it has become a truism that greatness is the legitimate result of labor, diligence, and perseverance.

. . . To you we would say, be true, be courageous, be steadfast in the discharge of your duty. The citadel of Error must yield to the unshrinking phalanx of truth. In our fireside circles, in the seclusion of our closets, we kneel in tearful supplication in your behalf. As Christian wives, mothers and daughters, we invoke the blessing of the King, Eternal and Immortal, "who sitteth upon the circle of the earth, who made the heavens with all their host," to rest upon you, and we pledge ourselves to exert our influence unceasingly in the cause of Liberty and Humanity.

Again we say, be courageous; be steadfast; unfurl your banner to the breeze—let its folds float proudly over you, bearing the glorious inscription, broad and brilliant as the material universe: *"God and Liberty!"*

Questions for Analysis

1. How did their elite status affect these women's choice of subjects, themes, and arguments?

2. How did their being female shape their arguments? How do they express a sense of unity with other women?

3. What role does religion play in their arguments?

4. What assumptions do these women make about women's role in society and politics? How are their arguments shaped by these assumptions? In arguing for black women's mental improvement, for example, why does Jennings say that "it is our duty . . . to make ourselves useful and pleasing to others"? In supporting the civil rights of black men, why doesn't Stanley argue for the civil rights of women?

5. Compare and contrast the arguments that Douglass and Stanton make for the cause of abolition. Why do they believe free black women must join the cause?

Former Slaves Speak Out on Slavery

Privileged free black and white abolitionists might condemn the institution of slavery, but none carried the authority of those who spoke from their own experience. Two of the most powerful black abolitionists were former slaves: Henry Highland Garnet and Frederick Douglass. Born into slavery in Maryland in 1815, Garnet escaped with his family to Pennsylvania when he was nine years old. Having moved with his family to New York City in 1925, he was apprenticed as a cabin boy for two years, during which time an accident left him disabled. Upon returning to his family in New York, he resumed his formal education at the African Free School, which had begun before his apprenticeship. His subsequent education continued at a series of institutions: Canal Street High School, Noyes Academy in Canaan, New Hampshire, and the Oneida Institute in Whitesboro, New York, from which he graduated in 1840. In 1842, he became pastor of the Liberty Street Presbyterian Church in Troy, New York. In 1843, he rocked a national black convention in Buffalo, New York, when he delivered a militant speech calling for slaves to revolt and overthrow slavery.

In an hour-long rebuttal, Frederick Douglass, also an escaped slave from Maryland, argued that "there was too much physical force, both in the address and the remarks of the speaker up last." The text of Douglass's response has not survived, but a report of the convention recorded his preference "for trying the moral means a little longer." Douglass feared that Garnet's speech might "be the occasion of an insurrection," and he wished "in no way to have any agency in bringing about, what we were called upon to avoid." When the convention voted whether to adopt Garnet's address and release it to the public, the motion failed by one vote.[40]

At the time, Douglass was relatively new to abolitionist organizing. He had been on the lecture circuit for only two years and a freeman for five, and he was still under the influence of the white abolitionist William Lloyd Garrison. After he published his autobiography in 1845, he feared capture as a fugitive slave and went to England. For two years, he lectured and made many friends among English abolitionists, who purchased his freedom. Returning to the United States in 1847, he was increasingly confident about formulating his own arguments against slavery. He broke with Garrison and by the early 1850s was arguing for political action, not just moral suasion, as the best means for abolishing slavery. In 1852, he delivered a speech in Rochester, New York, that electrified his listeners, much as Garnet's had nine years before.

The following excerpts from these two speeches show how Douglass and Garnet used contrasting techniques and rhetoric to advance the same cause.

documents

Henry Highland Garnet | An Address to the Slaves of the United States of America, 1843

At the time he delivered this speech, **Henry Highland Garnet (1815–1882)** had been involved in abolitionist activities for more than ten years. He had studied theology at Oneida Institute, where he sharpened his intellectual and rhetorical skills. As a pastor, he mastered public speaking. In 1843, he was one of seventy delegates from twelve states who attended the National Negro Convention in Buffalo, New York. There he gave a controversial speech that called on slaves to revolt. Notice a crucial rhetorical technique: He addressed his speech to slaves, although of course no slaves were present.

Brethren and fellow citizens: Your brethren of the North, East and West have been accustomed to meet together in national conventions, to sympathize with each other, and to weep over your unhappy condition. In these meetings we have addressed all classes of the free, but we have never, until this time, sent a word of consolation and advice to you. We have been contented in sitting still and mourning over your sorrows, earnestly hoping that before this day your sacred liberties would have been restored. But we have hoped in vain. Years have rolled on, and tens of thousands have been borne on streams of blood and tears to the shores of eternity. While you have been oppressed, we have also been partakers with you; nor can we be free while you are enslaved. We, therefore, write to you as being bound with you.

Many of you are bound to us, not only by the ties of a common humanity, but we are connected by the more tender relations of parents, wives, husbands and sisters and friends. As such we most affectionately address you. . . .

SOURCE: Philip S. Foner and Robert James Branham, eds., *Lift Every Voice: African American Oratory, 1787–1900* (Tuscaloosa: University of Alabama Press, 1998), 198–202, 204–5.

Two hundred and twenty-seven years ago the first of our injured race were brought to the shores of America. They came not with glad spirits to select their homes in the New World. They came not with their own consent, to find an unmolested enjoyment of the blessings of this fruitful soil. The first dealings they had with men calling themselves Christians exhibited to them the worst features of corrupt and sordid hearts, and convinced them that no cruelty is too great, no villainy and no robbery too abhorrent for even enlightened men to perform, when influenced by avarice and lust. Neither did they come flying upon the wings of Liberty to a land of freedom. But they came with broken hearts from their beloved native land and were doomed to unrequited toil and deep degradation. Nor did the evil of their bondage end at their emancipation by death. Succeeding generations inherited their chains, and millions have come from eternity into time, and have returned again to the world of spirits, cursed and ruined by American Slavery.

The propagators of the system, or their immediate successors, very soon discovered its growing evil and its tremendous wickedness, and secret promises were made to destroy it. The gross inconsistency of a people holding slaves, who had themselves "ferried o'er the wave" for freedom's sake, was too apparent to be entirely overlooked. The voice of Freedom cried, "Emancipate your slaves." . . . But all was [in] vain. Slavery had stretched its dark wings of death over the land, the Church stood silently by, the priests prophesied falsely, and the people loved to have it so. Its throne is established, and now it reigns triumphantly.

Nearly three millions of your fellow citizens are prohibited by law and public opinion (which in this country is stronger than law) from reading the Book of Life. Your intellect has been destroyed as much as possible, and every ray of light they have attempted to shut out from your minds. The oppressors themselves have become involved in the ruin. They have become weak, sensual and rapacious; they have cursed you; they have cursed themselves; they have cursed the earth which they have trod. . . .

Brethren, it is as wrong for your lordly oppressors to keep you in slavery as it was for the man thief to steal our ancestors from the coast of Africa. You should therefore now use the same manner of resistance as would have been just in our ancestors when the bloody footprints of the first remorseless soul thief was placed upon the shores of our fatherland. The humblest peasant is as free in the sight of God as the proudest monarch that ever swayed a scepter. Liberty is a spirit sent out from God and, like its great Author, is no respecter of persons.

Brethren, the time has come when you must act for yourselves. It is an old and true saying that, "if hereditary bondsmen would be free, they must themselves strike the blow."° You can plead your own cause and do the work of emancipation better than any others. The nations of the Old World are moving in the great cause of universal freedom, and some of them at least will, ere long, do you justice. The combined powers of Europe have placed their broad seal of disapprobation upon the African slave trade. But in the slaveholding parts of the United States the trade is as brisk as ever. They buy and sell you as though you were brute beasts. The North has done much; her opinion of slavery in the abstract is known. But in regard to the South, we adopt the opinion of the *New York Evangelist*—"We have advanced so far, that the cause apparently waits for a more effectual door to be thrown open than has been yet." We are about to point you to that more effectual door. Look around you and behold the bosoms of your loving wives heaving with untold agonies! Hear the cries of your poor children! Remember the stripes your fathers bore. Think of the torture and disgrace of your noble mothers. Think of your wretched sisters, loving virtue and purity, as they are driven into concubinage and are exposed to the unbridled lusts of incarnate devils. Think of the undying glory that hangs around the ancient name of Africa—and forget not that you are native-born American citizens, and as such

you are justly entitled to all the rights that are granted to the freest. Think how many tears you have poured out upon the soil which you have cultivated with unrequited toil and enriched with your blood; and then go to your lordly enslavers and tell them plainly that you *are determined to be free*. Appeal to their sense of justice and tell them that they have no more right to oppress you than you have to enslave them. Entreat them to remove the grievous burdens which they have imposed upon you, and to remunerate you for your labor. Promise them renewed diligence in the cultivation of the soil, if they will render to you an equivalent for your services. Point them to the increase of happiness and prosperity in the British West Indies since the Act of Emancipation.° Tell them, in language which they cannot misunderstand, of the exceeding sinfulness of slavery and of a future judgment and of the righteous retributions of an indignant God. Inform them that all you desire is freedom, and that nothing else will suffice. Do this, and forever after cease to toil for the heartless tyrants, who give you no other reward but stripes and abuse. If they then commence the work of death, they, and not you, will be responsible for the consequences. You had far better all die—*die immediately*—than live slaves and entail your wretchedness upon your posterity. If you would be free in this generation, here is your only hope. However much you and all of us may desire it, there is not much hope of redemption without the shedding of blood. If you must bleed, let it all come at once—rather *die freemen than live to be slaves*. . . .

Brethren, arise, arise! Strike for your lives and liberties. Now is the day and the hour. Let every slave throughout the land do this, and the days of slavery are numbered. You cannot be more oppressed than you have been; you cannot suffer greater cruelties than you have already. *Rather die freemen than live to be slaves*. Remember that you are three *millions*! . . .

Let your motto be Resistance! *Resistance!* RESISTANCE! No oppressed people have ever secured their liberty without resistance.

° Paraphrased from Lord Byron, *Childe Harold's Pilgrimage* (1818).

° Slavery had been abolished in the British West Indies by an act of Parliament in 1833.

documents

Frederick Douglass | What to the Slave Is the Fourth of July?, 1852

By the time **Frederick Douglass (1818–1895)** gave this speech, on July 5, 1852, he was as seasoned a speaker as Henry Highland Garnet, and more well known. This may be Douglass's most famous speech. He delivered it to the Ladies' Anti-Slavery Society of Rochester, New York, which had invited him to address an Independence Day celebration in Corinthian Hall. Some five hundred to six hundred people each paid 12½ cents to hear the renowned abolitionist. As with many community celebrations at the time, this one began with a prayer and a reading of the Declaration of Independence. Douglass made the most of the occasion to drive home his message. The audience, the local press reported, reacted with much applause.

Fellow-Citizens—Pardon me, and allow me to ask, why am I called upon to speak here to-day? What have I, or those I represent, to do with your national independence? Are the great principles of political freedom and of natural justice, embodied in that Declaration of Independence, extended to us? and am I, therefore, called upon to bring our humble offering to the national altar, and to confess the benefits, and express devout gratitude for the blessings, resulting from your independence to us?

Would to God, both for your sakes and ours, that an affirmative answer could be truthfully returned to these questions! . . .

But, such is not the state of the case. I say it with a sad sense of the disparity between us. I am not included within the pale of this glorious anniversary! Your high independence only reveals the immeasurable distance between us. The blessings in which you this day rejoice, are not enjoyed in common. The rich inheritance of justice, liberty, prosperity, and independence, bequeathed by your fathers, is shared by you, not by me. The

SOURCE: Frederick Douglass, *My Bondage and My Freedom*, Ebony Classics (Chicago: Johnson, 1970), 349–53.

sunlight that brought life and healing to you, has brought stripes and death to me. This Fourth of July is *yours*, not *mine. You* may rejoice, *I* must mourn. To drag a man in fetters into the grand illuminated temple of liberty, and call upon him to join you in joyous anthems, were inhuman mockery and sacrilegious irony. Do you mean, citizens, to mock me, by asking me to speak to-day? . . .

Fellow-citizens, above your national, tumultuous joy, I hear the mournful wail of millions, whose chains, heavy and grievous yesterday, are to-day rendered more intolerable by the jubilant shouts that reach them. If I do forget, if I do not faithfully remember those bleeding children of sorrow this day, "may my right hand forget her cunning, and may my tongue cleave to the roof of my mouth!" To forget them, to pass lightly over their wrongs, and to chime in with the popular theme, would be treason most scandalous and shocking, and would make me a reproach before God and the world. My subject, then, fellow-citizens, is AMERICAN SLAVERY. I shall see this day and its popular characteristics from the slave's point of view. Standing here, identified with the American bondman, making his wrongs mine, I do not hesitate to declare, with all my soul, that the character and conduct of this nation never looked blacker to me than on this Fourth of July. Whether we turn to the declarations of the past, or to the professions of the present, the conduct of the nation seems equally hideous and revolting. America is false to the past, false to the present, and solemnly binds herself to be false to the future. Standing with God and the crushed and bleeding slave on this occasion, I will, in the name of humanity which is outraged, in the name of liberty which is fettered, in the name of the constitution and the bible, which are disregarded and trampled upon, dare to call in question and to denounce, with all the emphasis I can command, everything that serves to perpetuate slavery—the great sin and shame of America! "I will not equivocate; I will not excuse"; I will use the severest language I can command; and yet not one word shall escape me that any man, whose judgment is not blinded by prejudice, or who is not at heart a slaveholder, shall not confess to be right and just.

But I fancy I hear some of my audience say, it is just in this circumstance that you and your brother abolitionists fail to make a favorable impression on the public mind. Would you argue more, and denounce less, would you persuade more and rebuke less, your cause would be much more likely to succeed. But, I submit, where all is plain there is nothing to be argued. . . .

For the present, it is enough to affirm the equal manhood of the Negro race. Is it not astonishing that, while we are plowing, planting, and reaping, using all kinds of mechanical tools, erecting houses, constructing bridges, building ships, working in metals of brass, iron, copper, silver, and gold; that, while we are reading, writing, and cyphering, acting as clerks, merchants, and secretaries, having among us lawyers, doctors, ministers, poets, authors, editors, orators, and teachers; that, while we are engaged in all manner of enterprises common to other men—digging gold in California, capturing the whale in the Pacific, feeding sheep and cattle on the hillside, living, moving, acting, thinking, planning, living in families as husbands, wives, and children, and, above all, confessing and worshiping the Christian's God, and looking hopefully for life and immortality beyond the grave—we are called upon to prove that we are men!

Would you have me argue that man is entitled to liberty? that he is the rightful owner of his own body? You have already declared it. Must I argue the wrongfulness of slavery? Is that a question for republicans? . . . There is not a man beneath the canopy of heaven that does not know that slavery is wrong *for him.*

What! am I to argue that it is wrong to make men brutes, to rob them of their liberty, to work them without wages, to keep them ignorant of their relations to their fellow-men, to beat them with sticks, to flay their flesh with the lash, to load their limbs with irons, to hunt them with dogs, to sell them at auction, to sunder their fam-ilies, to knock out their teeth, to burn their flesh, to starve them into obedience and submission to their masters? Must I argue that a system, thus marked with blood and stained with pollution, is wrong? No; I will not. I have better employment for my time and strength than such arguments would imply.

What, then, remains to be argued? Is it that slavery is not divine; that God did not establish it; that our doctors of divinity are mistaken? There is blasphemy in the thought. That which is inhuman cannot be divine. Who can reason on such a proposition! They that can, may! I cannot. The time for such argument is past.

At a time like this, scorching irony, not convincing argument, is needed. Oh! had I the ability, and could I reach the nation's ear, I would to-day pour out a fiery stream of biting ridicule, blasting reproach, withering sarcasm, and stern rebuke. For it is not light that is needed, but fire; it is not the gentle shower, but thunder. We need the storm, the whirlwind, and the earthquake. The feeling of the nation must be quickened; the conscience of the nation must be roused; the propriety of the nation must be startled; the hypocrisy of the nation must be exposed; and its crimes against God and man must be proclaimed and denounced.

What to the American slave is your Fourth of July? I answer, a day that reveals to him, more than all other days in the year, the gross injustice and cruelty to which he is the constant victim. To him, your celebration is a sham; your boasted liberty, an unholy license; your national greatness, swelling vanity; your sounds of rejoicing are empty and heartless; your denunciations of tyrants, brass-fronted impudence; your shouts of liberty and equality, hollow mockery; your prayers and hymns, your sermons and thanksgivings, with all your religious parade and solemnity, are to him mere bombast, fraud, deception, impiety, and hypocrisy—a thin veil to cover up crimes which would disgrace a nation of savages. There is not a nation on the earth guilty of practices more shocking and bloody, than are the people of these United States, at this very hour.

Questions for Analysis

1. Why did Garnet use the rhetorical technique of speaking directly to slaves? How do you think the free blacks in the audience reacted?

2. Why did Douglass choose the topic of slavery for his speech at a local Fourth of July celebration? The audience, which most likely included men and women, and at least some blacks, was said by the local press to applaud him. What do you think white listeners might have thought of the speech privately?

3. What role does Christianity play in Garnet's address? What role does the black family play?

4. What role does the Declaration of Independence play in Douglass's address?

5. Compare and contrast the rhetorical techniques used by the two speakers. Which one(s) do you find most persuasive? Explain.

documents

Minstrel Shows

Minstrel shows—white performances that ridiculed blacks through skits, variety acts, jokes, dancing, singing, and music—were the most popular form of mass entertainment in the nineteenth century. In this era in which white audiences found blacks onstage objectionable, the performers were white men who blackened their faces with burnt cork. "Blackface" and other stage makeup caricatured black features. Blacks were presented as having unruly woolly hair, gaping mouths, toothsome grins, wide noses, and big lips. Costumes distorted the performers' bodies to create huge hands, feet, and posteriors, as well as extra-long and extra-flexible limbs. To suggest an utter lack of style and refinement, clothes were ill fitting and outlandish. The characters also were presented as ignorant, childlike, lazy, and frivolous. They parodied African American dialect, mocking black English and belittling black people through absurd speech. In one routine, for example, a blackface minstrel said that he was "axed if I knowed anyting about dickshionary."[41]

White audiences found these routines funny, a response indicative of an attitude of superiority that helped to establish a theatrical tradition of demeaning and stereotyping blacks that has lasted into the present. Audiences were primarily working-class white men. Minstrel shows, however, were performed in Abraham Lincoln's White House as well as rowdy urban theaters throughout the North. At the height of their popularity between

DANCING FOR EELS, 1820 CATHARINE MARKET.

FIGURE 6.1
Dancing for Eels, 1820 *Courtesy of Sotheby's.*

FIGURE 6.2
Dancing for Eels, A Scene from the New Play of New-York as It Is, *as Played at the Chatham Theatre, N.Y.,* 1848 *Library of Congress, LC-USZC4-632.*

DANCING FOR EELS.

1845 and 1855, many whites assumed that these shows portrayed black people and black life and culture as they really were. Of course, they did not, but by elaborating on widely held notions of black inferiority, they confirmed a racial hierarchy and reinforced white supremacy in American society. Although a few serious black performers overcame white prejudice to be recognized for their talents, minstrel caricatures of blacks were etched in people's minds.

Minstrelsy grew out of 1820s urban street entertainments in which young black and white men performed for coins and food in public places such as wharves, markets, street corners, and parks. *Dancing for Eels* (Figure 6.1) is a folk drawing of a scene in Catharine Market, a fish market in lower Manhattan where free blacks and whites of various classes mingled. This image features a primary black male dancer in sailor's dress, a supporting dancer who is promoting clapping and cheering, and a drummer who appears to be a child. The performers are eliciting a highly enthusiastic response from the audience.

An 1848 lithograph with the same title depicts a similar scene at the same market (Figure 6.2), but here the single black dancer is dressed in tattered clothes, and the audience is far more diverse in terms of gender, age, class, and race. According to an 1849 fishing manual, black men still gathered at the market at dawn to skin eels and engage in dance competitions for bundles of fish. Those witnessing the spectacle, and betting on the winners, expressed approval with cheers and claps.[42] By this time, however, as the title of this lithograph indicates, spontaneous black singing and dancing had also been appropriated by white actors and turned into stage performances.

Starting in the 1820s, T. D. (Thomas Dartmouth) "Daddy" Rice, the white traveling actor most closely associated with early minstrelsy, developed blackface

FIGURE 6.3
Jim Crow, c. 1835

routines that featured singing, dancing, and humor. His most famous black character was a slave dressed in rags named Jim Crow (Figure 6.3), who, Rice claimed, was inspired by the dance of a disabled black man. When he performed at New York's Bowery Theatre as Jim Crow, he constantly changed the verses he sang to refer to celebrities and contemporary events. Some were published as sheet music that pictured Jim Crow on the cover. One went like this:

> Come listen all you gals and boys, I's jist from
>   Tuckyhoe,°
> I'm going to sing a little song, my name's Jim Crow,
> Weel about and turn about and do jis so,
> Eb'ry time I weel about and jump Jim Crow.
>
> Oh I'm a roarer on de fiddle, and down in old
>   Virginny,
> They say I play de skyentific like Massa Pagannini.°
> Weel about and turn about and do jis so,
> Eb'ry time I weel about and jump Jim Crow.[43]

Rice's Jim Crow character made him famous, and soon "Jim Crow" became a common racial epithet. By the late nineteenth century, the term was used to refer to the whole range of laws and customs related to racial segregation.

Another stock minstrel character was Zip Coon (Figure 6.4), a foolish and pretentious black dandy developed by George Washington Dixon, a white circus performer who also appeared at the Bowery Theatre. The following song, sung to the tune of "Turkey in the Straw," includes verses that distort and ridicule black speech:

> O ole Zip Coon he is a larned skoler
> Sings posum up a gum tree an coony in a holler.
> Posum up a gum tree, coony on a stump
> Den over dubbler trubble, Zip Coon will jump.[44]

° Tuckyhoe, likely the Tuckahoe Plantation where Thomas Jefferson grew up.

° Niccolò Paganini (1782–1840) was an Italian violinist. "Skyentific," a colloquial mix of "heavenly" and "scientific," refers to Paganini's virtuosity.

FIGURE 6.4
Zip Coon, c. 1834

In another vicious routine, Dixon performed as Coal Black Rose, an overweight and overdressed black woman (Figure 6.5). White audiences thought it funny that this character—an unattractive, masculine-looking woman (who was, of course, really a man)—would have two suitors, Sambo and Cuffee, whose rivalry is the subject of the song that tells her story.[45]

In the 1830s and 1840s, blackface minstrelsy evolved from solo song-and-dance routines, often presented between the acts of longer plays, into three-part ensemble performances. Groups such as the Virginia Serenaders (Figure 6.6) and (Edward) Christy's Minstrels (Figure 6.7) developed a standard format. Part 1 often consisted of caricatures of black songs, dances,

FIGURE 6.6
The Virginia Serenaders, 1844
Songs of the Virginia Serenaders, 1844/Box 018, item 33, Lester S. Levy Collection of Sheet Music, Department of Rare Books and Manuscripts, Sheridan Libraries, The Johns Hopkins University, http://levysheetmusic.mse.jhu.edu.

FIGURE 6.7
Christy's Minstrels,
c. 1847 *Library of
Congress, LC-DIG-
pga-02611.*

and humor, sometimes centered on the stereotype of the northern black dandy
who is mocked for his ineptness in manner and dress. Free black aspirations of
self-improvement and civil equality were thus held up to ridicule. Part 2, the
"olio," was a series of novelty acts, encompassing wild comic skits and loud
stump speeches rendered in ludicrous white versions of black dialect. Lectures

on contemporary topics were full of mispro-
nunciations and misused words that made the
speaker seem at once pompous and preposter-
ous. Part 3 was usually a lengthy skit built
around a view of southern plantation life, with
happy slaves and good masters, or a parody of
a Shakespearean play. The ensemble included
at least four performers seated in a semicircle.
The three most important were the interlocutor, called "the Ethiopian Delineator," in the
middle, and the performers at either end:
Mr. Tambourine, or simply Mr. Tambor, who
played the tambourine, and Mr. Bones, who
played the castanets, clackers, or even actual
bones. The interlocutor was the master of
ceremonies and the end men were his
sidekicks. The fast-paced give-and-take among
these characters pushed the lively show along.
Banjo and fiddle players rounded out the
instrumental accompaniment.

To clarify the distinction between their
blackface impersonations and their real-life
identities, white male performers sometimes
began their shows with a musical concert in
dressy attire before they put on their blackface, or they made sure their playbills and
sheet music included dignified images of
themselves (see Figure 6.7). These images
assured audiences of both the performers'
whiteness and their maleness and fixed the
difference between their real and their stage identities.

Christy's Minstrels specialized in performing songs by Stephen Foster,
whom they helped make famous. In the 1850 songbook *Christy's Nigga
Songster*, the figure who illustrates the lyrics to Foster's "Oh, Susanna" (Figure
6.8) resembles the overdressed Coal Black Rose (see Figure 6.5), an indication
of how whites increasingly stereotyped blacks. Such images were common-
place on sheet music, and playbills posted in cities across the North—and as
far west as San Francisco—made minstrel caricatures of blacks familiar to
many who never attended the shows.[46]

When *Uncle Tom's Cabin* was published in book form in 1852, illustrations
portraying black characters drew on minstrel types. George Cruikshank's
engraving of the wild child Topsy, for example, shows her in a dance that
resembles that of Jim Crow (Figure 6.9). This best-selling novel was soon
adapted to the stage, not only as a drama but also as "Tom shows"—minstrel
skits based loosely on the book's plot. In one famous dramatization, T. D. Rice
played Uncle Tom. More than twice as many people saw such minstrel shows

POPULAR SONGS

OH, SUSANNA.

AS SUNG BY CHRISTY'S CELEBRATED BAND OF
MINSTRELS.

I come from Alabama with my Banjo on my knee
I'm gwine to Louisiana my true lub for to see,
It rained all night de day I left, the wedder
        was dry,
De sun so hot, I froze to deff, Susanna don't you
        cry.

FIGURE 6.8
"Oh, Susanna," as Sung by
Christy's Celebrated Band of
Minstrels, c. 1850 Christy's Nigga
Songster, Containing Songs as Are
Sung by Christy's, Pierce's, White's
Sable Brothers, and Dumbleton's
Band of Minstrels (*M1628.C62
1850z*). *University of Virginia Library.*

TOPSY WITH MISS OPHELIA'S WARDROBE.

"On one occasion, Miss Ophelia found Topsy with her very best scarlet India Canton crape shawl wound round her head for a turban, going on with her rehearsals before the glass in great style—Miss Ophelia having, with carelessness most unheard-of in her, left the key for once in her drawer,"—Page 214.

FIGURE 6.9
Topsy in *Uncle Tom's Cabin,* 1852 *Library Company of Philadelphia.*

as read the book,[47] and Uncle Tom entered the lexicon of stock black characters. In the twentieth century, his name became synonymous with blacks who too easily accepted their inferior status and submissively deferred to whites.

More so than real-life images of blacks, caricatures of blacks became fixed in popular culture. Jim Crow and Uncle Tom are widely recognized today, for example, while the distinguished black Shakespearean actor Ira Aldridge (Figure 6.10) has been largely forgotten. Born in New York, Aldridge moved to England to escape discrimination. There his career flourished, and he gave notable performances in both white (Richard III) and black (Othello) roles. Another well-regarded black performer was Francis B. "Frank" Johnson (Figure 6.11), a bugler, bandleader, and composer. When his Philadelphia brass

FIGURE 6.10
Ira Aldridge, Shakespearean Actor, 1853
Schomburg Center, NYPL/Art Resource, NY.

FIGURE 6.11
Frank Johnson, Musician, Bandleader, and Composer
(undated) *Joseph Muller Collection of Music and Other
Portraits/The New York Public Library/Art Resource, NY.*

band toured England in 1838, the young Queen Victoria presented him with a silver bugle.

William Henry Lane, known as "Master Juba," began performing in dance halls and saloons in Manhattan's Five Points neighborhood, where, like the figure in *Dancing for Eels* (see Figures 6.1 and 6.2), he competed for food and coins. There he came to the attention of Charles Dickens, who was on a tour of America. Dickens described what he saw: "Single shuffle, double shuffle, cut and cross-cut; snapping his fingers, rolling his eyes, turning in his knees, presenting the backs of his legs in front, spinning about on his toes and heels like nothing but the man's fingers on the tambourine; dancing with two left legs, two right legs, two wooden legs, two wire legs, two spring legs—all sorts of legs and no legs."[48] Lane, a black man, later appeared with minstrel troupes, made up in blackface for routines in which he imitated white minstrel dancers caricaturing black dance. As a contemporary recalled, "There was not an audience in America that would not have resented, in a very energetic fashion, the insult of being asked to look at the dancing of a real negro."[49] Like Aldridge and Johnson, he found his greatest success in England, where, as Boz's Juba (Boz was one of Dickens's pen names), he created a sensation. In an image from a London newspaper (Figure 6.12), he is shown dressed in formal attire. Juba's dance routines, which seem to have combined African dance steps and the Irish jig, influenced tap dancing[50] and other dance styles,

"JUBA," AT VAUXHALL GARDENS.

FIGURE 6.12
Boz's Juba, 1848   *The Granger Collection, NYC. All rights reserved.*

from the nineteenth-century buzzard lope to twenty-first-century step teams. The career of "Master Juba" reflected the growing trend after the mid-nineteenth century of black males "blacking up" to perform as real, often plantation, minstrels.

Interpreting minstrelsy is difficult. It is an American original, not a tired takeoff on a European cultural form. And as an urban working-class entertainment, it represents popular culture in the era of the common man. On one hand, it conveys racial domination, portraying blacks as inferior, simple, and stupid. This stereotype and minstrelsy's stock characters persisted long after minstrelsy declined, adding support to the racist assumptions permeating American society. On the other hand, minstrelsy represents a grudging appreciation of black performance arts, from ragtime to rap, that have shaped American culture. Yet there is something profoundly disturbing about an entertainment form in which white men imitate black men to demean instead of dignify. Frederick Douglass called blackface minstrels "the filthy scum of white society, who have stolen from us a complexion denied to them by nature, in which to make money, and pander to the corrupt taste of their white fellow citizens."[51] His condemnation places minstrelsy in the middle of a persistent historical development: the exploitation of black culture and black bodies for white amusement and profit.

Questions for Analysis

1. What does minstrelsy reveal about black and white history and culture in the antebellum North? What does it suggest about antebellum notions of race, gender, and class?

2. In minstrelsy, black characters appeared onstage. What other instances can you think of in which people (or animals or objects) are or were placed onstage or displayed for viewing? What are or were the purposes and the effects of such situations?

3. Many have argued that blackface minstrelsy has had a strong impact on American popular culture. Do you agree? What specific evidence and broader cultural developments can you use to support your position? Do you see any evidence of the persistence of minstrelsy in contemporary American popular culture?

4. Compare and contrast the postures and dress shown in images of blackface minstrels and in images of authentic black performers. Recall Lewis Woodson's point that "the moral effect of mean dress is, to degrade us in our own eyes and in the eyes of all who behold us." He said this at a time when black impersonators and minstrelsy were becoming popular. Did minstrel caricatures affect black efforts in self-improvement? If so, how?

5. What are the particular ironies, and the implications, of the blackface black Juba imitating blackface white performers imitating black performers?

Notes

1. *North Star*, March 23, 1849, quoted in Jane Rhodes, *Mary Ann Shadd Cary: The Black Press and Protest in the Nineteenth Century* (Bloomington: Indiana University Press, 1998), 21.

2. *Frederick Douglass' Paper*, November 9, 1855, quoted ibid., 109.

3. Alexis de Tocqueville, *Democracy in America*, ed. Phillips Bradley (New York: Knopf, 1945), 1:359–60.

4. Quoted in Patrick Rael, *Black Identity and Black Protest in the Antebellum North* (Chapel Hill: University of North Carolina Press, 2002), 262.

5. George Wilson Pierson, *Tocqueville and Beaumont in America* (New York: Oxford University Press, 1938), 565.

6. James O. Horton and Lois E. Horton, *Black Bostonians: Family Life and Community Struggle in the Antebellum North* (New York: Holmes & Meier, 1979), 2; Ira Berlin, *Slaves without Masters: The Free Negro in the Antebellum South* (New York: New Press, 2007), 176.

7. George Foster, "Philadelphia in Slices" (1848–1849), quoted in Leonard P. Curry, *The Free Black in Urban America, 1800–1850: The Shadow of the Dream* (Chicago: University of Chicago Press, 1986), 49; George Foster, "New York in Slices" (1849), quoted ibid., 78.

8. Julie Winch, *A Gentleman of Color: The Life of James Forten* (New York: Oxford University Press, 2003), 84–85.

9. Leslie M. Alexander, *African or American? Black Identity and Political Activism in New York City, 1784–1861* (Urbana: University of Illinois Press, 2008), 158.

10. Martin R. Delany, *The Condition, Elevation, Emigration and Destiny of the Colored People of the United States* (1852; repr., New York: Arno Press, 1969), 45–46.

11. *Minutes and Proceedings of the Second Annual Convention, for the Improvement of the Free People of Color in These United States* (Philadelphia, 1832), 34.

12. *Proceedings of the National Convention of Colored People and Their Friends, Held in Troy, N.Y., on the 6th, 7th, 8th, and 9th October, 1847*, quoted in Leon Litwack, *North of Slavery: The Negro in the Free States, 1790–1860* (Chicago: University of Chicago Press, 1961), 135.

13. *Maria W. Stewart, America's First Black Woman Political Writer: Essays and Speeches*, ed. Marilyn Richardson (Bloomington: Indiana University Press, 1987), 21, 35, 59–60.

14. Ibid., 46.

15. Lewis Woodson [Augustine], "Moral Work for Colored Men," *Colored American*, August 12, 1837.

16. Howard H. Bell, "The American Moral Reform Society, 1836–1841," *Journal of Negro Education* 27, no. 1 (Winter 1958): 34–40; *Minutes and Proceedings of the First Annual Meeting of the American Moral Reform Society* (1837), quoted in Litwack, *North of Slavery*, 238.

17. *Report of the Proceedings of the Colored National Convention, Held at Cleveland, Ohio, on Wednesday, September 6, 1848* (Rochester, NY: John Dick, 1848), 18.

18. *Freedom's Journal*, March 16, 1827.

19. Quoted in Ronald L. F. Davis and B. J. Krekorian, "The Black Press in Antebellum America," Slavery in America, http://www.slaveryinamerica.org/history/hs_es_press.htm.

20. *Frederick Douglass' Paper*, March 9, 1855, quoted in Benjamin Quarles, *Black Abolitionists* (New York: Oxford University Press, 1969), 86.

21. In spite of several early positive reviews, Jacobs's text languished in obscurity, its authenticity questioned, until Jean Fagan Yellin convincingly demonstrated its authenticity in the 1980s. Jean Fagin Yellin, *Harriet Jacobs: A Life* (New York: Basic Books, 2005).

22. Nell Irvin Painter, *Sojourner Truth: A Life, a Symbol* (New York: Norton, 1996), 167.

23. Quoted ibid., 125.

24. Ibid.

25. "Legal Rights Vindicated," *Frederick Douglass' Paper*, March 2, 1855.

26. Charles Sumner, *Argument . . . against the Constitutionality of Separate Colored Schools, in the Case of Sarah C. Roberts vs. the City of Boston. Before the Supreme Court of Mass., Dec. 4, 1849*, quoted in Litwack, *North of Slavery*, 147.

27. Quoted in Quarles, *Black Abolitionists*, 23.

28. Winch, *A Gentleman of Color*, 241–42.

29. Lois E. Horton, "Kidnapping and Resistance: Antislavery Direct Action in the 1850s," in *Passages to Freedom: The Underground Railroad in History and Memory*, ed. David W. Blight (Washington, DC: Smithsonian Books, 2004), 166.

30. Quoted in Milton C. Sernett, "Jermain Wesley Loguen," in *African American Lives*, ed. Henry Louis Gates Jr. and Evelyn Brooks Higginbotham (New York: Oxford University Press, 2004), 542.

31. This information is drawn largely from Sarah H. Bradford's nineteenth-century biography *Harriet Tubman: The Moses of Her People* (New York: printed for author by G. R. Lockwood and Son, 1886). Recently, however, scholars have challenged several aspects of this text. For an overview of the debate, see Milton Sernett, *Harriet Tubman: Myth, Memory, and History* (Durham, NC: Duke University Press, 2007), 55–66.

32. Quoted in Quarles, *Black Abolitionists*, 212.

33. Taney, C. J., Opinion of the Court, Scott v. Sandford 60 U.S. 393 (1857).

34. All quoted in Quarles, *Black Abolitionists*, 231.

35. Martin R. Delany, *Official Report of the Niger Valley Exploring Party*, in *Search for a Place: Black Separatism and Africa*, ed. Howard H. Bell (1861; repr., Ann Arbor: University of Michigan Press, 1969), 35.

36. Quoted ibid.

37. All quoted in Quarles, *Black Abolitionists*, 240, 241.

38. Quoted in David S. Reynolds, *John Brown, Abolitionist: The Man Who Killed Slavery, Sparked the Civil War, and Seeded Civil Rights* (New York: Knopf, 2005), 395.

39. "The Destiny of Colored Americans," *North Star*, November 16, 1849.

40. Howard Holman Bell, *Minutes of the Proceedings of the National Negro Conventions, 1830–1864*, quoted in Henry Louis Gates Jr. and Jennifer Burton, eds., *Call and Response: Key Debates in African American Studies* (New York: Norton, 2011), 117–18.

41. Quoted in Robert Toll, *Blacking Up: The Minstrel Show in Nineteenth-Century America* (New York: Oxford University Press, 1974), 71.

42. Ben Phelan, "*Dancing for Eels* Explained," *Antiques Roadshow*, PBS Online, http://www.pbs.org/wgbh/roadshow/fts/washingtondc_201006A44.html, including a comment

with a quotation from John Jay Brown, *The American Angler's Guide, or Complete Fisher's Manual for the United States* (New York: H. Long & Brother, 1849), 275.

43. Verses quoted in Eric Lott, *Love and Theft: Blackface Minstrelsy and the American Working Class* (New York: Oxford University Press, 1993), 23–24. See T. D. Rice, *Jim Crow, American: Selected Songs and Plays,* ed. W. T. Lhamon Jr. (Cambridge: Belknap Press of Harvard University Press, 2009), 161.

44. Lester S. Levy, *Picture the Songs: Lithographs from the Sheet Music of Nineteenth-Century America* (Baltimore: Johns Hopkins University Press, 1976), 23.

45. "Coal Black Rose," America Singing: Nineteenth-Century Song Sheets, American Memory, Rare Book and Special Collections Division, Library of Congress, http://memory.loc.gov/cgi-bin/query/D?amss:1:./temp/~ammem_gphZ.

46. Minstrel playbills, Uncle Tom's Cabin and American Culture, http://utc.iath.virginia.edu/minstrel/mibillshp.html.

47. John Frick, "*Uncle Tom's Cabin* on the Antebellum Stage," Uncle Tom's Cabin and American Culture, http://utc.iath.virginia.edu/interpret/exhibits/frick/frick.html.

48. Charles Dickens, *American Notes, for General Circulation,* ed. Patricia Ingham (Harmondsworth, UK: Penguin Classics, 2000), 102.

49. Thomas Low Nichols, *Forty Years of American Life* (1864), quoted in Lott, *Love and Theft,* 112.

50. "Master Juba: The Inventor of Tap Dancing," http://www.masterjuba.com.

51. "The Hutchinson Family—Hunkerism," *North Star,* October 27, 1848.

Suggested References

The Boundaries of Freedom

Alexander, Leslie M. *African or American? Black Identity and Political Activism in New York City, 1784–1861.* Urbana: University of Illinois Press, 2008.

Curry, Leonard P. *The Free Black in Urban America, 1800–1850: The Shadow of the Dream.* Chicago: University of Chicago Press, 1986.

Harris, Leslie M. *In the Shadow of Slavery: African Americans in New York City, 1626–1863.* Chicago: University of Chicago Press, 2004.

Hodges, Graham Russell. *Root and Branch: African Americans in New York and East Jersey, 1613–1863.* Chapel Hill: University of North Carolina Press, 1999.

Horton, James O., and Lois E. Horton. *Black Bostonians: Family Life and Community Struggle in the Antebellum North.* New York: Holmes & Meier, 1979.

———. *In Hope of Liberty: Culture, Community, and Protest among Northern Free Blacks, 1700–1860.* New York: Oxford University Press, 1998.

Litwack, Leon. *North of Slavery: The Negro in the Free States, 1790–1860.* Chicago: University of Chicago Press, 1961.

Melish, Joanne Pope. *Disowning Slavery: Gradual Emancipation and "Race" in New England, 1780–1860.* Ithaca, NY: Cornell University Press, 2000.

Forging a Black Freedom Struggle

Bell, Howard H., ed. *A Survey of the Negro Convention Movement, 1830–1861.* New York: Arno Press, 1969.

Blackett, Richard. *Building an Antislavery Wall: Black Americans in the Atlantic Abolitionist Movement.* Ithaca, NY: Cornell University Press, 1989.

Hall, Stephen G. *A Faithful Account of the Race: African American Historical Writing in Nineteenth-Century America.* Chapel Hill: University of North Carolina Press, 2009.

McCarthy, Timothy Patrick, and John Stauffer, eds. *Prophets of Protest: Reconsidering the History of American Abolitionism.* New York: New Press, 2006.

Painter, Nell Irvin. *Sojourner Truth: A Life, a Symbol.* New York: Norton, 1996.

Pease, William H., and Jane H. Pease. *They Who Would Be Free: Blacks' Search for Freedom, 1830–1861.* New York: Atheneum, 1974.

Quarles, Benjamin. *Black Abolitionists.* New York: Oxford University Press, 1969.

Rael, Patrick. *Black Identity and Black Protest in the Antebellum North.* Chapel Hill: University of North Carolina Press, 2002.

Rhodes, Jane. *Mary Ann Shadd Cary: The Black Press and Protest in the Nineteenth Century.* Bloomington: Indiana University Press, 1998.

Winch, Julie. *Philadelphia's Black Elite: Activism, Accommodation, and the Struggle for Autonomy, 1787–1848.* Philadelphia: Temple University Press, 1988.

Yee, Shirley. *Black Women Abolitionists: A Study in Activism, 1828–1860.* Knoxville: University of Tennessee Press, 1992.

The Slavery Question and National Crisis

Bordewich, Fergus. *Bound for Canaan: The Underground Railroad and the War for the Soul of America.* New York: Amistad, 2005.

Fehrenbacher, Don. *The Dred Scott Case: Its Significance in American Law and Politics.* New York: Oxford University Press, 1978.

Finkelman, Paul. *Dred Scott v. Sandford: A Brief History with Documents.* Boston: Bedford/St. Martin's, 1997.

Foner, Eric. *Free Soil, Free Labor, Free Men: The Ideology of the Republican Party before the Civil War.* New York: Oxford University Press, 1970.

Holt, Michael F. *The Fate of the Country: Politicians, Slavery Extension, and the Coming of the Civil War.* New York: Hill and Wang, 2005.

McPherson, James M. *Battle Cry of Freedom: The Civil War Era.* New York: Oxford University Press, 1988.

Miller, Floyd J. *The Search for a Black Nationality: Black Emigration and Colonization, 1787–1863.* Urbana: University of Illinois Press, 1975.

Slaughter, Thomas P. *Bloody Dawn: The Christiana Riot and Violence in the Antebellum North.* New York: Oxford University Press, 1991.

Still, William. *The Underground Railroad.* 1871. Reprint. Chicago: Johnson, 1970.

Taylor, Quintard. *In Search of the Racial Frontier: African Americans in the American West, 1528–1990.* New York: Norton, 1998.

Freedom Rising: The Civil War, 1861–1865

AROUND THREE O'CLOCK in the morning on May 13, 1862, the *Planter*, a Confederate steamer loaded with supplies for nearby Confederate outposts, made its way up Charleston harbor with the slave pilot Robert Smalls at the helm. Confederate lookouts, accustomed to seeing black pilots, took little note of the fact that there were no white men on deck.

Once outside the harbor, Smalls revved up the steamer's engine and sped in the direction of the Union blockade. Hoisting a white flag of surrender, he hoped the Union navy would permit the *Planter* to enter Union lines as a fugitive vessel and, more important, that his family members and friends on board would be protected as fugitive slaves. After several tense moments, the Union sailors turned their guns and cannons away, receiving the surrender of the *Planter* and welcoming the fugitives as free men and women.

Smalls had devised a cunning plan to secure his own and his family's freedom. Smalls and those around him had heard that Union forces were using fugitive slaves to help fight the Confederacy. Once behind Union lines, he provided the Union navy with important information about Confederate units in Charleston harbor. Before long, he was piloting the *Planter* for the Union navy, transporting men and supplies within the Union zone. Not long afterward, Congress gave Smalls and his accomplices a financial reward for surrendering the *Planter* to Union forces.

The story of Smalls's daring escape captured the attention of African Americans and the northern white press. In October 1862, a meeting of blacks at New York City's Shiloh Baptist Church, pastored by the Reverend Henry Highland Garnet (see chapter 6), welcomed him "with deafening cheers." A resolution adopted by the meeting claimed that Smalls's bold action demonstrated "a faithful devotedness to the cause of the American union."[1] For blacks and their allies, the exploit became one of the most celebrated events of the Civil War. It is also just one instance in what turned out to be a massive defection of slaves from the Confederacy to Union lines. The ever-growing number of slave men, women, and children who seized their freedom by joining the Union cause ultimately contributed to the collapse of the Confederacy.

The Civil War began as a southern war for Confederate independence and a northern war to suppress the Confederate rebellion and restore the Union. At the outset, neither side thought that the war would last very long or eventually lead to the destruction of slavery. The Confederacy was founded to protect slavery. The Union was willing to accept slavery where it already existed, opposing only the extension of slavery into the territories.

The transformation of the Union cause from a war to restore the Union to a war also to abolish slavery owed much to the actions of the slaves. Their escape from slavery and their presence behind Union

1863 Continued

Union victory at Gettysburg ends Confederate offensive in North

Union army takes Vicksburg and splits Confederacy in two

Draft riots in New York City

Black army unit leads assault on Fort Wagner, South Carolina

Lincoln's Gettysburg Address

Lincoln announces "10 percent plan"

1864 Confederate troops murder black prisoners of war at Fort Pillow, Tennessee

Congress equalizes pay of black and white soldiers

National Equal Rights League founded

Lincoln reelected on National Union ticket, with former Democrat Andrew Johnson as vice president

1865 General William T. Sherman issues Special Field Order 15

Black lawyer John S. Rock accepted to argue cases before U.S. Supreme Court

Petition drive leads to repeal of Illinois law requiring black settlers to pay a fine

Congress establishes Freedmen's Bureau

Confederate Congress authorizes arming of slaves

Confederate general Robert E. Lee surrenders to Union general Ulysses S. Grant

Lincoln assassinated

Thirteenth Amendment abolishes slavery

lines, together with the advocacy of northern free blacks and their white abolitionist allies, put pressure on the Lincoln administration and the U.S. Congress for policy changes and new laws that would address the issue of slavery directly and end it. The Union victory also owed much to the black men—both free and recently freed—who served in the Union army and navy, as well as to the many black men and women who worked alongside the troops and, as civilians, supported the Union cause. Their dedication and service, they believed, would earn them the rights of U.S. citizens. But as free blacks in the North had known for decades, freedom did not mean fair treatment and equality, and it was apparent at the war's end that the black freedom struggle was far from over.

The Coming of War and the Seizing of Freedom, 1861–1862

In hindsight, the Civil War seems to have been inevitable, but following the election of Abraham Lincoln as president in November 1860, it came in a series of small steps, the consequences of which were not fully realized at the time. As the states of the Confederacy withdrew from the Union to protect the institution of slavery, northern free blacks and their allies began to hope that if war came, it would be a war to end slavery everywhere. That was not the Union's initial war aim, but when slaves began pressing the issue by fleeing to Union lines, Union commanders were forced to respond, and they moved to protect the refugees' freedom. Slowly, Lincoln and Congress, too, were forced to respond by putting in place policies and practices that pointed toward a general emancipation.

War Aims and Battlefield Realities

With the election of Abraham Lincoln, sectional tensions over slavery reached a point of crisis. Believing they owed no loyalty to a Union that could elect a president without any southern support, the slave states made plans to withdraw. On November 10, 1860, South Carolina called a secession convention, and on December 20 it declared that "the union now subsisting between South Carolina and other States, under the name of the 'United States of America' is hereby dissolved." Four days later, the convention passed a declaration listing the causes justifying secession: the North's interference with slavery; repeated northern condemnations of slavery as sinful; northern support for abolitionism; northerners' aiding and abetting the escape of southern fugitive slaves; northern promotion of slave insurrections through "emissaries, books, and pictures"; and the election of Lincoln, a leader "whose opinions and purposes are hostile to slavery."[2]

South Carolina's secession ordinance declared the state independent, but already a movement was under way for the formation of a confederacy. By February 1, 1861, Mississippi, Florida, Alabama, Georgia, Louisiana, and Texas also had seceded, and on February 4, delegates from these states met in Montgomery, Alabama, to create the **Confederate States of America**. They wrote a constitution that reads much like the U.S. Constitution, although the right to hold slaves as property was explicitly protected. Setting up a provisional government, they elected Mississippi senator Jefferson Davis as president.

Even as the Confederacy formed, two attempts were made to avert disunion. In Congress, Kentucky senator John J. Crittenden proposed to reinstate the 1820 Missouri Compromise and thus guarantee the protection of slavery in territories south of the southern border of Missouri. After a U.S. Senate committee failed to reach agreement on the proposal, the Virginia legislature called a peace convention. But the delegates in attendance, representing both free and slave states, also failed to find a compromise that would hold the Union together.

While some still hoped for peace, the Confederate States of America prepared for war. They began organizing an army and navy, and state militias seized federal forts, arsenals, and post offices. Most military posts in the South came under Confederate command. In Charleston, Union major Robert Anderson withdrew from Fort Moultrie to the more easily protected Fort Sumter, on an island in the harbor, and waited for provisions.

On March 4, 1861, Lincoln delivered his inaugural address to a fractured union. Speaking directly to "the Southern States," he reaffirmed, "I have no purpose, directly or indirectly to interfere with the institution of slavery in the States where it exists. I believe I have no lawful right to do so, and I have no inclination to do so." Furthermore, he explained, "no state upon its mere motion can lawfully get out of the Union." At the same time, Lincoln asserted that the Union was a binding and "perpetual" compact. He concluded, "Acts of violence, within any State or States, against the authority of the United States, are insurrectionary or revolutionary." Precisely because it was unlawful and thus intolerable, Lincoln believed that secession must be overturned. It was his position that the Union had to be respected and maintained.[3]

In his first cabinet meeting, Lincoln raised the issue of provisioning Fort Sumter, and the matter was discussed often in the following weeks. Eventually, the president determined that the fort should be resupplied, and he informed the governor of South Carolina of this intention. In turn, South Carolina demanded the fort's surrender. When Major Anderson refused, Confederate shore batteries opened fire early on the morning of April 12. The next day, Anderson surrendered. The Civil War had begun.

Anticipating that Anderson was ready to evacuate the fort, Confederate officials did not think their actions would lead to hostilities. After all, back in January, fire from Charleston's shore batteries had forced the withdrawal of a provision ship without further incident. But they miscalculated. On April 15, Lincoln called for 75,000 militia to put down the insurrection and "to repossess the forts, places, and property which have been seized from the Union."[4]

Virginia refused to answer the call. Its first secession convention had rejected leaving the Union, but now a second convention voted for it. By May 20, Arkansas, Tennessee, and North Carolina had also joined the Confederacy, making for a total of eleven Confederate states. The slave states of Delaware, Maryland, Kentucky, and Missouri, known as the border states, remained in the Union, but not without strife. Federal troops occupied Baltimore; guerrilla fighting ravaged Missouri; and a provisional Confederate government was formed in Kentucky, although the state officially declared its neutrality. Even as Virginia's state capital, Richmond, was selected as the new Confederate capital, the state's western counties seceded from Virginia and organized a Unionist government.

Patriotic fervor pervaded both North and South. Each side felt that its cause was just and it would soon prevail. Lincoln's call for volunteers had anticipated a three-month

Regimental Flag

This remnant of a handsome flag made by the Colored Ladies of Baltimore for the Fourth Regiment U.S. Colored Troops showcases black patriotism. It vividly illustrates the strong black civilian support for the Union war effort. Even more impressively, this regimental flag illustrates the deep black pride in and zealous support for black Union troops during and after the war. This support was particularly strong among women with male relatives and friends serving in the military. *Silk mounted on a wooden pole (with the eagle missing). Museum Department, Courtesy of the Maryland Historical Society, image ID 2004.22.*

commitment. With their superior economic, material, military, and manpower resources (close to two to one), northerners believed that the Confederate rebellion would be quickly put down. With fierce determination and confidence in their formidable military abilities, southerners believed that they would succeed in establishing the Confederate States of America as an independent nation. They would be defending their homeland, while the Union would be forced to take the war into the South.

Three months into the war, Union forces marched thirty miles into Virginia. On July 21, 1861, along a creek called Bull Run, the Confederates turned them back. Union officials had miscalculated. It was clear that the Confederacy would not back down in the face of Union advantages on and off the battlefield. It was also clear that the war would not be over soon.

Union Policy on Black Soldiers and Black Freedom

Free black men responded enthusiastically to Lincoln's call for volunteers. In Pittsburgh, the Hannibal Guards, a local black militia, pledged support for the Union cause: "As we consider ourselves American citizens . . . although deprived of all our political rights, we yet wish the government of the United States to be sustained against the tyranny of slavery and are willing to assist in any honorable way . . . to sustain the present administration."[5] In Albany, Ohio, free blacks organized the Attucks Guards, naming their regiment after Crispus Attucks, the fugitive slave who was the first person to die in the American Revolution. Albany's black women gave the volunteer company a handsome homemade flag. And at Boston's Twelfth Baptist Church, those assembled unanimously resolved that "we are ready to stand by and defend the Government with 'our lives, our fortunes, and our sacred honor.'" They resolved further that "the colored women could go as nurses, seamstresses, and warriors if need be."[6]

But in all cases, military service by black men was rejected. For many whites, black men serving in the Union forces evoked thoughts of slave insurrections and violated notions of white male superiority. When black men in Cincinnati met to organize a home guard to protect the city, white opposition was fierce. Instead of gratitude, these volunteers received "insults . . . for this simple offer." In Cincinnati, as throughout the North, blacks encountered a persistent refrain: "We want you d——d niggers to keep out of this: This is a white man's war."[7] In September 1862, President Lincoln observed that if the Union accepted black troops, he feared "that in a few weeks the arms would be in the hands of the rebels."[8] Despite the service of black men in the American Revolution and the War of 1812, the U.S. Army had generally excluded black soldiers, and they were barred from state militias as well.[9]

Nevertheless, from the outset, northern blacks and abolitionists engaged in a vigorous debate about the purposes, possible consequences, and larger meanings of the war. Many worked hard to make emancipation a central war goal. Shortly after the surrender of Fort Sumter, the *Anglo-African Magazine* prophesied that "out of this strife will come freedom, though the methods are not yet clearly apparent." "Justice to the slave," the magazine argued, was "the sure and permanent basis of 'a more perfect union.'"[10] Frederick Douglass expressed a similarly hopeful vision in May 1861: "Any attempt now to separate the freedom of the slave from the victory of the Government . . . any attempt to secure peace to the whites while leaving blacks in chains . . . will be labor lost. The American people and the Government at Washington may refuse to recognize it for a time; but the 'inexorable logic of events' will force it upon them in the end: that the war now being waged in this land is a war for and against slavery"[11] (See Documents: Wartime Opportunities and Dilemmas, pp. 351–54.)

Nevertheless, Lincoln continued to frame the conflict as a rebellion that must be put down so the Union could be preserved. As president and commander in chief, he refused to acknowledge slavery as the cause of the war, or abolition as its goal. He knew he could not afford to alienate the border states, where slavery still existed. The loyalty of Maryland—to the north of Washington, D.C.—was especially important to secure. Without it, the nation's capital would be surrounded by hostile territory. And Maryland's loyalty was uncertain. In Baltimore, federal troops had been shot at as they marched through the city. As riots and civil disorder continued, Lincoln suspended habeas corpus on April 27, 1861. Those suspected of disloyal acts could be taken into custody without the right to have a judge rule on the lawfulness of their imprisonment. In other words, they could be held in jail indefinitely without the authorities showing cause.

To help further secure border states' loyalty, Lincoln developed a plan for gradual, compensated slave emancipation that allowed the states, not the federal government, to take the initiative. He especially hoped that Delaware, with fewer than 2,000 slaves, would view such a plan favorably. But none of the border states adopted emancipation plans. Congress, however, took action to end slavery in the District of Columbia, and on April 16, 1862, Lincoln signed the act into law. It gave slave owners who could prove their loyalty to the Union up to $300 for each slave freed, and it gave each freed slave who chose emigration to Haiti, Liberia, or any country outside the United States up to $100. Nearly 3,000 slaves were freed by this act, and several hundred chose to accept payment to relocate to Haiti. In June, Congress ended slavery in U.S. territories—those areas west of the Mississippi River not yet organized as states—settling once and for all the issue that had caused such discord before the war.

The District of Columbia Emancipation Act showed Lincoln's two-pronged approach to the problem of slavery—compensation and colonization—but it did not prove to be the model that Lincoln had hoped it would. In the spring and summer of

1862, the war was not going well for the Union. Despite a massive effort, Union attempts to advance on Richmond failed, and by fall the Confederate Army of Northern Virginia was on the offensive. Calls for a general emancipation proliferated, but in a famous exchange with the journalist Horace Greeley of the *New York Tribune*, who urged Lincoln to commit himself to end slavery, Lincoln replied: "My paramount object in this struggle is to save the Union, and is not either to save or destroy Slavery. . . . What I do about Slavery and the colored race, I do because I believe it helps to save the Union. . . . I have here stated my purpose according to my view of official duty, and I intend no modification of my oft-expressed personal wish that all men, everywhere, could be free."[12]

Refugee Slaves and Freedpeople

Pressure to address emancipation directly mounted because some slaves had already freed themselves. Taking advantage of the unsettled conditions of wartime, slaves fled to Union lines and Union-controlled territory, where their presence forced military commanders to determine their status. The first to seize freedom in this way were Frank Baker, James Townsend, and Shepard Mallory, who, just after the hostilities began, had been sent by their owner to build Confederate fortifications in Hampton, Virginia. In the middle of the night on May 23, 1861, they commandeered a skiff and crossed the waters of Hampton Roads to Fortress Monroe, which was still in Union hands. There they received protection from the commander, General Benjamin F. Butler, who refused to return them to their owners. Instead, using the South's definition of slaves as property, Butler designated them **contraband** of war, or confiscated Confederate property. These three men were the first of thousands of fugitive slaves— men, women, and children—who would swell the population at Fortress Monroe. By July 1861, there were 900 refugees there, and by August 1862 there were 3,000. By the end of the war, in April 1865, some 10,000 former slaves lived in camps at Hampton, the village across from the fortress, which had been burned to the ground by retreating Confederates in August 1861.

In military terms, "contraband" designated nonhuman property and goods. Butler's use of it for refugee slaves was unconventional, but it shaped subsequent Union policy. It also implied subordinate status, as the former slaves were not yet fully emancipated. Butler put them to work as diggers and dockworkers, as servants and laundresses and cooks. They received army rations and eventually wages—$8 a month for males, $4 for females. These refugees deprived the Confederacy of a vital labor source that increasingly contributed to the Union cause.

Butler was not the only Union officer to be perplexed by the question of what to do with refugee slaves who fled to Union lines. In early August 1861, Congress sought to clarify the situation in the **First Confiscation Act**, which authorized the confiscation of slaves as Confederate property. This act voided masters' claims to slaves who—like the first three at Fortress Monroe—had been working directly for the Confederate military. Later that same month, John C. Frémont, the major general in charge of the Department of the West and an outspoken abolitionist, cited civil disorder in Missouri as the reason for declaring martial law and freeing the slaves of all disloyal owners. Lincoln, concerned about securing the loyalty of the border states, voided the order.

STAMPEDE AMONG THE NEGROES IN VIRGINIA—THEIR ARRIVAL AT FORTRESS MONROE.—FROM SKETCHES BY OUR SPECIAL ARTIST AT FORTRESS MONROE.—SEE PAGE 11.

Slave Contrabands
Enslaved blacks contributed to their emancipation by running away and seeking refuge at Union strongholds such as Fortress Monroe in Virginia, shown here. Union military policies and practices helped shape the freedom journey for tens of thousands of refugee slaves. By redefining their status as "contraband of war," and thus subject to seizure by the Union, military officials helped lay the groundwork for employing refugees as nonslave workers, further spurring the transition from slavery to freedom. *Library of Congress, LC-USZ62-31165.*

Nevertheless, African Americans, by running from slavery to freedom, were already shaping three related developments: the decisions of individual commanders about what to do with the refugees, Union military policy as a whole, and growing acceptance in the North of former slaves as laborers for the Union military. In March 1862, Congress passed an additional article of war that prohibited Union navy and army officers from returning fugitives to slavery. Even before that, however, Union officers in recaptured coastal South Carolina were developing their own innovative policies. Port Royal and the Sea Islands had been taken by Union troops in November 1861, as the Union naval blockade of the South proved increasingly successful. Fleeing plantation owners abandoned their land and some 10,000 slaves, who remembered November 7 as "the day of the big gun-shoot."[13]

In what came to be known as the **Port Royal Experiment**, these former slaves were designated contrabands and began working the abandoned cotton plantations under the supervision of Union military officials. They organized their own time and labor, received wages, and sold surplus crops. A few were able to purchase plots of abandoned land when U.S. Treasury officials auctioned it off, but most of the land went to northern businessmen who hired the contrabands to farm it. Their success in this endeavor could have been a model for the transition from slavery to freedom.

Assisting the contrabands were a group of idealistic missionaries and teachers sent by northern religious and charitable organizations such as the American Missionary Association. Most of the teachers were white women who saw themselves as civilizing and Christianizing a primitive and inferior people. Sea Island blacks may have resented their condescension and racial prejudice, but they were eager to be educated. At makeshift schools in churches and on outdoor benches, they learned to read and write, to understand the Bible and Christian principles, and to master the responsibilities of freedom. One who traveled to the Sea Islands to teach former slaves was Charlotte Forten, the granddaughter of the successful African American businessman James Forten. She subsequently published a revealing account of her experiences. (See From the Record: A School for Contrabands.)

Even as the Port Royal contrabands were building independent lives, their status was uncertain. On May 19, 1862, the Union commander General David Hunter issued a proclamation freeing all the slaves in Florida, Georgia, and South Carolina, but Lincoln again voided the order. Hunter set about organizing the freedmen into a regiment until the War Department forced him to abandon this plan. Finally, on July 17, 1862, Congress clarified the status of refugee slaves. The **Second Confiscation Act** declared freedom for all slaves employed in the rebellion and for refugee slaves able to make it to Union-controlled territory. It thereby freed all slaves who had been deserted by Confederate owners, as well as all those who took refuge behind Union lines or were captured, if their owners were waging war against the Union. Slavery in the border states, however, was protected. The act also empowered the federal government to seize and sell all other Confederate property. Finally, it gave the president the power to authorize the use of "persons of African descent" in any way he deemed necessary to put down the rebellion and "to make provision for the transportation, colonization, and settlement, in some tropical country beyond the limits of the United States, of such persons of the African race, made free by the provisions of this act, as may be willing to emigrate."[14]

Union forces in the West were more successful than those in the East, and by mid-1862 they had captured New Orleans and were moving up the Mississippi River. Here, as elsewhere, slaves fled to Union lines. Thousands of refugees arrived from the low-lying rice plantations near New Orleans, the cotton plantations around Baton Rouge, and the sugar plantations along the river and west of New Orleans. General Butler, now the military governor of New Orleans, initially followed a two-pronged policy: He welcomed the slaves of disloyal masters but returned the runaway slaves of pro-Union planters—some of whom had just recently sworn loyalty to the Union and were looking to Butler to protect their property. In the confusion of wartime conditions, however, it became increasingly difficult, if not impractical, to distinguish between the refugee slaves of loyal and disloyal masters. Butler's solution was to arrange for runaway

From the Record

Charlotte Forten | A School for Contrabands, 1864

Charlotte Forten (1837–1914), granddaughter of the wealthy black leader James Forten, had a privileged upbringing. She was educated by private tutors and at an academy in Salem, Massachusetts, where she taught grammar school after graduation. After the Civil War began, she applied to Philadelphia's Port Royal Relief Committee to teach newly freed slaves and in October 1862 arrived in the Sea Islands. She kept a journal of her experiences and in 1864 published an account in the *Atlantic Monthly*, from which the following excerpt is taken.

The first day at school was rather trying. Most of my children were very small, and consequently restless. Some were too young to learn the alphabet. These little ones were brought to school because the older children—in whose care their parents leave them while at work—could not come without them. We were therefore willing to have them come, although they seemed to have discovered the secret of perpetual motion, and tried one's patience sadly. But after some days of positive, though not severe treatment, order was brought out of chaos, and I found but little difficulty in managing and quieting the tiniest and most restless spirits. I never before saw children so eager to learn, although I had had several years' experience in New England schools. Coming to school is a constant delight and recreation to them. They come here as other children go to play. The older ones, during the summer, work in the fields from early morning until eleven or twelve o'clock, and then come into school, after their hard toil in the hot sun, as bright and as anxious to learn as ever.

Of course there are some stupid ones, but these are the minority. The majority learn with wonderful rapidity. Many of the grown people are desirous of learning to read. It is wonderful how a people who have been so long crushed to the earth, so imbruted as these have been,—and they are said to be among the most degraded negroes of the South,—can have so great a desire for knowledge, and such a capability for attaining it. One cannot believe that the haughty Anglo Saxon race, after centuries of such an experience as these people have had, would be very much superior to them. And one's indignation increases against those who, North as well as South, taunt the colored race with inferiority while they themselves use every means in their power to crush and degrade them, denying them every right and privilege, closing against them every avenue of elevation and improvement. Were they, under such circumstances, intellectual and refined, they would certainly be vastly superior to any other race that ever existed.

SOURCE: Charlotte Forten, "Life on the Sea Islands," *Atlantic Monthly*, May 1864, 591.

???   **What impressions of her students does Forten convey? How did her experience in teaching newly freed slaves inspire these reflections about white racism?**

slaves to provide wage labor for allegedly loyal plantation owners who sought the help, avoiding the question of the fugitives' status, which was neither slave nor free.

A growing body of refugee slaves took over and worked abandoned land and carved out hidden runaway settlements in the bayous. The widening slave exodus alarmed southern whites, who increasingly feared slave insurrections. As Union forces gained firmer control of the region, however, they instituted systems of labor that, like the Port Royal Experiment, allowed the former slaves to work the surrounding plantations as independent laborers under the supervision of Union officials.[15]

Turning Points, 1862–1863

In more than a year of fighting, neither side had achieved its aims. Union forces had secured some coastal areas of the Confederacy, but advances on the capital of Richmond had been checked. Fugitive slaves were creating turmoil for Union military officers and forcing the issue of freedom on a cautious Lincoln. But events began to take a decisive turn in the summer of 1862. Within the next twelve months, a military order by the president would decree formal emancipation for slaves under Confederate control and authorize black men to serve in the Union army. Following this change of policy, the use of black units would contribute to the Union's success, as significant military victories in the summer of 1863 marked a turning point in the war.

The Emancipation Proclamation

Abraham Lincoln fully understood the military and political advantages that freeing fugitive slaves and employing them as military labor and support personnel gave the Union cause. He was also aware that recasting the war as a fight against slavery could have diplomatic benefits. In Great Britain especially, where antislavery sentiment was strong, a war aim of ending slavery would enhance the political and moral weight of the Union's cause. It would also seriously undercut the Confederacy's push for diplomatic recognition in Europe.

Through the middle of 1862, Lincoln publicly continued his cautious, pragmatic approach to the question of slavery and the status of refugee slaves. Yet he was privately making plans to take a bolder step. On July 22, he surprised his cabinet by announcing his intention to free all the slaves of those in rebellion against the Union. This act would be a military proclamation issued under his authority as commander in chief. At the suggestion of one of his cabinet members, however, Lincoln agreed to withhold the announcement until after a Union victory on the battlefield, so as not to appear desperate or beholden in any way to the fugitive slaves or to abolitionist pressure.

The Union victory on September 17, 1862, at Antietam Creek, near Sharpsburg, Maryland, gave Lincoln the occasion he needed. Union forces repelled a Confederate offensive, and General Robert E. Lee's army retreated back into Virginia. The victory proved significant, not only for reversing Union military fortunes but also for dissuading Britain from recognizing the Confederacy. Ten days later, on September 22, 1862, Lincoln issued the **preliminary Emancipation Proclamation**.

This proclamation gave the Confederates one hundred days—until January 1, 1863—to cease their rebellion. If they did not, all their slaves would be freed on that date.

The proclamation drew its authority from the additional article of war approved in March 1862 and the Second Confiscation Act. The proclamation maintained Lincoln's two-pronged approach to the problem of slavery—compensation and colonization. It recommended that Congress offer monetary assistance to slave states not in rebellion that would enable them to adopt gradual or immediate emancipation plans. It also offered continued support for the colonization of freedpeople outside the United States.

The Confederacy scorned the preliminary Emancipation Proclamation, and no person or region ceased the rebellion. On January 1, 1863, Lincoln signed the final **Emancipation Proclamation** (see Appendix). This proclamation referenced the preliminary one, with its determination to free the slaves in states or parts of states still in rebellion against the United States as of January 1, and then listed the regions in which the slaves "shall be then, thenceforward, and forever free." It said nothing about compensation or colonization, only that military and naval authorities would recognize and maintain the freedom of "said persons," who were urged "to abstain from all violence" and to "labor faithfully for reasonable wages." Finally, it declared that "such persons of suitable condition" were to be "received into the armed service." Lincoln ended the proclamation with an invocation: "Upon this act, sincerely believed to be an act of justice, warranted by the Constitution upon military necessity, I invoke the considerate judgment of mankind and the gracious favor of Almighty God." The war to save the Union thus officially became a war also to free the slaves. It was clear that now, when the Union was restored, it would be a nation of free people, a nation in which slavery would not exist.

In the North, blacks and their allies ardently embraced the Emancipation Proclamation. At the grand celebration on January 1, 1863, at the Israel Bethel AME Church in Washington, D.C., Pastor Henry McNeal Turner witnessed a community overcome with joy: "Men squealed, women fainted, dogs barked, white and colored people shook hands, songs were sung. . . . Great processions of colored and white men marched to and fro and passed in front of the White House and congratulated President Lincoln on his proclamation. . . . It was indeed a time of times, and a half time, nothing like it will ever be seen again in this life."[16] (See Visual Sources: The Moment and Meaning of Emancipation, pp. 362–73.)

For blacks in captured Confederate territory now under Union control, Emancipation Proclamation celebrations also were widespread, joyous, and hopeful. In Hampton, Virginia, members of the large free black community that had grown up around Fortress Monroe gathered for a reading of the proclamation. They met under a large tree—now known as the Emancipation Oak and still standing on the campus of Hampton University—where a school for former slaves had been conducted since 1861 by Mary S. Peake. In the South Carolina Sea Islands, the high point of the long celebration was unplanned. Colonel Thomas Wentworth Higginson, an abolitionist from Massachusetts and commander of the First Regiment of South Carolina Volunteers, received a Union flag for his unit, which was composed of former slaves. As he received the flag, the freedpeople burst into a spontaneous rendition of "My Country, 'Tis of Thee." "It was a touching and beautiful incident, and sent a thrill through all our hearts," recalled Charlotte Forten.[17]

Slaves under Confederate control who got word of the Emancipation Proclamation kept their responses secret so as not to enrage Confederates and provoke retaliation. Many masters worked hard to prevent word of the proclamation from reaching their slaves, some even relocating their operations to more isolated or more secure Confederate areas, where plantation life continued as usual. The former Texas slave Felix Haywood recalled, "The War didn't change nothin'." In fact, he said, "sometimes you didn't knowed it was goin' on. It was the endin' of it that made the difference."[18]

Nevertheless, news of emancipation continued to spread as Union forces advanced. While the proclamation did not immediately free any slaves still under Confederate control, it transformed the conflict by making emancipation a central war aim, linking emancipation with Union victory. Outside the United States, emancipation was applauded in Britain and France, and it ended Confederate hopes for European diplomatic recognition.

The U.S. Colored Troops

At the beginning of the war, black men and black militia units had been officially excluded from service in the Union army, but some Union commanders in the field had seen the merit of turning contrabands into soldiers. In August 1862, General Hunter finally received permission to recruit freedmen in the Sea Islands, and one hundred signed up to become the First South Carolina Volunteers (later the Thirty-Third U.S. Colored Troops). In September, General Butler organized the First Louisiana by converting the Louisiana Native Guards—a unit of free blacks in New Orleans that had formed to serve in the Confederate army but been refused—into a federal unit. Neither saw action until after the Emancipation Proclamation officially declared that blacks would be received into the Union army and the War Department, on May 22, 1863, created a bureau to oversee the new **U.S. Colored Troops**.

In the North, recruitment of free blacks was slow at first. While some black men had already organized militia units, believing that wartime service would help promote emancipation and substantiate their claims to full citizenship, others were less confident. The *Liberator* reported that a well-attended recruitment meeting on April 27, 1863, in New York City's Shiloh Baptist Church had produced only one recruit, despite stirring speeches by Henry Highland Garnet and Frederick Douglass. One audience member explained that the problem "was not cowardice . . . but a proper respect for their own manhood. If the Government wanted their services, let it guarantee to them all the rights of citizens and soldiers, and, instead of one man, he would insure them 5,000 in twenty days."[19] That summer, Douglass stepped up his efforts to promote black military service, emphasizing its links with citizenship. "Once let the black man get upon his person the brass letters U.S.," he announced, "let him get an eagle on his button, and a musket on his shoulder, and bullets in his pocket, and there is no power on earth or under the earth which can deny that he has earned the right of citizenship in the United States."[20]

Ultimately, 179,000 black men enlisted in the U.S. Colored Troops, almost 10 percent of all who served in the Union army. A few, such as Martin R. Delany, were commissioned officers; 7,122 were noncommissioned officers. Another 29,500 black men served in the Union navy. Among them was Robert Smalls, who by the end of 1863 was captain of a Union vessel. In one estimate, blacks participated in almost 250 battles. They suffered more than 37,000 casualties. Seventeen black soldiers and four black sailors received the Congressional Medal of Honor. (See By the Numbers: African Americans in the Union Military.)

This distinguished record of black military wartime service evolved within the limits imposed by racial prejudice. The military hierarchy reinforced the racial

BY THE NUMBERS   African Americans in the Union Military

African Americans had a distinguished record of military service and played a significant role in Union victory. Of these, 33,000 were free blacks from Union states; 42,000 were former slaves and free men from border states; 99,000 were former slaves from Confederate states; and the rest were most likely southern free blacks. Another 29,500 black men served in the Union navy. Black troops accounted for 10 percent of the Union army and nearly 25 percent of the navy.

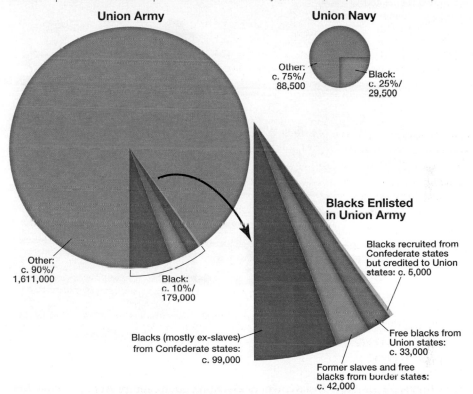

Union Army

Union Navy

Other:
c. 75%/
88,500

Black:
c. 25%/
29,500

Other:
c. 90%/
1,611,000

Black:
c. 10%/
179,000

**Blacks Enlisted
in Union Army**

Blacks recruited from
Confederate states
but credited to Union
states: c. 5,000

Blacks (mostly ex-slaves)
from Confederate states:
c. 99,000

Free blacks from
Union states:
c. 33,000

Former slaves and free
blacks from border states:
c. 42,000

hierarchy of American society at large. Black units were invariably led by white officers; the idea of black officers leading troops, especially white troops, was totally unacceptable. The white officers who led black troops varied in motivation, quality, and effectiveness, but most barely tolerated their black subordinates. One exception was Robert Gould Shaw, colonel of the Fifty-Fourth Massachusetts Volunteer Infantry Regiment, a unit raised by abolitionists. The first such black unit to be organized, it included two of Frederick Douglass's sons.

Black soldiers fighting for the Union endured many inequities. White officers, many of whom questioned the fitness and bravery of black soldiers, assigned them to the most difficult noncombat duties, such as building fortifications and manning supply lines. These officers often mismanaged their troops, resulting in inept battlefield maneuvers and excessive casualty rates. Lack of good training and equipment also contributed to the high number of black fatalities.

Black troops were also at greater risk than white troops because of Confederate policy, which regarded black Union soldiers as instigators of slave insurrections. As

Martin R. Delany

This hand-colored lithograph features the talented and ambitious Delany in full regalia as the Union military's highest-ranking African American. Toward the end of the war, Delany was appointed field commander and commissioned as a major in the 104th Regiment U.S. Colored Troops. Delany had been active in the northern campaign to recruit black soldiers, and in an earlier, less hopeful moment, he had advocated emigration to Africa. After the war, Delany became a prominent Reconstruction politician in South Carolina. *Martin Robinson Delany (1812–1885), Union army officer. c. 1865. Hand-colored lithograph, 55.2 x 43.8 cm (21¾ in. x 17¼ in.). National Portrait Gallery, Smithsonian Institution, Washington, DC, USA/ Art Resource, NY.*

MAJOR MARTIN R. DELANY, U.S.A.
PROMOTED ON THE BATTLE FIELD FOR BRAVERY

such, they were subject to enslavement or execution upon capture. At Fort Pillow, Tennessee, the killing of scores of black prisoners of war by their Confederate captors on April 12, 1864, sparked much controversy. The Confederates denied the incident, but the northern press called it a massacre and used it as propaganda to promote the war effort. The threat of capture and possible enslavement, torture, and murder at the hands of Confederates made enlistment in the Union army itself an act of courage.

Finally, pay inequities caused considerable resentment. Black soldiers received $10 a month, with $3 deducted for food and clothing, regardless of rank. By contrast, white privates received $13 and free food and clothing, and their pay increased with promotions. So strong was the resentment among the soldiers of the Fifty-Fourth Massachusetts Regiment that they refused to accept any pay at all until the pay for whites and blacks was equalized. In one black regiment in Jacksonville, Florida, the issue of pay inequity sparked a mutiny in which the leader, Sergeant William Walker, a former refugee slave, was executed. On June 15, 1864, Congress passed legislation that equalized the pay of black and white soldiers and offered back pay to all those who had been underpaid or had refused pay in protest. Following this remedy, the recruitment of black soldiers picked up significantly. (See From the Record: Are We Soldiers, or Are We Laborers?)

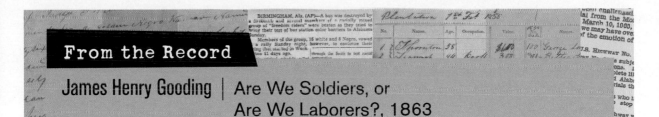

From the Record

James Henry Gooding | Are We Soldiers, or Are We Laborers?, 1863

Black men were not authorized to enlist in the U.S. army until after January 1863, when the Emancipation Proclamation declared them eligible. They were needed but not always welcome. They served in separate units, assigned primarily to manual labor, and as **Corporal James Henry Gooding (1837–1864)** complains in this letter to Abraham Lincoln, they were paid less than white soldiers. Gooding enlisted in the Fifty-Fourth Massachusetts Volunteer Infantry Regiment, fighting in 1863 at Fort Wagner, South Carolina, and the next year in Florida, where he was captured in battle. He died at Andersonville, a Confederate prison in Georgia.

Morris Island, S.C., September 28, 1863

Your Excellency, Abraham Lincoln:

Your Excellency will pardon the presumption of an humble individual like myself, in addressing you, but the earnest solicitation of my comrades in arms besides the genuine interest felt by myself in the matter is my excuse, for placing before the Executive head of the Nation our Common Grievance.

On the 6th of the last Month, the Paymaster of the Department informed us, that if we would decide to receive the sum of $10 (ten dollars) per month, he would come and pay us that sum, but that, on the sitting of Congress, the Regt. [regiment] would, in his opinion, be allowed the other 3 (three).° He did not give us any guarantee that this would be, as he hoped; certainly he had no authority for making any such guarantee. . . .

Now the main question is, are we Soldiers, or are we Laborers? We are fully armed, and equipped, have done all the various duties pertaining to a Soldier's life, have conducted ourselves to the complete satisfaction of General Officers, who were, if anything, prejudiced against us, but who now accord us all the encouragement and honors due us; have shared the perils and labor of reducing the first strong-hold that flaunted a Traitor Flag; and more, Mr. President, to-day the Anglo-Saxon Mother, Wife, or Sister are not alone in tears for departed Sons, Husbands and Brothers. . . .

Now your Excellency, we have done a Soldier's duty. Why can't we have a Soldier's pay? . . .

We appeal to you, Sir, as the Executive of the Nation, to have us justly dealt with. The Regt. do pray that they be assured their service will be fairly appreciated by paying them as American Soldiers, not as menial hirelings. Black men, you may well know, are poor; three dollars per month, for a year, will supply their needy wives and little ones with fuel.

° In July 1863, the War Department ruled that all black troops—regardless of rank—were to receive ten dollars per month, with three dollars deducted for clothing. This stood in stark contrast to the thirteen dollars per month paid to white troops.

Continued

Continued

If you, as Chief Magistrate of the Nation, will assure us of our whole pay, we are content. Our Patriotism, our enthusiasm will have a new impetus, to exert our energy more and more to aid our Country. Not that our hearts ever flagged in devotion, spite the evident apathy displayed in our behalf, but we feel as though our Country spurned us, now we are sworn to serve her. Please give this a moment's attention.

Source: Herbert Aptheker, ed., *A Documentary History of the Negro People in the United States* (New York: Citadel Press, 1951), 1:482–84.

??? **What arguments does Gooding advance in his request for equal pay for black soldiers?**

African Americans in the Major Battles of 1863

The U.S. Colored Troops helped the Union meet its mounting manpower needs, and when given the opportunity to fight, they fought heroically. The first black units in combat were the former Louisiana Native Guards, fighting for the Union as the African Brigade and soon designated the First Louisiana. Augmented by contrabands, the unit was assigned to the Mississippi River campaign that aimed to split the Confederacy in two. On May 27, these black soldiers participated in the assault on Port Hudson, Louisiana, where they proved they were as courageous as any white soldiers. "The undaunted . . . heroism, and the great endurance of the negro, as exhibited that day," the former slave William Wells Brown later wrote, "created a new chapter in American history for the colored man."[21] On June 7, armed only with old muskets, they defended the Union outpost at Milliken's Bend, Louisiana, causing Charles Dana, assistant secretary of war, to observe, "The bravery of the blacks in the battle of Milliken's Bend completely revolutionized the sentiment of the army with regard to the employment of negro troops. I heard prominent officers who . . . had sneered at the idea of the negroes fighting express themselves after that as heartily in favor of it."[22] Nevertheless, the battle at Milliken's Bend also revealed the risks black troops faced, as several who were captured by Confederates were sold as slaves, and a few were rumored to have been murdered.[23] On July 4, Vicksburg, Mississippi, the last major Confederate stronghold on the Mississippi River, surrendered to General Ulysses S. Grant, and a few days later Lincoln announced that the Mississippi River, now entirely in Union hands, "again goes unvexed to the sea."[24]

Lincoln had much to rejoice about on that Fourth of July. Just days before, Union armies had turned back another Confederate invasion. General Lee's march into Maryland and Pennsylvania was stopped at Gettysburg, where a three-day battle, on July 1–3, resulted in a decisive Union victory. No soldiers of the U.S. Colored Troops participated in the battle, and the services of black units organized in Philadelphia and Harrisburg by Octavius Catto and Thomas Morris Chester, respectively, were rejected. Nevertheless, large numbers of contrabands and free blacks aided the Army of the Potomac. Fearing capture and enslavement, hundreds of Pennsylvania free blacks fled in advance of Lee's march north, and a few were actually seized and sold.

PORT HUDSON.
Brilliant charge of the Phalanx upon the Confederate works.

The Battle of Port Hudson
Shown here with the U.S. flag held high as they make a valiant stand during this losing battle, the soldiers of the First and Third Louisiana Native Guards helped confirm for many northern whites that black troops were as competent and courageous as white troops. Their performance on the battlefield provided stirring evidence for establishing full U.S. citizenship for African Americans.
Schomburg Center, NYPL./Art Resource, NY.

The most notable battle that July for the U.S. Colored Troops took place in South Carolina, where on July 18 the Fifty-Fourth Massachusetts led a second assault on Fort Wagner, in Charleston harbor. Despite heavy losses, including the death of their commander, Colonel Shaw, they showed uncommon valor, charging the Confederate batteries in waves. Lewis Douglass, one of Frederick Douglass's sons, both of whom survived the conflict, wrote to his wife, "I wish we had a hundred thousand colored troops," because then "we would put an end to this war."[25] The bravery of the Fifty-Fourth excited the northern imagination. The unit's performance, said the *New York Tribune*, "made Fort Wagner such a name to the colored race as Bunker Hill has been for ninety years to the white Yankees"[26] (Map 7.1).

In November, Lincoln traveled to Gettysburg to dedicate a national cemetery honoring the fallen soldiers buried there. His short speech, delivered on November 19, 1863, is one of the best-known and most cherished speeches in American history. By announcing "a new birth of freedom" for an American nation "conceived in liberty and dedicated to the proposition that all men are created equal,"[27] it fixed forever

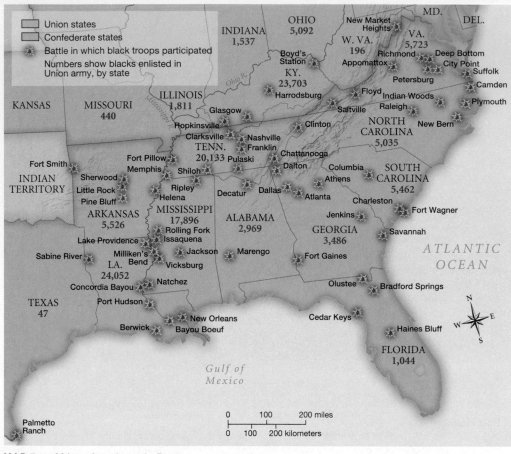

MAP 7.1   African Americans in Battle

Black troops played a pivotal role in the Union war effort, enlisting in the army and navy in significant numbers and participating in close to forty major battles. Their valiant efforts inspired black civilians to intensify their support for the Union cause. The impressive wartime service of black troops also sustained their claims and those of their people for full freedom and full U.S. citizenship. SOURCE: *The Atlas of African-American History and Politics: From the Slave Trade to Modern Times,* by Arwin Smallwood and Jeffrey Elliot. Copyright © 1998 The McGraw-Hill Companies, Inc. Used by permission of McGraw-Hill.

the noblest goal of the war. Originally aimed to suppress a rebellion and preserve the Union, it was now being fought to preserve democracy and make equality triumph.

Home Fronts and War's End, 1863–1865

Lincoln's words in the Gettysburg Address were reassuring to African Americans, but not to others. Northern Democrats objected to making emancipation a war goal, and in some areas of the North support for the war was faltering. As civilians and resources were increasingly mobilized for the war effort, war-weariness set in, and opposition to

Lincoln's conduct of the war grew. Congress tried to block his plans for reintegrating former Confederate land and people into the Union. At the same time, deaths, desertions, and declining numbers of white volunteers forced the imposition of a military draft, despite the addition of new black troops. In New York City, resistance to the draft turned violent, and roving mobs of white men targeted black neighborhoods and institutions. It was clear that any restoration of the Union would need to address civil rights and equality in the North as well as the end of slavery in the South. Black leaders renewed their efforts, recognizing that the freedom struggle would not end with emancipation. In 1865, freedom for the slaves was ensured by the Union victory and the passage of a constitutional amendment forbidding slavery forever. But for northern and southern blacks, both free and freed, the fight for citizenship and human dignity continued.

Riots and Restoration of the Union

Shortly after the decisive victories at Gettysburg and Vicksburg, and just before the assault on Fort Wagner, Union troops were hastily transferred to New York City to put down a riot. The violence was triggered by a military draft, instituted on March 3, 1863, that was not only unpopular but also inequitable, as the prosperous could pay $300 to purchase an exemption or hire a substitute, while the poor and working-class had no choice but to serve. On July 13, when newspapers published the names of the first draftees, chosen by lottery, a mob of white men attacked the Manhattan draft office.

The **New York City draft riots** spread quickly, and for four days roving white mobs, including large numbers of Irish and criminals, turned to ransacking black neighborhoods. They burned the Colored Orphan Asylum to the ground. Thousands of blacks were left homeless and destitute. Dozens were lynched; some were murdered in their homes. By July 15, as more federal troops arrived in the city, some directly from Gettysburg, the violence subsided.

The causes were deep-seated. Emancipation may have become a war aim, but for many whites it was not welcome. Many white soldiers resented being asked to fight and die to free the slaves. Many white working-class men and women feared that emancipation would mean a flood of black laborers coming north to take their jobs and undercut their wages and status.

The racist language of northern white Democratic politicians and the Democratic press inflamed these fears and tensions. Lincoln was denounced as a tyrant and the Emancipation Proclamation as unconstitutional. Democratic legislatures in Indiana, Illinois, and New Jersey raised formal objections to the war and passed peace resolutions. The language of the Illinois resolution revealed northern fears: After questioning the president's authority to proclaim emancipation, it argued that "the sudden, unconditional and violent liberation of 3,000,000 negro slaves" would have consequences that "cannot be contemplated without the most dismal foreboding of horror and dismay."[28]

The disturbances in New York City were not the only antiblack riots in the North during the war years. In 1862 and 1863, riots also rocked Brooklyn, New York—then a separate city—and Detroit. But the New York City riots were the worst, and black outrage was intense and widespread. "A gloom of infamy and shame will hang over New York for centuries," prophesied the AME Church's *Christian Recorder*.[29] After blasting

THE RIOTS IN NEW YORK : DESTRUCTION OF THE COLOURED ORPHAN ASYLUM.

The Destruction of the Colored Orphan Asylum
The New York City draft riots in March 1863 resulted in horrific violence against blacks and their property. Here the Colored Orphan Asylum is shown as it burns to the ground. The riots resulted from whites' outrage over a range of perceived wrongs, including being forced to serve in a war for the emancipation of black slaves. The vicious scapegoating of blacks by whites illustrates the destructive nature of antiblack prejudice and racist attitudes. *Private Collection/Peter Newark American Pictures/The Bridgeman Art Library International.*

local and state authorities for their failure to protect black people and black property, James W. C. Pennington called on blacks not to back down, but to redouble their efforts for full citizenship rights.[30] Events in New York City and elsewhere made it clear that emancipation would not mean racial equality.

These events also made it clear that the war's end would not mean harmony or even peace. Nevertheless, on December 8, 1863, Lincoln attempted to lay the groundwork for a stable postwar society in his **Proclamation for Amnesty and Reconstruction**. By this time, Louisiana, large stretches along the Mississippi River, and areas of Tennessee and Arkansas were in Union hands. To allow them to form pro-Union governments and reenter the Union, Lincoln officially pardoned all except high-ranking Confederate civil and military officials and decreed that their property should be restored to them, "except as to slaves." The proclamation directed that when voters equal to 10 percent of the votes cast in the 1860 election swore an oath of loyalty to the Union, they would be permitted to reestablish a state government. It also expressed the hope that the new state governments would recognize the needs of former slaves as "a laboring, landless, and homeless class" and would provide for their education.[31] This plan guided the reorganization of defeated Confederate areas until Lincoln's death a year and a half later.

African Americans Laboring for the Union
Here African American men are building a stockade in Alexandria, Virginia, to defend the Union Railroad Depot there and thus strengthen the defense of nearby Washington, D.C., against Confederate attack. Building such fortifications was essential to the Union war effort. In the Confederacy as well as the Union, African American civilians, both women and men, were an indispensable element of the labor force that performed such vital work as feeding and serving troops and building encampments and roads. © *Medford Historical Society Collection/Corbis.*

Civilians at Work for the War

The Union's 1863 military draft made it clear that the initial enthusiasm for the war was over. Even earlier, in April 1862, the Confederate army had sought to solve its manpower shortage through conscription. The war had gone on much longer than anyone had expected, and shortages in military manpower meant that civilians, too, had to be mobilized for the war effort. Resources were strained on both sides, but especially in the South. From the beginning, black labor—free and slave—had been vital to the Confederate war effort. Blacks grew most of the food for Confederate troops. They loaded and carted goods and supplies. Through coercion and impressment, as well as slave hiring and assignment, they worked for the military by building roads, entrenchments, and fortifications. Blacks served as personal servants, cooks, foragers, and spies for Confederate soldiers and officers. But as increasing numbers of slaves fled to the Union lines and Union troops controlled increasing amounts of Confederate territory, the Confederacy weakened. By mid-1864, roughly 400,000 slaves, or almost 10 percent of the slave population, were no longer under Confederate control, and many were laboring for the Union.

To stop slave flight and solidify the slave system, southern whites strengthened slave patrols, clamped down on slave and free black mobility, and moved their slaves away from nearby war zones and Union-controlled areas. At the same time, to quell slave unrest and defections, particularly in places near Union-held areas, masters often yielded to slave demands. These included continuing, or even expanding, previous understandings that allowed slaves to farm their own plots and market their own crops. Some masters and slaves made arrangements such as dividing or sharing harvests, trading wages for labor, and renting land and houses.

As most runaway slaves, at least early on, were males and wartime conditions further cut into the availability of male slave labor, the work of female slaves became increasingly important. Many shouldered additional field work in addition to the domestic work they traditionally performed. More than ever, they were responsible for sustaining their households. Like all slaves who remained under Confederate control, they weighed their options and waited for their chances. Toward the end of the war, increasing numbers of slave women, with their children, also began to seek freedom behind Union lines. Elizabeth Botume, a northern teacher sent to the Sea Islands by the New England Freedmen's Aid Society, remembered seeing a refugee mother "striding along with her hominy pot, in which was a live chicken, poised on her head. One child was on her back with its arms tightly clasped around her neck, and its feet about her waist, and under each arm was a smaller child."[32] In refugee camps, too, women tried to hold families together.

As an increasing number of slaves fled the Confederacy, their contributions to the Union war effort grew. Not only black soldiers and sailors but also another 200,000 black women and men labored in nonmilitary capacities, serving as cooks, laundresses, nurses, carpenters, wagon drivers, livestock tenders, foragers, servants, and spies. Black women often filled many roles at once, working in various capacities depending on what was needed. For example, Harriet Tubman was a scout, spy, teacher, and nurse during the war, even as she continued to assist slaves escaping to freedom. The former slave Susie King Taylor started a school in the Sea Islands and served as a teacher, nurse, and laundress for the all-black Thirty-Third U.S. Colored Troops. In the Confederate White House in Richmond, Mary Elizabeth Bowser worked undercover as a house servant and spied for the Union. Before she escaped toward the end of the war, she tried—unsuccessfully—to burn down the Confederate White House. In the Lincoln White House in Washington, Elizabeth Keckley served as the First Lady's dressmaker and confidante.

Using her connections, Keckley in 1862 established a charitable organization for assisting the contrabands who crowded into the Union capital. This Contraband Relief Association was supported by many prominent abolitionists, including Henry Highland Garnet, Frederick Douglass, and Sojourner Truth, who also raised food and money for black regiments. A report of the association explained, "Our work has been to provide shelter, food, clothing, medicines and nourishments for them, we have also buried their dead, and in fact, done all we could to alleviate their suffering, and help them on towards a higher plane of civilization."[33] Black women were prominent in the work of northern freedpeople's aid societies as well, such as the Contraband Committee of the Mother Bethel AME Church in Philadelphia and the Freedmen's Friend Society in Brooklyn. (See From the Record: The Contraband Relief Association.) From the battlefields and war-torn plantations of the South to the military hospitals and contraband camps in the North, it was often the unpaid work of black women that alleviated suffering and provided humanitarian aid. (See Documents: Black Women at Work during the War, pp. 355–61.)

From the Record

Elizabeth Keckley | The Contraband Relief Association, 1868

Born a slave in Virginia, **Elizabeth Keckley (1818–1907)** learned to sew and mastered the art of dressmaking. With the help of patrons, she purchased her own and her son's freedom and soon gained a notable reputation as a dressmaker. Settling in Washington, D.C., she was hired by First Lady Mary Todd Lincoln, and the two became confidantes and friends. In this excerpt from her memoirs of her White House years, Keckley describes her efforts to help contrabands in wartime Washington.

In the summer of 1862, freedmen began to flock into Washington from Maryland and Virginia. They came with a great hope in their hearts, and with all their worldly goods on their backs. Fresh from the bonds of slavery, fresh from the benighted regions of the plantation, they came to the Capital looking for liberty, and many of them not knowing it when they found it. Many good friends reached forth kind hands, but the North is not warm and impulsive. For one kind word spoken, two harsh ones were uttered; there was something repelling in the atmosphere. . . . The mute appeals for help too often were answered by cold neglect. Poor dusky children of slavery, men and women of my own race—the transition from slavery to freedom was too sudden for you! . . .

One fair summer evening I was walking the streets of Washington, accompanied by a friend, when a band of music was heard in the distance.

. . . It was a festival given for the benefit of the sick and wounded soldiers in the city. This suggested an idea to me. If the white people can give festivals to raise funds for the relief of suffering soldiers, why should not the well-to-do colored people go to work to do something for the benefit of the suffering blacks? I could not rest. The thought was ever present with me, and the next Sunday I made a suggestion in the colored church, that a society of colored people be formed to labor for the benefit of the unfortunate freedmen. The idea proved popular, and in two weeks "the Contraband Relief Association" was organized, with forty working members.

. . . The next morning I told Mrs. Lincoln of my project; and she immediately headed my list with a subscription of $200. I circulated among the colored people, and got them thoroughly interested in the subject. . . . We held a mass meeting at the Colored Baptist Church, Rev. Mr. Grimes, in Boston, raised a sum of money, and organized there a branch society. . . . This branch of the main society, during the war, was able to send us over eighty large boxes of goods, contributed exclusively by the colored people of Boston. Returning to New York, we held a successful meeting at the Shiloh Church, Rev. Henry Highland Garnet, pastor. . . . Mr. Frederick Douglass contributed $200, besides lecturing for us. Other prominent colored men sent in liberal contributions. From England a large quantity of stores was received. Mrs. Lincoln made frequent contributions, as also did the President. In 1863 I was re-elected President of the Association, which office I continue to hold.

Source: Elizabeth Keckley, *Behind the Scenes, or Thirty Years a Slave, and Four Years in the White House* (New York: Oxford University Press, 1988), 111–16.

???   **How does Keckley describe the condition of the newly arrived contrabands?**

Union Victory, Slave Emancipation, and the Renewed Struggle for Equality

Despite battlefield successes in 1864, Lincoln's reelection was by no means assured. Congressional opposition to the leniency of his "10 percent plan" for the reintegration of former Confederates and Confederate regions into the Union had culminated in the passage on July 2, 1864, of the **Wade-Davis Bill**, which challenged the president's authority. This bill required that before a state government could be reestablished, a majority of white male citizens had to take an ironclad oath that they had never supported the Confederacy. After Lincoln refused to sign the bill, its sponsors published a manifesto that signaled a looming constitutional crisis between the executive and legislative branches over what came to be called Reconstruction.

During the summer of 1864, opposition to the war and to Lincoln's conduct of it grew. Large numbers of Democrats pushed to end the war immediately. Within Lincoln's own Republican Party, John C. Frémont, who had been relieved of his command in Missouri, strenuously criticized the president for his overly cautious prosecution of the war. Frémont ran against Lincoln as a Radical Republican, splitting the party until withdrawing from the race in favor of Lincoln in September 1864. To gain Democratic and border state support, Lincoln chose as his vice presidential running mate the former Democratic senator and military governor of Tennessee, Andrew Johnson. Symbolically, and in opposition to the Radicals, this faction of the Republican Party renamed itself the National Union Party. The Democratic candidate was former Union general George B. McClellan. Lincoln and Johnson won by only 400,000 votes out of 4 million cast. General William Tecumseh Sherman's victories as he marched through Georgia contributed to Lincoln's slim margin of victory.

At Lincoln's second inauguration, on March 4, 1865, the proud black regiments that marched in front of him underscored how much had changed in four years of war. In his address, Lincoln acknowledged that slavery had been the cause of the war, which he cast as God's punishment for this national sin. Yet he ended with a vision of reconciliation: "With malice toward none, with charity for all, with firmness in the right as God gives us to see the right, let us strive on to finish the work we are in, to bind up the nation's wounds, . . . to do all which may achieve and cherish a just and lasting peace among ourselves and with all nations."[34]

While Lincoln's approach to former Confederates was conciliatory, allowing for pardons and the return of property, it was already being countermanded by his generals in the field. On January 16, 1865, General Sherman issued **Special Field Order 15**, which granted confiscated and abandoned Confederate land to former slaves. Each head of household could receive up to forty acres of land along the Florida, Georgia, and South Carolina coast, and later a few freedpeople received army mules for working the land. These arrangements granted the freedpeople possessory titles to the land until Congress ruled on the validity of the titles. These arrangements also aimed to facilitate the transition of the freedpeople to independent livelihoods by providing them with farms and a stable economic basis to sustain their freedom.

The same concerns moved Congress, in March 1865, to establish the **Freedmen's Bureau**, a new government agency charged with enabling the former slaves' transition to freedom, assisting them with food, clothing, and shelter. Ultimately, the bureau also supervised and enforced labor contracts, settled disputes, helped establish schools, and set up courts to protect their civil rights.[35]

Meanwhile, the Confederacy tried to avoid the defeat that now seemed inevitable by considering a plan to emancipate and arm slaves. Debate over the plan recognized the tremendous military advantage the Union had gained by arming fugitive slaves. President Davis initially resisted the idea, but General Robert E. Lee endorsed it. On March 13, the Confederate Congress passed the measure and Davis signed it, but by then the war was nearly over. On April 9, Lee surrendered to Grant at Appomattox Court House, Virginia, and other Confederate commanders soon followed suit. Before the Confederates' final capitulation, however, President Lincoln was shot on April 14 by Confederate sympathizer John Wilkes Booth and died the next morning. For a nation ravaged by four years of war, peace and reconciliation without a strong national leader would be even more difficult than it would have been with Lincoln at the helm.

With the Confederate surrender, slaves in the Confederate states were ostensibly freed, but many remained in bondage until Union soldiers reached them to enforce the terms of the Emancipation Proclamation. In Texas, slaves did not receive the news of freedom until June 19, 1865, now commemorated as the African American holiday Juneteenth. The former slaves' responses ran the gamut, from joyous celebrations to fear of the unknown. Texan Richard Carruthers recalled, "That the day I shouted," and fellow Texan Felix Haywood remembered that "everybody went wild." Many former slaves interpreted the moment of emancipation as evidence of God's deliverance. A Virginia woman claimed, "De Lord can make Heaven out of Hell any time, I do believe."[36] But mixed emotions, uncertainty, confusion, and anxiety were common. One former slave in Mississippi said, "Dey all had diffe'nt ways o' thinkin' 'bout it. Mos'ly though dey jus' lak me, dey didn't know zackly what it meant." A former slave in South Carolina remembered that "some were sorry, some hurt, but a few were silent and glad."[37] Some preferred the comfort of the familiar, even the patterns of mutual dependency between whites and blacks that slavery bred. "I was a-farin' pretty well in de kitchen," Texan Aleck Trimble said, "I didn't tink I eber see better times dan what dem was, and I ain't." But most freedpeople agreed with the Texas woman who concluded that "in slavery I owns nothin' and never owns nothin'. In freedom I's own de home and raise de family. All dat cause worriment and in slavery I have no worriment, but I takes de freedom."[38]

Between September 1864 and February 1865, new state constitutions in Louisiana, Maryland, Missouri, and Tennessee abolished slavery. In February, Congress approved the **Thirteenth Amendment**, which abolished slavery everywhere in the Union, and sent it to the states for ratification. When the amendment was ratified on December 18, 1865, slaves in Kentucky and Delaware were finally free (Map 7.2). The amendment was the culmination of a war initially undertaken to preserve the Union, then transformed into a war to end slavery.

But freedom did not mean equality. Free African Americans living in the North had struggled for civil rights for generations, and their efforts had continued during the war. In Philadelphia, for example, Octavius Catto launched a campaign to desegregate the streetcars, which finally succeeded in 1867. Black activism took place at the state and national levels as well. In California, blacks organized a petition campaign against a state law that prohibited blacks from testifying against whites in court. Similar laws existed in Oregon, Indiana, Illinois, and Iowa. This overtly discriminatory prohibition allowed unscrupulous whites to take advantage of blacks in shady court dealings. The California petition drive succeeded in 1863, when the state legislature voided the law.

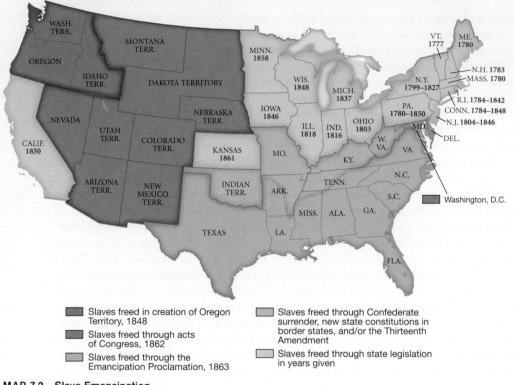

- Slaves freed in creation of Oregon Territory, 1848
- Slaves freed through acts of Congress, 1862
- Slaves freed through the Emancipation Proclamation, 1863
- Slaves freed through Confederate surrender, new state constitutions in border states, and/or the Thirteenth Amendment
- Slaves freed through state legislation in years given

MAP 7.2 Slave Emancipation

The role of the federal government in the abolition of slavery was neither simple nor straight-forward. This map illustrates key steps in the complex process of national state-sponsored emancipation as it unfolded between 1848 and 1865. In those states with gradual emancipation laws, the date spans show the year in which the initial emancipation statutes were passed followed by the year in which slavery actually ended.

In Illinois, blacks challenged an 1853 law that required African Americans settling in the state to pay a heavy fine. If they failed to do so, they were subject to arrest and forced labor for the highest bidder in order to pay the fine. Until 1863, the law was seldom enforced. That year, however, eight blacks were arrested under it, and seven were incarcerated and then further victimized as forced laborers. In response, the Repeal Association led by John Jones, the wealthiest black man in Chicago, mounted a vigorous campaign to have the law overturned. The campaign collected more than 11,000 signatures, and in February 1865 the Illinois legislature repealed the law.

At the national level, the National Convention of Colored Men, held in Syracuse, New York, in October 1864, revived the black convention movement. It had been initiated by Henry Highland Garnet, and Frederick Douglass served as president, but other black leaders, such as John S. Rock and John Mercer Langston, also made their presence felt. The 145 delegates, from both northern and southern states, endorsed emancipation, legal equality without regard to race, and black male suffrage. They also created the **National Equal Rights League** to advocate for these goals. Like the free black organizations of the antebellum era, the league emphasized moral reform and self-help, aiming "to encourage sound morality, education, temperance, frugality, industry, and promote everything that pertains to a well-ordered and dignified life."[39] To increase its influence, black leaders quickly formed state and local auxiliaries that attracted many members. The war correspondent Thomas Morris Chester, for example, was able to join the society in Harrisburg, Pennsylvania, directly upon his return from the front.

The U.S. government also took steps to reverse some inequities. The State Department ignored the nullification of black citizenship asserted in the *Dred Scott* decision (1857) by issuing passports to blacks. In 1865, Massachusetts senator Charles Sumner, a staunch ally of black citizenship rights, led the successful effort to end the forty-year prohibition against blacks carrying the U.S. mail. Sumner also paved the way for John S. Rock to become the first black man accepted to argue cases before the U.S. Supreme Court in early 1865.

Though important, these piecemeal triumphs did not dramatically alter antiblack prejudice and discrimination in the North. They did, however, solidify black commitment to the long freedom struggle that would define the next generations of African Americans, both north and south.

CONCLUSION

Emancipation and Equality

On New Year's Eve 1862, Frederick Douglass gathered with more than three thousand people at the Tremont Temple in Boston, and later at the Twelfth Baptist Church, to celebrate the Emancipation Proclamation. Speaking at Tremont, he called the gathering a "worthy celebration of the first step on the part of the nation in its departure from the thralldom of the ages."[40] As evidenced by this lukewarm statement, many abolitionists were disappointed in the proclamation for several reasons: It had been too long in coming; it pertained only to slaves in regions under Confederate control and so freed almost no one; and it seemed more a military necessity than an affirmation of moral right, aiming to harm slaveholders more than to help slaves. Yet others rejoiced that it made emancipation a war aim and held out hope for the future.[41]

At the beginning of the war, Lincoln avoided addressing slavery directly. He had to move cautiously to retain the loyalty of the border states, where slavery still existed. Although he pressured them to end slavery, none did so. Congress, however, acted to end slavery in all U.S. territories and in the District of Columbia, where Lincoln's preference for the compensation of slave owners and the colonization of slaves was written into the legislation.

Yet even as Lincoln moved cautiously, the slaves were themselves forcing the issue of emancipation. By taking advantage of wartime conditions to flee to Union lines in ever-increasing numbers, they compelled Union commanders to make decisions regarding their status. Weeks after the war began, General Benjamin Butler declared that the slaves who had fled to Fortress Monroe for protection were "contraband of war" and refused to return them to their owners. Other commanders made similar decisions. In the Sea Islands of coastal South Carolina and Georgia, Union commanders oversaw what came to be called the Port Royal Experiment, a system whereby contrabands worked the plantations abandoned by their former owners. Teachers and missionaries from the North helped them make the transition to independent livelihoods. General David Hunter organized black fighting units that were eventually recognized by the War Department. Now in Louisiana, General Butler did the same.

The Emancipation Proclamation authorized the military recruitment of black men, and eventually black units constituted one-tenth of the U.S. army. Although they gained distinction for their battlefield successes, many were assigned to work duties rather than to combat, and only when they protested did they receive the same pay as white troops. Over 68,000 African American men gave their lives for the Union victory; almost 2,800 were killed in combat. This ultimate sacrifice, the brave wartime service of black troops, and strong black civilian support proved crucial to the Union victory.

The Confederate defeat and the Thirteenth Amendment to the Constitution ended slavery forever. But as Frederick Douglass realized, emancipation was just "the first step"; it did not mean equality. Already, however, African Americans were renewing their efforts to achieve civil rights and citizenship. The fractured nation had to be reconstructed, and they were determined that it would incorporate them as equals.

CHAPTER REVIEW

Online Study Guide • bedfordstmartins.com/graywhite

Key Terms

Confederate States of America (p. 324)

contraband (p. 328)

First Confiscation Act (1861) (p. 328)

Port Royal Experiment (p. 330)

Second Confiscation Act (1862) (p. 330)

preliminary Emancipation Proclamation (1862) (p. 332)

Emancipation Proclamation (1863) (p. 333)

U.S. Colored Troops (p. 334)

New York City draft riots (1863) (p. 341)

Proclamation for Amnesty and Reconstruction (1863) (p. 342)

Wade-Davis Bill (1864) (p. 346)

Special Field Order 15 (1865) (p. 346)

Freedmen's Bureau (1865–1869) (p. 346)

Thirteenth Amendment (ratified 1865) (p. 347)

National Equal Rights League (p. 348)

Review Questions

1. Describe the attitudes and approaches of President Abraham Lincoln, Congress, and the Union military toward slavery and slave refugees in the early years of the war. How did blacks' actions shape their evolving policies and practices?

2. How did the war's aims shift from the suppression of the rebellion and the preservation of the Union to include emancipation? How might things have been different had the Confederate states responded differently to the preliminary Emancipation Proclamation?

3. How did the enlistment of black soldiers both challenge and reinforce existing racial hierarchies?

4. How did the Emancipation Proclamation promote black equality? In what ways did it fall short?

5. Describe the various contributions of African Americans to the Union war effort—both in the military and on the home front. How did their efforts further the war's aims and their own hopes of achieving freedom and citizenship rights?

For Web sites, images, and documents related to topics and places in this chapter, visit **Make History** at bedfordstmartins.com/graywhite.

Wartime Opportunities and Dilemmas

Wars often bring about huge and often unintended social changes, and for African Americans, the outbreak of the Civil War in 1861 was fraught with both opportunities and dilemmas. The central role of slavery in the crises that led to hostilities gave hope to many that the war would end that institution. Yet the uncertainty surrounding the status of slaves who sought freedom by running to Union lines, and the Union's official policy of refusing military service by African Americans through 1862, presented free blacks with dilemmas about how best to respond to, or even take charge of, events that had the potential to be revolutionary. The three documents excerpted here suggest the range of responses in Philadelphia, a city with a large and vigorous free black community.

Alfred M. Green acknowledges that black men have not been recognized as citizens, yet he urges them to support the Union cause and to respond to President Lincoln's call for volunteers. When Green spoke in April 1861, it was not yet clear that black units would not be accepted in the Union army. Later in 1861, as black volunteers were rejected in what was described by many, white and black, as "a white man's war," Green continued to urge black men to fight for the right to serve. Some black men agreed with him, but others questioned the wisdom of seeking to serve in a military that did not want them and considered them more fit for labor than for combat.

Isaiah C. Wears addresses the status of free black men in the American Republic more directly by challenging Lincoln's insinuations about black people as the cause of the war and his fondness for colonization schemes. Yet other free black men were, like Lincoln, supporters of colonization and concerned that blacks would never receive equal treatment in American society. One was Thomas Morris Chester, who in the third speech argues that if black people are to gain respect in the Republic, they must first build their own self-respect.

Alfred M. Green | Let Us . . . Take Up the Sword, 1861

Alfred M. Green, a Philadelphia schoolteacher, gave this speech to an assembly of black men in Philadelphia on April 20, 1861, just a few days after Lincoln's call for 75,000 volunteers to put down the insurrection. Green urges an enthusiastic response, pointing to the patriotism of black men who fought in previous wars, despite "past grievances." What other arguments does he give in support of black military service?

SOURCE: *Anglo African,* October 12, 1861, in Alfred M. Green, *Letters and Discussions on the Formation of Colored Regiments* (Philadelphia, 1969, orig. pub. 1862), 3–4.

The time has arrived in the history of the great Republic when we may again give evidence to the world of the bravery and patriotism of a race in whose hearts burns the love of country, of freedom, and of civil and religious toleration. It is these grand principles that enable men, however proscribed, when possessed of true patriotism, to say, "My country, right or wrong, I love thee still!"

It is true, the brave deeds of our fathers, sworn and subscribed to by the immortal Washington of the Revolution of 1776, and by Jackson and others in the War of 1812, have failed to bring us into recognition as citizens, enjoying those rights so dearly bought by those noble and patriotic sires.

documents

It is true that our injuries in many respects are great; fugitive-slave laws, Dred Scott decisions, indictments for treason, and long and dreary months of imprisonment. . . .

Our duty, brethren, is not to cavil over past grievances. Let us not be derelict to duty in the time of need. While we remember the past and regret that our present position in the country is not such as to create within us that burning zeal and enthusiasm for the field of battle which inspires other men in the full enjoyment of every civil and religious emolument, yet let us endeavor to hope for the future and improve the present auspicious moment for creating anew our claims upon the justice and honor of the Republic; and, above all, let not the honor and glory achieved by our fathers be blasted or sullied by a want of true

heroism among their sons. Let us, then, take up the sword, trusting in God, who will defend the right, remembering that these are other days than those of yore; that the world today is on the side of freedom and universal political equality.

That the war cry of the howling leaders of Secession and treason is: "Let us drive back the advance guard of civil and religious freedom; let us have more slave territory; let us build stronger the tyrant system of slavery in the great American Republic." Remember, too, that your very presence among the troops of the North would inspire your oppressed brethren of the South with zeal for the overthrow of the tyrant system, and confidence in the armies of the living God—the God of truth, justice and equality to all men.

Isaiah C. Wears | The Evil Injustice of Colonization, 1862

Lincoln's own racism and his keen awareness of the pervasiveness of white racism made him unable to envision a multiracial society. These realities shaped his views on emancipation. Until the Emancipation Proclamation of January 1863, his emancipation plans always involved promoting colonization. Meeting with black leaders on August 14, 1862, Lincoln stated, "But for your race among us, there could not be war, although many men engaged on either side do not care for you one way or the other. Nevertheless, I repeat, without the institution of slavery, and the colored race as a basis, the war could not have an existence. It is better for us to be separated."[42] The next day, at a meeting of the Statistical Association of the Colored People of Philadelphia, the group's president, **Isaiah C. Wears (1822–1900)**, challenged Lincoln's ideas. What reasons does Wears give for arguing that Lincoln is in error?

To be asked, after so many years of oppression and wrong have been inflicted in a land and by a people who have been so largely enriched by the black

man's toil, to pull up stakes in a civilized and Christian nation and to go to an uncivilized and barbarous nation, simply to gratify an unnatural wicked prejudice emanating from slavery, is unreasonable and anti-Christian in the extreme.

How unaccountably strange it seems, that wise men familiar with the history of this country, with the history of slavery, with the rebellion and its merciless outrages, yet are apparently totally ignorant of the true cause of the war—or, if not ignorant, afraid or ashamed to charge the guilt where it belongs. . . .

Says the President: The colored race are the cause of the war. So were the children of Israel the cause of the troubles of Egypt. So was Christ the cause of great commotions in Judea, in this same sense; and those identified with Him were considered of the baser sort, and really unfit for citizenship.

But surely the President did not mean to say that our race was the cause of the war, but the occasion thereof.

If black men are here in the way of white men, they did not come here of their own accord. Their presence is traceable to the white man's lust for power, love of oppression and disregard of the plain teachings of the Lord Jesus Christ, whose rule

SOURCE: Philip S. Foner and Robert James Branham, eds., *Lift Every Voice: African American Oratory, 1787–1900* (Tuscaloosa: University of Alabama Press, 1998), 375–77.

enjoins upon all men to "do unto others as they would be done by." . . .

But it is not the Negro that is the cause of the war; it is the unwillingness on the part of the American people to do the race simple justice. It is not social equality to be made the equal of the white man, to have kind masters to provide for him, or to find for him congenial homes in Africa or Central America that he needs, but he desires not to be robbed of his labor—to be deprived of his God-given rights.

The effect of this scheme of colonization, we fear, will be to arouse prejudice and to increase enmity against us, without bringing with it the remedy proposed or designed.

Repentance is more needed on the part of our oppressors than anything else. . . .

. . . And it seems reasonable to infer that the nation shall not again have peace and prosperity until prejudice, selfishness and slavery are sorely punished in the nation.

Thomas Morris Chester | Negro Self-Respect and Pride of Race, 1862

Speaking at the twenty-ninth anniversary of the Philadelphia Library Company of Colored Persons on December 9, 1862, the lawyer and educator **Thomas Morris Chester (1834–1892)** focused on a central theme in the black freedom struggle: the need for self-respect, or race pride. Chester supported colonization, leaving his family in Liberia during the Civil War. In June 1863, when invading Confederates threatened Harrisburg, Pennsylvania, he organized a company of African Americans to help defend the city, but Union commanders rejected their service. In 1864, he became a war correspondent for the *Philadelphia Press*. Based on this speech, why was Chester proud of his race, and what were his recommendations for achieving full rights and privileges for blacks?

While other speakers have very fully entertained you upon the troubled state of the country, and pointed out the cheering beacons which illuminate the political pathway of the Afro-American's future, I propose to make a few remarks upon SELF-RESPECT AND PRIDE OF RACE, in which I shall exhort the Library Company to contribute to the development of these virtues. . . .

When we consider that our fathers were dragged from their sunny homes and brutalized by an American institution, which exceeds in its unblushing outrages the combined villainies of christendom, and now look at their descendants who have advanced in intelligence and christianity, despite the malicious efforts of our unscrupulous foes, there is not a man with one drop of Negro blood in his veins but has cause to be proud of the superiority which the race has displayed under the most humiliating and disheartening circumstances. (Loud applause.) In direct opposition to the wishes and prejudices of our oppressors, to public sentiment and the laws of the land, we have come up from the house of bondage where every effort was made to brutalize and corrupt us; and as we advanced along the track of time, uncheered by the quickening beacons of good schools and churches we were nerved on by nothing else under Heaven but the transcendent superiority of our nature. (Applause.) The more they imposed heavy burdens upon us, the more we have increased and prospered. The greater the efforts to prevent the diffusion of knowledge, the more gratifying has been our intelligent growth. (Applause.) The deeper the curses for our degradation, the brighter have been the blessings for our elevation. (Applause.) The stronger the resolutions to perpetuate our servitude, the more transparent has been the power of God to break the yoke of the oppressed.—(Applause.) The more extensive the villainies to crush our impulses, the higher have sprung our aspirations of manhood.—(Applause.)

SOURCE: Richard Newman, Patrick Rael, and Phillip Lapsansky, eds., *Pamphlets of Protest: An Anthology of Early African American Protest Literature, 1790–1860* (New York: Routledge, 2001), 305–10.

documents

. . . There is one virtue, however, of which as a people we are somewhat deficient in this country, owing to the industrious efforts of the advocates of slavery to produce so unfortunate a result. It cannot be denied that we need a higher cultivation of self-respect and pride of race. Public sentiment and legislation have been sufficiently ungodly to somewhat distract the councils of Afro-Americans—to suppress every manly attribute, and cast doubts upon the superiority of our people. . . .

. . . But if you want to arouse our latent manhood, and see a grand development of moral courage in opposition to public sentiment and unjust laws—a love of race that is not surpassed by any people, and our united efforts supporting the principles of liberty,—let it be announced that a fugitive slave is arrested by the revolting vampires who exist by sucking our blood, and you will witness a magnificent gathering together of the Afro-Americans in their physical strength. (Loud applause.) . . .

. . . I do not counsel any violation of law, or breach of good order, but I beseech you to organize among all classes a more effective union upon every question which involves your rights, your privileges, or your happiness. I would not persuade you to like the white race less, but to love the black race more.—(Applause.) Remove as far as practicable, from all observation and association, every influence which tends to weaken your self-respect. . . . Tear down the large paintings in which only white faces are represented, and beautify your walls with scenes and landscapes connected with our history,

which shall win our praise and inspire our admiration.° . . .

The great and good men and women, with beautiful associated scenes in our history, looking down from the walls, will awaken a high degree of self-respect and an exalted pride of race. . . .

I am aware that your newspapers . . . express your sentiments on all the great questions under discussion, and that should be enough to commend them to your support. (Applause.) In subscribing for one, you not only encourage a sentinel guarding your liberties, but you manifest a laudable desire to contribute to the success of your own literature. (Applause.) . . .

In your libraries let the most conspicuous shelf be honored with the works of black authors, or the records which point to our worth and superiority. Place into the hands of the youths only those works which transmit the lives and public services of our eminent men, their heroic daring and unbending integrity. . . . Follow only the christianity of the Bible which diffuses good will to man, rally only in support of that policy which recognizes God as our Father and as all mankind as brethren, and study only that literature which enriches and ennobles the mind. (Applause.)

° Here Chester suggests that, among others, pictures of Frederick Douglass, Henry Highland Garnet, John Rock, Martin Delany, Charles Remond, Octavius Catto, Sarah [Mapps] Douglass, Crispus Attucks, Benjamin Banneker, Nat Turner, Joseph Cinque, and Robert Smalls also be displayed to increase self-respect and pride of race.

Questions for Analysis

1. In 1861 and 1862, what choices did the Civil War offer free black men in the North? Why did the speakers represented here take the positions they did?

2. From your reading of the documents, on what goals did all three men agree?

3. How does each speaker call on religious belief or use religious language to support his argument?

4. All three speakers addressed Philadelphia audiences. What other issues might have been addressed by free blacks in Baltimore or New Orleans?

5. Imagine how each speaker might have reacted when the war ended in 1865. Did he think his goals had been achieved or his views vindicated? Why or why not? Which arguments remain relevant today?

Black Women at Work during the War

While blacks debated the opportunities and dilemmas of the war, black women often responded to its uncertainties and demands by assuming new and expanded roles. In the South, as growing numbers of black men, particularly slaves and contrabands, joined the military and the war effort, black women, particularly slaves and contrabands, were called on to do more to keep households and plantations running and to keep their families together. Some used new responsibilities to gain greater control over their lives. Slave women who fled to Union lines took on new roles, too, working in a variety of ways to aid the Union cause. Similarly, free black women in the North strongly supported the war effort on the home front.

In the following documents, letters from Lucy Skipwith reveal the tasks and concerns of a literate slave woman on an Alabama plantation as she assumes new responsibilities and makes the transition to freedom. Susie King Taylor, a slave and then a contraband, served a black military unit in the Sea Islands as a teacher and nurse. Also working among contrabands in South Carolina was the famed underground railroad conductor Harriet Tubman, who left her home in New York to labor for the Union. Like many black women during the Civil War, these women took on new, expanded, and empowering roles even as they continued to perform the traditional women's role of serving the needs of others.

Lucy Skipwith | Letters to Her Master, 1861–1865

During the Civil War, **Lucy Skipwith (1830—?)** remained a privileged house slave on John H. Cocke's Hopewell Plantation near Greensboro, Alabama. She was literate, deeply religious, and conscientious, and Cocke entrusted her with the running of his household while he resided on his Virginia plantation. From 1854 to 1865, Skipwith wrote regularly to Cocke, reporting on the crops and gardens, the health of those on the plantation, local gossip, and the progress of her Sunday school, where she taught young slaves to read and write and to obey Christian teachings. Her letters offer insights into the everyday lives and concerns of plantation slaves. After the war, Skipwith disappears from the historical record. In the letters excerpted here—one from each year of the war—look for evidence of her concerns and the effect of the war on Hopewell Plantation.

Hopewell August the 5th 1861

my Dear Master

I received your letter two weeks ago, and was very glad to hear from you, and as Mr Beng Borden° expects to start to virginia in a few days I expects to send my letter by him.

we are all well at this time, and have had but little sickness this summer. I have heard of but very little sickness in the Neighborhood. I have nothing new to write about [.] every thing is going on as usual. the people are very busy at this time pulling Fodder. they commenced three days ago. we have had a long spell of rainny weather, but for the last week it has been quite fair. last night we had a good shower. the garden is quite grassy this rainny weather. we still have a plenty of vegatables to eat. we have more Tomattoes than we can destroy. . . . Etter° has a very

° The Bordens, Meltons, and Keys were white planters in the neighborhood.
° Etter (Isaetta Skipwith; d. 1863) was Lucy's sister, responsible for tending the garden. When Hopewell's overseer, Richard Powell, complained of her laziness and threatened to demote her to field hand, Lucy intervened and made a special effort to praise her performance when writing to John Cocke.

SOURCE: Randall M. Miller, ed., "Dear Master": Letters of a Slave Family (Ithaca and London: Cornell University Press, 1978), 237–38, 242–43, 256–57, 260–61, 262–63.

nice crop of onions. they are all dried and I think that they will keep. the peas that you had planted in the garden has turnd out very well, boath kind of them. we have enough of Josephs Corn for seed another year. we are saveing sunflower seed and other different kind of seed. . . . We have Preaching at the Church regularly three times a month. we also have family prayers regularly every morning. We have not heard from Mr Powell° since he went home from here the first of July, but we expect him here this week. I will do what I can at Clothing the people   my young Turkeys are growing very fast. . . . I often think of you, and fear sometimes that we shall never meet again, but should we fail to meet again on earth, I hope that we shall meet in heaven where parting shall be no more   remember me to master Charles, and to Berthier,° and to all of my relations, and believe me as ever your servant

Lucy Skipwith

Hopewell mar. 31 1862

Dear master

I would have writen to you before this, but as Smith° wrote to you after receiveing your letter I thought that I would wait untel the present time. Smith left us the 24th inst [the present month] for the War. he went from here to Mobile. we have hea[r]d nothing from him since. mr Powell has sent another young man down to take his place. his name is Sterling N. Hardy,° nephew of mrs Powell. he seem to be a very nice young man. he intend going to the College as Smith did, but not untell mr P comes down the 5th of april   Cain° is still planting corn   he commenced up at Meltons this morning. the whole of Meltons is to be put in corn. they have planted the Rye field and Evans field in corn. The weather is now beautiful for Farming and gardening. Etter is geting along very well gardening   she has very nice plants in the Hot Beds   she has Peas and other vegatables up.

the people are all well at New Hope. they are planting corn down there. mr Powell intend planting but very little Cotton. none of the people [abroad] here intend planting much   they intend planting the house field and the Lawn in cotton.

I surpose that mr Powell has written to you about Robt. at New Hope stealing Capt. Cockes° Hogs. it was a very bad act in him to do so, but mr P has setled with him for it. . . .

. . . the people all Joines me in love to you. your servant

Lucy Skipwith

Hopewell oct 21st 1863

my dear master

I wrote to you the last of September which letter I hope you have received. We have heard nothing from you for nearly too months. I hope that you are not sick. The health of the people is better than when I wrote last. . . . Cain is very busy geathering his corn   he will finish it this week. the Pea field is all that he has to geather. there is two cribs filled with corn & they are filling the third one.

Cain has picked a great many dry Peas, & there is a great many more to pick. he has not had much time to pick cotton, but he can pick it out before Christmas. the cotton patch is very white   there is beautiful cotton in the Lawn. it has been lately picked over. . . . mr Powell went away from here the 8th inst. he wrote to you from here & was disapointed at not receiveing a letter from you. he was very well. mr Smith Powell left here the 11th inst to Joine his company up at Chattanooga. his wound was a great deal better. he is looking very thin but says that he is willing to tuff it out untell the War ends. mr Borden has been very unwell for a week or two, but is better   mr Joe Borden is still at home in bad health. Capt John Cocke has got home after an absence of two months   I heard that the yankeys had him. he is looking very bad. . . .

° Richard Powell was John Cocke's overseer for all his properties in Alabama, including Hopewell and New Hope. He also had his own plantation near Columbus, Mississippi.

° Master Charles, on the Virginia plantation, is probably John Cocke's son. Berthier seems to be Lucy's nephew.

° Smith Powell was the young nephew of Richard Powell.

° Sterling Hardy quit Cocke's employ within a year. Richard Powell had increasing difficulty finding a white person to live at Cocke's plantations, but a white presence was required, and Cocke had earlier been fined $100 for not complying with that requirement.

° Cain Morse was a slave and foreman on Hopewell Plantation. He was literate and had previously been a field hand.

° Captain John Cocke, the absentee master and owner of New Hope.

I Am geting along very well Clotheing the people & manage to keep them from suffering. I make
cloth for both places. we have 8 men still workeing
in Mobile.° the people all desire to be rememberd to
you and says that they hope to see you again in Ala.
I must now bring my letter to a close hopeing soon
to hear from you   your servt

L Skipwith

March 28th 1864

dear master

I wrote to you a week ago which letter I hope
you have received. my business now is this. mr
Powell asked my consent to buy Maria° from you, &
I haveing so much respect for him hated to tell him
my mind upon the subject, but later [told] him that
he could perpose the thing to you & see what you
say about it.

I do not wish Maria sold to him, for she is a
child after my own heart & I hate to part from her.
if you think propper to hire her to him I will try to
make up my mind to that, but it goes hard with me
to think of parting with her. I would like to see him
acomadated but it seems that nothing will do for
him but Maria   if he must have her I would rather
be hired to him & go myself rather than be parted
from her.

my other poor child [Betsey] came very near
being ruined while liveing away from me. there is
nothing like a Mothers watchful eye over a child. I
hope that you will look into the matter & do what
you think best   let me hear from you on the subject   your servant

Lucy Skipwith

° *men still workeing in Mobile:* Lucy is referring to slaves from
Hopewell and New Hope who had been requisitioned to build
fortifications for the Confederate army in Mobile, Alabama. In a
letter of March 15, 1864, she reports the death of three of them.

° Maria (b. 1847?) was Lucy's daughter, later a house servant. In
the last paragraph of this letter, Lucy refers to her other daughter,
Betsey, who had been hired out to the Bordens and was caught
stealing. Lucy blamed the Bordens, who were not instructing
Betsey in Christian principles. Captain Cocke brought Betsey
back to Hopewell, where she was purchased by Julia Dorsey of
Mobile, a distant relative of Cocke who lived at Hopewell after
1863. She kept Betsey weaving and tending to household chores.
Betsey bore two children described as white. Both of Lucy's
daughters were fathered by white men.

Hopewell Dec 7th 1865

my dear Master

I Received your letter a few days ago dated oct
14th it being nearly two months on the way.

I was truly glad to see that you were still alive &
not yet gone the way of all the Earth & that you were
able to write to me once more. I was sorry that I had
to part from Armistead° but I have lived a life of
trouble with him, & a white man has ever had to
Judge between us, & now to be turned loose from
under a master, I know that I could not live with him
in no peace, therefore I left him for I wish to live a
life of peace & die a death of both Joy and peace & if
you have any hard feelings against me on the subject, I hope that you will forgive me for Jesus sake.

I Have a great desire to come to Va to see you & my
relations there & I hope that I maybe able some day to
do so. I have looked over my mind in regard to going to
Liberia but I cannot get my consent to go there, but I
thank you for your advice.° none of our people are willing to go. I am still carrying on my School on the plantation & the Children are learning very fast. I had a
notion of going up to Columbus another year to be
with my mother & Father, but as they have mooved
down here to mr Keys, I have given the notion out. I do
not know what Father done in Columbus but I have
not seen nor heard nothing of his drinking down here.°
I have been thinking of puting up a large School next
year as I can do more at that than I can at any thing elce,
& I can get more children than I can teach, but I do not
know yet whither I will be at liberty to do so or not. . . .

. . . mr Joseph Borden is not here as Mr Powell
have agreed to stay with us another year. our Turnip
patch failed this year. we have a small patch in the
Garden. our Crop of Potatoes were very small also.
Some of every bodys black people in this Neighbour-
hood have left their homes but us. we are all here so
far but I cannot tell how it will be another year.

I will now bring my letter to a Close hopeing soon
to hear from you again   I am as ever your Servant

Lucy Skipwith

° Armistead Hewitt, the headman at New Hope Plantation, was
Lucy's husband.

° *your advice:* In 1863, Cocke offered to free Lucy, provided that she and
Maria emigrate to Liberia. In case of his death, Cocke directed Mrs.
Dorsey to receive them if they chose to remain in America.

° *down here:* Lucy's parents had formerly been slaves on Powell's
plantation near Columbus, Mississippi.

documents

Susie King Taylor | Reminiscences of My Life in Camp, 1902

Susie King Taylor (1848–1912) was a Georgia slave who in 1862 ran away with her cousins and uncles to a contraband camp in the Sea Islands. Mature, well-spoken, and literate, she organized a school for contrabands. After she married Edward King, a black noncommissioned officer in the Thirty-Third U.S. Colored Troops, she was attached to the unit as a laundress. She also taught and nursed the soldiers. The following excerpt is from Taylor's memoir, published in 1902, which is the only published account of its kind. What did Taylor do for the soldiers and why?

When we arrived in Beaufort, Captain Trowbridge and the men he had enlisted went to camp at Old Fort, which they named "Camp Saxton." I was enrolled as laundress.

The first suits worn by the boys were red coats and pants, which they disliked very much, for, they said, "The rebels see us, miles away."

The first colored troops did not receive any pay for eighteen months, and the men had to depend wholly on what they received from the commissary, established by General Saxton. A great many of these men had large families, and as they had no money to give them, their wives were obliged to support themselves and children by washing for the officers of the gunboats and the soldiers, and making cakes and pies which they sold to the boys in camp. Finally, in 1863, the government decided to give them half pay, but the men would not accept this. They wanted "full pay" or nothing. They preferred rather to give their services to the state, which they did until 1864, when the government granted them full pay, with all the back pay due. . . .

On the first of January, 1863, we held services for the purpose of listening to the reading of President Lincoln's proclamation by Dr. W. H. Brisbane,

and the presentation of two beautiful stands of colors, one from a lady in Connecticut, and the other from Rev. Mr. Cheever. The presentation speech was made by Chaplain French. It was a glorious day for us all, and we enjoyed every minute of it, and as a fitting close and the crowning event of this occasion we had a grand barbecue. A number of oxen were roasted whole, and we had a fine feast. Although not served as tastily or correctly as it would have been at home, yet it was enjoyed with keen appetites and relish. The soldiers had a good time. They sang or shouted "Hurrah!" all through the camp, and seemed overflowing with fun and frolic until taps were sounded, when many, no doubt, dreamt of this memorable day. . . .

I taught a great many of the comrades in Company E to read and write, when they were off duty. Nearly all were anxious to learn. My husband taught some also when it was convenient for him. I was very happy to know my efforts were successful in camp, and also felt grateful for the appreciation of my services. I gave my services willingly for four years and three months without receiving a dollar. I was glad, however, to be allowed to go with the regiment, to care for the sick and afflicted comrades. . . .

I learned to handle a musket very well while in the regiment, and could shoot straight and often hit the target. I assisted in cleaning the guns and used to fire them off, to see if the cartridges were dry, before cleaning and reloading, each day. I thought this great fun. I was also able to take a gun all apart, and put it together again. . . .

Fort Wagner being only a mile from our camp, I went there two or three times a week, and would go up on the ramparts to watch the gunners send their shells into Charleston (which they did every fifteen minutes), and had a full view of the city from that point. Outside of the fort were many skulls lying about; I have often moved them one side out of the path. The comrades and I would have quite a debate as to which side the men fought on. Some thought they were the skulls of our boys; others thought they were the enemy's; but as there was no definite way to know, it was

Source: Susie King Taylor, *Reminiscences of My Life in Camp: An African American Woman's Civil War Memoir*, ed. Catherine Clinton (Athens: University of Georgia Press, 2006), 15–16, 18, 21, 26, 31–32, 34–35.

documents

never decided which could lay claim to them. They were a gruesome sight, those fleshless heads and grinning jaws, but by this time I had become accustomed to worse things and did not feel as I might have earlier in my camp life.

It seems strange how our aversion to seeing suffering is overcome in war,—how we are able to see the most sickening sights, such as men with their limbs blown off and mangled by the deadly shells, without a shudder; and instead of turning away, how we hurry to assist in alleviating their pain, bind up their wounds, and press the cool water to their parched lips, with feelings only of sympathy and pity. . . .

Finally orders were received for the boys to prepare to take Fort Gregg. . . . I helped as many as I could to pack haversacks and cartridge boxes. . . .

About four o'clock, July 2, the charge was made. The firing could be plainly heard in camp. I hastened down to the landing and remained there until eight o'clock that morning. When the wounded arrived, or rather began to arrive, the first one brought in was Samuel Anderson of our company. He was badly wounded. Then others of our boys, some with their legs off, arm gone, foot off,

and wounds of all kinds imaginable. They had to wade through creeks and marshes, as they were discovered by the enemy and shelled very badly. A number of the men were lost, some got fastened in the mud and had to cut off the legs of their pants, to free themselves. . . .

My work now began. I gave my assistance to try to alleviate their sufferings. I asked the doctor at the hospital what I could get for them to eat. They wanted soup, but that I could not get; but I had a few cans of condensed milk and some turtle eggs, so I thought I would try to make some custard. I had doubts as to my success, for cooking with turtle eggs was something new to me, but the adage has it, "Nothing ventured, nothing done," so I made a venture and the result was a very delicious custard. This I carried to the men, who enjoyed it very much. My services were given at all times for the comfort of these men. I was on hand to assist whenever needed. I was enrolled as company laundress, but I did very little of it, because I was always busy doing other things through camp, and was employed all the time doing something for the officers and comrades.

Sarah H. Bradford | Harriet Tubman: Ready for Service to the Union Cause, 1886

After the Civil War, supporters and friends of Harriet Tubman (c. 1820–1913) encouraged her to record her extraordinary life story for both posterity and financial support. **Sarah H. Bradford (1818–1912)**, an admirer and friend, wrote the account authorized by Tubman and based on interviews with Tubman herself, anecdotes, documents, letters, and newspaper articles. Tubman—slave and fugitive; conductor on the underground railroad; Union scout, spy, cook, and nurse; lecturer for woman suffrage; and caretaker and benefactor of indigent African Americans all her life—was a heroine in her own time and remains an iconic figure in the black

freedom struggle. Bradford's account, however, has been criticized as exaggerated. As you read the following excerpt, try to detect the real person behind Bradford's rhetoric and her transcription of Tubman's speech.

In the early days of the war, Governor Andrew of Massachusetts, knowing well the brave and sagacious character of Harriet, sent for her, and asked her if she could go at a moment's notice, to act as spy and scout for our armies, and, if need be, to act as hospital nurse, in short, to be ready to give any required service to the Union cause. . . .

. . . I received many letters . . . all testifying to her faithfulness and bravery, and her untiring zeal for the

SOURCE: Sarah H. Bradford, *Harriet Tubman: The Moses of Her People* (New York: printed for author by G. R. Lockwood, 1886), 93–95, 97–100.

welfare of our soldiers, black and white. She was often under fire from both armies; she led our forces through the jungle and the swamp, guided by an unseen hand. She gained the confidence of the slaves by her cheery words, and songs, and sacred hymns, and obtained from them much valuable information. She nursed our soldiers in the hospitals, and knew how, when they were dying by numbers of some malignant disease, with cunning skill to extract from roots and herbs, which grew near the source of the disease, the healing draught, which allayed the fever and restored numbers to health. . . .

. . . At this time her manner of life, as related by herself, was this:

"Well, missus, I'd go to de hospital, I would, early eb'ry mornin'. I'd get a big chunk of ice, I would, and put it in a basin, and fill it with water; den I'd take a sponge and begin. Fust man I'd come to, I'd thrash away de flies, and dey'd rise, dey would, like bees roun' a hive. Den I'd begin to bathe der wounds, an' by de time I'd bathed off three or four, de fire and heat would have melted de ice and made de water warm, an' it would be as red as clar blood. Den I'd go an' git more ice, I would, an' by de time I got to de nex' ones, de flies would be roun' de fust ones black an' thick as eber." In this way she worked, day after day, till late at night; then she went home to her little cabin, and made about fifty pies, a great quantity of ginger-bread, and two casks of root beer. These she would hire some contraband to sell for her through the camps, and thus she would provide her support for another day; for this woman never received pay or pension, and never drew for herself but twenty days' rations during the four years of her labors. At one time she was called away from Hilton Head, by one of our officers, to come to Fernandina [a town on Florida's northeast Amelia Island], where the men were "dying off like sheep," from dysentery. Harriet had acquired quite a reputation for her skill in curing this disease, by a medicine which she prepared from roots which grew near the waters which gave the disease. Here she found thousands of sick soldiers and contrabands, and immediately gave up her time and attention to them. At another time, we find her nursing those who were down by hundreds with small-pox and malignant fevers. She had never

had these diseases, but she seems to have no more fear of death in one form than another. "De Lord would take keer of her till her time came, an' den she was ready to go."

When our armies and gun-boats first appeared in any part of the South, many of the poor negroes were as much afraid of "de Yankee Buckra" [northern white soldiers and civilians] as of their own masters. It was almost impossible to win their confidence, or to get information from them. But to Harriet they would tell anything; and so it became quite important that she should accompany expeditions going up the rivers, or into unexplored parts of the country, to control and get information from those whom they took with them as guides.

General Hunter asked her at one time if she would go with several gun-boats up the Combahee River, the object of the expedition being to take up the torpedoes placed by the rebels in the river, to destroy railroads and bridges, and to cut off supplies from the rebel troops. . . . Harriet, with several men under her, . . . accompanied the expedition. Harriet describes in the most graphic manner the appearance of the plantations as they passed up the river; the frightened negroes leaving their work and taking to the woods, at sight of the gun-boats; then coming to peer out like startled deer, and scudding away like the wind at the sound of the steam-whistle. "Well," said one old negro, "Mas'r said de Yankees had horns and tails, but I nebber beliebed it till now." But the word was passed along by the mysterious telegraphic communication existing among these simple people, that these were "Lincoln's gun-boats come to set them free." In vain, then, the drivers used their whips in their efforts to hurry the poor creatures back to their quarters; they all turned and ran for the gun-boats. They came down every road, across every field, just as they had left their work and their cabins; women with children clinging around their necks, hanging to their dresses, running behind, all making at full speed for "Lincoln's gun-boats." Eight hundred poor wretches at one time crowded the banks, with their hands extended toward their deliverers, and they were all taken off upon the gun-boats, and carried down to Beaufort.

Questions for Analysis

1. Though hardly typical, what do Lucy Skipwith's letters suggest about the wartime labor, responsibilities, and authority of slave men and women in the Confederacy?

2. How did Skipwith look out for her own interests and those of her family?

3. What do Susie King Taylor's and Harriet Tubman's accounts reveal about the wartime labor of black women for the Union cause? What type of work did these women do? How are such tasks handled in the U.S. army today?

4. What do Taylor's and Tubman's accounts reveal about contraband camps and black military units in the South?

5. Taken together, what do these three documents indicate about social change during the Civil War?

The Moment and Meaning of Emancipation

The moment of emancipation lived long in African American memory. For contrabands, whose status was uncertain after they fled to Union lines, the Emancipation Proclamation of January 1, 1863, evoked both solemn and joyous celebrations. For slaves in the Confederate and border states, the news of final freedom came at various times and in various ways. Yet even seventy years later, when interviewed by workers in the Federal Writers' Project (1936–1938), many former slaves remembered exactly where they were when they learned they were free, what they thought, how they felt, and what they did. The moment of emancipation was not the same as its meaning, however. What freedom actually meant was much more complicated, emerging only as it was lived in the coming months and years. The images in this essay offer insights into both the moment and the meaning of emancipation, from a variety of perspectives.

Photography, invented in Europe in the 1830s and introduced in the United States in the 1840s, was prevalent enough by the Civil War to figure prominently in how people today perceive the conflict. Studio photographs of soldiers in uniform reveal their youth and sometimes their exuberance. Battlefield photographs of the dead convey war's terrible loss and sacrifice. For contemporaries, the former were cherished for preserving images of loved ones, and the latter brought home the horrors of war, never before seen by those who did not experience battle firsthand.

Photographs seem to document how a person actually looked or what was actually happening at the time the photograph was taken. It is important to remember, however, that they show only what the photographer chose to capture and, for studio photographs, how the subject chose to present himself or herself. Instead of being seen as documenting historical truth, photographs, like other art forms, must be understood as being selective and partial. As you analyze the following images, keep the creator of each in mind. Consider his or her purpose and historical context. All but one of the creators of these images were white; none was ever enslaved. Ask yourself what difference those things make. Whose memory of the moment and meaning of emancipation is being preserved in these images?

Arguably the most significant single moment of freedom in black memory—though it actually affected only a small number of slaves—was New Year's Day 1863, when the Emancipation Proclamation went into effect. Slaves and contrabands aware of the proclamation, as well as free blacks, and abolitionists—wherever they were in the United States and the Confederate States of America—grappled with the importance of this moment. In New England, the white painter William Tolman Carlton (1816–1888) envisioned how slaves or contrabands might have looked as they waited for midnight, when the new year would begin and slaves (at least in theory) would be freed (Figure 7.1). Not much is known about Carlton other than that he had a drawing school in Boston, where many of his students and patrons were

FIGURE 7.1
Watch Meeting—Dec. 31st—Waiting for the Hour, 1863
The Hour of Emancipation, *oil on canvas, 1863, by William Tolman Carlton (1816–1888). Private Collection/Photo © Christie's Images/The Bridgeman Art Library International.*

abolitionists. He was certainly aware of the traditional watch night services held in Christian churches on New Year's Eve that welcomed in the new year with prayers, worship, and thanksgiving.[43]

In this painting, titled *Watch Meeting—Dec. 31st—Waiting for the Hour* (also called *The Hour of Emancipation*), Carlton depicts a watch night congregation of slaves or contrabands located in a barn or outbuilding. About a dozen figures are gathered around a huge pocket watch illuminated by a flaring torch; the watch says five minutes to twelve. Notice the postures of those who have

WATCH MEETING DEC.31.1862

WAITING FOR THE HOUR.

Ent'd according to Act of Congress, A. D. 1863, by W. T. Carlton, in the Clerk's Office of the District Court of the District of Mass.

FIGURE 7.2
Watch Meeting Postcard, 1863 *Library of Congress, LC-USZCN4-153.*

gathered. What are they doing? What emotions do their expressions convey? There is one white woman present. Who is she, and why did the painter place her in the scene? The painting is full of symbols. What book is the central figure holding? What document is nailed to the wall? How do you interpret the figure of the torch holder with the coffle iron around his neck? After locating the cross in the upper left rafters, find a flag and a banjo. What do these objects symbolize? Although we can use this painting to understand the moment and meaning of emancipation as a New England abolitionist envisioned it,[44] how might the real moment for slaves and contrabands have been different?

Carlton's patrons purchased this painting, and William Lloyd Garrison arranged to have it delivered it to President Lincoln, who hung it in the White House. The image was widely circulated and popularized as a small postcard (Figure 7.2). This image is not quite identical to Carlton's painting. What differences can you detect? Where would it have circulated? What impact do you think it would have had on those who viewed it?

The influence of Carlton's image can also be seen in a steel engraving called *Reading the Emancipation Proclamation* (Figure 7.3), created by

FIGURE 7.3
Reading the Emancipation Proclamation, 1864   *The New York Public Library/Art Resource, NY.*

H. W. Herrick, a book illustrator, and published in Hartford, Connecticut, in 1864. Here the setting seems to be a home—note the fireplace and cradle—and the focus of attention is not a watch, but a Union soldier, who is reading aloud the Emancipation Proclamation. As the Union army advanced in the South, soldiers carried news of emancipation with them. Is this soldier black or white? What are the similarities and differences between this image and Figure 7.1?

In contrast to this intimate scene, two images that appeared in *Harper's Weekly,* a popular illustrated magazine, show Union soldiers bringing the news of freedom to large groups of slaves in outdoor settings. In *Colored Troops under General Wild, Liberating Slaves in North Carolina* (Figure 7.4), the artist shows the liberated slaves standing and rejoicing. One soldier is shaking the hand of a newly freed slave. In another image, *Arrival of a Federal Column at a Planter's House in Dixie* (Figure 7.5), white soldiers bring the

COLORED TROOPS, UNDER GENERAL WILD, LIBERATING SLAVES IN NORTH CAROLINA.

FIGURE 7.4
Colored Troops under General Wild, Liberating Slaves in North Carolina, 1864

ARRIVAL OF A FEDERAL COLUMN AT A PLANTER'S HOUSE IN DIXIE.—[See Page 215.]

FIGURE 7.5
Arrival of a Federal Column at a Planter's House in Dixie, 1863

FIGURE 7.6
Emancipated Slaves, 1863 *Library of Congress, LC-DIG-pga-03898.*

news to distressed plantation women and rejoicing slaves. Two slaves bow to a soldier. In the background, a soldier reaches to grasp the hand of a slave woman. Interpret the messages of these two images and the interactions they portray.

Figure 7.5 was the work of Thomas Nast (1840–1902), the era's most influential graphic artist and political cartoonist, who often exposed corruption to argue for political and moral reform. In *Emancipated Slaves* (Figure 7.6), a two-page spread in *Harper's Weekly* appearing three weeks after the Emancipation Proclamation, Nast presents images that suggest the meaning of emancipation. Why do you think the central portrait depicts a domestic scene? Look at the scenes that surround it. Images of slavery are on the left, and images of what life might be like in freedom are on the right. What aspects of slavery, and what benefits of freedom, did Nast choose to show the viewer?

Like Nast, many northerners believed that freedom would mean transformation. Two popular cartes de visite from 1864 are actually

AS WE FOUND THEM.

These children were owned by Thomas White, of Mathews Co., Va., until Feb. 20th, when Capt. Riley, 6th U. S. C. I., took them and gave them to the Society of Friends to educate at the Orphan's Shelter, Philadelphia.

Profits from sale, for the benefit of the children.

AS THEY ARE NOW.

The Mother of these children was beaten, branded and sold at auction because she was kind to Union Soldiers. As she left for Richmond, Va., Feb. 13th, 1864, bound down in a cart, she prayed "O! God send the Yankees to take my children away."

Profits from sale, for the benefit of the children.

FIGURE 7.7
Slave Children, "As We Found Them" and "As They Are Now," 1864 *Photos by Peregrine F. Cooper/George Eastman House/Getty Images.*

"before" and "after" portraits of two slave children from Mathews County, Virginia (Figure 7.7). The "before" portrait captured them in slavery, as they looked when liberated from their master by Union troops. The "after" portrait captured the difference emancipation made in their appearance. For being kind to Union soldiers, their mother had previously been separated from her children, brutalized, and taken to Richmond to be sold. The liberated children were sent to the Society of Friends in Philadelphia to be educated at the Friends' Orphan's Shelter. The cards were sold to help support the children.

Figure 7.8 shows Private Hubbard Pryor before and after enlisting in the U.S. Colored Troops. Compare the two images, especially taking note of Pryor's dress, facial expression, and posture in each photo. Keep in mind that

v i s u a l   s o u r c e s

FIGURE 7.8
Private Hubbard Pryor, before and after Enlisting in the U.S. Colored Troops, 1864   *Courtesy of the National Archives,*
Records of the Adjutant General's Office, c. 1775–c. 1928, ARC identifiers #849127 and #849136.

it was not yet a convention to smile for the camera. The paired portraits here
and in Figure 7.7 were consciously staged. Who might have staged them, and
what was their purpose? What effect might they have had on those who
viewed them?

At the very end of the war—after the Confederates withdrew from
Richmond but before they surrendered—Abraham Lincoln visited Richmond, taking his twelve-year-old son, Tad, with him. As he walked the streets
of the former Confederate capital, he was surrounded by African Americans,
who shouted "Glory! Glory!" "Bless the Lord!," and "The great Messiah!"
Said one onlooker, "I knowed him as soon as I seed him. He's been in my
heart four long years. Come to free his children from bondage." Overwhelmed, Lincoln said to a black man who had knelt before him, "Don't
kneel to me. That is not right. You must kneel to God only, and thank Him
for the liberty you will enjoy hereafter."[45] The scene was reported by war

FIGURE 7.9
President Lincoln Riding through Richmond, April 4, amid the Enthusiastic Cheers of the Inhabitants, 1865
Library of Congress, LC-USZ62-6931.

correspondents and envisioned by an artist in *President Lincoln Riding through Richmond, April 4, amid the Enthusiastic Cheers of the Inhabitants* (Figure 7.9). What similarities in representations of blacks and whites do you see in this image and the previous images?

Three years later, when Edmonia Lewis (c. 1843–after 1911) commemorated emancipation in a sculpture, she chose as her title *Forever Free*, words from the Emancipation Proclamation (Figure 7.10). The daughter of an African American father and a Chippewa–African American mother, Lewis was born free in New York. The subjects of her work reflect her multiracial heritage. Her style, however, is classical. After studying at Oberlin College, she moved to Rome, where she spent most of her career. Study the postures, expressions, and

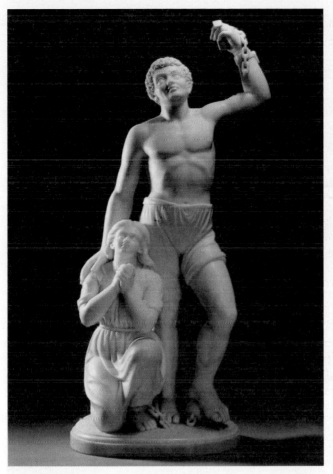

FIGURE 7.10
Forever Free, 1867

dress of the two figures in *Forever Free*. How are they similar to those in other images of emancipation? How are they different? What do they suggest about the moment and meaning of emancipation?

Another sculpture, titled *Emancipation* but also known as *Freedmen's Memorial* (Figure 7.11), stands in Lincoln Park on Capitol Hill in Washington, D.C. It was created by Thomas Ball (1819–1911), a white American artist best known for his monumental sculptures of American heroes. It was erected with contributions from African Americans, beginning with $5 entrusted to a former master by a former slave to build a monument to the martyred president.[46] Significantly, it portrays Lincoln as "the Great Emancipator," holding out his hand over a kneeling, nearly naked freedman. Is Lincoln offering the freedman a blessing? Is he urging him to rise?

FIGURE 7.11

Freedmen's Memorial, 1876   *The George F. Landegger Collection of District of Columbia Photographs in Carol M. Highsmith's America, Library of Congress, Prints and Photographs Division, LC-DIG-highsm-10341.*

A twenty-first-century critic has said, "It looks as if the 16th president is about to pet the man." What do you think? The monument has long been controversial. Frederick Douglass, who spoke at the dedication, was reported by one observer to have said that it "showed the Negro on his knees when a more manly attitude would have been indicative of freedom."[47]

Questions for Analysis

1. As the slaves depicted in the images here experience emancipation, what emotions do they display—at least according to the artists and photographers who created the images? What physical changes does emancipation seem to bring?

2. In these images, why are so many slaves kneeling? What does the kneeling posture suggest? Compare these images with those in Visual Sources: The Black Body in Early American Culture, pp. 199–207. Why was the kneeling slave a common convention in American art from the late eighteenth through the nineteenth century?

3. Compare and contrast the freedom monuments of Edmonia Lewis and Thomas Ball. What similarities and differences do you detect?

4. Whose perspective do the images in this essay portray? According to them, who freed the slaves? What influence do you think such images had on popular understanding of emancipation and on race relations following the Civil War?

5. This essay contains photographs, drawings, and monuments. Which type(s) of representation—monuments, drawings, or photographs—most accurately convey what happened? Among the three types of representations, which type(s) do you think have been more or less effective in conveying their messages? Why?

Notes

1. *New York Times*, October 3, 1862.
2. South Carolina Ordinance of Secession, December 20, 1860, in *Documents of American History*, ed. Henry Steele Commager and Milton Cantor (Englewood Cliffs, NJ: Prentice-Hall, 1988), Declaration of the Immediate Causes Which Induce and Justify the Secession of South Carolina from the Federal Union, December 24, 1860, in ibid., 1:372–74.
3. Abraham Lincoln, First Inaugural Address, March 4, 1861, in ibid., 385–88.
4. Quoted in Roy C. Basler, ed., *The Collected Works of Abraham Lincoln*, vol. 4 (New Brunswick, NJ: Rutgers University Press, 1953), 331–32.
5. Letter from Hannibal Guards to General James S. Negley, *Pittsburgh Gazette*, April 18, 1861, quoted in James M. McPherson, *The Negro's Civil War: How American Blacks Felt and Acted during the War for the Union* (New York: Pantheon, 1965), 19–20.
6. Benjamin Quarles, *The Negro in the Civil War* (Boston: Little, Brown, 1953), 28.
7. Peter H. Clark, *The Black Brigade of Cincinnati* (Cincinnati, 1864), 4–5.
8. Quoted in Basler, *The Collected Works of Abraham Lincoln*, 5:423.
9. James M. McPherson, *Battle Cry of Freedom: The Civil War Era* (New York: Oxford University Press, 1988), 563.
10. *Anglo-African Magazine*, April 20–27, 1861.
11. *Douglass' Monthly*, May 1861, 45–52.
12. Quoted in Basler, *The Collected Works of Abraham Lincoln*, 5:388–89.
13. Quoted in Willie Lee Rose, *Rehearsal for Reconstruction: The Port Royal Experiment* (Indianapolis: Bobbs-Merrill, 1964), xiii.
14. Second Confiscation Act, July 17, 1862, Freedmen and Southern Society Project, http://www.history.umd.edu/Freedmen/conact2.htm.
15. Ira Berlin et al., eds., *Freedom: A Documentary History of Emancipation, 1861–1867*, 1st ser., vol. 1, *The Destruction of Slavery* (New York: Cambridge University Press, 1985), 103–14; 187–99.
16. Henry M. Turner, *The Negro in Slavery, War and Peace* (Philadelphia, 1913), 6–7.
17. Charlotte Forten, "Life on the Sea Islands," *Atlantic Monthly*, June 1864, 4.
18. Interview with Felix Haywood, in *The American Slave: A Composite Autobiography, Texas Narratives*, ed. George P. Rawick, 2nd ser., vol. 4, part 2 (Westport, CT: Greenwood Press, 1972–1973), 131.
19. *Liberator*, May 22, 1863.
20. *Douglass' Monthly*, August 1863. Douglass said this in an address to a meeting for the promotion of colored enlistments on July 6, 1863.
21. William Wells Brown, *The Negro in the American Rebellion* (Boston: Lee and Shepard, 1867), 171.
22. McPherson, *Battle Cry of Freedom*, 634; Charles Dana, *Recollections of the Civil War* (New York: D. Appleton, 1899), 86.
23. McPherson, *Battle Cry of Freedom*, 634.
24. Quoted ibid., 638.
25. Lewis Douglass to Amelia Loguen, July 20, 1863, quoted in McPherson, *The Negro's Civil War*, 190–91.
26. *New York Tribune*, September 8, 1865.
27. Abraham Lincoln, Gettysburg Address, November 19, 1863, in *Documents of American History*, ed. Henry Steele Commager and Milton Cantor (Englewood Cliffs, NJ: Prentice-Hall, 1988), 1:428–29.
28. Resolutions of the Illinois State Legislature, January 7, 1863, in ibid., 1:421–22. See also New Jersey Peace Resolutions, March 18, 1863, in ibid., 1:427–28, and McPherson, *Battle Cry of Freedom*, 595–96.
29. *Christian Recorder*, July 25, 1863, quoted in McPherson, *The Negro's Civil War*, 74.
30. J. W. C. Pennington, "The Position and Duties of the Colored People," cited in Philip S. Foner and Robert James Branham, eds., *Lift Every Voice: African American Oratory, 1787–1900* (Tuscaloosa: University of Alabama Press, 1998), 397–407, 406, 401.
31. Abraham Lincoln, Proclamation of Amnesty and Reconstruction, December 8, 1863, in *Documents of American History*, ed. Henry Steele Commager and Milton Cantor (Englewood Cliffs, NJ: Prentice-Hall, 1988), 1:429–31.
32. Elizabeth Botume, *First Days amongst the Contrabands* (New York: Lee and Shepard, 1893; repr., New York: Arno Press, 1968), 15.
33. *Second Annual Report of the Freedmen and Soldiers Relief Association (Late Contraband Relief Association), Organized August 12, 1862*, quoted in McPherson, *The Negro's Civil War*, 139.
34. Abraham Lincoln, Second Inaugural Address, March 4, 1865, in *Documents of American History*, ed. Henry Steele Commager and Milton Cantor (Englewood Cliffs, NJ: Prentice-Hall, 1988), 1:442–43.
35. For information on the Freedmen's Bureau, see Mary Farmer-Kaiser, *Freedwomen and the Freedmen's Bureau: Race, Gender, and Public Policy in the Age of Emancipation* (New York: Fordham University Press, 2010).
36. Interview with Richard Carruthers, in *The American Slave: A Composite Autobiography, Texas Narratives*, ed. George P. Rawick, vol. 4, part 1 (Westport, CT: Greenwood Press, 1972–1973), 200; Haywood interview, in ibid., 133; interview with Virginia woman, in Virginia Writers Project, *The Negro in Virginia* (New York: Hastings House, 1940), 210.
37. Interview with a former Mississippi slave, in *The American Slave: A Composite Autobiography, Oklahoma and Mississippi Narratives*, ed. George P. Rawick, vol. 7 (Westport, CT: Greenwood Press, 1971), 94; interview with a former South Carolina slave, in *The American Slave: A Composite Autobiography, South Carolina Narratives*, ed. George P. Rawick, vols. 2–3 (Westport, CT: Greenwood Press, 1972), 54.
38. Interview with Aleck Trimble, in *The American Slave: A Composite Autobiography, Texas Narratives*, ed. George P. Rawick, vol. 5, part 4 (Westport, CT: Greenwood Press, 1972), 109; Texas woman, quoted in Edward D. C. Campbell Jr., with Kym S. Rice, eds., *Before Freedom Came: African-American Life in the Antebellum South* (Charlottesville: University of Virginia Press, 1991), xiii.

39. Thomas Morris Chester, *Black Civil War Correspondent. His Dispatches from the Virginia Front,* ed. R. J. M. Blackett (Baton Rouge: LSU Press, 1989), 46. See also Hugh Davis, "We Will Be Satisfied with Nothing Less": *The African American Struggle for Equal Rights in the North during Reconstruction* (Ithaca, NY: Cornell University Press, 2011), 17–26.

40. Quoted in John Hope Franklin, "The Emancipation Proclamation: An Act of Justice," *Prologue* 25, no. 2 (Summer 1993): 3.

41. Davis, *"We Will Be Satisfied,"* 11–12.

42. Quoted in Basler, *The Collected Works of Abraham Lincoln,* 5:370–75.

43. William Kloss and Doreen Bolger, *Art in the White House: A Nation's Pride,* 2nd ed. (Washington, DC: White House Historical Association, 2008), 158 59, 302 3.

44. Ibid.

45. All quoted in McPherson, *Battle Cry of Freedom,* 846–47.

46. Kirk Savage, *Standing Soldiers, Kneeling Slaves: Race, War, and Monument in Nineteenth-Century America* (Princeton, NJ: Princeton University Press, 1997), 90.

47. Aaron Lloyd, "Statue of Limitations: Why Does D.C. Celebrate Emancipation in Front of a Statue That Celebrates 19th-Century Racism?" *Washington City Paper,* April 28, 2000. Quoted in Freeman H. M. Murray, *Emancipation and the Freed in American Sculpture: A Study in Interpretation* (Washington, DC: published by author, 1916), 198.

Suggested References

The Coming of War and the Seizing of Freedom, 1861–1862

Berlin, Ira, Barbara J. Fields, Thavolia Glymph, Joseph P. Reidy, and Leslie S. Rowland, eds. *Freedom: A Documentary History of Emancipation, 1861–1867.* 1st ser., vol. 1, *The Destruction of Slavery.* New York: Cambridge University Press, 1985.

Gerteis, Louis. *From Contraband to Freeman: Federal Policy toward Southern Blacks, 1861–1865.* Greenwood, CT: Greenwood Press, 1973.

Litwack, Leon F. *Been in the Storm So Long: The Aftermath of Slavery.* New York: Knopf, 1979.

McPherson, James M. *The Negro's Civil War: How American Blacks Felt and Acted during the War for the Union.* 1965. Reprint. New York: Vintage, 2003.

Mohr, Clarence L. *On the Threshold of Freedom: Masters and Slaves in Civil War Georgia.* Baton Rouge: LSU Press, 2001.

Nieman, Donald G. *The Day of the Jubilee: The Civil War Experience of Black Southerners.* New York: Garland, 1994.

Quarles, Benjamin. *The Negro in the Civil War.* Boston: Little, Brown, 1953.

Robinson, Armstead. *Bitter Fruits of Bondage: The Demise of Slavery and the Collapse of the Confederacy.* Charlottesville: University of Virginia Press, 2005.

Rose, Willie Lee. *Rehearsal for Reconstruction: The Port Royal Experiment.* Indianapolis: Bobbs Merrill, 1964.

Ward, Andrew. *The Slaves' War: The Civil War in the Words of Former Slaves.* Boston: Houghton Mifflin, 2008.

Turning Points, 1862–1863

Berlin, Ira, Joseph P. Reidy, and Leslie S. Rowland, eds. *Freedom: A Documentary History of Emancipation, 1861–1867.* 2nd ser., *The Black Military Experience.* New York: Cambridge University Press, 1982.

Bernstein, Iver. *The New York City Draft Riots: Their Significance for American Society and Politics in the Age of the Civil War.* New York: Oxford University Press, 1990.

Cornish, Dudley Taylor. *The Sable Arm: Negro Troops in the Union Army, 1861–1865.* New York: Longmans, Green, 1956.

Franklin, John Hope. *The Emancipation Proclamation.* New York: Doubleday, 1963.

Glatthaar, Joseph T. *Forged in Battle: The Civil War Alliance of Black Soldiers and White Officers.* Baton Rouge: LSU Press, 2000.

Redkey, Edwin S., ed. *A Grand Army of Black Men: Letters from African American Soldiers in the Union Army, 1861–1865.* New York: Cambridge University Press, 1992.

Smith, John David, ed. *Black Soldiers in Blue: African American Troops in the Civil War Era.* Chapel Hill: University of North Carolina Press, 2007.

Trudeau, Noah A. *Like Men of War: Black Troops in the Civil War.* Boston: Little, Brown, 1998.

Home Fronts and War's End, 1863–1865

Bercaw, Nancy. *Gendered Freedoms: Race, Rights, and the Politics of Household in the Delta, 1861–1875.* Gainesville: University of Florida Press, 2003.

Berlin, Ira, and Leslie S. Rowland, eds. *Families and Freedom: A Documentary History of African-American Kinship in the Civil War Era.* New York: New Press, 1997.

Forbes, Ella. *African American Women during the Civil War.* New York: Garland, 1998.

Frankel, Nora Lee. *Freedom's Women: Black Women and Families in Civil War Era Mississippi.* Bloomington: Indiana University Press, 1999.

Jordan, Ervin L., Jr. *Black Confederates and Afro Yankees in Civil War Virginia.* Charlottesville: University of Virginia Press, 1995.

Levine, Bruce. *Confederate Emancipation: Southern Plans to Free and Arm Slaves during the Civil War.* New York: Oxford University Press, 2006.

Schwalm, Leslie A. *A Hard Fight for We: Women's Transition from Slavery to Freedom in South Carolina.* Urbana: University of Illinois Press, 1997.

Williams, Heather Andrea. *Self-Taught: African-American Education in Slavery and Freedom.* Chapel Hill: University of North Carolina Press, 2005.

CHAPTER 8

Reconstruction: The Making and Unmaking of a Revolution, 1865–1885

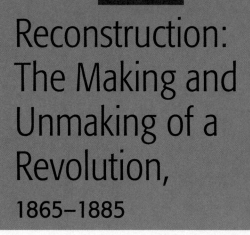

IN THE SUMMER AFTER the Civil War ended, freedman Jourdan Anderson of Dayton, Ohio, thought hard about the postwar prospects for himself and his wife, Mandy, and their three children. Colonel P. H. Anderson, their "Old Master" in Big Spring, Tennessee, "promising to do better for me than anybody else can," had asked Jourdan and his family to return to the "old place" to work for him. Free since 1864, Jourdan and Mandy had made a nice life for themselves and their family in Dayton. "I get $25 a month, with victuals and clothing; have a comfortable home for Mandy . . . and the children," Jourdan explained in his formal response to Colonel Anderson's invitation. Recalling that Anderson had more than once tried to shoot him, Jourdan demanded "some proof that you are sincerely disposed to treat us justly and kindly" as a condition of return. The terms Jourdan and Mandy laid out were clear and precise.

> We have concluded to test your sincerity by asking you to send us our wages for the time we served you. This will make us forget and forgive old scores, and

rely on your justice and friendship in the future. I served you faithfully for thirty-two years and Mandy twenty years. At $25 a month for me, and $2 a week for Mandy, our earnings would amount to $11,680. Add to this the interest for the time our wages has been kept back and deduct what you paid for our clothing and three doctor's visits to me, and pulling a tooth for Mandy, and the balance will show what we are in justice entitled to. Please send the money by Adams Express, in care of V. Winters, esq., Dayton, Ohio. If you fail to pay us for faithful labors in the past we can have little faith in your promises in the future. We trust the good Maker has opened your eyes to the wrongs which you and your fathers have done to me and my fathers, in making us toil for you without recompense.

Besides making sure that their economic situation would be solid, Jourdan and Mandy wanted to know that their domestic and social lives as free people would be protected and dignified. The old patterns of white dominance and black subordination were unacceptable. Jourdan observed that when "the folks here" talk to Mandy, they "call her Mrs. Anderson." Jourdan and Mandy demanded that their daughters Milly and Jane, "now grown up and both good-looking girls," be safe from rape and sexual exploitation at the hands of white men. "I would rather stay here and starve and die if it comes to that than have my girls brought to shame by the violence and wickedness of their young masters." In Dayton, Mandy and Jourdan made certain their children attended Sunday school and church, as well as grammar school, and they were proud that their son Grundy's teacher had told them he "has a head for a preacher." Committed to a good education for their children, they asked Colonel Anderson "if there has been any schools opened for the colored children in your neighborhood." Jourdan explained, "The great desire of my life now is to give my children an education, and have them form virtuous habits."[1]

Jourdan Anderson's extraordinary response to his former master's request that he and his family return to the old homestead to work for him reveals the concerns of African Americans as they built new lives for themselves in freedom. Family ties, church and community, dignified labor with fair compensation, and education for their children were top priorities. But these were neither safe nor protected in the immediate aftermath of the Civil War, as many white landowners sought to ensure that former slaves continued working the land and remained bound by white rules. The tension between black assertiveness and white racism made interracial conflict inevitable. Freedom brought a revolution in black economic, social, and political life, but it did not bring equality. As President Andrew Johnson and the Radical Republicans in Congress battled over executive and legislative power, the fate of the freedpeople hung in the balance. When Congress proved more powerful, laws and constitutional amendments sought to ensure African American civil and voting rights. For about a decade from 1867 to 1877, African Americans in the South, even more than in the North, actively and responsibly participated in public life. Intense, often violent, southern white opposition, coupled with a dwindling concern for freedpeople as the nation turned to economic development, undermined the revolutionary period of interracial democracy and the political gains black people had made during Reconstruction. Some left the South for other regions of the country, but wherever they tried to put down roots—in the U.S. military, in new all-black towns in Kansas and Oklahoma, and in northern and midwestern cities where they sought jobs in factories—they struggled to achieve equal rights and independent lives.

A Social Revolution

For the four million African Americans who had been enslaved, freedom brought new goals and responsibilities. Foremost for many was reuniting with family members from whom they had been separated. Economic independence wrought immediate changes in family structure and shifting gender roles for men and women, as well as hope for the future. Extended families and community structures such as new schools and independent black churches provided services and support in the new environment of freedom. Labor arrangements had to be renegotiated, even though for most freedpeople, the nature of their work—field work and domestic service—remained largely the same. In freedom, black people had the right to learn to read and write, and they eagerly pursued education. For those who had been enslaved, the first years of freedom involved a transition—from slave households to independent households and from slave labor to free labor—that constituted a social revolution.

Freedom and Family

Freedpeople's struggles to create independent and functional families gave meaning to their freedom. Under slavery, masters had exercised significant control over slave families. With freedom, black people gained control over their families, even as they tried to remake them. Often the first step was to reunite those who had been separated before the war. One government official observed that "the work of emancipation was incomplete until the families which had been dispersed by slavery were re-united."[2] The war also had separated families. As individuals fled to Union lines and traveled with Union armies or enlisted in the U.S. Colored Troops, they lost touch with parents, wives, children, and relatives who were themselves sometimes scattered. A Missouri official reported that after black men had enlisted in the military, their wives and children had been "driven from their masters' homes," and court records indicate that women separated from children sought help to get them back.[3] In short, wartime conditions had made it increasingly hard to hold black families together.

After the war, thousands of freedpeople traveled great distances at significant material and emotional costs seeking lost and displaced family members. One middle-aged North Carolina freedman who had been sold away from his wife and children traveled almost six hundred miles on foot to try to find them.[4] People inquired for missing relatives at former plantation homes, contraband camps, churches, and government agencies. Others wrote letters, with those who were not literate asking for help from teachers, preachers, missionaries, and government officials. Many took out ads in black newspapers. (See Documents: Letters to the Freedmen's Bureau, 1865–1868, pp. 409–13.)

Most searches were unsuccessful, owing to time and distance, death, and difficulties that were simply insurmountable given the lack of records. Family members who did find one another expressed relief and joy. Reunited after having been sold apart twenty years earlier, husband and wife Ben and Betty Dodson embraced, and Ben shouted, "Glory! Glory hallelujah." In some cases, people did not recognize one another after such a long absence. One former slave woman, sold away as a child, could identify the woman standing before her as her mother only by a distinctive facial scar.[5]

Sometimes new family ties had replaced old ones. Many forcibly separated partners and spouses over time had come to believe they would never see each other again, and they formed new attachments. For them, reunions were heartrending. Some chose their former spouse, others the new one. One woman gave each of her two husbands a two-week test run before settling on one. Many men stayed with and supported one wife while continuing to support the other.[6] Others remained torn between two loves. One freedman wrote to his first wife, "I thinks of you and my children every day of my life. . . . I do love you the same. My love to you have never failed. . . . I have got another wife, and I am very sorry. . . . You feels and seems to me as much like my dear loving wife, as you ever did."[7]

The tensions following from troubled reunions often proved overwhelming. Many spouses who accused their partners of infidelity or desertion now sought relief through the courts. The number of wives seeking support for their children and themselves from negligent fathers and husbands increased, as did the number of divorce cases and custody battles over children. Battles between birth parents and the adults who had raised their children were confusing and painful for all involved. During slavery, some white mistresses had taken young slaves from their mothers to be raised in the big house as part of the domestic staff. After emancipation, these children were reclaimed. As one freed mother told her former mistress, "You took her away from me an' didn' pay no mind to my cryin', so now I'se takin' her back home. We's free now, Miss Polly, we ain't gwine be slaves no more to nobody."[8]

Legalizing slave marriages was a critical step in confirming freedpeople's new identities. Some viewed marriage as a moral and a Christian responsibility, others as a means for legitimating children and becoming eligible for Union veterans' pensions. Preachers, missionaries, and public officials supported marriage as a way to anchor black families and enhance their moral foundation. The rites themselves varied widely, from traditional "jumping the broomstick" ceremonies, common under slavery, to church weddings. One freedwoman recalled that while she and her husband had had a broomstick ceremony as slaves, once freed they "had a real sho' nuff weddin' wid a preacher. Dat cost a dollar."[9] Mass weddings featuring as many as seventy couples were common. In 1866, seventeen North Carolina counties registered 9,000 marriages of freedpeople; four Virginia counties registered 3,000. Yet some couples remained together without formalizing their marriages, being accepted in their local communities as husband and wife.

Many former slaves took new names to recognize family ties or as a symbol of their independence and their desire for a new life characterized by dignity and respect. In slavery, "we hardly knowed our names," one ex-slave recalled. "We was cussed for so many bitches and sons of bitches and bloody bitches, and blood of bitches. We never heard our names hardly at all."[10] Masters had often assigned first names, such as Pompey and Caesar, and refused to recognize the surnames used within slave communities. Now, as independent people, former slaves legally claimed first and last names of their own choosing.

' MARRIAGE OF A COLORED SOLDIER AT VICKSBURG BY CHAPLAIN WARREN OF THE FREEDMEN'S BUREAU.

Marriage of a Colored Soldier at Vicksburg
This 1866 image of a formal Christian wedding uniting a young black Union soldier and his bride captures the sociocultural importance of the ceremonial ritual for both free and recently emancipated blacks. The dignified demeanor and elegant outfits of the entire wedding party reflect a deep love, seriousness, pride, and respectability. The image reveals not just the powerful commitment and bond between the wife and husband, but also the commitment and bond between the couple and their families and friends. Historically, strengthening black lives has demanded the strengthening of such relationships. *Library of Congress, LC-USZ62-138383.*

In form, freed families were flexible and adaptive Although the most common organization was the nuclear family—two parents and their children—families often included extended kin and nonrelated members. Ties of affection and economic need made extended families, as well as fictive kin (see chapter 5), important. Pooling resources and working collectively sustained these families. Even when dispersed in different households, families tended to live in communities among relatives. Close-knit communities defined women's and men's social and cultural worlds, nurturing a cooperative spirit and a communal folk culture.

Most newly freed families had to meet their household needs with very limited resources, and poverty rendered them fragile. Every person had to work. Immediately after emancipation, large numbers of freedwomen withdrew from field labor and domestic service to manage their own households, but most were soon forced to work outside the home for wages. Although traditional notions of women's and men's roles prevailed—woman as caretaker and homemaker; man as breadwinner and protector—black men rarely earned enough to support their families. One consequence was that black women who were contributing to the family income also participated more fully in family decision making. In addition, black women felt freer to leave dysfunctional relationships and to divorce or simply live apart from their husbands, as Lucy Skipwith from Hopewell Plantation chose to do. (See Documents: Black Women at Work During the War, pp. 355–57.) But female-headed households were almost always poorer than dual-headed households. Moreover, as legal protectors and guarantors of their wives and children, freedmen exercised the rights of contract and child custody. Men typically made and signed labor contracts on behalf of their wives, and they held the upper hand in child custody disputes.

Church and Community

The explosive growth of independent black churches in the South during this period reflects freedpeople's desire for dignity, autonomy, and self-expression. With emancipation, they rejected white Christianity and exited white churches by the thousands to form congregations of their own. As Matthew Gilbert, a Tennessee Baptist minister, noted, "The emancipation of the colored people made the colored churches and ministry a necessity, by virtue of the prejudice existing against us and of our essential manhood before the laws of the land."[11] Often with the assistance of missionaries from churches in the North, the major black denominations—Baptist, African Methodist Episcopal (AME), and African Methodist Episcopal Zion (AME Zion)—became established in the South. By 1880, nationwide there were more than 500,000 people in the Baptist Church; 400,000 in the AME Church; and 250,000 in the AME Zion Church. By 1890, more than half of those belonging to an independent black church were Baptists.[12]

Next to the family, the black church provided the most important institutional support in the transition from slavery to freedom. Joining a church was an act of physical and spiritual emancipation, and black churches united black communities. They also empowered blacks because they operated outside of white control. Men dominated church leadership, but women constituted most of the members and regular attendees, and they did most of what was called church work. Women gave and raised money, taught Sunday school, ran women's auxiliaries, welcomed visitors, and led social welfare programs for the needy, sick, and elderly. They were also prominent in

TABLE 8.1

Historically Black Colleges and Universities

College/University and Location	Year Founded	Sponsoring Organization
Cheyney State University; Cheyney, Pa.	1837	Quaker Church
Lincoln University; Lincoln, Pa.	1854	Presbyterian-Quaker Church
Wilberforce University; Wilberforce, Ohio	1856	Methodist Episcopal Church
Atlanta University; Atlanta, Ga.	1865	African Methodist Episcopal Church and Freedmen's Bureau
Bowie State University; Bowie, Md.	1865	Baltimore Association for the Moral and Educational Improvement of Colored People
Shaw University; Raleigh, N.C.	1865	American Baptist Home Mission Society and Freedmen's Bureau
Virginia Union University; Richmond, Va.	1865	American Baptist Home Mission Society
Edward Waters College; Jacksonville, Fla.	1866	African Methodist Episcopal Church
Fisk University; Nashville, Tenn.	1866	American Missionary Association and Freedmen's Bureau
Lincoln University; Jefferson City, Mo.	1866	62nd and 65th Colored Infantry
Rust College; Holly Springs, Miss.	1866	Methodist Episcopal Church and Freedmen's Aid Society
Fayetteville State University; Fayetteville, N.C.	1867	Black Private Founders
Alabama State University; Montgomery, Ala.	1867	American Missionary Association
Howard University; Washington, D.C.	1867	American Missionary Association and Freedmen's Bureau
Johnson C. Smith University; Charlotte, N.C.	1867	Presbyterian Church
Morehouse College; Atlanta, Ga.	1867	American Baptist Home Mission Society
Morgan State College; Baltimore, Md.	1867	Methodist Episcopal Church
Saint Augustine's College; Raleigh, N.C.	1867	Episcopal Church and Freedmen's Bureau
Talladega College; Talladega, Ala.	1867	American Missionary Association and Freedmen's Bureau
Hampton Institute; Hampton, Va.	1868	American Missionary Association and Freedmen's Bureau
Claflin College; Orangeburg, S.C.	1869	Methodist Church
Tougaloo College; Jackson, Miss.	1869	American Missionary Association
Allen University; Columbia, S.C.	1870	African Methodist Episcopal Church
Benedict College; Columbia, S.C.	1870	American Baptist Home Mission Society
Alcorn University; Lorman, Miss.	1871	State of Mississippi
LeMoyne College; Memphis, Tenn.	1871	American Missionary Association
Paul Quinn College; Dallas, Tex.	1872	African Methodist Episcopal Church
University of Arkansas at Pine Bluff; Pine Bluff, Ark.	1873	State of Arkansas
Bennett College; Greensboro, N.C.	1873	Methodist Episcopal Church and Freedmen's Aid Society
Wiley College; Marshall, Tex.	1873	Methodist Episcopal Church
Alabama A&M University; Normal, Ala.	1875	State of Alabama
Knoxville College; Knoxville, Tenn.	1875	Presbyterian Church
Stillman College; Tuscaloosa, Ala.	1876	Presbyterian Church
Jackson State University; Jackson, Miss.	1877	American Baptist Home Mission Society

Continued

Continued

College/University and Location	Year Founded	Sponsoring Organization
Philander Smith College; Little Rock, Ark.	1877	United Methodist Church
Prairie View A&M University; Prairie View, Tex.	1878	State of Texas
Selma University; Selma, Ala.	1878	Baptist Church
Florida Memorial College; Miami, Fla.	1879	Baptist Church
Livingstone College; Salisbury, N.C.	1879	African Methodist Episcopal Zion Church
Southern University and A&M College; Baton Rouge, La.	1880	State of Louisiana
Morris Brown College; Atlanta, Ga.	1881	African Methodist Episcopal Church
Spelman College; Atlanta, Ga.	1881	Woman's American Baptist Home Mission Society
Tuskegee Institute; Tuskegee, Ala.	1881	State of Alabama

domestic and foreign missionary activities. One grateful minister consistently offered "great praise" to the church sisters for all their hard work.[13]

Women derived their authority in churches from their roles as Christian wives, mothers, and homemakers. As "church mothers," they exercised informal yet significant influence in church affairs, including matters of governance typically reserved for male members, such as the selection of preachers and the allocation of church funds. Although women were not allowed to become preachers, many preached nevertheless, under titles such as "evangelist."

Black women were also leaders in and practitioners of African-derived forms of popular, or folk, religion—such as conjure (see chapter 3) and voodoo, or hoodoo (see chapter 5)—which had evolved during slavery and continued after emancipation. Focusing on magic and the supernatural, they involved healing and harming beliefs and practices. One celebrated voodoo "priestess" was Marie Laveau of New Orleans. Not surprisingly, black church leaders railed against folk religion as an ignorant and idolatrous relic of slavery. Still, these beliefs and practices were common, especially among rural people, but even in towns and cities and among Christians.

In black urban neighborhoods, church networks and resources helped fuel institutional growth, including hospitals, clinics, asylums for orphans and the mentally ill, mutual aid societies, lodges, and unions. Churches led black community efforts to deal with the epidemics of cholera, smallpox, and yellow fever that swept through the South after the war, especially as blacks who had never traveled much before became exposed to lethal diseases. With help from the Medical Division of the Freedmen's Bureau, former wartime army hospitals were converted into hospitals to serve African Americans. In Washington, D.C., Freedmen's Hospital was established during the war. In New Orleans and Richmond, Virginia, the existing black hospitals expanded. By the late 1860s, segregated asylums and hospitals served black communities in a number of southern cities.

In addition, black churches, northern white churches, and the American Missionary Association (AMA) founded black grade schools and high schools during this period. They also established colleges and teacher training institutes, known as normal schools (Table 8.1). These **historically black colleges and universities** reflected their founders' goals, giving great emphasis to religious instruction, Christian morality, and hard work, as well as academic and vocational training.

Through its networks and resources, the black church generated a range of economic organizations. The church itself operated as an economic enterprise, undertaking fund-raising, buying and maintaining buildings and real estate, promoting businesses, and supporting social programs for the needy. Mutual aid societies rooted in churches evolved into black insurance companies and banks in the late nineteenth and early twentieth centuries. Church social circles provided ready consumer bases for black products and services. Some churches sold Christian products, such as Bibles and religious pamphlets and lithographs. Black ministers served on the boards of black companies. Churches sponsored business expositions featuring products such as furniture, medicines, and handicrafts, in order to showcase African Americans' economic progress since emancipation.

The church was also the hub of black political life. At all levels—from within the church to local, state, and national politics—it functioned as the key forum for political debate and action. It was vital to black political education and activism, including participation in black community politics and the white-dominated political mainstream. Among black ministers' many roles, that of political leader proved central. Preacher-politicians saw themselves as both faithful servants to their congregations and representatives of their people to white politicians. They believed that their Christian-based leadership would improve the morality of both the political system and secular society. In the 1870s, the Reverend James Poindexter of the Second Baptist Church in Columbus, Ohio, explained that "all the help the preachers and all other good and worthy citizens can give by taking hold of politics is needed in order to keep the government out of bad hands and secure the ends for which governments are formed."[14]

Land and Labor

Landownership was fundamental to former slaves' aspirations for economic independence. Rebuilding families as independent households required land. Speaking for his people, particularly former slaves, in the summer of 1864, the AME missionary and minister Richard Cain explained, "We must possess the soil, be the owner of lands and become independent."[15] This message was repeated in January 1865, when several hundred blacks in the Sea Islands told General William T. Sherman, "We want to be placed on land until we are able to buy it, and make it our own."[16] Sherman settled more than 40,000 former slaves in coastal areas that had been abandoned by Confederate plantation owners, but what was known as Sherman's Reserve did not last. The Reconstruction plans of President Abraham Lincoln and his successor, Andrew Johnson, directed that former Confederates who swore allegiance to the United States would regain their land, and unclaimed land was auctioned to the highest bidder. Many former slaves were already working this land under federal supervision; others had simply squatted on abandoned land and worked it to sustain themselves. They were all evicted. Although the Freedmen's Bureau was able to help some enter into contracts to rent the land they were already farming, the bureau was not able to help them purchase land. Few freedpeople or free blacks possessed the capital or credit to buy land, and as a result, they lost out to returning ex-Confederate plantation owners and northern and southern investors. The Southern Homestead Act, passed by Congress in 1866, made public land available to freedmen, but it had little impact and was repealed a decade later. In the end, most land in the former Confederacy was returned to white control, often to the original owners. The rest went to northern white investors, former army officers, and Freedmen's Bureau officials.

This "landless emancipation" devastated freedpeople. "Damn such freedom as that," one angry freedman exclaimed, expressing the frustration of many.[17] Freedmen believed that they had earned the right to own the land they and their ancestors had worked as slaves. They argued that freedom without provision for self-sufficiency was a shocking violation of the federal government's economic and moral responsibility. A group of Mississippi blacks called it "a breach of faith on the part of the government."[18] Some simply refused to leave the property they now considered their own. The former slaves on the Taylor farm in Norfolk County, Virginia, mounted an armed resistance when their former owners returned to reclaim their prewar property, but to no avail. Forced evictions of freedpeople from land and farms they assumed now belonged to them were common.

Lacking the means to own land, most freedpeople were forced into tenancy. They rented and worked land that belonged to white landowners under terms that favored the owners. Black male heads of households entered into contracts with landowners that spelled out the paid labor, as opposed to slave labor, relationship. For their part, freedpeople sought fair compensation for their labor, work organized along family lines, and an end to physical punishment and gang-style labor with overseers. They also wanted guaranteed leisure time and the right to hunt, fish, gather wild food plants, raise farm animals, and cultivate designated plots for their own use. For white landowners, the aim of these contracts was to ensure a steady supply of farm labor so that their land holdings, planted in cash crops, would make a profit. That meant limiting wages, forbidding worker mobility, and suppressing competition. Labor contracts were difficult to break, and because most freedmen could neither read nor write, many relied on Freedmen's Bureau officials to look out for their best interests. The struggles between freedpeople and landowners were bitter and divisive, but in the end, the landowners were far more powerful, and labor contracts generally favored their interests.

Despite their landholdings, whites operated within cash-strapped southern economies after the war. Instead of paying farmworkers in cash, most negotiated **sharecropping** arrangements under which farmers worked the land for a "share" of the crop, typically one-third or one-half. Often the landowner supplied the cabin or house in which the family lived, as well as seed, work animals, and tools. If a "cropper" had his own mule and plow, he might warrant a larger share of the crop. This he would "sell" to the plantation owner or a local merchant—often the same person—following the harvest. But instead of cash changing hands, the sharecropper would get credit to use for buying food and clothing—or whatever his family might need—from the merchant. At the end of the year, when accounts were settled on "countin' day," the sharecropper usually got no more than a bill showing how much he still owed the landowner or merchant.

All too often, owners and merchants cheated workers, forcing them into a pattern of cyclical debt. Even black farmers who owned their own land were forced into debt. For example, in a system known as **crop lien**, they had to borrow against anticipated harvests for seed and supplies. Most black households were thus reduced to a kind of partial slavery, tied to the land they farmed as the only means they had to work off their debt, which grew larger, instead of smaller, every year. Debtors were also subject to imprisonment, and prisoners were subject to another form of slavery, for states contracted out their labor to landowners or businesses in need of a labor force. This **convict lease** system generated income for southern states, but it forced prisoners to work under conditions that blatantly disregarded their human rights.

Immediately after the war, the main goal for white southerners was to reassert control over blacks. State legislatures passed **black codes** that enforced the labor contracts that once again bound freedpeople, who had few other options, to the land. The codes mandated strict obedience to white employers and set work hours, usually sunup to sundown. Although the codes allowed freedpeople to legalize their marriages, own property, make contracts, and gain access to courts, their aim was to perpetuate a slave-like labor force in conditions of freedom. Thus vagrancy provisions were especially oppressive. Individuals without labor contracts who were unable to prove that they were employed risked fines, imprisonment, and forced labor, as did those who left a job before a contract ended or were unruly or simply lost. In Mississippi, freedpeople were prohibited from renting urban property, helping to ensure that they would stay on plantations and work in agriculture. In Florida, breaking a labor contract often resulted in physical punishment, such as a whipping, or being hired out for a year to a planter. As one southern white pointedly observed in November 1865, the purpose behind black codes and vagrancy laws was to "teach the negro that if he goes to work, keeps his place, and behaves himself, he will be protected by *our* white laws."[19]

Black codes also permitted the courts to order apprenticeships that removed children from families and bound them to white employers, often without their parents' or guardians' consent. In *Adeline Brown v. State* (1865), the Maryland Court of Appeals upheld the state's black apprentice law. Two years later, however, the case *In re Turner* (1867) overturned the law as unconstitutional because its educational provisions for black youths were different from those for white youths.

The Hope of Education

To operate as free and independent men and women, former slaves—more than 90 percent of whom were illiterate—recognized that they had to learn to read and write, and they did so eagerly. Some began their schooling in the Union military or in contraband camps, where they were sometimes taught by former slaves, such as Susie King Taylor, or by northern black women, such as Charlotte Forten, who went to the Sea Islands to teach (see chapter 7). After the war, makeshift classrooms grew into permanent institutions. On St. Helena Island, so many teachers were from Pennsylvania that the school was named the Penn School, and it expanded to accommodate 1,700 students on a campus that served black children into the 1940s. In Hampton, Virginia, where thousands of contrabands set up their own community soon after the Civil War began, the teacher was a free black woman named Mary S. Peake. Under the sponsorship of the American Missionary Association (AMA), she began her school under a tree later known as the Emancipation Oak. After she died of tuberculosis, General Benjamin Butler stepped in to build the Butler School for Negro Children, again with the assistance of the AMA. Frances Ellen Watkins Harper, who before the war had lectured on behalf of abolition and black education, captured in a poem the excitement and sense of independence that came with learning to read. (See From the Record: Learning to Read.)

Frances Ellen Watkins Harper | Learning to Read, 1872

Frances Ellen Watkins Harper (1825–1911) was born free in Baltimore, orphaned, and educated at the Academy for Negro Youth under the sponsorship of her uncle, the Reverend William Watkins, who founded the school. She supported herself as a seamstress and, at times, as a teacher. A champion for African American rights, women's rights, and woman suffrage, Harper was a well-regarded orator, activist, and writer. Her abolitionist poems in particular, published in *Poems on Miscellaneous Subjects* (1854), which indeed covered a range of subjects, proved very popular. In this poem from *Sketches of Southern Life* (1872), she assumes the voice of a southern black woman in order to express the impact that northern teachers had on blacks, enslaved and emancipated, and southern whites in the South.

Very soon the Yankee teachers
    Came down and set up school;
But, oh! how the Rebs did hate it,—
    It was agin' their rule.

Our masters always tried to hide
    Book learning from our eyes;
Knowledge didn't agree with slavery—
    'Twould make us all too wise.

But some of us would try to steal
    A little from the book,
And put the words together,
    And learn by hook or crook.

I remember Uncle Caldwell,
    Who took pot liquor fat
And greased the pages of his book,
    And hid it in his hat.

And had his master ever seen
    The leaves upon his head,
He'd have thought them greasy papers,
    But nothing to be read.

And there was Mr. Turner's Ben,
    Who heard the children spell,

And picked the words right up by heart,
    And learned to read 'em well.

Well, the Northern folks kept sending
    The Yankee teachers down;
And they stood right up and helped us,
    Though Rebs did sneer and frown.

And I longed to read my Bible,
    For precious words it said;
But when I begun to learn it,
    Folks just shook their heads,

And said there is no use trying,
    Oh! Chloe, you're too late;
But as I was rising sixty,
    I had no time to wait.

So I got a pair of glasses,
    And straight to work I went,
And never stopped till I could read
    The hymns and Testament.

Then I got a little cabin—
    A place to call my own—
And I felt as independent
    As the queen upon her throne.

SOURCE: Frances Ellen Watkins Harper, "Learning to Read," in *Sketches of Southern Life* (Philadelphia: Ferguson Bros. & Co., Printers, 1891), 17–19.

???

How does Harper describe the motivation of slaves and former slaves to achieve literacy? What obstacles did Chloe and the other slaves she describes have to overcome? With emancipation, who helped the former slaves in their quest to become literate and why did they do so? Once achieved, what did literacy mean for blacks, enslaved and freed?

Northern teachers, missionaries, and philanthropists helped found hundreds of schools for black children and adults. Some were set up in churches and homes. In other cases, freedpeople pooled their resources to buy land, build schoolhouses, and hire teachers. The Freedmen's Bureau assisted by renting facilities, providing books, and transporting teachers, while the AMA helped fund schools and hire teachers, white and black. The Pennsylvania Branch of the American Freedmen's Union Commission sent out 1,400 teachers to serve 150,000 students. In addition to these privately sponsored organizations, Reconstruction state governments, often led by black officials, began to establish public school systems—new for the South—that gave black children access to education, largely in segregated schools that operated only during the winter months, when children were not needed for planting and harvesting. Nevertheless, by 1880 black illiteracy had declined to 70 percent, and by 1910 it was 30 percent.[20]

In all these schools, the standard New England curriculum prevailed. The three R's—reading, writing, and arithmetic—were emphasized. In the best schools, instruction in history, geography, spelling, grammar, and music might also be available. Colleges offered a classical liberal curriculum that included math, science, Latin, and Greek. Given the pressing need for teachers, they usually emphasized teacher training, instructing young people in teaching methods and theory as well as diction, geometry, algebra, and map reading.

By 1868, more than half the teachers in black schools in the South were black, and most were women. For them, teaching was a calling, not just a job. "I am myself a colored woman," noted Sara G. Stanley, "bound to that ignorant, degraded, long enslaved race, by the ties of love and consanguinity: they are socially, and politically, 'my people.'"[21] The increasing preponderance of black teachers reflected a growing race consciousness and commitment to self-reliance. Despite the fact that white teachers may have had better training and more experience, black communities preferred black teachers. The Reverend Richard Cain observed that white "teachers and preachers have feelings, but not as we feel for our kindred."[22] In 1869, a group of blacks in Petersburg, Virginia, petitioned the school board to replace white teachers with black ones, asserting, "We do not want our children to be trained to think or feel that they are inferior."[23] Black female teachers became important community leaders and inspirational role models. Like black schools, they helped build racial solidarity and community identity.

Although the historically black colleges and universities emphasized teacher training, early on they took two different curricular paths that reflected the different expectations freedpeople had for themselves in light of their opportunities. The classical liberal arts model was followed by schools such as Fisk in Nashville, Tennessee, and the vocational-industrial model was adopted by Hampton Institute in Hampton, Virginia, and Tuskegee Institute in Tuskegee, Alabama. When Booker T. Washington helped found Tuskegee in 1881, he modeled it on Hampton, where he had been a student and teacher. In 1871, Alcorn Agricultural and Mechanical College (Alcorn A&M) opened as Alcorn University in Claiborne County, Mississippi. Alcorn was both the nation's first state-supported college for blacks and the first federal land-grant black college.

Fisk offered a well-rounded academic program to prepare the best and the brightest of the race for citizenship, leadership, and a wide range of careers. Founded in 1866, the school aimed for "the highest standards, not of Negro education, but of American education at its best."[24] Within six years, however, Fisk faced a serious financial crisis that threatened its survival. In an effort to raise money, George L. White, school treasurer and music professor, organized a choral ensemble to go on a fund-raising tour. Modeling their performances on European presentation styles, but singing slave songs and spirituals little known to white audiences, the Fisk Jubilee Singers were soon famous. In 1872, they performed for President Ulysses S. Grant at the White House, and the next year, while on a European tour, they sang for Britain's Queen Victoria. The money they raised saved the school from bankruptcy and enabled Fisk to build its first permanent building, Jubilee Hall, today a National Historic Landmark. Their performances built worldwide respect and admiration for African American music and culture, and inspired other black colleges to create similar groups.

Hampton Institute had a different mission: "to train selected Negro youth who should go out and teach and lead their people first by example, by getting land and homes; . . . to teach respect for labor, and in this way build up an industrial system

The Fisk Jubilee Singers
This 1880 photograph illustrates the middle-class refinement of the Fisk Jubilee Singers. This sense of middle-class respectability also revealed their commitment to racial uplift: the presentation of positive images of blacks as a way to enhance their freedom struggle. As former slaves and the children of former slaves, the Jubilee Singers pioneered an African American music tradition that relied on polished versions of slave spirituals. Their noble presentation of this black religious folk music provided a critical counterpoint and challenge to negative stereotypes of blacks resulting from the minstrel tradition (see Visual Sources: Minstrel Shows, pp. 309–19). Over time, the Jubilee Singers' performances for audiences around the world enhanced black and white respect for blacks and their culture. *The Granger Collection, NYC. All rights reserved.*

for the sake not only of self-support and intelligent labor, but also for the sake of character."[25] Samuel Chapman Armstrong, Hampton's white founder and Booker T. Washington's mentor, believed that training young people in skilled trades, rather than teaching a classical liberal arts curriculum, would best enable poverty-stricken former slaves to pull themselves up by their bootstraps. As skilled laborers and highly trained domestic servants, they would earn adequate wages, build self-respect, and win the admiration of whites. Students at Hampton paid their way by working on campus, all the while learning the occupational skills that would qualify them for jobs after graduation. Many learned to teach trade skills such as carpentry and sewing, and they practice-taught at the successor to the Butler School for Negro Children. The Hampton model of vocational training was akin to that of training schools for poor white children and immigrants at the time, but some black leaders feared that it would perpetuate black subordination. The *Louisianian*, a black newspaper, complained that Armstrong "seems to think we should only know enough to make good servants."[26] The debate over vocational training versus liberal arts intensified toward the end of the century, and at its center was Washington, the preeminent black leader of his day.

A Short-Lived Political Revolution

Even as black men and women built independent lives, they sought a place in American public life, and for a short period known as **Black Reconstruction**, black men were able to vote in the South and to participate in politics. Radical Republicans in Congress had taken charge of Reconstruction and forced the former Confederate states to hold democratically elected constitutional conventions, which wrote new state constitutions that protected black suffrage. The consequences were revolutionary. Nowhere else in the world had an emancipated people been integrated into the political system so quickly. Black men elected or appointed to state and local offices proved able and moderate, interested in compromise and progressive reforms such as public schools. But Black Reconstruction was short-lived. Outraged southern whites mobilized a violent and racist counterrevolution that restored white political dominance by 1877. Congress and the Republican Party abandoned black interests, and the U.S. Supreme Court reversed gains made by Reconstruction laws and amendments. In its retreat from Black Reconstruction, the national government reflected the expanding white opposition to the evolving black freedom struggle.

The Political Contest over Reconstruction

Andrew Johnson, who became president after Abraham Lincoln was assassinated, continued Lincoln's lenient policies toward former Confederates. Like Lincoln, Johnson insisted that the war was an insurrection, that the southern states were never out of the Union, and that the organization of a new civil authority in these states was an executive, not a legislative, function. His rapid restoration of civil government in the former Confederate states, amnesty for former Confederates, and lack of interest in protecting the civil rights of freedpeople angered the Radical Republicans in Congress. This faction, led by Representative Thaddeus Stevens and Senator Charles Sumner, had pressed for more aggressive military campaigns during the war and a quicker end to slavery.

Challenging Lincoln, it had run John C. Frémont against him for the presidency in 1864 and passed the Wade-Davis Bill aiming to reverse Lincoln's proposed leniency toward Confederates. In December 1865, when Johnson declared that the Union had been restored and it looked as though representatives and senators from former Confederate states would be reseated in Congress, the Radical Republicans balked. Concerned for the civil rights of the freedpeople, they quickly appointed a joint committee to examine issues of suffrage and representation for the former Confederate states. The struggle between the president and Congress escalated in early 1866 when Congress passed two bills over Johnson's veto—the reauthorization of the Freedmen's Bureau and the Civil Rights Act.

Established in March 1865, the Freedmen's Bureau aimed to help freedpeople in their economic, social, and political transition to freedom. To prevent them from becoming wards of the state and the bureau from becoming a permanent guardian, it remained a temporary agency that Congress had to renew annually. In reauthorizing the Freedmen's Bureau in February 1866, Congress expanded its powers by establishing military commissions to hear cases of civil rights abuses—of which there were many. The bureau heard shocking reports of whites violently beating and abusing blacks (even murdering them), cheating them out of their wages, shortchanging them on purchased goods, and stealing their crop shares. In September 1865, for example, the head of the Freedmen's Bureau in Mississippi reported, "Men, who are honorable in their dealings with their white neighbors, will cheat a negro without feeling a single twinge of their honor; to kill a negro they do not deem murder; to debauch a negro woman they do not think fornication; to take property away from a negro they do not deem a robbery. . . . They still have the ingrained feeling that the black people at large belong to the white people at large."[27] When Johnson vetoed the reauthorization bill, stating that the military commissions were unconstitutional, Congress passed the bill over his veto. The Freedman's Bureau was discontinued in 1869.

To further protect the civil rights of freedpeople, Congress passed the **Civil Rights Act of 1866**, again over Johnson's veto. This act defined U.S. citizenship for the first time and affirmed that all citizens were equally protected by the laws. It overturned black codes and ensured that blacks could make contracts and initiate lawsuits, but it did not protect black voting rights. In February 1866, Frederick Douglass and a delegation of other black leaders met with Johnson to try to convince him of the importance of black suffrage, but without success.

Tensions between the stubborn and increasingly isolated Johnson and an energetic Congress escalated over the **Fourteenth Amendment**, which Congress quickly proposed and sent to the states for ratification in 1866. Ratified in 1868, this amendment affirmed the Civil Rights Act's definition of citizenship and guarantee of "equal protection of the laws" to all citizens. Declaring that "all persons born or naturalized in the United States" are "citizens of the United States and of the State wherein they reside," it reversed the *Dred Scott* decision of 1857, which had ruled that blacks could not be citizens. To protect citizens against civil rights violations by the states, the amendment also declared that "no State shall make or enforce any law which shall abridge the privileges and immunities of citizens of the United States; nor shall any State deprive any person of life, liberty, or property without due process of law; nor deny to any person within its jurisdiction the equal protection of the laws." This clause would ultimately shape the black freedom struggle, but not before states found ways to

The First Vote, 1867

This image by A. R. Waud, which appeared in *Harper's Weekly*, evokes the revolutionary importance of African Americans' first opportunity to vote. The range of facial expressions, dress, status, and life experiences represented in the line of black male voters suggests the various meanings and expectations attached to the event. This all-male image captures the reality of the vote as a privilege of manhood. The flag overhead, as well as the serious expression of the white man overseeing the voting, reflect the profound political transformation represented by this very special moment. *Library of Congress, LC-DIG-ppmsca-31598.*

craft racially discriminatory laws in the areas in which states were sovereign, such as public education.

Outmaneuvered, Johnson took his case to the people, embarking on an unprecedented presidential speaking tour, which proved disastrous. In the midterm elections of 1866, the Radical Republicans captured two-thirds of both houses of Congress, and the next year they moved quickly to take charge of Reconstruction. Congress passed four Reconstruction Acts. The first **Reconstruction Act of 1867**, passed on March 2, 1867, dissolved state governments in the former Confederacy (except for Tennessee) and divided the old Confederacy into five military districts subject to martial law, each with a military governor. To reenter the Union, a state was required to call a constitutional convention, which would be elected by universal male suffrage (including black male suffrage); to write a new state constitution that guaranteed black suffrage; and to ratify the Fourteenth Amendment. The other three Reconstruction Acts passed in 1867 and early 1868 empowered the military commanders of each district to ensure that the process of reconstruction in each state went forward, in spite of strong ex-Confederate opposition.

On March 2, 1867, Congress also passed—and later passed again, over Johnson's veto—the Tenure of Office Act, which prohibited the president from removing any cabinet member from office without the Senate's approval. The act was designed to protect Secretary of War Edwin M. Stanton, a Radical Republican who was openly critical of the president. When Johnson dismissed Stanton in February 1868, the House of Representatives impeached Johnson for this violation of the act and other charges. The Senate failed to convict him, but thereafter the president was politically sidelined, and Congress assumed primary responsibility for Reconstruction.

Black Reconstruction

Meanwhile, the military Reconstruction of the South was already under way. Many former Confederates were ineligible to vote in elections for delegates to state constitutional conventions, and up to 30 percent of whites refused to participate in elections in which black men could vote. Thus in some states, black voters were in the majority. Of the little over 1,000 delegates elected to write new state constitutions, 268 were black. In South Carolina and Louisiana, blacks were in the majority. Black delegates advocated for the interests of freedpeople specifically, and the American people generally, and against the interests of caste and property. In South Carolina, for example, delegate Robert Smalls proposed that the state sponsor a public school system that was open to all.

The state constitutional conventions initiated a new phase of Reconstruction. Decades later, the black scholar and activist W. E. B. Du Bois called it "Black Reconstruction" in a book by that title. His subtitle, "An Essay toward a History of the Part Which Black Folk Played in the Attempt to Reconstruct Democracy in America," suggests a transformative and yet short-lived revolutionary moment during which African Americans participated in southern political life. (See Visual Sources: Portrayals of Reconstruction-Era African Americans, pp. 419–27.) The constitutions these conventions drafted provided for a range of "firsts" for the South: universal male suffrage, public schools, progressive taxes, improved court and judicial systems, commissions to promote industrial development, state aid for railroad development, and social welfare institutions such as hospitals and asylums for orphans and the mentally ill. In many ways, these were among the most progressive state constitutions and state governments the nation ever had, and they are why Du Bois called Reconstruction a "splendid failure"[28]—splendid for what could have been.

Du Bois also argued that Black Reconstruction was splendid because it did not fail due to alleged black incompetence and inferiority, as many whites expected. Instead Black Reconstruction clearly demonstrated African American competence and equality. From the first, white southerners who did not participate in the conventions denigrated the black delegates as incompetent and the white delegates as "carpetbaggers" and "scalawags." Carpetbaggers were northern white opportunity seekers who had come to the South (with all their belongings in travel bags made from carpet) to make money off plantation, railroad, and industrial interests. Scalawags were southern whites who turned on their fellow white southerners and tied their fortunes to the Republican Party. Such charges were ill founded. While Black Reconstruction politicians ranged from liberal to conservative, they were more centrist than radical, more committed to reintegrating former Confederates into the new state governments than punishing them for having waged war against the United States, and more than competent.

During Black Reconstruction, some 2,000 blacks served as officeholders at the various levels of government in the South.[29] Although a little over half for whom information is available had been slaves, they were now literate, and they were committed. Among them were artisans, laborers, businessmen, carpenters, barbers, ministers, teachers, editors, publishers, storekeepers, and merchants. They served as sheriffs, police officers, justices of the peace, registrars, city council members, county commissioners, members of boards of education, tax collectors, land office clerks, and

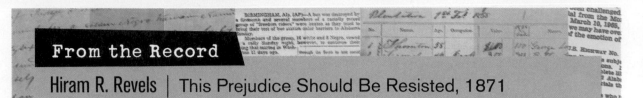

From the Record

Hiram R. Revels | This Prejudice Should Be Resisted, 1871

Hiram R. Revels (1822–1901), from Mississippi, was the first African American U.S. senator, serving from February 1870 to March 1871. In this speech delivered in the Senate, he opposes an amendment that would segregate public schools in the District of Columbia, which like the district itself, were under the jurisdiction of Congress. Despite his opposition, the amendment passed, and schools in the nation's capital were segregated until 1954, when the U.S. Supreme Court ruled segregated schools unconstitutional. At the end of his term, Revels returned to Mississippi to become president of Alcorn A&M, the first state-supported and first federal land-grant college for blacks.

Mr. President, I rise to express a few thoughts on this subject. It is not often that I ask the attention of the Senate on any subject, but this is one on which I feel it is my duty to make a few brief remarks.

In regard to the wishes of the colored people of this city, I will simply say that the trustees of colored schools and some of the most intelligent colored men of this place have said to me that they would have before asked for a bill abolishing the separate colored schools and putting all children on an equality in the common schools if they had thought they could obtain it. They feared they could not; and this is the only reason why they did not ask for it before.

I find that the prejudice in this country to color is very great, and I sometimes fear that it is on the increase. For example, let me remark that it matters not how colored people act, it matters not how they behave themselves, how well they deport themselves, how intelligent they may be, how refined they may be[;] . . . the prejudice against them is equally as great as it is against the most low and degraded man you can find in the streets of this city or in any other place. . . .

. . . Is this prejudice right? Have the colored people done anything to justify the prejudice against them that does exist in the hearts of so many white persons, and generally of one great political party in this country? Have they done anything to justify it? No, sir. . . .

Mr. President, if this prejudice has no cause to justify it, then we must admit that it is wicked, we must admit that it is wrong; we must admit that it has not the approval of Heaven. Therefore I hold it to be the duty of this nation to discourage it. . . . If the nation should take a step for the encouragement of this prejudice against the colored race, can they have any ground upon which to predicate a hope that Heaven will smile upon them and prosper them? . . .

Sir, this prejudice should be resisted. . . .

. . . Let me say that it is the wish of the colored people of this District, and of the colored people over this land, that this Congress shall not do anything which will increase that prejudice which is now fearfully great against them. If this amendment be adopted you will encourage that prejudice. . . .

Continued

Continued

... Let lawmakers cease to make the difference, let school trustees and school boards cease to make the difference, and the people will soon forget it.

SOURCE: "(1871) Senator Hiram Revels Calls for the End of Segregated Schools," *Cong. Globe*, 41st Cong., 3rd sess., part 2, 1059–60 (1871).

???

How does Revels describe white American attitudes toward African Americans throughout the nation? What arguments does he make for integrated schools and against antiblack prejudice? Do you find these arguments persuasive?

postmasters. Wherever they served, they sought to balance the interests of black and white southerners. In a political era marked by graft and corruption, black politicians proved to be more ethical than their white counterparts.

A few black Republicans achieved high state office. In Louisiana, Mississippi, and South Carolina, blacks served as lieutenant governor. Some were superintendents of education, a post with considerable power. More than six hundred state legislators were black, including Robert Smalls, who served in the South Carolina House of Representatives and Senate (Map 8.1). In 1874, Smalls was elected to the U.S. House of Representatives. Thirteen other black men served in the U.S. House during this era, and two in the Senate. Like their colleagues in local and state positions in the South, these black senators and congressmen were moderate politicians who tried hard to balance the often irreconcilable concerns of freedpeople and southern whites. Hiram R. Revels (1870–1871) and Blanche K. Bruce (1875–1881) were both senators from Mississippi. A minister in the AME Church, Revels was known for his oratorical ability and his amnesty program for disfranchised former Confederates, which would have allowed them to vote and hold office with limited penalties. (See From the Record: This Prejudice Should Be Resisted.) Bruce, a skilled Mississippi delta politician and planter, proved to be a far more vigorous champion of black civil rights and an unyielding opponent of white resistance to black political participation.

The widespread political involvement of blacks was unprecedented in the United States and unique among nineteenth-century post-emancipation societies, including Jamaica, Cuba, and Brazil. In the United States, many were former slaves who had never before had any political rights. Blacks' service in office, as well as the wide range of political activities of thousands of other black men and women, amounted to a political revolution. Black politics then and since has included innumerable local, grassroots, and community-based activities outside the realm of formal politics, activities aimed at enhancing black influence and control. Still, for the black community, political participation and the vote during Reconstruction represented key expressions of citizenship and national belonging. When black men voted, they cast a family vote—a choice that reflected the collective aspirations of their wives, children, relatives, and extended kin, as well as those of their neighbors and communities.

Freedpeople allied themselves with the Republican Party, the party of emancipation and Abraham Lincoln. They were actively recruited by the **Union League**, which had been created in 1862 in the North to support the Republican Party and after the war sent representatives to the South. Along with the Freedmen's Bureau,

THE FIRST COLORED SENATOR AND REPRESENTATIVES.
In the 41ˢᵗ and 42ⁿᵈ Congress of the United States.

The First Colored Senator and Representatives, 1872
This dignified group portrait represents the first black men to serve in Congress as statesmen as well as pioneering black political leaders. In the back row, from left to right, are Robert C. De Large (South Carolina) and Jefferson F. Long (Georgia). In the front row are Hiram R. Revels (Mississippi), Benjamin S. Turner (Alabama), Josiah T. Walls (Florida), Joseph H. Rainey (South Carolina), and Robert Brown Elliott (South Carolina). Except for Revels, who served in the Senate (1870–1871), all of these men served in the House of Representatives during the Forty-First (1869–1871) and/or Forty-Second Congress (1871–1873). *Library of Congress, LC-DIG-ppmsca-17564.*

southern branches of the Union League mobilized black support for the Republican Party and helped blacks understand their political rights and responsibilities as citizens.

African Americans viewed the right to vote as the most important of all civil rights and the one on which all the others depended. The vote made economic, social, and political liberties possible and helped protect them. To ensure this right, the overwhelmingly Republican U.S. Congress proposed the **Fifteenth Amendment** in 1869, and it was ratified the next year. It declared, "The right of citizens of the United States to vote shall not be denied or abridged by the United States or by any State on account of race, color, or previous condition of servitude." With this amendment, many—including the prominent white abolitionist William Lloyd Garrison—believed that the federal government's constitutional incorporation of blacks into the Union was complete and its formal responsibility to the former slaves fulfilled.

Enforcement of the amendment was a separate issue, however, and to help clarify what equality meant, Senator Charles Sumner introduced one more civil rights bill.

MAP 8.1   Black Political Participation in the Reconstruction South, 1867–1868

In the overlapping years of Congressional Reconstruction and Black Reconstruction, the states of the former Confederacy were reorganized into five military districts under the first Reconstruction Act of 1867. Within these districts, for the first time ever, thousands of newly enfranchised blacks participated in politics, voted, and held elected offices at all levels of the government. As this map illustrates, the percentages of African Americans elected to the first state legislatures as a result of the first Reconstruction Act and the three that followed were significant: a full half of Louisiana's elected state legislators were black, and in South Carolina, black legislators comprised a 61 percent majority. SOURCE: *The Atlas of African-American History and Politics: From the Slave Trade to Modern Times,* by Arwin Smallwood and Jeffrey Elliot. Copyright © 1998 The McGraw-Hill Companies, Inc. Used by permission of McGraw-Hill.

When passed after his death and partly in his memory, the **Civil Rights Act of 1875** required equal treatment in public accommodations and on public conveyances regardless of race. By this time, however, most Americans thought the freedpeople should be on their own and feared that further government efforts on their behalf would only undermine their self-reliance and make them wards of the state. Blacks, too, believed that they were responsible for their own future. Yet they knew all too well that the persistence of antiblack prejudice and discrimination, as well as the enduring legacy of slavery, required federal action. Only the federal government could ensure their freedom and their rights in the face of widespread and hostile white opposition.

The Defeat of Reconstruction

While northern whites thought that the Fifteenth Amendment completed Reconstruction, southern whites found black political involvement intolerable; they were shocked and outraged that their world had been turned upside down. For them, black political participation represented a "base conspiracy against human nature."[30] Even as many withdrew from the system, they immediately began planning a counterrevolution that would restore white rule and sought what they called "redemption" through the all-white Democratic Party.

White opposition movements proceeded differently in each state, but by the late 1860s they had begun to succeed. As soon as they gained sufficient leverage, southern whites ousted blacks from political office in an effort to bring back what they called "home rule" under the reinvigorated ideology of states' rights. Home rule and states' rights served as euphemisms for white domination of land, black labor, and state and local government. Under the guise of restoring fiscal conservatism—trimming taxes and cutting state government functions and budgets—southern Democrats scaled back and ended programs that assisted freedpeople, including ending South Carolina's land reform commission.

An essential element of white "redemption" was the intimidation of blacks through terror, violence, and even murder. White supremacist and vigilante organizations formed throughout the South. While the Ku Klux Klan (KKK), organized in Tennessee in 1865, was the most notable group, others were the '76 Association, Knights of the White Camelia, White Brotherhood, and Pale Faces. Members of the KKK, called night riders because they conducted their raids at night, wore white robes and hoods to hide their identity. People from all sectors of southern white society joined these groups.

The targets of white attacks were usually successful and economically independent black landowners, storeowners, and small entrepreneurs. Black schools, churches, homes, lodges, business buildings, livestock, barns, and fences were destroyed. Blacks were beaten, raped, murdered, and lynched. So widespread were these vicious attacks in the late 1860s and early 1870s that Congress held hearings to investigate the causes of this widespread lawlessness. "The object of it is to kill out the leading men of the Republican party . . . men who have taken a prominent stand," testified Emanuel Fortune, a delegate to Florida's constitutional convention and member of the state house of representatives who had been forced from his home and county by the KKK. In other testimony, Congress learned that Jack Dupree of Monroe County, Mississippi, the strong-willed president of a local Republican Club, had been lynched by the KKK in front of his wife and newborn twins.[31]

To restore order, Congress passed two **Force Acts**, in 1870 and 1871, to protect the civil rights of blacks as defined in the Fourteenth and Fifteenth Amendments. Federal troops rather than state militias were authorized to put down the widespread lawlessness, and those who conspired to deprive black people of their civil rights were to be tried in federal rather than state or local courts.

Nevertheless, the violence continued. In Colfax, Louisiana, a disputed election in 1873 prompted whites to use cannon and rifle fire to disband a group of armed freedmen, commanded by black militia and veterans, who were attempting to maintain Republican control of the town. On Easter Sunday, in the bloodiest racial massacre of the era, more than 280 blacks were killed, including 50 who had surrendered. The Colfax Massacre demonstrated the limits of armed black self-defense and the lengths to which whites would go to secure white dominance. A similar white attack occurred in 1876 in Hamburg, South Carolina, where skirmishes between black militiamen, armed by the state, and whites, acting on their own authority, escalated into a shoot out. Six black men died at the hands of the white mob. The Hamburg Massacre routed local black political authority and strengthened white resolve to "redeem" South Carolina.

In the end, the Republican Party, the federal government, and northern whites all accepted the return of white ex-Confederates to political and economic power. With the death of Thaddeus Stevens in 1868 and Charles Sumner in 1874, blacks lost their most effective spokesmen in Congress. Growing numbers of Republicans had wearied of the party's crusade on behalf of blacks and were happy to turn what they called the "Negro problem" over to southern whites, who were presumed to know best how to handle it. Republicans were confident that the Fifteenth Amendment had secured their black voting base in the South. As the party gathered strength in the Midwest and West, recruiting black Republicans—and securing a southern base for the Republican Party—became less important to the party. Instead, it turned its attention to economic issues, such as support for railroads and industry. Especially after the panic of 1873 set off a deep four-year depression, black Republicans in the South, and black civil rights in general, became expendable.

One indication of the federal government's abandonment of the freedpeople was its failure to back the Freedman's Savings and Trust Company, which collapsed during the depression. Chartered by Congress in 1865 to promote thrift and savings among freedpeople, it had many small savings accounts averaging less than $50 each. Its last president was Frederick Douglass, who deposited $10,000 of his own money to bolster the institution. When the bank failed, thousands of African Americans lost all they had. Eventually, half received reimbursements of about 60 percent of their deposits. The other half received nothing.

By 1877, southern whites had retaken political control of all the southern states. That same year, in a political deal that resolved the disputed 1876 presidential election between the Democrat Samuel Tilden and the Republican Rutherford B. Hayes, Black Reconstruction officially ended. In return for a Hayes victory, Republicans agreed to remove federal troops from the South. In April 1877, when the troops withdrew, blacks were left without federal protection.

The U.S. Supreme Court further undermined black civil rights. In the 1873 *Slaughterhouse cases*, the Court, distinguishing between national citizenship and state citizenship, ruled that the Fourteenth Amendment guaranteed only a narrow class of national citizenship rights and did not encompass the array of civil rights pertaining to state citizenship. A decade later, in the *Civil Rights cases* (1883), the Court overturned the Civil Rights Act of 1875, declaring that Congress did not have the authority to protect against the discriminatory conduct of individuals and private groups. As a result, private companies and businesses, such as hotels, restaurants, and theaters, could refuse to serve black people, and they did. The Court thus legitimized the power of states and private individuals and institutions to discriminate against black citizens and practically canceled the power of the federal government to intervene. AME bishop Henry McNeal Turner expressed pervasive black feelings of both outrage and despair. The decision, he proclaimed, "absolves the Negro's allegiance to the general government, makes the American flag to him a rag of contempt instead of a symbol of liberty."[32]

Opportunities and Limits outside the South

During the Civil War, roughly 100,000 blacks left the South permanently, relocating in the North, Midwest, and West, especially in areas bordering on the former Confederacy (Map 8.2).[33] During Reconstruction, the migration continued, as many African Americans believed they had to leave the South to improve their lives. Wherever they went, however, they encountered well-established patterns of antiblack prejudice and discrimination. Often new patterns developed as well. White military officials, factory owners, and union leaders limited black opportunities for dignified work and fair wages, further circumscribing black lives. By the mid-1880s, national indifference to the plight of blacks meant that wherever they lived, they knew that they themselves, not the states or the federal government, had to protect their rights and liberties.

Autonomy in the West

For African Americans, as for all Americans, the West beckoned as a land of opportunity. Some who envisioned a better future for themselves in the West were young men who joined the army. The U.S. Colored Troops were disbanded after the war, but new black units (again with white officers) were authorized. Between 1866 and 1917, 25,000 black men—some former Civil War soldiers and others with no prior military experience—served in the Ninth and Tenth Cavalry Regiments and the Twenty-Fourth and Twenty-Fifth Infantry Regiments (established in 1866), all assigned to military posts in the West. There they were engaged in the Indian wars that removed Native

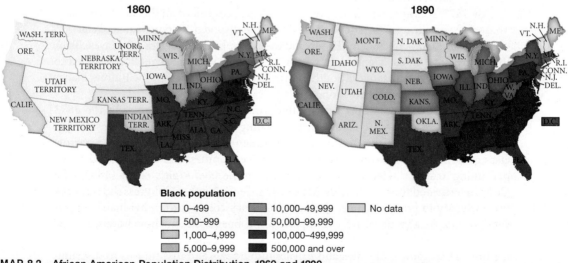

Black population

☐ 0–499	▨ 10,000–49,999 ☐ No data
☐ 500–999	▨ 50,000–99,999
☐ 1,000–4,999	▨ 100,000–499,999
☐ 5,000–9,999	■ 500,000 and over

MAP 8.2   African American Population Distribution, 1860 and 1890

In the years following the Civil War, the black population grew significantly and began to spread across the nation. Nevertheless, the vast majority of blacks remained wedded to the South. The states that witnessed the largest and most striking growth in their black populations from 1860 onward, and those with the largest total numbers of blacks in 1890, were those of the former Confederacy—the so-called Black Belt states of the antebellum and post-bellum South—and the states bordering them.

Buffalo Soldiers of the Twenty-Fifth Infantry Regiment
Four all-black U.S. army regiments were created after the Civil War. Given the name buffalo soldiers by Native Americans in the West, these black soldiers participated in the Indian wars of the late nineteenth century, the Spanish-American War of 1898, and subsequent U.S. wars. The soldiers shown here, some dressed in buffalo coats, illustrate these regiments' rough-and-ready image. While many have praised them for their military accomplishments, all achieved while they endured the injustices of separate and unequal civilian and military worlds, some have seen them as agents of U.S. imperialism and the genocidal policies of the U.S. government against the Indians. *Library of Congress, LC-DIG-ppmsca 11106.*

Americans onto reservations and placed their lands in the protection of white settlers, cattle herds, and railroad crews. Native Americans called them **buffalo soldiers**, apparently in reference to their fierce fighting abilities and their dark curly hair, which resembled a buffalo's mane. Thirteen enlisted men and six officers received the Congressional Medal of Honor for their service in the Indian wars. Private Henry McCombs of the Tenth Calvary bragged, "We made the West," having "defeated the hostile tribes of Indians; and made the country safe to live in."[34]

Buffalo soldiers led a rough life on remote military posts. Most were single, although over time, as camp life improved, some married or brought wives and children to join them. Unlike white soldiers, who rotated out of service in the West to posts in the South and East, buffalo soldiers remained in the West, where the army expected they would encounter less racial hostility. But tensions between them and whites, Native Americans, and Latinos were always evident, particularly in Kansas and in Texas along the Mexican border. Sometimes tensions erupted into violence, as when a black soldier was lynched in Sturgis, Dakota Territory, in 1885. In response, twenty men from the Twenty-Fifth Infantry shot up two saloons, killing one white civilian.

A few black men became officers, but not without enduring discrimination both within the ranks and from white officers. Henry O. Flipper is one example. Appointed to West Point by a Reconstruction Republican from Georgia, Flipper became the first black to graduate from the military academy, in 1877. As a second lieutenant in the Tenth Cavalry Regiment, he was often assigned to manual labor instead of command positions. Nevertheless, he served with distinction in the Apache War of 1880. Two years later, however, he was dismissed from the army on a controversial charge of embezzlement. For the rest of his life, he fought to be exonerated and reinstated.

Other African Americans went west as families. An especially notable migration took place from Tennessee and Kentucky to Kansas, where African Americans hoped to claim cheap public land available under the Homestead Act of 1862. In 1876, the Hartwell family of Pulaski, Tennessee, in 1866 the birthplace of the KKK, migrated to Kansas because Tennessee was "no place for colored people."[35] In Kansas, black migrants built all-black towns that promised freedom from white persecution and an opportunity for self-government. Nicodemus, incorporated in 1877, was the most famous. "Nicodemus is the most harmonious place on earth," proclaimed its newspaper in 1886. "Everyone works for the interest of the town and all pull together."[36] It grew out of a development proposal by W. J. Niles, a black businessman, and a white land developer named W. R. Hill. The first black settlers came from Lexington, Kentucky, and by 1880 the thriving town, which serviced a thriving county, had almost 260 black and almost 60 white residents, a bank, general stores, hotels, a pharmacy, a millinery, a livery, and a barbershop.[37] One resident was Edward P. McCabe, a talented and ambitious New Yorker and active Republican who, upon moving to Nicodemus, became a farmer, attorney, and land agent. During the years he served as state auditor (1883–1887), he was the highest-ranking black officeholder in the country.

Benjamin "Pap" Singleton, who detested sharecropping and promoted black landownership as the most viable basis for black self-improvement, became the most important proponent of the black migration to Kansas. Operating out of Edgefield, Tennessee, his Edgefield Real Estate and Homestead Association spread word of available land and a hospitable environment for blacks in Kansas. Black newspapers, mass meetings, circulars, and letters home from migrants also inspired "emigration fever." Singleton became known as "the Moses of the Colored Exodus." In the spring and summer of 1879, more than 6,000 blacks from Texas, Louisiana, and Mississippi—called **Exodusters**—migrated to Kansas, where they were able to settle on land that became theirs. John Solomon Lewis of Louisiana described the feeling: "When I landed on the soil, I looked on the ground and I says this is free ground. Then I looked on the heavens, and I says them is free and beautiful heavens. Then I looked within my heart, and I says to myself I wonder why I never was free before."[38]

Landownership made the difference, and the Exodusters established four all-black farming communities that grew into towns with businesses, churches, and schools. Most Exodusters decided for themselves to take a chance on the West, although grassroots leaders such as Singleton and Henry Adams, from Shreveport, Louisiana, helped inspire them. Adams's activities in politics and black labor organizing were indicative of a growing grassroots black nationalism. Involved in a variety of regional networks along the Mississippi River, Adams promoted migration to

Kansas and also supported the Colonization Council, which sought federal funds for black migration to Liberia.

Between 1865 and 1920, more than sixty all-black towns were created in the West, some fifty of them in Oklahoma, where new settlements of southern freedmen joined with former slaves owned by Native Americans in what had been designated Indian Territory. Tullahassee, for example, which began as a Creek settlement in 1850, had become mostly African American by 1881, as the Creeks moved elsewhere. In the late 1880s, when Indian land in Oklahoma was opened up for settlement, all-black towns boomed. They offered a freedom unknown elsewhere. But the five- to ten-acre plots on which most black migrants settled were too small for independent farms, and many ended up working for nearby ranches and larger farms owned by whites.[39] Eventually, most of the black towns that had boomed disappeared.

The Right to Work for Fair Wages

Like Jourdan Anderson, some former slaves left the South as soon as they were free, moving north in expectation of fair wages for their labor and a good education for their children. Many gravitated to cities, where the hope of better jobs soon faltered. Black newcomers ran into the prejudice and discrimination in hiring and wages that had long hobbled black workers there. Managers were reluctant to hire them, and white workers, who saw them as competition, were hostile, especially since blacks were often hired as strikebreakers. White labor unions characteristically excluded blacks.

Some individuals were able to set out on their own. In 1865, when white caulkers in the Baltimore shipyards went on strike to force the firing of more than a hundred black caulkers and longshoremen, Isaac Myers, a highly skilled black caulker, joined with other black labor activists and a small group of supportive whites to create the black-owned and cooperatively run Chesapeake Marine Railway and Dry Dock Company. It was a strong center of black union activism, and in 1869 Myers helped found the Colored National Labor Union to advance the cause of black workers. Myers was also a proponent of interracial labor solidarity. (See From the Record: The Freedom of Labor.) Yet his efforts were short-lived. By the mid-1870s, the Colored National Labor Union had dissolved due to internal dissension and the depression that followed the panic of 1873. By the mid-1880s, the company Myers had founded also had collapsed.

The idea of interracial labor solidarity was taken up by the Knights of Labor, a broad-based union founded in 1869 that welcomed both skilled and unskilled workers and eventually African Americans and women. With the rise of industry in the North during and after the war, the Knights believed that only a united and inclusive labor movement could stand up to the growing power of industrialists who, said the Knights, built profits through "wage slavery." The organization's motto was "An injury to one is the concern of all." At its height in 1886, the Knights had more than 700,000 members. Despite the fact that its assemblies in the South were segregated by race, the Knights' commitment to interracial unionism drew African American support. Black workers fully embraced the Knights' major goals: the eight-hour workday, the abolition of child and convict labor, equal pay for equal work, and worker-owned and managed cooperatives. By 1886, two-thirds of Richmond, Virginia's 5,000 tobacco workers—many of them black—belonged to the organization. But the Knights of Labor's quick decline followed its quick rise to prominence. Failed strikes and disputes between skilled and

From the Record

Isaac Myers | The Freedom of Labor, 1869

Isaac Myers (1835–1891) was born free in Baltimore and apprenticed by his parents to an African American ship caulker. He worked his way up in the trade to become a supervisor of caulkers in the Baltimore shipyards, where many free blacks were employed. He helped form the Colored Caulkers Trade Union Society, but he was also an advocate of interracial unionism, for which he makes a case in this excerpt from his speech to the white National Labor Union in Philadelphia in August 1869.

Gentlemen, silent but powerful and far-reaching is the revolution inaugurated by your act of taking the colored laborer by the hand and telling him that his interest is common with yours, and that he should have an equal chance in the race for life. . . . It is America and it is only Americans that can work up and work out such great revolutions in a day. God grant that it may be as lasting as the eternal hills. I speak today for the colored men of the whole country . . . when I tell you that all they ask for themselves is a fair chance; that you and they may make one steady and strong pull until the laboring man of this country shall receive such pay for time made [work done in a timely fashion] as will secure them a comfortable living for their families, educate their children and leave a dollar for a rainy day and old age. Slavery, or slave labor, the main cause of the degradation of white labor, is no more. And it is the proud boast of my life that the slave himself had a large share in the work of striking off the fetters that bound him by the ankle, while the other end bound you by the neck.

The white laboring men of the country have nothing to fear from the colored laboring man. We desire to see labor elevated and made respectable; we desire to have the highest rate of wages that our labor is worth; we desire to have the hours of labor regulated, as well to the interest of the laborer and the capitalist. And you, gentlemen, may rely on the support of the colored laborers of this country in bringing about this result. If they have not strictly observed these principles in the past, it was because the doors of the workshops of the North, East and West were firmly bolted against them, and it was written over the doors: "No Negro admitted here." Thus barred out, thus warned off, his only hope was to put his labor in the market to be controlled by selfish and unscrupulous speculators who will dare do any deed to advance their own ends.

Mr. President and gentlemen, American citizenship with the black man is a complete failure if he is proscribed from the workshops of this country, if any man cannot employ him who chooses, and if he cannot work for any man whom he will. If citizenship means anything at all, it means the freedom of labor, as broad and as universal as the freedom of the ballot.

Source: Philip S. Foner and Robert James Branham, eds., *Lift Every Voice: African American Oratory, 1787–1900* (Tuscaloosa: University of Alabama Press, 1998), 483–84.

???   According to Myers, in what ways did slavery and antiblack prejudice do a disservice to both black and white workers? How does he use this point to argue for interracial unions?

unskilled workers weakened it internally, and the 1886 Haymarket bombing—a deadly confrontation between striking workers and police in Chicago—damaged its reputation. In Richmond, the demise of the Knights doomed prospects for interracial unionism for decades.

The Struggle for Equal Rights

In the North and West, the struggle for the dignity of work and equal labor rights took place within a larger struggle for civil rights that had begun before the war. The National Equal Rights League (see chapter 7) continued to promote full legal and political equality, land acquisition as a basis for economic independence, education, frugality, and moral rectitude. Local, state, and national meetings kept the tradition of vigorous agitation alive, while petition campaigns and lobbying kept the pressure on the Republican Party to pass legislation and amendments guaranteeing black civil rights and suffrage.

On the local level, black campaigns against segregated seating in public conveyances continued, often initiated by women. In Philadelphia, Frances Ellen Watkins Harper and Harriet Tubman were among those who protested their forcible ejections from streetcars. The long campaign led by Octavius Catto, a teacher at the Institute for Colored Youth, and

THE NATIONAL COLORED CONVENTION IN SESSION AT WASHINGTON, D. C.—Sketched by Theo. R. Davis.

National Convention of Colored Men, 1869
Focused on advancing the cause of equal rights for blacks, particularly black male suffrage, the 1869 National Convention of Colored Men reflected the hopeful mood at the outset of Black Reconstruction. Looking ahead rather than back, a convention majority voted against reviving the defunct National Equal Rights League, which had been founded at the 1864 convention in Syracuse, New York (see chapter 7). *The Granger Collection, NYC. All rights reserved.*

William Still, the best-known "agent" on the underground railroad, finally succeeded in getting a desegregation law passed in 1867. Three days later, when a conductor told school principal Caroline Le Count that she could not board a streetcar, she lodged a complaint, and the conductor was fined. Thereafter, Philadelphia's streetcar companies abided by the new law, reversing decades of custom.[40] A similar protest, in which Sojourner Truth played a role, had ended streetcar segregation in Washington, D.C., in 1865.

Segregated schools were the norm in the North, and as in the South many blacks preferred all-black schools with black teachers who took the interests of black students to heart. Catto argued for this position. He also pointed out that white teachers assigned to black schools were likely to be those not qualified for positions in white schools, and thus "inferior."[41] In other communities, black fathers initiated suits so that their children could attend white schools. Cases in Iowa in 1875 and 1876 brought court rulings in the plaintiffs' favor, but local whites blocked their enforcement. In Indiana, despite an 1869 law permitting localities to provide schools for black children, communities with few black residents did not do so, and black children all too often went without an education. The same situation pertained in Illinois and California.[42]

During Black Reconstruction, educational opportunities for black children may have been more plentiful in the South than in the North, and opportunities for black voting were better, too. In 1865, black men could vote without restriction only in Maine, New Hampshire, Vermont, Massachusetts, and Rhode Island. Together these states accounted for just 7 percent of the northern black population. Some northern states actually took action to deny black men the vote: Minnesota, Kansas, and Ohio in 1867; Michigan and New York in 1868. Most northern whites viewed the vote as a white male prerogative. Even where blacks could vote, they were often intimidated and subjected to violence. In 1871, Octavius Catto was murdered on his way to the polls.

Thus, in 1869 and 1870, ratification of the Fifteenth Amendment proved to be as contentious in the North and West as it was in the South. The former slave states of Delaware, Kentucky, Maryland, and Tennessee rejected it, but so did California and New Jersey; New York rescinded its ratification; and Ohio waffled, first rejecting and then ratifying the amendment. Reasons for the opposition varied. Californians, for example, wanted to ensure that the amendment did not enfranchise Chinese residents. The debate in states that eventually ratified the amendment varied. Massachusetts and Connecticut had literacy requirements that they hoped would remain unaffected. Rhode Island wanted to retain its requirement that foreign-born citizens had to own property worth at least $134 to be eligible to vote. These restrictions narrowed the electorate in the North and West by making it difficult for poor and illiterate whites, as well as blacks, to vote. After the end of Reconstruction, some of the same and similar techniques would be used by southern states to disfranchise blacks.

Yet the Fifteenth Amendment proved most contentious among many northern women for what it did *not* do: It did not extend the vote to women. Supporters of woman suffrage felt betrayed that black men would get the vote before women. Abolitionists and feminists had long been allied in the struggle for equal rights, and women had actively worked for abolition, emancipation, and the Thirteenth Amendment. In 1866, to present a united front in support of universal suffrage, women's rights leaders Lucy Stone, Susan B. Anthony, and Elizabeth Cady Stanton joined with Frederick Douglass to found the American Equal Rights Association. But it soon became apparent that members of this organization had different priorities. (See Documents: Race,

Sex, and the Vote, pp. 414–18.) Douglass and Stone believed that the organization should work to secure the black male vote first and then seek woman suffrage. Stanton and Anthony detested the idea that the rights of women would take a backseat to those of black men. Stanton even resorted to using the racist epithet "Sambo" in reference to black men.[43] Black feminists such as Sojourner Truth and Frances Ellen Watkins Harper took Stanton to task for ignoring the reality of black women's lives. "You white women speak here of rights," Harper protested. "I speak of wrongs."[44]

Dissension over the Fifteenth Amendment divided old allies, destroyed friendships, and split the American Equal Rights Association—and ultimately the women's movement itself. In its wake, Anthony and Stanton organized the National Woman Suffrage Association, which focused on securing voting rights for women at the national level. That same year, Stone organized the rival American Woman Suffrage Association, which included among its members Harper, Truth, and Douglass and developed a state-by-state approach to woman suffrage. The bitter fight over the Fifteenth Amendment revealed deeper divisions in American politics and society over the rights and status of African Americans that would undercut their opportunities for decades to come.

CONCLUSION

Revolutions and Reversals

The end of slavery in the United States was revolutionary. For former slaves, now free, lives and livelihoods had to be remade. Foremost on the minds of many was reuniting with family members separated by slave sales and war. New black communities were built and old ones were renewed, centering on independent black churches, schools, and enterprises. Freedpeople knew that to live independently, they had to be literate, and they placed great faith in education. They learned eagerly, and within a decade dozens of black colleges were giving students a formal and expanded education, including the opportunity to acquire job skills, such as teacher training. Former slaves remade themselves, their families, and their communities, but their hopes for economic independence faded as the reality of emancipation, which had made them free but had not provided them with land, set in. Impoverished and pressed into labor patterns that resembled slavery, most became tenant farmers or sharecroppers, dependent on white landowners, and many became trapped in a cycle of debt.

When the Radical Republicans in Congress took control of Reconstruction in 1867, their efforts to guarantee civil rights for former slaves effected a political revolution in the South that had the potential for an economic and social revolution, too. With black votes and officeholding, southern states wrote new constitutions that created state aid for economic development, progressive tax and judicial systems, much-needed social welfare institutions, and the region's first public school systems. But this so-called Black Reconstruction proved short-lived. Southern white opposition was unrelenting and often violent. By 1877, whites had regained control of state and local governments in the South. As the Republican Party, now weary of the campaign for black rights, turned its attention to economic development, southern blacks in particular were left with shockingly little protection and dwindling numbers of effective white advocates of equal rights for blacks. "When you turned us loose," Frederick Douglass chastised the Republican National Convention in 1876, "you gave us no acres: you turned us loose to the sky, to the storm, to the whirlwind, and, worst of all, you turned us loose to the wrath of our infuriated masters."[45]

Some southern blacks went west to build new communities or serve in army units that fought the Indian wars. Others sought work in the expanding factories of the North. But wherever they went, they encountered prejudice and discrimination. Although campaigns for desegregating transportation and schools resulted in the passage of civil rights laws, those laws often went unenforced. U.S. Supreme Court rulings limited the impact of well-intentioned laws and constitutional amendments passed during Black Reconstruction. In 1883, a revived National Equal Rights League, meeting in Louisville, Kentucky, conceded "that many of the laws intended to secure us our rights as citizens are nothing more than dead letters."[46]

Abandoned by the government as they sought to carve out meaningful lives within an increasingly white supremacist nation, African Americans understood more clearly now than ever before what they had always known in their hearts: They were responsible for their own **uplift**. Thus freedom's first generations turned inward, practiced self-reliance, and focused even more intently on self-elevation and the building of strong communities that would sustain them going forward.

CHAPTER REVIEW

Online Study Guide ▪ bedfordstmartins.com/graywhite

Key Terms

historically black colleges and universities (p. 383)

sharecropping (p. 385)

crop lien (p. 385)

convict lease (p. 386)

black codes (p. 386)

Black Reconstruction (p. 390)

Civil Rights Act of 1866 (p. 391)

Fourteenth Amendment (ratified 1868) (p. 391)

Reconstruction Act of 1867 (first) (p. 392)

Union League (p. 395)

Fifteenth Amendment (ratified 1870) (p. 396)

Civil Rights Act of 1875 (p. 397)

Force Acts (1870, 1871) (p. 398)

Slaughterhouse cases (1873) (p. 399)

Civil Rights cases (1883) (p. 399)

buffalo soldiers (p. 401)

Exodusters (p. 402)

uplift (p. 408)

Review Questions

1. What practices, institutions, and organizations did former slaves develop to ease their transition to freedom? How successful were they, and what challenges did they face?

2. What factors resulted in the defeat of Reconstruction? Was it inevitable, or might things have turned out differently had any of these circumstances been different? Explain.

3. What kinds of opportunities did former slaves seek in the North and West? How did they attempt to realize their dreams? What obstacles did they have to overcome?

4. Should we judge Reconstruction on its initial promise or its ultimate failure? What is your assessment of this period?

For Web sites, images, and documents related to topics and places in this chapter, visit **Make History** at bedfordstmartins.com/graywhite.

Letters to the Freedmen's Bureau, 1865–1868

The **Freedmen's Bureau**, officially the Bureau of Refugees, Freedmen, and Abandoned Lands, was established by Congress in March 1865 to aid, protect, and manage the more than four million African Americans in the South in their transition from slavery to freedom. Its first task was to provide humanitarian relief. It also assisted freedmen in negotiating labor contracts and by promoting their education. The bureau was discontinued in 1869, although its educational activities and help for black veterans continued into the early 1870s.

From 1865 to 1869, the bureau's approximately nine hundred agents, operating out of field offices throughout the South, were like troops on the ground in the midst of great social upheaval—the social revolution wrought by emancipation and Reconstruction. Desperate blacks appealed to bureau agents for food, clothing, and medicine; for help in locating family members and arranging marriages; and for assistance with labor contracts. Agents received petitions for schools and applications for land. They settled labor disputes and heard testimony about outrages against blacks and even murder. Today the records of the Freedmen's Bureau in the National Archives are a rich documentary source for understanding the experiences of African Americans in these years. The following letters, arranged in chronological order, offer insight into the minds of black men and women as they made the transition from slavery to freedom. What was most important to them? Note that some wrote as committees, some as individuals, and one—a teacher—on behalf of others.

Joseph R. Johnson | The Need for Homes, 1865

Halls Hill Va   August 4th 1865.
Dear Sir: On Tuesday August 1st 1865, the Colored People of Halls Hill and vicinity, (near Camp Rucker, & Falls Church) Va—celebrated West India Emancipation, and American Emancipation.

During the business part of the celebration, the Rev Jacob Ross, (colored) of Georgetown—was chairman, and the following resolutions were unanimously adopted:—

1. "We feel it to be very important that we obtain HOMES—owning our shelters, *and the ground*, that we may raise fruit trees, concerning which our children can say—'*These are ours*'; also: that we may regularly and perseveringly educate our children, having our own school house in a central location, and also maintain public worship, and a Sabbath School, so that we may be an established and growing people, and be respected, and recognized by all loyal people, as welcome and efficient citizens of these United States—which is now *our* Country—made emphatically so by the blood of our brethren recently shed to save our Country."

2. Resolved: That we appoint a Committee of seven to visit the Freedmens Bureau, and enquire—"Can the Bureau give us any aid, or advice, in regard to obtaining Homes in this vicinity, or elsewhere?" . . .

I trust that they will receive such a response as may much encourage them, and those whom they represent. Yours for the Freedmen—

Joseph R. Johnson,
Missionary, and Teacher among Freedmen

SOURCE: Steven Hahn et al., eds., *Freedom: A Documentary History of Emancipation, 1861–1867*, 3rd ser., vol. 1, *Land and Labor, 1865*, Freedmen and Southern Society Project (Chapel Hill: University of North Carolina Press, 2008), 699–70.

Henry Bram, Ishmael Moultrie, and Yates Sampson | A Request for Homesteads, 1865

[Edisto Island, S.C., October 20 or 21, 1865]
General   It Is with painfull Hearts that we the committe address you,   we Have thoroughly considered the order which you wished us to Sighn,   we wish we could do so but cannot feel our rights Safe If we do so,°

General we want Homestead's; we were promised Homestead's by the government,°   If It does not carry out the promises Its agents made to us, If the government Haveing concluded to befriend Its late enemies and to neglect to observe the principles of common faith between Its self and us Its allies In the war you said was over, now takes away from them all right to the soil they stand upon save such as they can get by again working for *your* late and thier *all time ememies.*—If the government does so we are left In a more unpleasant condition than our former [condition]

we are at the mercy of those who are combined to prevent us from getting land enough to lay our Fathers bones upon. We Have property In Horses, cattle, carriages, & articles of furniture, but we are landless and Homeless,   from the Homes we Have lived In In the past we can only do one of three things   Step Into the public *road or the sea* or remain on them working as In former time and subject to thire will as then. We can not resist It In any way without being driven out Homeless upon the road.

You will see this Is not the condition of really freemen

You ask us to forgive the land owners of our Island,   *You* only lost your right arm In war and might forgive them. The man who tied me to a tree & gave me 39 lashes & who stripped and flogged my mother & my sister & who will not let me stay In His empty Hut except I will do His planting & be Satisfied with His price & who combines with others to keep away land from me well knowing I would not Have any thing to do with Him If I Had land of my own.—that man, I cannot well forgive. Does It look as If He Has forgiven me, seeing How He tries to keep me In a condition of Helplessness

General, we cannot remain Here In such condition and If the government permits them to come back we ask It to Help us to reach land where we shall not be slaves nor compelled to work for those who would treat us as such

we Have not been treacherous,   we Have not for selfish motives allied to us those who suffered like us from a common enemy & then Haveing gained *our* purpose left our allies In thier Hands There Is no rights secured to us   there Is no law likely to be made which our Hands can reach. The state will make laws that we shall not be able to Hold land even If we pay for It   Landless, Homeless. Voteless. we can only pray to god & Hope for *His Help*, *your Infuence & assistance*   With consideration of esteem your

Obt Servts
In behalf of the people
Henry Bram
Committe   Ishmael Moultrie
yates Sampson

Toney Golden William, Gabriel Andrews, and Toney Axon | The Terms of Work, 1865

Medway church Liberty county [Ga.]
Nov 28th 1865
Dear Sir   We the People of *Liberty county & State of georgia* Set Free from the oppression of Slavery, Desire through our *Delegates* . . . To appeal to you *asking aid* and *counsel* in this our *Distressed condition;* We *Learned*, from the Address of *general*

° General Oliver O. Howard, commissioner of the Freedmen's Bureau, had visited Edisto Island to inform the freedpeople settled there of President Andrew Johnson's order to restore the land to its former owners.

° The promise of homesteads had been made in General William T. Sherman's Special Field Order 15, which granted former slaves in the Sea Islands "possessory title" to tracts of up to forty acres until Congress ruled on the validity of the claims.

SOURCE: Steven Hahn et al., eds., *Freedom: A Documentary History of Emancipation, 1861–1867*, 3rd ser., vol. 1, *Land and Labor, 1865*, Freedmen and Southern Society Project (Chapel Hill: University of North Carolina Press, 2008), 440–42.

SOURCE: Steven Hahn et al., eds., *Freedom: A Documentary History of Emancipation, 1861–1867*, 3rd ser., vol. 1, *Land and Labor, 1865*, Freedmen and Southern Society Project (Chapel Hill: University of North Carolina Press, 2008), 942–43.

Howard that we were to *Return* to the *Plantation* and *work for our Former owners* at a *Reasonable contract as Freemen*; and find a *Home* and *Labour*,

Provided we can agree   But these owners of *Plantation* out here Says they only will Hire or Take the *Prime Hands* and our *old* and *Infirm Mothers*, and *Farthers* and our *children will not Be Provided for*; and this you will See Sir Put us in *confusion. . . . We cannot Labour for the Land owners and know that our Infirm and children are Not Provided for; and not Allowed to educate* or *Learn More than they were permitted in Slavery*; our *School* that was established in the county are *Broken up, and we are Destitute of Religious Worship, having No Home or Place to Live when we Leave the Plantations Returned* to *our Former owners; We are A Working class* of *People* and We are *Willing* and are *Desirous* to worke for *A Fair compensation*; But to *return to work opon the Terms, that are at Present offered to us, Would Be we Think going Backe into the State* of *Slavery that we have Just to some extent Been Delivered from*:

We *Appeal* to *you Sir and through you* to the *Rulers* of the *country* in our *Distressed state, and Declare that we feel, unsettled as Sheep Without A Shepard, and Beg you Advice* and *Assistance, and Believe Sir that this is an Earnest Appeal from A Poor But Loyal Earnest People*

Most Respectfully Submitted for your consideration—In Behalf of the People of Liberty county By

> *William, Toney Golden*
> *Gabriel Andrews*
> Toney Axon

James Herney | A Request for Furlough, 1866

Helena Ark   May. 15th 1866

Dear Sir   I imbrace this opertunity of writing you a few lines to inform you that I am well at present hoping those few lines may find you engoying the same gods blesing   I am a soldier of the 56th Colerd Infintry under Col— Benzona and have preformed my duty as a soldier should   since I inlisted I have never ben abesent at eny rool call   I inlisted January the 4th 1864 under Col Russel Culumbia boon County, Mo.   when I left my family I promised them that I would come home on furloe   in August last I lost two of my children   I asked for a leaf of absence and was refused   thare has ben but one man furloed in my comand and he was qtr master sargent and that was this year   in my redgement we have a large magority Christians and I thank god for it   thare has ben a grate meny of my felow soldiers who throgh grief and anziety about their familics have pined away and died   there has severl Redgements who inlisted one year after we did mustered out and gone home   we stood on the bank and shed teers to think that we who had batled for our country over two years should still be retained and deprived of the priviledge of seeing those who are so dear to us   my actions have proved that I have ben true to my government and I love it dearley   now the war is over and I now want to see those who are dearer to me than my life   thare is a great many of my Brother Soldiers who have ben out since the first Battle was faught in mo and have never seen their families   I have nothing more to say   hoping that you will lend a listening ear to an umble soldier I will close

ALS   James Herney

["ALS" signifies "a letter signed by the author."]

Cyntha NicKols | A Request for Custody, 1867

Clinton La.   Jary 10th 1867

Hon Sir   I am the mother of a woman Dina who is now dead   My Daughter Dina had a child boy by the name Porter. I am a Colored woman former slave of a Mr Sandy Spears of the parish of East Feliciana La. Said Porter is now about Eleven years of age. Mr Spears has had the little boy Porter bound over to him so I am told by the agent of the Freedmen in this parish   I was not informed of this fact untill after the matter of binding was consumated   I do not wish to wrongfully interfere with the arrangement of those who are endeavoring to properly control us black

SOURCE: Ira Berlin and Leslie S. Rowland, eds., *Families and Freedom: A Documentary History of African-American Kinship in the Civil War Era* (New York: New Press, 1997), 149.

SOURCE: Ira Berlin and Leslie S. Rowland, eds., *Families and Freedom: A Documentary History of African-American Kinship in the Civil War Era* (New York: New Press, 1997), 240, 242.

people   I feel confident they are doing the best they can for us and our present condition—but I am the Grand Mother of Porter—   his Father Andrew is now and has been for some time a soldier in the army of the U.S.   he is I am told some where in California   I do not know[,]only that he is not here to see to the interest of his child   I am not by any means satisfied with the present arrangement made for my Grand Child Porter. Mr Spears I have known for many years. I will say nothing of his faults, but I have the means of educating my Grand Child of doing a good part by him. his Uncle who has been lately discharged from the army of the U.S.—*Umphrey cold* who now resides in this parish is fully able to assist me in maintaining my Grand-Child Porter   we want him   we do not think Mr Spears a suitable person to control this boy   Mr Spears is very old and infirm   he is and has been for many years addicted to the use of ardent spirits   this fact I do not like to mention but truth requires me to speak   now is there no chance to get my little boy   the agent of this place will not listen to me, and I am required to call on you or I must let my Grand-Child go which greatly grieves me. will you be so kind after my statement to write to Elizabeth Collins f[*ree*]. w[*oman of*]. c[*olor*]. [,] Clinton La[,] the Step mother of Porter and advise her what I shall do to obtain my little Grand Child. please answer this letter and you will greatly oblige   Truly yours a poor old black woman

    Cyntha NicKols

ALS   f[*ree*]. w[*oman of*]. c[*olor*].

Milly Johnson | Seeking Information about Her Children, 1867

         Chapel Hill, N.C.   March, 26th 1867.
Sir:—. . . .

    It is my purpose, to advertise for my children,

    When I last knew them they were 2 of them in Esics county Va a girl and Boy, Living with their former owners.   The Boy Belonged to Hugh Billaps   The Girl Belonged to Dr Richards. The Boys name

SOURCE: Ira Berlin and Leslie S. Rowland, eds., *Families and Freedom: A Documentary History of African-American Kinship in the Civil War Era* (New York: New Press, 1997), 214–15.

was Musco Johnson—   The Girl Letty Johnson   This accounts for 2—

    There is another two a Girl and Boy.   They were sold to speculators at Richmond Va   Where they were carried I do not Know.   the girl's name was Henrietta Johnson   The Boy William Quals Johnson.   There is still another Anna Johnson° who is Living in Hertford Co., N.C. with Mr. Albert Elliott my former owner and since the [*Confederate*] surrender he took her from me   I protested against but of no avail   I have tried several times since to get her.   I wrote to him Last year and he would make no reply to my letters.   he said when he took my child that she belonged to him, and I herd that his wife said that she intended to Keep her till she was 21 years of age.   all this was done against my will.   Now Sir I want her.   if I cannot hear from the others she can be gotten I presume

    Now Sir:

    You will do me a lasting favor to attend to this matter for me as promptly as possible   I convey the Matter into your hands.—hopeing that there can some information be gained from my children

    Intrusting the matter with you sir I am Very Resptfully Sir:—

HLSr   Milly Johnson
["HLSr" signifies that the letter was written by someone else but signed with the author's designation.]

° The Freedmen's Bureau succeeded in restoring Anna to her mother and found information regarding the possible whereabouts of Letty and Musco, but information regarding Henrietta and William Quals had been burned with the slave traders' records.

Joe Easley | Persecution of the Freedpeople, 1868

       Hopkins County, Sulphur Springs, [Texas]
                         July 17, 1868.
Hon. M. L. Armstrong:

    Dear Sir—I am this morning situated like a mariner whose vessel is sinking, and he is dripping out slips of paper, hoping they may fall into some

SOURCE: Records of the Assistant Commissioner for the State of Texas, Bureau of Refugees, Freedmen, and Abandoned Lands, 1865–1869, National Archives Microfilm Publication M821, roll 32.

friendly hands, that the world may know what became of him.

The reign of terror is set up in this county. I will not undertake to give a minute description of it; time and space is not sufficient. Suffice it to say that the history of the darkest ages of the world does not, in my estimation, afford a parallel.

It commenced about the 1st of June, by brutally murdering Charles Grimes, the old freedman who was on the Board of Registrars [officials who register voters and verify voter eligibility]. This occurred on Sunday night, as well as I recollect, about the 17th of June. There was not the least semblance of any provocation for the outrage. Next, I ascertained beyond a doubt that the same parties were seeking an opportunity to kill me. I was cultivating my farm two and a half miles from town. I employed hands who agreed to assist me until I could wind up my farming. Just as I was nearly through, I was waylaid by the assassins as I was returning from my farm house, but happening to see them in time I made my escape and got home. . . .

I suppose you think strange of the murder of women and children. Ah, sir, it has already happened. About one week ago Minerva James was taken out of the house of Mr. Herman Spencer, four miles from this place, by five armed men, carried about one mile, and brutally murdered. [If I] had space to give you the particulars, you would say it was the most horrid murder you ever heard of.

Three days ago there was a man by the name of Flowers, taken out of his house at night and killed. The next day a party of men were carrying him to the burying ground, when they were fired into, and one man and a little boy killed, and another man dangerously wounded, receiving a shot through the lungs. . . .

The freed people have had all their arms taken away from them, and they are in the most deplorable condition of any people on earth. All that were living in the county by themselves, have been robbed of every thing of the least value—even taking the under dressing of freed women, their bed clothes; in a word every thing of the smallest value, and then driven from their homes into the woods. It is the most sickening sight I ever witnessed to see their fine corn crops now being destroyed by the stock. But I must close this sickening subject.

I am aiming to send this letter to Dallas, to have it mailed. It is impossible to have anything of the kind sent from this county by mail. The postmasters are all Ku Klux. . . .

I cannot leave my family to be murdered by them. I am bound to stay near them, so that I can give them protection at night.

Show this to any one you see proper, I care not who. I don't suppose I will be alive when this comes to hand; at least the chances look slim. I prefer a martyr's grave to living a slave. I shall die the same.

Joe Easley.

Questions for Analysis

1. Based on these letters, what were the main concerns of freedpeople? What did freedom mean to them?

2. All the letters describe acts of violence committed by whites against blacks, but what new concern does the final letter introduce? Who are the perpetrators in that letter?

3. Why did freedpeople write to the Freedmen's Bureau? What seems to have been the reputation of the bureau and its agents?

4. How do the letter writers express their loyalty to the Union?

5. Joe Easley describes himself as "a mariner whose vessel is sinking," and the delegates from Medway Church describe themselves as "*Sheep Without A Shepard*." Use these metaphors to interpret the experience of African Americans during Reconstruction. What had they lost? What did they fear?

Race, Sex, and the Vote

After the Thirteenth Amendment ended slavery in 1865, the Fourteenth Amendment, proposed in June 1866, sought to secure black civil rights by defining citizenship and guaranteeing the equal protection of the laws. In establishing the means by which representation in Congress would be apportioned, this amendment used the word *male* for the first time in the Constitution. Supporters of woman suffrage were dismayed, for they had hoped for universal suffrage—the right of every adult to vote without regard to race or sex. In August 1866, a group of women joined with Frederick Douglass to found the American Equal Rights Association (AERA), in an effort to create a united front for advancing the causes of black and women's rights. When it became evident that the Fifteenth Amendment, proposed in February 1869, would secure black male suffrage but not woman suffrage, the AERA split.

Some members, led by Douglass, believed that black male suffrage was the most immediate need. Others, including Susan B. Anthony and Elizabeth Cady Stanton, gave priority to woman suffrage. But what did black women think? Did they ally themselves with black men or white women? In the following documents, black women voice their opinions on suffrage, an issue that went to the core of their identities.

Sojourner Truth | Equal Voting Rights, 1867

Sojourner Truth (1797–1883) was nearly seventy years old when she spoke at the second meeting of the American Equal Rights Association in New York City in May 1867. She had begun life as a slave in New York and become one of the most famous African Americans of the nineteenth century. An abolitionist and a supporter of women's rights, Truth electrified audiences with her candor and forthright manner of expression.

I feel that if I have to answer for the deeds done in my body just as much as a man, I have a right to have just as much as a man. There is a great stir about colored men getting their rights, but not a word about the colored women; and if colored men get their rights, and not colored women theirs, you see the colored men will be masters over the women, and it will be just as bad as it was before. So I am for keeping the thing going while things are stirring;

because if we wait till it is still, it will take a great while to get it going again. White women are a great deal smarter, and know more than colored women, while colored women do not know scarcely anything. They go out washing, which is about as high as a colored woman gets, and their men go about idle, strutting up and down; and when the women come home, they ask for their money and take it all, and then scold because there is no food. I want you to consider on that, chil'n. I call you chil'n; you are somebody's chil'n, and I am old enough to be mother of all that is here. I want women to have their rights. In the courts women have no right, no voice; nobody speaks for them. I wish woman to have her voice there among the pettifoggers.° If it is not a fit place for women, it is unfit for men to be there.

I am above eighty years old;° it is about time for me to be going. I have been forty years a slave and forty years free, and would be here forty years more to have equal rights for all. I suppose I am kept here

SOURCE: Philip S. Foner and Robert James Branham, eds., *Lift Every Voice: African American Oratory, 1787–1900* (Tuscaloosa: University of Alabama Press, 1998), 464–65.

° Tricksters.
° She was actually about seventy.

because something remains for me to do; I suppose I am yet to help to break the chain. I have done a great deal of work; as much as a man, but did not get so much pay. I used to work in the field and bind grain, keeping up with the cradler;° but men doing no more, got twice as much pay; so with the German women. They work in the field and do as much work, but do not get the pay. We do as much, we eat as much, we want as much. I suppose I am about the only colored woman that goes about to speak for the rights of the colored women. I want to keep the thing stirring, now that the ice is cracked. What we want is a little money. You men know that you get as much again as women when you write, or for what you do. When we get our rights we shall not have to come to you for money, for then we shall have money enough in our own pockets; and may be you will ask us for money. But help us now until we get it. It is a good consolation to know that when we have got this battle once fought we shall not be coming to you any more. You have been having our rights so long, that you think, like a slave-holder, that you own us. I know that it is hard for one who has held the reins for so long to give up; it cuts like a knife. It will feel all the better when it closes up again. I have been in Washington about three years, seeing about these colored people. Now colored men have [will soon attain] the right to vote. There ought to be equal rights now more than ever, since colored people have got their freedom.

° A machine for binding and bunching grain.

Proceedings of the American Equal Rights Association | A Debate: Negro Male Suffrage vs. Woman Suffrage, 1869

The May 12, 1869, meeting of the **American Equal Rights Association** was its last. By this time, tensions between those who prioritized black male suffrage and those who prioritized woman suffrage had torn the association apart. In this excerpt from the meeting's proceedings, we hear from Frederick Douglass and Frances Ellen Watkins Harper, two of the most important African American leaders of the day and key advocates for abolition, African American rights, and women's rights. Susan B. Anthony, Lucy Stone, Pauline W. Davis, Julia Ward Howe, and Elizabeth Cady Stanton were key white advocates for both abolition and women's rights, and to differing extents, supporters of African American rights.

MR. DOUGLASS: I come here more as a listener than to speak and I have listened with a great deal of pleasure. . . . There is no name greater than that of Elizabeth Cady Stanton in the matter of woman's rights and equal rights, but my sentiments are tinged a little against [her remarks in] *The Revolution* [a magazine]. There was in the address to which I allude the employment of certain names,

---

SOURCE: Philip S. Foner, ed., *Frederick Douglass on Women's Rights* (New York: Da Capo Press, 1992), 86–89.

such as "Sambo," and the gardener, and the bootblack, and the daughters of Jefferson and Washington and other daughters. (Laughter.) I must say that I asked what difference there is between the daughters of Jefferson and Washington and other daughters. (Laughter.) I must say that I do not see how any one can pretend that there is the same urgency in giving the ballot to woman as to the negro. With us, the matter is a question of life and death, at least, in fifteen States of the Union. When women, because they are women, are hunted down through the cities of New York and New Orleans; when they are dragged from their houses and hung upon lampposts; when their children are torn from their arms, and their brains dashed out upon the pavement; when they are objects of insult and outrage at every turn; when they are in danger of having their homes burnt down over their heads; when their children are not allowed to enter schools; then they will have an urgency to obtain the ballot equal to our own. (Great applause.)

A VOICE:—Is that not all true about black women?

MR. DOUGLASS:—Yes, yes, yes; it is true of the black woman, but not because she is a woman, but because she is black. (Applause.) Julia Ward

Howe at the conclusion of her great speech delivered at the convention in Boston last year said: "I am willing that the negro shall get the ballot before me." (Applause.) Woman! why, she has 10,000 modes of grappling with her difficulties. I believe that all the virtue of the world can take care of all the evil. I believe that all the intelligence can take care of all the ignorance. (Applause.) I am in favor of woman's suffrage in order that we shall have all the virtue and vice confronted. Let me tell you that when there were few houses in which the black man could have put his head, this wooly head of mine found a refuge in the house of Mrs. Elizabeth Cady Stanton, and if I had been blacker than sixteen midnights, without a single star, it would have been the same. (Applause.)

MISS [Susan B.] ANTHONY:—The old anti-slavery school says women must stand back and wait until the negroes shall be recognized. But we say, if you will not give the whole loaf of suffrage to the entire people, give it to the most intelligent first. (Applause.) If intelligence, justice, and morality are to have precedence in the Government, let the question of woman be brought up first and that of the negro last. (Applause.) While I was canvassing the State with petitions and had them filled with names for our cause to the Legislature, a man dared to say to me that the freedom of women was all a theory and not a practical thing. (Applause.) When Mr. Douglass mentioned the black man first and the woman last, if he had noticed he would have seen that it was the men that clapped and not the women. There is not the woman born who desires to eat the bread of dependence, no matter whether it be from the hand of father, husband, or brother; for any one who does so eat her bread places herself in the power of the person from whom she takes it. (Applause.) Mr. Douglass talks about the wrongs of the negro; but with all the outrages that he to-day suffers, he would not exchange his sex and take the place of Elizabeth Cady Stanton. (Laughter and applause.)

MR. DOUGLASS: I want to know if granting you the right of suffrage will change the nature of our sexes? (Great laughter.)

MISS ANTHONY: It will change the pecuniary position of woman: it will place her where she can earn her own bread. (Loud applause.) She will not then be driven to such employments only as man chooses for her. . . .

MRS. LUCY STONE:—Mrs. Stanton will, of course, advocate the precedence for her sex, and Mr. Douglass will strive for the first position for his, and both are perhaps right. If it be true that the government derives its authority from the consent of the governed, we are safe in trusting that principle to the uttermost. If one has a right to say that you can not read and therefore can not vote, then it may be said that you are a woman and therefore cannot vote. We are lost if we turn away from the middle principle and argue for one class. . . . The gentleman who addressed you claimed that the negroes had the first right to the suffrage, and drew a picture which only his great word-power can do. He again in Massachusetts, when it had cast a majority in favor of Grant and negro suffrage, stood upon the platform and said that woman had better wait for the negro; that is, that both could not be carried, and that the negro had better be the one. But I freely forgave him because he felt as he spoke. But woman suffrage is more imperative than his own; and I want to remind the audience that when he says what the Ku-Kluxes did all over the South, the Ku-Kluxes here in the North in the shape of men, take away the children from the mother, and separate them as completely as if done on the block of the auctioneer. . . . Woman has an ocean of wrongs too deep for any plummet, and the negro, too, has an ocean of wrongs that can not be fathomed. There are two great oceans; in the one is the black man, and in the other is the woman. But I thank God for that XV. Amendment, and hope it will be adopted in every State. I will be thankful in my soul if *any* body can get out of the terrible pit. But I believe that the safety of the government would be more promoted by the admission of woman as an element of restoration and harmony than the negro. I believe that the influence of woman will save the country before every other power. (Applause.) I see the signs of times pointing to this consummation, and I believe that in some parts of the country women will vote for the President of the United States in 1872. . . .

MRS. PAULINE W. DAVIS said she would not be altogether satisfied to have the XVth Amendment passed without the XVIth, for woman would have a race of tyrants raised above her in the South, and the black women of that country would also receive worse treatment than if the Amendment was not passed. Take any class that have been slaves, and you will find that they are the worst when free, and become the hardest masters. The colored women of the South say they do not want to get married to the negro, as their husbands can take their children away from them, and also appropriate their earnings. The black women are more intelligent than the men, because they have learned something from their mistresses. She then related incidents showing how black men whip and abuse their wives in the South. One of her sister's servants whipped his wife every Sunday regularly. (Laughter.) She thought that sort of men should not have the making of the laws for the government of the women throughout the land. (Applause.)

MR. DOUGLASS said that all disinterested spectators would concede that this Equal Rights meeting had been pre-eminently a Woman's Rights meeting. (Applause.) They had just heard an argument with which he could not agree—that the suffrage to the black men should be postponed to that of the women. . . . "I do not believe the story that the slaves who are enfranchised become the worst of tyrants. (A voice, 'Neither do I.' Applause.) I know how this theory came about. When a slave was made a driver, he made himself more officious than the white driver, so that his master might not suspect that he was favoring those under him. But we do not intend to have any master over us. (Applause.)"

THE PRESIDENT (MRS. STANTON) argued that not another man should be enfranchised until enough women are admitted to the polls to outweigh those already there. (Applause.) She did not believe in allowing ignorant negroes and foreigners to make laws for her to obey. (Applause.)

MRS. [Frances Ellen Watkins] HARPER (colored) said that when it was a question of race, she let the lesser question of sex go. But the white women all go for sex, letting race occupy a minor position. She liked the idea of work-women, but she would like to know if it was broad enough to take colored women.

MISS ANTHONY and several others: Yes, yes.

MRS. HARPER said that when she was at Boston there were sixty women who left work because one colored woman went to gain a livelihood in their midst. (Applause.) If the nation could only handle one question, she would not have the black woman put a single straw in the way, if only the men of the race could obtain what they wanted. (Great applause.)

Mary Ann Shadd Cary | Woman's Right to Vote, early 1870s

Mary Ann Shadd Cary (1823–1893) was an educator, journalist, and reformer who was deeply committed to both black and women's rights. In the 1850s, she was also a proponent of emigration to Canada. Following the split of the AERA, she sided with Elizabeth Cady Stanton and Susan B. Anthony in founding the National Woman Suffrage Association. At the time she gave this speech, Cary was teaching in Washington, D.C. The speech captures the substance of remarks she made before the Judiciary Committee of the House of Representatives in support of a petition on behalf of enfranchising women in Washington, D.C. In 1883, Cary received her law degree from Howard University.

SOURCE: Philip S. Foner and Robert James Branham, eds., *Lift Every Voice: African American Oratory, 1787–1900* (Tuscaloosa: University of Alabama Press, 1998), 516–17.

By the provisions of the 14th & 15th amendments to the Constitution of the United States,—a logical sequence of which is the representation by colored men of time-honored commonwealths in both houses of Congress,—millions of colored *women*, to-day, share with colored men the responsibilities of freedom from chattel slavery. From the introduction of freedom° African slavery to its extinction, a period of more than two hundred years, *they shared equally* with fathers, brothers, denied the right to vote. This fact of their investiture with the privileges of free women of the same time and by the same amendments which disentralled their kinsmen and conferred upon the latter the right of franchise, without so endowing themselves is one of the

° The strikethroughs throughout are part of the original document.

documents

anomalies of a measure of legislation otherwise grand in conception and consequences beyond comparison. The colored women of this country though heretofore silent, in great measure upon this question of the right to vote by the women of the [copy missing], so long and ardently the cry of the noblest of the land, have neither been indifferent to their own just claims under the amendments, in common with colored men, nor to the demand for political recognition so justly made every where within its borders throughout the land.

The strength and glory of a free nation, is *not so much* in the size and equipments of its armies, as in the *loyal hearts* and willing hands of its *men* and *women*; And this fact has been illustrated in an eminent degree by well-known events in the history of the United States. To the white women of the nation conjointly with the men, it is indebted for arduous and dangerous personal service, and generous expenditure of time, wealth and counsel, so indispensable to success in its hour of danger. The colored *women* though humble in sphere, and unendowed with worldly goods, yet, led as by inspiration,—not only fed, and sheltered, and guided in *safety* the prisoner soldiers of the Union when escaping from the enemy, or the soldier who was compelled to risk life *itself* in the struggle to break the back-bone of rebellion, but gave their *sons* and brothers to the armies of the nation and their prayers to high Heaven for the success of the Right.

The surges of fratricidal war have passed we hope never to return; the premonitions of the future, are peace and good will; these blessings, so greatly to be desired, can only be made permanent, in responsible governments,—based as you affirm upon the consent of the governed,—by giving to both sexes practically the equal powers conferred in the provisions of the Constitution as amended. In the District of Columbia over which Congress has exclusive jurisdiction the women in common with the women of the states and territories, feel keenly the discrimination against them in the retention of the word *male* in the organic act for the same, and as by reason of its retention, all the evils incident to partial legislation are endured by them, they sincerely, hope that the word *male* may be stricken out by Congress on your recommendation without delay. Taxed, and governed in other respects, without their consent, they respectfully demand, that the principles of the *founders* of the government may *not* be disregarded in their case: but, as there are *laws* by which they are tried, with penalties attached thereto, that they may be invested with the right to vote as do men, that thus as in all Republics *indeed*, they may in future, be governed by their own consent.

Questions for Analysis

1. What economic arguments do Sojourner Truth and Susan B. Anthony present on behalf of women's rights?

2. What are the political arguments of Elizabeth Cady Stanton and Mary Ann Shadd Cary? How does Frederick Douglass counter such arguments? Does he take them seriously, or does he demean them?

3. Is Frances Ellen Watkins Harper a pragmatist? Why do you think she took the position she did?

4. Do you think Lucy Stone is being fair when she compares men in the North to "Ku-Kluxes"? Why or why not?

5. Would you have argued that black men should get the vote first, then women, as Douglass did? Or would you have argued for universal suffrage? Why? What if you thought a universal suffrage amendment would likely fail, thus leaving both blacks and women disfranchised? Would arguing for black male suffrage be more strategic?

Portrayals of Reconstruction-Era African Americans

For almost a hundred years after Reconstruction ended in 1877, popular and scholarly treatments represented the era negatively, as a time of dishonest government and a disastrous attempt to integrate freedpeople into civic life. In this narrative, Reconstruction's failure was a result of black inferiority. Incapable of shouldering the responsibilities of freedom, the former slaves once again had to be put under white rule.

D. W. Griffith's cinematic masterpiece *The Birth of a Nation* (1915), which offered a lurid treatment of the southern white rationale for overthrowing Black Reconstruction, boldly portrayed this widely held view. According to the script, black misrule, abetted by corrupt and vindictive Republicans, wrought so much suffering on the defeated white South that a valiant and heroic Ku Klux Klan finally arose to take charge and restore order. In Figure 8.1, note the stereotypical portrayal of white and black men, particularly the notion of chivalrous southern white men duty-bound to protect the honor of white women and the white South from the beastly, bug-eyed black man.

FIGURE 8.1
The Birth of a Nation, 1915
Epic/The Kobal Collection at Art Resource, NY.

FIGURE 8.2
Democratic Party Broadside, 1866 *Library of Congress, LC-USZ62-40764.*

The film was wildly popular. In fact, it was the first movie ever to be shown at the White House, where it received the endorsement of President Woodrow Wilson. In popular literature, Claude G. Bowers's highly dramatic *The Tragic Era: The Revolution after Lincoln* (1929) offered the same view, and in scholarly studies historians also interpreted Reconstruction as a "tragic era" of black incompetence and abuse of federal power. At Columbia University, the work of William A. Dunning, a founder of the American Historical Association, and John W. Burgess, a leader in the field of political science, gave this view intellectual respectability. Their scholarship and that of their students—the so-called Dunning School—portrayed white southerners as heroically overturning the colossal mistake of Black Reconstruction, saving both the South and the nation.

In 1935, W. E. B. Du Bois, one of the founders of the National Association for the Advancement of Colored People and himself a scholar as well as an activist, countered the Dunning School with his pathbreaking *Black Reconstruction in America*. In it, he argued that Dunning's version of Reconstruction was "a cheap and false myth" constructed by southerners and northerners alike to heal the "terrible wounds" of civil strife. He continued:

> In order to paint the South as a martyr to inescapable fate, to make the North the magnanimous emancipator, and to ridicule the Negro as the impossible joke in the whole development, we have in fifty years by libel, innuendo and silence, so completely misstated and obliterated the history of the Negro in America and his relation to its work and government that today it is almost unknown. This may be fine romance, but it is not science. It may be inspiring, but it is certainly not the truth. And beyond this it is dangerous.

Titling his final chapter "The Propaganda of History," Du Bois reported a survey of textbooks that portrayed blacks in Reconstruction as ignorant, lazy, dishonest, and extravagant. "It is propaganda like this," he concluded, "that has led men in the past to insist that history is 'lies agreed upon.'"[47]

The civil rights and black power movements of the mid-twentieth century sparked a major scholarly revision of the dominant view of Reconstruction. Inspired by the indispensable work of Du Bois and led by eminent historians such as John Hope Franklin and Kenneth M. Stampp, a new consensus far more sympathetic to Black Reconstruction began to emerge. Capped by Eric Foner's *Reconstruction: America's Unfinished Revolution* (1988), this view now dominates both the scholarly and popular understanding of Black Reconstruction.

It is not hard to find the origins of the myth that Du Bois repudiated. It was present, for example, in campaign literature of the Reconstruction era, which drew on minstrel-style stereotypes (see Visual Sources: Minstrel Shows, pp. 309–19) to degrade freedmen. Figure 8.2 is a Democratic Party broadside from the 1866 congressional elections. Examine the image of the black man and the surrounding text. What prejudices are they appealing to? What were the issues in these elections? What was at stake? Note that the Democratic Party portrays itself as a "white man's" party both here and in a campaign badge from the 1868 presidential election (Figure 8.3).

In the late 1860s, the Radical Republicans were still in their ascendancy, but by 1874 their heyday was over. Within the party, support for freedpeople and their civil rights had diminished. Even Thomas Nast, the political cartoonist for *Harper's Weekly* whose drawings had often been sympathetic to the cause of black rights (see Visual Sources: The Moment and Meaning of

FIGURE 8.3
Campaign Badge Supporting Horatio Seymour and Francis P. Blair Jr. for President and Vice President, 1868 *Schomburg Center, NYPL./Art Resource, NY.*

FIGURE 8.4
Colored Rule in a Reconstructed(?) State, 1874
Library of Congress, LC-USZ62-102256.

Emancipation, pp. 362–73), now presented a very different view. His *Colored Rule in a Reconstructed(?) State* (Figure 8.4) appeared on the cover of the March 14, 1874, issue of *Harper's* with this caption: "The members call each other thieves, liars, rascals, and cowards." Columbia, the goddess at the podium under the banner that says "Let us have peace," is reprimanding the legislators: "You are Aping the lowest Whites. If you disgrace your Race in this way you had better take Back Seats." What does this image of the South Carolina legislature and the accompanying text suggest about popular views of Black Reconstruction? *Harper's* did include this disclaimer referring to Joseph Hayne Rainey, who served four congressional terms, from 1870 through early 1879:

"If we may trust the following report, taken from a recent number of the *Charleston News*, some of the colored members of the South Carolina Legislature must be men of very different stamp from the cultivated and able gentleman who represents the State in the Congress of the United States." The editors urged that if the *Charleston News* report was true, "these ignorant and incompetent legislators must give place to those who will more faithfully represent the worth and intelligence of the people of the State, both white and colored,"[48] like Joseph Hayne Rainey.

Compare this 1874 view of the South Carolina legislature with the 1869 image of the National Convention of Colored Men (see p. 405), also published in *Harper's Weekly*, and to other images of dignified black men and women in this chapter. Which image or images make the most powerful impression?

In December 1876, just after the presidential election, Nast's *The Ignorant Vote* appeared on the cover of *Harper's Weekly* (Figure 8.5). It conveys the idea that the ignorant voters in the North, represented by a belligerent, apish Irishman, are evened out by the ignorant voters in the South, represented by a smiling, apish black man. Compare this image of the black voter with A. R. Waud's *The First Vote* (1867) on page 392. In Waud's drawing, the black voters are individualized—a poor laborer, a well-dressed city man, a soldier. In Nast's portrayal, created nine years later, the black voter is a dehumanized stereotype.

One final image by Nast that depicts Reconstruction as an era of corrupt government is *The "Practical" Politician's Love for the Negro* (Figure 8.6), which appeared in 1885. What, according to this image, was the motivation of white politicians who allied themselves with black voters?

The images that appear earlier in chapter 8 offer a stark contrast to the blatantly racist caricatures of blacks that appeared in Democratic Party campaign literature and the mass media, yet it was the caricatures that came to predominate. Currier & Ives, the firm that printed *The First Colored Senator and*

FIGURE 8.5
The Ignorant Vote, 1876 *Library of Congress, LC-USZ62-57340.*

THE "PRACTICAL" POLITICIAN'S LOVE FOR THE NEGRO.

FIGURE 8.6
The "Practical" Politician's Love for the Negro, 1885   Harper's Weekly, *July 25, 1885, provided courtesy HarpWeek.*

Representatives in 1872 (see p. 396), initiated the Darktown Series in 1879. This series made fun of freedpeople who moved north after the Civil War. Currier & Ives was the most famous lithography firm in nineteenth-century America, and its hand-colored, sentimental images of American life, sold for pennies by street vendors, decorated the walls of millions of homes. The seventy-five prints in the Darktown Series were among its most profitable images. The firm sold more than 73,000 copies of just one of the prints.[49] Figures 8.7 and 8.8 are representative of the series. Blacks are portrayed as buffoons, engaged in comic actions that seem staged, not unlike the characters in the minstrel show skits that had amused audiences in the North since the 1830s (see Visual Sources: Minstrel Shows, pp. 309–19). Note the minstrel-style facial characteristics. Note, too, the aftermath of a Darktown Club literary debate.

THE DARKTOWN FIRE BRIGADE - HOOK AND LADDER GYMNASTICS.
Brace her up dar! and cotch her on de fly!

FIGURE 8.7
The Darktown Fire Brigade,
1887 © Swiss Ink 2, LLC/Corbis.

A LITERARY DEBATE IN THE DARKTOWN CLUB.
The Question Settled.

FIGURE 8.8
A Literary Debate in the
Darktown Club, 1885 *Library*
of Congress, LC-USZC2-2922.

CRUMPLED.

DRUSILLA (*to Cousin Miriam, down from Little Rock*). "Why, Mir'm, yo' dress is all crumpled up in de back whey yo's set on't. Trabellin's ha'd on clo'es, any—"
MIRIAM. "Laws, hain' yo' folks eber been out de woods? Dat's draped like de style is, yo' know."

FIGURE 8.9

Crumpled, 1886 *The Granger Collection, NYC. All rights reserved.*

Earlier, in 1874, *Harper's Weekly* began publishing intermittently black caricatures by a series of white artists. These Blackville prints revealed common white perceptions of African Americans. With a Reconstruction circulation of up to 300,000, these caricatures of black men and women may have reached an even wider audience than the Currier & Ives lithographs. *Crumpled* (Figure 8.9), which appeared in *Harper's* on October 9, 1886, is typical. The caption reads: "Drusilla (*to Cousin Miriam, down from Little Rock*). 'Why, Mir'm, yo' dress is all crumpled up in de back whey yo's set on't. Trabellin's ha'd on clo'es, any—' Miriam. 'Laws, hain' yo' folks eber been out de woods? Dat's draped like de style is, yo' know.'" Compare the dress and deportment of these caricatures with those of the women who attended the National Convention of Colored Men in 1869 (see p. 405) or who sang with the Fisk Jubilee Singers (see p. 389).

For enslaved black men and women, emancipation sparked a revolution. But when W. E. B. Du Bois reconsidered Reconstruction, he proposed that it was the end of Black Reconstruction that was the "revolution," for it estab-
~hed "a new dictatorship of property in the South through the color line. It

was a triumph of men who in their effort to replace equality with caste and to build inordinate wealth on a foundation of abject poverty have succeeded in killing democracy, art, and religion." How did images like those in this essay contribute to the killing of democracy? What might have happened if Black Reconstruction had survived? "If the Reconstruction of the Southern states," Du Bois mused, "from slavery to free labor, and from aristocracy to industrial democracy, had been conceived as a major national program of America, whose accomplishment at any price was well worth the effort, we should be living today in a different world." He concluded, "The attempt to make black men American citizens was in a certain sense all a failure, but a splendid failure."[50]

Questions for Analysis

1. How do the images presented here reinforce racial stereotypes? Compare them to the minstrelsy images in chapter 6 (see Visual Sources: Minstrel Shows, pp. 309–19).

2. Contrast these images to the reality of black life and black participation in politics in the South. Give specific examples. Use Hiram R. Revels's speech in the Senate (see From the Record: This Prejudice Should Be Resisted, p. 394) to amplify your response.

3. What political and social functions might the different portrayals of Reconstruction have served for different groups of people, even well after the period?

4. Discuss Reconstruction as a success, a failure, a "splendid failure," and an "unfinished revolution."

5. In *Black Reconstruction in America*, Du Bois states, "If . . . we are going to use history for our pleasure and amusement, for inflating our national ego, and giving us a false but pleasurable sense of accomplishment, then we must give up the idea of history either as a science or as an art using the results of science, and admit frankly that we are using a version of historic fact in order to influence and educate the new generation along the way we wish."[51] Du Bois was attacking what he called the "myth" of Reconstruction. Is his observation still valid today? Consider the popular and scholarly interpretations of history that you have encountered in the media (television, movies, the Internet) or have studied in your history classes.

visual sources

Notes

1. Jourdan Anderson to Colonel P. H. Anderson, August 7, 1865, quoted in Leon F. Litwack, *Been in the Storm So Long: The Aftermath of Slavery* (New York: Knopf, 1979), 333–35.

2. Quoted ibid., 230.

3. Provost Marshal to Superintendent of the Organization of Missouri Black Troops, March 21, 1864, in *Freedom: A Documentary History of Emancipation, 1861–1867*, ed. Ira Berlin et al., 1st ser., vol. 1, *The Destruction of Slavery* (New York: Cambridge University Press, 1985), 481–82; Clarissa Burdett, affidavit filed before J. M. Kelley, March 27, 1865, Camp Nelson, Kentucky, in ibid., 615, 616.

4. Litwack, *Been in the Storm So Long*, 230.

5. Ibid., 229.

6. Tera Hunter, *To 'Joy My Freedom: Southern Black Women's Lives and Labors after the Civil War* (Cambridge: Harvard University Press, 1997), 39.

7. Quoted in Henry L. Swint, ed., *Dear Ones at Home: Letters from Contraband Camps* (Nashville: Vanderbilt University Press, 1966), 242–43.

8. Interview, in *The American Slave: A Composite Autobiography, North Carolina Narratives*, ed. George P. Rawick, vol. 14, part 1 (Westport, CT: Greenwood Press, 1972–1973), 248–52.

9. Interview, in *The American Slave: A Composite Autobiography, Unwritten History of Slavery*, ed. George P. Rawick, vol. 18 (Westport, CT: Greenwood Press, 1972), 124.

10. Interview, in *The American Slave: A Composite Autobiography, Arkansas Narratives*, ed. George P. Rawick, vol. 8, part 2 (Westport, CT: Greenwood Press, 1972), 52.

11. Matthew Gilbert, "Colored Churches: An Experiment," quoted in William E. Montgomery, *Under Their Own Vine and Fig Tree: The African-American Church in the South, 1865–1900* (Baton Rouge: LSU Press, 1993), 54.

12. C. Eric Lincoln and Lawrence H. Mamiya, *The Black Church in the African American Experience* (Durham, NC: Duke University Press, 1990), 25, 66.

13. Leslie A. Schwalm, *Emancipation's Diaspora: Race and Reconstruction in the Upper Midwest* (Chapel Hill: University of North Carolina Press, 2009), 144.

14. Quoted in Carter G. Woodson, *The History of the Negro Church* (Washington, DC: Associated Publishers, 1921), 202.

15. Quoted in Reginald F. Hildebrand, *The Times Were Strange and Stirring: Methodist Preachers and the Crisis of Emancipation* (Durham, NC: Duke University Press, 1995), 65.

16. Quoted in Steven Hahn et al., eds., *Freedom: A Documentary History of Emancipation, 1861–1867*, 3rd ser., vol. 1 (Chapel Hill: University of North Carolina Press, 2008), 396.

17. Quoted in Manuel Gottlieb, "The Land Question during Reconstruction," *Science and Society* 111 (1939): 364.

18. Quoted in Hahn, *Freedom*, 51–52.

19. Quoted in Litwack, *Been in the Storm So Long*, 366.

20. *The 2003 National Assessment of Adult Literacy*, Institute of Education Sciences, National Center for Education Statistics, U.S. Department of Education.

21. Quoted in Adam Fairclough, *A Class of Their Own: Black Teachers in the Segregated South* (Cambridge: Harvard University Press, 2007), 42.

22. Quoted in Clarence Walker, *A Rock in a Weary Land: The AME Church during the Civil War and Reconstruction* (Baton Rouge: LSU Press, 1982), 51.

23. Quoted in Fairclough, *A Class of Their Own*, 69.

24. Quoted in "Fisk's Storied Past," Fisk University, http://www.fisk.edu/AboutFisk/HistoryOfFisk.aspx.

25. Quoted in "History," Hampton University, http://www.hamptonu.edu/about/history.cfm.

26. *Louisianian*, May 10, 1879, quoted in James D. Anderson, *The Education of Blacks in the South, 1860–1935* (Chapel Hill: University of North Carolina Press, 1988), 64.

27. Samuel Thomas to O. O. Howard, September 6, 1865, quoted in Eric Foner, *Reconstruction: America's Unfinished Revolution, 1863–1877* (New York: Harper & Row, 1988), 150.

28. W. E. B. Du Bois, *Black Reconstruction in America: An Essay toward a History of the Part Which Black Folk Played in the Attempt to Reconstruct Democracy in America, 1860–1880* (1935; repr., New York: Atheneum, 1970), 708. See also W. E. B. Du Bois, "Reconstruction and Its Benefits," *American Historical Review* 15 (July 1910): 781–99.

29. Eric Foner, *Freedom's Lawmakers: A Directory of Black Officeholders during Reconstruction* (Baton Rouge: LSU Press, 1993), xi. This book includes entries for the 1,500 officials for whom Foner found documentation. The 2,000 figure in the text includes those for whom documentation was lacking.

30. Quoted in James M. McPherson, *Ordeal by Fire: The Civil War and Reconstruction* (New York: Knopf, 1982), 536.

31. Emanuel Fortune, quoted in Foner, *Reconstruction*, 426; Jack Dupree story, cited ibid., 426.

32. *Christian Recorder*, November 8, 1883, quoted in Henry M. Turner, "The Barbarous Decision of the Supreme Court," in *Respect Black: The Writings and Speeches of Henry McNeal Turner*, ed. Edwin Redkey (New York: Arno Press, 1971), 60.

33. Schwalm, *Emancipation's Diaspora*, 46.

34. Quoted in Quintard Taylor, *In Search of the Racial Frontier: African Americans in the American West, 1528–1990* (New York: Norton, 1998), 164.

35. Quoted in Nell Irvin Painter, *Exodusters: Black Migration to Kansas after Reconstruction* (New York: Knopf, 1977), 158.

36. *Nicodemus Western Cyclone*, March 24, 1886, quoted in Taylor, *In Search of the Racial Frontier*, 140.

37. "Go to Kansas": History and Culture, Nicodemus National Historic Site, National Park Service, http://www.nps.gov/nico/index.htm.

38. Quoted in Painter, *Exodusters*, 4.

39. Taylor, *In Search of the Racial Frontier*, 138.

40. "Caroline Le Count," Pennsylvania Civil War 150, http://www.pacivilwar150.com/people/africanamericans/Story.aspx?id=1.

41. Quoted in Hugh Davis, *"We Will Be Satisfied with Nothing Less": The African American Struggle for Equal Rights in the North during Reconstruction* (Ithaca, NY: Cornell University Press, 2011), 78.

42. Davis, *"We Will Be Satisfied,"* 95.

43. Foner, *Reconstruction*, 448.

44. Frances Ellen Watkins Harper, "We Are All Bound Up Together," speech, Eleventh National Women's Rights Conven-

tion, New York, May 1866, http://www.blackpast.org/?q
=1866-frances-ellen-watkins-harper-we-are-all-bound-
together-0. In this speech, Harper goes on to describe her
humiliation at not being allowed to ride Philadelphia's
streetcars.

45. Frederick Douglass, *Proceedings of the Republican National
Convention, Held at Cincinnati, Ohio . . . June 14, 15, and
16, 1876,* http://quod.lib.umich.edu/cgi/t/text/text-idx?c
=moa&cc=moa&q1=republican%20national%20
convention&view=text&rgn=main&idno=
AEW7097.0001.001.

46. Quoted in August Meier, *Negro Thought in America, 1880–
1915: Racial Ideologies in the Age of Booker T. Washington*
(Ann Arbor: University of Michigan Press, 1963), 69.

47. Du Bois, *Black Reconstruction in America,* 713, 723, 711, 714.

48. All quoted in "Colored Rule in a Reconstructed(?)
State," HarpWeek.com, http://blackhistory.harpweek.com
/4Reconstruction/ReconLevelOne.htm.

49. Robert Kipp, *Currier's Price Guide to Currier & Ives* (Brock-
ton, MA: Currier Publications, 1989), 27. See also Stephen J.
Gertz, "The Dark Side of Currier & Ives," Booktryst, February 28, 2011, http://www.booktryst.com/2011/02/dark
-side-of-currier-ives.html.

50. Du Bois, *Black Reconstruction in America,* 707, 708.

51. Ibid., 714.

Suggested References

A Social Revolution

Anderson, James D. *The Education of Blacks in the South,
1860–1935.* Chapel Hill: University of North Carolina Press,
1988.

Berlin, Ira, and Leslie S. Rowland, eds. *Families and Freedom: A
Documentary History of African-American Kinship in the Civil
War Era.* New York: New Press, 1997.

Fairclough, Adam. *A Class of Their Own: Black Teachers in the
Segregated South.* Cambridge: Harvard University Press,
2007.

Hunter, Tera. *To 'Joy My Freedom: Southern Black Women's Lives
and Labors after the Civil War.* Cambridge: Harvard
University Press, 1997.

Litwack, Leon F. *Been in the Storm So Long: The Aftermath of
Slavery.* New York: Knopf, 1979.

Montgomery, William E. *Under Their Own Vine and Fig Tree: The
African-American Church in the South, 1865–1900.* Baton
Rouge: LSU Press, 1993.

Rachleff, Peter J. *Black Labor in the South: Richmond, Virginia,
1865–1890.* Philadelphia: Temple University Press, 1984.

Saville, Julie. *The Work of Reconstruction: From Slave to Wage
Laborer in South Carolina, 1860–1870.* New York:
Cambridge University Press, 1994.

Schwalm, Leslie A. *A Hard Fight for We: Women's Transition from
Slavery to Freedom in South Carolina.* Urbana: University of
Illinois Press, 1997.

Williams, Heather Andrea. *Self-Taught: African American
Education in Slavery and Freedom.* Chapel Hill: University of
North Carolina Press, 2005.

A Short-Lived Political Revolution

Benedict, Michael Les. *A Compromise of Principle: Congressional
Republicans and Reconstruction.* New York: Norton, 1974.

Du Bois, W. E. B. *Black Reconstruction in America: An Essay
toward a History of the Part Which Black Folk Played in the
Attempt to Reconstruct Democracy in America, 1860–1880.*
1935. Reprint, New York: Atheneum, 1970.

Foner, Eric. *Freedom's Lawmakers: A Directory of Black
Officeholders during Reconstruction.* Baton Rouge: LSU Press,
1993.

———. *Reconstruction: America's Unfinished Revolution,
1863–1877.* New York: Harper & Row, 1988.

Gillette, William. *The Retreat from Reconstruction, 1869–1879.*
Baton Rouge: LSU Press, 1979.

Hahn, Steven. *A Nation under Our Feet: Black Political Struggles
in the Rural South from Slavery to the Great Migration.*
Cambridge: Harvard University Press, 2003.

McKitrick, Eric L. *Andrew Johnson and Reconstruction,
1865–1867.* Chicago: University of Chicago Press, 1960.

Rabinowitz, Howard N., ed. *Southern Black Leaders of the
Reconstruction Era.* Urbana: University of Illinois Press, 1982.

Opportunities and Limits outside the South

Athearn, Robert G. *In Search of Canaan: Black Migration to
Kansas.* Lawrence: Regents Press of KS, 1978.

Davis, Hugh. *"We Will Be Satisfied with Nothing Less": The
African American Struggle for Equal Rights in the North during
Reconstruction.* Ithaca, NY: Cornell University Press, 2011.

Painter, Nell Irvin. *Exodusters: Black Migration to Kansas after
Reconstruction.* New York: Knopf, 1977.

Richardson, Heather Cox. *The Death of Reconstruction: Race,
Labor, and Politics in the Post–Civil War North, 1865–1901.*
Cambridge: Harvard University Press, 2001.

Schwalm, Leslie A. *Emancipation's Diaspora: Race and
Reconstruction in the Upper Midwest.* Chapel Hill: University
of North Carolina Press, 2009.

Taylor, Quintard. *In Search of the Racial Frontier: African
Americans in the American West, 1528–1990.* New York:
Norton, 1998.

The Declaration of Independence

IN CONGRESS, JULY 4, 1776, THE UNANIMOUS DECLARATION OF THE THIRTEEN UNITED STATES OF AMERICA

When in the Course of human events, it becomes necessary for one people to dissolve the political bands which have connected them with another, and to assume among the Powers of the earth, the separate and equal station to which the Laws of Nature and of Nature's God entitle them, a decent respect to the opinions of mankind requires that they should declare the causes which impel them to the separation.

We hold these truths to be self-evident, that all men are created equal, that they are endowed by their Creator with certain unalienable rights, that among these are Life, Liberty, and the pursuit of Happiness. That to secure these rights, Governments are instituted among Men, deriving their just powers from the consent of the governed. That whenever any Form of Government becomes destructive of these ends, it is the Right of the People to alter or to abolish it, and to institute new Government, laying its foundation on such principles and organizing its powers in such form, as to them shall seem most likely to effect their Safety and Happiness. Prudence, indeed, will dictate that Governments long established should not be changed for light and transient causes; and accordingly all experience hath shown, that mankind are more disposed to suffer, while evils are sufferable, than to right themselves by abolishing the forms to which they are accustomed. But when a long train of abuses and usurpations, pursuing invariably the same Object evinces a design to reduce them under absolute Despotism, it is their right, it is their duty, to throw off such Government, and to provide new Guards for their future security.—Such has been the patient sufferance of these Colonies; and such is now the necessity which constrains them to alter their former Systems of Government. The history of the present King of Great Britain is a history of repeated injuries and usurpations, all having in direct object the establishment of an absolute Tyranny over these States. To prove this, let Facts be submitted to a candid world.

He has refused his Assent to Laws, the most wholesome and necessary for the public good.

He has forbidden his Governors to pass Laws of immediate and pressing importance, unless suspended in their operation till his Assent should be obtained; and, when so suspended, he has utterly neglected to attend to them.

He has refused to pass other Laws for the accommodation of large districts of people, unless those people would relinquish the right of Representation in the Legislature, a right inestimable to them and formidable to tyrants only.

He has called together legislative bodies at places unusual, uncomfortable, and distant from the depository of their public Records, for the sole purpose of fatiguing them into compliance with his measures.

He has dissolved Representative Houses repeatedly, for opposing with manly firmness his invasions on the rights of the people.

He has refused for a long time, after such dissolutions, to cause others to be elected; whereby the Legislative powers, incapable of Annihilation, have returned to the People at large for their exercise; the State remaining in the mean time exposed to all the dangers of invasion from without and convulsions within.

He has endeavoured to prevent the population of these States; for that purpose obstructing the Laws of Naturalization of Foreigners; refusing to pass others to encourage their migrations hither, and raising the conditions of new Appropriations of Lands.

He has obstructed the Administration of Justice, by refusing his Assent to Laws for establishing Judiciary powers.

appendix

He has made Judges dependent on his Will alone, for the tenure of their offices, and the amount and payment of their salaries.

He has erected a multitude of New Offices, and sent hither swarms of Officers to harass our People, and eat out their substance.

He has kept among us, in times of peace, Standing Armies without the Consent of our legislature.

He has combined with others to subject us to a jurisdiction foreign to our constitution, and unacknowledged by our laws; giving his Assent to their Acts of pretended Legislation:

For quartering large bodies of armed troops among us:

For protecting them, by a mock Trial, from Punishment for any Murders which they should commit on the Inhabitants of these States:

For cutting off our Trade with all parts of the world:

For imposing taxes on us without our Consent:

For depriving us, in many cases, of the benefits of Trial by jury:

For transporting us beyond Seas to be tried for pretended offences:

For abolishing the free System of English Laws in a neighbouring Province, establishing therein an Arbitrary government, and enlarging its Boundaries so as to render it at once an example and fit instrument for introducing the same absolute rule into these Colonies:

For taking away our Charters, abolishing our most valuable Laws, and altering fundamentally the Forms of our Governments:

For suspending our own Legislatures, and declaring themselves invested with Power to legislate for us in all cases whatsoever.

He has abdicated Government here, by declaring us out of his Protection and waging War against us.

He has plundered our seas, ravaged our Coasts, burnt our towns, and destroyed the lives of our people.

He is at this time transporting large armies of foreign mercenaries to compleat the works of death, desolation, and tyranny, already begun with circumstances of Cruelty & perfidy scarcely parallelled in the most barbarous ages, and totally unworthy the Head of a civilized nation.

He has constrained our fellow Citizens taken Captive on the high Seas to bear Arms against their Country, to become the executioners of their friends and Brethren, or to fall themselves by their Hands.

He has excited domestic insurrections amongst us, and has endeavoured to bring on the inhabitants of our frontiers, the merciless Indian Savages, whose known rule of warfare, is an undistinguished destruction of all ages, sexes, and conditions.

In every stage of these Oppressions We have Petitioned for Redress in the most humble terms: Our repeated Petitions have been answered only by repeated injury. A Prince, whose character is thus marked by every act which may define a Tyrant, is unfit to be the ruler of a free people.

Nor have We been wanting in attention to our British brethren. We have warned them from time to time of attempts by their legislature to extend an unwarrantable jurisdiction over us. We have reminded them of the circumstances of our emigration and settlement here. We have appealed to their native justice and magnanimity, and we have conjured them by the ties of our common kindred to disavow these usurpations, which, would inevitably interrupt our connections and correspondence. They too have been deaf to the voice of justice and of consanguinity. We must, therefore, acquiesce in the necessity, which denounces our Separation, and hold them, as we hold the rest of mankind, Enemies in War, in Peace Friends.

We, therefore, the Representatives of the United States of America, in General Congress, Assembled, appealing to the Supreme Judge of the world for the rectitude of our intentions, do, in the Name, and by Authority of the good People of these Colonies, solemnly publish and declare, That these United Colonies are, and of Right ought to be FREE AND INDEPENDENT STATES; that they are Absolved from all Allegiance to the British Crown, and that all political connection between them and the State of Great Britain, is and ought to be totally dissolved; and that as Free and Independent States, they have full Power to levy War, conclude Peace, contract Alliances, establish Commerce, and to do all other Acts and Things which Independent States may of right do. And for the support of this Declaration, with a firm reliance on the Protection of Divine Providence, we mutually pledge to each other our Lives, our Fortunes, and our sacred Honor.

John Hancock

Button Gwinnett	George Wythe	James Wilson	Josiah Bartlett
Lyman Hall	Richard Henry Lee	Geo. Ross	Wm. Whipple
Geo. Walton	Th. Jefferson	Caesar Rodney	Matthew Thornton
Wm. Hooper	Benja. Harrison	Geo. Read	Saml. Adams
Joseph Hewes	Thos. Nelson, Jr.	Thos. M'Kean	John Adams
John Penn	Francis Lightfoot Lee	Wm. Floyd	Robt. Treat Paine
Edward Rutledge	Carter Braxton	Phil. Livingston	Elbridge Gerry
Thos. Heyward, Junr.	Robt. Morris	Frans. Lewis	Step. Hopkins
Thomas Lynch, Junr.	Benjamin Rush	Lewis Morris	William Ellery
Arthur Middleton	Benja. Franklin	Richd. Stockton	Roger Sherman
Samuel Chase	John Morton	John Witherspoon	Sam'el Huntington
Wm. Paca	Geo. Clymer	Fras. Hopkinson	Wm. Williams
Thos. Stone	Jas. Smith	John Hart	Oliver Wolcott
Charles Carroll	Geo. Taylor	Abra. Clark	
of Carrollton			

The Constitution of the United States of America

AGREED TO BY PHILADELPHIA CONVENTION, SEPTEMBER 17, 1787
IMPLEMENTED MARCH 4, 1789

We the People of the United States, in Order to form a more perfect Union, establish Justice, insure domestic Tranquility, provide for the common defence, promote the general Welfare, and secure the Blessings of Liberty to ourselves and our Posterity, do ordain and establish this Constitution for the United States of America.

ARTICLE I

SECTION 1. All legislative Powers herein granted shall be vested in a Congress of the United States, which shall consist of a Senate and a House of Representatives.

SECTION 2. The House of Representatives shall be composed of Members chosen every second Year by the People of the several States, and the Electors in

Note: The Constitution became effective March 4, 1789. Provisions in italics are no longer relevant or have been changed by constitutional amendment. Copy highlighted in yellow pertains to African Americans.

each State shall have the Qualifications requisite for Electors of the most numerous Branch of the State Legislature.

No Person shall be a Representative who shall not have attained to the Age of twenty-five Years, and been seven Years a Citizen of the United States, and who shall not, when elected, be an Inhabitant of that State in which he shall be chosen.

Representatives and direct Taxes shall be apportioned among the several States which may be included within this Union, according to their respective Numbers, *which shall be determined by adding to the whole Number of free Persons, including those bound to Service for a Term of Years, and excluding Indians not taxed, three fifths of all other Persons.*[1]

The actual Enumeration shall be made within three Years after the first Meeting of the Congress of the United States, and within every subsequent Term of ten Years, in such Manner as they shall by Law

1. Changed by Section 2 of the Fourteenth Amendment.

direct. The Number of Representatives shall not exceed one for every thirty Thousand, but each State shall have at Least one Representative; and *until such enumeration shall be made, the State of New Hampshire shall be entitled to chuse three, Massachusetts eight, Rhode Island and Providence Plantations one, Connecticut five, New-York six, New Jersey four, Pennsylvania eight, Delaware one, Maryland six, Virginia ten, North Carolina five, South Carolina five, and Georgia three.*

When vacancies happen in the Representation from any State, the Executive Authority thereof shall issue Writs of Election to fill such Vacancies.

The House of Representatives shall chuse their Speaker and other Officers; and shall have the sole Power of Impeachment.

SECTION 3. The Senate of the United States shall be composed of two Senators from each State, *chosen by the Legislature thereof,*[2] for six Years; and each Senator shall have one Vote.

Immediately after they shall be assembled in Consequence of the first Election, they shall be divided as equally as may be into three Classes. The Seats of the Senators of the first Class shall be vacated at the Expiration of the second Year, of the second Class at the Expiration of the fourth Year, and of the third Class at the Expiration of the sixth Year, so that one-third may be chosen every second Year; and if Vacancies happen by Resignation, or otherwise, during the Recess of the Legislature of any State, the Executive thereof may make temporary Appointments until the next Meeting of the Legislature, which shall then fill such Vacancies.[3]

No person shall be a Senator who shall not have attained to the Age of thirty Years, and been nine Years a Citizen of the United States, and who shall not, when elected, be an Inhabitant of that State for which he shall be chosen.

The Vice President of the United States shall be President of the Senate, but shall have no Vote, unless they be equally divided.

The Senate shall chuse their other Officers, and also a President pro tempore, in the absence of the Vice President, or when he shall exercise the Office of President of the United States.

The Senate shall have the sole Power to try all Impeachments. When sitting for that Purpose, they shall be on Oath or Affirmation. When the President of the United States is tried, the Chief Justice shall preside: And no Person shall be convicted without the Concurrence of two thirds of the Members present.

Judgment in Cases of Impeachment shall not extend further than to removal from Office, and disqualification to hold and enjoy any Office of honor, Trust or Profit under the United States: but the Party convicted shall nevertheless be liable and subject to Indictment, Trial, Judgment and Punishment, according to Law.

SECTION 4. The Times, Places and Manner of holding Elections for Senators and Representatives, shall be prescribed in each State by the Legislature thereof; but the Congress may at any time by Law make or alter such Regulations, except as to the Places of Chusing Senators.

The Congress shall assemble at least once in every Year, and such Meeting *shall be on the first Monday in December, unless they shall by Law appoint a different Day.*[4]

SECTION 5. Each House shall be the Judge of the Elections, Returns and Qualifications of its own Members, and a Majority of each shall constitute a Quorum to do Business; but a smaller number may adjourn from day to day, and may be authorized to compel the Attendance of absent Members, in such Manner, and under such Penalties, as each House may provide.

Each House may determine the Rules of its Proceedings, punish its Members for disorderly Behavior, and, with the Concurrence of two thirds, expel a Member.

Each House shall keep a Journal of its Proceedings, and from time to time publish the same, excepting such Parts as may in their Judgment require Secrecy; and the Yeas and Nays of the Members of either House on any question shall, at the Desire of one-fifth of those Present, be entered on the Journal.

Neither House, during the Session of Congress, shall, without the Consent of the other, adjourn for more than three days, nor to any other Place than that in which the two Houses shall be sitting.

SECTION 6. The Senators and Representatives shall receive a Compensation for their Services, to be ascertained by Law, and paid out of the Treasury of the United States. They shall in all Cases, except Treason,

---

2. Changed by Section 1 of the Seventeenth Amendment.
3. Changed by Clause 2 of the Seventeenth Amendment.

---

4. Changed by Section 2 of the Twentieth Amendment.

Felony and Breach of the Peace, be privileged from Arrest during their Attendance at the Session of their respective Houses, and in going to and returning from the same; and for any Speech or Debate in either House, they shall not be questioned in any other Place.

No Senator or Representative shall, during the Time for which he was elected, be appointed to any civil Office under the Authority of the United States, which shall have been created, or the Emoluments whereof shall have been increased, during such time; and no Person holding any Office under the United States, shall be a Member of either House during his Continuance in Office.

SECTION 7. All Bills for raising Revenue shall originate in the House of Representatives; but the Senate may propose or concur with Amendments as on other Bills.

Every Bill which shall have passed the House of Representatives and the Senate, shall, before it becomes a Law, be presented to the President of the United States; If he approve he shall sign it, but if not he shall return it, with his Objections to that House in which it shall have originated, who shall enter the Objections at large on their Journal, and proceed to reconsider it. If after such Reconsideration two thirds of that House shall agree to pass the Bill, it shall be sent, together with the Objections, to the other House, by which it shall likewise be reconsidered, and if approved by two thirds of that House, it shall become a Law. But in all such Cases the Votes of both Houses shall be determined by Yeas and Nays, and the Names of the Persons voting for and against the Bill shall be entered on the Journal of each House respectively. If any Bill shall not be returned by the President within ten Days (Sundays excepted) after it shall have been presented to him, the Same shall be a Law, in like Manner as if he had signed it, unless the Congress by their Adjournment prevent its Return, in which Case it shall not be a Law.

Every Order, Resolution, or Vote to which the Concurrence of the Senate and the House of Representatives may be necessary (except on a question of Adjournment) shall be presented to the President of the United States; and before the Same shall take Effect, shall be approved by him, or being disapproved by him, shall be repassed by two thirds of the Senate and House of Representatives, according to the Rules and Limitations prescribed in the Case of a Bill.

SECTION 8. The Congress shall have Power to lay and collect Taxes, Duties, Imposts and Excises, to pay the Debts and provide for the common Defence and general Welfare of the United States; but all Duties, Imposts and Excises shall be uniform throughout the United States;

To borrow money on the credit of the United States;

To regulate Commerce with foreign Nations, and among the several States, and with the Indian Tribes;

To establish an uniform Rule of Naturalization, and uniform Laws on the subject of Bankruptcies throughout the United States;

To coin Money, regulate the Value thereof, and of foreign Coin, and fix the Standard of Weights and Measures;

To provide for the Punishment of counterfeiting the Securities and current Coin of the United States;

To establish Post Offices and post Roads;

To promote the Progress of Science and useful Arts, by securing for limited Times to Authors and Inventors the exclusive Right to their respective Writings and Discoveries;

To constitute Tribunals inferior to the supreme Court;

To define and punish Piracies and Felonies committed on the high Seas, and Offenses against the Law of Nations;

To declare War, grant Letters of Marque and Reprisal, and make Rules concerning Captures on Land and Water;

To raise and support Armies, but no Appropriation of Money to that Use shall be for a longer Term than two Years;

To provide and maintain a Navy;

To make Rules for the Government and Regulation of the land and naval Forces;

To provide for calling forth the Militia to execute the Laws of the Union, suppress Insurrections and repel Invasions;

To provide for organizing, arming, and disciplining the Militia, and for governing such Part of them as may be employed in the Service of the United States, reserving to the States respectively, the Appointment of the Officers, and the Authority of training the Militia according to the discipline prescribed by Congress;

appendix

To exercise exclusive Legislation in all Cases whatsoever, over such District (not exceeding ten Miles square) as may, by Cession of particular States, and the acceptance of Congress, become the Seat of Government of the United States, and to exercise like Authority over all Places purchased by the Consent of the Legislature of the State in which the Same shall be, for the Erection of Forts, Magazines, Arsenals, dock-Yards, and other needful Buildings;—And

To make all Laws which shall be necessary and proper for carrying into Execution the foregoing Powers, and all other Powers vested by this Constitution in the Government of the United States, or in any Department or Officer thereof.

SECTION 9. The Migration or Importation of such Persons as any of the States now existing shall think proper to admit, shall not be prohibited by the Congress prior to the Year one thousand eight hundred and eight but a tax or duty may be imposed on such Importation, not exceeding ten dollars for each Person.

The privilege of the Writ of Habeas Corpus shall not be suspended, unless when in Cases of Rebellion or Invasion the public Safety may require it.

No Bill of Attainder or ex post facto Law shall be passed.

No capitation, or other direct, Tax shall be laid, unless in Proportion to the Census or Enumeration herein before directed to be taken.[5]

No Tax or Duty shall be laid on Articles exported from any State.

No Preference shall be given by any Regulation of Commerce or Revenue to the Ports of one State over those of another: nor shall Vessels bound to, or from, one State, be obliged to enter, clear, or pay Duties in another.

No Money shall be drawn from the Treasury, but in Consequence of Appropriations made by law; and a regular Statement and Account of the Receipts and Expenditures of all public Money shall be published from time to time.

No Title of Nobility shall be granted by the United States: And no Person holding any Office of Profit or Trust under them, shall, without the Consent

of the Congress, accept of any present, Emolument, Office, or Title, of any kind whatever, from any King, Prince, or foreign State.

SECTION 10. No State shall enter into any Treaty, Alliance, or Confederation; grant Letters of Marque and Reprisal; coin Money; emit Bills of Credit; make any Thing but gold and silver Coin a Tender in Payment of Debts; pass any Bill of Attainder, ex post facto Law, or Law impairing the Obligation of Contracts, or grant any Title of Nobility.

No State shall, without the Consent of the Congress, lay any Imposts or Duties on Imports or Exports, except what may be absolutely necessary for executing its inspection Laws: and the net Produce of all Duties and Imposts, laid by any State on Imports or Exports, shall be for the Use of the Treasury of the United States; and all such Laws shall be subject to the Revision and Control of the Congress.

No State shall, without the Consent of the Congress, lay any duty of Tonnage, keep Troops, or Ships of War in time of Peace, enter into any Agreement or Compact with another State, or with a foreign Power, or engage in War, unless actually invaded, or in such imminent Danger as will not admit of delay.

ARTICLE II

SECTION 1. The executive Power shall be vested in a President of the United States of America. He shall hold his Office during the Term of four Years, and, together with the Vice President, chosen for the same Term, be elected, as follows:

Each State shall appoint, in such Manner as the Legislature thereof may direct, a Number of Electors, equal to the whole Number of Senators and Representatives to which the State may be entitled in the Congress; but no Senator or Representative, or Person holding an Office of Trust or Profit under the United States, shall be appointed an Elector.

The Electors shall meet in their respective States, and vote by Ballot for two Persons, of whom one at least shall not be an Inhabitant of the same State with themselves. And they shall make a List of all the Persons voted for, and of the Number of Votes for each; which List they shall sign and certify, and transmit sealed to the Seat of the Government of the United States, directed to the President of the Senate. The President of the Senate shall, in the Presence of the Sen-

---

5. Changed by the Sixteenth Amendment.

ate and House of Representatives, open all the Certificates, and the Votes shall then be counted. *The Person having the greatest Number of Votes shall be the President, if such Number be a Majority of the whole Number of Electors appointed; and if there be more than one who have such Majority, and have an equal Number of Votes, then the House of Representatives shall immediately chuse by Ballot one of them for President; and if no Person have a Majority, then from the five highest on the List the said House shall in like Manner chuse the President. But in chusing the President, the Votes shall be taken by States, the Representation from each State having one Vote; a quorum for this Purpose shall consist of a Member or Members from two thirds of the States, and a Majority of all the States shall be necessary to a Choice. In every Case, after the Choice of the President, the Person having the greatest Number of Votes of the Electors shall be the Vice President. But if there should remain two or more who have equal Votes, the Senate shall chuse from them by Ballot the Vice President.*[6]

The Congress may determine the Time of chusing the Electors, and the Day on which they shall give their Votes; which Day shall be the same throughout the United States.

No Person except a natural born Citizen, or a Citizen of the United States, at the time of the Adoption of this Constitution, shall be eligible to the Office of President; neither shall any Person be eligible to that Office who shall not have attained to the Age of thirty five Years, and been fourteen Years a Resident within the United States.

In Case of the Removal of the President from Office, or of his Death, Resignation, or Inability to discharge the Powers and Duties of the said Office, *the same shall devolve on the Vice President, and the Congress may by Law provide for the Case of Removal, Death, Resignation, or Inability, both of the President and Vice President, declaring what Officer shall then act as President, and such Officer shall act accordingly, until the Disability be removed, or a President shall be elected.*[7]

The President shall, at stated Times, receive for his Services a Compensation, which shall neither be increased nor diminished during the Period for which he shall have been elected, and he shall not receive within that Period any other Emolument from the United States, or any of them.

Before he enter on the Execution of his Office, he shall take the following Oath or Affirmation:—"I do solemnly swear (or affirm) that I will faithfully execute the Office of President of the United States, and will to the best of my Ability, preserve, protect and defend the Constitution of the United States."

SECTION 2. The President shall be Commander in Chief of the Army and Navy of the United States, and of the Militia of the several States, when called into the actual Service of the United States; he may require the Opinion, in writing, of the principal Officer in each of the executive Departments, upon any Subject relating to the Duties of their respective Offices, and he shall have Power to Grant Reprieves and Pardons for Offences against the United States, except in Cases of Impeachment.

He shall have Power, by and with the Advice and Consent of the Senate, to make Treaties, provided two thirds of the Senators present concur; and he shall nominate, and by and with the Advice and Consent of the Senate, shall appoint Ambassadors, other public Ministers and Consuls, Judges of the supreme Court, and all other Officers of the United States, whose Appointments are not herein otherwise provided for, and which shall be established by Law: but the Congress may by Law vest the Appointment of such inferior Officers, as they think proper, in the President alone, in the Courts of Law, or in the Heads of Departments.

The President shall have Power to fill up all Vacancies that may happen during the Recess of the Senate, by granting Commissions which shall expire at the End of their next Session.

SECTION 3. He shall from time to time give to the Congress Information of the State of the Union, and recommend to their Consideration such Measures as he shall judge necessary and expedient; he may, on extraordinary Occasions, convene both Houses, or either of them, and in Case of Disagreement between them, with Respect to the Time of Adjournment, he may adjourn them to such Time as he shall think proper; he shall receive Ambassadors and other public Ministers; he shall take Care that the Laws be faithfully executed, and shall Commission all the Officers of the United States.

---

6. Superseded by the Twelfth Amendment.
7. Modified by the Twenty-fifth Amendment.

SECTION 4. The President, Vice President and all civil Officers of the United States, shall be removed from Office on Impeachment for, and Conviction of, Treason, Bribery, or other high Crimes and Misdemeanors.

ARTICLE III

SECTION 1. The judicial Power of the United States, shall be vested in one supreme Court, and in such inferior Courts as the Congress may from time to time ordain and establish. The Judges, both of the supreme and inferior Courts, shall hold their Offices during good Behaviour, and shall, at stated Times, receive for their Services a Compensation, which shall not be diminished during their Continuance in Office.

SECTION 2. The judicial Power shall extend to all Cases, in Law and Equity, arising under this Constitution, the Laws of the United States, and Treaties made, or which shall be made, under their Authority;—to all Cases affecting Ambassadors, other public Ministers and Consuls;—to all Cases of admiralty and maritime Jurisdiction;—to Controversies to which the United States shall be a Party;—to Controversies between two or more States;—*between a State and Citizens of another State;*[8]—between Citizens of different States;—between Citizens of the same State claiming Lands under Grants of different States, and between a State, or the Citizens thereof, and foreign States, Citizens or Subjects.

In all Cases affecting Ambassadors, other public Ministers and Consuls, and those in which a State shall be Party, the supreme Court shall have original Jurisdiction. In all the other Cases before mentioned, the supreme Court shall have appellate Jurisdiction, both as to Law and Fact, with such Exceptions, and under such Regulations as the Congress shall make.

The trial of all Crimes, except in Cases of Impeachment, shall be by Jury; and such Trial shall be held in the State where said Crimes shall have been committed; but when not committed within any State, the Trial shall be at such Place or Places as the Congress may by Law have directed.

SECTION 3. Treason against the United States, shall consist only in levying War against them, or in adhering to their Enemies, giving them Aid and Comfort. No Person shall be convicted of Treason unless on the Testimony of two Witnesses to the same overt Act, or on Confession in open Court.

The Congress shall have Power to declare the Punishment of Treason, but no Attainder of Treason shall work Corruption of Blood, or Forefeiture except during the Life of the Person attainted.

ARTICLE IV

SECTION 1. Full Faith and Credit shall be given in each State to the public Acts, Records, and judicial Proceedings of every other State. And the Congress may by general Laws prescribe the Manner in which such Acts, Records, and Proceedings shall be proved, and the Effect thereof.

SECTION 2. The Citizens of each State shall be entitled to all Privileges and Immunities of Citizens in the several States.

A Person charged in any State with Treason, Felony, or other Crime, who shall flee from Justice, and be found in another State, shall on demand of the executive Authority of the State from which he fled, be delivered up, to be removed to the State having Jurisdiction of the Crime.

No Person held to Service or Labour in one State, under the Laws thereof, escaping into another, shall, in Consequence of any Law or Regulation therein, be discharged from such Service or Labour, but shall be delivered up on Claim of the Party to whom such Service or Labour may be due.[9]

SECTION 3. New States may be admitted by the Congress into this Union; but no new State shall be formed or erected within the Jurisdiction of any other State; nor any State be formed by the Junction of two or more States, or parts of States, without the Consent of the Legislatures of the States concerned as well as of the Congress.

The Congress shall have Power to dispose of and make all needful Rules and Regulations respecting the Territory or other Property belonging to the United States; and nothing in this Constitution shall be so construed as to Prejudice any Claims of the United States, or of any particular State.

8. Restricted by the Eleventh Amendment.

9. Superseded by the Thirteenth Amendment.

SECTION 4. The United States shall guarantee to every State in this Union a Republican Form of Government, and shall protect each of them against Invasion; and on Application of the Legislature, or of the Executive (when the Legislature cannot be convened) against domestic Violence.

ARTICLE V

The Congress, whenever two thirds of both Houses shall deem it necessary, shall propose Amendments to this Constitution, or, on the Application of the Legislatures of two thirds of the several States, shall call a Convention for proposing Amendments, which, in either Case, shall be valid to all Intents and Purposes, as Part of this Constitution, when ratified by the Legislatures of three fourths of the several States, or by Conventions in three fourths thereof, as the one or the other Mode of Ratification may be proposed by the Congress; Provided that no Amendment which may be made prior to the Year One thousand eight hundred and eight shall in any Manner affect the first and fourth Clauses in the Ninth Section of the first Article; and that no State, without its Consent, shall be deprived of its equal Suffrage in the Senate.

ARTICLE VI

All Debts contracted and Engagements entered into, before the Adoption of this Constitution, shall be as valid against the United States under this Constitution, as under the Confederation.

This Constitution, and the Laws of the United States which shall be made in Pursuance thereof; and all Treaties made, or which shall be made, under the Authority of the United States, shall be the supreme Law of the Land; and the Judges in every State shall be bound thereby, any Thing in the Constitution or Laws of any State to the Contrary notwithstanding.

The Senators and Representatives before mentioned, and the Members of the several State Legislatures, and all executive and judicial Officers, both of the United States and of the several States, shall be bound by Oath or Affirmation, to support this Consti-tution; but no religious Test shall ever be required as a Qualification to any Office or public Trust under the United States.

ARTICLE VII

The Ratification of the Conventions of nine States shall be sufficient for the Establishment of this Constitution between the States so ratifying the Same.

Done in Convention by the Unanimous Consent of the States present the Seventeenth Day of September in the Year of our Lord one thousand seven hundred and Eighty seven and of the Independence of the United States of America the Twelfth. In Witness whereof We have hereunto subscribed our Names.

Go. Washington
President and deputy from Virginia

NEW HAMPSHIRE
John Langdon
Nicholas Gilman

MASSACHUSETTS
Nathaniel Gorham
Rufus King

CONNECTICUT
Wm. Saml. Johnson
Roger Sherman

NEW YORK
Alexander Hamilton

NEW JERSEY
Wil. Livingston
David Brearley
Wm. Paterson
Jona. Dayton

PENNSYLVANIA
B. Franklin
Thomas Mifflin
Robt. Morris
Geo. Clymer
Thos. FitzSimons
Jared Ingersoll
James Wilson
Gouv. Morris

DELAWARE
Geo. Read
Gunning Bedford jun
John Dickinson
Richard Bassett
Jaco. Broom

MARYLAND
James McHenry
Dan. of St. Thos. Jenifer
Danl. Carroll

VIRGINIA
John Blair
James Madison, Jr.

NORTH CAROLINA
Wm. Blount
Richd. Dobbs Spaight
Hu Williamson

SOUTH CAROLINA
J. Rutledge
Charles Cotesworth
Pinckney
Pierce Butler

GEORGIA
William Few
Abr. Baldwin

AMENDMENT I [1791][1]

Congress shall make no law respecting an establishment of religion, or prohibiting the free exercise thereof; or abridging the freedom of speech, or of the press; or the right of the people peaceably to assemble, and to petition the government for a redress of grievances.

AMENDMENT II [1791]

A well-regulated militia being necessary to the security of a free State, the right of the people to keep and bear arms shall not be infringed.

AMENDMENT III [1791]

No soldier shall, in time of peace, be quartered in any house without the consent of the owner, nor in time of war, but in a manner to be prescribed by law.

AMENDMENT IV [1791]

The right of the people to be secure in their persons, houses, papers, and effects, against unreasonable searches and seizures, shall not be violated, and no warrants shall issue but upon probable cause, supported by oath or affirmation, and particularly describing the place to be searched, and the persons or things to be seized.

AMENDMENT V [1791]

No person shall be held to answer for a capital, or otherwise infamous crime, unless on a presentment or indictment of a grand jury, except in cases arising in the land or naval forces, or in the militia, when in actual service in time of war or public danger; nor shall any person be subject for the same offence to be twice put in jeopardy of life or limb; nor shall be compelled in any criminal case to be a witness against himself, nor be deprived of life, liberty, or property, without due process of law; nor shall private property be taken for public use without just compensation.

AMENDMENT VI [1791]

In all criminal prosecutions, the accused shall enjoy the right to a speedy and public trial, by an impartial jury of the State and district wherein the crime shall have been committed, which district shall have been previously ascertained by law, and to be informed of the nature and cause of the accusation; to be confronted with the witnesses against him; to have compulsory process for obtaining witnesses in his favor, and to have the assistance of counsel for his defence.

AMENDMENT VII [1791]

In suits at common law, where the value in controversy shall exceed twenty dollars, the right of trial by jury shall be preserved, and no fact tried by a jury shall be otherwise reexamined in any court of the United States, than according to the rules of the common law.

AMENDMENT VIII [1791]

Excessive bail shall not be required, nor excessive fines imposed, nor cruel and unusual punishments inflicted.

AMENDMENT IX [1791]

The enumeration in the Constitution, of certain rights, shall not be construed to deny or disparage others retained by the people.

AMENDMENT X [1791]

The powers not delegated to the United States by the Constitution, nor prohibited by it to the States, are reserved to the States respectively, or to the people.

AMENDMENT XI [1798]

The judicial power of the United States shall not be construed to extend to any suit in law or equity, commenced or prosecuted against one of the United States by citizens of another State, or by citizens or subjects of any foreign state.

---

1. The date in brackets indicates when the amendment was ratified.

AMENDMENT XII [1804]

The electors shall meet in their respective States, and vote by ballot for President and Vice-President, one of whom, at least, shall not be an inhabitant of the same State with themselves; they shall name in their ballots the person voted for as President, and in distinct ballots the person voted for as Vice-President, and they shall make distinct lists of all persons voted for as President, and of all persons voted for as Vice-President, and of the number of votes for each, which lists they shall sign and certify, and transmit sealed to the seat of government of the United States, directed to the President of the Senate;—the President of the Senate shall, in the presence of the Senate and House of Representatives, open all the certificates and the votes shall then be counted;—the person having the greatest number of votes for President shall be the President, if such number be a majority of the whole number of electors appointed; and if no person have such majority, then from the persons having the highest numbers not exceeding three on the list of those voted for as President, the House of Representatives shall choose immediately, by ballot, the President. But in choosing the President, the votes shall be taken by States, the representation from each State having one vote; a quorum for this purpose shall consist of a member or members from two-thirds of the States, and a majority of all the States shall be necessary to a choice. And if the House of Representatives shall not choose a President whenever the right of choice shall devolve upon them, before *the fourth day of March* next following, then the Vice President shall act as President, as in the case of the death or other constitutional disability of the President.[2]

The person having the greatest number of votes as Vice-President shall be the Vice-President, if such number be a majority of the whole number of electors appointed; and if no person have a majority, then from the two highest numbers on the list the Senate shall choose the Vice-President; a quorum for the purpose shall consist of two thirds of the whole number of Senators, and a majority of the whole number shall be necessary to a choice. But no person constitutionally ineli-

---

2. Superseded by Section 3 of the Twentieth Amendment.

gible to the office of President shall be eligible to that of Vice-President of the United States.

AMENDMENT XIII [1865]

SECTION 1. Neither slavery nor involuntary servitude, except as a punishment for crime whereof the party shall have been duly convicted, shall exist within the United States, or any place subject to their jurisdiction.

SECTION 2. Congress shall have power to enforce this article by appropriate legislation.

AMENDMENT XIV [1868]

SECTION 1. All persons born or naturalized in the United States, and subject to the jurisdiction thereof, are citizens of the United States and of the State wherein they reside. No State shall make or enforce any law which shall abridge the privileges or immunities of citizens of the United States; nor shall any State deprive any person of life, liberty, or property, without due process of law; nor deny to any person within its jurisdiction the equal protection of the laws.

SECTION 2. Representatives shall be appointed among the several States according to their respective numbers, counting the whole number of persons in each State, excluding Indians not taxed. But when the right to vote at any election for the choice of electors for President and Vice-President of the United States, Representatives in Congress, the executive and judicial officers of a State, or the members of the legislature thereof, is denied to any of the male inhabitants of such State, being twenty-one years of age and citizens of the United States, or in any way abridged, except for participation in rebellion, or other crime, the basis of representation therein shall be reduced in the proportion which the number of such male citizens shall bear to the whole number of male citizens twenty-one years of age in such State.

SECTION 3. No person shall be a Senator or Representative in Congress, or Elector of President and Vice-President, or hold any office, civil or military, under the United States, or under any State, who, having previously taken an oath, as a member of Congress, or as an officer of the United States, or as a member of any

State legislature, or as an executive or judicial officer of any State, to support the Constitution of the United States, shall have engaged in insurrection or rebellion against the same, or given aid or comfort to the enemies thereof. Congress may, by a vote of two-thirds of each house, remove such disability.

SECTION 4. The validity of the public debt of the United States, authorized by law, including debts incurred for payment of pensions and bounties for services in suppressing insurrection or rebellion, shall not be questioned. But neither the United States nor any State shall assume or pay any debt or obligation incurred in aid of insurrection or rebellion against the United States, or any claim for the loss or emancipation of any slave; but all such debts, obligations, and claims shall be held illegal and void.

SECTION 5. The Congress shall have power to enforce, by appropriate legislation, the provisions of this article.

AMENDMENT XV [1870]

SECTION 1. The right of citizens of the United States to vote shall not be denied or abridged by the United States or by any State on account of race, color, or previous condition of servitude.

SECTION 2. The Congress shall have power to enforce this article by appropriate legislation.

AMENDMENT XVI [1913]

The Congress shall have power to lay and collect taxes on incomes, from whatever source derived, without apportionment among the several States, and without regard to any census or enumeration.

AMENDMENT XVII [1913]

SECTION 1. The Senate of the United States shall be composed of two Senators from each State, elected by the people thereof, for six years; and each Senator shall have one vote. The electors in each State shall have the qualifications requisite for electors of [voters for] the most numerous branch of the State legislatures.

SECTION 2. When vacancies happen in the representation of any State in the Senate, the executive authority of such State shall issue writs of election to fill such vacancies: Provided, that the Legislature of any State may empower the executive thereof to make temporary appointments until the people fill the vacancies by election as the Legislature may direct.

SECTION 3. This amendment shall not be so construed as to affect the election or term of any Senator chosen before it becomes valid as part of the Constitution.

AMENDMENT XVIII [1919; Repealed 1933 by Amendment XXI]

SECTION 1. After one year from the ratification of this article the manufacture, sale, or transportation of intoxicating liquors within, the importation thereof into, or the exportation thereof from the United States and all territory subject to the jurisdiction thereof, for beverage purposes, is hereby prohibited.

SECTION 2. The Congress and the several States shall have concurrent power to enforce this article by appropriate legislation.

SECTION 3. This article shall be inoperative unless it shall have been ratified as an amendment to the Constitution by the legislatures of the several States, as provided by the Constitution, within seven years from the date of the submission thereof to the States by the Congress.

AMENDMENT XIX [1920]

SECTION 1. The right of citizens of the United States to vote shall not be denied or abridged by the United States or by any State on account of sex.

SECTION 2. Congress shall have the power to enforce this article by appropriate legislation.

AMENDMENT XX [1933]

SECTION 1. The terms of the President and Vice-President shall end at noon on the twentieth day of January, and the terms of Senators and Representatives at noon on the third day of January, of the years in which such terms would have ended if this article had not been ratified; and the terms of their successors shall then begin.

SECTION 2. The Congress shall assemble at least once in every year, and such meeting shall begin at noon on the third day of January, unless they shall by law appoint a different day.

SECTION 3. If, at the time fixed for the beginning of the term of the President, the President-elect shall have died, the Vice-President-elect shall become President. If a President shall not have been chosen before the time fixed for the beginning of his term, or if the President-elect shall have failed to qualify, then the Vice-President-elect shall act as President until a President shall have qualified; and the Congress may by law provide for the case wherein neither a President-elect nor a Vice-President-elect shall have qualified, declaring who shall then act as President, or the manner in which one who is to act shall be selected, and such person shall act accordingly until a President or Vice-President shall have qualified.

SECTION 4. The Congress may by law provide for the case of the death of any of the persons from whom the House of Representatives may choose a President whenever the right of choice shall have devolved upon them, and for the case of the death of any of the persons from whom the Senate may choose a Vice-President whenever the right of choice shall have devolved upon them.

SECTION 5. Sections 1 and 2 shall take effect on the 15th day of October following the ratification of this article.

SECTION 6. This article shall be inoperative unless it shall have been ratified as an amendment to the Constitution by the Legislatures of three-fourths of the several States within seven years from the date of its submission.

AMENDMENT XXI [1933]

SECTION 1. The eighteenth article of amendment to the Constitution of the United States is hereby repealed.

SECTION 2. The transportation or importation into any State, Territory, or Possession of the United States for delivery or use therein of intoxicating liquors, in violation of the laws thereof, is hereby prohibited.

SECTION 3. This article shall be inoperative unless it shall have been ratified as an amendment to the Constitution by conventions in the several States, as provided in the Constitution, within seven years from the date of the submission thereof to the States by the Congress.

AMENDMENT XXII [1951]

SECTION 1. No person shall be elected to the office of the President more than twice, and no person who has held the office of President, or acted as President, for more than two years of a term to which some other person was elected President shall be elected to the office of President more than once. But this article shall not apply to any person holding the office of President when this Article was proposed by the Congress, and shall not prevent any person who may be holding the office of President, or acting as President, during the term within which this Article becomes operative from holding the office of President or acting as President during the remainder of such term.

SECTION 2. This article shall be inoperative unless it shall have been ratified as an amendment to the Constitution by the legislatures of three-fourths of the several States within seven years from the date of its submission to the States by the Congress.

AMENDMENT XXIII [1961]

SECTION 1. The District constituting the seat of Government of the United States shall appoint in such manner as the Congress may direct: A number of electors of President and Vice-President equal to the whole number of Senators and Representatives in Congress to which the District would be entitled if it were a State, but in no event more than the least populous State; they shall be in addition to those appointed by the States, but they shall be considered for the purposes of the election of President and Vice-President, to be electors appointed by a State; and they shall meet in the District and perform such duties as provided by the twelfth article of amendment.

SECTION 2. The Congress shall have the power to enforce this article by appropriate legislation.

AMENDMENT XXIV [1964]

SECTION 1. The right of citizens of the United States to vote in any primary or other election for President or Vice-President, for electors for President or Vice-President, or for Senator or Representative in Congress, shall not be denied or abridged by the United States or any State by reason of failure to pay any poll tax or other tax.

appendix

SECTION 2. The Congress shall have the power to enforce this article by appropriate legislation.

AMENDMENT XXV [1967]

SECTION 1. In case of the removal of the President from office or of his death or resignation, the Vice-President shall become President.

SECTION 2. Whenever there is a vacancy in the office of the Vice-President, the President shall nominate a Vice-President who shall take office upon confirmation by a majority vote of both Houses of Congress.

SECTION 3. Whenever the President transmits to the President pro tempore of the Senate and the Speaker of the House of Representatives his written declaration that he is unable to discharge the powers and duties of his office, and until he transmits to them a written declaration to the contrary, such powers and duties shall be discharged by the Vice-President as Acting President.

SECTION 4. Whenever the Vice-President and a majority of either the principal officers of the executive departments or of such other body as Congress may by law provide, transmit to the President pro tempore of the Senate and the Speaker of the House of Representatives their written declaration that the President is unable to discharge the powers and duties of his office, the Vice-President shall immediately assume the powers and duties of the office as Acting President.

Thereafter, when the President transmits to the President pro tempore of the Senate and the Speaker of the House of Representatives his written declaration that no inability exists, he shall resume the powers and duties of his office unless the Vice-President and a majority of either the principal officers of the executive department[s] or of such other body as Congress may by law provide, transmit within four days to the President pro tempore of the Senate and the Speaker of the House of Representatives their written declaration that the President is unable to discharge the powers and duties of his office. Thereupon Congress shall decide the issue, assembling within forty-eight hours for that purpose if not in session. If the Congress, within twenty-one days after receipt of the latter written declaration, or, if Congress is not in session, within twenty-one days after Congress is required to assemble, determines by two-thirds vote of both Houses that the President is unable to discharge the powers and duties of his office, the Vice-President shall continue to discharge the same as Acting President; otherwise, the President shall resume the powers and duties of his office.

AMENDMENT XXVI [1971]

SECTION 1. The right of citizens of the United States, who are eighteen years of age or older, to vote shall not be denied or abridged by the United States or by any State on account of age.

SECTION 2. The Congress shall have power to enforce this article by appropriate legislation.

AMENDMENT XXVII [1992]

No law, varying the compensation for the services of the Senators and Representatives, shall take effect, until an election of Representatives shall have intervened.

The Emancipation Proclamation [1863]

BY THE PRESIDENT OF THE UNITED STATES OF AMERICA: A PROCLAMATION.

Whereas, on the twenty-second day of September, in the year of our Lord one thousand eight hundred and sixty-two, a proclamation was issued by the President of the United States, containing, among other things, the following, to wit:

"That on the first day of January, in the year of our Lord one thousand eight hundred and sixty-three, all persons held as slaves within any State or designated part of a State, the people whereof shall then be in rebellion against the United States, shall be then, thenceforward, and forever free; and the Executive Government of the United States, including the military and naval authority thereof, will recognize and maintain the freedom of such persons, and will do no act or acts to repress such persons, or any of them, in any efforts they may make for their actual freedom.

"That the Executive will, on the first day of January aforesaid, by proclamation, designate the States and parts of States, if any, in which the people thereof, respectively, shall then be in rebellion against the United States; and the fact that any State, or the people thereof, shall on that day be, in good faith, represented in the Congress of the United States by members chosen thereto at elections wherein a majority of the qualified voters of such State shall have participated, shall, in the absence of strong countervailing testimony, be deemed conclusive evidence that such State, and the people thereof, are not then in rebellion against the United States."

Now, therefore I, Abraham Lincoln, President of the United States, by virtue of the power in me vested as Commander-in-Chief, of the Army and Navy of the United States in time of actual armed rebellion against the authority and government of the United States, and as a fit and necessary war measure for suppressing said rebellion, do, on this first day of January, in the year of our Lord one thousand eight hundred and sixty-three, and in accordance with my purpose so to do publicly proclaimed for the full period of one hundred days, from the day first above mentioned, order and designate as the States and parts of States wherein the people thereof respectively, are this day in rebellion against the United States, the following, to wit:

Arkansas, Texas, Louisiana, (except the Parishes of St. Bernard, Plaquemines, Jefferson, St. John, St. Charles, St. James Ascension, Assumption, Terrebonne, Lafourche, St. Mary, St. Martin, and Orleans, including the City of New Orleans) Mississippi, Alabama, Florida, Georgia, South Carolina, North Carolina, and Virginia, (except the forty-eight counties designated as West Virginia, and also the counties of Berkley, Accomac, Northampton, Elizabeth City, York, Princess Ann, and Norfolk, including the cities of Norfolk and Portsmouth[)], and which excepted parts, are for the present, left precisely as if this proclamation were not issued.

And by virtue of the power, and for the purpose aforesaid, I do order and declare that all persons held as slaves within said designated States, and parts of States, are, and henceforward shall be free; and that the Executive government of the United States, including the military and naval authorities thereof, will recognize and maintain the freedom of said persons.

And I hereby enjoin upon the people so declared to be free to abstain from all violence, unless in necessary self-defence; and I recommend to them that, in all cases when allowed, they labor faithfully for reasonable wages.

And I further declare and make known, that such persons of suitable condition, will be received into the armed service of the United States to garrison forts, positions, stations, and other places, and to man vessels of all sorts in said service.

And upon this act, sincerely believed to be an act of justice, warranted by the Constitution, upon military necessity, I invoke the considerate judgment of mankind, and the gracious favor of Almighty God.

In witness whereof, I have hereunto set my hand and caused the seal of the United States to be affixed.

Done at the City of Washington, this first day of January, in the year of our Lord one thousand eight hundred and sixty three, and of the Independence of the United States of America the eighty-seventh.

By the President: ABRAHAM LINCOLN
WILLIAM H. SEWARD, Secretary of State.

Presidents of the United States

Years in Office	President	Party
1789–1797	George Washington	No party designation
1797–1801	John Adams	Federalist
1801–1809	Thomas Jefferson	Democratic-Republican
1809–1817	James Madison	Democratic-Republican
1817–1825	James Monroe	Democratic-Republican
1825–1829	John Quincy Adams	Democratic-Republican
1829–1837	Andrew Jackson	Democratic
1837–1841	Martin Van Buren	Democratic
1841	William H. Harrison	Whig
1841–1845	John Tyler	Whig
1845–1849	James K. Polk	Democratic
1849–1850	Zachary Taylor	Whig
1850–1853	Millard Fillmore	Whig
1853–1857	Franklin Pierce	Democratic
1857–1861	James Buchanan	Democratic
1861–1865	Abraham Lincoln	Republican
1865–1869	Andrew Johnson	Republican
1869–1877	Ulysses S. Grant	Republican
1877–1881	Rutherford B. Hayes	Republican
1881	James A. Garfield	Republican
1881–1885	Chester A. Arthur	Republican
1885–1889	Grover Cleveland	Democratic
1889–1893	Benjamin Harrison	Republican
1893–1897	Grover Cleveland	Democratic
1897–1901	William McKinley	Republican
1901–1909	Theodore Roosevelt	Republican
1909–1913	William H. Taft	Republican
1913–1921	Woodrow Wilson	Democratic
1921–1923	Warren G. Harding	Republican
1923–1929	Calvin Coolidge	Republican
1929–1933	Herbert C. Hoover	Republican
1933–1945	Franklin D. Roosevelt	Democratic
1945–1953	Harry S. Truman	Democratic
1953–1961	Dwight D. Eisenhower	Republican
1961–1963	John F. Kennedy	Democratic
1963–1969	Lyndon B. Johnson	Democratic
1969–1974	Richard M. Nixon	Republican
1974–1977	Gerald R. Ford	Republican
1977–1981	Jimmy Carter	Democratic
1981–1989	Ronald W. Reagan	Republican
1989–1993	George H. W. Bush	Republican
1993–2001	William Jefferson Clinton	Democratic
2001–2009	George W. Bush	Republican
2009–	Barack Obama	Democratic

appendix

Selected Legislative Acts

The following four pieces of legislation touched myriad aspects of African American life: unjust employment practices, discrimination in public facilities, black voter disfranchisement, and the ability of blacks to immigrate to the United States from elsewhere in the world. From opening new work opportunities and spurring black voter participation to paving the way for one million new black immigrants, these acts had profound consequences for African Americans. The brief excerpts that follow provide some of the key provisions of the acts. As you read them, consider the specific impact these words had on the lives of African Americans—both individually and as a group.

The Civil Rights Act of 1875

The Civil Rights Act of 1875, introduced by Senator Charles Sumner and passed after his death, stipulated that all individuals were to receive equal treatment in public facilities—such as hotels, trains, and places of public amusement—regardless of race. The act made discrimination in such facilities a criminal offense and established monetary damages for those who were victims of discrimination. The law was not well enforced, however. It was finally struck down altogether in the 1883 *Civil Rights* cases, in which the Supreme Court ruled that Congress lacked the authority to outlaw discriminatory practices by private individuals and businesses.

Whereas it is essential to just government we recognize the equality of all men before the law, and hold that it is the duty of government in its dealings with the people to mete out equal and exact justice to all, of whatever nativity, race, color, or persuasion, religious or political; and it being the appropriate object of legislation to enact great fundamental principles into law: Therefore,

Be it enacted, That all persons within the jurisdiction of the United States shall be entitled to the full and equal enjoyment of the accommodations, advantages, facilities, and privileges of inns, public conveyances on land or water, theaters, and other places of public amusement; subject only to the conditions and limitations established by law, and applicable alike to citizens of every race and color, regardless of any previous condition of servitude.

SECTION 2. That any person who shall violate the foregoing section . . . shall, for every offense, forfeit and pay the sum of five hundred dollars to the person aggrieved thereby, to be recovered in an action of debt, with full costs; and shall also, for every such offense, be deemed guilty of a misdemeanor, and, upon conviction thereof, shall be fined not less than five hundred nor more than one thousand dollars, or shall be imprisoned not less than thirty days nor more than one year. . . .

SECTION 3. That the district and circuit courts of the United States shall have . . . cognizance of all crimes and offenses against, and violations of, the provisions of this act; and actions for the penalty given by the preceding section may be prosecuted in the territorial, district, or circuit courts of the United States wherever the defendant may be found, without regard to the other party; and the district attorneys, marshals, and deputy marshals of the United States, and commissioners appointed by the circuit and territorial courts of the United States . . . are hereby specially authorized and required to institute proceedings against every person who shall violate the provisions of this act, and cause him to be arrested and imprisoned or bailed, as the case may be, for trial before such court of the United States, or territorial court, as by law has cognizance of the offense, except in respect of the right of action accruing to the person aggrieved; and such district attorneys shall cause such proceedings to be prosecuted to their termination as in other cases . . . and any district attorney who shall willfully fail to institute and prosecute the proceedings herein required, shall, for every such offense, forfeit and pay the sum of five hundred dollars to the person aggrieved thereby, to be recovered by an action of debt, with full costs, and shall, on conviction thereof, be deemed guilty of a misdemeanor, and be fined not less than one thousand nor more than five thousand dollars. . . .

SECTION 4. That no citizen possessing all other qualifications which are or may be prescribed by law shall be disqualified for service as grand or petit juror in any court of the United States, or of any State, on account of race, color, or previous condition of servitude; and any officer or other person charged with any duty in the selection or summoning of jurors who shall exclude or fail to summon any citizen for the cause aforesaid shall, on conviction thereof, be deemed guilty of a misdemeanor, and be fined not more than five thousand dollars.

The Civil Rights Act of 1964

The Civil Rights Act of 1964 was a watershed for both African Americans and women. It prohibited discrimination on the basis of race, color, religion, sex, or national origin in employment and voting practices, federally assisted programs, public education, and places of public accommodation; authorized the Justice Department to institute desegregation suits; and provided technical and financial aid to assist communities in the desegregation of their schools. The act's fundamental Title VII, which dealt with discrimination in the workplace, established the Equal Employment Opportunity Commission to investigate cases of job discrimination.

AN ACT

To enforce the constitutional right to vote, to confer jurisdiction upon the district courts of the United States to provide injunctive relief against discrimination in public accommodations, to authorize the Attorney General to institute suits to protect constitutional rights in public facilities and public education, to extend the Commission on Civil Rights, to prevent discrimination in federally assisted programs, to establish a Commission on Equal Employment Opportunity, and for other purposes. . . .

TITLE I—VOTING RIGHTS

. . .

"(2) No person acting under color of law shall—

"(A) in determining whether any individual is qualified under State law or laws to vote in any Federal election, apply any standard, practice, or procedure different from the standards, practices, or procedures applied under such law or laws to other individuals . . . who have been found by State officials to be qualified to vote;

"(B) deny the right of any individual to vote in any Federal election because of an error or omission on any record or paper relating to any application, registration, or other act requisite to voting, if such error or omission is not material in determining whether such individual is qualified under State law to vote in such election; or

"(C) employ any literacy test as a qualification for voting in any Federal election unless (i) such test is administered to each individual and is conducted wholly in writing, and (ii) a certified copy of the test and of the answers given by the individual is furnished to him within twenty-five days of the submission of his request. . . ."

TITLE II—INJUNCTIVE RELIEF AGAINST DISCRIMINATION IN PLACES OF PUBLIC ACCOMMODATION

. . . (a) All persons shall be entitled to the full and equal enjoyment of the goods, services, facilities, and privileges, advantages, and accommodations of any place of public accommodation, as defined in this section, without discrimination or segregation on the ground of race, color, religion, or national origin.

(b) Each of the following establishments which serves the public is a place of public accommodation within the meaning of this title if its operations affect commerce, or if discrimination or segregation by it is supported by State action:

(1) any inn, hotel, motel, or other establishment which provides lodging to transient guests, other than an establishment located within a building which contains not more than five rooms for rent or hire and which is actually occupied by the proprietor of such establishment as his residence;

(2) any restaurant, cafeteria, lunchroom, lunch counter, soda fountain, or other facility principally engaged in selling food for consumption on the premises. . . .

(3) any motion picture house, theater, concert hall, sports arena, stadium or other place of exhibition or entertainment; and

(4) any establishment (A)(i) which is physically located within the premises of any establishment otherwise covered by this subsection, or (ii) within the premises of which is physically located any such covered establishment, and (B) which holds itself out as serving patrons of such covered establishment. . . .

(d) Discrimination or segregation by an establishment is supported by State action within the meaning of this title if such discrimination or segregation (1) is carried on under color of any law, statute, ordinance, or regulation; or (2) is carried on under color of any custom or usage required or enforced by officials of the State or political subdivision thereof; or (3) is required by action of the State or political subdivision thereof.

(e) The provisions of this title shall not apply to a private club or other establishment not in fact open to the public, except to the extent that the facilities of such establishment are made available to the customers or patrons of an establishment within the scope of subsection (b). . . .

TITLE III — DESEGREGATION OF PUBLIC FACILITIES

SECTION 301. (a) Whenever the Attorney General receives a complaint in writing signed by an individual to the effect that he is being deprived of or threatened with the loss of his right to the equal protection of the laws, on account of his race, color, religion, or national origin . . . the Attorney General is authorized to institute for or in the name of the United States a civil action in any appropriate district court of the United States against such parties and for such relief as may be appropriate. . . .

TITLE IV — DESEGREGATION OF PUBLIC EDUCATION . . .

Survey and Report of Educational Opportunities

SECTION 402. The Commissioner shall conduct a survey and make a report to the President and the Congress, within two years of the enactment of this title, concerning the lack of availability of equal educational opportunities for individuals by reason of race, color, religion, or national origin in public educational institutions at all levels in the United States, its territories and possessions, and the District of Columbia.

Technical Assistance

SECTION 403. The Commissioner is authorized, upon the application of any school board, State, municipality, school district, or other governmental unit legally responsible for operating a public school or schools, to render technical assistance to such applicant in the preparation, adoption, and implementation of plans for the desegregation of public schools. Such technical assistance may, among other activities, include making available to such agencies information regarding effective methods of coping with special educational problems occasioned by desegregation, and making available to such agencies personnel of the Office of Education or other persons specially equipped to advise and assist them in coping with such problems. . . .

TITLE V — COMMISSION ON CIVIL RIGHTS . . .

"**SECTION 104.** (a) The Commission shall—

"(1) investigate allegations . . . that certain citizens of the United States are being deprived of their right to vote and have that vote counted by reason of their color, race, religion, or national origin; . . .

"(2) study and collect information concerning legal developments constituting a denial of equal protection of the laws under the Constitution because of race, color, religion or national origin or in the administration of justice;

"(3) appraise the laws and policies of the Federal Government with respect to denials of equal protection of the laws under the Constitution because of race, color, religion or national origin or in the administration of justice;

"(4) serve as a national clearinghouse for information in respect to denials of equal protection of the laws because of race, color, religion or national origin, including but not limited to the fields of voting, education, housing, employment, the use of public facilities, and transportation, or in the administration of justice;

"(5) investigate allegations . . . that citizens of the United States are unlawfully being accorded or denied the right to vote, or to have their votes properly counted, in any election. . . ."

TITLE VI — NONDISCRIMINATION IN FEDERALLY ASSISTED PROGRAMS

SECTION 601. No person in the United States shall, on the ground of race, color, or national origin, be excluded from participation in, be denied the benefits of, or be subjected to discrimination under any program or activity receiving Federal financial assistance. . . .

TITLE VII — EQUAL EMPLOYMENT OPPORTUNITY . . .

Discrimination Because of Race, Color, Religion, Sex, or National Origin

SECTION 703. (a) It shall be an unlawful employment practice for an employer—
(1) to fail or refuse to hire or to discharge any individual, or otherwise to discriminate against any individual with respect to his compensation, terms, conditions, or privileges of employment, because of such individual's race, color, religion, sex, or national origin; or
(2) to limit, segregate, or classify his employees in any way which would deprive or tend to deprive any individual of employment opportunities or otherwise adversely affect his status as an employee, because of such individual's race, color, religion, sex, or national origin.
(b) It shall be an unlawful employment practice for an employment agency to fail or refuse to refer for employment, or otherwise to discriminate against, any individual because of his race, color, religion, sex, or national origin, or to classify or refer for employment any individual on the basis of his race, color, religion, sex, or national origin.
(c) It shall be an unlawful employment practice for a labor organization—
(1) to exclude or to expel from its membership, or otherwise to discriminate against, any individual because of his race, color, religion, sex, or national origin;
(2) to limit, segregate, or classify its membership, or to classify or fail or refuse to refer for employment any individual, in any way which would deprive or tend to deprive any individual of employment opportunities, or would limit such employment opportunities or otherwise adversely affect his status as an employee or as

an applicant for employment, because of such individual's race, color, religion, sex, or national origin; or
(3) to cause or attempt to cause an employer to discriminate against an individual in violation of this section.
(d) It shall be an unlawful employment practice for any employer, labor organization, or joint labor-management committee controlling apprenticeship or other training or retraining, including on-the-job training programs to discriminate against any individual because of his race, color, religion, sex, or national origin in admission to, or employment in, any program established to provide apprenticeship or other training.
(e) Notwithstanding any other provision of this title, (1) it shall not be an unlawful employment practice for an employer to hire and employ employees, for an employment agency to classify, or refer for employment any individual, for a labor organization to classify its membership or to classify or refer for employment any individual, or for an employer, labor organization, or joint labor-management committee controlling apprenticeship or other training or retraining programs to admit or employ any individual in any such program, on the basis of his religion, sex, or national origin in those certain instances where religion, sex, or national origin is a bona fide occupational qualification reasonably necessary to the normal operation of that particular business or enterprise, and (2) it shall not be an unlawful employment practice for a school, college, university, or other educational institution or institution of learning to hire and employ employees of a particular religion if such school, college, university, or other educational institution or institution of learning is, in whole or in substantial part, owned, supported, controlled, or managed by a particular religion or by a particular religious corporation, association, or society, or if the curriculum of such school, college, university, or other educational institution or institution of learning is directed toward the propagation of a particular religion. . . .

Equal Employment Opportunity Commission

SECTION 705. (a) There is hereby created a Commission to be known as the Equal Employment Opportunity Commission, which shall be composed of five members, not more than three of whom shall be members of the same political party, who shall be appointed by the President by and with the advice and consent of the Senate. . . .

(g) The Commission shall have power—

(1) to cooperate with and, with their consent, utilize regional, State, local, and other agencies, both public and private, and individuals;

(2) to pay to witnesses whose depositions are taken or who are summoned before the Commission or any of its agents the same witness and mileage fees as are paid to witnesses in the courts of the United States;

(3) to furnish to persons subject to this title such technical assistance as they may request to further their compliance with this title or an order issued thereunder;

(4) upon the request of (i) any employer, whose employees or some of them, or (ii) any labor organization, whose members or some of them, refuse or threaten to refuse to cooperate in effectuating the provisions of this title, to assist in such effectuation by conciliation or such other remedial action as is provided by this title;

(5) to make such technical studies as are appropriate to effectuate the purposes and policies of this title and to make the results of such studies available to the public;

(6) to refer matters to the Attorney General with recommendations for intervention in a civil action brought by an aggrieved party under section 706, or for the institution of a civil action by the Attorney General under section 707, and to advise, consult, and assist the Attorney General on such matters. . . .

TITLE VIII – REGISTRATION AND VOTING STATISTICS

SECTION 801. The Secretary of Commerce shall promptly conduct a survey to compile registration and voting statistics in such geographic areas as may be recommended by the Commission on Civil Rights.

The Voting Rights Act of 1965

The 1965 Voting Rights Act eliminated the practices responsible for the widespread disfranchisement of blacks in the South, such as poll taxes and literacy tests. It also established a strict system of enforcement, providing federal oversight for the administration of elections—particularly in states that had consistently engaged in discriminatory voting practices. The impact of the act was tremendous: Blacks registered in droves, and black voter participation skyrocketed throughout the South.

SECTION 2. No voting qualification or prerequisite to voting, or standard, practice, or procedure shall be imposed or applied by any State or political subdivision to deny or abridge the right of any citizen of the United States to vote on account of race or color.

SECTION 3. (a) Whenever the Attorney General institutes a proceeding under any statute to enforce the guarantees of the fifteenth amendment in any State or political subdivision the court shall authorize the appointment of Federal examiners by the United States Civil Service Commission . . . to serve for such period of time and for such political subdivisions as the court shall determine is appropriate to enforce the guarantees of the fifteenth amendment. . . .

(b) If in a proceeding instituted by the Attorney General under any statute to enforce the guarantees of the fifteenth amendment in any State or political subdivision the court finds that a test or device has been used for the purpose or with the effect of denying or abridging the right of any citizen of the United States to vote on account of race or color, it shall suspend the use of tests and devices in such State or political subdivisions as the court shall determine is appropriate and for such period as it deems necessary. . . .

SECTION 4. (a) To assure that the right of citizens of the United States to vote is not denied or abridged on account of race or color, no citizen shall be denied the right to vote in any Federal, State, or local election because of his failure to comply with any test or device in any State. . . .

appendix

SECTION 7. (a) The examiners for each political subdivision shall, at such places as the Civil Service Commission shall by regulation designate, examine applicants concerning their qualifications for voting. An application to an examiner shall be in such form as the Commission may require and shall contain allegations that the applicant is not otherwise registered to vote.

(b) Any person whom the examiner finds, in accordance with instructions received under section 9(b), to have the qualifications prescribed by State law not inconsistent with the Constitution and laws of the United States shall promptly be placed on a list of eligible voters. . . . The examiner shall certify and transmit such list, and any supplements as appropriate, at least once a month, to the offices of the appropriate election officials, with copies to the Attorney General and the attorney general of the State, and any such lists and supplements thereto transmitted during the month shall be available for public inspection on the last business day of the month and, in any event, not later than the forty-fifth day prior to any election. The appropriate State or local election official shall place such names on the official voting list. Any person whose name appears on the examiner's list shall be entitled and allowed to vote in the election district of his residence unless and until the appropriate election officials shall have been notified that such person has been removed from such list. . . .

(c) The examiner shall issue to each person whose name appears on such a list a certificate evidencing his eligibility to vote. . . .

SECTION 8. Whenever an examiner is serving under this Act in any political subdivision, the Civil Service Commission may assign, at the request of the Attorney General, one or more persons, who may be officers of the United States, (1) to enter and attend at any place for holding an election in such subdivision for the purpose of observing whether persons who are entitled to vote are being permitted to vote, and (2) to enter and attend at any place for tabulating the votes cast at any election held in such subdivision for the purpose of observing whether votes cast by persons entitled to vote are being properly tabulated. . . .

SECTION 9. (a) Any challenge to a listing on an eligibility list prepared by an examiner shall be heard and determined by a hearing officer appointed by and responsible to the Civil Service Commission and under such rules as the Commission shall by regulation prescribe. . . .

SECTION 10. (a) The Congress finds that the requirement of the payment of a poll tax as a precondition to voting (i) precludes persons of limited means from voting or imposes unreasonable financial hardship upon such persons as a precondition to their exercise of the franchise, (ii) does not bear a reasonable relationship to any legitimate State interest in the conduct of elections, and (iii) in some areas has the purpose or effect of denying persons the right to vote because of race or color. Upon the basis of these findings, Congress declares that the constitutional right of citizens to vote is denied or abridged in some areas by the requirement of the payment of a poll tax as a precondition to voting. . . .

SECTION 11. (a) No person acting under color of law shall fail or refuse to permit any person to vote who is entitled to vote under any provision of this Act or is otherwise qualified to vote, or willfully fail or refuse to tabulate, count, and report such person's vote.

The Immigration and Nationality Act of 1965

Also known as the Hart-Cellar Act, the Immigration and Nationality Act of 1965 was a substantial revision of the immigration policy that had prevailed in the United States since 1924, when a quota system was established that limited immigration by nation of origin. The new system used different criteria to determine eligibility, such as immigrants' skills, family connections within the United States, and potential benefit to the national economy. As a result of the act, immigration surged, bringing one million immigrants from Africa—as well as large numbers from Asia and Latin America—to the United States.

"(1) Visas shall be first made available, in a number not to exceed 20 per centum of the number specified in section 201(a)(ii), to qualified immigrants who are the unmarried sons or daughters of citizens of the United States.

"(2) Visas shall next be made available, in a number not to exceed 20 per centum of the number specified in section 201(a)(ii), plus any visas not required for the classes specified in paragraph (1), to qualified immigrants who are the spouses, unmarried sons or unmarried daughters of an alien lawfully admitted for permanent residence.

"(3) Visas shall next be made available, in a number not to exceed 10 per centum of the number specified in section 201(a)(ii), to qualified immigrants who are members of the professions, or who because of their exceptional ability in the sciences or the arts will substantially benefit prospectively the national economy, cultural interests, or welfare of the United States.

"(4) Visas shall next be made available, in a number not to exceed 10 per centum of the number specified in section 201(a)(ii), plus any visas not required for the classes specified in paragraphs (1) through (3), to qualified immigrants who are the married sons or the married daughters of citizens of the United States.

"(5) Visas shall next be made available, in a number not to exceed 24 per centum of the number specified in section 201(a)(ii), plus any visas not required for the classes specified in paragraphs (1) through (4), to qualified immigrants who are the brothers or sisters of citizens of the United States.

"(6) Visas shall next be made available, in a number not to exceed 10 per centum of the number specified in section 201(a)(ii), to qualified immigrants who are capable of performing specified skilled or unskilled labor, not of a temporary or seasonal nature, for which a shortage of employable and willing persons exists in the United States.

"(7) Conditional entries shall next be made available by the Attorney General, pursuant to such regulations as he may prescribe and in a number not to exceed 6 per centum of the number specified in section 201(a)(ii), to aliens who satisfy an Immigration and Naturalization Service officer at an examination in any non-Communist or non-Communist-dominated country, (A) that (i) because of persecution or fear of persecution on account of race, religion, or political opinion they have fled (I) from any Communist or Communist-dominated country or area, or (II) from any country within the general area of the Middle East, and (ii) are unable or unwilling to return to such country or area on account of race, religion, or political opinion, and (iii) are not nationals of the countries or areas in which their application for conditional entry is made; or (B) that they are persons uprooted by catastrophic natural calamity as defined by the President who are unable to return to their usual place of abode. For the purpose of the foregoing the term 'general area of the Middle East' means the area between and including (1) Libya on the west, (2) Turkey on the north, (3) Pakistan on the east, and (4) Saudi Arabia and Ethiopia on the south: *Provided*, That immigrant visas in a number not exceeding one-half the number specified in this paragraph may be made available, in lieu of conditional entries of a like number, to such aliens who have been continuously physically present in the United States for a period of at least two years prior to application for adjustment of status."

Selected Supreme Court Decisions

The cases that follow were landmarks in African American legal history, bringing about both immediate and long-term change and establishing vital precedents for future cases. Grappling with issues as diverse as the right of Congress to limit slavery, the citizenship status of slaves, the permissibility of state-sanctioned segregation, discrimination in the workplace, and the constitutionality of affirmative action, these cases exerted a tremendous impact on both black citizens and the nation as a whole. The following brief excerpts have been carefully selected from the full opinions of the U.S. Supreme Court. As you read them, consider how they are reflective of the specific historical and social contexts in which they were written.

Dred Scott v. Sandford [1857]

In 1846, the Missouri slave couple Dred and Harriet Scott sued for their freedom, claiming that their temporary residence with their master on free soil had rendered them free. Eleven years later, in *Dred Scott v. Sandford*, the Supreme Court ruled that the Scotts were to remain enslaved. In its decision, the Court harked back to the original intent of the writers of the Declaration of Independence and the U.S. Constitution, arguing that this was of paramount importance in interpreting the meaning of those documents for slaves and others of African descent. The Court argued that neither Scott nor any other person of African descent was entitled to U.S. citizenship and thus could not legitimately bring suit in court. Further, the Court asserted that slaves were property and emphasized that Congress lacked the authority to deny slaveholders their property. With this decision, the Court made it clear that Congress could not prevent slaveholding anywhere, rendering all laws that forbade slavery in the territories—including the Missouri Compromise of 1820—unconstitutional.

The question is simply this: Can a negro whose ancestors were imported into this country, and sold as slaves, become a member of the political community formed and brought into existence by the Constitution of the United States, and as such become entitled to all the rights and privileges and immunities guaranteed to the citizen? One of which rights is the privilege of suing in a court of the United States in the cases specified in the Constitution. . . .

In the opinion of the court, the legislation and histories of the times, and the language used in the Declaration of Independence, show, that neither the class of persons who had been imported as slaves, nor their descendants, whether they had become free or not, were then acknowledged as a part of the people, nor intended to be included in the general words used in that memorable instrument.

It is difficult at this day to realize the state of public opinion in relation to that unfortunate race, which prevailed in the civilized and enlightened portions of the world at the time of the Declaration of Independence, and when the Constitution of the United States was framed and adopted. But the public history of every European nation displays it in a manner too plain to be mistaken.

They had for more than a century before been regarded as beings of an inferior order, and altogether unfit to associate with the white race, either in social or political relations; and so far inferior, that they had no rights which the white man was bound to respect; and that the negro might justly and lawfully be reduced to slavery for his benefit. He was bought and sold, and treated as an ordinary article of merchandise and traffic, whenever a profit could be made by it. This opinion was at that time fixed and universal in the civilized portion of the white race. It was regarded as an axiom in morals as well as in politics, which no one thought of disputing. . . .

The language of the Declaration of Independence . . . would seem to embrace the whole human family, and if [these words] were used in a similar instrument at this day would be so understood. But it is too clear for dispute, that the enslaved African race were not intended to be included, and formed no part of the people who framed and adopted this declaration. . . .

. . . The right of property in a slave is distinctly and expressly affirmed in the Constitution. . . .

Upon these considerations, it is the opinion of the court that the act of Congress which prohibited a citizen from holding and owning property of this kind in the territory of the United States north of the line therein mentioned, is not warranted by the Constitution, and is therefore void; and that neither Dred Scott himself, nor any of his family, were made free by being carried into this territory; even if they had been carried there by the owner, with the intention of becoming a permanent resident.

Plessy v. Ferguson [1896]

In this landmark case, a shoemaker named Homer Plessy, who was seven-eighths white, argued that he had been denied equal protection under the Fourteenth Amendment when a Louisiana train conductor forced him to ride in the "colored car" rather than in the first-class car for which he had purchased a ticket. Plessy was arrested and charged with violating Louisiana's Separate Car Act. The Court found the act to be constitutional, arguing that separate facilities did not violate one's right to equal protection under the laws or imply the inferiority of blacks. In protecting local custom and state-sanctioned discrimination and establishing the legal doctrine of separate but equal, the decision effectively legitimized and legalized Jim Crow, paving the way for new and ever more sweeping laws. In 1954, the Court would take up the issue once again in *Brown v. Board of Education of Topeka*, this time with a very different outcome.

A statute which implies merely a legal distinction between the white and colored races—a distinction which is founded in the color of the two races, and

which must always exist so long as white men are distinguished from the other race by color—has no tendency to destroy the legal equality of the two races, or re-establish a state of involuntary servitude. . . .

. . . The object of the [fourteenth] amendment was undoubtedly to enforce the absolute equality of the two races before the law, but, in the nature of things, it could not have been intended to abolish distinctions based upon color, or to enforce social, as distinguished from political, equality, or a commingling of the two races upon terms unsatisfactory to either. Laws permitting, and even requiring, their separation, in places where they are liable to be brought into contact, do not necessarily imply the inferiority of either race to the other, and have been generally, if not universally, recognized as within the competency of the state legislatures in the exercise of their police power. . . .

We consider the underlying fallacy of the plaintiff's argument to consist in the assumption that the enforced separation of the two races stamps the colored race with a badge of inferiority. If this be so, it is not by reason of anything found in the act, but solely because the colored race chooses to put that construction upon it. The argument necessarily assumes that if, as has been more than once the case, and is not unlikely to be so again, the colored race should become the dominant power in the state legislature, and should enact a law in precisely similar terms, it would thereby relegate the white race to an inferior position. We imagine that the white race, at least, would not acquiesce in this assumption. The argument also assumes that social prejudices may be overcome by legislation, and that equal rights cannot be secured to the negro except by an enforced commingling of the two races. We cannot accept this proposition. If the two races are to meet upon terms of social equality, it must be the result of natural affinities, a mutual appreciation of each other's merits, and a voluntary consent of individuals. . . . Legislation is powerless to eradicate racial instincts, or to abolish distinctions based upon physical differences, and the attempt to do so can only result in accentuating the difficulties of the present situation. If the civil and political rights of both races be equal, one cannot be inferior to the other civilly or politically.

Brown v. Board of Education of Topeka [1954]

In the 1954 *Brown v. Board of Education of Topeka* decision, the Supreme Court unanimously declared the establishment of separate public schools for black and white children unconstitutional, thereby reversing its 1896 ruling in *Plessy v. Ferguson.* While the case dealt specifically with education, it was designed to have larger repercussions for the system of segregation as a whole. The NAACP lawyer Thurgood Marshall, who served as lead counsel on the case—and later became the first African American Supreme Court justice—argued successfully that segregation violated the equal protection clause of the Fourteenth Amendment, rendering *Plessy v. Ferguson* unconstitutional. The Court did not strike down the entire 1896 decision, but it did rule that race-based segregated facilities were inherently unequal in their psychological effects on black children.

Today, education is perhaps the most important function of state and local governments. . . . It is the very foundation of good citizenship. Today it is a principal instrument in awakening the child to cultural values, in preparing him for later professional training, and in helping him to adjust normally to his environment. In these days, it is doubtful that any child may reasonably be expected to succeed in life if he is denied the opportunity of an education. Such an opportunity, where the state has undertaken to provide it, is a right which must be made available to all on equal terms.

We come then to the question presented: Does segregation of children in public schools solely on the basis of race, even though the physical facilities and other "tangible" factors may be equal, deprive the children of the minority group of equal educational opportunities? We believe that it does. . . .

. . . To separate them from others of similar age and qualifications solely because of their race generates a feeling of inferiority as to their status in the community that may affect their hearts and minds in a way unlikely ever to be undone. The effect of this separation on their educational opportunities was well stated by a finding . . . by a court which nevertheless felt compelled to rule against the Negro plaintiffs:

["]Segregation of white and colored children in public schools has a detrimental effect upon the colored children. The impact is greater when it has the sanction of the law, for the policy of separating the races is usually interpreted as denoting the inferiority of the negro group. A sense of inferiority affects the motivation of a child to learn. Segregation with the sanction of law, therefore, has a tendency to [retard] the educational and mental development of negro children and to deprive them of some of the benefits they would receive in a racial[ly] integrated school system.["]

Whatever may have been the extent of psychological knowledge at the time of *Plessy v. Ferguson*, this finding is amply supported by modern authority. Any language in *Plessy v. Ferguson* contrary to this finding is rejected.

We conclude that, in the field of public education, the doctrine of "separate but equal" has no place. Separate educational facilities are inherently unequal. Therefore, we hold that the plaintiffs and others similarly situated for whom the actions have been brought are, by reason of the segregation complained of, deprived of the equal protection of the laws guaranteed by the Fourteenth Amendment.

Griggs v. Duke Power Co. [1971]

In *Griggs v. Duke Power Co.*, an employment discrimination case, the Supreme Court decided unanimously that under Title VII of the Civil Rights Act of 1964, intelligence and other tests that did not measure one's ability to perform a job were discriminatory. The NAACP filed the case on behalf of Willie Griggs and thirteen other black janitors, whose employer had begun to require IQ tests or high school diplomas as prerequisites for promotion. These requirements affected African Americans disproportionately, and the able performance of workers hired before the institution of the requirements made it clear that the tests were unnecessary to perform the work. In its verdict, the Court placed the burden of proof on the employer: Unless intelligence or other tests were "demonstrably a reasonable measure of job performance," employers could not require them under Title VII

The objective of Congress in the enactment of Title VII is plain from the language of the statute. It was to achieve equality of employment opportunities and remove barriers that have operated in the past to favor an identifiable group of white employees over other employees. Under the Act, practices, procedures, or tests neutral on their face, and even neutral in terms of intent, cannot be maintained if they operate to "freeze" the *status quo* of prior discriminatory employment practices.

The Court of Appeals' opinion, and the partial dissent, agreed that, on the record in the present case, "whites register far better on the Company's alternative requirements" than Negroes. . . . This consequence would appear to be directly traceable to race. Basic intelligence must have the means of articulation to manifest itself fairly in a testing process. Because they are Negroes, petitioners have long received inferior education in segregated schools. . . . Congress did not intend by Title VII, however, to guarantee a job to every person regardless of qualifications. In short, the Act does not command that any person be hired simply because he was formerly the subject of discrimination, or because he is a member of a minority group. Discriminatory preference for any group, minority or majority, is precisely and only what Congress has proscribed. What is required by Congress is the removal of artificial, arbitrary, and unnecessary barriers to employment when the barriers operate invidiously to discriminate on the basis of racial or other impermissible classification.

. . . The Act proscribes not only overt discrimination, but also practices that are fair in form, but discriminatory in operation. The touchstone is business necessity. If an employment practice which operates to exclude Negroes cannot be shown to be related to job performance, the practice is prohibited. . . .

The Court of Appeals held that the Company had adopted the diploma and test requirements without any "intention to discriminate against Negro employees." . . . We do not suggest that either the District Court or the Court of Appeals erred in examining the employer's intent; but good intent or absence of discriminatory intent does not redeem employment procedures or testing mechanisms that operate as "built-in headwinds" for minority groups and are unrelated to measuring job capability. . . .

Nothing in the Act precludes the use of testing or measuring procedures; obviously they are useful. What Congress has forbidden is giving these devices and mechanisms controlling force unless they are demonstrably a reasonable measure of job performance. Congress has not commanded that the less qualified be preferred over the better qualified simply because of minority origins. Far from disparaging job qualifications as such, Congress has made such qualifications the controlling factor, so that race, religion, nationality, and sex become irrelevant. What Congress has commanded is that any tests used must measure the person for the job, and not the person in the abstract.

Regents of the University of California v. Bakke [1978]

In this case, the Supreme Court ruled that the medical school of the University of California, Davis, had discriminated against Allan Bakke, a white prospective student, when it denied him admission. Bakke believed he was the victim of reverse discrimination. The school maintained an admissions quota, overseen by a special committee, in which sixteen out of one hundred seats in each entering class were reserved for racial minorities. The justices were divided over the case. Ultimately, in a 5–4 decision, the Court argued that a system of racial "quotas" was unconstitutional, whereas a more flexible policy of affirmative action—with educational diversity as its goal—could, under some circumstances, be constitutional. The Court believed that the medical school's system did not meet the requirements for constitutionality and thus ordered Bakke's admission.

Racial and ethnic classifications of any sort are inherently suspect and call for the most exacting judicial scrutiny. While the goal of achieving a diverse student body is sufficiently compelling to justify consideration of race in admissions decisions under some circumstances, petitioner's special admissions program, which forecloses consideration to persons like respondent, is unnecessary to the achievement of this compelling goal, and therefore invalid under the Equal Protection Clause. . . .

The concept of "discrimination," like the phrase "equal protection of the laws," is susceptible of varying interpretations, for as Mr. Justice Holmes declared, "[a] word is not a crystal, transparent and unchanged, it is the skin of a living thought and may vary greatly in color and content according to the circumstances and the time in which it is used." . . .

. . . The parties fight a sharp preliminary action over the proper characterization of the special admissions program. Petitioner prefers to view it as establishing a "goal" of minority representation in the Medical School. Respondent, echoing the courts below, labels it a racial quota.

This semantic distinction is beside the point: The special admissions program is undeniably a classification based on race and ethnic background. To the extent that there existed a pool of at least minimally qualified minority applicants to fill the 16 special admissions seats, white applicants could compete only for 84 seats in the entering class, rather than the 100 open to minority applicants. Whether this limitation is described as a quota or a goal, it is a line drawn on the basis of race and ethnic status.

Selected Speeches and Letters

These documents, penned by three of history's most influential African Americans, are revealing of the state of black America at three key points in the nation's history. In each document, the author lays out the circumstances as he sees them and provides his thoughts on how best to address the situation. As you read these documents, consider how they would have been received by their audiences and what they have to tell us about the evolution of race relations in the nineteenth, twentieth, and twenty-first centuries.

Booker T. Washington, *The Atlanta Compromise Speech* [1895]

When Booker T. Washington delivered the following speech at the Cotton States and International Exposition in Atlanta, he managed to speak to multiple audiences. Washington urged that blacks remain in the South, start at the bottom, and advance within the confines of the prevailing system. White employers, he argued, should do their part by recognizing blacks' contributions and hiring them rather than foreign laborers. Washington's emphasis on black self-help and economic uplift as the keys to race advancement proved a hopeful message for many blacks. Whites, however, focused on Washington's accommodationism and acceptance of the racial status quo, drawing encouragement from his admonition that blacks should struggle for their own economic prosperity rather than agitate for social equality.

Mr. President and Gentlemen of the Board of Directors and Citizens.

One-third of the population of the South is of the Negro race. No enterprise seeking the material, civil, or moral welfare of this section can disregard this element of our population and reach the highest success. I but convey to you, Mr. President and Directors, the sentiment of the masses of my race when I say that in no way have the value and manhood of the American Negro been more fittingly and generously recognized than by the managers of this magnificent Exposition at every stage of its progress. It is a recognition that will

do more to cement the friendship of the two races than any occurrence since the dawn of our freedom.

Not only this, but the opportunity here afforded will awaken among us a new era of industrial progress. Ignorant and inexperienced, it is not strange that in the first years of our new life we began at the top instead of at the bottom; that a seat in Congress or the state legislature was more sought than real estate or industrial skill; that the political convention or stump speaking had more attractions than starting a dairy farm or truck garden.

A ship lost at sea for many days suddenly sighted a friendly vessel. From the mast of the unfortunate vessel was seen a signal, "Water, water; we die of thirst!" The answer from the friendly vessel at once came back, "Cast down your bucket where you are." A second time the signal, "Water, water; send us water!" ran up from the distressed vessel, and was answered, "Cast down your bucket where you are." And a third and fourth signal for water was answered, "Cast down your bucket where you are." The captain of the distressed vessel, at last heeding the injunction, cast down his bucket, and it came up full of fresh, sparkling water from the mouth of the Amazon River. To those of my race who depend on bettering their condition in a foreign land or who underestimate the importance of cultivating friendly relations with the Southern white man, who is their next-door neighbour, I would say: "Cast down your bucket where you are"—cast it down in making friends in every manly way of the people of all races by whom we are surrounded.

Cast it down in agriculture, mechanics, in commerce, in domestic service, and in the professions.

SOURCE: Booker T. Washington, *Up from Slavery* (New York: Doubleday, Page, 1907), 218–25.

appendix

And in this connection it is well to bear in mind that whatever other sins the South may be called to bear, when it comes to business, pure and simple, it is in the South that the Negro is given a man's chance in the commercial world, and in nothing is this Exposition more eloquent than in emphasizing this chance. Our greatest danger is that in the great leap from slavery to freedom we may overlook the fact that the masses of us are to live by the productions of our hands, and fail to keep in mind that we shall prosper in proportion as we learn to dignify and glorify common labour and put brains and skill into the common occupations of life; shall prosper in proportion as we learn to draw the line between the superficial and the substantial, the ornamental gewgaws of life and the useful. No race can prosper till it learns that there is as much dignity in tilling a field as in writing a poem. It is at the bottom of life we must begin, and not at the top. Nor should we permit our grievances to overshadow our opportunities.

To those of the white race who look to the incoming of those of foreign birth and strange tongue and habits for the prosperity of the South, were I permitted I would repeat what I say to my own race, "Cast down your bucket where you are." Cast it down among the eight millions of Negroes whose habits you know, whose fidelity and love you have tested in days when to have proved treacherous meant the ruin of your firesides. Cast down your bucket among these people who have, without strikes and labour wars, tilled your fields, cleared your forests, builded your railroads and cities, and brought forth treasures from the bowels of the earth, and helped make possible this magnificent representation of the progress of the South. Casting down your bucket among my people, helping and encouraging them as you are doing on these grounds, and to education of head, hand, and heart, you will find that they will buy your surplus land, make blossom the waste places in your fields, and run your factories. While doing this, you can be sure in the future, as in the past, that you and your families will be surrounded by the most patient, faithful, law-abiding, and unresentful people that the world has seen. As we have proved our loyalty to you in the past, in nursing your children, watching by the sick-bed of your mothers and fathers, and often following them with tear-dimmed eyes to their graves, so in the future, in our humble way, we shall stand by you with a devotion that no foreigner can approach, ready to lay down our lives, if need be, in defence of yours, interlacing our industrial, commercial, civil, and religious life with yours in a way that shall make the interests of both races one. In all things that are purely social we can be as separate as the fingers, yet one as the hand in all things essential to mutual progress.

There is no defence or security for any of us except in the highest intelligence and development of all. If anywhere there are efforts tending to curtail the fullest growth of the Negro, let these efforts be turned into stimulating, encouraging, and making him the most useful and intelligent citizen. Effort or means so invested will pay a thousand per cent interest. These efforts will be twice blessed—"blessing him that gives and him that takes."

There is no escape through law of man or God from the inevitable:—

> The laws of changeless justice bind
> Oppressor with oppressed;
> And close as sin and suffering joined
> We march to fate abreast.

Nearly sixteen millions of hands will aid you in pulling the load upward, or they will pull against you the load downward. We shall constitute one-third and more of the ignorance and crime of the South, or one-third its intelligence and progress; we shall contribute one-third to the business and industrial prosperity of the South, or we shall prove a veritable body of death, stagnating, depressing, retarding every effort to advance the body politic.

Gentlemen of the Exposition, as we present to you our humble effort at an exhibition of our progress, you must not expect overmuch. Starting thirty years ago with ownership here and there in a few quilts and pumpkins and chickens (gathered from miscellaneous sources), remember the path that has led from these to the inventions and production of agricultural implements, buggies, steam-engines, newspapers, books, statuary, carving, paintings, the management of drug-stores and banks, has not been trodden without contact with thorns and thistles. While we take pride in what we exhibit as a result of our independent efforts, we do not for a moment forget that our part in this exhibition would fall far short of your expectations but for the constant help that has come to our educational life, not only from the Southern states, but especially from Northern philanthropists, who have made their gifts a constant stream of blessing and encouragement.

The wisest among my race understand that the agitation of questions of social equality is the extremest folly, and that progress in the enjoyment of all the privileges that will come to us must be the result of severe and constant struggle rather than of artificial forcing. No race that has anything to contribute to the markets of the world is long in any degree ostracized. It is important and right that all privileges of the law be ours, but it is vastly more important that we be prepared for the exercise of these privileges. The opportunity to earn a dollar in a factory just now is worth infinitely more than the opportunity to spend a dollar in an opera-house.

In conclusion, may I repeat that nothing in thirty years has given us more hope and encouragement, and drawn us so near to you of the white race, as this opportunity offered by the Exposition; and here bending, as it were, over the altar that represents the results of the struggles of your race and mine, both starting practically empty-handed three decades ago, I pledge that in your effort to work out the great and intricate problem which God has laid at the doors of the South, you shall have at all times the patient, sympathetic help of my race; only let this be constantly in mind, that, while from representations in these buildings of the product of field, of forest, of mine, of factory, letters, and art, much good will come, yet far above and beyond material benefits will be that higher good, that, let us pray God, will come, in a blotting out of sectional differences and racial animosities and suspicions, in a determination to administer absolute justice, in a willing obedience among all classes to the mandates of law. This, this, coupled with our material prosperity, will bring into our beloved South a new heaven and a new earth.

Martin Luther King Jr., *Letter from Birmingham City Jail* [1963]

While imprisoned during the civil rights demonstrations in Birmingham, Alabama, in April 1963, Martin Luther King Jr. wrote the following letter. It addresses a group of Alabama clergymen who had, days earlier, penned a statement criticizing King and the other "outsiders" who had come to Birmingham to protest. The clergymen argued that the protesters should cease to practice "extreme" tactics that "incite to hatred and violence"; exercise patience; negotiate with local leaders and work through the court system rather than protest publicly; and let Birmingham locals grapple with their own issues, rather than attempting to exert influence from the outside. Drawing on the Bible as well as powerful examples from history, philosophy, and literature, King refutes the clergymen's objections and asserts the rectitude of nonviolent direct-action protest. He also expresses his disappointment with the response of white church leaders and white political moderates to the plight of African Americans and the realities of segregation.

My dear fellow clergymen:

While confined here in the Birmingham City Jail, I came across your recent statement calling our present activities "unwise and untimely." Seldom, if ever, do I pause to answer criticism of my work and ideas. If I sought to answer all the criticisms that cross my desk, my secretaries would be engaged in little else in the course of the day, and I would have no time for constructive work. But since I feel that you are men of genuine goodwill and your criticisms are sincerely set forth, I would like to answer your statement in what I hope will be patient and reasonable terms.

appendix

I think I should give the reason for my being in Birmingham, since you have been influenced by the argument of "outsiders coming in." I have the honor of serving as president of the Southern Christian Leadership Conference, an organization operating in every Southern state, with headquarters in Atlanta, Georgia. We have some eighty-five affiliate organizations all across the South—one being the Alabama Christian Movement for Human Rights. Whenever necessary and possible we share staff, educational and financial resources with our affiliates. Several months ago our local affiliate here in Birmingham invited us to be on call to engage in a nonviolent direct action program if such were deemed necessary. We readily consented and when the hour came we lived up to our promises. So I am here, along with several members of my staff, because I have basic organizational ties here.

Beyond this, I am in Birmingham because injustice is here. Just as the eighth century prophets left their little villages and carried their "thus saith the Lord" far beyond the boundaries of their home towns; and just as the Apostle Paul left his little village of Tarsus and carried the gospel of Jesus Christ to practically every hamlet and city of the Graeco-Roman world, I too am compelled to carry the gospel of freedom beyond my particular home town. Like Paul, I must constantly respond to the Macedonian call for aid.

Moreover, I am cognizant of the interrelatedness of all communities and states. I cannot sit idly by in Atlanta and not be concerned about what happens in Birmingham. Injustice anywhere is a threat to justice everywhere. We are caught in an inescapable network of mutuality, tied in a single garment of destiny. Whatever affects one directly affects all indirectly. Never again can we afford to live with the narrow, provincial "outside agitator" idea. Anyone who lives inside the United States can never be considered an outsider anywhere in this country.

You deplore the demonstrations that are presently taking place in Birmingham. But I am sorry that your statement did not express a similar concern for the conditions that brought the demonstrations into being. I am sure that each of you would want to go beyond the superficial social analyst who looks merely at effects, and does not grapple with underlying causes. I would not hesitate to say that it is unfortunate that so-called demonstrations are taking place in Birmingham at this time, but I would say in more emphatic terms that it is even more unfortunate that the white power structure of this city left the Negro community with no other alternative.

In any nonviolent campaign there are four basic steps: 1) Collection of the facts to determine whether injustices are alive. 2) Negotiation. 3) Self-purification and 4) Direct action. We have gone through all of these steps in Birmingham. There can be no gainsaying of the fact that racial injustice engulfs this community.

Birmingham is probably the most thoroughly segregated city in the United States. Its ugly record of police brutality is known in every section of this country. Its unjust treatment of Negroes in the courts is a notorious reality. There have been more unsolved bombings of Negro homes and churches in Birmingham than any city in this nation. These are the hard, brutal and unbelievable facts. On the basis of these conditions, Negro leaders sought to negotiate with the city fathers. But the political leaders consistently refused to engage in good faith negotiation.

Then came the opportunity last September to talk with some of the leaders of the economic community. In these negotiating sessions certain promises were made by the merchants—such as the promise to remove the humiliating racial signs from the stores. On the basis of these promises Rev. [Fred] Shuttlesworth and the leaders of the Alabama Christian Movement for Human Rights agreed to call a moratorium on any type of demonstrations. As the weeks and months unfolded we realized that we were the victims of a broken promise. The signs remained. Like so many experiences of the past we were confronted with blasted hopes, and the dark shadow of a deep disappointment settled upon us. So we had no alternative except that of preparing for direct action, whereby we would present our very bodies as a means of laying our case before the conscience of the local and national community. We were not unmindful of the difficulties involved. So we decided to go through a process of self-purification. We started having workshops on nonviolence and repeatedly asked ourselves the questions: "Are you able to accept blows without retaliating?" "Are you able to endure the ordeals of jail?" We decided to set our direct-action program around the Easter season, realizing that with the exception of Christmas, this was the largest shopping period of the year. Knowing that a strong economic withdrawal program would be the by-product of direct action, we felt that this was the best time to bring pressure on the merchants for the needed changes. Then it occurred to us that the March election was ahead and so we speedily decided to postpone action until after election day. When we discovered that Mr. [Eugene "Bull"] Connor was in the run-off, we decided again to postpone action so that the demonstrations could not be used to cloud the issues. At this time we agreed to begin our nonviolent witness the day after the run-off.

This reveals that we did not move irresponsibly into direct action. We too wanted to see Mr. Connor defeated; so we went through postponement after postponement to aid in this community need. After this we felt that direct action could be delayed no longer.

You may well ask: "Why direct action? Why sit-ins, marches, etc.? Isn't negotiation a better path?" You are exactly right in your call for negotiation. Indeed, this is the purpose of direct action. Nonviolent direct action seeks to create such a crisis and establish such creative tension that a community that has constantly refused to negotiate is forced to confront the issue. It seeks so to dramatize the issue that it can no longer be ignored. I just referred to the creation of tension as a part of the work of the nonviolent resister. This may sound rather shocking. But I must confess that I am not afraid of the word tension. I have earnestly worked and preached against violent tension, but there is a type of constructive nonviolent tension that is necessary for growth. Just as Socrates felt that it was necessary to create a tension in the mind so that individuals could rise from the bondage of myths and half-truths to the unfettered realm of creative analysis and objective appraisal, we must see the need of having nonviolent gadflies to create the kind of tension in society that will help men to rise from the dark depths of prejudice and racism to the majestic heights of understanding and brotherhood. So the purpose of the direct action is to create a situation so crisis-packed that it will inevitably open the door to negotiation. We, therefore, concur with you in your call for negotiation. Too long has our beloved Southland been bogged down in the tragic attempt to live in monologue rather than dialogue.

One of the basic points in your statement is that our acts are untimely. Some have asked, "Why didn't

you give the new administration time to act?" The only answer that I can give to this inquiry is that the new Birmingham administration must be prodded about as much as the outgoing one before it acts. We will be sadly mistaken if we feel that the election of Mr. [Albert] Boutwell will bring the millennium to Birmingham. While Mr. Boutwell is much more articulate and gentle than Mr. Connor, they are both segregationists, dedicated to the task of maintaining the status quo. The hope I see in Mr. Boutwell is that he will be reasonable enough to see the futility of massive resistance to desegregation. But he will not see this without pressure from the devotees of civil rights. My friends, I must say to you that we have not made a single gain in civil rights without determined legal and nonviolent pressure. History is the long and tragic story of the fact that privileged groups seldom give up their privileges voluntarily. Individuals may see the moral light and voluntarily give up their unjust posture; but as Reinhold Niebuhr has reminded us, groups are more immoral than individuals.

We know through painful experience that freedom is never voluntarily given by the oppressor; it must be demanded by the oppressed. Frankly, I have never yet engaged in a direct action movement that was "well timed," according to the timetable of those who have not suffered unduly from the disease of segregation. For years now I have heard the words [sic]"Wait!" It rings in the ear of every Negro with a piercing familiarity. This "Wait" has almost always meant "Never." We must come to see with the distinguished jurist of yesterday that "justice too long delayed is justice denied."

We have waited for more than three hundred and forty years for our constitutional and God-given rights. The nations of Asia and Africa are moving with jet-like speed toward the goal of political independence, and we still creep at horse and buggy pace toward the gaining of a cup of coffee at a lunch counter. I guess it is easy for those who have never felt the stinging darts of segregation to say, "Wait." But when you have seen vicious mobs lynch your mothers and fathers at will and drown your sisters and brothers at whim; when you have seen hate-filled policemen curse, kick, brutalize and even kill your black brothers and sisters with impunity; when you see the vast majority of your twenty million Negro brothers smothering in an airtight cage of poverty in the midst of an affluent society; when you suddenly find your tongue twisted and your speech stammering as you seek to explain to your six-year-old daughter why she can't go to the public amusement park that has just been advertised on television, and see tears welling up in her eyes when she is told that Funtown is closed to colored children, and see the depressing clouds of inferiority begin to form in her little mental sky, and see her begin to distort her little personality by unconsciously developing a bitterness toward white people; when you have to concoct an answer for a five-year-old son asking in agonizing pathos: "Daddy, why do white people treat colored people so mean?"; when you take a cross-country drive and find it necessary to sleep night after night in the uncomfortable corners of your automobile because no motel will accept you; when you are humiliated day in and day out by nagging signs reading "white" and "colored"; when your first name becomes "nigger," your middle name becomes "boy" (however old you are) and your last name becomes "John," and your wife and mother are never given the respected title "Mrs."; when you are harried by day and haunted by night by the fact that you are a Negro, living constantly at tip-toe stance never quite knowing what to expect next, and plagued with inner fears and outer resentments; when you are forever fighting a degenerating sense of "nobodiness"; then you will understand why we find it difficult to wait. There comes a time when the cup of endurance runs over, and men are no longer willing to be plunged into an abyss of despair. I hope, sirs, you can understand our legitimate and unavoidable impatience.

You express a great deal of anxiety over our willingness to break laws. This is certainly a legitimate concern. Since we so diligently urge people to obey the Supreme Court's decision of 1954 outlawing segregation in the public schools, it is rather strange and paradoxical to find us consciously breaking laws. One may well ask: "How can you advocate breaking some laws and obeying others?" The answer is found in the fact that there are two types of laws: There are just and there are unjust laws. I would agree with Saint Augustine that "An unjust law is no law at all."

Now, what is the difference between the two? How does one determine when a law is just or unjust? A just law is a man-made code that squares with the moral law

or the law of God. An unjust law is a code that is out of harmony with the moral law. To put it in the terms of Saint Thomas Aquinas, an unjust law is a human law that is not rooted in eternal and natural law. Any law that uplifts human personality is just. Any law that degrades human personality is unjust. All segregation statutes are unjust because segregation distorts the soul and damages the personality. It gives the segregator a false sense of superiority, and the segregated a false sense of inferiority. To use the words of Martin Buber, the Jewish philosopher, segregation substitutes an "I-it" relationship for an "I-thou" relationship, and ends up relegating persons to the status of things. So segregation is not only politically, economically and sociologically unsound, but it is morally wrong and sinful. Paul Tillich has said that sin is separation. Isn't segregation an existential expression of man's tragic separation, an expression of his awful estrangement, his terrible sinfulness? So I can urge men to disobey segregation ordinances because they are morally wrong.

Let us turn to a more concrete example of just and unjust laws. An unjust law is a code that a majority inflicts on a minority that is not binding on itself. This is difference made legal. On the other hand a just law is a code that a majority compels a minority to follow that it is willing to follow itself. This is sameness made legal.

Let me give another explanation. An unjust law is a code inflicted upon a minority which that minority had no part in enacting or creating because they did not have the unhampered right to vote. Who can say that the legislature of Alabama which set up the segregation laws was democratically elected? Throughout the state of Alabama all types of conniving methods are used to prevent Negroes from becoming registered voters and there are some counties without a single Negro registered to vote despite the fact that the Negro constitutes a majority of the population. Can any law set up in such a state be considered democratically structured?

These are just a few examples of unjust and just laws. There are some instances when a law is just on its face and unjust in its application. For instance, I was arrested Friday on a charge of parading without a permit. Now there is nothing wrong with an ordinance which requires a permit for a parade, but when the ordinance is used to preserve segregation and to deny citizens the First-Amendment privilege of peaceful assembly and peaceful protest, then it becomes unjust.

I hope you can see the distinction I am trying to point out. In no sense do I advocate evading or defying the law as the rabid segregationist would do. This would lead to anarchy. One who breaks an unjust law must do it openly, lovingly, (not hatefully as the white mothers did in New Orleans when they were seen on television screaming "nigger, nigger, nigger") and with a willingness to accept the penalty. I submit that an individual who breaks a law that conscience tells him is unjust, and willingly accepts the penalty by staying in jail to arouse the conscience of the community over its injustice, is in reality expressing the very highest respect for law.

Of course, there is nothing new about this kind of civil disobedience. It was seen sublimely in the refusal of Shadrach, Meshach and Abednego to obey the laws of Nebuchadnezzar because a higher moral law was involved. It was practiced superbly by the early Christians who were willing to face hungry lions and the excruciating pain of chopping blocks, before submitting to certain unjust laws of the Roman empire. To a degree academic freedom is a reality today because Socrates practiced civil disobedience.

We can never forget that everything Hitler did in Germany was "legal" and everything the Hungarian freedom fighters did in Hungary was "illegal." It was "illegal" to aid and comfort a Jew in Hitler's Germany. But I am sure that if I had lived in Germany during that time I would have aided and comforted my Jewish brothers even though it was illegal. If I lived in a Communist country today where certain principles dear to the Christian faith are suppressed, I believe I would openly advocate disobeying these anti-religious laws. I must make two honest confessions to you, my Christian and Jewish brothers. First, I must confess that over the last few years I have been gravely disappointed with the white moderate. I have almost reached the regrettable conclusion that the Negro's great stumbling block in the stride toward freedom is not the White Citizen's Counciler or the Ku Klux Klanner, but the white moderate who is more devoted to "order" than to justice; who prefers a negative peace which is the absence of tension to a positive peace which is the presence of justice; who constantly says "I agree with you in the goal you seek, but I can't agree with your methods of direct action"; who paternalistically feels

he can set the timetable for another man's freedom; who lives by the myth of time and who constantly advises the Negro to wait until a "more convenient season." Shallow understanding from people of goodwill is more frustrating than absolute misunderstanding from people of ill will. Lukewarm acceptance is much more bewildering than outright rejection.

I had hoped that the white moderate would understand that law and order exist for the purpose of establishing justice, and that when they fail to do this they become dangerously structured dams that block the flow of social progress. I had hoped that the white moderate would understand that the present tension in the South is merely a necessary phase of the transition from an obnoxious negative peace, where the Negro passively accepted his unjust plight, to a substance-filled positive peace, where all men will respect the dignity and worth of human personality. Actually, we who engage in nonviolent direct action are not the creators of tension. We merely bring to the surface the hidden tension that is already alive. We bring it out in the open where it can be seen and dealt with. Like a boil that can never be cured as long as it is covered up but must be opened with all its pus-flowing ugliness to the natural medicines of air and light, injustice must likewise be exposed, with all of the tension its exposing creates, to the light of human conscience and the air of national opinion before it can be cured.

In your statement you asserted that our actions, even though peaceful, must be condemned because they precipitate violence. But can this assertion be logically made? Isn't this like condemning the robbed man because his possession of money precipitated the evil act of robbery? Isn't this like condemning Socrates because his unswerving commitment to truth and his philosophical delvings precipitated the misguided popular mind to make him drink the hemlock? Isn't this like condemning Jesus because His unique God-Consciousness and never-ceasing devotion to His will precipitated the evil act of crucifixion? We must come to see, as the federal courts have consistently affirmed, that it is immoral to urge an individual to withdraw his efforts to gain his basic constitutional rights because the quest precipitates violence. Society must protect the robbed and punish the robber.

I had also hoped that the white moderate would reject the myth of time. I received a letter this morning from a white brother in Texas which said: "All Christians know that the colored people will receive equal rights eventually, but it is possible that you are in too great of a religious hurry. It has taken Christianity almost 2000 years to accomplish what it has. The teachings of Christ take time to come to earth." All that is said here grows out of a tragic misconception of time. It is the strangely irrational notion that there is something in the very flow of time that will inevitably cure all ills. Actually time is neutral. It can be used either destructively or constructively. I am coming to feel that the people of ill-will have used time much more effectively than the people of good will. We will have to repent in this generation not merely for the vitriolic words and actions of the bad people, but for the appalling silence of the good people. We must come to see that human progress never rolls in on wheels of inevitability. It comes through the tireless efforts and persistent work of men willing to be co-workers with God, and without this hard work time itself becomes an ally of the forces of social stagnation. We must use time creatively, and forever realize that the time is always ripe to do right. Now is the time to make real the promise of democracy, and transform our pending national elegy into a creative psalm of brotherhood. Now is the time to lift our national policy from the quicksand of racial injustice to the solid rock of human dignity.

You spoke of our activity in Birmingham as extreme. At first I was rather disappointed that fellow clergymen would see my nonviolent efforts as those of the extremist. I started thinking about the fact that I stand in the middle of two opposing forces in the Negro community. One is a force of complacency made up of Negroes who, as a result of long years of oppression, have been so completely drained of self-respect and a sense of "somebodiness" that they have adjusted to segregation, and, of a few Negroes in the middle class who, because of a degree of academic and economic security, and because at points they profit by segregation, have unconsciously become insensitive to the problems of the masses. The other force is one of bitterness, and hatred comes perilously close to advocating violence. It is expressed in the various black nationalist groups that are springing up over the nation, the largest and best-known being Elijah Muhammad's Muslim movement. This movement is nourished by the contemporary frustration over the continued existence of racial discrimination. It is made up of people who have lost faith in America, who have absolutely repudiated Christianity, and who have concluded that the white man is an incurable "devil." I have tried to stand between these two forces saying that we need not follow the "do-nothingism" of the complacent or the hatred and despair of the black nationalist. There is the more excellent way of love and nonviolent protest. I'm grateful to God that, through the Negro church, the dimension of nonviolence entered our struggle. If this philosophy had not emerged, I am convinced that by now many streets of the South would be flowing with floods of blood. And I am further convinced that if our white brothers dismiss as "rabble rousers" and "outside agitators" those of us who are working through the channels of nonviolent direct action and refuse to support our nonviolent efforts, millions of Negroes, out of frustration and despair, will seek solace and security in black-nationalist ideologies, a development that will lead inevitably to a frightening racial nightmare.

Oppressed people cannot remain oppressed forever. The urge for freedom will eventually come. This is what happened to the American Negro. Something within has reminded him of his birthright of freedom; something without has reminded him that he can gain it. Consciously and unconsciously, he has been swept in by what the Germans call the Zeitgeist, and with his black brothers of Africa, and his brown and yellow brothers of Asia, South America and the Caribbean, he is moving with a sense of cosmic urgency toward the promised land of racial justice. Recognizing this vital urge that has engulfed the Negro community, one should readily understand public demonstrations. The Negro has many pent up resentments and latent frustrations. He has to get them out. So let him march sometime; let him have his prayer pilgrimages to the city hall; understand why he must have sit-ins and freedom rides. If his repressed emotions do not come out in these nonviolent ways, they will come out in ominous expressions of violence. This is not a threat; it is a fact of history. So I have not said to my people "get rid of your discontent." But I have tried to say that this normal and healthy discontent can be channelized through the creative outlet of nonviolent direct action. Now this approach is being dismissed as extremist. I must admit that I was initially disappointed in being so categorized.

But as I continued to think about the matter I gradually gained a bit of satisfaction from being considered an extremist. Was not Jesus an extremist for love—"Love your enemies, bless them that curse you, pray for them that despitefully use you." Was not Amos an extremist for justice—"Let justice roll down like waters and righteousness like a mighty stream." Was not Paul an extremist for the gospel of Jesus Christ "I bear in my body the marks of the Lord Jesus." Was not Martin Luther an extremist—"Here I stand; I can do none other so help me God." Was not John Bunyan an extremist—"I will stay in jail to the end of my days before I make a butchery of my conscience." Was not Abraham Lincoln an extremist—"This nation cannot survive half slave and half free." Was not Thomas Jefferson an extremist— "We hold these truths to be self-evident, that all men are created equal." So the question is not whether we will be extremist but what kind of extremist will we be. Will we be extremists for hate or will we be extremists for love? Will we be extremists for the preservation of injustice—or will we be extremists for the cause of justice? In that dramatic scene on Calvary's hill, three men were crucified. We must not forget that all three were crucified for the same crime—the crime of extremism. Two were extremists for immorality, and thusly fell below their environment. The other, Jesus Christ, was an extremist for love, truth and goodness, and thereby rose above his environment. So, after all, maybe the South, the nation and the world are in dire need of creative extremists.

I had hoped that the white moderate would see this. Maybe I was too optimistic. Maybe I expected too much. I guess I should have realized that few members of a race that has oppressed another race can understand or appreciate the deep groans and passionate yearnings of those that have been oppressed and still fewer have the vision to see that injustice must be rooted out by strong, persistent and determined action. I am thankful, however, that some of our white brothers have grasped the meaning of this social revolution and committed themselves to it. They are still all too small in quantity, but they are big in quality. Some like Ralph McGill, Lillian Smith, Harry Golden and James Dabbs have written about our struggle in eloquent, prophetic and understanding terms. Others have marched with us down nameless streets of the South. They have languished in filthy roach-infested jails, suffering the abuse and brutality of angry policemen who see them as "dirty nigger lovers." They, unlike so many of their moderate brothers

and sisters, have recognized the urgency of the moment and sensed the need for powerful "action" antidotes to combat the disease of segregation.

Let me rush on to mention my other disappointment. I have been so greatly disappointed with the white church and its leadership. Of course, there are some notable exceptions. I am not unmindful of the fact that each of you has taken some significant stands on this issue. I commend you, Rev. [Earl] Stallings, for your Christian stand on this past Sunday, in welcoming Negroes to your worship service on a non-segregated basis. I commend the Catholic leaders of this state for integrating Spring Hill College several years ago.

But despite these notable exceptions I must honestly reiterate that I have been disappointed with the church. I do not say that as one of those negative critics who can always find something wrong with the church. I say it as a minister of the gospel, who loves the church; who was nurtured in its bosom; who has been sustained by its spiritual blessings and who will remain true to it as long as the cord of life shall lengthen.

I had the strange feeling when I was suddenly catapulted into the leadership of the bus protest in Montgomery several years ago, that we would have the support of the white church. I felt that the white ministers, priests and rabbis of the South would be some of our strongest allies. Instead, some have been outright opponents, refusing to understand the freedom movement and misrepresenting its leaders; all too many others have been more cautious than courageous and have remained silent behind the anesthetizing security of the stained-glass windows.

In spite of my shattered dreams of the past, I came to Birmingham with the hope that the white religious leadership of this community would see the justice of our cause, and with deep moral concern, serve as the channel through which our just grievances would get to the power structure. I had hoped that each of you would understand. But again I have been disappointed. I have heard numerous religious leaders of the South call upon their worshippers to comply with a desegregation decision because it is the law, but I have longed to hear white ministers say, "follow this decree because integration is morally right and the Negro is your brother." In the midst of blatant injustices inflicted upon the Negro, I have watched white churches stand on the sideline and merely mouth pious irrelevancies and sanctimonious trivialities. In the midst of a mighty struggle to rid our nation of racial and economic injustice, I have heard so many ministers say, "Those are social issues with which the gospel has no real concern." And I have watched so many churches commit themselves to a completely other-worldly religion which made a strange distinction between body and soul, the sacred and the secular.

So here we are moving toward the exit of the twentieth century with a religious community largely adjusted to the status quo, standing as a tail-light behind other community agencies rather than a headlight leading men to higher levels of justice.

I have traveled the length and breadth of Alabama, Mississippi and all the other southern states. On sweltering summer days and crisp autumn mornings I have looked at her beautiful churches with their lofty spires pointing heavenward. I have beheld the impressive outlay of her massive religious education buildings. Over and over again I have found myself asking: "What kind of people worship here? Who is their God? Where were their voices when the lips of [Mississippi] Governor [Ross] Barnett dripped with words of interposition and nullification? Where were they when [Alabama] Governor [George] Wallace gave the clarion call for defiance and hatred? Where were their voices of support when tired, bruised and weary Negro men and women decided to rise from the dark dungeons of complacency to the bright hills of creative protest?"

Yes, these questions are still in my mind. In deep disappointment, I have wept over the laxity of the church. But be assured that my tears have been tears of love. There can be no deep disappointment where there is not deep love. Yes, I love the church; I love her sacred walls. How could I do otherwise? I am in the rather unique position of being the son, the grandson and the great-grandson of preachers. Yes, I see the church as the body of Christ. But, oh! How we have blemished and scarred that body through social neglect and fear of being nonconformists.

There was a time when the church was very powerful. It was during that period when the early Christians rejoiced when they were deemed worthy to suffer for what they believed. In those days the church was not merely a thermometer that recorded the ideas and principles of popular opinion; it was a thermostat that transformed the mores of society. Whenever the early Christians entered a town the power structure got disturbed and immediately sought to convict them for being "disturbers of the peace" and "outside agitators." But they went on with the conviction that they were "a colony of heaven," and had to obey God rather than man. They were small in number but big in commitment. They were too God-intoxicated to be "astronomically intimidated." They brought an end to such ancient evils as infanticide and gladiatorial contest.

Things are different now. The contemporary church is often a weak, ineffectual voice with an uncertain sound. It is so often the arch supporter of the status quo. Far from being disturbed by the presence of the church, the power structure of the average community is consoled by the church's silent and often vocal sanction of things as they are.

But the judgement of God is upon the church as never before. If the church of today does not recapture the sacrificial spirit of the early church, it will lose its authentic ring, forfeit the loyalty of millions, and be dismissed as an irrelevant social club with no meaning for the twentieth century. I am meeting young people every day whose disappointment with the church has risen to outright disgust.

Maybe again, I have been too optimistic. Is organized religion too inextricably bound to status-quo to save our nation and the world? Maybe I must turn my faith to the inner spiritual church, the church within the church, as the true ecclesia and the hope of the world. But again I am thankful to God that some noble souls from the ranks of organized religion have broken loose from the paralyzing chains of conformity and joined us as active partners in the struggle for freedom. They have left their secure congregations and walked the streets of Albany, Georgia, with us. They have gone through the highways of the South on tortuous rides for freedom. Yes, they have gone to jail with us. Some have been kicked out of their churches, and lost support of their bishops and fellow ministers. But they have gone with the faith that right defeated is stronger than evil triumphant. These men have been the leaven in the lump of the race. Their witness has been the spiritual salt that has preserved the true meaning of the Gospel in these troubled times. They have carved a tunnel of hope th[r]ough the dark mountain of disappointment.

I hope the church as a whole will meet the challenge of this decisive hour. But even if the church does not come to the aid of justice, I have no despair about the future. I have no fear about the outcome of our struggle in Birmingham, even if our motives are presently misunderstood. We will reach the goal of freedom in Birmingham and all over the nation, because the goal of America is freedom. Abused and scorned though we may be, our destiny is tied up with the destiny of America. Before the pilgrims landed at Plymouth we were here. Before the pen of Jefferson etched across the pages of history the majestic words of the Declaration of Independence, we were here. For more than two centuries our fore-parents labored in this country without wages; they made cotton king; and they built the homes of their masters in the midst of brutal injustice and shameful humiliation—and yet out of a bottomless vitality they continued to thrive and develop. If the inexpressible cruelties of slavery could not stop us, the opposition we now face will surely fail. We will win our freedom because the sacred heritage of our nation and the eternal will of God are embodied in our echoing demands.

I must close now. But before closing I am impelled to mention one other point in your statement that troubled me profoundly. You warmly commended the Birmingham police force for keeping "order" and "preventing violence." I don't believe you would have so warmly commended the police force if you had seen its angry violent dogs literally biting six unarmed, nonviolent Negroes. I don't believe you would so quickly commend the policemen if you would observe their ugly and inhuman treatment of Negroes here in the city jail; if you would watch them push and curse old Negro women and young Negro girls; if you would see them slap and kick old Negro men and young boys; if you will observe them, as they did on two occasions, refuse to give us food because we wanted to sing our grace together. I'm sorry that I can't join you in your praise for the police department.

It is true that they have been rather disciplined in their public handling of the demonstrators. In this sense they have been rather publicly "nonviolent." But for what purpose? To preserve the evil system of segregation. Over the last few years I have consistently preached that nonviolence demands that the means we use must be as pure as the ends we seek. So I have tried to make it clear that it is wrong to use immoral means to attain moral ends. But now I must affirm that it is just as wrong, or even more so, to use moral means to preserve immoral ends. Maybe Mr. Connor and his policemen have been rather publicly nonviolent, as [Police] Chief [Laurie] Pritchett was in Albany, Georgia, but they have used the moral means of nonviolence to maintain the immoral end of flagrant racial injustice. T. S. Eliot has said that there is no greater treason than to do the right deed for the wrong reason.

I wish you had commended the Negro sit-inners and demonstrators of Birmingham for their sublime courage, their willingness to suffer and their amazing discipline in the midst of the most inhuman provocation. One day the South will recognize its real heroes. They will be the James Merediths, courageously and with a majestic sense of purpose, facing jeering and hostile mobs and with the agonizing loneliness that characterizes the life of the pioneer. They will be old oppressed, battered Negro women, symbolized in a seventy-two-year-old woman of Montgomery, Alabama, who rose up with a sense of dignity and with her people decided not to ride the segregated buses, and responded to one who inquired about her tiredness with ungrammatical profundity; "my feet is tired, but my soul is rested." They will be the young high school and college students, young ministers of the gospel and a host of their elders courageously and nonviolently sitting-in at lunch counters and willingly going to jail for conscience's sake. One day the South will know that when these disinherited children of God sat down at lunch counters they were in reality standing up for the best in the American dream and the most sacred values in our Judaeo-Christian heritage, and thusly, carrying our whole nation back to those great wells of democracy which were dug deep by the founding fathers in the formulation of the Constitution and the Declaration of Independence.

Never before have I written a letter this long, (or should I say a book?). I'm afraid it is much too long to take your precious time. I can assure you that it would have been much shorter if I had been writing from a comfortable desk, but what else is there to do when you are alone for days in the dull monotony of a narrow jail cell other than write long letters, think strange thoughts, and pray long prayers?

If I have said anything in this letter that is an overstatement of the truth and is indicative of an unreasonable impatience, I beg you to forgive me. If I have said anything in this letter that is an understatement of the truth and is indicative of my having a patience that makes me patient with anything less than brotherhood, I beg God to forgive me.

I hope this letter finds you strong in the faith. I also hope that circumstances will soon make it possible for me to meet each of you, not as an integrationist or a civil rights leader, but as a fellow clergyman and a Christian brother. Let us all hope that the dark clouds of racial prejudice will soon pass away and the deep fog of misunderstanding will be lifted from our fear-drenched communities and in some not too distant tomorrow the radiant stars of love and brotherhood will shine over our great nation with all their scintillating beauty.

Yours for the cause of Peace and Brotherhood,
Martin Luther King, Jr.

Barack Obama, *A More Perfect Union* [2008]

In March 2008, during the presidential primaries, presidential hopeful Senator Barack Obama delivered the following speech. He addressed the issue of race head-on, partially in response to public concern over controversial statements made by his former pastor, the Reverend Jeremiah Wright. Quoting the preamble of the Constitution, Obama laid out the lingering problems and divisions that characterized both black and white America. Americans could either focus on divisiveness, he said, or they could move forward by addressing their shared concerns in a unified way. This, Obama argued, would be the first step toward improving the American lot and creating as perfect a union as possible.

"We the people, in order to form a more perfect union."

Two hundred and twenty one years ago, in a hall that still stands across the street, a group of men gathered and, with these simple words, launched America's improbable experiment in democracy. Farmers and scholars; statesmen and patriots who had traveled across an ocean to escape tyranny and persecution finally made real their declaration of independence at a Philadelphia convention that lasted through the spring of 1787.

The document they produced was eventually signed but ultimately unfinished. It was stained by this nation's original sin of slavery, a question that divided the colonies and brought the convention to a stalemate until the founders chose to allow the slave trade to continue for at least twenty more years, and to leave any final resolution to future generations.

Of course, the answer to the slavery question was already embedded within our Constitution—a Constitution that had at its very core the ideal of equal citizenship under the law; a Constitution that promised its people liberty, and justice, and a union that could be and should be perfected over time.

And yet words on a parchment would not be enough to deliver slaves from bondage, or provide men and women of every color and creed their full rights and obligations as citizens of the United States. What would be needed were Americans in successive generations who were willing to do their part—through protests and struggle, on the streets and in the courts, through a civil war and civil disobedience and always at great risk—to narrow that gap between the promise of our ideals and the reality of their time.

This was one of the tasks we set forth at the beginning of this campaign—to continue the long march of those who came before us, a march for a more just, more equal, more free, more caring and more prosperous America. I chose to run for the presidency at this moment in history because I believe deeply that we cannot solve the challenges of our time unless we solve them together—unless we perfect our union by understanding that we may have different stories, but we hold common hopes; that we may not look the same and we may not have come from the same place, but we all want to move in the same direction—towards a better future for our children and our grandchildren.

This belief comes from my unyielding faith in the decency and generosity of the American people. But it also comes from my own American story.

I am the son of a black man from Kenya and a white woman from Kansas. I was raised with the help of a white grandfather who survived a Depression to serve in Patton's Army during World War II and a white grandmother who worked on a bomber assembly line at Fort Leavenworth while he was overseas. I've gone to some of the best schools in America and lived in one of the world's poorest nations. I am married to a black American who carries within her the blood of slaves and slaveowners—an inheritance we pass on to our two precious daughters. I have brothers, sisters, nieces, nephews, uncles and cousins, of every race and every hue, scattered across three continents, and for as long as I live, I will never forget that in no other country on Earth is my story even possible.

It's a story that hasn't made me the most conventional candidate. But it is a story that has seared into my genetic makeup the idea that this nation is more than the sum of its parts—that out of many, we are truly one.

Throughout the first year of this campaign, against all predictions to the contrary, we saw how hungry the American people were for this message of unity. Despite the temptation to view my candidacy through a purely racial lens, we won commanding victories in states with some of the whitest populations in the country. In South Carolina, where the Confederate Flag still flies, we built a powerful coalition of African Americans and white Americans.

This is not to say that race has not been an issue in the campaign. At various stages in the campaign, some commentators have deemed me either "too black" or "not black enough." We saw racial tensions bubble to the surface during the week before the South Carolina primary. The press has scoured every exit poll for the latest evidence of racial polarization, not just in terms of white and black, but black and brown as well.

And yet, it has only been in the last couple of weeks that the discussion of race in this campaign has taken a particularly divisive turn.

On one end of the spectrum, we've heard the implication that my candidacy is somehow an exercise in affirmative action; that it's based solely on the desire of wide-eyed liberals to purchase racial reconciliation on the cheap. On the other end, we've heard my former pastor, Reverend Jeremiah Wright, use incendiary language to express views that have the potential not only to widen the racial divide, but views that denigrate both the greatness and the goodness of our nation; that rightly offend white and black alike.

I have already condemned, in unequivocal terms, the statements of Reverend Wright that have caused such controversy. For some, nagging questions remain. Did I know him to be an occasionally fierce critic of American domestic and foreign policy? Of course. Did I ever hear him make remarks that could be considered controversial while I sat in church? Yes. Did I strongly disagree with many of his political views?

Absolutely—just as I'm sure many of you have heard remarks from your pastors, priests, or rabbis with which you strongly disagreed.

But the remarks that have caused this recent firestorm weren't simply controversial. They weren't simply a religious leader's effort to speak out against perceived injustice. Instead, they expressed a profoundly distorted view of this country—a view that sees white racism as endemic, and that elevates what is wrong with America above all that we know is right with America; a view that sees the conflicts in the Middle East as rooted primarily in the actions of stalwart allies like Israel, instead of emanating from the perverse and hateful ideologies of radical Islam.

As such, Reverend Wright's comments were not only wrong but divisive, divisive at a time when we need unity; racially charged at a time when we need to come together to solve a set of monumental problems—two wars, a terrorist threat, a falling economy, a chronic health care crisis and potentially devastating climate change; problems that are neither black or white or Latino or Asian, but rather problems that confront us all.

Given my background, my politics, and my professed values and ideals, there will no doubt be those for whom my statements of condemnation are not enough. Why associate myself with Reverend Wright in the first place, they may ask? Why not join another church? And I confess that if all that I knew of Reverend Wright were the snippets of those sermons that have run in an endless loop on the television and YouTube, or if Trinity United Church of Christ conformed to the caricatures being peddled by some commentators, there is no doubt that I would react in much the same way.

But the truth is, that isn't all that I know of the man. The man I met more than twenty years ago is a man who helped introduce me to my Christian faith, a man who spoke to me about our obligations to love one another; to care for the sick and lift up the poor. He is a man who served his country as a U.S. Marine; who has studied and lectured at some of the finest universities and seminaries in the country, and who for over thirty years led a church that serves the community by doing God's work here on Earth—by housing the homeless, ministering to the needy, providing day care services and scholarships and prison ministries, and reaching out to those suffering from HIV/AIDS.

In my first book, *Dreams from My Father*, I described the experience of my first service at Trinity:

"People began to shout, to rise from their seats and clap and cry out, a forceful wind carrying the reverend's voice up into the rafters. . . . And in that single note—hope!—I heard something else; at the foot of that cross, inside the thousands of churches across the city, I imagined the stories of ordinary black people merging with the stories of David and Goliath, Moses and Pharaoh, the Christians in the lion's den, Ezekiel's field of dry bones. Those stories—of survival, and freedom, and hope—became our story, my story; the blood that had spilled was our blood, the tears our tears; until this black church, on this bright day, seemed once more a vessel carrying the story of a people into future generations and into a larger world. Our trials and triumphs became at once unique and universal, black and more than black; in chronicling our journey, the stories and songs gave us a means to reclaim memories that we didn't need to feel shame about . . . memories that all people might study and cherish—and with which we could start to rebuild."

That has been my experience at Trinity. Like other predominantly black churches across the country, Trinity embodies the black community in its entirety—the doctor and the welfare mom, the model student and the former gang-banger. Like other black churches, Trinity's services are full of raucous laughter and sometimes bawdy humor. They are full of dancing, clapping, screaming and shouting that may seem jarring to the untrained ear. The church contains in full the kindness and cruelty, the fierce intelligence and the shocking ignorance, the struggles and successes, the love and yes, the bitterness and bias that make up the black experience in America.

And this helps explain, perhaps, my relationship with Reverend Wright. As imperfect as he may be, he has been like family to me. He strengthened my faith, officiated my wedding, and baptized my children. Not once in my conversations with him have I heard him talk about any ethnic group in derogatory terms, or treat whites with whom he interacted with anything but courtesy and respect. He contains within him the contradictions—the good and the bad—of the community that he has served diligently for so many years.

I can no more disown him than I can disown the black community. I can no more disown him than I can my white grandmother—a woman who helped raise me, a woman who sacrificed again and again for me, a woman who loves me as much as she loves anything in this world, but a woman who once confessed her fear of black men who passed by her on the street, and who on more than one occasion has uttered racial or ethnic stereotypes that made me cringe.

These people are a part of me. And they are a part of America, this country that I love.

Some will see this as an attempt to justify or excuse comments that are simply inexcusable. I can assure you it is not. I suppose the politically safe thing would be to move on from this episode and just hope that it fades into the woodwork. We can dismiss Reverend Wright as a crank or a demagogue, just as some have dismissed Geraldine Ferraro, in the aftermath of her recent statements, as harboring some deep-seated racial bias.

But race is an issue that I believe this nation cannot afford to ignore right now. We would be making the same mistake that Reverend Wright made in his offending sermons about America—to simplify and stereotype and amplify the negative to the point that it distorts reality.

The fact is that the comments that have been made and the issues that have surfaced over the last few weeks reflect the complexities of race in this country that we've never really worked through—a part of our union that we have yet to perfect. And if we walk away now, if we simply retreat into our respective corners, we will never be able to come together and solve challenges like health care, or education, or the need to find good jobs for every American.

Understanding this reality requires a reminder of how we arrived at this point. As William Faulkner once wrote, "The past isn't dead and buried. In fact, it isn't even past." We do not need to recite here the history of racial injustice in this country. But we do need to remind ourselves that so many of the disparities that exist in the African American community today can be directly traced to inequalities passed on from an earlier generation that suffered under the brutal legacy of slavery and Jim Crow.

Segregated schools were, and are, inferior schools; we still haven't fixed them, fifty years after *Brown v. Board of Education*, and the inferior education they provided, then and now, helps explain the pervasive achievement gap between today's black and white students.

Legalized discrimination—where blacks were prevented, often through violence, from owning property, or loans were not granted to African American business owners, or black homeowners could not access FHA mortgages, or blacks were excluded from unions, or the police force, or fire departments—meant that black families could not amass any meaningful wealth to bequeath to future generations. That history helps explain the wealth and income gap between black and white, and the concentrated pockets of poverty that persist in so many of today's urban and rural communities.

A lack of economic opportunity among black men, and the shame and frustration that came from not being able to provide for one's family, contributed to the erosion of black families—a problem that welfare policies for many years may have worsened. And the lack of basic services in so many urban black neighborhoods—parks for kids to play in, police walking the beat, regular garbage pick-up and building code enforcement—all helped create a cycle of violence, blight and neglect that continues to haunt us.

This is the reality in which Reverend Wright and other African Americans of his generation grew up. They came of age in the late fifties and early sixties, a time when segregation was still the law of the land and opportunity was systematically constricted. What's remarkable is not how many failed in the face of discrimination, but rather how many men and women overcame the odds; how many were able to make a way out of no way for those like me who would come after them.

But for all those who scratched and clawed their way to get a piece of the American Dream, there were many who didn't make it—those who were ultimately defeated, in one way or another, by discrimination. That legacy of defeat was passed on to future generations—those young men and increasingly young women who we see standing on street corners or languishing in our prisons, without hope or prospects for the future. Even for those blacks who did make it, questions of race, and racism, continue to define their worldview in fundamental ways. For the men and women of Reverend Wright's generation, the memories of humiliation and doubt and fear have not gone away; nor has the anger and the bitterness of those years. That anger may not get expressed in public, in front of white co-workers or white friends. But it does find voice in the barbershop or around the kitchen table. At times, that anger is exploited by politicians, to

gin up votes along racial lines, or to make up for a politician's own failings.

And occasionally it finds voice in the church on Sunday morning, in the pulpit and in the pews. The fact that so many people are surprised to hear that anger in some of Reverend Wright's sermons simply reminds us of the old truism that the most segregated hour in American life occurs on Sunday morning. That anger is not always productive; indeed, all too often it distracts attention from solving real problems; it keeps us from squarely facing our own complicity in our condition, and prevents the African American community from forging the alliances it needs to bring about real change. But the anger is real; it is powerful; and to simply wish it away, to condemn it without understanding its roots, only serves to widen the chasm of misunderstanding that exists between the races.

In fact, a similar anger exists within segments of the white community. Most working- and middle-class white Americans don't feel that they have been particularly privileged by their race. Their experience is the immigrant experience—as far as they're concerned, no one's handed them anything, they've built it from scratch. They've worked hard all their lives, many times only to see their jobs shipped overseas or their pension dumped after a lifetime of labor. They are anxious about their futures, and feel their dreams slipping away; in an era of stagnant wages and global competition, opportunity comes to be seen as a zero sum game, in which your dreams come at my expense. So when they are told to bus their children to a school across town; when they hear that an African American is getting an advantage in landing a good job or a spot in a good college because of an injustice that they themselves never committed; when they're told that their fears about crime in urban neighborhoods are somehow prejudiced, resentment builds over time.

Like the anger within the black community, these resentments aren't always expressed in polite company. But they have helped shape the political landscape for at least a generation. Anger over welfare and affirmative action helped forge the Reagan Coalition. Politicians routinely exploited fears of crime for their own electoral ends. Talk show hosts and conservative commentators built entire careers unmasking bogus claims of racism while dismissing legitimate discussions of racial injustice and inequality as mere political correctness or reverse racism.

Just as black anger often proved counterproductive, so have these white resentments distracted attention from the real culprits of the middle class squeeze—a corporate culture rife with inside dealing, questionable accounting practices, and short-term greed; a Washington dominated by lobbyists and special interests; economic policies that favor the few over the many. And yet, to wish away the resentments of white Americans, to label them as misguided or even racist, without recognizing they are grounded in legitimate concerns—this too widens the racial divide, and blocks the path to understanding.

This is where we are right now. It's a racial stalemate we've been stuck in for years. Contrary to the claims of some of my critics, black and white, I have never been so naïve as to believe that we can get beyond our racial divisions in a single election cycle, or with a single candidacy—particularly a candidacy as imperfect as my own.

But I have asserted a firm conviction—a conviction rooted in my faith in God and my faith in the American people—that working together we can move beyond some of our old racial wounds, and that in fact we have no choice if we are to continue on the path of a more perfect union.

For the African American community, that path means embracing the burdens of our past without becoming victims of our past. It means continuing to insist on a full measure of justice in every aspect of American life. But it also means binding our particular grievances—for better health care, and better schools, and better jobs—to the larger aspirations of all Americans—the white woman struggling to break the glass ceiling, the white man who's been laid off, the immigrant trying to feed his family. And it means taking full responsibility for own lives—by demanding more from our fathers, and spending more time with our children, and reading to them, and teaching them that while they may face challenges and discrimination in their own lives, they must never succumb to despair or cynicism; they must always believe that they can write their own destiny.

Ironically, this quintessentially American—and yes, conservative—notion of self-help found frequent expression in Reverend Wright's sermons. But what my former pastor too often failed to understand is that embarking on a program of self-help also requires a belief that society can change.

The profound mistake of Reverend Wright's sermons is not that he spoke about racism in our society. It's that he spoke as if our society was static; as if no progress has been made; as if this country—a country that has made it possible for one of his own members to run for the highest office in the land and build a coalition of white and black; Latino and Asian, rich and poor, young and old—is still irrevocably bound to a tragic past. But what we know—what we have seen—is that America can change. That is [the] true genius of this nation. What we have already achieved gives us hope—the audacity to hope—for what we can and must achieve tomorrow.

In the white community, the path to a more perfect union means acknowledging that what ails the African American community does not just exist in the minds of black people; that the legacy of discrimination—and current incidents of discrimination, while less overt than in the past—are real and must be addressed. Not just with words, but with deeds—by investing in our schools and our communities; by enforcing our civil rights laws and ensuring fairness in our criminal justice system; by providing this generation with ladders of opportunity that were unavailable for previous generations. It requires all Americans to realize that your dreams do not have to come at the expense of my dreams; that investing in the health, welfare, and education of black and brown and white children will ultimately help all of America prosper.

In the end, then, what is called for is nothing more, and nothing less, than what all the world's great religions demand—that we do unto others as we would have them do unto us. Let us be our brother's keeper, Scripture tells us. Let us be our sister's keeper. Let us find that common stake we all have in one another, and let our politics reflect that spirit as well.

For we have a choice in this country. We can accept a politics that breeds division, and conflict, and cynicism. We can tackle race only as spectacle—as we did in the OJ trial—or in the wake of tragedy, as we did in the aftermath of Katrina—or as fodder for the nightly news. We can play Reverend Wright's sermons on every channel, every day and talk about them from now until the election, and make the only question in this campaign whether or not the American people think that I somehow believe or sympathize with his most offensive words. We can pounce on some gaffe by a Hillary supporter as evidence that she's playing the race card, or we can speculate on whether white men will all flock to John McCain in the general election regardless of his policies.

We can do that.

But if we do, I can tell you that in the next election, we'll be talking about some other distraction. And then another one. And then another one. And nothing will change.

That is one option. Or, at this moment, in this election, we can come together and say, "Not this time." This time we want to talk about the crumbling schools that are stealing the future of black children and white children and Asian children and Hispanic children and Native American children. This time we want to reject the cynicism that tells us that these kids can't learn; that those kids who don't look like us are somebody else's problem. The children of America are not those kids, they are our kids, and we will not let them fall behind in a 21st century economy. Not this time.

This time we want to talk about how the lines in the Emergency Room are filled with whites and blacks and Hispanics who do not have health care; who don't have the power on their own to overcome the special interests in Washington, but who can take them on if we do it together.

This time we want to talk about the shuttered mills that once provided a decent life for men and women of every race, and the homes for sale that once belonged to Americans from every religion, every region, every walk of life. This time we want to talk about the fact that the real problem is not that someone who doesn't look like you might take your job; it's that the corporation you work for will ship it overseas for nothing more than a profit.

This time we want to talk about the men and women of every color and creed who serve together, and fight together, and bleed together under the same proud flag. We want to talk about how to bring them home from a war that never should've been authorized and never should've been waged, and we want to talk about how we'll show our patriotism by caring for them, and their families, and giving them the benefits they have earned.

I would not be running for President if I didn't believe with all my heart that this is what the vast majority of Americans want for this country. This union may never be perfect, but generation after generation has shown that it can always be perfected. And today, whenever I find myself feeling doubtful or cynical about this possibility, what gives me the most hope is the next generation—the young people whose attitudes and beliefs and openness to change have already made history in this election.

There is one story in particular that I'd like to leave you with today—a story I told when I had the great honor of speaking on Dr. King's birthday at his home church, Ebenezer Baptist, in Atlanta.

There is a young, twenty-three year-old white woman named Ashley Baia who organized for our campaign in Florence, South Carolina. She had been working to organize a mostly African American community since the beginning of this campaign, and one day she was at a roundtable discussion where everyone went around telling their story and why they were there.

And Ashley said that when she was nine years old, her mother got cancer. And because she had to miss days of work, she was let go and lost her health care. They had to file for bankruptcy, and that's when Ashley decided that she had to do something to help her mom.

She knew that food was one of their most expensive costs, and so Ashley convinced her mother that what she really liked and really wanted to eat more than anything else was mustard and relish sandwiches. Because that was the cheapest way to eat.

She did this for a year until her mom got better, and she told everyone at the roundtable that the reason she joined our campaign was so that she could help the millions of other children in the country who want and need to help their parents too.

Now Ashley might have made a different choice. Perhaps somebody told her along the way that the source of her mother's problems were blacks who were on welfare and too lazy to work, or Hispanics who were coming into the country illegally. But she didn't. She sought out allies in her fight against injustice.

Anyway, Ashley finishes her story and then goes around the room and asks everyone else why they're supporting the campaign. They all have different stories and reasons. Many bring up a specific issue. And finally they come to this elderly black man who's been sitting there quietly the entire time. And Ashley asks him why he's there. And he does not bring up a specific issue. He does not say health care or the economy. He does not say education or the war. He does not say that he was there because of Barack Obama. He simply says to everyone in the room, "I am here because of Ashley."

"I'm here because of Ashley." By itself, that single moment of recognition between that young white girl and that old black man is not enough. It is not enough

to give health care to the sick, or jobs to the jobless, or education to our children.

But it is where we start. It is where our union grows stronger. And as so many generations have come to realize over the course of the two hundred and twenty-one years since a band of patriots signed that document in Philadelphia, that is where the perfection begins.

James Weldon Johnson and John Rosamond Johnson, *Lift Every Voice and Sing* [1900]

Also known as the Negro National Anthem, "Lift Every Voice and Sing" was written by James Weldon Johnson and set to music by his brother John Rosamond Johnson. Black schools and churches across the country took up the anthem, which is still sung by students and choirs today. James Weldon Johnson noted a feeling of special joy at hearing his song sung by black children.

1

Lift ev'ry voice and sing
Till earth and heaven ring,
    Ring with the harmonies of Liberty;
Let our rejoicing rise
High as the list'ning skies,
Let it resound loud as the rolling seas;
Sing a song full of the faith that the dark past has
    taught us,
Sing a song full of the hope that the present has
    brought us;
Facing the rising sun
Of our new day begun,
Let us march on till victory is won.

2

Stony the road we trod,
Bitter the chast'ning rod
Felt in the days when hope had died;
Yet, with a steady beat,
Have not our weary feet
    Come to the place for which our fathers sighed,
We have come over a way that with tears has been
    watered,
We have come, treading our path thro' the blood of the
    slaughtered,

Out from the gloomy past,
Till now we stand at last
Where the white gleam of our bright star
    is cast.

3

God of our weary years,
God of our silent tears,
    Thou who hast brought us thus far on the way;
Thou who hast by Thy might,
Led us into the light,
Keep us forever in the path, we pray,
Lest our feet stray from the places, our God, where we
    met Thee,
Lest, our hearts drunk with the wine of the world, we
    forget Thee,
Shadowed beneath Thy hand,
May we forever stand,
True to our God, true to our Native Land.

SOURCE: Tuskegee Institute Department of Records and Research, Monroe N. Work, ed., *Negro Year Book: An Annual Encyclopedia of the Negro, 1918–1919* (Tuskegee, AL: Negro Year Book, 1919).

Tables and Charts

African American Population of the United States, 1790–2010

Year	Black Population	Percentage of Total Population	Number of Slaves	Percentage of Blacks Who Were Enslaved
1790	757,208	19.3	697,681	92
1800	1,002,037	18.9	893,602	89
1810	1,377,808	19.0	1,191,362	86
1820	1,771,656	18.4	1,538,022	87
1830	2,328,642	18.1	2,009,043	86
1840	2,873,648	16.1	2,487,355	87
1850	3,638,808	15.7	3,204,287	88
1860	4,441,830	14.1	3,953,731	89
1870	4,880,009	12.7	—	—
1880	6,580,793	13.1	—	—
1890	7,488,788	11.9	—	—
1900	8,833,994	11.6	—	—
1910	9,827,763	10.7	—	—
1920	10,463,131	9.9	—	—
1930	11,891,143	9.7	—	—
1940	12,865,518	9.8	—	—
1950	15,044,937	10.0	—	—
1960	18,871,931	10.6	—	—
1970	22,580,289	11.1	—	—
1980	26,482,349	11.8	—	—
1990	29,986,060	12.0	—	—
2000	34,658,190	12.3	—	—
2010	38,929,319	12.6	—	—

SOURCES: U.S. Census Bureau, *Historical Statistics of the United States, Colonial Times to 1970* (1975); *Statistical Abstract of the United States*, 2010.

Historically Black Colleges and Universities, 2013

College/University	Location	College/University	Location
Alabama A & M University	Normal, Alabama	Bluefield State College	Bluefield, West Virginia
Alabama State University	Montgomery, Alabama	Bowie State University	Bowie, Maryland
Albany State University	Albany, Georgia	Central State University	Wilberforce, Ohio
Alcorn State University	Alcorn State, Mississippi	Cheyney University of Pennsylvania	Cheyney, Pennsylvania
Allen University	Columbia, South Carolina	Claflin University	Orangeburg, South Carolina
Arkansas Baptist College	Little Rock, Arkansas	Clark Atlanta University	Atlanta, Georgia
Benedict College	Columbia, South Carolina	Clinton Junior College	Rock Hill, South Carolina
Bennett College for Women	Greensboro, North Carolina	Coahoma Community College	Clarksdale, Mississippi
Bethune-Cookman University	Daytona Beach, Florida	Concordia College–Selma	Selma, Alabama
Bishop State Community College	Mobile, Alabama	Coppin State University	Baltimore, Maryland

Continued

Historically Black Colleges and Universities, 2013 *Continued*

College/University	Location	College/University	Location
Delaware State University	Dover, Delaware	North Carolina Central University	Durham, North Carolina
Denmark Technical College	Denmark, South Carolina	Oakwood University	Huntsville, Alabama
Dillard University	New Orleans, Louisiana	Paine College	Augusta, Georgia
Edward Waters College	Jacksonville, Florida	Paul Quinn College	Dallas, Texas
Elizabeth City State University	Elizabeth City, North Carolina	Philander Smith College	Little Rock, Arkansas
Fayetteville State University	Fayetteville, North Carolina	Prairie View A & M University	Prairie View, Texas
Fisk University	Nashville, Tennessee	Rust College	Holly Springs, Mississippi
Florida Agricultural and Mechanical University	Tallahassee, Florida	Saint Augustine's College	Raleigh, North Carolina
Florida Memorial University	Miami Gardens, Florida	Saint Paul's College	Lawrenceville, Virginia
Fort Valley State University	Fort Valley, Georgia	Savannah State University	Savannah, Georgia
Gadsden State Community College	Gadsden, Alabama	Selma University	Selma, Alabama
Grambling State University	Grambling, Louisiana	Shaw University	Raleigh, North Carolina
H Councill Trenholm State Technical College	Montgomery, Alabama	Shelton State Community College	Tuscaloosa, Alabama
Hampton University	Hampton, Virginia	South Carolina State University	Orangeburg, South Carolina
Harris-Stowe State University	Saint Louis, Missouri	Southern University and A & M College	Baton Rouge, Louisiana
Hinds Community College–Utica	Utica, Mississippi	Southern University at New Orleans	New Orleans, Louisiana
Howard University	Washington, D.C.	Southern University at Shreveport	Shreveport, Louisiana
Huston-Tillotson University	Austin, Texas	Southwestern Christian College	Terrell, Texas
Interdenominational Theological Center	Atlanta, Georgia	Spelman College	Atlanta, Georgia
J. F. Drake State Technical College	Huntsville, Alabama	St. Philip's College	San Antonio, Texas
Jackson State University	Jackson, Mississippi	Stillman College	Tuscaloosa, Alabama
Jarvis Christian College	Hawkins, Texas	Talladega College	Talladega, Alabama
Johnson C. Smith University	Charlotte, North Carolina	Tennessee State University	Nashville, Tennessee
Kentucky State University	Frankfort, Kentucky	Texas College	Tyler, Texas
Lane College	Jackson, Tennessee	Texas Southern University	Houston, Texas
Langston University	Langston, Oklahoma	Tougaloo College	Tougaloo, Mississippi
Lawson State Community College–Birmingham Campus	Birmingham, Alabama	Tuskegee University	Tuskegee, Alabama
Le Moyne-Owen College	Memphis, Tennessee	University of Arkansas at Pine Bluff	Pine Bluff, Arkansas
Lincoln University	Jefferson City, Missouri	University of Maryland Eastern Shore	Princess Anne, Maryland
Lincoln University of Pennsylvania	Lincoln University, Pennsylvania	University of the District of Columbia	Washington, D.C.
Livingstone College	Salisbury, North Carolina	University of the Virgin Islands	Charlotte Amalie, Virgin Islands
Meharry Medical College	Nashville, Tennessee	University of the Virgin Islands–Kingshill	St. Croix, Virgin Islands
Miles College	Fairfield, Alabama	Virginia State University	Petersburg, Virginia
Mississippi Valley State University	Itta Bena, Mississippi	Virginia Union University	Richmond, Virginia
Morehouse College	Atlanta, Georgia	Virginia University of Lynchburg	Lynchburg, Virginia
Morehouse School of Medicine	Atlanta, Georgia	Voorhees College	Denmark, South Carolina
Morgan State University	Baltimore, Maryland	West Virginia State University	West Virginia
Morris College	Sumter, South Carolina	Wilberforce University	Wilberforce, Ohio
Norfolk State University	Norfolk, Virginia	Wiley College	Marshall, Texas
North Carolina A & T State University	Greensboro, North Carolina	Winston-Salem State University	Winston-Salem, North Carolina
		Xavier University of Louisiana	New Orleans, Louisiana

SOURCE: National Center for Education Statistics, U.S. Department of Education.

appendix

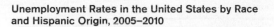

Unemployment Rates in the United States by Race and Hispanic Origin, 2005–2010

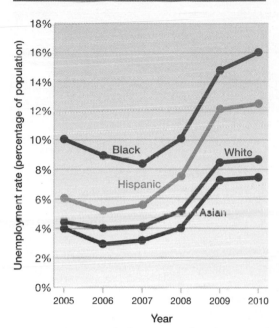

SOURCE: U.S. Bureau of Labor Statistics, "Employment and Earnings Online," January 2011 issue, March 2011, http://www.bls.gov/opub/ee/home.htm and http://www.bls.gov/cps/home.htm.

African American Educational Attainment in the United States, 2011

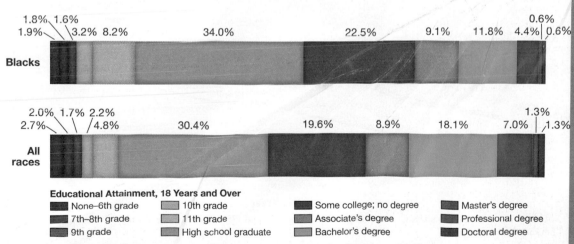

SOURCE: U.S. Census Bureau, Current Population Survey, 2011 Annual Social and Economic Supplement.

Educational Attainment in the United States, 1960–2010

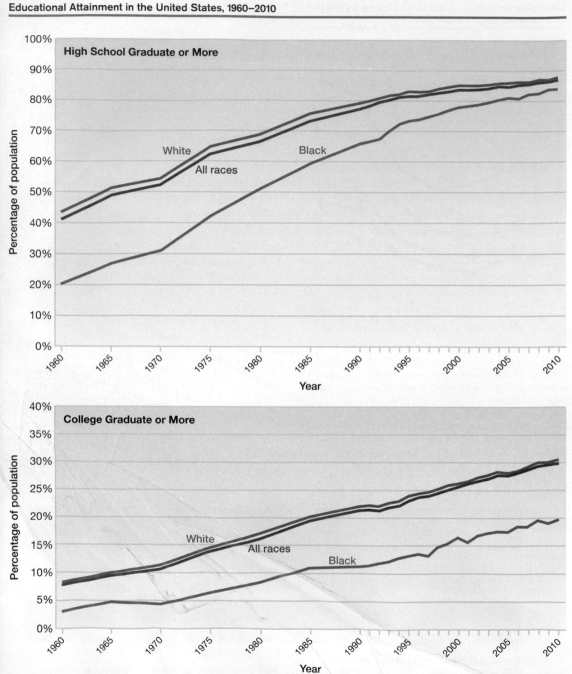

SOURCES: U.S. Census Bureau, U.S. Census of Population, 1960, 1970, and 1980, Summary File 3; Current Population reports and "Educational Attainment."

African American Occupational Distribution, 1900 and 2010

1900	
Occupation/Industry	Percentage of African American Laborers
Agricultural laborers	33.7
Farmers, planters, and overseers	19.0
Unspecified laborers	13.7
Servants and waiters	11.7
Launderers	5.5
Draymen, hackmen, and teamsters[1]	1.7
Steam railroad employees	1.4
Miners and quarrymen	0.9
Sawmill and planing mill employees	0.8
Porters and helpers (in stores etc.)	0.7
Teachers and professors	0.5
Carpenters and joiners	0.5
Turpentine farmers and laborers	0.5
Barbers and hairdressers	0.5
Nurses and midwives	0.5
Clergymen	0.4
Tobacco and cigar factory operatives	0.4
Hostlers[2]	0.4
Bricklayers and stonemasons	0.4
Dressmakers	0.3
Iron- and steelworkers	0.3
Seamstresses	0.3
Janitors and sextons[3]	0.3
Housekeepers and stewards	0.3
Fishermen	0.3
Engineers and firemen	0.2
Blacksmiths	0.2
Other occupations	4.6

2010	
Occupation/Industry	Percentage of African American Laborers
Educational and health services	30.1
Retail trade	11.2
Leisure and hospitality	8.9
Manufacturing	8.4
Transportation and utilities	7.6
Government	7.2
Professional and business services	5.7
Financial activities	5.6
Other services	4.1
Construction	3.3
Information	2.3
Wholesale trade	1.9
Agriculture and related industries	0.4
Mining	0.2

SOURCES FOR BOTH TABLES: U.S. Census Bureau, 1900 Census of Population and Housing, Bulletin 8: Negroes in the United States, table LXII; U.S. Bureau of Labor Statistics, "Employment and Earnings Online," January 2011 issue, March 2011, http://www.bls.gov/opub/ee/home.htm and http://www.bls.gov/cps/home.htm.

1. Drivers of horses, cabs, and trucks.
2. Those who look after horses or service vehicles.
3. Those who maintain graveyards.

appendix

African American Regional Distribution, 1850–2010

Year	Percentage of Total Population			
	Northeast	Midwest	South	West
1850	1.7	2.5	37.3	0.7
1860	1.5	2.0	36.8	0.7
1870	1.5	2.1	36.0	0.6
1880	1.6	2.2	36.0	0.7
1890	1.6	1.9	33.8	0.9
1900	1.8	1.9	32.3	0.7
1910	1.9	1.8	29.8	0.7
1920	2.3	2.3	26.9	0.9
1930	3.3	3.3	24.7	1.0
1940	3.8	3.5	23.8	1.2
1950	5.1	5.0	21.7	2.9
1960	6.8	6.7	20.6	3.9
1970	8.9	8.1	19.1	4.9
1980	9.9	9.1	18.6	5.2
1990	11.0	9.6	18.5	5.4
2000	11.4	10.1	18.9	4.9
2010	11.8	10.4	19.2	4.8

SOURCES: U.S. Census Bureau; U.S. Census Bureau, *Census 2000 Redistricting Data (Public Law 94-171) Summary File*, table PL1; U.S. Census Bureau, *2010 Census Redistricting Data (Public Law 94-171) Summary File*, table P1; U.S. Census Bureau, *Census 2000 Redistricting Data (Public Law 94-171)* Population Characteristics (1990 CP-1).

Glossary of Key Terms

This glossary of key terms contains definitions of words and ideas that are central to your understanding of the material covered in this textbook. Each term in the glossary is in **boldface** in the text when it is first defined. We have included the page number(s) on which the full discussion of the term appears so that you can easily locate the complete explanation. We have also included the page numbers for documents that appear in the Appendix.

For words not defined here, two additional resources may be useful: the index, which will direct you to many more topics discussed in the text, and a good dictionary.

abolitionist movement (283): A loose coalition of organizations with black and white members that worked in various ways to end slavery immediately.

abroad marriages (238): Marriages between slaves who belonged to different owners and lived on different plantations.

American Missionary Association (284): A Protestant missionary organization resulting from the merger of black and white missionary societies in 1846 to promote abolition and black education.

Amistad **case** (227): An 1839 slave insurrection aboard the *Amistad*, a Spanish ship, in international waters near Cuba. The case became a widely publicized abolitionist cause and ultimately reached the U.S. Supreme Court, which freed the rebels in 1841.

asiento (18): A contract or trade agreement created by the Spanish crown.

barracoons (22): Barracks or sheds where some slaves were confined before boarding the slave ships.

bilboes (26): Iron hand and leg cuffs used to shackle slaves.

black codes (386): Laws regulating the labor and behavior of freedpeople passed by southern states in the immediate aftermath of emancipation. These laws were overturned by the Civil Rights Act of 1866.

black convention movement (277): A series of national, regional, and local conventions, starting in 1830, where black leaders addressed the concerns of free and enslaved blacks.

black laws (177): Laws adopted in some midwestern states requiring all free black residents to supply legal proof of their free status and post a cash bond of up to $1,000 to guarantee their good behavior.

black nationalism (293): A diffuse ideology founded on the idea that black people constituted a nation within a nation. It fostered black pride and encouraged black people to control the economy of their communities.

Black Reconstruction (390): The revolutionary political period from 1867 to 1877 when, for the first time ever, black men actively participated in the mainstream politics of the reconstructed southern states and, in turn, transformed the nation's political life.

Bobalition (184): A rendition of the word *abolition*, based on what whites heard as a mispronunciation by blacks. It was used on broadsides and in newspapers to mock free black celebrations of abolition.

bozales (16): A term used by the Spanish for recently imported African captives.

buffalo soldiers (401): Black soldiers who served in U.S. army units in the West.

carracks/caravels (11): Small sailing ships used by the Portuguese to explore Africa and the Atlantic world. Lightweight, fast, and easy to maneuver, they generally had two to four masts.

cash crops (25, 82, 163, 213): Readily salable crops grown for commercial sale and export, rather than local use.

chattel slavery (59): A system by which slaves were considered portable property and denied all rights or legal authority over themselves or their children.

civil disobedience (288): The refusal to obey a law that one believes is unjust.

Civil Rights Act of 1866 (391): An act defining U.S. citizenship and protecting the civil rights of freedpeople.

Civil Rights Act of 1875 (397, A 17 A 18): An act requiring equal treatment regardless of race in public accommodations and on public conveyances.

Civil Rights cases (1883) (399): The U.S. Supreme Court ruling overturning the Civil Rights Act of 1875.

Code Noir (77): The slave code used in France's New World colonies.

coffle (20): A group of animals, prisoners, or slaves chained together in a line.

colonization (186): The idea that blacks should be sent back to Africa or moved to another territory outside the United States.

Compromise of 1850 (286): A compromise aimed at reducing sectional tensions by admitting California as a free state; permitting the question of slavery to be settled by popular sovereignty in New Mexico and the Utah Territories; abolishing the slave trade in the District of Columbia; resolving the Texas debt issue; and enacting a new fugitive slave law.

Confederate States of America (324): The eleven southern states that seceded from the United States in 1860 and 1861, precipitating the Civil War.

conjure (116): Traditional African folk magic in which men and women called conjurers draw on the powers of the spirit world to influence human affairs.

contraband (328): A refugee slave seeking protection behind Union lines. This designation recognized slaves' status as human property and paved the way for their emancipation.

convict lease (386): A penal system in which convict labor is hired out to landowners or businesses to generate income for the state.

country marks (66): Facial scars indicating particular African origins.

creole (63): A language that originated as a combination of other languages; the term *creole* can also refer to people who are racially or culturally mixed.

***Creole* insurrection** (227): An 1841 slave insurrection aboard the *Creole*, a ship carrying 135 slaves from Hampton Roads, Virginia, to New Orleans, Louisiana.

crop lien (385): An agricultural system in which a farmer borrows against his anticipated crop for the seed and supplies he needs and settles his debt after the crop is harvested.

diaspora (4): The dispersion of a people from their homeland. Applied to Africans, this term usually describes the mass movement of Africans and their descendants to the Americas during the slave trade.

Dred Scott v. Sandford (1857) (291, A-24–A-25): The controversial U.S. Supreme Court decision ruling that Scott, a slave, was not entitled to sue in the Missouri courts and was not free even though he had been taken into a free territory; that no person of African descent could be a citizen; that slaves were property; and that Congress had no authority to regulate slavery in the territories.

driver (64): A slave assigned to oversee the work of other slaves.

Elmina Castle (16): A fortress in present-day Ghana, built by the Portuguese as a trading post in 1482 and used as a major slave trading center by the Dutch from 1637 to 1814.

Emancipation Proclamation (1863) (333, A-15): A presidential proclamation, issued by Abraham Lincoln, freeing all slaves under Confederate control and authorizing the use of black troops in the Civil War.

encomienda (12): A labor system used by the Spanish in their colonization of the Americas. Under this system, the crown granted colonists control over a specified number of Native Americans from whom they could extract labor.

Exodusters (402): Black migrants who left the South to settle on federal land in Kansas.

fictive kin (239): People regarded as family even though they were not related by blood or marriage.

Fifteenth Amendment (ratified 1870) (396, A-12): The constitutional amendment that enfranchised black men.

First Confiscation Act (1861) (328): A congressional act authorizing the confiscation of Confederate property, including slaves employed in the rebellion, who were then considered free.

Force Acts (1870, 1871) (398): Two laws providing federal protection of blacks' civil rights in the face of white terroristic activities.

Fourteenth Amendment (ratified 1868) (391, A-11–A-12): The constitutional amendment that defined U.S. citizenship to include blacks and guarantees citizens due process and equal protection of the laws.

Freedmen's Bureau (1865–1869) (346): The federal agency created to aid freedpeople in their transition to freedom.

freedom suits (122): Legal actions by which slaves sought to achieve freedom in British and American courts.

Fugitive Slave Act of 1850 (286): Part of the Compromise of 1850, this law strengthened federal authority over fugitive slaves.

fugitive slave clause (163): The constitutional clause permitting slave owners of any state to retrieve their fugitive slaves from any other state.

gag rule (226): A series of congressional resolutions passed by the House of Representatives between 1836 and 1840 that tabled, without discussion, petitions regarding slavery; the gag rule was instituted to silence dissent over slavery. It was repealed in 1844.

Great Awakening (116): A multidenominational series of evangelical revivals that took place in North America between the 1730s and the 1780s.

Guanches (11): The aboriginal inhabitants of the Canary Islands.

Gullah (116): A creole language composed of a blend of West African languages and English.

habeas corpus (122): A feature of English common law that protects prisoners from being detained without trial. Translated literally, the Latin phrase means "you should have the body."

half-freedom (71): A status allotted primarily to Dutch-owned slaves who helped defend New Netherland against Indian attacks. Half-freedom liberated adult slaves but not their children.

hiring out (174): The practice of owners contracting out their slaves to work for other employers.

historically black colleges and universities (383): Separate institutions of higher learning for African Americans. Most of them were founded in the post-emancipation era.

indentured servants (59): White laborers who came to the English North American colonies under contract to work for a specified amount of time, usually four to seven years.

Indian Removal Act (1830) (216): An act signed into law by President Andrew Jackson forcing Indians living east of the Mississippi River to relocate to Indian Territory (present-day Oklahoma).

invisible church (233): A term used to describe groups of African American slaves who met in secret for Christian worship.

John Brown's raid (1859) (295): An unsuccessful attempt by the white abolitionist John Brown to seize the federal arsenal at Harpers Ferry, Virginia, and incite a slave insurrection.

Kansas-Nebraska Act (1854) (290): A law that allowed the residents of Kansas and Nebraska Territories to decide whether slavery should be allowed.

ladinos (15): Latinized blacks who were born or raised in Spain, Portugal, or these nations' Atlantic or American colonies and who spoke fluent Spanish or Portuguese.

living out (174): The practice of allowing slaves who were hired out in urban areas to keep part of their wages to pay for their rented lodgings.

Lord Dunmore's Proclamation (1775) (128): A document issued by Virginia's royal governor, John Murray, the Earl of Dunmore, in November 1775, offering freedom to "rebel" colonists' slaves who joined his forces.

Louisiana Purchase (1803) (171): The federal government's purchase of Louisiana from France, which doubled the size of the United States and fostered the spread of slavery.

loyalists (127): Colonists who remained loyal to Britain during the American Revolution.

lying out (228): A form of resistance in which slaves hid near their home plantations, often to escape undesirable work assignments or abusive treatment by their owners.

maroons (57): Members of runaway slave communities; also known as cimarrons, from the Spanish *cimarrón*.

Missouri Compromise (1820) (215): An agreement balancing the admission of Missouri as a slave state with the admission of Maine as a free state and prohibiting slavery north of latitude 36°30′ in any state except Missouri.

moral suasion (281): A primary strategy in the abolitionist movement that relied on vigorous appeals to the nation's moral and Christian conscience.

mulatto (63): A person with mixed white and African ancestry.

mutual aid society (179): An organization or voluntary association in which members agreed to assist one another in securing benefits such as insurance.

National Equal Rights League (348): An organization established by black leaders in 1864 to promote emancipation, legal equality, and black male suffrage.

Naturalization Act of 1790 (177): The nation's first immigration law, which instituted a two-year residency requirement for immigrants who wished to become U.S. citizens and limited naturalization to free white people.

Negro Election Day (115): An annual New England celebration in which black communities elected their own kings and governors in elaborate ceremonies that included royal processions, political parades, and inaugural parties.

New Lights (117): Protestant ministers who, during the Great Awakening, challenged traditional religious practices by delivering emotional sermons that urged listeners to repent and find salvation in Christ.

New York City draft riots (1863) (341): Antiblack riots sparked by white working-class opposition to the Union's military draft.

North Star (231): A star, also known as Polaris, that always points north and was used by escaped slaves to navigate their way to freedom.

Northwest Ordinance (1787) (163): An act of the Second Continental Congress organizing the region known as the Old Northwest, which included U.S. territories north of the Ohio River and east of the Mississippi River. Slavery was banned in these territories.

personal liberty laws (286): A series of state laws in the North aimed at preventing the return of fugitive slaves to the South.

political action (283): A primary strategy in the abolitionist movement that relied on working through political channels to force changes in the law and political practices.

popular sovereignty (286): An approach to resolving the question of whether to allow slavery in new states by letting residents of the territories decide.

Port Royal Experiment (330): An attempt by government officials and civilian volunteers to assist Sea Island slaves, who had been abandoned by their owners, in their transition to freedom.

preliminary Emancipation Proclamation (1862) (332): A presidential proclamation giving the Confederacy one hundred days to cease the rebellion. If it did not, all its slaves would be freed.

Proclamation for Amnesty and Reconstruction (1863) (342): Lincoln's proposal for the reorganization and readmission into the Union of the defeated Confederate states.

Quaker (74): A member of the Religious Society of Friends, a pacifist Protestant sect known for its commitment to social justice.

Reconstruction Act of 1867 (first) (392): An act dividing the South into military districts and requiring the former Confederate states to write new constitutions at conventions with delegates elected by universal male suffrage.

ring shout (233): A religious ritual developed by slaves in the West Indies and North America that involved forming a circle and shuffling counterclockwise while singing and praying.

Second Confiscation Act (1862) (330): A congressional act declaring freedom for all slaves employed in the rebellion and for refugee slaves able to make it to Union-controlled territory.

Second Great Awakening (225): A Christian revival movement that took place during the first half of the nineteenth century.

sharecropping (385): An agricultural system that emerged during Reconstruction in which a landowner contracts with a farmer to work a parcel of land in return for a share of the crop.

silent march (1917) (501): A mass march orchestrated by the NAACP down New York City's Fifth Avenue on July 28, 1917, to protest the horrific East St. Louis, Illinois, race riot of July 2.

Slaughterhouse cases (1873) (399): The U.S. Supreme Court ruling limiting the authority of the Fourteenth Amendment. The ruling expanded the scope of state-level citizenship at the expense of U.S. citizenship.

Somerset case (1772) (122): A British legal case that freed an American slave named James Somerset and inspired other slaves to sue for their freedom.

southern strategy (131): An unsuccessful British military plan, adopted in late 1778, that was designed to defeat the patriots by recapturing the American South.

Special Field Order 15 (1865) (346): A military order by Union general William T. Sherman distributing confiscated and abandoned Confederate land to freedmen.

Stono rebellion (1739) (80): A slave rebellion that took place near South Carolina's Stono River in 1739. It was led by slaves who hoped to find freedom in Spanish Florida. The rebels killed about twenty whites before they were captured and subdued.

Taino Indians (12): One of the indigenous peoples of the Caribbean.

task system (64): A system of slave labor in which enslaved workers were assigned daily tasks and permitted to work unsupervised as long as they completed their tasks.

Thirteenth Amendment (1865) (347, A-11): The constitutional amendment that officially outlawed slavery everywhere in the Union.

Three-Fifths Compromise (164): A compromise between the northern and southern states, reached during the Constitutional Convention, establishing that three-fifths of each state's slave population would be counted in determining federal taxes and representation in the House of Representatives.

tight packing (26): Crowding the human cargo carried on slave ships to maximize profits. By contrast, "loose packing" involved carrying fewer slaves in better conditions in an effort to keep mortality rates low.

triangle trade (18): The trade system that propelled the transatlantic slave trade, in which European merchants exchanged manufactured goods for enslaved Africans, whom they shipped to the Americas to exchange for New World commodities, which they then shipped back to European markets.

truant (228): A slave who ran away for a limited period of time to visit loved ones; attend religious meetings or other social events; or escape punishment, abusive treatment, or undesirable work assignments.

Uncle Tom's Cabin (1852) (290): A best-selling novel by Harriet Beecher Stowe that portrayed the horrors of slavery, boosted the abolitionist cause, and angered the proslavery South.

underground railroad (231): A network of antislavery activists who helped fugitive slaves escape to the North and Canada.

Union League (395): An organization founded in 1862 to promote the Republican Party. During Reconstruction, the league recruited freedpeople into the party and advanced their political education.

uplift (271, 408): The idea that racial progress demands autonomous black efforts; especially seen as the responsibility of the more fortunate of the race to help lift up the less fortunate.

U.S. Colored Troops (334): The official designation for the division of black units that joined the U.S. army beginning in 1863.

vigilance committees (287): Groups led by free blacks and their allies in the North to assist fugitive slaves.

Wade-Davis Bill (1864) (346): A congressional proposal for the reorganization and readmission into the Union of the defeated Confederate states. Lincoln refused to sign the bill.

Wilmot Proviso (1846) (286): A controversial congressional proposal that sought to prohibit slavery in the new territories gained as a result of the Mexican-American War. Although it did not pass the Senate, it sparked angry debate between the North and South.

Acknowledgments

FROM THE RECORD AND DOCUMENTS BANNER ARTIFACTS

Left to right: Payment for a Negro woman; Library of Congress, LC-USZ62-125-135. AP article excerpt, "Bus Mixers Are Beaten," Associated Press, May 15, 1961. Mss1 D5607a 6 p.82, Inventory of Negroes at Berry Plain Plantation, owned by John Fayette Dickinson, 1855, King George County, Virginia. Virginia Historical Society, Richmond, Virginia, USA/The Bridgeman Art Library International. *Congressional Record* excerpt: *Congressional Record.*

TITLE PAGE, CONTENTS, AND TIMELINE IMAGES

Page v: Left to right: F & A Archive/The Art Archive at Art Resource, NY. *Antislavery Cameo, late eighteenth century* Wedgwood jasper medallion, 1790s/© Wilberforce House, Hull City Museums and Art Galleries. UK/The Bridgeman Art Library International. Inventory of Negroes at Berry Plain Plantation, owned by John Fayette Dickinson, 1855, King George County, Virginia. Virginia Historical Society, Richmond Virginia, USA/The Bridgeman Art Library International. Library of Congress, LC-USZ62-7816 © North Wind Picture Archives/Alamy. Library of Congress, LC-DIG-ppmsca-17564. **Page xvii:** From *L'Afrique,* by R. Geoffrey, 1814/Bibliothèque de L'Arsenal, Paris, France/Archives Charmet/The Bridgeman Art Library International. **Page xviii:** The Granger Collection, NYC. All rights reserved. **Page xix:** Portrait of Elizabeth "Mumbet" Freeman (c. 1742–1829), watercolor on ivory, Sedgwick, Susan Anne Livingston Ridley III (f. 1811)/© Massachusetts Historical Society, Boston, MA, USA/The Bridgeman Art Library International. **Page xx:** © North Wind Picture Archives/Alamy. **Page xxi:** Library of Congress. **Page xxii:** Library of Congress, LC-USZ62-79305. **Page xxiii:** Private Collection/Peter Newark American Pictures/The Bridgeman Art Library International. **Page xxiv:** Library of Congress, LC-DIG-ppmsca-17564. **Page 2:** Top: From *L'Afrique,* by R. Geoffrey, 1814/Bibliothèque de L'Arsenal, Paris, France/Archives Charmet/The Bridgeman Art Library International. Bottom: © Roger-Viollet/The Image Works. **Page 3:** Top left: From John Barbot, *A Description of the Coasts of North and South-Guinea,* 1732/© The British Library Board, Shelf mark Add.28788 f45. Bottom left: Museum of Ife Antiquities, Lagos, Nigeria/photograph © Andrea Jemolo. Right: *Antislavery Cameo, late eighteenth century* Wedgwood jasper medallion, 1790s/© Wilberforce House, Hull City Museums and Art Galleries, UK/The Bridgeman Art Library International. **Page 54:** Left: The Granger Collection, NYC. All rights reserved. Right: *Lucy Parke Byrd,* c. 1716, oil on canvas by

studio of Sir Godfrey Kneller/Lent anonymously to the Virginia Historical Society, Richmond, VA/The Bridgeman Art Library International. **Page 55:** Top: Private Collection/The Bridgeman Art Library International. Bottom: Charles de Rochefort, *Histoire naturelle et morale des îles Antilles de l'Amérique*/Private Collection/The Bridgeman Art Library International. **Page 110:** Top: *La déstruction de la statue royale à Nouvelle York/Die Zerstorung der Koniglichen Bild Saule zu Neu Yorck,* published in Paris, 1777-/Library of Congress LC-USZC4-1476. Bottom left: Paul Revere, *The Bloody Massacre,* 1770. Library of Congress LC-DIG-ppmsca-01657. Bottom right: Portrait of Elizabeth "Mumbet" Freeman (c. 1742–1829), watercolor on ivory, Sedgwick, Susan Anne Livingston Ridley III (f. 1811)/© Massachusetts Historical Society, Boston, MA, USA/The Bridgeman Art Library International. **Page 111:** Top: Title page and frontispiece to *Poems on Various Subjects, Religious and Moral* by Phillis Wheatley (1753–1784), published in London, 1773 (engraving)/© Massachusetts Historical Society, Boston, MA, USA/The Bridgeman Art Library International. Bottom left: John Singleton Copley (1738–1815), *The Death of Major Peirson, January 6, 1781.* Painted 1783. Oil on canvas/Tate, London/Art Resource, NY. Bottom right: Marie-Joseph Paul Yves Roch Gilbert Motier (1757–1834), *Portrait of the Marquis de Lafayette with an Aide-de-Camp during the American War of Independence,* oil on canvas, eighteenth century/Musée de la Ville de Paris, Musée Carnavalet, Paris, France/Archives Charmet/The Bridgeman Art Library International. **Page 160:** Top left: 1827 broadside/Library of Congress LC-USZ62-34025. Bottom left: James Akin, *A Philosophic Cock,* c. 1804, hand-colored aquatint, Newburyport, Massachusetts/Courtesy American Antiquarian Society/The Bridgeman Art Library International. Right: Oliver Goldsmith, *A History of the Earth and Animated Nature* (Philadelphia, 1795). Courtesy American Antiquarian Society/The Bridgeman Art Library International. **Page 161:** Top left: 1812 engraving/Library of Congress LC-USZ62-26174. Bottom left: Boston Public Library. Right: © North Wind Picture Archives/Alamy. **Page 210:** Top: Private Collection/Peter Newark American Pictures/The Bridgeman Art Library International. Bottom left: Friedrich Schulz (1823–1875), *The Slave Market,* 19th century, oil on canvas/Hirshhorn Museum and Sculpture Garden, Washington, DC, USA/The Bridgeman Art Library International. Bottom right: Library of Congress. **Page 211:** Top left: F & A Archive/The Art Archive at Art Resource, NY. Bottom left: *Aunt Phillis's Cabin, or Southern Life As It Is*/Eastman (PS646.F53.E27A8 1852). Clifton Walker Barrett Library of American Literature, Special Collections,

University of Virginia Library. Right: Library of Congress, LC-USZ62-7816. **Page 264:** Top: *The Five Points, Junction of Baxter, Worth and Park Streets, New York,* hand-colored engraving by George Catlin (1796–1872) © Museum of the City of New York, USA/The Bridgeman Art Library International. Bottom left: Newberry Library, Chicago, IL, USA/The Bridgeman Art Library International. Bottom right: Library of Congress, LC-USZC4-6165. **Page 265:** Top: *Songs of the Virginia Serenaders,* 1844/Box 018, item 33, Lester S. Levy Collection of Sheet Music, Department of Rare Books and Manuscripts, Sheridan Libraries, The Johns Hopkins University, http://levysheetmusic.mse.jhu.edu. Bottom left: Library of Congress, LC-USZ62-126131. Right: Library of Congress, LC-USZ62-79305. **Page 322:** Top: Library of Congress, LC-DIG-pga-03898. Bottom: Private Collection/Peter Newark American Pictures/The Bridgeman Art Library International. **Page 323:** Top left: Courtesy of the National Archives, Records of the Adjutant General's Office, c. 1775–c. 1928, ARC identifiers #849127 and #849136. Bottom left: The Granger Collection, NYC. All rights reserved. Right: Courtesy of the National Archives, Records of the Adjutant General's Office, c. 1775–c. 1928, ARC identifiers #849127 and #849136. **Page 376:** Top left: Library of Congress, LC-DIG-ppmsca-31598. Top right: Library of Congress, LC-USZ62-138383. Bottom: Library of Congress, LC-DIG-ppmsca-17564. **Page 377:** Top: Library of Congress, LC-DIG-ppmsca-11406. Bottom left: Library of Congress, LC-USZ62-57340. Bottom right: Library of Congress, LC-USZC2-2922.

TEXT ACKNOWLEDGMENTS
CHAPTER 1

"Black Conquistadors: Armed Africans in Early Spanish America" by Matthew Restall. From *The Americas* 57, no. 2 (2000): 171. Copyright © AAFH. Used by permission.

The African Past, translated by Basil Davidson. Curtis Brown Ltd., 1964. Copyright © 1964 by Basil Davidson. Reprinted by permission of Curtis Brown, Ltd.

CHAPTER 5

Vilet Lester, Letter to Miss Patsey Patterson, Joseph Allred Papers, David M. Rubenstein Rare Book & Manuscript Library, Duke University.

APPENDIX

Martin Luther King Jr. "Letter from Birmingham Jail." Reprinted by arrangement with the Heirs to the Estate of Martin Luther King Jr., c/o Writers House as agent for the proprietor New York, NY. Copyright © 1963 by Dr. Martin Luther King, Jr.; copyright © renewed 1991 by Coretta Scott King.

Index

KEY TO FIGURES ON THE COVER

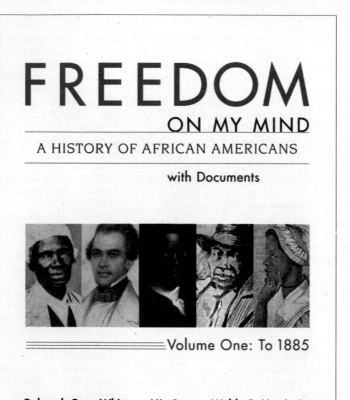

FREEDOM

ON MY MIND

A HISTORY OF AFRICAN AMERICANS

with Documents

Volume One: To 1885

Deborah Gray White ☐ Mia Bay ☐ Waldo E. Martin Jr.

Left to right

Sojourner Truth

William Wells Brown

Olaudah Equiano

Nat Turner

Phillis Wheatley